V&R

Ellert R. S. Nijenhuis

The Trinity of Trauma: Ignorance, Fragility, and Control

The Evolving Concept of Trauma / The Concept and Facts of Dissociation in Trauma

Vandenhoeck & Ruprecht

With 26 figures and 12 tables.

Bibliographical information published by the Deutsche Nationalbibliothek

The Deutsche Nationalbibliothek lists this publication in the Deutsche Nationalbibliografie; detailed bibliographic data available online: http://dnb.d-nb.de.

ISBN 978-3-525-40247-4
You can find alternative editions of this book and additional material on our website: www.v-r.de

Cover image: Balancing of pebbles on the top of a triangle stone/shutterstock.com

Printed in Germany.
Typesetting: Satzspiegel, Nörten-Hardenberg
Managing Editor: Joseph A. Smith
Printed and bound in Germany by ⊕ Hubert & Co., Göttingen

Printed on non-aging paper.

Table of Contents

Volume I: The Evolving Concept of Trauma

Volume I

The Evolving Concept of Trauma

Preface

One of the pitfalls of childhood is that one doesn't have to understand something to feel it. By the time the mind is able to comprehend what has happened, the wounds of the heart are already too deep.
Carlos Ruiz Zafón (2005, p. 33)

The trinity of trauma is a trilogy: Volume I, *The Evolving Concept of Trauma*, and Volume II, *The Concept and Facts of Dissociation in Trauma*, are predominantly conceptual, theoretical, and empirical in nature. Volume III, *Assessment and Treatment of Dissociation in Trauma*, which builds on the first two volumes, addresses clinical practice.

The first seven chapters of Volume I present a selective history of the concept of trauma, revealing the capricious understanding of trauma and trauma-related disorders from ancient to modern times. It also identifies several recurrent and persistent conceptual flaws that have plagued the issue. Chapters 8 and 9 reveal that these relate in part to philosophical matters that have hardly, if at all, been considered or realized in the trauma field. Philosophical wisdom – mainly but not exclusively treated in Chapter 10 – shows that (1) there are *intrinsic* relationships between the brain, the body, and the environment, that (2) subject and object are co-constitutive, co-dependent, and co-occurrent, that (3) causation is dynamic, and that (4) matter – hence neuroscience – cannot explain consciousness and will outside of experience. All science and clinical practice depends on two irreducible fibers: will and consciousness. Any human action starts and ends with consciousness and is propelled by will such as desires to live, love, explore, care, dominate, compete, play, and defend. Grounded in these insights, Chapter 11 fulfills the primary aim of Volume I: to formulate new definitions of trauma and traumatic experience, traumatic events, traumatizing events, and traumatic memory.

The secondary aim of Volume I – one closely related to its primary aim – is to demonstrate and critique the age-old 'dissociation' of two groups of disorders that are more alike than different. In the course of medical and psychiatric history these two have been described and contrasted using a wide variety of names, such as 'melancholia' versus 'hysteria,' or 'traumatic neurosis' versus 'traumatic hysteria.' In the most recent version of the *Diagnostic and Statistical Manual of Mental Disorders* (DSM-5; APA, 2013), the two are now called (1) trauma- and stressor-related disorders, which prominently includes acute stress disorder and posttraumatic stress disorder (PTSD), and (2) dissociative disorders. Another 'dissociation' in the DSM-5 that should be rejected and mended is the division of dissociative disorders and conversion disorders.

The reasons for proposing a single category of trauma-related disorders to capture the trauma- and stressor-related disorders, dissociative disorders, and conversion disorders of the DSM-5 are conceptual, theoretical, and empirical. Whereas these various disorders are not identical, they do have the classic causes in common that Aristotle formulated many ages ago: material, efficient, formal, and final causality. Their common efficient causes include particular patterns of psychophysiological and brain activation, and the material causes include common structural brain abnormalities. Their common formal cause is a more or less complex dissociative organization of the personality, that is, a division of this biopsychosocial system in two or more conscious and self-conscious subsystems or 'parts.' This dissociative organization is intimately related to two common final goals: the desire to live (a happy) daily life and the desire to survive adverse events. Children have an evolutionary-grounded, deep-felt need to attach to their parents, other important caregivers, or relatives on which they depend. Children are also defined by an equally natural and strong urge to defend themselves against individuals who molest, harass, rape, hit, kick, confine, betray, manipulate, degrade, and/or neglect them. These two very different wills are exceptionally hard to integrate when the will to attach and the will to defend themselves pertain to the same individual(s). In this light, it is easy to understand that these conflicting wills can fissure the developing child's personality.

Postulating that the formal causality of these disorders involves a dissociation of the personality requires a solid definition of the concept of dissociation (Chapter 13). The definition provided balances the clinical and scientific interests of sensitivity and specificity, and thus includes phenomena that characterize individuals whose personality is dissociated and excludes phenomena that also typify individuals with other mental disorders. The distinctive features of the dissociative parts is that they are both conscious and self-conscious. They include the unique conceptions of who they are ('I'), what the world is like, and how their 'I' relates to itself ('me, myself, mine'), to other people ('You'), and to 'things' and 'events.' In other words, what distinguishes dissociative parts is that they include their own person perspectives. To get a firm grip on the nature of these perspectives, Chapter 12, the opening chapter of Volume II, analyzes the concepts of consciousness and self-consciousness, and examines the differences between the two in individuals with and without dissociative disorders. To substantiate the concept of dissociation of the personality, the chapter also includes an analysis and definition of the concept of personality.

Chapter 13 presents a meticulous definition of dissociation in trauma. Several authors have criticized the proposal to delimit the concept of dissociation to a division of the personality and the manifestations of this partition, but their objections are less than persuasive (Chapter 14). Another criticism implies that the dissociative parts of the personality are artifacts rather than natural, trauma-related phenomena. These parts stem from factors such as suggestibility as well as self-suggestion and hetero-suggestion, fantasy proneness and engagement in fantasy, and prescribed and enacted social roles. Chapter 15 formulates and examines the contrasting hypotheses of these 'sociocognitive models' of dissociation and trauma-related views of dissociation, particularly those that emerge from the theory of (trauma-related) structural dissociation of the personality (TSDP; Nijenhuis, Van der Hart, & Steele, 2002; Van der Hart, Nijenhuis, & Steele, 2006). The empirical evidence generally supports the trauma models and rejects the sociocognitive models. In fact, the scientific base of TSDP has strengthened with every new study exploring its hypotheses.

Chapters 16–19 present, examine, and test several biopsychosocial hypotheses of the theory of structural dissociation of personality. The findings are consistent with the essential formulations of this perspective regarding the material and efficient causality of this dissociation. Chapters 16–18 present the psychophysiological and neurophysiological research; Chapter 19 details structural brain abnormalities. The empirical evidence gathered to date contradicts the sociocognitive models and clearly strengthens the stance that PTSD in its various forms (APA, 2013) and complex dissociative disorders are indeed one of a kind. The crucial conceptual, theoretical, and empirical link lies in the common dissociation of personality as a whole 'embrained,' embodied, and environmentally embedded system. This system does not exist and function, and cannot be comprehended, at the exclusion of a material and social environment, as explained in Volume I. The division of this organism-environment system in conscious and self-conscious biopsychosocial organism-environment subsystems is simple in PTSD (APA, 2013) and intricate in more complex dissociative disorders, particularly in dissociative identity disorder (DID).

This division of the personality in trauma involves a trinity, that is, three major prototypical subsystems or parts of traumatized individuals' personality: more or less trauma-ignorant and trauma-ignoring apparently normal parts (ANP), fragile emotional parts (fragile EP), and controlling emotional parts (controlling EP). The core theme of Chapter 20 is that this trinity, these three major modes of existence and functioning, also seem to characterize perpetrators and their partners in crime: professionals such as physicians, psychologists, and psychiatrists, and the general public when it comes to trauma, particularly chronic childhood traumatization. The link, thus, lies in the difficulty to integrate and realize traumatic experiences and their consequences, particularly when it comes to the immense problem of chronic childhood traumatization.

The various concepts developed, and the insights gained, in the first two volumes are then applied in the third. This volume presents and analyzes in detail the different phases of assessment and the treatment of chronically traumatized individuals. Several strategies and interventions are suggested, analyzed, and discussed at a microlevel. One major theme is the continual challenge of helping the different dissociative parts – each involving person perspectives that are unique in at least some crucial regards – to recognize, acknowledge, understand, and accept each other. It is also a demanding task to get these different parts to cooperate with each other. Healing requires an individual who, in manageable steps, as a whole organism environment system learns to integrate his or her different dissociative parts:

1. the first-person perspective, the unreflected 'I' with a point of view that involves *past and present phenomenal experience*;

2. the quasi-second-person perspectives, the 'I-me, myself, mine' relationships that involve *past and present phenomenal judgment*;
3. the second-person perspectives, the 'I-You' relationships that also involve specific *past and present phenomenal judgment*, as well as
4. the third-person perspectives, the 'I-object' relationships that involve *past and present physical judgment*.

Therapists help patients to initiate, execute, and complete these integrative actions. In order to be effective, therapists must pursue and model the integration of their own different person perspectives:
1. the first-person perspective (e.g., "I feel apprehensive"),
2. the quasi-second-person perspective (e.g., "My body tells me I'm stressed"; "I'm pleased with the result of my intervention"; "Was my judgment correct?"),
3. the second-person perspective (e.g., "I like her"; "He resists my good intentions"; "How does she perceive me?"; "I find it hard that she still mistrusts me"), and
4. the third-person perspective (e.g., "The patient has a dissociative disorder"; "The way the patient reacts to me suggests she is re-enacting the traumatic relationship with her mother"; "What intervention could lessen the self-cutting?").

In this context, therapists become attuned to their patients' phenomenal experiences and judgments. They meticulously and empathically pace their patients' dissociative part-dependent conceptions of the self, the world, and the self-of-the-world in order to achieve a consensus how 'things are.' They join their patient's conceptions, but they do not give up their own. Rather, they aim at integrating the two. This ongoing integration process constitutes the relational foundation for therapeutic stimulation, for inviting the patient to engage in new, more efficient actions that are within their reach. The actions proposed are more efficient, are better suited, because the execution thereof fulfills the patient's desires (e.g., to reduce or end their suffering) more than the ones they replace. Therapy, thus, concerns the stepwise improvement of the patient's actions effecting the gradual realization of their goals.

The joint enterprise called therapy may be seen in fact as 'therapeutic dancing.' This creative action comprises three levels of action:
1. the therapist's ongoing attunement to the patient's phenomenal experience and phenomenal conceptions of him- or herself, of the world, and of his or her being a part of that world;
2. the therapist's ongoing effort to reach a consensus regarding these phenomenal realities; and
3. the therapist's invitations to the patient to make a particular 'move' in a direction defined by the patient's interests, not by those of the therapist. The trauma therapist is thus a guide and model, not a controlling authority.

Healing trauma involves two interacting persons: the 'dividuum' injured by adverse life circumstances but willing to mend the division; the blessed, or in any case less unfortunate, 'individuum' willing to guide whatever actions this recovery may take.

I am most grateful to Arne Blindheim, Stephen Braude, Fredrik Garpe, Onno van der Hart, Annica Ljung, Isabel Lopez-Fiestas, Timo Järvilehto, Sebastian Lorenz, Winja Lutz, Klaus Matthess, Yolanda Schlumpf, Simona Seidmann, Hans Peter Sondergaard, Sander van Straten, Esther Veerman-Renkema, Ekaterina Weder, and Fabian Wilmers for their thoughtful comments on the original version of the current text, their discussions with me on the themes of the present two volumes, and for their sympathy.

Joseph Smith's linguistic and technical corrections of the original text have been invaluable. It was great working with you, Joe, thank you very much. It is an immense privilege that Vandenhoeck & Ruprecht was willing to accept my lengthy text for publication. Franco Biondi and Inge Liebel-Fryszer paved the way to the V&R author Rainer Schwing, who helped me persuade Günter Presting and his V&R team that publishing the *Trinity of Trauma* might be a worthwhile venture.

I sincerely thank the deeply wounded individuals I have encountered for their eventual trust in me and for everything I learned from them. The thoughts on the 'trinity of trauma' would not have evolved without the many hours we shared together. The book could also not have been written had not participants in courses on trauma and dissociation and other colleagues shown an eager interest in my ideas. Like anyone else, I am indeed an organism-environment system. Rainy, my beloved wife, even though contemporary philosophers doubt essences exist, love is all.

Westerbork, The Netherlands; Cuidad Quesada, Spain, Fall 2014

Chapter 1

A Horrible Kind of Melancholia

> *Trauma tends to exceed human understanding. It disrespects boundaries, interrupts all kinds of units and makes them blend, it disrupts bodily and psychic organisms and upsets social and historical organizations.*
> Esther Fischer-Homburger

The beginning of wisdom, Socrates taught us, lies in the definition of terms. Since terms point to concepts, to ways of grasping something, defining terms yields conceptual clarity. Establishing a clarity of complex concepts can be an intellectual and, as the history of trauma illustrates, emotional struggle as well. Part of the challenge is that thought is subject to perspective, interest, and ongoing development. How we as individuals, groups, nations, and indeed as a species perceive and understand our world and ourselves is influenced by many different and ever evolving personal, social, political, cultural, and historical contexts. For these reasons our concepts may tend to drift. The goal, then, is less the love of wisdom – the literal meaning of the term 'philosophy' – than the desire to gain wisdom. The Dutch word for philosophy *wijsbegeerte* aptly expresses this insight. *Wijs* means wise and *begeerte* a desire or urge. *Wijsbegeerte* thus means the desire or will to gain wisdom. The 19th-century German philosopher Arthur Schopenhauer (1958, 1813/2007) taught that will is extremely powerful and everlasting, including the desire to explore. Indeed, the quest for wisdom is eternal, and the invention and definition of terms a continual venture. Originally, the term 'trauma' pertained to an open physical wound or a violent rupture to the surface of the skin, and carried no psychological meaning. Although the concept of 'physical trauma' had been around since the ancient Greeks, the concept of 'psychic trauma' was proposed only in the last quarter of the 19th century (Eulenburg, 1878). Psychic trauma has been defined in a variety of ways during its relatively brief history, and as we shall see different perspectives have persevered. The concept and its derivatives such as 'traumatic experiences' and 'traumatic events' continue to be used in a confusing variety of ways in the general, clinical, and scientific literature and discourse. The historian Donna Trembinski (2011, p. 82) observed that "the terminology and theoretical parameters of trauma theory have never been definitively settled and differ from scholar to scholar." Whereas achieving a consensus definition of trauma is essential for progress in the field of traumatic stress (Weathers & Keane, 2007), the definitions offered to date are, as leading traumatologists Julian Ford and Christine Courtois (2009) remarked, not particularly clear.

One major reason for the difficulty in making progress, I admit, is that the conceptualization – and hence the definition of trauma – relate to basic, albeit unresolved philosophical conundrums as well as to some 'tough' themes in psychology and psychiatry. Daunting questions include the following:

- Are traumatic experiences caused by inherently traumatizing events? Or are they rather due to subjective features? In other words, do particular events cause trauma-related disorders and diseases by their very nature – or does the impact of events relate foremost to personal, social, cultural, political, and historical features?
- Do events exist objectively, that is, do they exist at all independent of experiencing and knowing subjects? Is our whole world, including traumatizing events, perhaps in essence just an idea? Is it but a shadow of something else that we cannot perceive or know – much as Plato contended?
- Is there a natural class of events that are inherently traumatizing? Or is any category of trauma necessarily a human, and hence an artificial, construction?
- Is trauma and are human experience, thought, and behavior generally more fully explicable in terms of the brain (at least in principle)? Will we come to understand trauma in all respects the day we know everything about the brain? Or is this hope a mere tragic illusion?
- Is the mind simply an epiphenomenon of the working brain? That is, is the mind a secondary phenomenon caused by, and thus unable to affect, the brain? Is its activity a primary phenomenon, and is therefore the study of the mental features of trauma in the end irrelevant?
- Or is the mind different from the brain? Does the mind constitute a different substance altogether than brain matter? Does it possess properties that are different from those of the brain? Can we therefore understand trauma in full only by also considering the mind?
- Or are the brain and the mind perhaps in fact identical? Applied to trauma, would a complete description of the brain in trauma be identical to a complete description of the mind in trauma?
- Is the head the seat of the mind? Does trauma thus lie between the ears? Or is our mind somewhere out of our head? Is trauma as much a phenomenon beyond our head and body as within it?
- Is our body (minus the brain) sufficient unto itself? Or can it be understood only in relation to the brain as well as in relation to the individual's current and past experience and environment?
- Is it possible to understand and change human experience and thought, including trauma, in terms of the classic Western methods of science, that is, from an 'objective' third-person perspective? Or must we explore the first-person perspective, that is, the sub-

jective experience, using, say, Buddhist methods? Or would it be possible and necessary to use a combination of these traditions?

Any attempt to develop definitions of trauma and related concepts must consider these puzzles, which have been and still are often cast in terms of dichotomies. Is trauma best understood in terms of

- philosophical *materialism* (= all that really counts is matter; physics and biology, notably including materialistic neuroscience, suffice) or philosophical *idealism* (= all that exists are ideas; the world is like a dream)?
- philosophical *realism* (= there is an objective, knowable world with eternal laws that can be directly known [naïve realism]) or philosophical *constructionism* (= all we can experience and know are our own constructions of reality)?
- philosophical *dualism* (= matter – hence body – and mind are different substances or have different properties) or philosophical *monism* (= matter and mind are different attributes of a single substance)?
- *natural and universal laws* (= trauma has always existed among all cultures and is here to stay) or as a *product of modern culture* (= the phenomenon did not exist prior to the 'modern' invention of trauma, the disorder is culturally bound)?
- *exogenesis* (= trauma, understood as a psychic injury, is caused primarily by objectively existing events that are like a sharp knife inducing multiple cuts to the skin) or *endogenesis* (= trauma, the mental wound, is essentially due to subjective factors)?
- *genuine effects* (= trauma involves a real injury) or *artifacts* (= 'trauma' is about matters such as attention seeking, avoiding responsibility, seeking economic gain, suggestion, simulation, and fantasy)?

Or would some of these matters, or perhaps even all of them, somehow be simultaneously entangled?

To get a deeper feel for the conceptual and definitional problems at hand as well as for their clinical, scientific, and societal relevance, in the first chapters of this book I sketch the history of trauma (this history is thus not presented solely for its own sake). This history shows that the struggle to conceptualize, understand, and define trauma has often strongly pertained to the puzzles and apparent dichotomies mentioned above.

Within this framework, I examine in the present chapter whether in the course of written history it has been recognized that particular environmental events can cause, co-determine, or at least crucially relate to a particular kind of psychopathology? Has it been postured that psychopathology involves exogenesis (= external event induces pathology) or has the focus regarding psychopathology typically been on matters internal to individuals, thus on endogenesis (= internal condition induces pathology') rather than on environmental influences (cf. Fischer-Homburger, 1999)? Was it thought in former times that the world can be an injurious, unbearable place? Or was it rather believed that some people – whether men, women, or children – are incapable or unwilling to cope with common life and with environmental conditions that seem not to trouble other individuals?

A second issue I explore in the present chapter is whether the core features of the pathology, which according to contemporary insight are often related to experiencing adverse events, have remained relatively stable across time? And if so, have these features been associated with one disorder or rather with various disorders, whether across historical time and/or within a particular historical phase?

Still another matter that demands attention from the start is whether throughout the ages trauma-related symptoms and disorders have been foremost seen as *psycho*pathology, thus as a pathology of the mind, or whether they have been more commonly understood as *bio*pathology, for example, as an imbalance of humors or neurotransmitters?

Trauma Through the Ages

Do we function today as our ancestors once did? Is trauma the same at all times and at all places? Some philosophers, anthropologists, and psychiatrists doubt it and instead contend that trauma is a culture-bound phenomenon (Bracken, 2001; Hacking, 1995, 2002; Jones et al., 2003; Young, 1997). Within the wider debate in the history of psychology, they variously emphasize that applying modern psychological categories to individuals from the past is most problematic. In their view, trauma-related disorders came into existence only in the last decades of the 19th century. They claim that this was the time when the concept and the diagnosis of psychic trauma and its symptoms were 'invented' or at least formalized, and that a language of trauma developed. Other authors maintain that, although our experiences are colored by cultural beliefs, our ancestors were no different from us in psychological, biological, and social regards (Trembinski, 2011). They thus assert that trauma is quintessentially a phenomenon of all times and all places.

Even in remote times, it was recognized that there are relationships of all kinds between adverse events, body, and mind. However, the various ideas that scholars, survivors, and laymen have crafted regarding the kind of relationships that apply have sometimes been as capricious as the symptoms of the individuals injured by the hardships they met up with. The current selective review of the history of melancholia and hysteria attests to this. I start with melancholia, a disorder that, from the 18th century and in particular from the 19th century onward, became defined ever more in terms of sadness and depression, thus preparing the way for our contemporary understanding (Jackson, 1987). However, originally and for many ages after its first appearance in written history melancholia also captured a condition of intense anxiety.

Traumatic Melancholia

Throughout history, melancholia has been associated with any number of causes, some of which were largely endogenic in nature: The disorder was caused by factors residing within the affected individual. Other explanations focused more on changes in the environment leading to intense fear and deep sorrow. The melancholia of present interest is (1) a mental disorder that, by whatever name we call it, was or is no longer classified as hysteria or by some other name with the same referents, which includes (2) overwhelming fear or other vehement emotions (3) during and after experiencing, witnessing, or hearing about one or more adverse events, as well as (4) a subjective inability to overcome the experience, which (5) exhibits in a variety of often long-lasting physical and mental symptoms. In this sense a number of disorders that went or go by various other names – some of which refer to the kind of adverse event under consideration (e.g., "a horrible kind of melancholia," irritable heart, railway spine, traumatic neurosis, war neurosis, battered child syndrome, PTSD (American Psychiatric Association (APA), 1994, 2013) – are intimately related. While they capture at least highly similar, if not identical, conditions, it seems warranted to conveniently collect them under the label 'traumatic melancholia,' even though experiencing highly adverse events and a lack of integration of these experiences was not instantly, consistently, or uniformly seen in all cases as a main or contributing causal factor of the disorder.

Suffering from an Excess of Black Bile, Strong Emotions, and Dissociation of the Personality

The foundational works of the Hippocratic School documented that leading ancient Greek philosophers and physicians understood the body and mind as inseparable entities. This philosophical monism also applied to prominent Roman doctors such as the physician and philosopher Galen of Pergamum (129–199/217?) and medieval philosophy and medicine. Illness, it was felt, affected the body and the soul (= mind) in equal measure. The received idea was that physical and mental health was achieved by balancing the four humors: blood, phlegm, black bile, and yellow bile. In addition to this endogenic physiological interpretation, Galen and other physicians from late antiquity also believed that mental health was supported by avoiding all overwhelming emotions because these could cause a humoral imbalance. Whereas this psychological advice disappeared in medical literature by the 5th century, it would later reappear, among others in the seminal works of Spinoza in the 17th century. Spinoza may have been the first to emphasize the importance of symbolizing intense emotional experiences ("passions"), of putting them in words or other symbols ("clear and distinct ideas") rather than re enacting them recurrently. As he stated in his magnum opus *Ethica* (Part V, proposition 3): "An affect that is a passion ceases to be a passion as soon as we form a clear and distinct idea thereof." Because Spinoza thought affects are intrinsically related to environmental influences, which means that the one (affects) cannot exist without the other (environmental events), his understanding of passions involved a mixture of endogenic and exogenic influences that presuppose each other. As I shall detail later, this view reemerged in the work of some 19th-century thinkers and has been taken to its deep implications in the writings of a number of contemporary authors.

The *Internal Affections*, a collection of works by different authors, published under the name of Hippocrates (circa 400 BC), was known to Galen and copied and commented on throughout the Middle Ages. It describes the symptoms of a 'thick disease.' Black bile, it was said, initially collects in the liver, then moves upward, and finally reaches the head. The initial headache might later become complicated by a loss of clear vision and hearing as well as by hallucinations, nightmares, the inability to stand and speak, heavy breathing, and bouts of somnambulism. Yet periods of melancholic madness could be interrupted by periods of lucidity, showing that the disorder involved transitions between quite different ways of being. With respect to our understanding of trauma, these shifts in the way and level of functioning will be a recurring and essential theme. Melancholia, it was further claimed, could eventually evolve into a still graver condition called mania.

Greek, Roman, and medieval thinkers (e.g., Vincent of Beauvais, circa 1190–1264) suggested that melancholia involves an excess of black bile (melancholia literally means an [over]abundance of black bile) that might result from an individual's constitutional temperament, illness, or strong emotions. Vincent of Beauvais believed that individuals suffering from melancholy sometimes feared death – and sometimes desired it – and often killed themselves. This changeability and other capricious symptoms of melancholia Vincent observed indicate that the disorder apparently implied profound shifts between opposite affects, desires, and actions.

These shifts may have related – and continue to be related – to a crucial observation by Magister Lorentius near the end of the 13th century. He suggested that the interior, intellectual soul wanders during night terrors (Lawn, 1979). The part of a human's soul that resembles the souls of animals controls the individual's movements. Yet the intellectual soul does not wake up and indeed remains completely unaware of the bodily movements. Cast in modern terms, Lorentius thus felt that melancholia involves a dissociation of the whole, normally integrated system of biopsychosocial functions that constitutes an individual's personality. The division was between a terrified dissociative part of the personality with strong sensorimotor and emotional features, and a dissociative part that was more cognitively and less physically and emotionally oriented.

Suffering from Terror

The Ancient Greeks and Romans recognized that emotional shocks may have lasting effects. Herodotus (*The History of Herodotus*, 440 BC, Liber 6, caput 117, translation by George Rawlinson) recorded how an Athenian soldier became permanently blind after the following incident during the Battle of Marathon:

> Epizelus, the son of Cuphagoras, an Athenian, was in the thick of the fray, and behaving himself as a brave man should, when suddenly he was stricken with blindness, without blow of sword or dart; and this blindness continued thenceforth during the whole of his after life. The following is the account which he himself, as I have heard, gave of the matter: He said that a gigantic warrior, with a huge beard, which shaded all his shield, stood over against him; but the ghostly semblance passed him by, and slew the man at his side. Such, as I understand, was the tale which Epizelus told.

According to Plutarch (46–120 CE), such events as war scenes can elicit vehement fear. This terror, he contended, is most usually caused from some imminent danger, when a terrible object is at hand, heard, seen, or conceived, whether physically present or in a dream.

Ancient Arabic physicians and psychologists agreed on this matter. They categorized melancholia, which they called *huzn,* as a disease that included mental symptoms such as sadness, sorrow, and mental pain (e.g., Radden, 2000). Al-Kindi (circa 801–873 CE) linked melancholia with intense emotions such as anger, passionate love, hatred, and depression; and for Ibn Sina (980–1037 CE), known in the Western world as Avicenna, the various causes for melancholia included catastrophic events such as intrigues surrounding one's life and lost love.

Several centuries later the Oxford University scholar Robert Burton (1577–1640) would also link melancholia, at least in a number of cases, with catastrophe. In his *Anatomy of Melancholia* (1621), he emphasized that "many times the more sudden the accident, it is the more violent." Plutarch and Burton thus realized, very independently, that particularly sudden, imminent, and recurrent danger may elicit dramatic physical and emotional reactions that can take the form of melancholia.

But not just the events involved are of a special kind, Burton emphasized. The overwhelming fear that horrific events may trigger is in some regards also different from other fears. Burton reminded us that Cicero and Patritius had distinguished between fears that can arise from observing or hearing about terrible events and other fears. He quoted the Swiss physician and Basel professor Felix Plater (1536–1614; *Praxis Medica*, 1602–1608, cap. 3, de mentis alienatio), who observed that

> [of] all fears they are most pernicious and violent, and so suddenly alter the whole temperature of the body, move the soul and spirits, strike such a deep impression, that the parties can never be recovered, causing more grievous and fiercer melancholy, than any inward cause whatsoever, and imprints itself so forcibly in the spirits, brain, humours, that if all the mass of blood were let out of the body, it could hardly be extracted.

It is this type of melancholia, which relates to dreadful environmental conditions and involves the whole human organism, that I refer to as *traumatic melancholia.*

Suffering from Sadness, Terror, Nightmares, and Guilt Without a Cause?

For several centuries the writings of Plater, Burton, and André Du Laurens (1558–1609) came to strongly influence the understanding of melancholia, with little progress being make in actually grasping the causes of the disorder. Whereas, as discussed above, Plater related the most severe type of melancholia he knew to experiencing terrifying events, more generally experts had a hard time explaining the overwhelming sadness and fear that beset the patients. Du Laurens (1597; quoted in Jackson, 1987) defined melancholia as "delirium" and "a kind of dotage without any fever, having as its ordinarie companions, feare and sadness, without any apparent occasion." This lack of apparent causation was to become the standard description for a long time.

Following Plater's statement that melancholia includes feelings and thoughts of being bad, being damned, and fearing punishment, in addition to experiences of fear, sadness, despondency, and social withdrawal, in the 17th and 18th centuries the disorder became linked to guilt (Jackson, 1987). It was also observed that the patient's unfounded imaginations of beliefs might relate to a single particular theme or be only intermittent. For example, DuLaurens (quoted in Jackson, 1987) described a patient who "had not his imagination troubled, otherwise than in this one only thing, for he could speak mervailouslie well of any other thing." Still other symptoms Plater and Du Laurens listed were sleeplessness and disturbed sleep as well as hypochondria.

Melancholia long continued to be generally understood in merely physiological terms. Thomas Willis gave up the humoral explanation near the end of the 17th century and replaced it by the idea that the disorder involves abnormalities regarding the motions and proportions in mixtures of the five principles of the chemist: spirit, sulphur, salt, water, and earth. Over time, melancholia became ever more comprehended in terms of genetic and brain abnormalities as well as nervous forces. In the 20th century, psychological explanations as well as a surge of new (neuro)physiological causal interpretations came to the forefront.

Suffering from Uncontrollable Bodily and Metaphysical Forces

What about the symptoms of melancholia? Is there any ground for assuming that these included, in at least some cases, symptoms that we understand today as features of PTSD and dissociative disorders (APA, 1994, 2013)? According to Trembinski (2011), there is. While Greek, Roman, medieval, and early 'modern' practitioners had very different philosophical languages and theories of health, in her view "they nonetheless recognized similar causes of trauma and its consequent symptoms under the rubrics of melancholia and mania" (p. 86).

For example, Trembinski (2011) relates recurrent war-related night terrors of the monk Guibert of Nogent (1055–1124) in which Guibert saw the images of men being slaughtered by the sword of those whose deaths he had heard about in some detail (described in his book *Monadiae*, 1115). As a result, he developed a sleep phobia, a feature pertaining to many survivors who experience trauma-related nightmares.

Trembinski (2011) also presents the haunting nightly episodes of Sir Pierre de Béarn, who arose and even armed himself, drew his sword, and fought with someone or something. He cursed his servants who tried to wake, calm, and reorient him from his spells and called them liars. In the morning, Sir Pierre could not explain his odd behavior. The day before the onset of these frequently recurring dissociative episodes, the knight had been fighting with a bear and had only been able to kill the animal with tremendous difficulty and great danger to his own life. It seems quite likely that he was re-experiencing and re-enacting the gruesome experience at night. But because he had not, or not sufficiently, integrated the dangerous encounter into his personality, he was unable to understand his night terrors by day. Francesco Petrarch, an Italian who lost many dear ones in the plague of 1361 including his son Giovanni and his muse Laura, subsequently fell into a state of melancholy or weariness of the soul, a condition known as *acedia*.

Guibert, Sir Pierre, and Petrarch did not think to ascribe their symptoms to their terrible experiences. Guibert rather believed he was possessed by demons who were trying to keep him from living a religious life; and Sir Pierre thought he was being punished for killing a magical bear: two metaphysical, exogenic interpretations. While Petrarch did relate his sorrow to his losses, he felt that his inability to overcome his acedia involved a triumph of the desires of his body over the needs of his soul. His interpretation thus involves a form of endogenesis.

At the time Guibert's, Sir Pierre's and Petrarch's symptoms were certainly seen as manifestations of melancholia. According to current insight, the three men had symptoms of PTSD and trauma-related dissociative disorders following their terrible earthly experiences. Trembinski (2011) therefore maintains that melancholia bore similarities to the notion of trauma, both in the sense of causation (traumatizing events as an exogenic cause) and symptoms (trauma as a psychobiological injury). In my view, this conclusion is best limited to traumatic melancholia.

Suffering Men, Women, and Children

Guibert, Sir Pierre, and Petrarch – all men. Was melancholia perhaps seen largely as a male affair? Apparently not. In the second century CE Rufus of Ephesus had asserted that the disorder was more common in men, but more serious in women. According to Plater (1602–1608), the "horrible kind of melancholy," the condition that supposedly involved the body as much as the mind, "had been often brought before him, and troubles and affrights commonly men and women, young and old of all sorts." Still, many authors associated melancholia, as well as hysteria, two commonly ill-defined and overlapping disorders throughout history with the female sex (Gosling, 1987, quoted in Radden, 2000).

Suffering Previously Stable and Able Individuals

Even men of acknowledged stability and ability such as one Samuel Pepys might develop the disorder (Daly, 1983). From Pepys' detailed diary we learn how the plague caused him less stress than London's Great Fire of 1666. He wrote: "it is strange to think how to this day I cannot sleep a night without great terrors of the fire; and this very night I could not sleep to almost two in the morning through great terrors of the fire." The fear the "... horrid, malicious, blood fire ..." evoked was so great that it "... was enough to put us out of our wits" (see Daly, 1983). Pepys had recurrent nightmares about the fire, attempted to avoid reminders of the fire, developed memory problems and insomnia, became irritable, and showed some evidence of self-defense against his guilt about having saved himself and his property.

Although it is risky to diagnose mental disorders in historical figures, there is some evidence that influential persons including Achilles (Shay, 1995), Alexander the Great, Captain James Cook, the 19th-century poet Emily Dickinson, Charles Dickens, as well as Florence Nightingale had trauma-related disorders (Mackowiak & Batten, 2008). Following adverse events, all had become hypervigilant. Some turned irritable and had angry outbursts, most lost interest in activities and matters they previously enjoyed, and all developed other striking behavioral or even characterological changes. Alexander and Cook became incompetent leaders, Dickinson isolated herself to avoid cues that reminded her of overwhelming experiences, and Dickens suffered from numerous traumatic symptoms after witnessing a tragic rail accident outside of London (Trimble, 1981). Voisin (1883) described several previously well-functioning individuals who had developed a trauma-related mental disorder with dissociative symptoms when exposed to bombardments during the siege of Paris and subsequent violence in 1870–1871 (see Dorahy & Van der Hart, 2007). In literature, Henry IV and Macbeth both suffered from trauma-related psychopathology, suggesting that the features of this pathology existed and were recognized in Shakespeare's time (1564–1616). Trauma, it would seem, was not limited to commoners.

Suffering from a Secret Self

Possibly in reference to dissociation of the personality, a phenomenon often related to early childhood neglect and abuse to be discussed later, Emily Dickinson (1975) wrote that there can be an utterly scary, haunting self-lurking behind our ordinary self:

> One need not be a chamber to be haunted,
> One need not be a house;
> The brain has corridors surpassing
> Material place.

Far safer, of a midnight meeting
External ghost,
Than an interior confronting
That whiter host.

Far Safer, through an Abbey gallop,
The Stones a'chase –
Than Unarmed, one's a'self encounter -
In lonesome Place –

Ourself behind ourself, concealed –
Should startle most –
Assassin hid in our Apartment
Be Horror's least.

The Body – borrows a Revolver –
He bolts the Door –
O'erlooking a superior spectre –
Or More –

What self, what frightening, and perhaps also frightened experiencing and knowing part of the organism we are can lurk behind the 'I, myself, and me' we are more comfortable with? Would it be too wild to relate the haunted self to structures like the animalistic soul that Lorentius observed, to structures like Sir Pierre's nightly self in self-defense? Would the haunted self, the better known and more cherished self, be Lorentius' intellectual soul? And would the shifting ways of being that, in the view of a number of authors, characterize (traumatic) melancholia and the changeable presentation of affected patients more generally, perhaps relate to the existence of insufficiently integrated parts of the personality, each with its own at least rudimentary identity?

Answers to these pertinent questions require a solid understanding of what a self, what 'I, myself, me, mine' are in the first place. The effort necessary to achieve this comprehension is a returning theme of this book. For example, it reemerges when discussing hysteria, when considering commonalities between traumatic melancholia, traumatic and grand hysteria, and when defining dissociation of the personality. Chapter 12 discusses the issues involved in detail.

Suffering from a Broken Heart

If traumatic melancholia is a natural phenomenon, then the core features of this disorder must be present under whatever name employed – at all times, in all places, and in relationship to all types of terrifying events, including obviously war. Indeed, throughout the ages military physicians have documented the mental disorders of soldiers. Here are some brief examples from the 17th and 19th century. Later I will offer more elaborate examples from the 19th century as well as specifically address war trauma in the 20th century.

Soldiers suffering from 'el mal de corazon' in the 30 Years War (1614–1648) were broken and in despair ('estar roto'). Johannes Hofer (1678) described how some Swiss mercenaries who fought in France or other European countries developed symptoms such as dejection, continuing melancholy, disturbed sleep, weakness, loss of appetite, anxiety, cardiac palpitations, stupor, and fever. Believing that the condition related to homesickness, he called it 'nostalgia' (literally 'homesickness'). Whereas nostalgia would also become known as the 'Swiss disease,' *Heimweh* (a longing for home) also afflicted a number of German soldiers in the 18th century.

Similarly, American Civil War soldiers (1861 ff.) developed 'Da Costa's syndrome (nostalgia): Confronted with casualties of the American Civil War, army physician Da Costa (1871) observed symptoms of increased arousal, irritability, and elevated heart rate in combat-exposed soldiers. He called it 'irritable heart,' but the condition was later generally referred to as 'Da Costa's syndrome' or 'soldier's heart.' It also became known as 'neurasthenia,' 'nervous exhaustion,' or 'nervous debility' (Beard, 1869).

The term 'soldier's heart' stands for a set of symptoms that suggest, but do not in fact pertain, to heart disease. Apart from heart palpitations, the men might also suffer from intense fear, tremors, paralysis, and any number of other symptoms now recognized as reactions to the horrors of the battlefield. So many soldiers were affected, that the US military had to establish the first military hospital. Probably guided mainly by military interests, they were not generally seen as brave men who broke under tremendous pressure at some point, but as cowards or otherwise inadequate individuals. The cause of nostalgia, neurasthenia, and the soldier's heart was thus not sought in extreme environmental conditions (an exogenic interpretation), but in the affected individual (an endogenic view). The men were at fault, not the harsh world forced upon them.

Suffering from a Shaken Spine or Brain

A seemingly new, adverse, event-related syndrome would emerge in the course of the 19th century. Had until that age wars mostly affected army personnel, and had dramas at sea remained largely invisible to the public at large, the now widespread railway system might bring its own particular joys and sorrows to anyone. Riding the trains was generally safe, but major accidents did happen (Harrington, 2010). Along with the surgeons Sir Benjamin Brodie (1837) and John Erichsen (1866), many physicians believed that the bodily and mental symptoms some individuals developed following these accidents were due to a somatic injury (The Lancet, 1862), more specifically to a concussion of the spine (see Caplan, 1995, 2010; Harrington, 1994, 2010). Hence the name of the disorder: 'railway spine.' The trouble was, however, that this exogenic, biological understanding did not fit the observation that individuals' whose spine has *not* been shaken also developed the condition's symptoms. *The Lancet*, a leading journal, carefully noted at the time that the accidents might cause primary and secondary effects. The primary symptoms involved evident physical injuries such as broken bones, lacerations, and burns; the secondary mental and physical effects, largely hidden from direct view, included an astounding broad range of symptoms such as "giddiness, loss of memory, pain in the back and head" (The Lancet, 1862, p. 157), "tingling and numbness of the extremities, local paralysis, paraplegia, functional leasions of the kidney and bladder" as well as "slowly ensuing symptoms of intellectual derangement" (The Lancet, 1862, p. 156). Erichsen also listed concentration problems, fear, sleeping disorders, nightmares, stiffening of the extremities, and speech problems.

Feeling that almost all railway collisions could have been prevented, many blamed the railway companies. Some victims took these companies to court and pressed financial charges. If only in this context, victims and their lawyers had an interest in finding a somatic cause to the illness. Pure mental causation was neither charming nor convincing for the major part of the 19th century. At this time, physicians were so dedicated to reducing the mind to the body, the mental to the physical, that in their view only a physical explanation of mental phenomena counted as a true scientific explanation (Fisher-Homburger, 1999). Diseases that did not appear to have a physical cause could not possibly be authentic, real disorders. Throughout history the line from beliefs in mental causation to accusations of moral weakness, simulation, suggestion, and fantasy has never been long, certainly never winding, and always tempting. As I discuss in later chapters, some professionals and citizens travel this road to this very day.

Physicians and lawyers hired to defend the interests of the railway companies were thus motivated to reject any somatic interpretation of railway spine and replace it by a mental explanation. It was peculiarly felt that, if the problem was in the mind, then the railway companies were not responsible for the survivors' pathology and suffering. *The Lancet*'s position on the matter of physical and mental causation was ambivalent, but eventually included aspects of both physical disruption of the nervous system and organic damage. As the journal stated (cited in Harrington, 2010, p. 42), the severe physical shock during the accident results "in the nervous system being shaken, and, for a time, sometimes considerably weakened" (January 18, 1862, p. 84). This weakening, this "impairment of nervous forces" (February 8, 1862, p. 158) results in a disruption of the action of muscles and organs throughout the body. In this context, railway spine became so to speak 'railway brain.'

Suffering from Intense Fear

Erichsen came to change his original view in 1875 (see Harrington, 2010). Faced with the frequent lack of evidence of spinal or other organic lesions, he started to favor the idea of fright-related unconscious mental or moral causation. The recognition of the possibility that railway spine had both physical and mental origins would have a major impact on both the medical and legal thought of the day (e.g., Jordan, 1873; Le Gros Clark, 1868). Railway company surgeon Herbert Page (1891) particularly emphasized the role of fear; he did not deny that fright may relate to an underlying physiological process of some kind, but stressed that intense fear as a mental phenomenon came first.

In this regard, Page (1891) was strongly influenced by views of another popular disorder, hysteria. By the end of the 19th century, hysteria had come to be seen as a disorder that essentially involved one or more 'fixed ideas.' These fixed ideas pertained to strong fear-related mental impressions that have become rigid and dominant, and that affect the nervous system. Page thus regarded railway spine and hysteria as disorders that primarily involve mental causation. In fact he felt that posttraumatic disorders and hysteria involved the same psychological and biological processes.

Whereas Page was influenced by this late-19th century perspective on hysteria, Jean-Martin Charcot (1889) in the last years of his life showed a particular interest in Page's views on railway spine. This French-English cross-fertilization invites an examination of the historical understanding of hysteria, as well as of the relationship between traumatic melancholia (and its descendants including railway spine) and hysteria (and its offspring). This exploration forms the topic of the next chapter on the evolution of the trauma concept.

Chapter 2

Traumatic Hysteria and Grand Hysteria

Hysteria is of all times and places.
Jean-Martin Charcot

Hysteria is dead.
Étienne Trillat

The history of hysteria is as long as it is enlightening for our understanding of the human struggle to come to terms with a whimsical condition that defies the body-mind distinction, and it raises deep questions regarding causation by environmental and personal features.

Suffering from a Dry Womb

It has long been believed that Hippocrates, the "Father of Medicine," first described hysteria (Littré, 1839–1861; Veith, 1965). However, the writings subsumed under his name include the works of various authors who did not use the term 'hysteria' at all (King, 1993; Trillat, 1986). What appears in these texts is the adjective *hysterikos* (hysteric), a purely physical description of cause meaning 'coming from the womb' and 'suffering from the womb.' As the historian Helen King (1993) details, the *hysterikos* conditions involved a variety of diseases that the Hippocratic authors regarded as real and organic. They believed that the womb (Gr.: *hystera*) can become light and dry due to a lack of bodily fluids. A prominent cause of this fluid shortage was menstrual suppression, but it might also relate to insufficient food, exhaustion, and sexual abstinence. The ancient Greek thus combined an endogenic view (troubles of the uterus) with an exogenic perspective (lack of moisturizing food and semen). Looking for moisture, the womb would move to different parts within the body. It was this "dislocation" that generated the symptoms of the *hysterikos* ailments. For the Hippocratic authors many disorders thus related to uterine abnormalities. According to one of them, the "wandering womb" even constituted the essence of *all* female illnesses.

The cure was achieved by stimulation of various kinds: intercourse, marriage, pregnancy, scent therapy, irritant pessaries, and various herbal mixtures that were administered per mouth or nose – or direct to the woman's vulva. Despite appearances the point of the treatment was not sexual gratification – as the psychoanalyst and classicist Simon (1978) believed – but the moistening of the dry womb and the restoration of blood circulation.

In the second century BC post-Hippocratic writers introduced the expression *hysterike pnix*, which means 'suffocation of the womb' (King, 1993). Pliny the Elder stated how a mixture of mustard and vinegar might rouse women from *vulvarum conversione suffocatas*, that is, from suffocation by the turning of the womb (see King, 1983). Many ancient authors discuss how difficult it could be to know whether the suffocated woman was in fact dead or still alive. The mixture could make her sneeze, a welcome sign of life. Sneezing was also provoked to expel various kinds of matter that at the time were presumed to cause illness. It is tempting to relate *hysterike pnix* to the contemporary temporal lobe epilepsy and pseudoepilepsy, also described as dissociative convulsions and loss of consciousness (World Health Organization, 1992).

Suffering from Black Bile, the Devil, or Demons

Other descriptions and explanations of hysterical conditions would follow. For example, Galen proposed they were due to uterine retention of substances such as blood and seed. Also, retention of black bile would lead to despondency. Although Galen was highly influential, womb movement remained the dominant description for centuries to come. Only at the end of the 16th century and in the early decades of the 17th century were uterus-centered views seriously challenged. In the same epoch, the tragic medieval exogenic belief that hysterical women were possessed by devils and demons started to lose ground, which would eventually put an end to these patients' persecution as witches. The last were tried in the 1730s (Rousseau, 1993).

Not all hysterical women were persecuted, though. Less horrible, though still appalling, were efforts to exorcize the Devil or demons who, it was believed, had taken possession of their body and mind. Demonic possession would later be reinterpreted as trauma-related hysteria in 19th-century French psychiatry (Ellenberger, 1970; Van der Hart, Lierens, & Goodwin, 1996). According to this view, the personality of individuals with hysteria had become divided in two or more subsystems or parts, commonly in the context of childhood abuse and neglect. Some of these parts imitate perpetrators and verbally or physically attack other parts. In particular in the Middle Ages – but not only then – for many patients, the clergy, and still others, it was precisely these features that signaled the presence and works of malevolent metaphysical entities.

Jeanne Fery, a 25-year-old nun who described her own exorcism in 1584 and 1585, is probably the first known case of severe and chronic dissociation of the personality that relates to childhood traumatization (Bourneville, 1886; Van der Hart et al., 1996). Her exorcists gave an even more detailed account of the treatment that proved to be effective. Jeanne had the classic 19th-century major symptoms of hysteria, as Bourneville recognized. They are currently known as cognitive-emotional or psychoform dissociative symptoms as well as sensorimotor or somatoform dissociative symptoms. She also had other trauma-related symptoms such as various tendencies toward self-mutilation and suicide attempts. As Van der Hart et al. (1996) recount, several dissociative parts influenced Jeanne or took full control over her consciousness and behavior. For example, she sometimes acted in a child-like manner, was mute, sobbed on end, suffered intense physical pain, displayed dissociative blindness, or apparently lost consciousness in pseudoepileptic attacks.

Whereas a trauma-related interpretation of possession thus evolved only in 19th-century French thought, near the end of the 17th century the idea took hold that hysteria is a natural physical disease, not a matter of supernatural possession (see Trimble, 1982). In his book *The Suffocation of the Mother*, Edward Johnson (1569–1632) explained that hysteria is

> ... an affect of the mother or wombe wherein the principle parts of the bodie by consent do suffer ... [These] ... are the seates of the three faculties which do govern the whole bodie. The brain of the animal, the hart of the vital, the liver of the naturall ... these parts are affected in this disease and do suffer in their functions as they are diminished, depraved or abolished, according to the nature and plenty of the humor and temperament and situation of the mother.

Suffering from the Whole Body

Although hysteria was still considered to be centered in the womb, with Johnson the disease came to be seen as a functional disease of the whole body, including the brain. In this he followed the 16th-century Dutch physician Jan Wier (1515 or 1516–1588; see Cobben, 1976), who had stated that hysteria was not a matter of devils and witches, but rather a bodily disease that had to be understood solely through its signs and symptoms. With Wier hysteria became medicalized.

A further change and widening of the concept of 'hysteria' was soon to follow. Charles Lepois (1563–1633), a personal physician to Henry II of France, agreed that hysteria was not only an anatomic condition; all symptoms would rather "come from the head" (see Jackson, 1987). This change in perspective allowed *men* to enter hysteria's picture. As Lepois described in the 1620s, hysterical symptoms were now not foreign to the strong sex. Before long the ancient idea that the womb is prime mover of hysteria would meet empirical falsification. Postmortem examinations informed Thomas Willis (1612–1673) and Thomas Sydenham (1624–1689) that the womb of afflicted women was completely normal. Along with this reformulation of organic causes, Robert Burton linked hysteria to the male condition of hypochondria, in which the spleen was believed to emit 'vapors.' In his view, hypochondria and hysteria constituted forms of melancholia.

Willis followed and extended Jordan's lead in stating that the nerves of hysterical, melancholic, hypochondriacal individuals were abnormal. Building on concepts introduced by Galen, he proposed that the brain excretes animal spirits, a fictitious entity largely analogous to the contemporary concept of 'nerve impulse' (Eadie, 2003a). In his view, the nerves had the capacity to transmit the 'sensitive soul' (a concept dating back to Aristotle) via neural conductors and animal spirits. These intrinsically normal material spirits, thus, bridge the feeling mind and the body. In hysteria, the animal spirits possess explosive features, whereas in melancholia they are nonexplosive in nature. With Lepois and Willis, not the moisture-seeking womb moved upward, but the presumed spatial center of the disorder. Hysteria had started to be seen as a disorder of the central and peripheral nervous system.

As noted before, the ancient Greeks did not distinguish between body and mind, believing that individuals constitute one system. Their understanding of hysterical ailments and their treatment thereof was basically materialistic in nature. Apart from the medieval persuasion that supernatural forces were involved, the organic view of hysterical disorders had dominated the field up to the 17th century. Willis' body-mind dualism fits this perspective quite well.

Suffering from the Emotional Mind

Sydenham, however, recognized that in many cases hysteria involved an emotional disturbance that runs parallel to physical disease and depression (Dewhurst, 1966). Whereas he probably overdiagnosed mental disorder – patients with apparent hysteria may have had physical diseases more often than he suspected – Sydenham was a pioneer in the understanding that hysteria can result from mental causes. In fact he regarded hysteria as a disease of the whole person, whether male or female, as a disorder that somehow related to the convergence of the mind and nerves. This mysterious convergence, he felt, was mediated by the elusive 'animal spirits.' If hysteria were more prevalent among women than among men, then this was because of their weaker constitution, their more sensitive nervous system.

Sydenham was also the first to suggest that hysteria imitates other diseases, and that it is itself in fact somehow an imitation of civilization (Rousseau, 1993). He observed that the disorder related to tensions and stresses within the culture surrounding the patient, a feature foreign to other disorders. This thought involves a move in the direction of a mixed endogenic (sensitive nervous system, psychological factors)-exogenic (environmental influences) view of hysteria. Whereas the symptoms of hysteria, such as involuntary loss of consciousness, fits, twitching, nervous tics, as well as eating and sleeping disorders, remain constant over time, Sydenham claimed that the cultural stressors eliciting this pathology varied.

Still, despite his groundbreaking view of hysteria as a quintessentially psychological disorder rather than a physical disease, and despite the recognition that hysterical conditions could afflict men – Sydenham concurred with Lepois in this regard – the idea of uterine causation would survive two more centuries. Some (bad) ideas are simply die-hards.

Suffering from Sensibility Gone Awry

By the early 18th century it was felt that the main cause of hysteria would involve less environmental stressors than the state of the individual's nerves and the animal spirits that control the nervous system (Cheyne, 1733; Rousseau, 1993). George Cheyne and other medical authors of the time studied what they called "The English Malady," also known as hysteria in women and hypochondria in men, as a disorder relating to overstrained 'nerves.' They believed that some individuals had ultrasensitive nerves, a feature more common in women than in men.

'Sensibility of nerves' is a concept that emerged in Britain following John Locke's *Essay Concerning Human Understanding* (1689/1836). As Locke (1632–1704) wrote (p. 60):

> [i]f it shall be demanded then, when a man begins to have any ideas? I think the true answer is, when he first has any sensation. For since there appear not to be any ideas in the mind, before the senses have conveyed any in, I conceive that Ideas in the Understanding, are coeval with Sensation; which is such an Impression or Motion, made in some part of the Body, as makes it be taken notice of in the Understanding.

Locke was probably inspired by the Dutch philosopher Spinoza (1632–1677), who had conceded that "[t]he human mind does not know the human body itself, nor does it know that it exists, except through the ideas of affections by which the body is affected" (1677/1996, p. 47).[1] At the time, sensibility was generally perceived as a virtue, albeit a fragility. It provided a keener perception, such as a delicate appreciation of the feelings of another, as well as a higher awareness of beauty and moral truth. However, sensibility that went over the top caused physical and emotional weakness.

Influenced by Newtonian mechanics, Cheyne and like-minded physicians felt that "no reflex, no disturbance of consciousness, no sensation or motor response, was to be admitted without presuming some prior organic disturbance communicated via the senses and the nerves" (Rousseau, 1993, p. 151). Within this mechanical, philosophical materialistic edifice, the nerve doctors were not blind to psychogenic causation of hysteria, but strongly focused on "a neurology of solids, an iatromathematics of forces, a neural web of nerves, spirits, and fibers" (Rousseau, 1993, p. 165). "Every change of the Mind indicates a change in the Bodily Organs," Robinson asserted in 1729. Hysteria, it was felt, required the anal-

1 Spinoza (see Nadler, 1999) had a major influence on the representatives of the Enlightenment (Israel, 2001) such as Locke. Locke lived in Rotterdam during his exile and, although they were banned, he possessed Spinoza's books.

ysis of the human nervous system and need not be concerned with mental issues that were not open to a mechanical understanding.

The gain was twofold. First, the well-to-do that filled Cheyne's practice and those of other leading physicians of the time could suffer from hysteria without being seen as lunatics or as malingerers seeking economic gains. They were not mad or fraudulent, but had a real, organic ailment. Second, medicine became respectable. Following the successful path of Newtonian physics, the nerve doctors were less likely to be regarded as quacks and mountebanks. They were studying the physics of the body, not the mysteries of the mind. The patients were respectable, and so were their healers. Still, in the 18th century there existed no clear boundary between madness and hysteria. Even if the term 'hysteria' was not used in books on madness – an acknowledged mind disease – the symptoms being presented were very similar, and the language used to describe madness and hysteria was practically the same. It was sensed that hysteria might be somehow close to madness, while realizing the bridge was apparently too dangerous.

With the physician Andrew Combe (1797–1847) and the phrenologists, the notion that hysteria is due to a functional disorder in "the action of the organs of the mind" gained ground (Combe, 1831; Trimble 1981). But the crucial notion to evolve in the 19th century was that hysteria can, in at least a very considerable number of cases, be related to emotional reactions to adverse life events that came to be seen as traumatizing (Briquet, 1859; Carter, 1853; Charcot, 1889; Mitchell, 1885; Janet, 1889; Breuer & Freud, 1893–1895). The understanding of some kind causal link between hysteria and adverse events had taken thousands of years to emerge, and this newborn creature was to have a conflicted childhood and adolescence extending, as I will discuss later, to this day.

Suffering from Abuse and Neglect, or from Imaginary Movements of the Womb?

Pierre Briquet (1796–1881) joined his predecessors, such as the physicians Jordan, Willis, Cheyne, and Combe, in understanding hysteria as a disorder of the nervous system. Women were particularly at risk: Due to their highly sensitive nervous system, they are more impressionable and sensitive by nature than men. Briquet thus also concurred with the physicians of the Enlightenment that female sensibility was, at least in principle, as noble as it was important. He specifically emphasized that it furthered the caretaking of children, the elderly, and the poor and the sick, which he regarded as women's primary societal role. In this he anteceded contemporary insights regarding the major role of empathy with respect to the development of secure attachment in the child as well as the parental regulation of affects of infants, toddlers, and older children who are unable to regulate themselves. Empathy puts Shakespeare's line "Frailty, thy name is woman!" in perspective.

Based on his empirical study of hysteria, later also labeled Briquet's syndrome or somatization disorder, Briquet (1859) asserted that intense and chronic bouts of sadness and fear, or still other hurtful 'affective impressions' elicited by adverse events, can exert a negative influence on the 'affective part' of the brain. In this he reiterated observations made by Sydenham and the 18th-century physician Joseph Raulin (1758) that hysteria relates to vehement and distressing emotions. Thus affected, Briquet proposed, the patient develops a natural sensibility that can increase to great heights and provoke manifold, capricious as well as intense bodily and emotional reactions to hysteria. These reactions included the ones that Pierre Janet would soon classify as "dissociative symptoms." The adverse life events particularly included abuse, maltreatment, and emotional neglect of children by their parents, maltreatment of women by their husbands, molestation, and relational upsets. Briquet found that one third of the children he studied had been maltreated by their father and/or mother, treated harshly, or strongly deprived.

He could find nothing wrong with the patients' body, implying that the problem had to be of a mental nature. However, mental functioning related to brain functioning. Briquet's ideas and empirical findings were sufficiently powerful to put the longstanding belief that hysterical conditions involve an exclusively or predominantly endogenous disease of the female reproductive organs finally to rest.

In complete contrast to Cheyne and his colleagues, who had contended that hysteria is a disease of upper classes, Briquet documented the fact that hysteria was actually far more prevalent in the lower classes. A quarter of all lower-class women, he determined, were afflicted, but only a small proportion of lower-class men. It appeared that women of the lower classes were sensible enough to be afflicted by hysteria after all. Children could develop hysteria before puberty, but the disorder was most frequent among adolescents between 12 and 24 years, and rarely emerged beyond those years. There might also be a hereditary component because a quarter of the girls whose mother had hysteria developed the condition themselves. Another finding was that the disorder was as prevalent in urban environments as in rural areas.

Had the stubborn belief in the uterine causation of hysteria finally been halted, a new idea was eager to take its place: the thought that the disorder was not real, but somehow imaginary. This new idea was to be as persistent as the old idea it replaced. It is ironic that the Hippocratic corpus includes neither the idea of hysteria as a singular disorder nor the view that hysterical afflictions can involve imaginary disorders. These ideas, says Helene King (1993), are rather 19th-century distortions. It was Emile Littré, the French translator of the Hippocratic corpus, who inserted the heading *Hystérie* to several passages in the three volumes of the *Gynaikeia* (1851–1853; translated as Diseases of Women, Robb, 1892). Subsequent authors, including Littré's translator in English, Robb (1892), and Veith (1965) seem to have followed Littré's rewriting blindly. More serious distortions of the original texts relate to Littré's inserted beliefs that hysteria pertains to *imaginary* movement of the womb, and that hysteria must be distinguished from an organic disorder that involves actual uterine displacement. As King (1993) reports, he thus added comments to the original texts such as "This section appears to be a confusion of imaginary with real movements of the womb," mystifying the original Hippocratic corpus.

Suffering from *tare nerveuse, agents provocateurs,* and Fixed Ideas

Jean-Martin Charcot (1825–1893) concurred with Briquet that hysteria might relate to events that had been traumatizing for the individual. He believed that these *nevroses traumatiques* (traumatic neuroses) or *hystéro-traumatiques* (traumatic hysteria) were the combined result of a *tare nerveuse,* that is, a constitutional predilection to nervous degeneration, and an environmental *agent provocateur.* The idea of a *tare nerveuse* can be seen as a mental version of the idea of a physical vulnerability, that had been developed by surgeons at the beginning if the 19th century. This physical vulnerability, so it was thought, influenced how an organism reacts to a physical injury. The organism's reaction to such wounds would also be negatively influenced by mental disorders that included hysteria and melancholia as well as drunkenness and pregnancy. Surgeons, thus, had started to look beyond the physical rupture and were now open to the idea that the mental affects the physical (mental causation). It was in this emerging climate that Charcot developed his views on hysteria and melancholia.

The agent provocateur was deemed not to be traumatizing in itself, but rather it elicited the development of the disorder in individuals with the hereditary weakness. Charcot came to this conclusion because not all individuals exposed to some agent provocateur in fact developed traumatic hysteria: This happened only in those who experienced or recalled the event as traumatic. There could thus be no direct causal link between an agent provocateur and traumatic hysteria. Rather, Charcot contended that an agent provocateur can provoke a hypnotic-like state of mind in which the individual develops particular ideas that become rigid (agent provocateur → hereditary weakness → hypnotic state → fixed ideas = hysteria). In his ideogenetic view, these fixed ideas constitute the very heart of the symptoms of the disorder. A patient with traumatic hysteria with a paralyzed leg would thus have developed the fixed idea that his leg had become paralyzed in the context of the accident.

The symptoms of traumatic hysteria included the phenomena that had been observed for ages, and that had been linked to hysterical afflictions, melancholia, and hypochondria. For Charcot the most common ones were anesthesias including loss of consciousness, hyperesthesias (e.g., chest pain, headache), paralyses, and contractures. In addition to these motor and sensory disturbances of the arms and legs (or even other body parts), the manifestations pertained mostly to heart palpitations and irregular pulse, dizziness, constipation, trembling, and fatigue. In many cases, the patients also had emotional symptoms such as insomnia and nightmares, all kinds of phobias, confusion, and concentration problems as well as memory problems and low intellectual performance.

The agents provocateurs that Charcot described included foremost working-place accidents in railway, industrial, and artisan settings, other physical accidents such as a dogbite or burns, assaults, war scenes, unrequited love, a disruption of romantic life, dissolution of a marriage, and even fright from thunder and lightning. Charcot also recognized that a recent provocative event might trigger nightmares and other symptoms related to earlier adverse events such as wartime experiences.

But what about childhood abuse and neglect and abuse by the patient's spouse, the adversities that Briquet had marked as a frequent cause of hysteria in impressionable individuals? Charcot mentioned only in passing that some female patients with hysteria had suffered abusive sexual experiences in childhood and adolescence, or even rape. He neither recognized nor acknowledged that these events constituted agents provocateurs nor did he classify the cases involved as traumatic hysteria, but rather regarded them as cases of *grande hystérie*. A telling example is Charcot's famous patient Augustine, who came to him with a variety of symptoms that included paralysis and anesthesia of particular body parts, right abdominal pain, and dissociative convulsions. She had been boarded out to relatives until the age of 6 years, had received severe punishments at the hands of priests and nuns, and had experienced repeated attempts at exorcism which included dousing in ice-cold water, when it was believed that her symptoms were signs of possession by the Devil. When it appeared that the exorcism had failed, her mother took her 15-year-old daughter to the Salpêtrière, the hospital where Charcot worked as a doctor and educator, and abandoned her there.

Photographs of her body positions and facial expressions during her 'hysterical crises' have been interpreted by some as a sheer effect of Charcot's suggestions and of watching other patients' hysterical crises. However, it has also been conjected that her symptoms included at least in part re-enactments of her traumatic experiences, and that her symptoms of anesthesia and pain related to the abuse. Whereas Augustine told Charcot that her mother's employer and lover had raped her several times from the time she was 13 years old, and whereas he knew about her other ordeals, it seems he never realized that her peculiar behaviors during the crises might be intimately related to her horrible life experiences, that they might be fixed ideas grounded in the abuse and neglect she had suffered.

The photographs show that Augustine sometimes had a normal appearance, and that she in fact looked older than she was at the time. During her crises, she was sometimes frightened and sometimes enraged. Did her personality perhaps include different subsystems, different parts that were insufficiently integrated with each other, and that some of these were fixated in traumatic memories, as Pierre Janet might have felt (see below)? The expression of frightened and frightening selves behind her cooler, calmer, and more collected self? This possibility fits the fact that, dissatisfied with Charcot's treatment, she eventually escaped the Salpêtrière dressed as a man. Is it a wild conjecture that her personality included one or more dissociative parts with a male identity who refused to be an abused female? Or was the cross-dressing merely a disguise to escape the famous man and his staff, who neither understood nor helped her to recover? Was Augustine trying to please Charcot and the public that attended his demonstrations of patients when she was producing her doctor's idea on what constituted the features of grand hysteria? Was she seeking acceptance by a caretaker when she fell in love with Charcot? Adopting pleasing behavior characterizes many girls and women like Augustine who attempt to gain the love of their emotionally neglectful and abusive caretakers or other perpetrators. Some please them in sexualized ways to gain at least some control over them.

In any case, there may not have been any essential differences between traumatic hysteria and grand hysteria. Perhaps Charcot was selectively blind to sexual abuse and emotional neglect as potential agents provocateurs. He had a keen eye for the role of other potentially traumatizing events and clearly knew Briquet's pioneering observations in this regard. Moreover, Briquet was not a lone 19th-century voice addressing child abuse and its consequences. In 1857, two years prior to the publication of Briquet's magnum opus, the first edition of Auguste Ambroise Tardieu's (1818–1879) book *Etude médico-légale sur les attentats aux moeurs* saw the light of day. Six more elaborate editions were to follow (e.g., Tardieu, 1860, 1878). A physician and pre-eminent medical forensic specialist, Tardieu described sex crimes, including the sexual abuse of children by relatives and others, and the physical damage they might cause. The 1878 edition of the book includes the finding that over 75% of all the rapes or attempted rapes tried in French courts were being committed against children under 16 years old. Most of them were girls under 12 years old.

It seems that psychogenic blindness and *belle indifference* – in Charcot's case, overlooking or ignoring childhood emotional, sexual, and physical abuse as interpersonal agents provocateurs – are not limited to patients with hysteria. They can apparently also affect brilliant minds. In fact, it can happen to whole professions, cultures, and humankind as a whole. For example, why did the concept of 'psychic trauma' only come to be formally invented in the 19th century? And why did most professionals, institutions, and laymen continue to overlook and ignore childhood traumatization even when this concept eventually emerged in human thought? Some legal authorities and other clinicians sharply criticized Tardieu's empirical findings and conclusions, whereas others preferred to ignore it (Labbé, 2005; Masson, 1984). As Tardieu himself wrote in 1878 (p. 70), "[t]his study, undertaken eighteen years ago, is the first to have been attempted on this subject, about which writers in the field of legal medicine have subsequently remained completely silent." The sad fact is that the field would remain mostly silent for another century before directing its attention to childhood neglect and abuse on any significant scale. Discovering childhood abuse and neglect does not come easy. Tardieu's publications on the terrible working conditions of young boys and girls in mines and factories were far more influential (Labbé, 2005). For example, his study of child and adult copper workers led to a radical improvement in their working conditions.

Just as there may not have been essential differences between traumatic hysteria and grand hysteria, Charcot and Page noticed strong commonalities between traumatic hysteria and railway spine. However, Page was not fond of hysteria because of the vagueness of the term. Charcot, in turn, did not think that there was anything special about the potential pathological consequences of railway collisions. While largely overlooking or ignoring sexual abuse and childhood traumatization, he emphasized that *any* adverse event might act as an agent provocateur.

Suffering from Adverse Events, Vehement Emotions, and Dissociation of the Personality

Pierre Janet (1889) concurred with Charcot that adverse events can trigger 'vehement' emotions and dissociation of the personality, but he did not overlook sexual abuse (Van der Hart Nijenhuis, & Steele, 2006; Van der Kolk & Van der Hart, 1989). His clinical observations taught him that two major and closely related factors determined the outcome. By their very nature some events can be more or less threatening and distressing for practically anyone and in this context lower the subject's capacity to integrate the experience in his or her life history. In his words, vehement emotions evoked by adverse events "produce their disintegrative effects in proportion to their intensity, duration, and repetition" (Janet, 1909, p. 1556). However, just how disintegrating the events are also depends on the individual's pre-existing integrative capacity. Janet (1907, p. 332) noted that, when the capacity to integrate the experiences is insufficient, a dissociation of the survivor's personality in two or more "systems of ideas and functions" is bound to follow. Each of these subsystems of an individual's personality is characterized by a 'retraction of the field of consciousness,' that is, by an unduly small attentional field. In trauma, one or more 'systems of ideas and functions' are fixated in, that is, excessively focused on the traumatic memory that continues to exist in a largely sensorimotor and highly emotional, thus non-symbolized form. Janet suggested that the typical, rather simple reflex-like actions and reactions of these kinds of dissociative subsystems may relate to a trauma-related regression of brain functioning to phylogenetically earlier phases.

These subsystems of the traumatized individual's personality remain dissociated from the rest of the personality, which typically entails a (far) more complex system of ideas and functions, at least some of which are fixed. A crucial feature of this 'rest' is that it fears and avoids the dissociative part (or parts) that is (are) fixed in the traumatic experience(s). Janet (1904) described this fear and avoidance as the phobia of the traumatic memory.

He explained that integrative actions can be demanding. For example, it is hard to be fully attentive at all times and to keep the mind from drifting from the present to the past or some anticipated future. Integrative actions become excessively difficult when they pertain to adverse events, in particular when the adversity is chronic and severe, and when the affected individual is young and requires the assistance of trusted others to succeed.

The integration of any experience and fact includes several actions: 'synthesis,' 'personification,' and 'presentification' (see Van der Hart et al., 2006). Synthesis stands for creating cohesion and coherence among current sensorimotor, emotional, cognitive, and behavioral actions (Janet, 1907; Kant, 1787/1998). For example, an abused child must synthesize pain, fear, freeze reactions, and thoughts like "this is horrible." Personification entails linking these syntheses so that they become the agent ("I freeze") and owner ("The experience happens to me"). Presentification is the action of connecting one's personified syntheses with each other to form a life history (Janet, 1928a). The connection must be such that the actual present is experienced and perceived as the most real. The near past and anticipated future should also be quite real for the individual, and generally more real than the distant past and anticipated future. Presentification of the past commonly implies a symbolization that entails putting experiences in symbols. Normal autobiographical memories are thus mostly stories told, that is, narratives. 'Realization' is more than experiencing and judging whether an event or fact is real. It also involves acting responsibly on the basis of the experienced and known reality.

Trauma involves major problems of integration (Van der Hart et al., 2006). For example, bodily anesthesia and emotional anesthesia reflect incomplete syntheses. Depersonalization symptoms involve a lack of personification, and sensorimotor and emotional re-enactment of traumatic memories constitute a lack of presentification. These symptoms relate to a lack of integration of the personality, because what traumatized individuals do not synthesize, personify, presentify, and realize is in fact not gone from them.

Janet categorized the symptoms of this dissociation of the personality in two major groups (Janet, 1901/1977; Nijenhuis, 2004; Van der Hart, Van Dijke, Van Son, & Steele, 2000). By expressing that negative symptoms or losses such as dissociative amnesia and dissociative anesthesia are invariable features of hysteria, he referred to them as 'mental stigmata.' Positive symptoms or intrusions are more variable across different patients; these he called 'mental accidents.' The most extreme mental accident actually included a behavioral accident, that is, a shift in the dominance of behavior and consciousness from one dissociative part to another. Less profound accidents pertained to intrusions of features of one dissociative part into the experiential, perceptual, emotional, cognitive, and motor domain of another part. For example, one dissociative part may hear the voice, experience the bodily and emotional feelings, and perceive the perceptions that 'belong to' another part. One dissociative subsystem may be unable to control particular bodily movements, which happens when these are controlled by another dissociative subsystem.

In sum, according to Janet, hysteria involves low integrative capacity, overly selective attention, and a division of the personality as a whole system in two or more subsystems. This condition is caused by an intricate combination of exogenic and endogenic factors. The division can be more or less complex, and it manifests itself in mental stigmata (losses) and mental accidents (intrusions). Janet formulated his theory of hysteria in psychological terms and resisted the tendency to come up with physiological explanations that may sound impressive, but that in fact explain very little (1907, pp. 321–322):

> Thus, I shall perhaps surprise you by telling you that there is no opposition between the definitions [of hysteria] that gloriously entitle themselves physiological and those that modestly call themselves psychological. No doubt, there would be a great difference if these authors had seen, really seen, a lesion characteristic of the neurosis, and if they had connected the evolution of the disease with this lesion. Never fear, one can make, nowadays, a so-called physiological definition at smaller cost. It is enough to take the most commonplace psychological definitions and replace their terms with words vaguely borrowed from the language of anatomy and the current physiological hypotheses. Instead of saying, "The function of language is separated from the personality," one will proudly say, "The centre of speech has no longer any commu-

nication with the higher centres of association." Instead of saying, "The mental synthesis appears to be diminished," one will say, "The higher centre of association is benumbed," and the feat will be done.

Suffering from Hypnoid States Containing Reminiscences of Sexual Abuse

In their *Studien über Hysterie*, Breuer and Freud (1893–1895) held a position that included many of Charcot's and Janet's essential ideas on the disorder. Freud was strongly influenced at the time by these French conceptualizations of hysteria and brought them to Vienna following his Parisian excursion. For example, Breuer and Freud stated that patients with hysteria include a 'hypnoid state' or *condition seconde*, as Charcot had called it. This state can intrude on "waking life" (p. 64) or "normal consciousness" (p. 67). During a hysterical attack, a hypnoid state has even become dominant. Hypnoid states involve nonintegrated reminiscences, highly emotional, sensorimotor re-enactments of traumatic experiences that tend to be reactivated by salient reminders of the involved events. Both ideas stemmed from Janet, as did the idea that a dissociation of different states of consciousness is the hallmark of hysteria, whatever its degree of severity:

> The longer we have been occupied with these [hysterical phenomena from psychical traumas, p. 62] the more we have become convinced that *the splitting of consciousness which is so striking in the well-known classical cases under the form of* 'double conscience' *is present to a rudimentary degree in every hysteria, and that a tendency toward such a dissociation, and with it the emergence of abnormal states of consciousness (which we shall bring together under the term 'hypnoid'), is the basic phenomenon of this neurosis.* (pp. 62–63)

Breuer and Freud (1893, p. 63) added that "[i]n these views we concur with Binet and the two Janets, though we have had no experience of the remarkable findings they have made on anaesthetic patients." Apart from this statement, and despite the major influence of Janet's ideas on Breuer and Freud's understanding of hysteria, particularly Freud hardly referred to Janet's work. There were also considerable differences between 'Paris' and 'Vienna.' For example, Breuer and Freud emphasized that patients with hysteria repressed their traumatic reminiscences. In the case of women, these memories pertained to sexual abuse in their childhood, often by a close relative, and female hysteria could be caused by this abuse as well as by the repression of the memory of the event(s). Janet did not use the concept of 'repression,' but observed that traumatized individuals have a phobia of their traumatic memories. They fear and attempt to avoid (the reactivation of) these sensorimotor and highly emotional experiences (1904/1911). He certainly did not feel that *all* individuals with hysteria necessarily had been sexually abused. In his view, sexual abuse is one type of event among many that challenge our integrative capacity. For example, severe lack of sleep and illness might imply a profound 'mental depression,' that is, a reduction of our capacity to integrate life experiences.

Suffering from the Infantile Sexual Body, Inner Conflicts, and Wish-Fulfilling Fantasies

Freud's understanding of trauma would change constantly throughout his working life, but according to Verhaeghe (2001) three elements remained stable amid all shifts: The first element is the inability to cast an overwhelming experience in words – this may relate to internal and/or external events. The second stable element in Freudian thought is that the trauma is always of a sexual nature (although, as discussed below, there is an exception). The third involves the idea that trauma always relates to an inner conflict and a psychological defense in reaction to the conflict.

Lack of Verbalization and Conflicts

Freud believed that our neuronal system commonly 'discharges' our experiences by verbalizing them. Adverse experiences, however, can induce an *Erregungszuwachs*, that is, an increase in excitation that interferes with this verbalization, so that the experience remains represented in an undischarged nonverbal or 'antithetical' form. Whereas one might have expected that this excitation concerns intense fear and pain, Freud felt that sexually violated children do not experience fear and therefore do not engage in physical defensive action. In his view, the violation generates in them an untimely eruption of extreme sexual agitation that they register only unconsciously. The result is that there remains within them *bewusstseinsunfähige Vorstellungen*, that is, event-related ideas they are unable to experience consciously. These ideas remain as encapsulated, unassimilated, unbound unconscious energy seeking discharge. In this context, for Freud the trauma of sexually abused children was not the violation in itself, but the sexually charged and unconscious 'imprints' left by this violation. Furthermore, the essence of hysteria lies not in these mental 'traces,' but in their repression by 'the Ego' that fears the unbearable sexual affects. So, "we are to understand that trauma is no longer an [external] event, but rather a violent internal disturbance within the Ego" (Nasio, 1998, p. 15).

In line with this largely endogenic interpretation of trauma, Freud renamed hysteria 'defense hysteria' and later 'conversion hysteria.' The psychological defense would have a paradoxical effect in that the intensity of the repressed sexual affect would increase in reaction to the Ego's attempts to isolate the unbearable affects. The repressed would thus be lurking, just waiting to intrude on the Ego, hence, to become conscious. In this battle of psychological forces, the repressed sexual affect attempts to evade the repression of the Ego by converting itself into a secondary somatic form, that is, to hysterical conversion symptoms. For example, once a perceived part of the body has become hurt during the original worldly event, then the body part becomes associated with an unbearable and repressed image of the hurting, and finally, due to conversion, the body part is left anesthetic or paralyzed.

The repressed imprints encompass more than a mental version of what happened to the subject in the world. Freud had learned from Charcot as well as – although he underplayed this – foremost from Janet (1892; see Macmillan, 1990) that sometimes it is not the event, such as a blow to an arm, that constitutes the essence of the traumatization, but the idea of what *might* have happened, such as a physical injury. Charcot had called this phenomenon *suggestion traumatique* , and Freud became convinced that traumatization was a consequence of recurrent imagination of this kind. He referred to it as 'deferred suggestion': "It is found everywhere that a memory is repressed, which only has become a trauma by deferment" (Freud, 1895/1962, p. 356). The deferment entailed a 'repetition compulsion,' by which he meant that traumatized individuals tend to re-experience a stressful event, time and again (Freud, 1981). This compulsion to repeat the fateful experience turns a singular event into a series of imagination-based events, and it is this mental repetition that constitutes the trauma. It involves a biological fixation: "After severe shock . . . the dream life continually takes the patient back to the situation of his disaster from which he awakens with renewed terror . . . the patient has undergone a physical fixation to the trauma" (Freud, 1919, 1954, p. 207). Hence, event → deferred action → trauma as physical fixation → hysteria.

Infantile Sexuality and Conflicts

The second constant element in Freud's understanding of trauma is the idea that trauma always involves a conflict. As is well-known and as has often been described, Freud (1905/1958) was to switch from the one extreme – all women with hysteria have been incestuously abused – to another, namely, to the belief that memories of patients with hysteria are in most cases not historically true. Rather, they would often be wish-fulfilling sexual fantasies. This he wrote in the *New Introductory Lectures on Psychoanalysis* (1933/1960, p., 120):

> In the period in which the main interest was directed to discovering of infantile sexual traumas, almost all of my women patients told me[2] that they had been seduced by their father. I was driven to recognise in the end that those reports were untrue and so came to understand that the hysterical symptoms are derived from phantasies and not from real occurrences . . . It was only later that I was able to recognise in this phantasy of being seduced by the father the expression of the typical Oedipus complex in women.

Freud's theoretical conversion of a predominant endogenic interpretation of trauma and hysteria (sexual abuse → sexual overstimulation, deferred action, repression → hysteria) in an extreme endogenic view (Oedipal sexual wishes → fantasy, repression → hysteria)

2 Actually, the majority of his patients did not offer Freud actual narratives of incestuous abuse. The telling rather pertains to Freud's *interpretation* of their memories, thoughts, associations, and symptoms. See Steele, 1982.

had major clinical implications. Not sexual overstimulation, but sexual desires were being repressed; not the free-floating unconscious sexual affect, but Oedipal sexual desires had to be brought to conscious awareness. And because these desires are essentially of a biological nature, the essence of hysteria would also be biological.

Freud's thesis in this regard started with the assumption that the child's body includes erogenous zones. Because the child's physical and psychological means to regulate the libidinal tensions that are bound to arise in these zones are immature, these tensions, these *desires*, are traumatizing and must be repressed. The moderation of the sexual desires must be checked by the Ego, which takes the form of fantasies of sexual violation. Infantile sexuality, thus, is a trauma, an unconscious center of suffering in anyone, and fantasy is its manifestation. This conceptualization of trauma implies an almost boundless category; worse, it removes real perpetrators from any moral responsibility. It is not an abusive individual who inflicts a mental wound, but rather the injury is due to the child's own libido.

Psychoanalysts, therefore, would not need to be concerned much with real violation. Freud (1928) acknowledged that factual events can traumatize an individual, but he was not much concerned with their 'objective reality.' What counted for him as a psychoanalyst more was how a person constructs and experiences what happened. The focus had to be on the recurrent subjective mental reworking and distortion of an 'objective' event, not on its 'objective' characteristics. The facts of events such as war, accidents, or child abuse and neglect were of little interest to psychoanalytic thinking, because at the subjective level there would be no difference of meaning between facts and the way in which facts were experienced or distorted. In 1914, Freud still characterized an 'original scene' (*Urszene*) as a "reproduction of a reality experienced by the child" (p. 172), but in 1918 he held that these are "... mostly not true, and in some cases [are] directly opposed to historical truth ... The fact remains that the patient produces these fantasies, and this fact has scarcely less importance for his neurosis as if he had really gone through the content of these fantasies" (p. 358). Inasmuch as this conception was furthered not only by psychoanalysis but also by mainstream psychiatry toward the end of World War I, psychic trauma lost its status as accident injury. Subsequent to this shift there existed only '*so-called* war neurosis' and '*so-called* traumatic neurosis' (Schäffner, 2001, p. 86). Suffering and mental disorder became more or less isolated from the world. The patient's mind was troubled, not the world in which the patient had been thrown.

Suffering from Conflicts Between Eros and Thanatos

To save his sexual theory of the neuroses, Freud initially tried to explain the traumatization of soldiers who took part in the Great War (as World War I was originally called) in sexual terms. When that idea proved most unlikely, he proposed a view in terms of a presumed natural 'death drive'. This propensity toward destruction contrasted with Eros, a natural inclination to survival, propagation, and sex as well as other creative and life generating drives – and the pleasures all of these life drives entail. The tendency of traumatized soldiers to re-experience and re-enact their horrific experiences did not fit the 'pleasure principle'; re-experiencing and re-enacting traumatizing events did not provide any pleasure. In addition, Freud was not completely content with his interpretation that the 'repetition compulsion' involves an attempt to master traumatic experiences. To explain the repetition compulsion, as well as other destructive and self-destructive tendencies in trauma, the idea became that these phenomena constitute manifestations of a presumed basic death drive, an inclination to self-directed aggression, a striving toward a cold inanimate state. Later psychoanalysts would refer to this drive as Thanatos. In a word, Freud proposed that traumatized individuals repeat their horrific experiences because they unconsciously strive to destroy themselves, and that this basic striving is countered by their unconscious basic drive to live.

I already pointed out that an important element in Freudian thinking involves the notion that individuals are not passive recipients of life events, but actively react to it in a mental sense, which Charcot among others had also emphasized. The downside of this move toward philosophical idealism was that hysteria in women became associated with fantasized traumatization rather than real sexual, physical, and emotional abuse, and emotional neglect. The horrors of war became of less concern than traumatized soldiers' inner reworking of what happened. That is, Freud was much more concerned with endogenic explanations of trauma than with recognizing and acknowledging exogenic components in traumatization, and his understanding of female hysteria and male hysteria or traumatic neurosis diverged.

Furthermore, trauma became linked with a vertical model of mind, with the *Ego* repressing unbearable experiences and ideas into the *Unconscious*, where these experiences and ideas became disguised in a different, apparently somatic form (conversion). At this juncture, Freud abandoned the Janetian notion that hysteria involves a division of personality in two or more different *conscious and self-conscious* dissociative parts, as well as Breuer's notion that some of these parts function at a hypnoid level. This theoretical conversion implied the loss of the understanding that the patient and the therapist can communicate with these parts in any direct fashion. Their difficult assignment became tracing and making sense of idealistic, conflict-laden trauma in disguise.

Suffering from a Confusion of Tongues Between Children and Adults

Ferenczi (1929, 1932, 1933, 1949), a military psychiatrist during the Great War and perhaps Freud's most gifted collaborator, was not convinced that women with hysteria had not actually been sexually abused. In his view, there exists an intimate, a-symmetrical relationship between children and their parents. In this context children engage in infantile sexual and Oedipal behavior that normally remains on the level of tenderness, imagination, and play. Parents (or other adults), however, can misperceive these erotic behaviors as full-blown sexual invitations. There would in this sense be a 'confusion of tongues,' a semantic misapprehension – between children and adults. Ferenczi asserted that particularly perverse, drunk, or feeble-minded adults can become confused in this sense and respond with adult sexual confrontations.

The 'passion' and 'seduction' of the adult overwhelms the child, because of his or her immature sexuality. Moreover, it is not only the rape as such, or whatever other forms the sexual abuse may take, that the child cannot assimilate. It is also the corruption of the tender bond between the adult and the child by the mature sexuality of the adult (commonly the father), as well as the lack of care of a nonabusive parent (usually the mother). In the context of this emotional unavailability and neglect, the child cannot afford to lose the father's affection as well. For these reasons, Ferenczi thought, the abused and neglected child identifies with the active aggressor, more specifically with the *desires* of the aggressor, and also introjects the guilt feelings that the aggressor does not feel or realize.

The social environment commonly denies and/or disregards the violation. Children who convey what has happened and perhaps is still happening to them, are often told that they are lying, that they are making things up, that they are nuts. To cope with these false accusations, they may start to disbelieve their own memory and may eventually feel that it is better to remain silent; if that is not possible, to forget the whole thing. Ferenczi bridged psychoanalysis and Janetian dissociation theory by saying that the personality of traumatized children can become divided, particularly when the traumatization is perpetual. In his words (Ferenczi, 1929, p. 121),

> [i]n every case of neurotic amnesia, and possibly also in the ordinary childhood-amnesia, it seems likely that a psychotic splitting of a part of the personality occurs under the influence of shock. The dissociated part, however, lives on hidden, ceaselessly endeavouring to make itself felt, without finding any outlet except in neurotic symptoms.

In 1933, he added (p. 13–14, my translation),

> [i]f such shocks accumulate during the life of the developing person, the number and variety of [personality] splits will increase, and soon it will be rather difficult to maintain contact without confusion with the fragments, which all act as if they were separate personalities, though they mostly do not know each other.

Still another development in abused and neglected children is that they tend to develop a 'curious adulthood,' that is, they become prematurely wise, careful, and seductive (Ferenczi, 1949; see Van Haute & Geyskens, 2004). Might this tendency explain Augustine's apparently normal face?

Ferenczi's grounding of hysteria in a 'confusion of tongues,' or rather a confusion of infantile and full-blown, mature sexual intentions, reintroduced the psychological interpretation of hysteria, including a mixed exogenic and endogenic causation. Despite all its virtues, his work did not acknowledge the fact that an adult can abuse a child in absence of any preceding infantile erotic behavior that may confuse the adult. Most perpetrators indeed do not need such incentives.

Like Briquet's and Tardieu's empirical findings, medicine, psychiatry, and society did not graciously receive Ferenczi's insights. Freud tried to save his theory by controlling Ferenczi, whose ideas had started to dangerously resemble those of Janet – Freud's archrival. For example, Freud tried but failed to prevent Ferenczi from sharing his insights at the XII. Internationaler Psychoanalytischer Kongress in Wiesbaden in 1932 (Ferenczi, 1932). Most psychoanalysts chose to follow Freud's lead by rejecting or ignoring the new insights for decades. Ferenczi died in 1933, the year in which his unwelcome message appeared in the *Internationale Zeitschrift für Psycho-analyse*. Real sexual or other abuse of children and women would have to wait for recognition in medicine, psychiatry, and society for another 50 years. Moreover, this development would not emerge from a shift in psychiatric and psychological thought, and it would be slow and conflicted.

Back to Traumatic Melancholia

We have looked at developments concerning an understanding of hysteria until the 1930s, now it is time to pick up the developmental path of traumatic melancholia. I left this path with a review of the work of Erichsen from the last quarter of the 19th century. What kinds of traumatic melancholia emerged after railway spine and railway brain? Would, following Charcot and Page, traumatic melancholia (including railway spine, railway brain, and traumatic neurasthenia), and traumatic hysteria become united in one diagnostic category? And would, following Janet, traumatic hysteria and grand hysteria come to be seen as a single disorder that, perhaps, can entail different degrees of severity?

Chapter 3

Traumatic Neurosis and Traumatic Hysteria

Common notions
1. Things that equal the same thing also equal one another.
2. If equals are added to equals, then the wholes are equal.
3. If equals are subtracted from equals, then the remainders are equal.
4. Things that coincide with one another equal one another.
5. The whole is greater than the part.
Euclid

The emerging 19th-century British notion (e.g., Erichsen and Page) and the French idea (e.g., Briquet, Charcot, and Janet) that adverse events can injure vulnerable individuals also surfaced in Germany. Although it is often believed that Breuer and Freud originally proposed the term 'psychological trauma' in 1893, as Van der Hart and Brown (1990) wrote, it had earlier antecedents. In 1878 (p. 589) the German neurologist Albert Eulenburg contended that 'psychic shock' in the form of sudden vehement emotions such as terror or intense anger could better be called 'psychic trauma.' In his view, these emotions are due to a molecular concussion of the brain. Psychic trauma – a mental phenomenon – would thus have a biological cause, a position that reflects philosophical materialism (matter → causes → mind).

Suffering from Physical and Mental Concussion

Eulenburg's view that the symptoms of psychic trauma are due to lesions of the brain is similar to Erichsen's idea that railway spine is caused by a concussion of the nervous system in the context of railway disasters and, for that matter, other accidents. Proposing a clinical syndrome of 'traumatic neurosis,' the Berlin neurologist Herman Oppenheim (1884, 1889; Lerner, 2001, 2003) also suggested that the physically jarring experience of accidents could cause minute lesions in the brain or in the nervous system more generally. These lesions would lead to the symptoms of traumatic neurosis such as pain, sensory losses, inability to stand, paralysis, and various shaking and sleeping disorders (matter →

causes → mental alterations). When the Great War erupted in 1914, Oppenheim added war situations to the list of accidents that might cause a physical trauma. However, in agreement with Page, who stressed the importance of psychological factors in the development of railway spine, Oppenheim (1889, pp. 123–124) also held that

> [i]n the genesis of this illness, the physical trauma is only partially responsible. The major role is played by the psyche: the terror, the emotional shock. The [physical] injury has direct consequences, but these would normally take on no great importance, if the sickly altered mind did not create a lasting illness on the basis of its abnormal way of reacting to the physical symptoms.

He then went on to even introduced a purely psychological explanation for traumatic neurosis (mind → causes → alterations of matter [e.g., paralyses, physical pain]):

> In our view, the most important instant is the mental shock. The fearful aroused state of mind that arises during the accident is often so intense that it causes an ongoing mental alteration. This alteration can immediately express itself in psychogenic paralyses, or the continuing pains and abnormal sensations provide the disturbed mind to a certain degree with the nutrition from which it generates the pathological ideas, that gradually become one of its lasting features. (p. 124)

From the other side of the Atlantic, the North American neurologist Charles Dana (1892, p. 461) concurred that it "is the mental impression, the shock much more than the physical injury, which produces neurosis or psychosis." Frank Ely (1903) also stressed that the traumatic neurosis might have psychological causes, and Morton Prince observed in 1897–1898 that, whereas originally the cause of the disorder was thought to be foremost physical, over time emotional factors came to be emphasized more (see Cardyn, 2001).

Referring to Charcot's demonstrations that hypnotically induced ideas can cause bodily paralysis and sensory alterations, Oppenheim explored the role of ideas (*Vorstellungen*) in trauma. The symptoms of traumatic neurosis, he felt by 1889, were in the majority of cases not due to macroscopically large or microscopically small anatomical injuries. Rather, they were to be found in *functional* disorders that most probably had their seat in the neocortex, and that pertain to the psyche as well as to brain centers for movement, sensibility, and sensory functions (1889, p. 127). Traumatic neurosis could, at least in some cases, also involve a combination of structural and functional changes. Oppenheim added that, given the state of neurological knowledge of the time, saying to what degree anatomic damage might be involved was very difficult.

Oppenheim did not concur with the French 'Napoleon of the neuroses' and Page that traumatic neurosis and traumatic hysteria are identical. Whereas he did not specify any symptom or symptoms that could distinguish the two disorders, he feared that regarding all functional disorders as instances of traumatic hysteria would generate an overinclusive category. (Oppenheim apparently disregarded that Charcot, for better or for worse, had made a distinction between traumatic hysteria and grand hysteria.) Oppenheim's (1889) text does not clearly state what would cause this overinclusiveness; perhaps he wanted to

Table 3.1. Negative and positive symptoms of traumatic neurosis according to Oppenheim, and of hysteria according to Janet.

Negative sensorimotor (somatoform) symptoms	Traumatic neurosis	Hysteria (mental stigmata)
Analgesia	+	+
Loss* of bodily feelings	+	+
Loss of hearing	+	+
Loss of speech (difficulty or inability to speak)	+	+
Loss of vision/narrowing of the visual field/tunnel vision	+	+
Loss of taste (includes loss or alteration of taste preferences)	+	+
Loss of smell	+	+
Loss of muscle tension motor weakness/paralysis	+	+
Loss of consciousness /pseudoepileptic seizures	+	+
Loss of sexual feelings/impotence	+	+
Urinary retention	+	+
Negative cognitive-emotional symptoms	**Traumatic neurosis**	**Hysteria (mental stigmata)**
Loss of concentration	+	+
Loss of memory	+	+
Loss of consciousness	+	+
Loss of willpower	unclear	+
Loss of emotions/emotional liveliness	unclear	+
Difficulty making decisions	+	+
Positive sensorimotor (somatoform) symptoms	**Traumatic neurosis**	**Hysteria (mental accidents)**
Hypervigilance	+	+
Palpitations, durable increase of heart rate	+	+
Dizziness	+	+
Pain (headache, somatic pain)	+	+
Sleeplessness	+	+
Contractures	+	+
Abnormal movements, including gait	+	+
Trembling	+	+
Double vision	+	+
Positive cognitive-emotional (psychoform) symptoms	**Traumatic neurosis**	**Hysteria (mental accidents)**
Fear	+	+
Nightmares, tendency toward re-experience or re-enact traumatizing events	+	+
Identity alteration/somnambulism	not stated	+
Psychotic-like confusion, hallucinations	+	+
Hearing voices	not stated	+
Paraesthesias	+	+
Alternating moods (particularly depressive, withdrawn mood versus bouts of hyperemotionality as related to traumatic memories)	+	+
Suicidality	+	+

Note. *The term 'loss' pertains to a partial or complete, temporary or durable loss of the sensory function.

express that some functional disorders do not pertain to traumatizing events. If there is any truth to this conjecture, the pertinent question becomes: What distinguishes environmental conditions that are directly traumatizing (traumatizing event → causes → psychobiological injury, functional disorder) or indirectly traumatizing (adverse event → causes → pathogenic idea → causes → psychobiological injury, functional disorder) from environmental conditions that do not play a causal role regarding a functional disorder (functional disorders unrelated to injurious environmental conditions)? As I detail in upcoming chapters, answering this question is not at all simple.

Oppenheim's (1889) description of the symptoms of traumatic neurosis allows us to compare his list to that of the major symptoms of hysteria that Janet (1901, 1907; see Chapter 2) described under the headings of 'mental stigmata' (losses or negative symptoms) and 'mental accidents' (intrusion and alternations between different dissociative parts or positive symptoms).

Table 3.1 shows that there is so much overlap between traumatic neurosis and hysteria, making it highly improbable that these disorders are indeed different. To roughly test the idea that the two disorders are highly similar if not identical, I used a contemporary tool to check how many sensorimotor dissociative symptoms manifested in the 33 cases that Oppenheim detailed in his book from 1889. Most items of this Somatoform Dissociation Questionnaire (SDQ-20; Nijenhuis, Spinhoven, Van Dyck, Van der Hart, & Vanderlinden, 1996), which my colleagues and I developed on the basis of our consistent clinical observations of sensorimotor symptoms of patients with complex dissociative disorders, concern Janetian mental stigmata – and some address mental accidents. The range of possible scores per item on the SDQ-20 is 1 (*absent*) to 5 (*very severe*). The minimum score is thus 20, and the maximum score is 100. If Oppenheim mentioned a particular symptom regarding a case, I scored a 3, which yielded an average total SDQ-20 score of 31,8. This score is slightly above 29, the cutoff value in the screening for DSM-IV dissociative disorders (Nijenhuis, Spinhoven, Van Dyck, Van der Hart, & Vanderlinden, 1997), and is similar to the score of the contemporary patients with PTSD or conversion disorder (for a review, see Nijenhuis, 2009; see also Chapter 6, Table 6.1). Out of the 33 cases, 26 had an estimated SDQ-20 score over the cutoff. (Mind that DSM-IV dissociative disorders do not include the ICD-10 [WHO, 1992] dissociative disorders of movement and sensation; in DSM-IV and DSM-5 these disorders are listed as 'conversion disorder' [see Chapter 6].) The results of this exploration, however crude, fit the idea that traumatic neurosis and hysteria were one of a kind.

Suffering from Bad Morals and a Weak Will

Apart from the concern discussed in the previous section, there may have been an additional reason why Oppenheim rejected the view that traumatic neurosis and (traumatic) hysteria are intimately related, if not identical disorders. The mainstream German understanding of hysteria differed significantly from Janet's and like-minded clinicians' view of the disorder. Whereas Janet asserted that hysteria involves a subject's inability to integrate potentially traumatizing events – and was in his understanding hysteria due to a combination of subjective and environmental factors – many German physicians and neurologists downplayed the influence of adverse events. Instead they emphasized the decisive influence of endogenic subjective features, and for the most part quite negative ones at that.

One of their ideas was that individuals who had experienced accidents might develop *Rentenneurose* (pension neurosis). For example, following ideas of neurologist Adolf Strümpell (1895, see also Fischer-Homburger, 1975), psychiatrist Alfred Hoche claimed in 1910 (see Lerner, 2003) that accident survivors might easily become beset by *Begehrungsvorstellungen*, that is, by powerful imaginative desires such as the wish to avoid working or to collect a pension. The idea and diagnosis of 'traumatic neurosis' would foster these semiconscious pathological wishes. Hoche agreed that these individuals were ill, but dismissed Oppenheim's claim that adverse events can harm body and mind. Many colleagues joined Hoche's refusal of the concept and diagnosis of traumatic neurosis by claiming that it was the cause of an epidemic of pension hysteria among 'work-shy' members of the working class. This opinion was based on politics and propaganda rather than on facts, because in fact only 1% to 2% of all accident insurance claims at the time pertained to traumatic neurosis.

Another, but closely related concern regarding the concept of 'traumatic neurosis' was that the symptoms of the disorder would be easy to fake. The neurologist Adolf Seeligmüller at a medical conference in Berlin in 1890 estimated that a quarter of all cases of traumatic neurosis were simulators. His colleague Friedrich Schultze (1890; see also Fischer-Homburger, 1975; Lerner, 2003) argued that patients diagnosed with traumatic neurosis actually had hysteria, neurasthenia, or hypochondria, and that some were simulators.

In light of the presumed pension neurosis and risks of simulation, traumatic neurosis came to be seen as a major threat to Germany's treasury, public health, and national strength (Lerner, 2001, 2003). The rejection of the concept and diagnosis of traumatic neurosis reached its crescendo at a medical congress in Munich in 1916. Many German physicians and psychiatrists claimed that the 'war neuroses' did not relate to the ongoing war, but involved hysterical reactions of inferior men with a 'will to sickness' (Bonhoeffer, 1911) as well as a desire for safety and a pension. The parallel with popular causal interpretations of Da Costa's syndrome and railway spine is striking: Not a cruel world was to blame, not leaders and their supporters, who had taken nations down paths to destruction and misery, but the survivors' weakness. However, confronted with numerous mental casualties of war, psychiatrist Ernst Kretschmer (1923) wondered: "Why does such a man lie whimpering in bed year after year for a couple of pennies, when he could earn good money every day and sing, drink, and dance by night?"

In addition to alleged inferiority, wish fulfillment, and simulation, still another argument was raised against traumatic neurosis when it was found that very few prisoners of war developed the symptoms of the alleged disorder, but that these might occur in individuals who had never been at the front. Leading physicians and psychiatrists such as Max Nonne (1915, 1971) and Robert Gaupp (1911, 1918) concluded that the disorder could therefore not possibly be due to physical lesions, but that it had to be seen as hysteria or as hysterical reactions that, in their view, involved only the mental (see Lerner, 2003). However, they and many others set up a straw man by claiming that, according to Oppenheim, traumatic neurosis in war was due solely to the somatic effects of shelling. As discussed above, Oppenheim had stated as early as 1889 that traumatic neurosis in the majority of cases involved mental reactions to adverse events. His rebuttal at the dramatic Munich conference that his opponents overlooked or ignored this fact was to no avail. Almost every speaker agreed that traumatic neurosis reflected hysteria and involved psychogenesis in the form of negative personal features. That, they felt, should be the end of it. German psychiatry crucified a brilliant son. Devastated, Oppenheim died only two years later.

Hysteria was not an autonomous illness, Robert Gaupp (1911) contended, but an abnormal way of reacting in the individual. However, Karl Bonhoeffer (1911) felt that hysteria was more than a psychological reaction in that the tendency toward hysterical reactions would relate to a mental constitution or disposition, more specifically to a 'will to sickness.' In contrast, 'strength of will' involved the ability of self-control, discipline, and calmness, the ability to cope with adverse events by inhibiting the kind of emotional, hysterical reactions that characterized the weak-willed (Gaupp, 1911). Women, effeminate men, children, the uneducated, and individuals from non-Western cultures would be particularly prone to loss of self-control and to 'fleeing into' hysterical symptoms (Lerner, 2003). With the introduction of the vague *psychiatric* concept of 'will' – will had a different and much clearer meaning in Schopenhauer's philosophy, to be discussed later – pathological reactions to adverse events, including war, ominously became linked with morality. This link opened the door for using will and the pathology of will for military, economic, and political purposes (Lerner, 2003). For example, it was said, and not only in Germany, that war might actually *lift* an individual's functioning: "In the field all neurotic symptoms disappear as by magic, and one's whole system is charged with energy and vitality," Kreisler exclaimed (1915, p. 63). War became portrayed as glory.

Whereas some individuals may indeed start to function better in challenging circumstances, they constitute a minority, and even the sturdiest of individuals are not immune to traumatization. As several witnesses of the horrors of war have observed, every man has a breaking point (e.g., War Office Committee, 1922, p. 5). The psychiatrist T. A. Ross (1941, p. 66) agreed: "[N]o man probably can stand the stress of warfare for an unlimited time. All of us have our breaking-point. To some it comes sooner than to others."

These insights, however, did not exist among the military authorities in the early stages of the Great War (e.g., Stone, 1985; Van der Hart et al., 2000), so that army physicians and psychiatrist were totally unprepared for the high number of soldiers who developed acute and chronic mental disturbances. And some believed, or rather hoped, that the disorders would simply vanish with the silencing of the guns and canons. As Van der Hart et al. (2000, p. 37) noted "[i]t was believed, even by Freud (1919), that with the end of the war most of the neurotic diseases that had been brought about by the war disappeared" (p. 1).

Reality was quite different, with long-term psychiatric disability for thousands of soldiers on all sides of the Great War. In 1917, the German psychiatrist Robert Gaupp concluded that *Kriegsneurosen* (war neuroses) constituted the largest category of wounded soldiers in the German army: more than 613,000 men. Entire German companies suffered from constant vomiting or unceasing fits of crying (Van Bergen, 1999, p. 211). The numbers within the British ranks are less clear, but one thing is certain: The official number of 80,000 is a vast underestimation (Van Bergen, 1999).

These high numbers precluded interpretations of war neurosis as hysteria or hysterical reactions in the sense of moral inferiority, emotional weakness, simulation, and the like. There was no way around the uncomfortable fact: Oppenheim had been right after all in claiming that the development of mental disorders can be directly related to war situations, hence to highly adverse events. As the leading British psychiatrist Hart (cited in Van der Hart & Broeze, 2012, p. 64) asserted in 1929:

> During the recent War a great mass of illness occurred which, christened at first by the misleading name of "shell shock," came ultimately to be known as the psychoneuroses of war. This change in nomenclature was due to the rapidly won recognition of the psychological origin of these conditions. Indeed it may be said that, whatever else the War has done, it has at least conclusively demonstrated the existence and importance of psychogenic disorder.

Any individual, no matter how strong-willed, masculine, and educated, can collapse.

Suffering from Ringing Bells of Danger and a Sensitive Temperament

Amid the understanding of hysteria as an emotional and moral inferiority, the idea of physical fixation on traumatizing events and the Janetian analysis of hysteria as a dissociation of the personality did not get completely lost. Janet had stated that adverse events can trigger continued emergency reactions, which he described in psychological as well as in biological terms. The 'vehement emotions,' he wrote, include excessive physiological components that could become associated with crucial reminders of the traumatizing events (e.g., Janet, 1904/1911; 1928). Ivan Pavlov (1927) and his followers came to understand these automatic reactions in terms of classical conditioning theory. Pavlov started from the observation that serious threats to physical integrity and life tend to trigger innate defensive reflexes or reactions that animals and human beings share. They include the startle, flight, freeze, fight, and playing dead. In terms of the theory, unconditional threat stimuli (US) unleash unconditioned responses (UR). Under particular conditions, US can become associated with stimuli that the individual originally did not experience as threatening or otherwise adverse. For example, the individual may learn that stimuli that precede the US by a brief and critical time interval 'signal' the upcoming US. Following this associative signal learning, we respond with physical defensive reactions to the now conditioned stimulus (CS). What defensive reaction this will be depends on the personal and environmental context. That is, the reactions to the CS may, but need not, be of the same type as the UR. For example, a physically maltreated child may, depending on the context, engage in startle responses, flight, freeze, or playing dead (all conditioned reactions) to a particular facial expression, when that expression signals onset of the abuse (CS). During his extensive laboratory experiments Pavlov also observed that dogs with different temperaments tended to react to US in different ways. This suggested to him that sensitivity to classical conditioning is influenced by 'constitutional factors.'

Suffering from Instinctive Defenses

Kretschmer (1923, 1927, 1944) concurred that adverse events, such as war situations, as well as salient reminders of these events can trigger defensive reactions, something human beings share with other animals. Apart from other 'instinctive' (inborn) physical defensive actions such as flight, the reactions include the phylogenetically very old *Bewegungssturm* (i.e., the storm of movements), and the *Totstellreflex* (i.e., playing dead, also known as death feigning or tonic immobility).

All species, from one-cellular organisms to human beings, can engage in vigorous and rather chaotic movements when they are under threat. This storm of movements (*Bewegungssturm*) involves a primitive attempt to get rid of or escape from the aversive stimulation, whose effectiveness may depend more on coïncidence than on any deliberate goal-directed action. It is the kind of behavior that individuals engage in when they panic.

Death-feigning involves immobilization, low muscle tension and heart rate, slow breathing, loss of speech, and low consciousness, including sensory and emotional numbing. This behavioral pattern can serve survival interests in that attack by predators is initiated more by moving prey (suggesting sound meat) than by prey that are corpse-like (the flesh of a corpse may be toxic to the predator). Kretschmer and other authors noted that death-feigning, which has also been described as hysterical or dissociative stupor, can happen in a variety of adverse life events. Many World War I soldiers with hysteria displayed these reactions, and Stierlin (cited in Kretschmer, 1927, p. 14) recounted the tragic case of a woman who remained numb and immobile in her bed for three full days following an earthquake while her child was dying.

Kretschmer (1927) observed that *Bewegungssturm* and *Totstellreflex* belong to the kind of actions that patients with hysteria tend to engage in when they remain in a dissociative condition that he described as 'hyponoic.' Following Janet, he contended that hysteria involves a dissociation of the personality, which is characterized by a lack of integration between higher and lower types of 'will' (basic desires, urges), along with higher and lower levels of mental and behavioral functioning. One type, for example, may involve a will to heal, reflective thinking, and deliberate behavior; the other type pertains to hyponoic conditions marked by a different, more primitive will, clouded or retracted consciousness, and a relatively low mental level of functioning observed in the form of 'hysterical attacks.' A common hyponoic condition or hysterical attack is the re-enactment of a traumatic experience, Kretschmer wrote in full consonance with Janet's numerous observations of the phenomenon. During these attacks, survivors mentally return to a former time, place, and conception of self, feel a need and will to defend themselves against threats they perceive, and engage in defensive behaviors. Meanwhile, they tend to lose the awareness of their posttraumatic life, including their posttraumatic idea of self. Thus, in this kind of hyponoic condition, there is a re-enactment of a traumatic past. The painful past becomes the present, and the actual present gets lost. Along with this shift in time and place, a former identity is re-enacted and the present identity becomes deactivated.

The views of Kretschmer and Pavlov that psychopathology can relate to instinctive defensive reactions to major threat were not unprecedented. Writing on traumatic neurasthenia, the British army psychiatrist W. H. Rivers had proposed in 1920 that the disorder involves a lack of integration of different instincts. He grouped the different instincts in three main classes: Apart from instincts of self-preservation, there are species-preservation instincts and instincts that serve the cohesion of smaller and larger social groups. Sexuality and parental caretaking of their children, providing feelings of attachment, constitute major species-preservation instincts. Some instincts of self-preservation involve our attractions. They pertain to nutrition and exploration. Whereas the nutrition instinct provides feelings of attraction (hunger and thirst) and repulsion (disgust), the exploration instinct implies feelings of curiosity. Other self-preservation instincts are about reactions to danger. According to Rivers, they include flight, aggression, complex behavioral actions to cope with threat that he referred to as 'manipulative actions,' immobilization, and collapse. Flight is associated with fear, aggression with anger, manipulative actions with a lack of emotionality, immobilization with suppression of fear and pain (i.e., analgesia), and collapse with terror.

These different evolutionary inventions not only awake particular actions under fitting circumstances, but also suppress noncompatible actions. Reciprocal suppression of different instincts – this happens automatically and thus does not require conscious mental action – is a fine thing because it prevents, or in any case reduces, conflicts of different basic interests and motivations. A soldier under threat has no appetite for dinner or sex; and flight and immobilization do not interfere with each other's businesses. The downside of reciprocal suppression of core biopsychosocial functions is the difficulty involved in integrating these functions. However, integration is the key to achieving and maintaining mental health. According to Rivers, "mental health depends on the presence of a state of equilibrium between different instinctive tendencies and the forces by which they are controlled. The psycho-neuroses in general are failures in the maintenance of this equilibrium" (1920, p. 119). Because shock, strain, illness, and fatigue lower the individual's integrative and controlling forces, the integrative capacity of individuals who are exposed to adversities becomes seriously compromised, particularly when these events are prolonged and recurrent.

Rivers (1920) conceded that anesthesia and paralysis, in his view the major symptoms of hysteria, point to the essential role of the danger instinct of defensive immobility in this disorder. As he stated, "hysteria is primarily due to the activity of a danger-instinct, to the coming into action of an instinct whose primary function is protection from danger." However, hysteria would not involve dissociation. When trying to grasp Rivers' position, it is important to realize that he defined dissociation as a suppression-based, and thus unconscious and automatic, lack of integration of different centers of conscious action:

> If, in place of regarding dissociation as a state of independent activity [i.e., unconscious, automatic action], we hold independent consciousness to be a necessary part of the concept of dissociation, it is evident that hysteria wholly fails to answer to the definition, for there is no evidence whatever of such independent consciousness. In the absence of any evidence of alternate consciousness, it is doubtful whether anything is gained by bringing hysteria within the category of dissociation.
>
> I have, therefore, no hesitation in excluding dissociation from the connotation of hysteria, and in regarding this state as a [...] product of the two processes of suppression and suggestion. I have already pointed out its close relation to hypnotism, from which it differs in being unaccompanied by independent consciousness, thus bringing it still nearer than the hypnotic state to the instinctive reaction to danger by means of immobility. I have pointed out that the paralyses and anæsthesias, which are the most characteristic manifestations of hysteria, may be regarded as localised manifestations of the suppression of the instinct of immobility, of which sleep and hypnotism are other forms. According to this view the symptoms of hysteria are due to the substitution, in an imperfect form, of an ancient instinctive reaction in place of other forms of reaction to danger.

Rivers' contention that hysteria does not involve conscious centers of instinct-mediated action sharply contrasts with ample demonstrations of the existence of self- and world-conscious dissociative parts of the personality in hysteria by scholars such as Janet. Why did Rivers not, in line with the French understanding of hysteria, propose that the re-enactment of traumatic memories often involves instinctive defensive (re)actions such as immobility of conscious dissociative subsystems of the survivor's personality? Did he not observe major alterations in consciousness in the veterans who were in treatment with him? Did he not notice that they were in a very different state of mind and body when they re-enacted traumatic memories? Did their shifts in consciousness, their recurrent alternations between being oriented to the present and getting lost in the traumatic past, not include alternations of anesthesia and pain, of paralysis and trembling? Rivers' texts indicate that indeed he *did* observe these alterations and alternations. However, he did not regard these phenomena as features of hysteria, but rather as symptoms of traumatic neurasthenia. Hysteria would involve automatic, unconscious action subject to suggestion – and traumatic neurasthenia was different.

In Rivers' view, traumatic neurasthenia involves a conflict between danger instincts and instincts for functioning in daily life. Under the influence of the instincts for functioning of daily life, survivors would consciously and ardently try to get rid of intruding, nonintegrated traumatic memories that involve dominance of the danger instincts. Rivers referred to this intentional and conscious mental avoidance as 'repression.' (Freud originally proposed that repression was a conscious effort, but later suggested it was an unconscious defense.) Focusing on traumatic neurasthenia in World War I veterans, Rivers stated:

> In those who suffer thus from the effect of war-experience, one party in the original conflict is usually the re-awakened danger-instinct in some form or other with its accompanying affect of fear, but this is often wholly displaced by the affect of horror associated with some peculiarly painful incident of war, or by the affect of shame following some situation which the sufferer fears that he has failed to meet in a proper manner. Whether the dominant affect be fear, horror or shame, the sufferer strives with all his strength to banish it from his consciousness. The process of witting repression is often assisted greatly by the occupations and activities of the day, and may be apparently successful so long as occupation is able to fill the day and the fatigue it brings leads to sleep at night. But if sleep fails, the repressed content may acquire such power as wholly to gain the upper hand, and when sleep abrogates control, the repressed content finds expression in the form of painful dreams or nightmares. On these occasions the painful affect, together with the experience round which it has crystallised, dominates the mind. The disturbed sleep only exhausts the sufferer's strength and makes still more unequal the struggle between the fear, horror or shame, and the forces by which the attempt is made to subdue the ever-rising storm. The sufferer may throw himself into still greater activity or may attempt to drown the conflict by excesses of various kinds, but only succeeds in still further sapping his strength till some comparatively trivial shock, illness or wound, removes him from the possibilities of such attempts to solve the conflict. He [p. 124] becomes the victim of the fully-developed state, formerly called neurasthenia, but now, following Freud, more generally known as anxiety-neurosis from the special exaggerated anxiety, the Angst of the German language, which forms one of its most striking and characteristic symptoms.

Writing these sentences, Rivers must have had the conditions of Craiglockhart in mind, the Scottish hospital where he worked as a psychologist and anthropologist during the Great War. Van der Hart (www.istss.org/publications/TS/summer01/edinburgh.htm) described Craiglockhart as a

> monstrous building with a depressing interior, but located in a lovely and serene countryside. Walking through its dark, deserted corridors, it was not hard to feel the echo of Sassoon's[1] portrayal of the suffering there: "The doctors did everything to counteract gloom. The place had melancholy . . ., redeemed only by its healthy situation and pleasant view of the Pentland Hills. By day, the doctors dealt successfully with these disadvantages. But by night they lost control and the hospital became sepulchral and oppressive with saturations of war experience.

1 Siegfried Loraine Sassoon (1886–1967) was a leading English poet of the Great War, author, and soldier decorated for bravery on the Western front.

> One lay awake and listened to feet padding along passages . . . One became conscious that the place was full of men whose slumbers were morbid and terrifying – men muttering uneasily or suddenly crying out in their sleep. Around me was that underworld of dreams haunted by submerged memories of warfare and its intolerable shocks and self-lacerating failures to achieve the impossible."

According to Rivers, an army psychologist who admitted that he knew little about civil traumatization, war trauma-related conflicts stem from conflicts between two different instinct-guided 'parts.' One part of the conflict was instinct-mediated defense, the other instinct-mediated interests of daily life. Sassoon's (1961) words describe how the part strongly mediated by instinctive defense – and immersed in "that underworld" of haunting traumatic memories – tends to be become dominant at night.

For Rivers traumatic neurasthenia, (Oppenheim's) traumatic neurosis, and (Freud's) anxiety neurosis or repression-neurosis were synonyms. Did it ever cross his mind to suggest that traumatic neurasthenia, with its roots in melancholia, and trauma-related hysteria, are in fact one and the same disorder, and that this disorder involves a dissociation of personality in two different instinct-mediated systems? Did he not in fact say that functioning in daily life as supported by conscious attempts to evade traumatic memories and the repressed, that is, mentally and behaviorally avoided traumatic memories, involves different conscious centers of action? Rivers' clear definition of dissociation, and his most important evolutionary and psychobiological perspectives on traumatization, actually strongly point to such a merger. By proposing a fusion of traumatic neurosis (in my term of convenience, 'traumatic melancholia') and hysteria, he might have said that (war) traumatization involves a suppression-based and a fear-based lack of integration of a survivor's personality, with one conscious part guided by instincts for species preservation, social cohesion, and appetitive self-preservation (nutrition, sleep, curiosity), and a different conscious part influenced, if not almost completely guided by, the danger instincts.

Perhaps Rivers was so focused on Freud's original idea of conscious repression that he forgot about Janet's understanding of hysteria, including his concept 'phobia of traumatic memories.' As discussed above, similar to Freud's notion of 'repression,' this phobia consists of the survivors' fear and their attempts to mentally avoid integrating their terrible memories – which they fear more than anything else. Rivers might have added that, to paraphrase Emily Dickinson, the self of daily life dreads the self of the horrific past, thus maintaining the dissociation of the survivor's personality along with the symptoms that this division implies.

Yet he may have had another reason for distinguishing traumatic neurasthenia and hysteria (Onno van der Hart, personal communication, June 5, 2012). During the Great War, he was an attending psychologist and anthropologist at Craiglockhart, the hospital where traumatized *officers* were treated. Higher ranked men were presumed not to suffer from hysteria – an illness of the lower ranks – but from neurasthenia. This political bias was not, however, specific to Rivers, as the next section shows.

Suffering from Apparently Normal and Emotional Parts of the Personality

Although they did not know or include Rivers' ideas on suppression-based instincts[2], several other psychiatrists and psychologists did in fact understand (war) trauma in terms of a dissociation of the personality or of psychophysiological functions, and in terms of the results of this division (Brown, 1919a, 1919b; Ferenczi, 1919; McDougall, 1926; Myers, 1940; Simmel, 1919). For example, McDougall (p. 545) conceded in close harmony with Janet that

> [n]ormal personality, as we know it in ourselves and in our neighbours, is the product of an integrative process ... and is susceptible to disintegration that results in the manifestation of two or more personalities in and through the one bodily organism.

McDougall (1926) also made the important point that this dissociation does not involve dissociation or splitting of consciousness – an expression that Breuer and Freud had used in 1893, and that many contemporary authors on dissociation still apply – because normal cognition does not involve a compound of elements of consciousness capable of independent existence. Hart (1926, p. 247) agreed with Janet that dissociation involves a division of different 'systems of ideas and functions.' Using an (imperfect) metaphor, he made the important comment that the mind is not a dividable thing:

> Dissociation does not separate the mind into pieces, it only produces more or less independently acting functional units, each such unit comprising material which may be peculiar to itself, but which may just as well form a part of any number of other functional units. The distinguishing character does not lie in the material of which it is composed, but in the set or pattern. Instead of regarding dissociation as the splitting of conscious material into separate masses, it must be regarded as an affair of gearing, the various elements of mental machinery being organized into different functional systems by throwing in of the appropriate gear.

A major representative of the position that trauma involves a division of personality was World War I army physician Charles Myers (1940). Whereas he stated that the personality of traumatized soldiers encompassed two different, insufficiently integrated 'personalities,' his descriptions reveal that he actually did not have full-blown personalities in mind, but less complex structures. These structures match Janet's dissociative systems as parts of the whole biopsychosocial system that an individual's personality consists of.

Myers (1940) distinguished an 'apparently normal personality' (ANP) and an 'emotional personality' (EP). The adjective 'apparently normal' constitutes an improvement over Breuer and Freud's (1893) term 'normal consciousness,' the state that can be intruded on by a hypnoid state. As contemporary biopsychosocial research has confirmed (see

---

2 William McDougall (1926, p. 138] referred to Rivers' ideas on traumatic memories in a footnote.

Chapters 17 and 18), and as will be discussed later in detail, 'normal consciousness' in patients with dissociative disorders is in fact abnormal (see Chapter 12).

As EP the soldier with hysteria re-experienced traumatizing events, and as ANP he attempted to avoid these unnerving experiences. Both involve abnormal levels of consciousness (LOC) and sensorimotor/somatoform (e.g., kinesthetic anesthesia, paralysis, contracture) and cognitive-emotional/psychoform (e.g., amnesia, different identities) dissociative symptoms. Van der Hart et al. (2000) sampled several descriptions of alternations between these different ways of being from the World War I literature. Here is one of them (the italicized insertions involve comments by Van der Hart et al., pp. 41–42):

> Dissociative deaf-muteness (Mott, 1916, pp. xv): A deafmute, aged 24, with no history of a neurotic temperament or neuropathic predisposition, was admitted under my care on November 16, 1915. He wrote the following account of himself: "I left England the 8th of March and went to Gallipoli on the 26th May, and about the middle of August one of our monitors fired short. I felt something go in my head, then I went to the Canada hospital; they said it was concussion" *[reduction in LOC]*. In answer to questions he says the last thing he remembers is seeing the monitors firing. He came to a dug-out about one hour later. He could see and speak a little, but was quite deaf, and his head felt as if it would burst. He lost his speech completely when Bárány's tests (hot and cold-water tests) were applied. He does not now complain of headache, but is quite deaf and dumb. Captain Jenkins reports that the ears are normal; it is therefore a functional deafness *[somatoform: ANP]*. He is able to cough and whistle, but cannot speak *[somatoform: ANP]*. His wife says that she has letters from him, in one of which he described how he killed a Turkish woman sniper. He does not remember writing this letter, but there is evidently some retrograde amnesia *[psychoform: ANP]*. He says he does not dream, but it seems certain that he has dreams but does not recollect them *[psychoform: ANP]*, for the sister of the ward says that while asleep he *[EP]* assumes the attitude of shooting with his rifle, and he gives a jerk as if pulling the trigger, then he assumes the attitude of using his bayonet; the other men in the ward tell her that he gives the movement of the right parry, then the left parry, and lastly the thrust, as if he were in action *[somatoform: EP]*. He sometimes jumps his whole body as if he heard or saw a shell coming, and he catches his right elbow as if he were hit there. He was then observed to open his eyes wide, get up, and look under the bed *[somatoform: EP]*. Apparently he is not conscious of this *[psychoform: ANP]*. He then awakens and begins to cry, but there is no sound *[somatoform: ANP]*.

Myers missed the opportunity to link ANP and EP to Rivers' ideas on suppression-based instincts. Yet his work clearly shows that ANP and EP serve different wills, different basic desires, or motivations. As EP, the men engaged in defensive actions; as ANP, they focused on daily life – and in this frame attempted to evade EP's world.

The different dissociative personalities, or rather the different *parts* of the singular personality that each individual has (Nijenhuis, 2012; Nijenhuis & Van der Hart, 2011; Van der Hart et al., 2006), include their own conception of self, however rudimentary (McDougall, 1926; Mitchell, 1922). No matter how 'hyponoic' EPs may be, no matter how low and retracted their consciousness, they have their own ideas of who they are, what the world (situation, time, place) in which they are is like, and how they relate to that world. I discuss this important feature of dissociative parts of the personality in more detail in Chapters 4, 12, and 13, and there give more substance and clarity to the vague expression 'sense of self.'

Myers observed that traumatized soldiers had symptoms of hysteria such as amnesia and impaired vision. Associating hysteria with feminine troubles, he wanted a different term for male war trauma. He introduced the masculine-sounding term 'shell shock' in 1915 while describing several soldiers who had become traumatizing due to nearby exploding bombs. He would regret this name following observations that the disorder also appeared in men who had not been 'shelled' (Myers, 1940): The history of the understanding and naming of railway spine repeated itself. Shell shock, Myers (1940) emphasized, did not pertain to a concussion of the spine, the nervous system, or the brain, but rather constituted a mental shock. The shock involved mental and not physical causation of symptoms, including the division of personality.

Suffering from Neurochemics

It would not last long before the seat of trauma was taken from the mind back to the body. That is, a foremost psychogenic interpretation of trauma (mind → causes → alterations of the body/brain) was substituted for a biogenetic and thus philosophically materialistic understanding (matter → causes → mental alterations). Later, studying North American World War II veterans, Kardiner and Spiegel (1945) observed that the men had a variety of intense physical reactions to war situations and reminders of these events. This led them to propose that traumatic neurosis is a 'physioneurosis.' Kardiner (1941) had earlier emphasized the unconditioned and conditioned startle response and aggressive outbursts in this regard, and Grinker and Spiegel suggested that traumatic neurosis involves physical symptoms that suggest neurochemical changes of the catecholamine system. These symptoms, such as violent startle reflex, flexor changes in posture, hyperkinesis, tremor in rest, 'violently propulsive gait,' and gastric distress, seem related to Kretschmer's *Bewegungssturm*. Kardiner also noted that physioneurosis involves striking alternations between phases of unpremeditated aggression and 'moods of extreme tenderness' (p. 97). However, he did not relate these alternations to shifts between Myers' EP and ANP, nor he did not mention that, apart from hyperarousal, traumatic neurosis might also include hypoarousal or death feigning. In other words, Kardiner did not link trauma-related physioneurosis to dissociation of the personality or hysteria.

As detailed in the next chapter, the work of Kardiner would be a major impetus to the development of the concept and diagnosis of PTSD (APA, 1980). PTSD would come to be seen and classified as an anxiety disorder, hence as a form a traumatic melancholia. However, traumatic melancholia and hysteria were not to remain dissociated forever.

Suffering from Childhood Traumatization, Particularly Sexual Abuse

Although it has been recognized across the ages that terrible events can be mentally injurious, this insight has been exceptionally slow and problematic. Gains in understanding and acceptance in one epoch became more than once lost in the next. Society and psychiatry were not at all eager to know and understand the mental wounds that public and private disasters can cause. From the 19th century, developments regarding the concept of 'trauma' occurred when it became practically impossible to ignore the psychopathology that severe accidents and war could cause in previously healthy individuals. World War I revealed that even the brave are frail when life becomes excessively grim. And, as described above, even under those circumstances, society and psychiatry were generally more eager to *control* the wounded than to help them heal.

Slower and more conflicted still was the recognition of the existence and pathogenic traces of much less visible horrific events: childhood sexual, physical, and emotional abuse, emotional neglect, as well as sexual abuse and other kinds of maltreatment of adults, mostly women. In spite of the development of the concept of 'psychic trauma' in the last quarter of the 19th century, medicine, psychology, psychiatry, and society at large continued to ignore, overlook, deny, or downplay occasional, but recurrent observations and documentation of chronic interpersonal traumatization (Cardyn, 2001). Briquet's and Tardieu's observations of childhood traumatization were not welcomed. Charcot mostly overlooked that child abuse and neglect also constitute major agents provocateurs. Janet and some other like-minded 19th-century clinicians did notice the harmful effects of these events, but sadly their voices did not carry far. Freud declared that most memories of childhood traumatization were morbid fantasies, and he and the psychoanalytic community silenced Ferenczi's opposing view. In this context, hysteria and childhood traumatization were kept at a safe distance from traumatic neurosis as elicited by tragic accidents and war.

However, is it really true that very little was known about child abuse and neglect in society until the 1980s? For example, was childhood sexual abuse (CSA) a big societal unknown – or was it perhaps simply an accepted practice? Historians suggest otherwise. They have traced that, from early written history onward, sexual relations with children were well known, legally prohibited, and prosecuted at some times and in some places. Whereas some legal systems included the idea that these relations were (or at least could be) harmful, it would last ages and ages before this awareness was to garner clinical, scientific, and general societal recognition.

In the Byzantine Empire, which lasted from 324 to 1453 A. D., girls had to be at least 12 years old and boys 14 years old to be legally wedded. Both the Law and the Church strictly forbade having sexual relations with children younger than these ages. Yet, as documented by Byzantine historians, chroniclers, and ecclesiastical authors, rapes under the cover of premature marriage as well as child prostitution, incest, and pederasty were not at all seldom, and indeed happened in all social classes (Lascaratos & Poulakou-Rembelakou, 2000). There are some historical indications that these forms of sexual abuse impacted the mental health of the involved children, which may have been one reason why transgressors, and pedophiles in particular, were punished. Some even received capital punishment, and the Church included CSA among the major sins (Kukules, 1955).

Another example of the awareness and prohibition of CSA in former centuries may be found in the long list of prohibited sexual behaviors and recommended punishments of offenders known as *The Penitentials* (Lalor, 1998; Payer, 1984), which emerged in Ireland in the 6th century. From there, it spread to England and throughout Western Europe, and was used until the 12th century. It included the following:

> adultery, incest, homosexuality, lesbianism, bestiality, masturbation, sodomy, fellatio, touching, kissing with and without "pollution" (ejaculation), adultery at the urging of a husband, the use of aphrodisiacs (frequently semen based) and the use of "quasdam machinas" (certain instruments) by lesbians. Proscriptions on incest included sexual relations with daughters, sisters, brothers, step-daughters, god-daughters, aunts, god-mothers, mothers, infant sons, the sister of a wife and the fiancée of a son. (Lalor, 2001, p. 3)

Later generations did not lose the existing knowledge of sexual abuse of children in the Byzantine Empire and Western Europe. For example, in the 19th century the Church was well aware of this (e.g., Niebuhr, 1828). Yet knowing that something exists is very different from *acting on it*, in this case, realizing how harmful CSA can be, how this harm is expressed, how the abuse can be prevented or reduced, and engaging in prevention and in lessening the suffering the abuse implies. Tardieu (1878) communicated his findings in writing, but to the extent that the contents of his book were known, physicians, psychiatrists, psychologists failed to realize that CSA in fact related to subsequent traumatic neurosis and hysteria. It seems that, in at least some countries, the Ministry of Justice realized more than these professionals that sexual relationships between an adult and a child are commonly harmful to the child. Tardieu thus stated that between 1858 and 1869 in France, 9,125 people were accused of rape or attempted rape on children, and Bernard (1886) reported 36,176 cases of sexual abuse of French children 15 years and younger between 1827 and 1870. Tardieu (1878) himself focused on the physical consequences of CSA and did not know or discuss its psychological sequelae.

Not knowing and not realizing veracious sexual abuse feeds false ideas, as several examples may illustrate. Thoinot (1919, p. 66) erred in assuming that "[u]nder the age of six . . . a child cannot be raped, the penis cannot enter the internal genital organs." He also felt that children under 10 years would hardly ever be raped. Some 19th-century physicians similarly conceded that women cannot be raped, because they can resist by firmly crossing their legs (Robinson, 1917; Williams, 1913). When doctors found objects that had been inserted in some women's vagina, with few exceptions (Parvin, 1885; Robinson, 1917), they did not consider the possibility that a man could have done this (e.g., Jinkins, 1905).

In 1847, Sir Matthew Hale stated that "[r]ape is an accusation easily to be made and hard to be proved, and harder to be defended by the party accused, tho' never so innocent" (cited in Cardyn, 2001). The myth that reports of rape by women and children are in most cases inventions than facts has been circling in medicine, psychiatry, and society for a long time. It erupted time and again when the problem of sexual abuse was addressed. Near the end of the 19th century and at the beginning of the 20th century, there was a discussion on how often allegations of rape involved fabrications. Cardyn (2001) asserted that North American medical authorities of the time contributed immensely to the promulgation of the idea that most allegations were in fact false (Southard & Jarrett, 1922; Thoinot, 1919). For example, Robinson (1931) claimed that 90% of cases were fictitious. Williams (1913) estimated the rate at 12:1. In a climate in which men feared false accusations of rape by "vicious hysterics" (Robinson, 1931, p. 307; Ross, 1882), "women are never portrayed as more duplicitous and conniving that when they brand the physician himself as the rapist" (Cardyn, 2001, p. 197).

A variation of the clinical and scientific nonrealization of sexual abuse is the assumption that a woman's involuntary physical sexual arousal meant that she had consented physiologically (Talmey, 1919). Talmey's condescending belief reflects a mereological error, that is, a violation of the logic of part-whole relationships. Only individuals can consent, not their body. If a raped woman was at all believed, physicians were concerned more with the physical wounds, with the local somatic trauma – not with her mental condition. This one-sided interest reveals a failure to realize that the quintessential problem of sexual violation lies in its mental sequelae.

Prior to the start of systematic studies of sexual abuse from the 1980s, estimations of its prevalence varied immensely. Whereas Alfred Kinsey et al. wrote in 1953 that the prevalence of incest is one case per hundred, Weinberg (1955) stated that it is only one case per million. These very different estimations of the prevalence of sexual abuse should have lead to an examination and improvement of the methods to assess the prevalence of incest and other kinds of sexual violation, but they did not. Two decades later, Freedman, Kaplan, and Sadock (1975) would still adhere to Weinberg's dramatic underestimation in their influential psychiatric textbook. Trainees in psychology and psychiatry were sent into the real world ignorant of the prevalence, nature, and treatment of CSA.

This also applies to my own case, which is very similar to that of many colleagues. As a young psychologist and psychotherapist of children, adolescents, and adults in 1978, I knew *practically nothing* about sexual abuse and any kinds of childhood traumatization. Dissociation? I was unaware that the term even had a meaning in psychiatry. My teachers had not even mentioned the terms 'trauma' or 'dissociation' during all my years of training, let alone address them. Thus, when I met Paula in 1982, my first patient with a dissociative disorder – or at least the first patient who left me no chance to overlook the severe dissociation of her personality – I did not have the faintest idea how to be of professional help to her. Since there was no one else around who was any better prepared and equipped for assessing and treating Paula's disorder, we decided to embark on an uncertain voyage together.

I studied hard and learned a lot along the way, mostly from Paula. Sometimes the learning came the hard way. For example, Paula believed she had been a bad girl. That's why her parents had to punish her, she said. One day, she advanced to the conviction that she had been a good child after all. "Yes," I told her, "and you were also a good girl." "No," she emphasized, intensely irritated, "I was a good *child*." I was stupid enough to miss her point and voiced my opinion once more. Two days later, as an angry, controlling dissociative part of her, she severely cut her vagina: She was a good *child*, not a good *girl*. Fifteen years later, we had reached our therapeutic goals and could terminate our contacts. In 2011, her husband told me that Paula had died. She left 13 grandchildren who had been a major compensation for the ice-cold and horrific childhood and adolescent world she had managed to survive. Our therapeutic efforts had not been in vain.

An important step toward the recognition and acknowledgment of childhood interpersonal traumatization was made in the form of a brief but seminal paper by Kempe, Silverman, Steele, Droegemueller, and Silver (1962) on what they chose to call battered child syndrome. This work was to significantly raise clinical and scientific interest in physical abuse, leading to a major body of knowledge. Regarding sexual abuse, it mostly took abused women who spoke out to make a change. They and the feminist movement that emerged in the 1970s forced professionals and society alike to start attending to this traumatization and associated psychopathology (Cardyn, 2001; Herman, 1992).

Another movement had also been set in motion in those years: the reemergence of a professional interest in hysteria under the generic label 'dissociative disorders' in the DSM-III (APA, 1980). Many patients with these disorders reported the kinds of injury-precipitating life events that psychiatry and society more generally had rather not heard. Their reports of traumatization in childhood, adolescence, and adulthood received serious attention and study from a minority of clinicians and scientists. Others were quick to contend that their memories of childhood traumatization are generally false, and that complex dissociative disorders are sad, deplorable conditions caused by suggestion (self-suggestion, but mostly suggestion by therapists and the media), fantasy proneness, suggestibility, and role-playing. And once again a societal and professional climate emerged in which an intimate relationship between traumatic melancholia – under the label of PTSD – and traumatic and grand hysteria – under the label of dissociative disorders – was ignored or denied. Still, the theme would not completely vanish, as will be pointed out in the next chapter.

Chapter 4

Dissociation of the Personality as a Core Feature of Trauma

Empirical sciences prosecuted purely for their own sake, and without philosophic tendency are like a face without eyes.
Arthur Schopenhauer (*The World as Will and Idea,* Vol. 2, 318–319)

Kardiner's (1941) work on what he called the 'traumatic neuroses of war' greatly contributed to the development of the concept and diagnosis of stress response syndrome in the first version of the *Diagnostic and Statistical Manual of Mental Disorders* (DSM-I; APA, 1952). In DSM-II (1968) the disorder was presented as a mere example of situational disorders, but under pressure of forensic psychiatrists it eventually regained full status as posttraumatic stress disorder (PTSD) in DSM-III and DSM-IV (APA, 1980, 1994). Kardiner (1941) described its core characteristics, such as fixation on traumatic memories, constriction of personality functioning as well as atypical dream life, features that Janet and like-minded clinicians had regarded as symptoms of hysteria.

Along with the contributions of Abram (1970), the seminal work of John Henry Krystal (1968) on World War II concentration camp survivors was also of great importance to the emergence of the concept of PTSD. Mardi J. Horowitz (1976) specifically sought to define the nature and process of stress-response syndromes. He proposed that survivors tend to oscillate between different 'phases' or 'episodes' that remain insufficiently integrated. The logical implication is that these 'phases' constitute dissociative conditions. As described in this chapter, this fact was and is not generally or consistently recognized or acknowledged. The two major phases pertain to denial, numbing, and avoidance as well as to intrusion of trauma-related imagery and affect.

Horowitz described the different phases or stages also as 'states.' Thus, Zilberg, Weiss, and Horowitz (1982) distinguished three different forms of pathological stress response syndromes, namely, 'frozen and avoidant states,' 'stuck in undercontrolled intrusion,' and 'oscillating . . . between states of high intrusion and high avoidance.' Individuals frozen in avoidance effectively prevent avoidance of traumatic memories, which blocks the 'working through process' as Horowitz (1986, 1988) called it. Those who are 'stuck in undercontrolled intrusion' fail to keep their traumatic memories at bay. Often and intensely intruded on by these memories, they are caught in hyperarousal.

The disorder appears when traumatized individuals do not integrate their traumatic memories, but rather attempt to mentally escape from these sensorimotor and affectively charged re-enactments of terrible experiences as quickly and as effectively as possible. Indeed, despite recurrent re-experiences and other re-enactments of their traumatic memories, PTSD patients do not manage or sometimes even dare to integrate their traumatic memories into their overarching personality as an ever-developing, biopsychosocial, and historical system. The consequences are that these recollections continue to exist in a nonintegrated, that is, dissociative form; the patients continue to alternate between Horowitz's different 'phases.'

Following the lead of Kardiner, Abram, Krystal, and Horowitz, in DSM-III PTSD included three primary symptom groups that have been retained in later versions of this classificatory system: (1) intrusion and re-experiencing of nonintegrated traumatic memories, (2) mental avoidance of these memories and other reminders of the traumatic experiences, numbing, and (3) general hyperarousal. Acute stress disorder (ASD) was added in DSM-IV (APA, 1994). In addition to these symptoms, the formulation of ASD and PTSD in DSM-IV included the statement that ASD and PTSD applies only to individuals who experienced, witnessed, or were otherwise confronted with "an event or events that involved actual or threatened death or serious injury, or a threat to the physical integrity of self or others" (APA, 1994, pp. 427 and 431).

The introduction of PTSD in DSM-III represents a major step toward a better recognition and treatment of traumatized individuals. It was also a courageous step because relatively little was known about this "new kid on the DSM block" at the time of its introduction. And it was a wise step at that, because the very formulation and introduction of the disorder fostered clinical and theoretical wisdom, and sparkled a tremendous amount of psychological, psychobiological, and psychosocial research.

PTSD: Traumatic Melancholia or Hysteria? Traumatic Neurosis or Dissociative Disorder?

At the time of the introduction of PTSD in DSM, there was a discussion whether the disorder was perhaps best conceptualized and classified as a dissociative disorder (rather than as an anxiety disorder) along with the other dissociative disorders that DSM-III introduced. There were indeed excellent reasons to conceptualize and classify PTSD as a dissociative disorder. Horowitz' 'phases' had been described and comprehended by Janet as dissociative systems of ideas and functions, each with their own idea of who they are (Janet, 1907). As previously discussed, Breuer and Freud (1893–1895) had referred to some of these dissociative subsystems of the personality as a whole system as dissociative hypnoid states, and Kretschmer (1923) had talked about hyponoic states. Like Janet, Rivers (1920, Chapter 10) defined dissociation as a division among different conscious centers of activity. In his words,

> if we accept the fugue as a characteristic example of dissociation, the question arises whether we should not include in . . . its definition the character of alternate consciousness, and I believe that we shall best be meeting the needs of the situation by doing so. I propose therefore to use the term 'dissociation,' not merely for a process and state in which suppressed experience acquires an independent activity, but shall assume that this independent activity carries with it independent consciousness. In some cases in which we have obviously to do with independent activity as shown by behaviour, it may not be possible to demonstrate the existence of independent and dissociated consciousness, but I believe it will be convenient to limit the term 'dissociation' to cases where there is evidence of this independent consciousness.

In the previous chapter, I noted that Rivers (1920), however, felt that conscious dissociative centers around characterized traumatic neurasthenia – a precursor of PTSD – but not hysteria. As mentioned before, Myers (1940) had proposed the terms 'apparently normal personality' (ANP) and 'emotional personality' (EP) to describe veterans with shell shock, another precursor of PTSD. He observed and formulated, in accord with Janet, Rivers, and still others, that these different 'personalities' were conscious as well as self-conscious. But like Rivers, Myers did not link these different ways of being to hysteria. In my term of convenience, shell shock became another derivate of traumatic melancholia. Had the lack of integration of the personality in traumatized individuals been fully and broadly appreciated when PTSD was introduced in DSM-III, Charcot and Page would have been most pleased: At last traumatic neurosis, melancholia, or neurasthenia (i.e., PTSD) and hysteria (i.e., dissociative disorders) might have been united. Consistent with Janet's ideas, PTSD might have become seen as relatively simple dissociative disorder. It might have been stated that PTSD involves a relatively simple dissociation of the personality, and that this division increases with the complexity of the dissociative disorder with DID; APA, 2013) as an extreme. Alas, Charcot was not granted the favor. In DSM-III and DSM-IV as well as in ICD-10 (WHO, 1992) PTSD became classified as an anxiety disorder. ASD – introduced in DSM-IV (APA, 1994) – was also categorized as an anxiety disorder. Kardiner's emphasis on posttraumatic *aggression* was largely ignored when it came to categorizing the disorder, as were major other frequent emotions in PTSD such as intense sadness, shame, and disgust. Consistent with DSM-III, in ICD-9 (WHO, 1977) and ICD-10 (WHO, 1992) acute stress reaction and PTSD were classified as reactions to severe stress, not as dissociative disorders.

Still, Page's and Charcot's understanding that traumatic neurosis and (traumatic) hysteria essentially comprise one disorder – or at least belong to one category of disorders – did not get completely lost. Since the 1980s there have been recurrent proposals to bring ASD, PTSD, and the DSM-IV and ICD-10 dissociative disorders under one conceptual and classificatory heading. Since the introduction of PTSD several authors have suggested that complex dissociative disorders are best understood as complex forms of PTSD (Kluft,

1987; Spiegel, 1984; Van der Hart et al., 2006), just as complex dissociative disorders constitute complex forms of PTSD (Dorahy & Van der Hart, 2014; Nijenhuis, 2014a, 2014b; Van der Hart et al., 2006). Some experts on PTSD suggested that the disorder was best classified in the DSM-5 with the dissociative disorders in a singular category of trauma-related disorders (Friedman et al., 2011). These proposals are fully consonant with our understanding that there exists a dimension of trauma-related disorders, with PTSD as the simplest form, and DID as the most complex (Nijenhuis, 2014a, 2014b; Nijenhuis et al., 2002b; Van der Hart, Nijenhuis, & Steele, 2005; Van der Hart et al., 2006). The feature that links the various disorders is a dissociation of the personality, which can be more or less complex.

Indeed, Horowitz was certainly not the last to observe that the personality of traumatized individuals, including patients with PTSD, is dissociated. For example, according to Wilson (1995, cited in Wang, Wilson, & Zigelbaum, 1986, p. 250), PTSD is a disorder "in which the core injury is to the individual's ego-states that results in a re-configuration of personality processes and psychobiological adaptation." Consistent with this formulation, Wang et al. (1996) documented that Vietnam veterans with PTSD alternate between different 'stages of decompensation.' As they relate, "[o]ne of the strongest clinical impressions we have had working with Vietnam veterans with PTSD is the tremendous variability in functioning over time" (p. 239). Each of the stages includes its own characteristic affects, cognitions, preferences, sense of self, attachment patterns, memories, coping styles, capacity for insights, reinforcement value of stimuli, and response to medication. In Stage 1, "the PTSD patient can appear to be very normal" (p. 240), in Stage 2 the orientation is toward survival, and Stage 3 involves decompensation that may involve sensation seeking but also total shutting down. Stage 4 pertains to regrouping or giving up, with suicidal tendencies. Like Myers (1940), Wilson and Zigelbaum (1986) observed that the patient tends to alternate between a mode of (apparent) normality and a survivor mode. Several other authors proposed similar 'modes.' For example, Raftery (2003) distinguished between a daily life self and a war marked self. According to Wilson and Walker (1986), these different conditions involve state-dependent learning and memory. Brewin, Dalgleish and Joseph (1996) proposed a duality between different memory systems in trauma, which they refer to as 'situationally accessible memories and verbal accessible memories.'

Near the turn of the century, Onno van der Hart, Kathy Steele, and I started to develop the concept of (trauma-related) structural dissociation of the personality (TSDP) (Nijenhuis, Vanderlinden, & Spinhoven, 1998d; Nijenhuis & Van der Hart, 1999; Nijenhuis et al., 2002b; Steele, Van der Hart, & Nijenhuis, 2001, 2005; Van der Hart, Nijenhuis, Steele, & Brown, 2004; Van der Hart, Nijenhuis, & Steele, 2005; Van der Hart, 1995; Van der Hart et al., 2006). Inspired by our long-term and extensive clinical observations of traumatized individuals, Janet's, Rivers,' Myers' and other pioneers' work, ideas on classical and operant conditioning and attachment as well as wider theoretical reflections (e.g., Hurley, 1998; Panksepp, 1998) and emerging research findings, we proposed that trauma is an injury that crucially involves a dissociation of the personality as a historical and ever-developing whole system. This dissociation occurs when adverse events demand more integrative capacity than the individual can muster, so that the actions of synthesis, personification, presentification, and realization that Janet described so well (see Chapter 2; Van der Hart et al., 2006) falter. The dissociation pertains to a lack of integration of two or more self-aware and world-aware subsystems or 'parts.' Each of these dissociative parts tends to integrate some sensations, affects, thoughts, memories, and behaviors, but none integrates them all. This lack of integration and the implied realization manifests itself in dissociative symptoms and in some other phenomena such as a low or retracted consciousness.

In our view, the basic division is between one prototypical subsystem, metaphorically referred to as an 'apparently normal part' (ANP), and one different prototype, metaphorically addressed as an 'emotional part of the personality' (EP). These different prototypes emerge when individuals who are confronted with an adverse event do not manage to integrate the experience in their personality either in part or in full. They cease to operate as an individual. The individual, the *individuum,* becomes a 'dividual' – a *dividuum.*

The Theory of Structural Dissociation of the Personality

Some essentials. The basic idea of TSDP is that the division of the personality in trauma is not coincidental, but relates to the core structure of a person's personality as a whole biopsychosocial system. This basic structure is not primarily cognitive, but emotional and behavioral. To ground and explain this statement, a brief philosophical excursion is in place.

Spinoza on Desire and Appetite, Kant on 'The Thing in Itself,' and Schopenhauer on the Will

The German philosopher Arthur Schopenhauer (1788–1860) pointed out that the will (*der Wille*) in its various manifestations precedes cognition (Schopenhauer, 1813/2007, 1818/1844/1958). Immanuel Kant (1724–1804), the philosopher who changed the world of thought though never traveling any further than ten kilometers from his native town of Königsberg, analyzed that anything we perceive or think is cast in terms of space, time, and causality because as a species we are constructed that way (Kant, 1781/1998). This implies, Kant said, that we cannot know the world as it is in itself. He called this world 'the thing in itself' (*das Ding an sich*). All we can perceive and think remains limited to 'the thing for me' (*das Ding für mich*). We cannot escape the human world of 'phenomena,' for what we experience and what we know are all phenomena, 'the thing for me/us.' The noumenon, 'the thing in itself' or the world as it may exist independent from our senses and remains hidden from us. We cannot know it. Whatever we may say about it is mere speculation.

Schopenhauer (1788–1860) described the phenomenal[1] world as the domain of our *Vorstellungen. Sich (etwas) vorstellen* is a German verb that literally means 'to place (something) before oneself.' In English translations, the noun *Vorstellung* has come to be translated as 'representation,' sometimes as 'idea.' Translating *Vorstellung* as representation, however, is problematic. The term *Vorstellung* did not involve the thought that there is an objective world that presents itself to us and that we 're-present,' or that we bring to the present and to ourselves once more. The term also did not involve the thought that we generate representations in the sense of symbols that stand for something else that exists in the independently existing objective world. What Schopenhauer did want to express, however, is that we perceive and think about the world, and regardless of how we can perceive and think about it, "the world is my idea" thereof (1958, Vol. II, p. 3). For this reason, *Vorstellung* may in my view be better translated as 'idea.' Ideas include perceptions, as in the perception of an object or a situation. They also include conceptions, that is, abstract ideas. The Latin verb *capere* stands for 'to take, to take to oneself.' Linguistic constructions with '-ception' thus beautifully and efficiently indicate that *we take something to ourselves in a particular way*. 'Per-' stands for 'by,' 'through,' and 'by means of,' and 'con-' for 'with' and 'together.' The German/Dutch words for the noun 'perception' and the verb 'to perceive' are *Wahrnehmung/waarneming* and *wahrnehmen/waarnemen*, respectively. They are even more telling than the English term. The verbs *wahrnehmen* and *waarnemen* are composed of *Wahr* (resp. *waar*) which means 'true,' and *nehmen* (resp. *nemen*) meaning 'to take.' Hence, when we perceive something, *we take something to ourselves and take it to be true.*

Schopenhauer concurred with Kant that we are caught in our phenomenal world, but he added that we do get glimpses of 'the thing in itself' in the form of what he called the will (*der Wille*). Benedictus de Espinoza or Baruch Spinoza (1632–1677) had already prepared the way for this insight by postulating that "desire is man's very essence, insofar as it is conceived to be determined, from any given affection of it, to do something" (1677/1996, p. 104). Hence, man is a willing organism, that is, an organism that engages in actions that relate to desire. Spinoza defined desire as "need together with the consciousness of it" (hence the phrase "insofar as it is conceived to be determined"), and appetite as "the very essence of man, insofar as it is determined to do what promotes his preservation" (pp. 76 and 104). Desire thus implies being conscious of one's strivings, one's urges, and appetite pertains to the will to life, to persevere in one's being. Appetite thus had a far wider meaning than our contemporary notion of appetite. For example, it also included the will to defend in the face of threat. Man is "determined to do those things" (p. 76). Spinoza added that "by the word *desire* I understand any of man's strivings, impulses, appetites, and volitions, which vary as the man's constitution varies, and which are not infrequently so opposed to one another that the man is pulled in different directions and knows not

1 The term 'phenomenal' stems from Kant, who distinguished between the world phenomena, 'the things for me,' and 'the thing in itself,' the noumenal world.

where to turn" (p. 104). This statement clarifies that desire is not one thing, but a differentiated manifold. There are different ways to preserve our being, so that we do not want one thing, but many different things, and these different desires can be conflicting. Spinoza also concluded that we do not strive for something because we judge it to be good, but that "we judge something to be good because we strive for it, will it, want it, and desire it" (p. 76). Will thus precedes cognition. Will is also primarily bodily, that is, grounded in our embodiment: ". . . since the human mind is necessarily conscious of itself through the ideas of the body's affections, the mind . . . is conscious of its strivings" (p. 76), that is, insofar as they are conscious. Differentiating between desire (conscious) and appetite (unconscious), Spinoza emphasized that we are not necessarily consciously aware of all urges that guide our actions.

There are many major parallels with respect to will between Spinoza and Schopenhauer, and far more than Schopenhauer indicates in his work. As applies to Spinoza's philosophy and psychology, for Schopenhauer the will is radically different from knowledge and from cognition. The will is primary, whereas knowledge, our intellect, is secondary. The organism that we are is the will itself, that is, the will as perceived in the brain, as perceived by our intellect, first of all in the form of the acts of the will. No matter how clever our intellect may be, the energetic embodied will beats it: "The intellect grows tired, the will is untiring" (Schopenhauer, 1958, Vol. II, p. 211) and will "gives all things, whatever they may be, the power to exist and to act" (Schopenhauer, 2007, p. 217). The organism we are never stops wanting something. We endlessly desire and strive to get the good things of life, and we wish and struggle on end to evade or get rid of the bad things. We long, cling, hope, love, play, rejoice, please, cry for attachment, startle, flee, freeze, fight, submit, or control. The will thus expresses itself in any degree of affect and passion, as Augustine (354–430; 1950, p. 179) already recognized:

> For what are desire and joy but a volition of consent to the things we wish? And what are fear and sadness but a volition of aversion from the things which we do not wish? But when consent takes the form of seeking to possess the things we wish, this is called desire; and when consent takes the form of enjoying the things we wish, this is called joy. In like manner, when we turn with aversion from that which we do not wish to happen, this volition is termed fear; and when we turn away from that which has happened against our will, this act of will is called sorrow. And generally in respect of all that we seek or shun, as a man's will is attracted or repelled, so it is changed and turned into these different affections.

The will we experience prior to any thought is the same will that manifests itself in all inorganic and organic structures, in all physical and chemical phenomena, and in all physical laws (e.g., gravity). Hence, the will is not dependent on our brain or on our cognitions. It is not caused by cognition though cognition is conditioned by the will (will → causes → thought). In beings like us gifted with intellect, the individual manifestations of the will, and hence its appearances in our phenomenal world, are often initially experienced in our body and set in motion by what we know as motives. The intellect, the understanding, "furnishes the will with motives; but only subsequently, and thus wholly *a posteriori*, does it know how these have acted ..." (Schopenhauer, 1813/2007, p. 209). The intellect "does not penetrate into the secret workshop of the will's decisions. It is, of course, a confidant of the will, yet a confidant that does not get to know everything" (p. 210). At best, our intellect operates as a timid regulator of the will. The will is set in motion by stimuli in animals and plants, and in inorganic nature by causes "in the narrowest sense of the word" (p. 217). Undifferentiated in the very beginning of life on earth, the will became more differentiated over evolutionary time and started to manifest in a variety of essential desires, strivings, efforts, or urges, and associated affects.

Spinoza's philosophical insights regarding appetites and desires, and Schopenhauer's emphasis on the will were to be lost and found again. For example, they reemerged in phenomenology (Merleau-Ponty, 1945/1962). Like Schopenhauer, Merleau-Ponty stressed that the will is primarily lived experience, and that this experience is intimately tied to our embodiment, to our lived body (*corps propre*) as well as to the intimate relationship between our lived body and our perceived and conceived world. According to the philosopher Jonas (1973), feeling is the first unfolding of the world, and Weber (2002) added that we may find an emotive background as the deepest underlying structure in all concepts of reality:

> The first fission of the world, the first discontinuity in the homogenous equilibrium of eternity has no structure, it is nothing but the amorphous cry of highest urgency uttered by the organism: vital or deadly.

Schopenhauer's ideas on will survived the behavioral and cognitive revolutions in psychology. The intellect would and could obviously not silence the will for long. Basic affects, basic urges or desires were to re-enter philosophy and psychology from the turn of the century. Thus, Panksepp (1998; Panksepp & Biven, 2012) – who may not have been aware of Spinoza's and Schopenhauer's philosophies; in any case, he does not refer to their seminal works – proposes that basic affects are the core of emotional operating systems that mammals developed in evolution. Lang, Bradley, and Cuthbert (1998) as well as Liotti (2006) refer to these evolutionary achievements as motivational systems. Carver and Scheier (2000) call them 'affect systems,' whereas Van der Hart, Steele, and I (Nijenhuis et al., 2002; Van der Hart et al., 2006) introduced the term 'action systems.' The idea that mammals are mediated by evolutionarily derived systems that precede, support, and constrain learning were similarly proposed by Bolles (1970), Bolles and Fanselow (1980), Fanselow and Lester (1988), and Timberlake and Lucas (1989) (see Chapter 6).

Action systems are thus systems that involve basic wills. These essential wills guide cognition and behavior. They could just as well, or perhaps even better, be called 'will systems'[2]. These teleofunctional[3] systems include systems for achieving something that, as determined

2 I use the terms 'action system' and 'will system' as synonyms.

3 'Teleos' (Greek) means 'goal.' 'Teleofunctional' expresses the hypothesis that the intended systems have evolved across evolutionary time because they served survival interests. It certainly does not refer

by these systems, is subjectively experienced and known to be attractive (e.g., pleasurable, exciting). These will systems comprise everything we really desire to get, everything we wish to achieve. The will also includes systems for avoiding or escaping from whatever (as established by these defensive systems) is subjectively experienced and known to be aversive (e.g., painful, dangerous, disgusting). These will systems comprise everything we really want to get rid of or evade. As Panksepp's work strongly suggests, "primal affects are internal valuative processes that promote survival" (Panksepp & Biven, 2012, p. 480). These 'primary-process' affects

> . . . coax us to treasure and detest various events and objects of the world, many of which would have no psychological depth, no profoundness, without our affective capacities. Thus, whatever *basic* values do exist in this human psychological world of ours, they reside inside human brains, and to a substantial degree, in the ancestral minds we inherited from earlier animals.

Spinoza's appetites, Schopenhauer's will, Panksepp's primal affects – they all pertain to the striving to life that we share with many other animals, and that manifests itself as the desire to explore, play, attach, make friends, eat, relax, have sex, and influence one's fate, as well as the urge to defend ourselves when faced with threat. These various wills and their implied raw emotional feelings are *deeply* felt and enacted, and are, in a literal sense, associated with the deep parts of the brain. That is, they are primarily mediated by the brainstem. For example, even decorticated animals passionately work to obtain the pleasurable raw emotional feelings of excitation and likewise work to avoid or escape from adverse events (Panksepp & Biven, 2012). Congenitally decorticate children also show basic emotions (Shewmon, Holmes, & Byrne, 1999).

The will systems involved are thus primarily emotional. They strongly influence what we experience and regard as important. They guide how we perceive ourselves, other individuals, objects, situations, and our world in general. And they powerfully influence what we think, remember, and do. In this context, basic affects tend to precede, constrain, and support cognition. They are also integrative, because the particular form the will takes integrates sensations, emotions, perceptions, cognitions and behaviors relevant to it.

An inherent problem of the will is that it is a manifold phenomenon. Our various wills encompass different mental actions (e.g., experiencing a desire to eat, sleep, play, attach, or an urge to defend; thinking appropriate thoughts and remembering relevant previous experiences) and behavioral actions. In some cases these actions may be related and compatible, as happens when we are hungry: We have a will to eat and therefore search for food. The will systems of energy management and exploration generally go quite well together. However, there are also will systems that are hard to reconcile with each other, or even practically incompatible, particularly when they concern the same object (a ma-

to the idea that these systems were created by design (e.g., God's plans). Varela (1991) conceded that teleology concerns meaning making, that is, a coupling between the individual organism and his or her environment.

terial object, another individual, a situation). Strong but contrary wills imply contrary actions. For example, what should children do who have chronically been traumatized by their parents? One will tells them to defend themselves in one fashion or another; another will commands them to attach, because how can children exist and mature without their parents? They are prone to swing back and forth between these different strivings they cannot integrate, which manifests itself in shifting, dissociative attachment patterns (Liotti, 2004, 2006; Van der Hart et al., 2006). Hence, the motto of the next chapter will be: "Men can disagree in nature insofar as they are torn by affects which are passions; and to that extent also one and the same man is changeable and inconstant" (Spinoza, 1677, Proposition 33, p. 131). Structural dissociation of the personality is the one extreme of this inconstancy that stems from the difficulty to reconcile and coordinate contrary wills. Different Janetian dissociative 'systems of ideas and functions' thus tend to involve contrary wills (functions) and implied behaviors as well as ideas: affects, sensations, perceptions, thoughts, and memories.

ANP: Ignorance

According to our consistent clinical observations, as a prototypical ANP, traumatized patients are mainly focused on concerns of daily life. They strive to eat, drink, sleep, explore, play, attach (e.g., to their parents), have sex perhaps (though following sexual abuse, many will certainly try to avoid it as much as possible), have children, care for children, and have partners and friends. Such is their differentiated primary will. These observations lead us to hypothesize that, as ANP, traumatized individuals are primarily mediated by action systems for functioning in daily life, such as energy management, exploration, reproduction, care taking, sociability, and play.

Anyone who has been confronted with adverse events and who has not yet been able to integrate the experience (i.e., synthesize, personify, and presentify it) will be intruded on by the hurtful memories of these occasions. These involuntary confrontations with the terrifying past and with the person they were at the time are considered adverse events and may lead to classically conditioned fear and avoidance. That is, ANP develops phobias of traumatic memories and the associated idea of self that involves EP. Traumatic memories are mostly sensorimotor and highly affectively charged. These "passions" lack symbolization (Spinoza's "clear and distinct ideas"). The implication is that, by means of generalization learning, ANP may also develop phobias of bodily feelings and of the body as such as well as a phobia of affects. And to the extent that the traumatization involved interpersonal betrayal, ANP may also develop a phobia of attachment and/or attachment loss. A particular form of classical conditioning involves evaluative conditioning: By means of this type of associative learning, ANP may start to dislike or even detest EP and everything this part encompasses, such as a strong awareness of a hurt or filthy body, aversive bodily sensations, affects such as the feeling of being utterly fragile and terrified, and many other things as well (for a more detailed description of these forms of associative learning, see Van der Hart et al., 2006).

Trying to function in daily life, ANP preconsciously and consciously attempts to avoid the feared and detested EP and the hurting traumatic memories where this part of his or her personality is stuck. Trying to act as if nothing is wrong, ANP ignores EP and what this part or these parts encompass as much as possible. This ignorance, this avoidance, is mediated by the will to avoid or escape from any physical and mental pain ANP cannot or does not want to integrate (or both). Unwilling or unable to integrate EP and the associated overwhelming sensorimotor and highly affectively charged re-enactments that traumatic memories are, ANP includes the features of Horowitz's phases of denial, numbing, and avoidance.

Some poets poignantly express clinical realities in their works. Rainer Maria Rilke (2005), for example, captured the truncated life that remains when an individual, as ANP, is forced to hide behind a mask and must put EP and authenticity away:

> No one lives his life.
> Disguised since childhood, haphazardly assembled from voices and fears and little pleasures,
> we come of age as masks.
> Our true face never speaks.
>
> Somewhere there must be storehouses where all these lives are laid away
> like suits of armor and old carriages or clothes hanging limply on the walls.
> Maybe all the paths lead us there to the repository of unlived things.
> And yet, though you and I struggle against this deathly clutch of daily necessity,
> sense there is this mystery
> All life is being lived
> Who is living it then?

According to TSDP, ANP is not primarily characterized by thoughts and ideas. As this part of the personality, traumatized individuals predominantly *desire* to have a daily life, and they strive to avoid traumatic memories and the associated dissociative subsystems of the personality. It is their deep will that conditions what they as ANP tend to feel, perceive, think, imagine, and do, and what they, for their part, *wish* to feel perceive, think, imagine, and do not.

Fragile EP

According to TSDP, EP is fixed in traumatizing events. In this prototypical part, traumatized individuals are oriented toward the traumatizing past they take for the present. In this part, they feel fragile and victimized, hence the term 'fragile EP.' Whereas some EPs have a desperate urge to seek safety in a caretaking relationship, which may include desperately craving attachment, most EPs are primarily mediated by one or more subsystems of a more general action system for defense that mammals have developed in evolution. To understand fragile EPs, it is important to know the will or action system of mammalian defense and to appreciate that the ideas of this dissociative part are conditioned by the will to defend.

Mammalian Defense

Like other mammals, humans respond to potential and perceived threat to the integrity of the body and to life itself in a complex and coordinated manner (Bovin & Marx, 2010; Nijenhuis et al., 1998d; Nijenhuis et al., 2002b). The reaction patterns involve efforts to avoid confrontations with predators or threatening members of one's own species. When a predator is spotted, the prey engages in a series of different reactions. A common first reaction is an orientation reflex or startle response. When the predator gets closer in terms of space and time, the prey shift to different defenses. These include pre-encounter defenses such as freezing and flight, circa-strike defenses such as appeasement and fight, as well as tonic immobility, also known as playing dead, playing possum, or death feigning (Cantor, 2009; Fanselow & Lester, 1988). Freezing involves the will to survive threat by staying immobile (Fendt & Fanselow, 1999). Freezing is often confused with death feigning. However, whereas death feigning involves a type of mammalian defense in which the mammal becomes passive, freezing mammals are activated and alert. For example, their muscle tension is high, and they can readily shift to flight or fight if they preconsciously or consciously decide that these defensive actions are more effective. The evolutionary value of freezing is that predators have a sharp eye for moving prey, and they have difficulty detecting immobile prey that, thanks to their camouflage colors, may merge with the environment. Moreover, at least some predatory taxa are less likely to attack still prey, that is, they attack only when prey is on the move. Freezing is not per se associated with inescapable threat, because prey may also freeze in situations that afford flight or other defensive strategies. Freezing is strongly associated with analgesia. Analgesia allows prey to focus on defensive concerns should it become injured during an attack rather than on struggling with pain and minding tissue damage. Flight is about the will to survive by moving away from the source of threat; defensive fight is the will to survive by warding off the predator.

Whereas active defenses including freezing involve dominance of the sympathetic nervous system, in death feigning/tonic immobility the parasympathetic nervous system, more specifically the dorsal vagal complex reigns (Porges, 1995, 2001, 2007, 2009; Reed, Ohel, David, & Porges, 1999). Tonic immobility is often described as a defense of last resort. However, it rather ensues when prey estimate that sympathetically mediated defensive actions are less likely to save their skin. When an animal engages in this passive type of defensive action, it is more or less paralyzed. Completely immobile, the animal looks as if it were dead. The breathing is slowed, the heart rate and the sensitivity to pain drop. Apart from being analgesic, the animal may also become anesthetic in the sense that it becomes insensitive to touch.

Consistent with Schopenhauer's view that the will has become ever more differentiated in evolution, Porges (1995, 2001, 2007, 2009) suggests that mammalian defenses involving the sympathetic nervous system emerged later in evolution than the passive defense of tonic immobility. He hypothesizes that this type of mammalian defense is associated with the dorsal vagal nerve, which is a part of the parasympathetic nervous system that much later in evolution came to include a ventral branch supporting social engagement (see Chapter 16; Nijenhuis & Den Boer, 2009).

Some prototypical fragile EPs are stuck in active kinds of defense to real or perceived threat that involve the sympathetic nervous system and that imply hyperarousal. In these dissociative parts, traumatized individuals want to escape from threat by stilling, hiding, running, appeasing, or warding off. Other EPs predominantly engage in tonic immobility, which includes hypoarousal.

In sum, according to TSDP, some prototypical fragile EPs are stuck in active kinds of defense to real or perceived threat that include activation of the sympathetic nervous system and imply hyperarousal. In these dissociative parts, traumatized individuals have the urge to escape from threat by active behavioral means. Other fragile EPs predominantly engage in tonic immobility including subjective and physiologic hypoarousal. When ANPs manage to keep traumatic memories and associated EPs at bay, they do not become hyperaroused, but rather experience symptoms of depersonalization, derealization, bodily numbing, and emotional detachment. Did Emily Dickinson perhaps describe the intense pains of EP, and trance of forgetting found in ANP?

There is a pain – so utter –
It swallows substance up –
Then cover the Abyss with Trance –
So memory can step
Around – across – upon it –
As one within a Swoon –
Goes safely – where an open eye –
Would drop Him – Bone by Bone.

Controlling EP

Utter helplessness is antithetical to health. All children, adolescents, and adults want to be able to influence, to control their fate whenever possible. In a social frame, the will to power implies a striving to have an influence on other individuals. In humans, it manifests itself as achievement, ambition, and the striving to reach the highest possible position in life. Nietzsche (1968) even conceded that the will to power is fundamental[4].

4 The Nazis abused Nietzsche's philosophy, whereby Nietzsche's own sister Elisabeth Förster-Nietzsche paved the path to this sad development, reformulating her brother's ideas to make them more compatible with Nazi ideology.

In ANP, a child that is chronically traumatized by caretakers or other significant individuals may be able to attend school, have a hobby, engage in sports, and have some friends, but will also be more or less depersonalized, numbed, and avoidant. As one or more EPs engaged in active or passive defense, the child survives threat but feels fragile and victimized. So how should a child develop or maintain a sense of control?

Consistent clinical observations suggest that children may develop a prototypical EP that seems to be mediated by an action system of social ranking or dominance, by a will to control, a will to power. I call this prototype 'controlling EP'. Much of what children learn comes by learning to imitate models. Chronically abused and neglected children are chronically exposed to vicious models for social dominance, and these are the models that tell them how to gain influence in life (cf. Liotti, 2006). To achieve at least some sense of control, these children may start to imitate their perpetrator's actions. As controlling EPs, they hide their fragility, powerlessness, and dependency on their perpetrators – their deepest nightmares – behind a display of strength and aggression (Draijer & Van Zon, 2013).

As found with the other prototypes of dissociative parts, the way in which controlling EPs perceive and conceive of the world and themselves is guided by their will. As one or more controlling EPs, they reject and attack fragile EPs by calling them names, by mutilating their body, or even by attempting to kill them. controlling EPs typically want to get rid of fragile EPs – in any case they do not want to be associated with any part of these "weak" EPs. Controlling EPs tend to despise ANPs as well. For example, one controlling EP said: "Sonja [the ANP] is a sissy. She only talks for hours and hours and achieves nothing. Words are no good. Words are for pussies and don't mean a thing. I am angry, I am strong, I want to hit people as hard as I can when I can. That's what you have to do." This part, which called herself "The Devil," also despised the therapist because he too used only words.

When reactivated, fragile EPs and controlling EPs can intrude on the domains of ANPs, just as these different prototypical EPs can intrude on each other's domains. These intrusions include Horowitz's phase of intrusion of trauma-related imagery and affect. The hurting felt by fragile EPs is plainly present when these parts step forward and re-enact the uncompleted horrific past. Their pain becomes the pain of the ANPs during intrusions.

Integration of Will Systems

Coordinating and integrating sensations, affects, thoughts, memories, and behaviors can be difficult. However, the coordination and integration between different will systems is an even greater challenge, especially when the involved wills are antithetical. Children who want to play may not be thrilled to hear that it is bedtime. The natural urge to attach to parents is at odds with an equally natural striving to run from or otherwise defend themselves against abusive, maltreating, or neglectful parents. Adults who have been sexually abused may detest sex but still long for a partner and children. In conflicts, we may want to assert ourselves, but fear rejection and abandonment, and hence withhold our critical feelings.

We need to learn to regulate and coordinate our different wills, our different desires. This regulation is not a given, but rather constitutes a developmental task. According to Schore (2001, 2003), one primary function of parents and other primary caretakers is to help children regulate their affects. In the present terms, this regulation involves the coordination and integration of components of will systems as well as of different wills. Individuals who enjoy and have enjoyed good parenting will therefore, *ceteris paribus*, have a higher integrative capacity and better affect/will regulation skills than those who have not been enjoyed affective guidance and support.

Because of the stress that adverse events may evoke – exactly how stressful adverse events turn out to be is in part dependent on the exposed subject (see Chapters 6 and 7) – the individual's integrative capacity may diminish. Chronically traumatized individuals, and children in particular, are thus placed in double trouble. They must coordinate and integrate extreme emotional experiences, which lowers their integrative capacity; and the parents or other primary caretakers who should be assisting them to come to terms with the terrifying experience(s) ignore the fragility of the ones they abuse, maltreat, and neglect. Dominated by, or obsessed with, their own needs for control in interpersonal sexual, physical, and/or emotional regards, such parents victimize in a double sense: They abuse, maltreat, and neglect as well as disregard their victims' need for assistance in bearing, integrating, and realizing what has been done to them.

Individuals who have a greater integrative capacity and who are confronted with less adverse events (relatively speaking, of course) are generally better equipped to deal with such adversities. However, anyone with social support during and following the adverse events will fare better.

Who Develops a Dissociation of the Personality?

According to TSDP, the difficulty of coping with and integrating adverse experiences thus relates to factors that limit the exposed individual's integrative capacity. They include the developmental stage and the implied degree of brain maturation, attachment style, severity, and chronicity of adverse events, lack of peritraumatic and posttraumatic social recognition and affective support and regulation, prior adverse event exposure, adverse event-related structural and functional changes of the brain, and perhaps also some particular genetic endowment as Charcot suspected (see Chapter 6).

In sum, an unfavorable constellation of these factors compromises the individual's ability to integrate such experiences into their personality. When this integration does not occur, in at least one EP, patients become fixed in their traumatic experiences, and in at least one ANP, they wish to mentally avoid the traumatic memory in order to meet the interests of daily life. EPs will not have a normal narrative autobiographical memory of the traumatizing event, but rather re-enact it in a sensorimotor and highly emotional, nonsymbolized form. These passionate re-enactments commonly include a retracted field of consciousness (cf. Bob, Golla, Epstein, & Konopka, 2011) or, as in the context of tonic immobility, a low level of consciousness. The abnormal field and level of consciousness interfere with EP's ability to grasp the actual present as the experienced present. EP is thus bound to remain stuck in the traumatic memory under these circumstances, particularly when ANP – who can in principle reach a wider field and higher level of consciousness – avoids integrating the aversive memory in which EP is fixed. For example, when ANPs are occasionally intruded upon by EP, as happens during flashbacks and nightmares, ANPs may retract their field of consciousness and panic and/or lower their level of consciousness, leaving the traumatic memory non-integrated and largely unaltered. The maintenance of the dissociation is also due to EP's avoidance of ANP. For example, in EP, the patient may become phobic of ANP when ANP rejects EP. This phobia can become particularly severe when emotional neglect and rejection are part of EP's life experiences with caretakers and other significant others.

Sooner or later the continued efforts of ANP at mental avoidance exhaust this part, compromising its ability to ignore. ANP's faltering ignorance or other avoidant actions lead to ever more frequent and powerful intrusions of EP and the traumatic memories of this part in ANP's crumbling domain.

These theoretical concepts are consistent with the hypothesis of Ehlers and Clark (2000) that emotional avoidance may maintain PTSD because it impedes the extinction[5] of emotional responses that are part and parcel of traumatic memories. In concert with these ideas, in one study (Kumpula, Orcutt, Bardeen, & Varkovitzky, 2011) emotional avoidance predicted the maintenance of PTSD better than peritraumatic dissociation+[6] (discussed in Chapter 6).

5 However, there are problems with the idea of extinction. There is evidence that learned associations between conditioned and unconditioned aversive stimuli remain intact when an individual has overcome conditioned emotional and behavioral reactions to conditioned stimuli. What can be learned is that the association between conditioned and unconditioned stimuli does not apply in every context. This theme will be taken up in Volume III.

6 The reason for writing 'dissociation+' is that for most authors the term 'dissociation' also captures alterations of the quality and quantity of mental contents. However, these alterations do not imply a dissociation of the personality, and they are not specific to trauma-related disorders. The '+' symbol expresses this, in my view, overinclusive domain of dissociative symptoms. Much more on the conceptualization of dissociation is to follow, particularly in Chapters 12–14 (Volume II). For writing style regarding the term 'dissociation,' see Chapter 5, p. 107.

A Dimension of Severity of Personality Division

According to TSDP, the basic division of one ANP and one EP marks most cases of simple PTSD and dissociative disorders of movement and sensation (ICD-10, WHO 1992; see Chapter 5). Complex PTSD (also discussed in Chapter 5) commonly entails one ANP and several fragile EPs, as well as one or more controlling EPs. This organization of the traumatized individual's personality also characterizes many cases of "chronic and recurrent syndromes of mixed dissociative symptoms" (APA, 2013). These disorders often involve cases of what I call 'minor DID,'[7] that is, lesser but *certainly not insignificant forms* of full-blown (major) DID (see Chapter 6). The personality of patients with major DID typically encompasses more than one ANP and more than one EP. The more complex the dissociative disorder is, the more at least some of the patient's EPs will tend to be evolved.

Personality as a Biopsychosocial System

The personality constitutes a whole biopsychosocial system. The rather awkward adjective 'biopsychosocial' communicates the metaphysical position that living individuals can be described and studied in biological, psychological, and psychosocial terms. René Descartes (1596–1650; 1637) proposed that matter and mind constitute essentially different substances. His philosophical dualism presents the insoluble enigma how matter and mind, being essentially different, can influence or communicate with each other. An interesting correspondence between Descartes and the brilliant Princess Elisabeth of Bohemia reveals how she humbly, but clearly and persistently, confronted Descartes with the puzzle the philosopher had created and his futile attempts to solve it (Bennett, 2005; see Chapter 8).

Spinoza, who like Descartes worked and lived in the Netherlands, was also quick to protest:

> I cannot wonder enough that a philosopher of his caliber – one who had firmly decided to deduce nothing except from principles known through themselves, and to affirm nothing which he did not perceive clearly and distinctly, one who had so often censured the Scholastics for wishing to explain obscure things by occult qualities – that such a philosopher should assume a hypothesis more occult than any occult quality. (1677/1996, p. 162)

Spinoza alternatively suggested a philosophical monism in which matter and mind are metaphysically comprehended as different attributes of one substance that he called God

7 The World Health Organization working group, whose task it is to propose a classification and typology for dissociative disorders in ICD-11 (Nijenhuis, Lewis-Fernandez, Moskowitz, & Moreira-Almeida, 2014) recently suggested the term "Complex Dissociative Intrusion Disorder" as an alternative name for the term Minor DID. This proposed name captures very well that ANP in Minor DID is currently intruded on by EPs that do not, or only rather exceptionally, take full control over the patient's consciousness and behavior. Hence, when I use the term Minor DID in the present text, one may read Complex Dissociative Intrusion Disorder.

or Nature. This singular substance may have manifold attributes, though mankind knows only two of them: matter – what appears to humans as being extended, that is, as having volume – and mind – what appears to humans as having no extension.

I discuss these philosophical issues in more detail later (e.g., Chapter 8). Here, I want to make only some preliminary remarks. One comment is that the term 'biopsychosocial' can be discarded if personality is understood as a living system that includes matter and mind as different attributes of one substance. A related provisional statement is that this system includes a brain that is an intrinsic part of a wider body, and that this wider body is intrinsically tied to that brain. The embodied and 'embrained' system is in part aware of itself and of the world it finds around it. A fruit of ongoing phylogenic evolution and ontogenic development, this conscious organism cannot exist in a materially, socially, and culturally environmental void. Whereas there is thus an environment, this environment only exists because a subject experiences and knows it in a particular way. Whatever individuals experience and know, it is of necessity confined to what they can experience and know – and what they can experience and know is subject to evolutionary changes. Without objects, there would be no subjects, and without experiencing and knowing subjects, there would be no objects. In a word, subject and object constitute and depend on each other (Northoff, 2003; Schopenhauer, 1958). Although personality can be seen as a living system, a conscious organism is necessarily part of a wider system that Järvilehto (1998a, 1998b, 1999, 2000a, 2000b, 2000c, 2001a, 2001b) calls the organism-environment system. The personality constitutes an intrinsic part of this wider system because neither the personality nor the environment exists or could exist independent of each other. It is this organism-environment system that defines the individual's characteristic actions, that is, his or her *personality*. As Faust (von Goethe, 1808/1959, p. 394) marveled:

> How all things weave one whole together,
> And live and work in one other!
> How heavenly beings sink and rise
> Exchanging golden chalices!

Dissociative Symptoms: Manifestations of a Dissociation of the Personality

In terms of TSDP, the existence of a division in the individual's personality as a living system that constitutes an intrinsic part of an organism-environment system manifests itself in dissociative symptoms. Whereas some of these symptoms present in the body, they may also be of a mental nature, just as mental symptoms imply the brain, the rest of the body, as well as the material environment. To speak with Spinoza, the mental and the physical are attributes of one substance.

The symptoms can be classified as positive and negative and as psychoform/cognitive-emotional and somatoform/sensorimotor (Nijenhuis & Van der Hart, 2011a). Positive symptoms pertain to 'something that is there, that should not be there [anymore].' This 'something' entails particular mental/behavioral actions and their implied contents. For example, re-experiencing traumatizing events is a positive dissociative symptom because there is a subsystem or part of the personality, metaphorically described as EP, that recurrently engages in the action of recollecting the past in the form of a traumatic memory. Rather than relive the traumatic past, the individual is challenged to integrate and symbolize it. Negative symptoms, on the other hand, indicate that 'something is missing.' For example, the bodily numbing of ANP or EP is a negative symptom, because the involved dissociative part does not engage in the action of feeling one or more parts the body.

Cognitive-emotional dissociative symptoms involve the contents of cognitive-emotional actions such as an EP recollecting the traumatic past in the form of a traumatic memory, and an ANP avoiding to integrate these painful recollections as a personal experience, which can present as being depersonalized and emotionally detached. Sensorimotor dissociative symptoms involve the contents of sensorimotor actions such as an EP engaging in the action of re-enacting tonic immobility (playing dead) under massive threat that tends to imply a degree of sensory anesthesia, paralysis, and lowering, or even loss of consciousness.

Chapter 5

Dissociation of the Personality in PTSD

Men can disagree in nature insofar as they are torn by affects which are passions; and to that extent also one and the same man is changeable and inconstant.
Spinoza (1677)

Following our discussion of the theme of structural dissociation of the personality in general, it is now time to return to the discussion at the time of formulating and classifying PTSD in the DSM-III (APA, 1980) whether the disorder is best comprehended as a form of traumatic melancholia (anxiety disorder), or whether it is perhaps better understood as a form of hysteria, that is, as a dissociative disorder. The dispute did not find its completion with the classification of PTSD as an anxiety disorder in DSM-III.

According to the standard view of PTSD, re-experiencing involves spatiotemporal confusion and a lack of symbolization or at least insufficient symbolization of the traumatizing event. That is, when PTSD patients re-experience the traumatizing events they once experienced, they do not recollect these as an autobiographical narrative, but rather re-enact them in a sensorimotor form that may or may not be highly affectively charged. While re-experiencing and re-enacting an event that injured or traumatized them, they do not (or at least not sufficiently) realize that their experience pertains to the past. They conceive the terrible past as a present occurrence, as a horrible event that is occurring here and now, rather than as an event that happened 'there and then.'

What this view conspicuously overlooks or ignores is that the spatiotemporal confusion involved includes a shift in the individual's subjective conception of who he or she *is*. Is the person who re-experiences and re-enacts the traumatic memory the same person who avoids that memory but who gets recurrently intruded? Observers might say that they are, indeed, the same individual. But they can only come to that superficial conclusion by ignoring the individual's subjective experience. If they were to consider subjectivity and take it seriously, a different answer would emerge. What they soon discover is that traumatized individuals lose their subjective experience and conception of who they presently are during the re-experiencing and re-enactment. Their present 'I' becomes replaced by a former 'I,' which they then experience and think of as if it were their present 'I.'

Some clinicians and researchers have noted these shifts. For example, Wang et al. (1996)

found that each of the different 'stages' of PTSD patients include their own phenomenal sense of self. Several traumatized individuals expressed this truth very clearly. Having been chronically sexually abused by her father in her childhood, Marilyn Van Derbur (2003) developed a 'day child' (ANP) and a 'night child' (fragile EP). The day child had matured and developed the identity of an adult. Whereas she was academically and professionally successful, she was practically unable to engage in a normal intimate relationship. When the day child, she managed to function in daily life until she became haunted by the night child that was stuck in the traumatic past, which this part of her experienced as the present. Rejected and avoided by the day child, the night child had stayed phenomenally locked in the terrible abuse by her father, and in the emotional neglect by her mother – who knew about her husband's malign deeds, but who did not interfere. The night child was not only stuck in re-experiencing and re-enacting the abuse and neglect, she also was stuck in the experience, perception, and conception of who she was: a child. Indeed, for EP, traumatizing events, time, place and identity are static.

Charlotte Delbo (1985) also described the existence of more than one identity in PTSD. As quoted in *The Haunted Self* by Van der Hart et al. (2006), she wrote

> I have the feeling that the 'self' who was in the camp isn't me, isn't the person who is here, opposite you. No, it's too unbelievable. And everything that happened to this other 'self,' the one from Auschwitz, doesn't touch me now, *me*, doesn't concern me, so distinct are deep memory and common memory. (p. 13)

As EP, Delbo (1985) re-experienced her terror at times. Unable to integrate her concentration camp life, as ANP she ran from it whenever she could, seeking refuge in a depersonalized existence:

> Fortunately, in my anguish, I cry out. The cry awakens me, and I emerge from the nightmare, exhausted. It takes days for everything to return to normal, for memory to be "refilled" and for the skin of memory to mend itself. I become myself again, the one you know, who can speak to you of Auschwitz without showing any sign of distress or emotion. (1985, p. 13–14)

Like Van Derbur's night child, Delbo's Auschwitz-fixated existence did not mature, certainly not subjectively.

Individuals with PTSD thus harbor more than one sense of self. 'Sense of self' is a common but vague expression, as is the term 'self.' So, what is our 'sense' of 'self'? Chapter 12 is an attempt to answer to this intriguing, complex, and important question. As a prelude, it can be said that 'self' is not given, and that it is absent when we are asleep and not dreaming. It is not a little child, a man, or a woman in the head that guides our actions. If it were, the instant question would become: What is that mannekin's self? An endless regress would follow. There are good reasons to contend that our 'I' does not appear in and of itself, but that it is generated by the dreaming or conscious individual in ongoing, largely unconscious actions in the interest of that individual as a whole organism (Metzinger, 2003). According to Metzinger, 'self,' then, is a phenomenal model[1] of self, or as I prefer, a phenomenal conception of self. *It is a conception of who one is.* This phenomenal conception is not static but dynamic, because, aside from unconscious states such as dreamless sleep, it is continuously generated. The unconscious and ongoing generation of a phenomenal conception of self can explain why mentally healthy individuals experience and think they have or are a self. It is in this sense that our self is not the cause, but the phenomenal *result* of particular conceptual actions (Loevinger, 1976).

This hypothesis is supported by the phenomenon of trauma. From the time of their traumatization, PTSD patients and patients with a more complex dissociation of their personality as a whole system encompass two or more different subsystems, each of which generates its own phenomenal conception of self. Anyone who closely and recurrently observes individuals with PTSD and who on this basis reflects on the disorder cannot miss the point that these patients generate more than one idea of who they are, and that these different conceptions do not or only insufficiently become integrated among each other. The patients experience that they have or are a self, but they then lose this present 'I' and replace it by a different experience and idea of who they are when they re-experience their nonintegrated horrors. This loss is not like the voluntary loosening of the phenomenal conception of self that, for example, can be achieved in meditation. It is rather a phenomenon that, as patients experience and report, happens beyond their voluntary control. For example, 'the day child' and Delbo's daily life self became recurrently and involuntary deactivated when 'the night child' and 'the one from Auschwitz,' respectively, emerged for a stretch of time. It also happened to Van Derbur and Delbo that their daily life selves became intruded on by their other phenomenal selves that were fixed in traumatic experiences. In that case, two different phenomenal conceptions of self were activated in parallel. As ANP, PTSD patients tend to be more or less depersonalized and detached; as EP, they are hyperaroused (e.g., while engaging in flight or freeze) or hypoaroused (e.g., when engaging in tonic immobility) when re-enacting traumatic memories. In this context, ANPs often prefer to feel and believe that they are not the one who became traumatized, that they are not the 'night child,' not 'the one from Auschwitz.' ANPs can achieve this goal by engaging in mental avoidance of the feared EPs. They can completely deactivate themselves or reduce their level of consciousness, which results in a weak phenomenal self-conception – and which presents in negative symptoms of depersonalization, derealization, and bodily as well as emotional detachment.

In order to recognize and acknowledge that PTSD includes more than one 'I,' a condition that is not overcome for the duration of the disorder, one need not accept TSDP or a similar persuasion at blind sight. What *is* needed, however, is a serious appreciation and examination of subjectivity in PTSD, more specifically, of shifting phenomenal selves and the mental and behavioral actions of these selves. This includes studying their different conceptions of the world and the place in the world they conceive for themselves.

---

1 For a critique of the term 'model,' and grounds for replacing the term model by the terms 'idea' or 'conception,' see Chapters 8 and 12.

A small but meaningful step in this direction was to ask seasoned trauma therapists whether, according to their experiences with and observations of PTSD patients, re-enactment of traumatizing events only involves spatiotemporal shifts, or whether these shifts also comprise a shift in the patient's phenomenal self and in the patient's will(s). All agreed that these re-enactments do include a shift toward a felt, perceived, and conceived self that fits the re-enacted traumatic experience, with a loss or serious weakening of the patient's present phenomenal conception of self. The consistent and recurrent observation of these spatiotemporal and identity shifts led Myers, Horowitz, Wilson, Wang and still other pioneers to propose that shell shock, PTSD, or any other descendent of Burton's "horrible kind of melancholia" involve a division or recurrent reconfiguration of personality. The existence of more than one phenomenal conception of self in PTSD can be empirically tested by systematically examining patients with PTSD in this regard, particularly by systematically exploring these different conceptions in intimate interaction with these individuals.

The First-Person Perspective

The shifts between different conceptions of phenomenal self in trauma-related disorders including PTSD involve various epistemic perspectives, various ways of experiencing and knowing both oneself and one's world. As applies to any individual, ANP and EP do not 'have' a self, but rather engage in the action of experiencing, perceiving, and conceiving of a self. They generate their own phenomenal self in this context, their own first-person perspective: *the phenomenal experience of being an 'I' with particular bodily feelings, emotions, perceptions, and thoughts, and of having a point of view regarding oneself, other people, and objects.* A first-person perspective thus includes the experience, the ongoing perception, and the more general conception of an 'I,' of being an experiencing and knowing subject. It involves phenomenal experience, that is, access to one's mental states (Northoff, 2003).

The injury that trauma is involves more than one first-person perspective – more than one 'I.' More specifically, alternating between an ANP and an EP implies shifts between the different first-person perspectives that these different subsystems of the personality generate. For example, traumatized individuals who re-enact a traumatic experience as a fragile EP may feel "I am terribly afraid" and "I am hurting." This re-enactment includes the partial or complete deactivation of the phenomenal self-conception of the ANP. As ANP, the patient may experience and appreciate that he or she is presently safe, mature, physically recovered, married, or the father of a child, but as EP they may fail to experience, know, or realize this. What is more, reactivation of, or intrusion by, the EP does not lead to the integration of the 'I' of this dissociative part and the 'I' of the ANP for the duration of the disorder. As EP, traumatized individuals are unable to integrate the present that includes their existence as ANP. As ANP, they neither wish nor dare, or are simply unable to integrate EP.

The first-person perspective includes 'I-object' relationships[2]. Different dissociative parts of the personality experience, know, and evaluate objects in their own way. Particularly as EP do individuals with PTSD or a different trauma-related disorder experience and conceive numerous objects in terms of the traumatic past. They may regard a desk as a place to hide, sounds in the corridor as footsteps of a perpetrator, utensils as weapons, and a helmeted man as an exceptionally dangerous individual. For example, as ANP, traumatized individuals may conceive of a knife as a household utensil; as a fragile EP, they may regard the knife as a weapon that will be used against them, and as a controlling EP, they might perceive it as a tool for mutilating the fragile EP's body.

Only when the patient integrates his or her traumatic memories do the different conscious and self-conscious subsystems become integrated. This integration leads to the ongoing generation of one largely coherent and cohesive phenomenal self. The integrated individual realizes that the terrible experiences in fact happened in the past, that they happened to him or her, and that the past experience and the implied past self have come to an end. Only then do the previously nonintegrated past and the associated 'I' become integrated with the ANP's 'I' and personal history. Following this realization, the individual is basically healed, becomes a whole, and generates only a single 'I' that has overcome prior apparent normality and emotionality.

The Quasi-Second-Person Perspective

Mentally healthy individuals also have the experience that they have a 'me,' 'mine,' and 'myself.' These concepts refer to the *phenomenal experience and conception of ownership* (e.g., "This is my hand") *and agency* (e.g., "My hands are trembling"). 'Myself' appears in relational conceptions such as "I am proud of myself." I propose to use the term 'quasi-second-person perspective'[3] to capture these 'I-me,' 'I-myself,' and 'I- mine' relationships. In these relationships, the phenomenal 'I' experiences and knows. And 'me' is the object of attention that reflects the 'I,' or at least some of the features of the 'I.' Whereas the first-person perspective concerns phenomenal experience, the quasi-second-person perspective involves *phenomenal judgment* (Northoff, 2003). The judgment is phenomenal because it involves the judgment of phenomenal experiences, that is, of mental states the owner can consciously access. Like the first-person perspective, the quasi-second-person perspective is not a given, but depends on ongoing mental action. To judge is to act.

Re-experiencing the injurious past as an EP often includes a partial or more complete

2 These relationships will be technically renamed and defined in Chapter 12 as phenomenal conceptions of intentionality relationships.

3 Northoff (2003) refers to 'I-me, myself, mine' relationships as the second-person perspective. However, he also uses this term to denote 'I-You' relationships. To avoid confusion, I use the term quasi-second-person perspective for 'I-me, myself, mine' phenomenal relationships and reserve the term second-person perspective for 'I-You' phenomenal relationships.

re-enactment of the quasi-second-person perspective that the individual generated during the actual traumatization. For example, survivors who re-enact the past may re-experience or phenomenally judge that "my body is dirty and hurting"; they may say "I hate myself" (for example, for obeying the perpetrator's demands), or when talking about the perpetrator, "that is not my mother; my mother loves me." Referring to an EP they may as ANP say "that child does not belong to me."

The quasi-second-person perspective also relates to autobiographical memory. Many authors feel that these memories pertain to experiences that individuals 'encode,' 'store,' and 'retrieve.' A different view is that they involve functional links between what an individual once wanted and what that individual presently wants to achieve. As the neurophilosopher Georg Northoff (2003, p. 156) put it,

> [p]ast 'goal-orientations' are simulated in order to become 'available' for the actual i.e., present 'goal-orientation.' Nonetheless, the simulation of 'past-goal-orientation' cannot be considered as a mere copying since, due to the orientation on present 'goal-orientation,' it may be slightly modified. Feelings and emotions provide the linkage between past and present 'goal-orientation.' This is reflected in the comparison between past and actual feelings and emotions. If both past and actual feelings are compatible with each other, a feeling of 're-experiencing' and 're-living' arises. This feeling characterizes the retrieval of a past event within the context of the actual event.
>
> Accordingly, [autobiographical] memories may be regarded as 're-vival' rather than 'storage.' Nonetheless, the 're-vival' is not simply 're-vival' since the original contents may be modified by the action context and its respective emotions. This has already been pointed out by Locke (1690, Book II, Chapter X, 2): '... this laying up of our ideas in the repository of the memory signifies no more but this – that the mind has a power in many cases to revive perceptions which it once had, with this additional perception annexed to them, that it has had them before. And in this sense it is that our ideas are said to be in our memories, when indeed they are actually nowhere – but only there is an ability in the mind when it will to revive them again, and as it were paint them anew on itself, though some with more, some with less difficulty; some more lively, and others more obscurely.'

Re-experiencing traumatic memories means a lack of orientation toward present goals. EP experiences and conceives the 'past 'goal-orientation' as the present 'goal-orientation,' and combines a first-person and quasi-second-person perspective into one: "I am hurting. Horrible things happen to me." The context of the actual present is lacking, so that there is no comparison of the real past and present. ANP experiences and conceives the revived past 'goal-orientation' as not-me, or disowns a traumatic revival when it is over as soon as possible. In both cases, ANP does not compare past and present goals either, so that they do not experience and conceive the traumatic past in terms of a quasi-second-person perspective.

The Second-Person Perspective

The first-person and quasi-second-person perspectives are often also associated with (and probably to a considerable degree dependent on) a 'second-person perspective.' The second-person perspective pertains to 'I-You' relationship[s], such as "I would like to have dinner with you" and "You and I have different views on the matter." Like the quasi-second-person perspective, the second-person perspective involves *phenomenal judgment* (Northoff, 2003).

There are recurrent and consistent clinical observations that dissociative parts of the personality create and maintain their own second-person perspectives and implied goal-orientations. For example, mediated by the action system of attachment cry, fragile EPs can be fixed in the desperate second-person perspective that they must be close to the therapist in order to survive. Many controlling EPs experience and believe the opposite, and vehemently express that they neither need anyone nor should trust anyone.

When re-experiencing traumatizing events, traumatized individuals thus tend to partially or completely revive a former second-person perspective and its implied goal-orientation. As an EP, they do not tend to perceive and relate to perpetrators and others as the ones they are presently, but regard them as the ones they were at the time of the perpetration. For example, as EPs who experience and believe they are hurt children, traumatized individuals tend to perceive a perpetrator as the person he or she was at the time of the traumatization. The present context with the individual's present goal-orientations is lacking completely; there is no comparison of the past and present goal-orientations. The past is the phenomenal present. In response to a hallucinated presence of a former perpetrator who may actually be living at a great geographical distance, or who is long dead, an EP may tell in agony "She beats me up," "He wants to kill me," "She does not care about me at all," or "I cry for help, but she just stands there, doing nothing."

Patients with PTSD can encompass different second-person perspectives regarding the same individual(s). A married couple was severely tortured by two burglars who wore helmets. As ANP, the husband knew that policemen who ride a motorbike and for that reason wear a helmet are generally trustworthy. However, when stopped by a policeman, the sight of a helmeted head in front of him instantly took him back to the past that then became the phenomenal present. This reorientation implied the regeneration of a former second-person perspective and an implied goal-orientation regarding helmeted men. That is, as a reactivated fragile EP, the patient perceived the policeman as one of his torturers and felt his life was at stake once again. He panicked and pushed the throttle. A dangerous pursuit followed that culminated in an upsetting arrest.

Many individuals who have been abused and neglected by caretakers or other significant others develop a deep mistrust of adults. They tend to re-enact this distrust in intimate relationships, including their relationships with therapists. No matter how reliable and trustworthy the involved therapists may prove themselves to be, traumatized individuals can be caught in fixed second-person perspectives such as "You will sooner or later leave me," "I am of no interest to you," "You will abuse me as well, I only have to wait for the day it happens." Some patients cognitively concede at some point in time that these kinds of beliefs are inaccurate, but they may nonetheless continue to feel that their fearful anticipations hold true.

The Third-Person Perspective

The second-person perspective involves phenomenal judgment and thus presupposes a feeling or emotional relationship between the judging 'I' and the judged 'You.' When this kind of relationship is impossible or resisted, the possibility of *physical judgment* remains. Physically judging someone or something involves taking a third-person perspective (Northoff, 2003). In this perspective, the judging (part of a) subject does not engage in a phenomenal (e.g., empathic) relationship with the subject or some part of the subject he or she judges, but rather regards the judged (dissociative part of a) subject as if he or she were a physical *object* or *thing.* That is, physical judgment resembles the way in which someone judges the physical or formal features of an object.

Imitating perpetrators and avoiding the realization that they too are fragile and hurt, controlling EPs may resist entering a second-person perspective relationship with other parts of the personality. This seriously limits their epistemic abilities in that they can only judge the other person or dissociative part of a person as if he or she were a physical thing. For example, from an experiential and emotional distance a controlling EP may judge that a ten-year-old fragile EP is responsible for the sexual abuse "because she is a dirty thing wearing sexy garments." In such cases, the controlling EP does not relate to the fragile EP in the form of second-person perspective in which the controlling EP would phenomenally relate to the fragile EP as a feeling being. Rather, the controlling EP judges the physical or formal features of the fragile EP.

To the degree that ANP resists entering a feeling relationship with EP, ANP also tends to physically judge EP. As Van Derbur (2004, p. 98) explained, "I was unable to explain to anyone why I was so tied up, walled off and out of touch with my feelings . . . To be in touch with my *feelings* would have meant opening Pandora's box." Since the Night Child was flooded with emotion, the Day Child kept her at a far emotional distance:

> While extolling my father's virtues, my night child was screaming at my refusal to even acknowledge her, much less comfort and love her. She was like the child who goes into the kitchen and says, "Mommy can you help me with this?" And the mother replies perfunctionarily, "In a minute." "Please now, Mommy?" "I said in a minute" . . . My night child kept her part of the deal. She had "taken it" until I was strong and secure enough to come back and rescue her. Now, instead of gratitude for her sacrificing herself, I loathed, despised and blamed her. (p. 191)

In sum, PTSD patients or other traumatized individuals tend to alternate between being oriented to the real present and being fixed in a traumatic past that they take for the actual 'here and now.' These alternating spatiotemporal perceptions include shifts of the first-person, quasi-second person, second-person, and third-person perspectives. In other words, these patients alternate between present and former, albeit re-enacted experiences and ideas of who they and who other people are, what the world is like, and how they relate to themselves, other people, and the world more in general. As EP, they do not generate perspectives on themselves, others, and the environment that fit the actual present. As ANP, they do not generate and integrate EP's perspectives. ANP's and EP's first-person, quasi-second-person, second-person, and, if applicable, third-person perspectives may also (re)activated in parallel.

Conclusion: PTSD thus involves a lack of integration of at least two different organized and cohesive sets of first-person, quasi-second-person, second-person, and third-person perspectives. These different person-perspectives and the implied subject-object relationships exist because of ongoing mental and behavioral action. Action (e.g., the ongoing action of generating an 'I') and content (e.g., the particular conception of 'I') are two sides of a coin. Each set of perspectives and implied actions includes at least some important perceptions, sensations, affects, memories, thoughts, and behavioral actions that are not shared by one or more other sets. The involved sets of mental and behavioral actions are not random samples of action, but are internally coordinated. That is, the intra-set coordination is significantly higher than the inter-set coordination. The different action sets can be comprehended as different subsystems of the personality as a whole system, each with a different basic will or set of wills as their predominant guiding principles or goal orientations. The insufficiently coordinated, divided subsystems can be labeled dissociative parts of the individual's personality as a whole, yet insufficiently integrated living organism-environment system.

According to TSDP, in PTSD there commonly are one strongly evolved ANP and one EP that may be a rudimentary or more evolved subsystem. For example, EP may only encompass one traumatic experience or perhaps even only a part of a traumatic memory. Rudimentary dissociative parts engage only in a quite limited range of mental and behavioral actions. Hence, they have few 'mental contents.' The more evolved these parts are, the more mental and behavioral actions they engage in, and the richer their 'contents' will be. To illustrate, here is an example of a rudimentary dissociative conscious and self-conscious subsystem or part of the personality.

> Case report: Rita (22 years) developed a phobia of sleeping since having had a recurrent nightmare three years ago. Rita did not dare to fall asleep, because "something" was threatening her in the dream. In her dreams, scared to death, she would scream and suddenly get up. Then there was a blank. She found herself back in the living room or in the street, dressed in her nightgown (or less), having no idea how she had got there and why. Her friend told her that she left the bed during these episodes, bumped into things, and rushed down the stairs. Exhausted and ever more depressed, Rita lost her job. She was despondent. "Something had to

be done," both she and her physician said. Still, she was quite reluctant to see a psychotherapist and remained emotionally distant when she eventually did.

Rita had had a happy, regular childhood and a normal adolescence. The only remarkable developmental fact was that the nightmares had started when her friend had an innocuous motor vehicle accident. Sure, she had been overrun by a car when she was three years old, but in her mind this accident was unrelated to her nightmare.

Since Rita had nothing else to say, I decided to use ideomotor finger signaling as an exploratory hypnotic method[4]. Given her screaming and flight behavior, "something inside" might know what was going on, and why. If that were the case, I told her, this "something inside" might indicate this by moving a thumb. When her right thumb moved, Rita denied it. Repeated clear thumb movements were required before she acknowledged that something had happened, and that the thumb movements did not seem to be coincidental. Then, I invited "whatever it was that reacted" to use a different digit to signal "no." The left thumb moved. Simultaneous right and left thumb movement signalled "I do not know."

A history unfolded. The signals came from a scared three-year-old. She had been playing, had run after her ball, had fallen in front of a car, and had disappeared under it. Next she had been hit by some part of the car – it might have been the muffler. The last thing the three-year-old remembered was that there was a blow to her head and then everything turned black. The event encompassed the complete life of this EP. She relived it at night, time and again.

Rita was not thrilled but followed my instructions to start taking care of "the three-year-old." The next step in her therapy was to share the experience of the car accident with this inner child, while Rita stayed oriented to the present day with my help. The toddler was glad that Rita, the adult, finally acknowledged her existence. I suggested that Rita would take care of the little girl, and that she would share her agony. By the fourth session, the adult and the child were ready to become one, to "fuse," to become an individuum. When Rita returned for the fifth and last session, she impressed me for the first time as a warm person. The cold and distant presentation had only involved an apparently normal self. Her nightmares vanished and her battery recharged. Rita felt fine and was ready to look for a new job.

The case shows that the young woman's personality encompassed one major shareholder – i.e, Rita as ANP – and one rudimentary fragile EP. All this EP contained was a traumatic experience that may have only lasted a minute or so. This dormant emotional subsystem of her personality had been awakened when Rita's friend had a motor vehicle accident. From that time onwards, the EP intruded on Rita's adult existence in the form of nightmares and in flight behavior for which Rita as ANP was in part amnestic. ANP's recognition and acknowledgment of the EP, her caretaking of the 3-year-old and sharing of the traumatic experiences, led to a rapid reintegration of the patient's personality and the practically instant return to mental health. With these previously feared and avoided recollected actions, she turned her dissociative apparent normality and emotionality into full normality. With these actions, ANP no longer related to the EP in a second-person or third-person perspective. EP and ANP became one whole personality that Rita phenom-

4 This technique will be explained in more detail in Volume III.

enally experienced and judged in first-person and associated person perspectives. As this whole person, she could remember the car accident and the implied goal-orientation as a part of her personal past. When she revived the accident as this whole, she was consciously aware that the revival was a simulation of the past, not the event in itself.

Rita's case shows that dissociation of the individual's personality is maintained when recurrent reactivations and intrusions of EP into ANP's domain do not lead to the integration of the traumatic memories in which the EP is fixed. However, when the patient as ANP manages to integrate (i.e., synthesize, personify, presentify) these memories and the associated EP, which implies a realization of what happened, the patient as a whole personality can plant the traumatic experience firmly in the past (Van der Hart et al., 2006). Upon the completion of these actions, patients feel and can say that "it is all over now." Continuing or overcoming the dissociation of the personality is thus the difference between the continuation and resolution of the injury that trauma is. Indeed, the core of any treatment of trauma-related disorders, including PTSD and ASD, is the integration of the traumatic memories, including a former experience and conception of self, others, and the rest of the world, into the individual's current existence.

As to the structure of the personality, PTSD constitutes a relatively simple dissociative disorder. In the prototypical case, the patient's personality encompasses one major structure, metaphorically described as ANP, and one far smaller structure, metaphorically referred to as EP. The preponderant dynamic of this structure is that ANP avoids EP because of EP's actions and contents, in particular EP's re-enacting and reliving traumatic memories. Although ANP and EP are dissociated from each other, they are not split. Further, they are not fragments, but rather constitute *sets of actions and associated contents* that are internally coordinated, but not or not sufficiently coordinated among each other.

PTSD and Dissociation of the Personality: Some Hypotheses

TSDP includes the idea that PTSD is a dissociative disorder. Several hypotheses can be derived from this theory:

- Hypothesis (H)1. The complexity of the dissociation of the personality is proportional to the complexity of the dissociative disorder.
  - H1.1. PTSD involves a less complex dissociation of the personality than dissociative disorders such as minor and major DID.
  - H1.2. Simple forms of PTSD are associated with a lesser dissociation of the personality than complex PTSD discussed below.
  - H1.3. Minor forms of DID are associated with lesser complex dissociation of the personality than major forms of DID.
- H2. The severity of cognitive-emotional and sensorimotor dissociative symptoms is proportional to the complexity of dissociation of the personality.

- H3. Abnormal volume of the whole brain and particular brain areas is proportional to the complexity of the dissociative disorder insofar as the involved brain regions are volumetrically dependent on chronic stress.
- H4. Different prototypes of dissociative parts of the personality (e.g., ANP, fragile EP, controlling EP) are associated with their own kinds of subjective, physiological and neural reaction patterns to reminders of traumatizing events.
  - H4.1. Abnormal physiological reactions to reminders of adverse events in PTSD and in more complex dissociative disorders are similar.
  - H4.2. Abnormal neural reactions to reminders of adverse events in PTSD and in more complex dissociative disorders are similar.
- H5. The complexity of the dissociation of the personality is relative to the severity and duration of adverse events as well as to the developmental phase and setting in which they occur(red).
  - H5.1. Adverse events involving abuse, maltreatment and neglect by primary caretakers and significant others are associated with more complex dissociation of the personality than traumatization by strangers, accidents, and natural disasters.
- H6. PTSD is associated with less severe attachment problems and less severe caretaker malfunctioning than disorders that involve a more severe dissociation of the personality.

Each of these hypotheses meets conceptual, theoretical, clinical, and emergent scientific evidence that I shall present in the due course of the present Volume and Volume II. Accumulating support for TSDP strengthens the view that "[a]dvances in the field critically depend on theoretical predictions with respect to the kind of differences that exist among different types of dissociative [parts of the personality]" (Nijenhuis, Van der Hart, & Steele, 2002, p. 1086). My colleagues and I concluded at the time that

> [t]o date, research of PTSD and most research of dissociative disorders has largely overlooked that findings may depend on the type of dissociative psychobiological system that dominates the functioning of the patient at the time of measurement. (It must be noted that in parallel dissociation, two or more dissociative [parts of the personality] may be activated simultaneously, and conflicts among them may occur.) In this regard, at a minimum, the theory of structural dissociation can serve as a heuristic for future research of trauma-related dissociation. ... As the theory predicts, EPs engaged in flight, freeze, fight, or total submission would have different psychobiological reactivity to threat cues and, for example, ANPs engaged in work or reproduction and caretaking would have different responses to attachment cues. [2002, p. 1093]

Several years later we (Nijenhuis & Den Boer, 2009, p. 359) added that

> at a minimum, the theory of structural dissociation can serve as a heuristic for future research of trauma-related dissociation. More specifically, the theory may be of help (1) in selecting minimal sets of variables needed to assess the different types of dissociative parts that patients

with trauma-related dissociative disorders encompass; (2) in conceptualizing and studying the features of these different types of parts in terms of these essential variables; and (3) in conceptualizing dynamics of transitions between these different dissociative parts that constitute these patients' personality (cf. Vaitl et al., 2005).

If TSDP is accurate, samples of PTSD patients should show different subjective, behavioral, physiological, and neural reactions to cues that signify threats for them. Technically, these samples should be characterized by heterogeneous reactions, resulting in notable within-group variability as well as modest test-retest reliability, both effects due to changeable reactions to these cues between and within subjects. The most general phenomenon should be patterns of defensive mammalian hyperarousal (hyperaroused fragile EP), hypoarousal (hypoaroused fragile EP engaging in a degree of tonic immobility), and lack of arousal or hypoarousal that reflects ANP's ignorance/avoidance of EP's terrifying world.

PTSD: Hyperarousal and Hypoarousal

PTSD researchers did not contemplate the involved issues when they set out to explore the disorder from its introduction in DSM-III. In apparent oblivion or disregard of the work of pioneers such as Janet, Rivers, Kretschmer, and Myers, and in disregard for clinical observations of hypoarousal reactions in traumatized individuals (e.g., in patients with complex dissociative disorders), the standard idea of PTSD in the 1980s and 1990s became that confrontations with reminders of traumatic experiences cause subjective and psychophysiological hyperarousal reactions that tend to be associated with hyperaroused re-experiencing of traumatizing events. To speak with Pavlov, these reminders can be understood as classically conditioned stimuli. Researchers thus hypothesized that (sets of) conditioned stimuli such as personalized trauma scripts would cause classically conditioned sympathetic nervous system reactions in PTSD patients as well as activations in brain areas implied in emotional reactivity (e.g., Rauch et al., 1996). Whereas it appeared that the majority of these patients show an increase in heart rate and neural activity in brain areas associated with emotional reactions in these circumstances, it became ever more apparent that some patients reacted quite differently.

PTSD and Tonic Immobility

Whereas Kretschmer had linked death feigning/tonic immobility to hysteria, increasing evidence suggested that this defense could also play a role in PTSD. For example, in a sample of sexually assaulted female undergraduates, "tonic immobility fully mediated relations between perceived inescapability and overall PTSD symptom severity, as well as re-experiencing and avoidance/numbing symptom clusters. Tonic immobility also fully mediated the relation between fear and re-experiencing symptoms, and partially mediated relations between fear and overall PTSD symptom severity, and avoidance/numbing symptoms" (Bovin, Jager-Hyma, Gold, Marx, & Sloan, 2008, p. 402). Patients reporting tonic immobility had the most severe PTSD symptoms as well as a worse treatment prognosis than those reporting peritraumatic panic or peritraumatic dissociation+ (Fiszman et al., 2008; Lima et al., 2010). Furthermore, there was a significant association between peritraumatic tonic immobility, i.e., tonic immobility during or briefly after a traumatizing event, and PTSD symptoms in nonclinical samples exposed to various potentially traumatizing events (Abrams, Carleton, Taylor, & Asmundson, 2009; Portugal et al., 2012; Rocha-Rego et al., 2009). The association was upheld in these studies after controlling for peritraumatic panic reactions, negative affect, gender, type of potentially traumatizing event, as well as elapse of time since the potentially traumatizing event that triggered the tonic immobility. To the extent that tonic immobility includes derealization, it is of note that the link between peritraumatic panic and the severity of PTSD was mediated by derealization in one study (Bryant et al., 2011).

We found that sensorimotor dissociative symptoms that fit the features of tonic immobility (i.e., analgesia, anesthesia, paralysis) are excellent statistical predictors of complex dissociative disorders (Nijenhuis et al., 1997b; Nijenhuis, Spinhoven, Vanderlinden, Van Dyck, & Van der Hart, 1998c). Our clinical observations of patients with these disorders taught us that this subtype of defense implies bodily and verbal stilling, emotional and bodily anesthesia, low muscle tone, low heart rate frequency as well as low levels of consciousness. For example, a patient with a lesser form of DID who had been sexually raped by his father for many years was unable to defend himself effectively when he felt threatened by other individuals. As his psychotherapist, I invited him to say "stop" or to raise his hand to indicate whenever a harmless object slowly moved in the direction of his face came too close for comfort. Consistent with his reports of his reactions to situations in daily life in which he felt threatened or pressured, it appeared that he was unable to actively defend himself. During the exposure, his heart rate dropped from 68 to 40, his body became limp, his speech became blocked, and he had great difficulty concentrating.

The level of consciousness becomes very low in patients who engage in dissociative stupor, also described as pseudoepileptic attacks. As described above, death feigning in the fact of a major threat can be advantageous. Writing on depersonalization disorder, Stein and Simeon (2009, p. 467) concur that "attenuation of emotional responses, mediated by deactivation of limbic structures, may sometimes be advantageous in response to inescapable stress." However, playing dead in circumstances that are actually safe or in threatening situations that allow for active mammalian defenses is highly maladaptive.

In conclusion, patients with trauma-related disorders including PTSD can become mentally and physiologically hypoaroused when they perceive a threat. This hypoarousal may in at least some cases be a feature of tonic immobility, death feigning, or whatever other term is used to describe the involved subsystem of mammalian defense. In other cases, hypoarousal to reminders of traumatizing events may involve an ANP who is more or less depersonalized, derealized, and hence emotionally detached.

PTSD: A Dynamic Interplay of Hyperarousal and Hypoarousal Reaction Patterns

In light of the described theoretical considerations, clinical observations, and research findings, it is not surprising that from the last years of the 20th century onward researchers started to notice that some PTSD patients do not or not always become physiologically hyperaroused and do not tend to re-experience traumatizing events when exposed to reminders of traumatizing events, or that they only sometimes engage in such re-enactments. For example, using psychophysiological responses to trauma-related cues as a classificatory criterion of PTSD yielded a substantial number of false positives and false negatives (Keane et al., 1998). Keane et al. also found that 'physiologic nonresponders' with PTSD manifested less re-experiencing symptoms. Bremner (1999) suggested there could be two subtypes of reactions to acutely traumatizing events that involve unique pathways to chronic stress-related psychopathology. Apart from a predominant 'intrusive and hyperaroused,' there could be another that is primarily 'dissociative' (Bremner, 1999).

In the interest of increasing the homogeneity of their subject population, initially only PTSD patients with hyperarousal responses to trauma-related cues were included in psychophysiological and neuroimaging studies (Bremner et al. 1999a, 1999b; Rauch et al., 1996; Pissiota et al., 2002; Shin et al., 1999). This approach clearly misses considerable naturally existing variation in the population of interest. As Osuch et al. (2001) found

> [p]henomenologically, subjects had one of three responses to the auditory trauma script: They either were calm despite the eliciting stimulus, became acutely disturbed by it, or had some increased disturbance on a baseline of already moderate distress. Autonomically, subjects either had an acute elevation of their heart rate with the script or did not.

Seven participants in their study had an increased heart rate while listening to the trauma script, whereas four participants did not. The 'physiologic responders' and 'physiologic nonresponders' also had different patterns of neural activity in reaction to the trauma script. Osuch et al. (2001) concluded that different PTSD patients have different subjective, physiological, and neural reactions to individualized trauma scripts. They also suggested that a PTSD patient can have different psychobiological reaction patterns at different time points.

Since the beginning of the 21st century, numerous psychobiological studies of traumatized individuals have started to document strikingly different types of subjective, physiologic, and neural reactions to reminders of traumatizing events (Frewen & Lanius, 2006; Hopper, Frewen, Van der Kolk, & Lanius, 2007; Lanius, Bluhm, Lanius, & Pain, 2006; Lanius, Hopper, & Menon, 2003; Lanius et al., 2010; Wolf et al., 2012a, 2012b). It appeared that some become hyperaroused and relived traumatic experiences, whereas others were not affected much or became hypoaroused. Referring to our work (Nijenhuis et al., 1998d; Nijenhuis et al., 2002; see Chapter 16), Frewen and Lanius (2006) proposed that the hyperaroused reliving of traumatic experiences pertains to sympathetically related mammalian flight and freeze reactions. They also concurred with us that detached responding could relate to tonic immobility or to emotional numbing as a means of avoiding traumatic memories.

In this context and also inspired by Bremner (1999), Lanius and colleagues (2010; Lanius, Brand, Vermetten, Frewen, & Spiegel, 2012) suggested a few years later that there are two subtypes of PTSD. They conceded that individuals with the 're-experiencing/hyperarousal subtype' may become hyperaroused and may tend to relive traumatic experiences when confronted with reminders of these experiences. Those with the 'dissociative subtype,' on the other hand, remain physiologically stable or become hypoaroused. In this context, they may also become subjectively detached. Lanius et al. (2010, p. 640) added that these subtypes are "involved in a dynamic interplay and lead to alternating symptom profiles in PTSD." *They thus suggested that PTSD patients (can) encompass both subtypes of response patterns, and that these patterns can alternate.*

The evidence for the existence of different patterns of subjective, physiologic, and neural reactions to reminders of traumatizing events is convincing (Lanius et al., 2006, 2010; Reinders et al., 2003, 2006; Reinders, Willemsen, Vos, Den Boer, & Nijenhuis, 2012; Wolf et al., 2012a, 2012b). This will be discussed further in Chapters 17 and 18. The findings are in full consonance with TSDP, which predicts these differences, and which offers hypotheses about what form these different response patterns can take, why they exist, and how and why they are maintained. This theory also includes the idea and fits the observation that "these [re-experiencing/hyperarousal and dissociative] response patterns are not completely distinct and that individual patients with PTSD may show both response patterns either simultaneously or at different time points" (Lanius et al., 2010, p. 641). Their remark that the different response patterns can exist simultaneously communicates even more clearly than their statement that these response patterns can alternate, that PTSD is dissociative *pur sang*. We describe these two phenomena as parallel and sequential dissociation of the personality (Van der Hart et al., 2006). The evidence for the involved shifts in response patterns in patients with PTSD is clinical to date (which is not to say that clinical evidence is of no importance; see Chapter 6). Yet it is implied in the very criteria for PTSD in DSM-IV (and DSM-5; see below) that include positive symptoms (i.e., forms of reliving traumatic experiences) and negative symptoms (i.e, markers of emotional detachment, as well as behavioral and mental avoidance of trauma-related cues) (Dorahy & Van der Hart, 2014; Nijenhuis, 2014a, 2014b; see Chapter 18).

It is remarkable that Bremner (1999) and Lanius et al. (2006, 2010, 2012) do not state that these recurrent and profound shifts in response patterns involve dissociation. In their concepts of dissociation+ (Bremner) and a dissociative subtype of PTSD (Lanius et al.), dissociation+ exclusively refers to a set of negative symptoms. Following Schore (2001, 2003), Lanius and colleagues (2006) initially defined dissociation as disengagement from *external* stimuli, and distinguished the concept from emotional numbing (Frewen & Lanius, 2006) and avoidance (Hopper et al., 2007). However, they later expanded the domain of dissociative phenomena, proposing the 'dissociative subtype' of PTSD to include depersonalization and being at a subjective distance from one's emotional experiences.

These latter phenomena pertain to disengagement from *internal* stimuli. Lanius et al. (2010) also included phenomena involving "overmodulation to trauma-related emotional and somatosensory information" (p. 645) to the house of dissociation, that is, intentional mental avoidance of perceived trauma-related cues. They did not specify that the dissociative subtype can also pertain to detachment in the context of tonic immobility. However, this would have been consistent with their previous publications (e.g., Frewen & Lanius, 2006).

One might be tempted to think that the proposal by Bremner (1999) and Lanius and colleagues (2010, 2012) of a dissociative subtype of PTSD is a step toward integrating traumatic melancholia/traumatic neurosis (PTSD) and hysteria (dissociative disorders). However, their suggestion includes an understanding of dissociation that significantly differs from the original concept. Charcot, Janet, Myers, and other pioneers certainly regarded hyperaroused re-experiencing traumatic memories as a dissociative symptom when the individual does not integrate the relived memories in his or her personality as a whole system. The question is thus: Why, according to Bremner and Lanius and colleagues, would the 're-experiencing/hyperarousal' subtype of PTSD not be dissociative?

The Concept of 'Dissociation'

It is important to realize that

> [a]ny evaluation of the dissociation-PTSD literature depends upon defining and measuring dissociation consistently; however, the extant literature reveals wide-ranging definitions for dissociation (DePrince, Chu, & Visvanathan, 2006, p. 1)

The idea of a 'dissociative' and nondissociative 'hyperarousal' subtype of PTSD does not fit the original concept of 'dissociation' encompassing two elements. The first element was that dissociation pertains to a division of the personality as a whole system in two or more (sub)systems of ideas and functions. The second component involved the understanding that hysterical/dissociative symptoms are manifestations of the existence of this organization of the personality (e.g., Janet, 1907; Nijenhuis & Van der Hart, 2011a, 2011b; see Chapter 13). The classical concept of 'dissociation' fits the more general meaning of the term 'dissociation.' As the Merriam-Webster online dictionary teaches, dissociation involves the idea of division of a complex in two or more elements. It is

> 1. the act or process of dissociating or the state of being dissociated:
> a: the process by which a chemical combination breaks up into simpler constituents; *especially*: one that results from the action of energy (as heat) on a gas or of a solvent on a dissolved substance
> b: the separation of whole segments of the personality (as in multiple personality disorder) or of discrete mental processes (as in the schizophrenias) from the mainstream of consciousness or of behavior with loss of integrated awareness and autonomous functioning of the separated segments or parts

> 2: the process by which some biological stocks (as of certain bacteria) differentiate into two or more distinct and relatively permanent strains; *also*: such a strain

Dissociation thus concerns the act of disassociating, disconnecting, or discoordinating elements, segments, or strains from a whole as well as the result of this act, which is the existence of insufficiently associated, connected, or coordinated parts of a whole.

From the 1980s, the constraints on the concept in the trauma and dissociation field became liberalized in some regards and tightened in others. The liberalization then reached very far. A view that has become rather popular among clinicians and scientists is that there are two qualitatively different types of dissociation: One type is described as 'compartmentalization' and the other as 'detachment' (Holmes et al., 2005). Whereas many authors feel that common alterations of field and level of consciousness involve one type of dissociation (Holmes et al., 2005; Lawton, Baker, & Brown, 2008; Spitzer, Barnow, Freyberger, & Grabe, 2006; Vogel, Braungardt, Grabe, Schneider, & Klauer, 2013), others use only the term 'dissociation' as a mere placeholder for detachment phenomena (Perry & Pollard, 1998; Schore, 2001, 2003).

Compartmentalization pertains to Janet's original definition of dissociation; detachment captures alterations in consciousness such as absorption, depersonalization, and derealization. It is not clear what criterion or principle links the phenomena of compartmentalization and detachment phenomena so tightly that they would be best seen and classified as instances of one more generic phenomenon – under whatever name. What *is* clear is that detachment phenomena do not necessarily imply disconnection or discoordination. For example, an episode of absent-mindedness while driving on the highway is presently often referred to as an instance of 'normal dissociation.' However, the individuals involved forget how they drove the car and what traffic situations they perceived during the episode. They leave nothing behind concerning their driving experience in a disconnected or discoordinated form that they can later connect and coordinate, that is, integrate. They cannot revive (i.e., simulate) the past. 'Normal dissociation' does not involve 'breaking up of a unity in simpler constituents,' 'separation of segments of the personality,' or 'differentiation in different strains.'

Grave and recurrent absent-mindedness has become labeled and classified as 'pathological dissociation.' Like 'normal dissociation,' episodes involving a pathological low level of consciousness do not imply the existence of simpler constituents, segments, or strains of a former unity. For example, depressed patients may stare in space and lose track of time. Should these and similar pathological phenomena qualify as dissociation? Episodes involving low consciousness are lost forever, *unless* there are one or more conscious segments of the individual's personality that *do* experience, perceive, know, and remember what escapes the absent-minded segment of his or her personality. In dissociation, the ability to revive the past is not gone, but has become dependent on particular dissociative parts of the personality.

The same observation applies to phenomena that involve a retraction of the field of consciousness. Whatever individuals who are not divided in different simpler constituents, segments, or strains fail to notice *does not exist for them.* They do not dissociate, do not disconnect or discoordinate whatever it is that they do not attend to. They do not perceive it at all, their attention was elsewhere: It was focused on other objects. When authors write, they tend to forget time and do not attend much to what is happening around them or in their body, they are focused on the task, so that their orientation to the environment and to themselves narrows. Their selective attention is functional, because it supports the writing aims. One might say that states of selective attention involve a lack of integration of particular cues (e.g., passage of time, thirst), and that it therefore involves dissociation. However, if that were the case, *any perception would qualify as dissociative. Any perception is necessarily selective.* Individuals need only notice what is important to them in a particular context. Absorbing more than what is needed for the task at hand implies in fact inefficient action, confusion, or even chaos. Some individuals generate an unduly narrow field of attention, which can be pathological. For example, obsessed patients attend only to particular thoughts and feelings far too much and to important other things far too little (or not at all). Undue selective attention is in fact a ubiquitous feature of many mental disorders. Consistent with this critique, compartmentalization and detachment phenomena have different correlates (Lawton et al., 2008; Vogel et al., 2013). For example, Lawton et al. found that patients with epilepsy and pseudo-epilepsy were distinguished by compartmentalization but not by detachment/depersonalization.

There are profound conceptual, empirical, and clinical differences between individuals' whose personality is integrated but who *fail to notice or recall* something, and individuals' who *fail to integrate* something that exists within them as a whole in a dissociative form. Still, like any activated conscious system, activated dissociative parts of the personality have a particular field and level of consciousness as well as shifting fields and levels of consciousness over time. For example, as a particular ANP, an individual can be wide awake and personalized at some times, but drowsy, absorbed, depersonalized, and bodily and emotionally anesthetic at other times. While an ANP is anesthetic, an EP can be in pain.

In sum, the idea that the concept of 'dissociation' should include ubiquitous alterations of level and field of consciousness is inconsistent with the general concept of 'dissociation' as defined in the Merriam Webster dictionary. Including omnipresent phenomena such as selective attention, forgetfulness, lack of concentration, losing track of time, absorption, daydreaming, fantasizing, absentmindedness, and forgetfulness in the domain of dissociation creates an oceanic category (Frankel, 1994; Nijenhuis & Van der Hart, 2011a, 2011b). Huge categories are commonly of little clinical or scientific interest and use. The power of valuable clinical and scientific concepts lies in their provision of a solid balance between sensitivity – the power to include in the conceptual domain what is relevant in one or more important regards – and specificity – the power to exclude what is irrelevant with respect to one's classificatory, clinical, or scientific goals. It is unclear what useful classificatory, clinical, or scientific purposes the inclusion of phenomena involving low levels of consciousness and selective attention in the province of dissociation serve. It is also unclear what principle or structure would link these phenomena and the (symptoms of) dissociation of the personality. Pointing out that these different phenomena are associated does not suffice. Many phenomena are correlated, but correlation does not in fact prove conceptual unity. For example, all intact horses, cows, crocodiles, and mice have four legs. All healthy individuals have a working brain and a heart that beats. Do these perfect correlations force us to say that these various animals belong to one category, and that the brain and the heart constitute one class? High correlations meet the requirement of sensitivity. Patients with a dissociative disorder tend to have significant shifts in their level and field of consciousness, but so do many patients with a different mental disorder. High correlations, thus, do not at all imply or prove specificity.

Janet would not have been pleased with the expanding conceptual domain of dissociative phenomena. He was clear that alterations in consciousness that do not pertain to a division of personality differ from dissociative phenomena, and that they have their own clinical and scientific implications. These different phenomena therefore require their own conceptualization. For example, a clinical interest is that an individual who is unduly forgetful but who does not encompass dissociative parts needs a *different treatment* than an individual who does not recall a particular episode as one dissociative part, but who does know it as a different dissociative part. These different symptoms are bound to have a *different meaning* for the individual who experiences them. One scientific interest is that dissociation of the personality, selective attention, and low levels of consciousness involve *different mental and behavioral actions*. For example, these different actions will be associated with *different patterns of neural and physiological activation*. Another scientific interest is that the manifestations of a dissociation of the personality and alterations in consciousness will probably entail *different correlates*. Still another interest is *clarity of expression*. When clinicians or scientists use the term 'dissociation,' it should be clear to their audience – and to themselves – what they actually mean. Grasping the meaning of a spoken or written text should not be a guessing game.

Janet, Myers, and other pioneers would also have been unhappy with the idea that hyperaroused re-experiencing of traumatizing events does not constitute a dissociative phenomenon when that re-experiencing does not lead to the integration of the involved memories. As Charcot taught before them, nonintegrated traumatic memories act like parasites in the mind. To speak with Kretschmer, it must be asked why nonintegrative recurrent re-experiencing involving *Totstellung*, dissociative stupor, dissociative reduction, and loss of consciousness would be dissociative, but not equally disconnected and discoordinated conditions involving startle reflex, *Bewegungssturm*, freeze, flight, fight (e.g., aggression observed by Kardiner in veterans with traumatic neurosis)? The view that hyperaroused re-experiencing of traumatizing events is not a dissociative phenomenon conflicts with the fact that this re-experiencing is a core feature of one or more conscious and self-conscious subsystems that remain insufficiently integrated in the personality as a whole system.

The view that the hyperaroused reliving of traumatizing events is not dissociative is also fully inconsistent with the DSM-IV notion of 'dissociative flashbacks' in PTSD, which are seen as instances of "acting or feeling as if the traumatic event were recurring" (APA, 1994, p. 428). These flashbacks and other forms of re-experiencing traumatizing events do not pertain to a nonintegrated state of hypoarousal, but rather to a nonintegrated state of hyperarousal. The ICD-10 (WHO 1992, p. 148) includes the view that typical symptoms of PTSD include episodes of hyperaroused repeated reliving of the traumatizing event in the form of intrusive memories as in flashbacks or dreams. The intruding memories do not become integrated for the duration of the disorder and thus continue to exist in a dissociative form. In conclusion, there is every reason to say that recurrent hyperaroused re-experiencing of traumatizing events, hence the re-experiencing hyperaroused subtype of PTSD, are dissociative phenomena.

One can define one's concepts as one pleases as long as the definition details what the concept actually entails. However, in addition to meeting the requirements of specificity (so that it can be of clinical, scientific, or practical use), concepts should also be internally consistent. That is what logic demands. Lanius et al.'s (2010, 2012) concept of 'dissociation' in the context of the dissociative subtype of dissociation is limited to the indicated set of negative symptoms. However, more generally they recognize the existence of dissociative disorders and, in that framework, positive dissociative symptoms. As noted above, these positive dissociative symptoms include dissociative parts of the personality and intrusion phenomena such as one dissociative part's voice, feelings, memories, thoughts, or motor actions that invade the phenomenal domain of a different dissociative part. These symptoms obviously include dissociative flashbacks.

Lanius et al. (2010, 2012) thus use two contradictory definitions of 'dissociation.' In the context of the 'dissociative' subtype, 'dissociation' stands only for certain negative symptoms; in other contexts (e.g., when they are considering complex dissociative disorders), their concept of 'dissociation' pertains to negative as well as positive symptoms. This lack of internal consistency is unacceptable. If Lanius et al. were to stay true to the definition that dissociation also pertains to positive symptoms, they would have to acknowledge that the hyperaroused re-experiencing of traumatizing event is as dissociative as is hypoaroused re-experiencing. One cannot have it both ways. One resolution is to stick to the concept of 'dissociation' as negative symptoms such as depersonalization, distinguish this concept from the concept of 'division of personality' and its manifestations, and invent new terms for these two latter concepts. The other way out is to substitute the term 'dissociative subtype of PTSD' for a term such as 'emotionally detached subtype of PTSD' and define both subtypes of PTSD as dissociative on the grounds that the disorder involves a basic dissociation of the personality.

The Concept of 'Dissociation' in DSM-5

The conceptual, definitional, and classificatory problems regarding dissociation are continued in the DSM-5 (APA, 2013). However, there is also some progress.

Progress

First the positive news: PTSD is now classified in the new chapter on trauma- and stressor-related disorders. This move brings the disorder so to speak home to the category of adjustment and stress reactions that were included in the DSM I (APA, 1952) and DSM-II (APA, 1968). The reclassification is an improvement over PTSD's classification as an anxiety disorder in the DSM-III and DSM-IV. As detailed above, anxiety was classically regarded as a core feature of PTSD and its predecessors such as traumatic melancholia (Burton, 1621), railway spine (Erichsen, 1875), traumatic neurosis (Oppenheim, 1889), and shell shock (Myers, 1940). However, the disorder includes other intense emotions such as anger (Kardiner, 1941), disgust (Badour, Bown, Adams, Bunaciu, & Feldner, 2012), survivor guilt (Koranyi, 1969) and other types of guilt, as well as shame (Kubany, 1994; Wilson, Drozdek, & Turkovic, 2006). In light of the pluriform affects in PTSD, its primary comprehension and classification as an anxiety disorder is problematic.

The dissociative disorders that DSM-5 recognizes are placed next to, but are not a part of, the trauma- and stressor-related disorders. This organization reflects "the close relationship between these diagnostic categories. Both acute stress disorder and posttraumatic stress disorder contain dissociative symptoms, such as amnesia, flashbacks, numbing, and depersonalization/derealization" (p. 291). The link between these two groups of disorders also pertains to the fact that particularly, albeit not exclusively, patients with complex dissociative disorders, like patients with acute stress disorder (ASD) and PTSD, have experienced adverse events. Traumatic melancholia and hysteria have thus become close neighbors in DSM-5.

Stagnation

The question remains whether trauma- and stressor-related disorders and dissociative disorders are in fact at all different, and if so in what sense are they alike and dissimilar? Are they, indeed must they, remain neighbors, or are they rather members of one family? An inquiry into this matter can be successful only when the concepts of 'dissociation,' 'dissociative symptoms,' and 'dissociative disorders' are crystal clear, consistent, and meaningful. As discussed above, however, this clarity and consistency do not exist in the field to date, and DSM-5 only continues the fuzzy status quo. The system defines and uses the terms 'dissociation,' 'dissociative symptoms,' and 'dissociative disorders' in confusing and contradictory ways. For example, the manual includes two subtypes of PTSD with dissociative symptoms, one for individuals older than six years and one for younger children. These subtypes clearly involve Lanius et al.'s (2012) dissociative subtype of PTSD. In this conceptualization, 'dissociative' does not stand for a lack of integration of different subsystems of the personality, but for the negative symptoms of depersonalization and derealization. The common form of PTSD would not be dissociative, because patients with this condition do not respond to reminders of traumatizing events with these negative symptoms.

But what about positive dissociative symptoms such as intrusions of nonintegrated traumatic memories, voices, feelings, affects, thoughts, and actions that belong to those parts of traumatized individuals' personality they have not integrated (i.e., synthesized, personified, presentified, realized)? The authors of DSM-5 accept the existence of these positive dissociative symptoms. For example, they also use the term 'dissociation' in the sense of a dissociation of the personality (as in the criteria for DID, APA, 2013, p. 291). They explicitly recognize and describe "positive dissociative symptoms" (APA, 2013, p. 291) and "dissociative reactions (e.g., flashbacks) in which the individual feels or acts as if traumatic events were recurring" (APA, 2013, criterion B3, p. 271).[5] These dissociative reactions "may occur on a continuum with the most extreme expression being a complete loss of awareness of present surroundings" (APA, 2013, criterion B3, p. 271). Criterion B1 states that the patients have "[r]ecurrent, involuntary, and intrusive distressing memories of the traumatic event(s)." Criterion B2 is that they experience "[r]ecurrent distressing dreams in which the content and/or affect of the dream are related to the traumatic event(s)."

The B1–3 forms of re-enactment of traumatic memories do not concern a bundle of isolated reactions to isolated stimuli, but are rather organized actions in the context of experienced and perceived events. Major questions in this regard are: What organization within the personality is intruding, what organization is intruded, and what are the first-, quasi-second-, second-, and third-person perspectives of these organizations?

To reiterate what has already been detailed in this chapter, the organization of traumatic memories can take various forms. The reliving can be highly emotional and sensorimotor, but it may also involve biopsychosocial hypoarousal with emotional and bodily anesthesia, depersonalization, and derealization. Both forms can coexist (e.g., the patient is first hyperaroused and then becomes hypoaroused) and both include disorientation in time and place. The patients lose the orientation on the 'here and now' and become emotionally and physically immersed in a 'here and now' that actually involves a 'there and then.' These "dissociative reactions" (APA, 2013, p. 271) are not mere symptoms or conditioned reactions, but involve their own person perspectives.

---

5 ICD-10 dissociative disorders of movement and sensation are categorized in DSM-5 as conversion disorders, as if these disorders were not primarily characterized by sensorimotor dissociative symptoms. For a review of somatoform (sensorimotor) dissociation see Nijenhuis (2009). Although DSM-5 mentions that DID includes 'disruption' of 'sensory-motor functioning,' this disruption is not described as somatoform or sensorimotor dissociative symptoms. Empirically speaking, somatoform dissociative symptoms are extreme in DID and as indicative of the disorder as psychoform (cognitive-emotional) dissociative symptoms.

The intrusions thus entail an organization of a set of syntheses that traumatized individuals have not or not sufficiently presentified. The syntheses involved are personified because there is an 'I' who is the subject of the relived phenomenal experiences (first-person perspective), and this subject phenomenally judges himself or herself (quasi-second-person perspective) and other individuals (second-person perspective), and physically judges objects (third-person perspective). However, this subject is not the patient's present 'I,' but the 'I' that person was at the time. It is this latter 'I' that the patient re-enacts and relives, however rudimentary or elaborate (the actions and contents of) that 'I' may be.

This 'I' and the mental and behavioral actions of this 'I,' this organization of the personality, is EP. EP can be rudimentary or more evolved. That is, this dissociative conscious subsystem can encompass only a few or a larger set of states. The organization of the personality that does not integrate the traumatic memories and the associated multiple person perspectives is ANP or at least includes ANP. (In the case of the existence of more than one EP, the different EPs may not have integrated each other's traumatic memories.)

When the reliving is massive, the patients become the person they were when they became injured and lose their present person perspectives that would tell them that they are actually safe. In terms of TSDP, the patients' ANP becomes deactivated and their EP takes control (assuming there is one EP; in more complex forms of dissociation, there can be more than one EP, and more than one EP can become simultaneously reactivated). For example, as DSM-5 recognizes, PTSD can involve dissociative amnesia. That is, ANP can be more or less amnestic for EP and this part's traumatic memories, just as EP may not or not completely know ANP, at least not the current ANP (e.g., EP may regard ANP as a teenager, whereas she is actually an adult woman). During lesser intrusions, the patients remain present as ANP, but become influenced or even flooded by dynamic traumatic states of EP(s). For example, ANP may hear EP's voice – which does not necessarily mean that ANP realizes that the voice belongs to a dissociative part of them.

More Confusion Regarding the Concept of 'Dissociation'

The term 'dissociation' can stand for still other phenomena in current psychiatry and psychology than I have discussed so far. For example, it is also used to describe a mental defense that may or may not maintain a particular dissociation of the personality. Some authors even intend the term 'dissociation' in different ways within one text without a clarification of the different referents they have in mind.

The current situation is like asking for apples in a grocery by saying, "I'd like to have a kilo of fruits." The servant's face becomes a question mark: "Fruits"? "Yes, fruits." Shaking his head, the servant hands the customer a kilo of pears. But now it is the customer who shakes his head – and points at apples. "Why didn't you tell me straight away that you wanted apples?" The next time that the customer asks for 'fruit' the servant smiles, says "I got it," and provides juicy, shiny apples. "No," is the reply, "I had pears in mind"! No one would talk like this in common life, unless in a silly effort to be funny. Then why do clinicians and scientists talk like this when it comes to dissociation? The point should be clear: This custom is in sore need of repair.

One resolution would be to specify what kind of dissociation one has in mind every time one uses the term. However, that would be a most impractical, cumbersome method, and it is unlikely that clinicians and scientists are so disciplined that they would consistently adhere to this practice. A by far better solution is to give the term 'dissociation' in psychiatry and psychology one clear and specific meaning – or else bury it forever. If dissociation is given a single, clear meaning, the phenomena that become excluded from the domain must obviously be given their own name. Wouldn't it be helpful to name apples apples, pears pears, and cauliflower cauliflower?

I will specify and use the term 'dissociation' and its derivate terms as follows. *Dissociation* (without an added + symbol) stands for a division of personality in two or more conscious subsystems. The term 'dissociative' thus stands for manifestations of this dissociation of the personality. When authors use the term 'dissociation,' but mean symptoms of 'depersonalization,' 'derealization,' and 'emotional detachment,' that may or may not involve manifestations of dissociation of the personality, I will write (as before) 'dissociation+,' and 'dissociative+ symptoms'. When they use the term to denote 'mental avoidance,' I will point this out. Further, 'cognitive-emotional dissociative symptoms' and 'sensorimotor dissociative symptoms' shall denote evident or presumed manifestations of a dissociation of the personality. 'Cognitive-emotional dissociation' and 'sensorimotor dissociation' are synonyms. Other synonyms are 'psychoform dissociation' or 'psychoform dissociative symptoms' and 'somatoform dissociation' or 'somatoform dissociative symptoms'. According the present conceptualization, 'depersonalization,' 'derealization,' and 'cognitive-emotional' or 'sensorimotor detachment' are only dissociative when they are core features of one or more dissociative parts of the personality, but not of one or more other dissociative parts. For example, 'amnesia' qualifies as 'dissociative amnesia' when autobiographical memories that one dissociative part recollects are not recollected by another dissociative part. Only in these cases shall I write 'dissociative symptoms.' 'Amnesia' that does pertain to this division of the personality is not dissociative, but involves 'forgetting.' When authors use the terms 'dissociation' and 'dissociative symptoms' to capture a mixture of 'cognitive-emotional' and 'sensorimotor dissociative symptoms' and 'symptom of retracted and low consciousness,' as before I will write 'dissociation+,' and 'dissociative+ symptoms.' I will place the word 'dissociation' in quotation marks in two constructions: (1) the term 'dissociation,' and (2) the concept of 'dissociation.' In Chapter 13, the concept of 'dissociation' will be carefully defined. The reason for postponing this definition that long relates to other conceptual problems that need to be dealt with first. When quotes include the terms 'dissociation' and 'dissociative symptoms,' I will leave the original text unaltered.

Conceptualizing, Classifying, and Studying PTSD

The conceptual and classificatory concerns regarding PTSD can be overcome given a solid and specific definition of the concept of 'dissociation.' The following position can serve as a good heuristic by offering a clear and coherent set of hypotheses open to empirical testing:

1) PTSD involves a dissociation of the personality in at least two insufficiently integrated biopsychosocial subsystems that are conscious and self-conscious – hence, the disorder constitutes a dissociative disorder.
2) The personality of an individual with PTSD can include a dissociative subsystem
   - that is fixed in traumatic memories,
   - that tends to re-experience and re-enact traumatizing events when confronted with cues that remind this subsystem of these events,
   - that is predominantly mediated by actions systems of defense when exposed to reminders of traumatizing events,
   - the actions of which involve dominance of the sympathetic nervous system, thus subjective and physiological hyperarousal, and concomitant neural activation patterns and behaviors,
   - that in this context engages in flight, freeze, or defensive fight, and/or attachment cry,
   - that may be quite rudimentary or somewhat more evolved,
   - that can be metaphorically described as a hyperaroused fragile EP.
3) The personality of an individual with PTSD may also, or alternatively, include a dissociative subsystem
   - that is fixed in traumatic memories,
   - that tends to re-experience and re-enact traumatizing events when confronted with cues that remind this subsystem of these events,
   - that is predominantly mediated by action systems of defense involving dominance of the parasympathetic nervous system, thus including subjective and physiologic hypoarousal as well as concomitant neural activation patterns and behaviors,
   - hence engages in more or less complete forms of mammalian defense described as tonic immobility or death feigning,
   - that may be quite rudimentary or more evolved,
   - and that can be metaphorically described as a hypoaroused fragile EP.
4) The personality of an individual with PTSD additionally includes a dissociative subsystem
   - that, mediated by actions systems for functioning in daily life, strives to function in daily life,
   - that tends to ignore/mentally avoid EP and associated traumatic memories,
   - that in this framework tends to respond to reminders of traumatic experiences and reminders of traumatizing events with forms of emotional and sensory detachment,

and concomitant physiological and neural activation patterns as well as behavioral avoidance,
- that, when intruded on by #2, may become temporarily hyperaroused,
- or that, when intruded on by #3, may become temporarily hypoaroused,
- that is commonly far more evolved than the other subsystem(s),
- and that can be metaphorically described as ANP.

5) The involved dissociative subsystems
   - are different in some but not all respects, hence they are not distinct,
   - can become dominant at different point in time,
   - can be activated in parallel,
   - and can intrude on each other.
6) The dissociation of the personality in PTSD, as in any dissociative disorder, manifests itself in
   - cognitive-emotional dissociative symptoms, and
   - sensorimotor dissociative symptoms
   - that can be of the negative kind, and
   - of the positive kind.
7) Integration of the different dissociative subsystems (#2, #3, #4) and the traumatic memories that dissociative subsystems #2 and #3 encompass, constitutes the core of the therapeutic aims as well as the major cause of recovery from the disorder.

Developmental Trauma Disorder: Suffering from Much More than the Primary Symptoms of PTSD

There is a growing concern that patients who meet the criteria for DSM-IV and DSM-5 PTSD commonly have a far more elaborate and complex set of symptoms (D'Andrea, Ford, Stolbach, Spinazzola, & Van der Kolk, 2012). To some extent, this was recognized by the authors of the DSM-IV, who mentioned that patients with PTSD may have other symptoms in addition to the disorder's primary symptoms. They listed survival guilt feelings and interpersonal problems that relate to phobic avoidance of traumatic reminders, and they stated that particularly interpersonal traumatization may relate to a host of still other symptoms. Other listed symptoms included impaired affect regulation, self-destructive and impulsive behavior, dissociative symptoms, somatic complaints, feelings of ineffectiveness, shame, despair, or hopelessness, feeling permanently damaged, a loss of previously sustained beliefs, hostility, social withdrawal, feeling constantly threatened, impaired relationships with others, or a change from the individual's previous personality characteristics (APA, 1994, p. 425). It was furthermore stated that there may be an increased risk of a variety of other mental disorders.

The text on PTSD in DSM-5 similarly states that individuals with PTSD are 80% more likely than those without PTSD to have symptoms that meet diagnostic criteria for at least one other mental disorder (APA, 2013, p. 280). It also mentions that most young children with PTSD have at least one other diagnosis with oppositional defiant and separation anxiety disorder predominant. PTSD patients who have lived prolonged, repeated, and severe traumatizing events such as childhood abuse or torture may additionally have "difficulty regulating emotions or maintaining social relationships, or dissociative symptoms" (p. 276).

The remark that the comorbidity may include "dissociative symptoms" is puzzling because it is not stated what these other dissociative symptoms would be. One must assume that different "dissociative symptoms" are meant than the "dissociative reactions" given in the B Criterion (p. 271) and the "dissociative" symptoms that characterize the dissociative subtype (p. 272). Clarification and conceptual housecleaning regarding the term and concept of 'dissociation' in the DSM-5 are therefore urgent.

In any case, the PTSD diagnosis is underinclusive in the large majority of cases. Since individuals are whole organisms, it is most unlikely that the various symptoms and disorders that beset severely traumatized individual in particular are isolated phenomena. The question that must thus be posed is: What links the symptoms of PTSD and of the 'comorbid' symptoms? What exactly is the essence of the injury called trauma?

Observing and documenting the complex injury of chronic childhood traumatization, Van der Kolk and colleagues (2005) proposed the diagnosis disorders of extreme stress not otherwise specified for DSM-IV, now more commonly known as Complex PTSD. The proposal *almost* made it into DSM. Despite the rejection of the concept in DSM-IV, many clinicians and scientists started to use it, be it under the name complex PTSD or some other name. For example, Cloitre et al. (2009) documented that exposure to multiple adverse events, and childhood adversities in particular, can result in combined symptoms of PTSD and disturbance of self-regulation in adults and children. In adults, symptom complexity was associated with cumulative childhood adversity, but not with adversity in adulthood. Symptom complexity in children was statistically predicted by cumulative adversity. Ford, Conner, and Hawke (2009) found that childhood adversity was associated with externalizing behavior problems and psychosocial impairment among psychiatrically hospitalized children. They noted that this association cannot be accounted for completely by existing psychiatric diagnoses, gender, or ethnicity.

Van der Kolk and colleagues (D'Andrea et al., 2012; Van der Kolk, 2005, 2010; Van der Kolk & D'Andrea, 2010) more recently proposed 'developmental trauma disorder,' a new name for essentially the same concept. As Van der Kolk (2009, p. 572) wrote,

> [l]ess than eight years after the establishment of the National Child Traumatic Stress Network in 2001 it has become evident that the current diagnostic classification system is inadequate for tens of thousands of traumatized children. While the inclusion of PTSD in the psychiatric classification system in 1980 led to extensive scientific studies of that diagnosis, over the past 25 years there has been a parallel emergence of the field of Developmental Psychopathology, which has documented the effects of interpersonal trauma and disruption of caregiving systems on the development of affect regulation, attention, cognition, perception, and interper-

> sonal relationships. Another significant development has been the increasing documentation of the effects of adverse early life experiences on brain development. The goal of introducing the diagnosis of Developmental Trauma Disorder is to capture the reality of the clinical presentations of children and adolescents exposed to chronic interpersonal trauma.

The proposed A Criterion of developmental trauma disorder involves experienced or witnessed multiple or prolonged adverse events over a period of time of at least 1 year beginning in childhood or early adolescence. The events include interpersonal violence and significant disruptions of protective caregiving as the result of repeated changes in primary caregiver, repeated separation from the primary caregiver, or exposure to severe and persistent emotional abuse. In light of the documented harmfulness of emotional neglect by and emotional unavailability of the primary caregiver(s), it is curious that these environmental conditions were not included in the proposal.

The symptoms of the disorder involve various kinds of dysregulation: affective and physiological (B Criterion), attentional and behavioral (C Criterion), and self and relational (D Criterion). The duration of the disturbance must be at least 6 months (E Criterion), and the functional impairment pertains to the scholastic, familial, peer group, legal, health, and vocational functioning (at least two must apply; F Criterion).

Dorahy et al. (2013) documented that complex PTSD is associated with difficulties in intimate relationships. Dissociative+ symptoms made an independent contribution to these relational difficulties in their study, and they had an organizing effect on complex PTSD symptoms. Complex PTSD (or developmental trauma disorder) involves more severe dissociative+ symptoms than in simple PTSD (Zucker, Spinazzola, Blastein, & Van der Kolk, 2006). Discussing the disturbances of attention, cognition, and consciousness that characterize developmental trauma disorder, Van der Kolk (2010) drew attention to the fact that over 400 cross-sectional and prospective longitudinal studies have documented an association between childhood traumatization and dissociative symptoms (e.g., Trickett, Noll, & Putnam, 2011; for a review, see Dalenberg et al., 2012). The association exists for cognitive-emotional (psychoform) dissociative+ symptoms as well as for sensorimotor (somatoform) dissociative symptoms (a longitudinal study may be found in Diseth, 2006; see Chapter 6, as well as Nijenhuis, 2009). Consistent with this, Van der Kolk (2010, p. 60) proposed that "diminished awareness/dissociation of sensations, emotions, and bodily states" be part of the B Criterion for developmental trauma disorder. However, he does not clearly define the concept of 'dissociation,' so it remains unclear whether the phrase "dissociation of sensations, emotions, and bodily states" captures a dissociation of the personality, a low level of consciousness, a retracted field of consciousness, a combination of these phenomena, or still something else altogether. Whereas the distinction between (simple) PTSD and developmental trauma disorder or complex PTSD received support from seasoned clinicians and researchers (e.g., Sar, 2011), DSM-5 does not include developmental trauma disorder or complex PTSD. This outcome relates to the controversy regarding the status of complex PTSD (Bryant, 2012; Goodman, 2012; Herman, 2012; Lindauer, 2012; Resick et al., 2012). PTSD and complex PTSD are proposed as two related disorders within a spectrum of trauma and stressor-related disorders for the upcoming 11th version of the ICD. The distinction seems clinically useful, because complex PTSD includes pathology not addressed in standard PTSD treatment (e.g., Landes, Garovoy, & Burkman, 2013; Litt, 2013). The clinical utility of the division is now to be tested in field trials (Cloitre, Garvert, Brewin, Bryant, & Maercker, 2013).

Using a latent profile analysis, Cloitre et al. (2013) found three classes of individuals. One class had complex PTSD, that is, PTSD symptoms as well as disturbances in three domains of self-organization: affective dysregulation, negative self-concept, and interpersonal problems. Another class had only PTSD symptoms. There was also a group that had low scores for PTSD and complex PTSD symptoms and problems. They also found that chronic traumatization to be more strongly predictive of complex PTSD. Conversely, PTSD was better predicted by single adverse events. As might be expected, complex PTSD was associated with greater impairment than (simple) PTSD.

Zoladz and Diamond (2013, p. 860) also noted that PTSD may not be a single disorder:

> . . . factors involved in the susceptibility and expression of PTSD symptoms are more complex and heterogeneous than is commonly stated, with extensive findings which are inconsistent with the stereotypic behavioral and biological profile of the PTSD patient. A thorough assessment of the literature indicates that interactions among myriad susceptibility factors, including social support, early life stress, sex, age, peri- and post-traumatic dissociation, cognitive appraisal of trauma, neuroendocrine abnormalities and gene polymorphisms, in conjunction with the inconsistent expression of the disorder across studies, confounds attempts to characterize PTSD as a monolithic disorder.

Even complex PTSD may not be a monolith. For example, Dorrepaal et al. (2013) found two main subtypes: adaptive and nonadaptive. Characterized by different levels of introversion and disinhibition, the nonadaptive subtype could be further differentiated into withdrawn, alienated, suffering, and aggressive subtypes. These subtypes did not differ regarding PTSD symptoms, trauma history, or parental bonding characteristics, but they were associated with different levels of dissociative+ symptoms and depression.

Chapter 6

Adverse Events and Their Consequences

> *The scars you can't see are the hardest to heal.*
> Astrid Alauda

Apart from the historical and current problems regarding our comprehension, conceptualization, and classification of trauma-related disorders, there have been and continue to be similar difficulties regarding the events that cause, or at least significantly contribute to, their emergence.

The A Criterion for ASD and PTSD in DSM-IV and DSM-5

The DSM-IV A1 Criterion for ASD and PTSD comprised the idea that some types of 'traumatic events' – but not others – can cause these disorders, or are at least required for these conditions to emerge (traumatic event → [i.e., causes/is required for the emergence of] ASD, PTSD). Emphasizing physical death, injury, and threat, the A1 Criterion can be traced to the fact that, like its immediate forerunners such as traumatic neurosis, traumatic neurasthenia, anxiety-neurosis, repression-neurosis, and combat neurosis or combat fatigue, PTSD primarily involves an attempt to capture the mental disturbances of 'men at war,' in the case of PTSD, male Vietnam veterans. In fact, none other than Henry Kissinger coined the label Post-Vietnam Syndrome for what was to become PTSD.

The A Criterion: Overinclusive?

However, the recognition of exogenic causation of some kinds of psychopathology would be challenged. Some authors were concerned that the A1 Criterion was insufficiently stringent. For example, McNally (2003a) asserted that, in times of peace and prosperity, the definition of what counts as a traumatic stressor gets liberalized. In his view, in the absence of "catastrophic stressors" such as war, specialists in traumatic stress would direct their attention toward "noncatastrophic events deemed capable of producing PTSD"

(p. 280). McNally feared that the more inclusive the category of traumatic stressors becomes, the less likely it is that the common mechanisms that mediate PTSD are detected – and the more PTSD becomes a "valued idiom of distress rather than as a genuine disease entity" (see also Brewin, McNally, & Taylor, 2004, p. 101).

In response to these apprehensions, Brewin (Brewin et al., 2004) mentioned that individuals only fulfill the complete DSM-IV A Criterion if they have responded to an A1 Criterion event with extreme fear, helplessness, or terror. This additional A2 Criterion expressed the idea that PTSD includes an endogenic cause (traumatic event → extreme emotionality → ASD, PTSD). For example, a motor vehicle accident did not count as a traumatic event if the involved individual adaptively regulates his or her emotions during and after the crash.

However, several authors raised concerns regarding the validity of DSM-IV Criterion A2 (Bedard-Gilligan & Zoellner, 2008; Bovin & Marx, 2011; Kilpatrick, Resnick, & Acierno, 2009; Resick & Miller, 2009). Some suggested that the A2 Criterion was better deleted in DSM-5 (Brewin, Lanius, Novac, Schnyder, & Galea, 2009). Indeed, it is *overinclusive* in that some individuals who experience extreme fear, helplessness, or terror during 'traumatic events' do not show long-term psychopathology (traumatic event → despite extreme emotionality → no ASD, no PTSD). The A2 Criterion is *underinclusive* in a different regard, because individuals who do not experience strong emotions during the event may nonetheless become mentally injured by what happened to them (traumatic event → despite lack of extreme emotionality in the proximity of the event → ASD, PTSD). Subdued emotionality relates to the topic of what became known as 'peritraumatic dissociation+,' discussed below.

In other words, the DSM-IV A2 Criterion appeared to be a weak statistical predictor for PTSD diagnosis. Whereas many patients with PTSD experienced extreme fear, helplessness, or terror during an A1 Criterion 'traumatic event,' and although responding with extreme fear, helplessness, or terror is associated with greater PTSD severity (Boals & Schuettler, 2009; Osei-Bonsu et al., 2012; Schnurr, Spiro III, Vielhauer, Findler, & Hamblen, 2002), the presence or absence of this emotionality does not tell whether exposed individuals will in fact develop PTSD. Because the absence or presence of the A2 Criterion does not increase the diagnostic accuracy, it was dropped in DSM-5.

The DSM-5 A Criterion for PTSD and ASD reads:

A. Exposure to actual or threatened death, serious injury, or sexual violence in one or more of the following ways:
   1. Directly experiencing the traumatic event(s).
   2. Witnessing, in person, the event(s) as it occurred to others.
   3. Learning that the traumatic event(s) occurred to a close family member, or close friend. In cases of actual or threatened death of a family member or friend, the event(s) must have been violent or accidental.
   4. Experiencing repeated or extreme exposure to aversive details of the traumatic

event(s) (e.g., first responders collecting body parts; police officers repeatedly exposed to details of child abuse). A4 does not apply to exposure through electronic media, television, movies, or pictures, unless this exposure is work related.

As this text shows, the DSM-5 A Criterion events are referred to as "traumatic events" (pp. 271 ff.). The DSM-5 also includes the term 'trauma' (e.g., pp. 275 and 277). While the DSM-5 leaves 'trauma' undefined, it is used as a synonym for 'traumatic event.' This use of the terms 'traumatic event' and 'trauma' deviates from the original meaning of the word 'trauma,' which is wound or injury. The concept of 'psychic trauma' originally pertained to particular *consequences* of an adverse event (adverse event → trauma in the sense of injury). However, many authors presently use the terms 'trauma' and 'traumatic event' as synonyms for an event that has been injurious – i.e., traumatic – rather than as a term that captures the injury as such. Even more troublesome is that many clinicians and scientists currently talk about particular events (e.g., motor vehicle accidents, sexual abuse) as traumas *irrespective of the exposed individual's immediate and later reactions to these events* (e.g., ASD, PTSD, other dissociative disorders).

This practice creates a confusion of tongues. Without specification, it is unclear whether the term 'trauma' denotes a mental wound, an adverse event that caused this injury, or an adverse event that may or may not have caused some kind of pathology of the individual as a living system. It also creates an almost boundless category of traumas in the sense of events. The unchecked liberalization of events that are called traumas as well as the conceptual confusion of an injurious event and the injury that particular events may cause are in need of repair. The terminological and definitional problems involved cannot be easily resolved because of philosophical complexities that deserve more attention than they have received to date in the trauma field. I will briefly indicate the difficulties here and discuss them in more detail later.

Can Science Be at All Objective?

I remarked that McNally (2003a) talks about "traumatic stressors." In his view, war is a "catastrophe" and for that reason counts as a traumatic stressor. He describes particular peacetime stressors as "noncatastrophic," and suggests that these events should not be seen as traumatic stressors. This type of thinking includes the idea that whatever is and is not deemed "catastrophic" can be objectively defined. McNally seems to hold the position that scientists can observe reality in an objective fashion and hence can find and define naturally existing categories of catastrophic and noncatastrophic events. This persuasion can be described as philosophical realism about events and their meaning (e.g., Lakoff & Johnson, 1999). It entails the assumptions that there is some objectively existing world including a natural class of traumatic stressors, and that this class can be objectively known. However, is there in fact such a thing as 'objective knowledge'? A scientific perspective like any other view is not a view from nowhere, it is someone's inescapably *subjective* perspective. As Järvilehto (2001b, statement 53) asserted,

> [t]he fall of man was the beginning of the illusion that a human being can lift himself above the nature to the position of an "objective" observer and judge, being able with his descriptions to determine what the nature really is like. In reality this illusion represents only an absolutization of the human point of view and requires loss of the points of view of the other creatures of nature (also of other men!).

Scientists cannot rise beyond the given human ways of knowing themselves and their surroundings. Like all others, they have their epistemic[1] limitations. No matter how sophisticated it may be, a scientist's view of nature is of necessity a human perspective – no more and no less. However, the common idea in science and beyond is that scientists can in principle access 'objective reality,' that they can assess what objectively exists, that they can resolve deep ontological[2] riddles. Scientists would therefore at least in principle be able to generate and provide an objective view of nature.

This idea is as tempting as it is treacherous. Scientific views involve a third-person perspective. As explained before, this perspective entails an 'I-object' relationship in which a subject, the 'I' (or groups of 'I''s), engages in a formal, physical judgment of an object: I → physically judge → that there is an object with particular properties. The 'object' of concern may be an individual, an event, a feeling or thought, a thing, process, or whatever. The fact that a scientific view necessarily involves the view of a scientist or group of scientists who engage in this physical judgment is commonly removed from consideration. The formula "I or we physically judge that there exists an object with particular properties" then becomes "there exists an object with particular properties." This condensation of the event is unwarranted as it masks that the physical judgment is a human judgment. It hides that human epistemology (i.e., that which human individuals know and can know) provides a human ontology (i.e., that which according to human individuals exists

1 Epistemology is the philosophical study or a theory of the nature and grounds of knowledge especially with reference to its limits and validity. Epistemological puzzles include questions such as what is knowledge, how is knowledge acquired, to what extent is it possible for a particular subject or entity to be known, and who can know the involved subject or entity.

2 Ontology is the philosophical study of the nature of being and existence in general. The focus is on the basic categories of being and their relations, and on the question in what sense the items in those categories can be said to "be." Ontology can thus generally be described as "a philosophical discipline that encompasses besides the study of what there is and the study of the general features of what there is also the study of what is involved in settling questions about what there is in general, especially for the philosophically tricky cases" (see Section 3.1 at http://plato.stanford.edu/entries/logic-ontology/). Whereas there is a theoretical distinction between ontology and epistemology, it is doubtful if there is a practical difference in the sense that for us as human beings there only exists what we can know (Järvilehto, 2004; see Chapters 8, 9, and 10). We can imagine that there is probably far more between Heaven and Earth than we know (Shakespeare; Spinoza, 1677), but we can only guess what else may exist than what we know or can know, as indeed Kant taught.

and can exist), not an absolute ontology (i.e., that which presumably exists irrespective of human experience and knowledge).

A related problem is that a scientific physical judgment is grounded in the judging scientist's first-person perspective (the scientist as a phenomenally experiencing 'I'), quasi-second (a phenomenal judgment yielding 'I-me, myself, mine' relationships), and second-person perspective (a phenomenal judgment generating 'I-You' relationships). It is these person perspectives that allow the physically judging individual to experience and know in the first place. Without these perspectives, they would not be an 'I,' that is, there would be no 'I.' Individuals would be unable to have experiences, know themselves, other individuals, objects, and the world more generally. They would not be able to relate to themselves and their social and material environment. Without the involved bodily and emotional feelings and without these intrapersonal and interpersonal relationships, scientists (and clinicians) would not be human and would not be capable of any sensible judgment of someone else's feelings and emotions. They would have no clue as to what 'fear' and 'helplessness' are, and they would remain unaware that another person can experience these emotions. Only a feeling and social individual can *phenomenally and physically judge* another individual's subjective reactions in a meaningful way. A machine may be programmed to analyze an individual's actions, but it is dependent on such programming by a human being, and it is unable to feel and understand anything. In short, any third-person perspective is based and dependent on thus presupposes the physically judging individual's phenomenal experience and phenomenal judgment, hence, subjectivity. Pure 'objective' knowledge and 'objective' physical judgment are fables.

The third-person perspective does not allow for a classification of events that are catastrophic and those that are not for still another reason. The formula "I → physically judge as a scientist → that some events are catastrophic but not others, and that I know the difference" is false. The third-person perspective does not give access to the minds of other individuals. An empathic second person may to a degree feel along with an individual who lives or lived one or more adverse events, but how 'catastrophic' the experience is can in fact only immediately be phenomenally experienced and judged by the individual who lives or lived the event(s). The meaning and impact of an event therefore depends on the individual who experienced, witnessed, or was otherwise confronted with it.

Moreover, first, second, and third persons cannot fathom the exposed individuals' reactions *a priori*, at least not for certain. For example, a third-person judgment might be that particular events will be catastrophic to particular individuals. However, some individuals considered to be at risk of developing a trauma-related disorder may not develop this condition following such 'catastrophes,' and individuals who were not considered to be at risk may surprisingly have pathological reactions to an event. Further, some individuals may develop a trauma-related condition following an event that third persons did not regard as a 'catastrophe.'

The same misjudgment may apply to the quasi-second-person and second-person perspectives. Particular individuals may not have expected that they would stay mentally healthy following a particular adverse event, but in fact they do. The faulty prediction may also work the other way: Individuals who had expected that they would manage to cope with an adverse event may in fact become traumatized. Second persons (i.e., individuals that engage in a second-person relationship with the individual of concern) may similarly err in either direction.

The point is that it cannot be precisely defined *a priori* how a particular individual will respond to a particular adverse event. This phenomenal or physical judgment can only be made with any certainty *a posteriori*. Whatever is catastrophic or noncatastrophic eventually depends in part on a subject's experience and evaluation of the event(s) (events → as phenomenally experienced and judged by the exposed individual → presence or absence of ASD/PTSD or some other trauma-related disorder). Phenomenal experience and judgment thus influence to what degree the B to H criteria for PTSD apply to an exposed individual. These criteria involve several phenomena that are associated with an adverse event(s): intrusions (B), persistent avoidance of stimuli (C), negative alterations in cognitions and mood (D), and marked alterations in arousal and reactivity (E). The phenomena need to last more than one month (F) and cause clinically significant distress or impairment in important areas of functioning (G). Finally, they should not be attributable to the physiological effects of a substance or another medical condition (H).

The A Criterion: Too Narrow?

This subject dependency precludes a strict third-person *a priori* determination of the kind of events that can be traumatizing for an individual. For example, as DSM-5 has it, a threat to an individual's *physical* integrity can certainly be a potential exogenic cause of PTSD. However, so can threats to his or her *mental* integrity, a fact DSM-5 does not recognize. To illustrate, having been sexually abused as a child and adolescent by her father, Van Derbur (2003, 2012) felt even more injured by her mother's behavior, who knew but ignored what happened, than by her father's recurrent perpetration. Furthermore, she felt more traumatized by his French kissing than by his vaginal penetration. Her phenomenal traumatic experiences and judgments of these experiences are clearly at odds with the DSM-5 A criterion's emphasis on threat to *physical* integrity.

The point should be clear: DSM-5 A Criterion for PTSD has to fulfill a job it cannot do. The personal impact of whatever event is crucially co-dependent on the way in which the exposed individual phenomenally experiences and evaluates the event, and this reaction cannot be precisely predicted *a priori* by first, second, and third persons. Whereas A Criterion events can obviously be precursors to PTSD or some other trauma-related disorder, empirical evidence demonstrates that trauma-related disorders can be elicited by adversities that are not included in the DSM-5 A Criterion. What is deemed adverse depends on phenomenal experience and the meaning a particular event assumes for the exposed individual. This is not to say that this meaning is restricted to conscious reactions:

Preconscious and unconscious evaluations are also included, which are as subject-dependent as the individual's conscious evaluations.

Subject and Object

The philosophical problem of the A Criterion is even more complex *because it cannot be meaningfully defined from a third-person perspective whatever constitutes an 'event.'* In Chapter 4 I mentioned that it is not just the meaning of an event that is dependent on the involved individual's first-person perspective on the event, that is, on the necessarily subjective ways in which he or she experiences and knows it. In addition to this epistemological issue, what is also at stake is that whatever constitutes 'an event' is *subject-dependent.* That is, there is also a problem of ontology. 'An event' is not an objective reality, it is not 'information' that is 'out there,' just waiting for us to experience and 'process' it. It is not an object or constellation of objectively existing things or processes (i.e., movements between objects) that we discover and to which we respond. The crucial point is that an event does not exist in isolation of an experiencing and knowing individual. Rather, it constitutes a perception and/or conception of an individual whose brain is embodied, and who is a biopsychosocial whole, a whole living system, intrinsically embedded in an environment (Järvilehto, 1998a, 1998b, 1999, 2000a, 2000b, 2000c, 2001a, 2001b; Fuchs, 2008, 2010; Northoff, 2003; Schopenhauer, 1818/1844/1958; Spinoza, 1677/1996; Thompson, 2007). *Without an experiencing and knowing subject, there would not be any event.*

This understanding does not imply Platonic ontological idealism, that is, the idea that we 'dream' an otherwise nonexistent material world. If there were no physical environment, our mind would remain 'empty,' as Northoff (2003) contends. A brain could not exist without a living body, and a living body/brain unity could not exist without an environment. However, whatever we can experience and know about that environment, it is necessarily dependent on our human and our personal perceptions and conceptions. These perceptions and conceptions are influenced by our evolution as a species as well as by our shared and personal history, culture, and subculture.

In other words, and as briefly mentioned before, subject and object are ontologically and epistemologically co-dependent: The one cannot exist and be known without the other. Subject and object are also co-constitutive in that the subject conceives his or her world, albeit not out of the blue. We are not like the Holy Virgin Mary capable of Immaculate Conception. There are objects that affect us – bodily, experientially, emotionally, and rationally – or else there would be nothing to experience or know. Whatever we experience and know, it is subjective (Spinoza, 1677/1996).

I will examine these complexities in more detail later. For now let me reiterate that individuals are co-dependently and co-constitutively related to events, some of which can injure and traumatize them as a living system. These philosophical insights have consequences for the definition and use of the term 'trauma,' including the formulation of what kind of events may injure an individual. They also have consequences for science, including a science of trauma and a scientifically based clinical practice of trauma.

One implication of the involved philosophical deliberations that can already be formulated here is the realization that events other than those defined in the A Criterion can be traumatizing. Indeed, whereas adult and childhood sexual harassment and abuse includes threats to the *physical* integrity which clearly fit the A Criterion, there is mounting clinical and empirical evidence that much more can be traumatizing than the experienced or witnessed threats to the actual or perceived physical integrity of self or others.

For example, cross-sectional and prospective longitudinal studies show that attachment disruptions in early childhood as well as emotional unavailability of the mother, including emotional neglect in the first years of life, can be severely traumatizing and constitute a major precursor of dissociative symptoms up to 20 years later (Akyuz, Sar, Kugu, & Dogan, 2005; Dutra, Bureau, Holmes, Lyubchik, & Lyons-Ruth, 2009; Frewen, Pain, Dozois, & Lanius, 2006; Lyons-Ruth, 2008; Nijenhuis et al., 1998b; Ozcetin et al., 2009; Ogawa, Sroufe, Weinfield, Carlson, & Egeland, 1997; Sar, Akyuz, Kugu, Ozturk, & Ertem-Vehid, 2006; Wright, Crawford, & Del Castillo, 2009). Dissociative disorders are also associated with emotional abuse (Nijenhuis et al., 1998b; Sar, Akyuz, & Dogan, 2007a, 2007b). These studies support clinical observations that the severity of child sexual abuse as well as dissociative and other trauma-related symptoms are in part dependent on emotional neglect and abuse, and on the emotional unavailability of the child's caretakers (Blizard, 1997, 2003; Bowlby, 1980; Jones, 1986; Howell, 2005; Kluft, 1984a; Liotti, 2004; Van der Kolk, Perry, & Herman, 1991). Studies have also documented that emotional neglect and emotional abuse are associated with symptoms of PTSD, dissociative+ symptoms, and dissociative disorders (Draijer & Langeland, 1999; Nijenhuis et al., 1998b; Ozcetin et al., 2009; Pederson & Wilson, 2009; Spertus, Yehuda, Wong, Halligan, & Seremetis, 2003; Watson, Chilton, Fairchild, & Whewell, 2006; Wright et al., 2009). Evidence for the potential pathogenic effects of caretaker betrayal (Freyd, 2008; Goldsmith, Freyd, & DePrince, 2011) is also at odds with the A Criterion for PTSD.

These empirical findings demonstrate that far more can be traumatizing than just threats to the integrity of the body and life itself. Given the persuasive evidence for the underinclusiveness of the A Criterion, one may wonder why the authors of DSM-5 have disregarded it (see Chapter 20).

The Proposed A Criterion for Developmental Trauma Disorder: Too Narrow?

The proposed A Criterion for developmental trauma disorder involves experienced or witnessed multiple or prolonged adverse events over a period of time of at least 1 year beginning in childhood or early adolescence. The events include interpersonal violence and significant disruptions of protective caregiving as the result of repeated changes in primary caregiver, repeated separation from the primary caregiver, or exposure to severe and persistent emotional abuse. The formal recognition of the adversity and potentially traumatizing effects of early childhood emotional abuse and of early childhood emotional caregiving and attachment disruptions is certainly a profound advancement. However, in the light of the documented harmfulness of emotional neglect by and emotional unavailability of the primary caregiver(s), it is curious that these environmental conditions are not, at least not explicitly, included in the proposal.

Causes Among Causes: 'Risk Factors' for Trauma-Related Disorders

A cause is only a cause in a context of preceding other causes (Spinoza, 1677/1996; Schopenhauer, 1814/2007). Therefore, however significant an A Criterion event or any other adverse event may be, it constitutes only one among several factors that influence the effects and meaning these event(s) will have for an individual. Events do not exist in a historical vacuum; they are not isolated from other events, but constitute an episode in an individual's life. Hence, to the extent that adverse events can be considered as causes of pathology, the presumed causal connection becomes as follows: adverse event(s) plus contextual factors → codetermine → mental disorder. The involved contextual causal factors that may precede, accompany, or follow adversities are commonly described as 'risk factors.'

Risk Factors for Adult Psychiatric Disorders

With the growing recognition of PTSD and other trauma-related disorders during the 1980s, it became important to study what features of exposed subjects and adverse or potentially traumatizing events as well as what circumstantial factors are associated with the emergence of the injury such a trauma is. For example, what differences exist between individuals who do and those who do not become traumatized when they experience an adverse, potentially traumatizing event? Is it true that 'any man has his breaking point?' Are some kinds of events more injurious than others, and does it matter how other people respond to survivors?

Consistent with the present analysis that the terms 'traumatic events' or 'trauma' in the sense of an event are misleading, upon reviewing childhood determinants of adult psychiatric disorder Fryers and Brugha (2013, p. 39) concluded that

> [s]ubstantial proportions of children and young people are apparently subjected to serious verbal, physical and sexual abuse, severe maltreatment and neglect in every community where it has been investigated. But also many children are resilient and, achieve healthy, adjusted adult lives even even after child abuse, dependent also upon the type, degree and circumstances of abuse.

Fryers and Brugha found clear evidence that serious childhood adversity increases the risk of recurrent psychiatric disorder throughout life. The most serious risk seems to be child abuse, especially child sexual abuse. The evidence suggests that this abuse is surprisingly and disturbingly common, and that in particular multiple adversities and multiple experiences of abuse tend to be associated with multiple serious biopsychosocial consequences affecting individuals, families, and communities. These causes, Fryers and Brugha (2013, p. 41) emphasize,

> must be considered among the most important potentially preventable 'causes' of psychiatric disorder throughout life. It is, of course, not a single 'cause' but an accumulation of several or many 'causes,' which appear to be cumulative in their ultimate effects on children, and families with the highest levels of multiple adversity should be a very high priority for early identification and relief.

The documented risk factors in parents include young parental age, low academic achievement, and adverse childhood experiences, particularly parental exposure to abuse and neglect in their own childhood, and parental psychiatric history, including a history of substance abuse. The review also found that the relationship between long-term psychopathology and childhood adversity is to a degree related to the severity and type of the abuse, frequency, timing, and relationship with the perpetrator. The harming effects of childhood adversities can last at least into middle age. Attachment disorders and specifically disorganized attachment are common in individuals who are or were chronically abused and neglected as children (Cyr, Euser, Bakermans-Kranenburg, & Van IJzendoorn, 2010).

Under the leadership of Robert Anda and Vincent Felitti, the Adverse Childhood Events (ACE) studies have also documented relationships between childhood adversity and many mental disorders and physical diseases, suicide attempts, substance (ab)use, as well as academic and occupational underachievement (Anda et al., 2006, 2008). Prospective, longitudinal work of Cathy Spatz Widom and her colleagues (Currie & Widom, 2010; Widom, 1999; Widom, Czaja, Bentley, & Johnson, 2012; Widom, Czaja, & Paris, 2009) shows how psychologically, physically, and economically damaging physical and sexual abuse as well as emotional neglect can be in the short and (very) long run. A most impressive 23-year multigenerational longitudinal study similarly demonstrated the detrimental impact of intrafamilial sexual abuse on female biopsychosocial development (Trickett et al., 2011, p. 453). In the authors' words,

> [r]esults of many analyses, both within circumscribed developmental stages and across development, indicated that sexually abused females (on average) showed deleterious sequelae across a host of biopsychosocial domains including: earlier onsets of puberty, cognitive deficits, depression, dissociative symptoms, maladaptive sexual development, hypothalamic – pituitary – adrenal attenuation, asymmetrical stress responses, high rates of obesity, more major illnesses and healthcare utilization, dropping out of high school, persistent posttraumatic stress disorder, self-mutilation, Diagnostic and Statistical Manual of Mental Disorders diagnoses, physical and sexual revictimization, premature deliveries, teen motherhood, drug and alcohol abuse,

and domestic violence. Offspring born to abused mothers were at increased risk for child maltreatment and overall maldevelopment.

Trickett and colleagues also found a pattern of considerable within-group variability, suggesting there is not a direct, one-to-one relationship between sexual abuse and outcome. There must be mediating causal factors in play. One factor is that the relationship between experiencing adverse events and outcome might for at least some variables not be linear, but exponential (see Figures 6.1–6.4).[3] Individuals may be able to integrate adversities that hap-

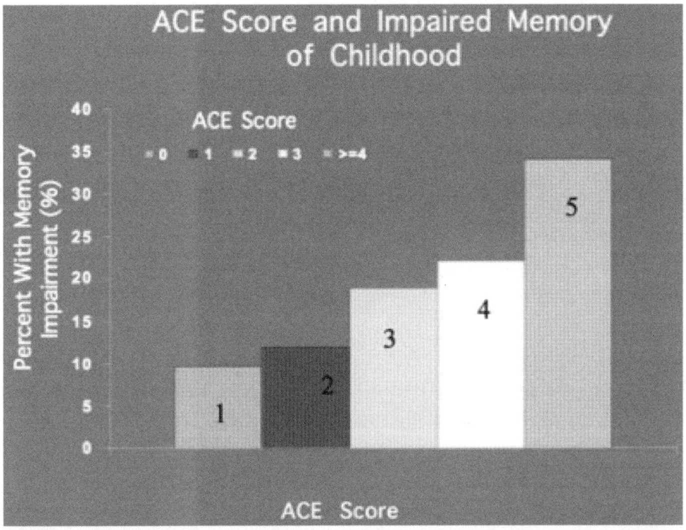

Figure 6.1. Reported childhood adversity and impaired memory of childhood.

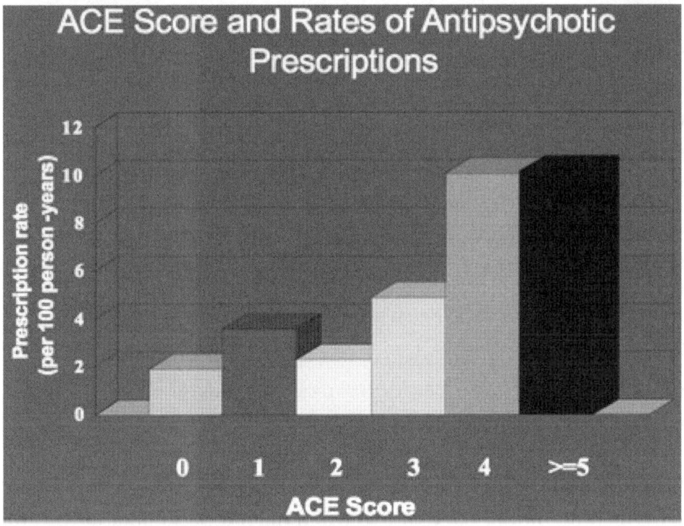

Figure 6.2. Reported childhood adversity and the rate of antipsychotic prescriptions.

3 The major ACE Study findings may be downloaded as a PDF at http://www.theannainstitute.org/ACE%20STUDY%20FINDINGS.html

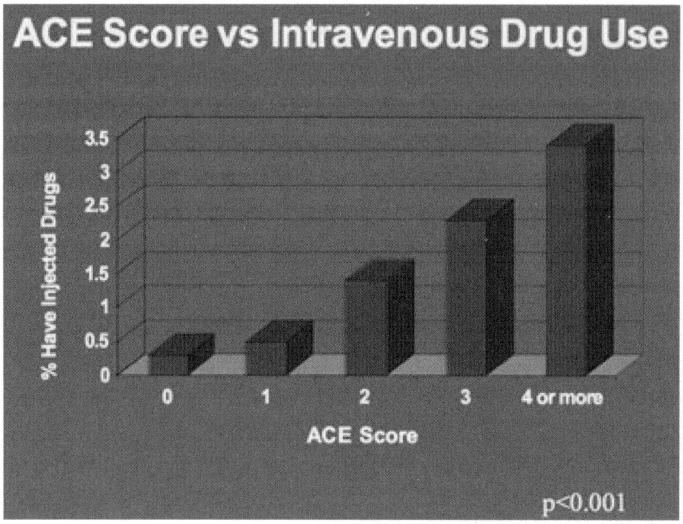

Figure 6.3. Reported childhood adversity and intravenous drug abuse.

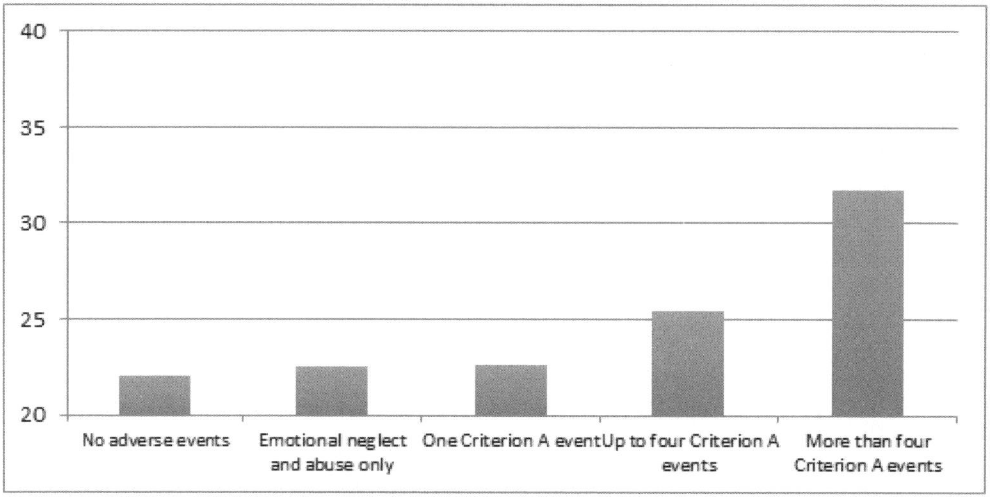

Figure 6.4. Sensorimotor dissociation and adverse events as reported by general psychiatric outpatients.

pen to them up to a particular point. Beyond that critical point, they will start to develop a mental disorder. Thus, the relationships between the degree of childhood traumatization and pathology might be exponential with regard to at least some outcome variables.

For example, Felitti and Anda (2008, p. 82) stated that

> [t]he relationship of intravenous drug use with ACE Score is particularly striking, given that male children with ACE Score 6 or more have a 46-fold increased likelihood of later becoming an injection drug user, compared to a male child with an ACE Score 0; this moves the probability from an arithmetic to an exponential progression. Relationships of this magnitude are rare in epidemiology.

Risk Factors for PTSD

A meta-analysis of risk factors for PTSD (Brewin, Andrew, & Valentine, 2000) found that the individual effect size of all examined 14 risk factors was modest. Factors such as psychiatric history, reported childhood abuse, and family psychiatric history had the most uniform predictive effects across different populations. However, factors operating during or after the adverse event (e.g., severity of the adverse event, lack of social support, additional life stress) were somewhat stronger associated with PTSD than pretrauma factors. In another meta-analysis, Ozer, Best, Lipsey, and Weiss (2003) also concluded that peritraumatic psychological factors are more strongly correlated with PTSD than pretrauma characteristics. Still, prior adverse events, prior psychological adjustment, and family history of psychopathology also yielded significant effect sizes. Among the peritraumatic psychological factors, which included perceived life threat during the adverse event, posttrauma social support, peritraumatic emotional responses, and peritraumatic dissociation+, peritraumatic dissociation+ was most strongly associated with later PTSD.

Reviewing risk factors for PTSD, DiGangi et al. (2013) included only prospective, longitudinal studies comprising assessments that preceded and followed the exposure to the adverse event(s). They found six categories of predictor variables: cognitive abilities, coping and response styles, personality factors, psychopathology, psychophysiological factors, and social ecological factors. Many of these variables had previously been considered *outcomes* of adverse event exposure. There is also evidence that use of benzodiazepines and duration of sedation, along with fear, stress and delirium are risk factors for PTSD in individuals who are taken to an intensive care unit (Wade, Hardy, Howell, & Mythen, 2013).

Peritraumatic Dissociation+ as a Risk Factor for Trauma-Related Disorders

The concept of 'peritraumatic dissociation+' pertains to a broad collection of mental phenomena. For example, Cardeña and Spiegel (1993) studied the mental reactions of university students and faculty members to the Loma Prieta earthquake that hit San Francisco in 1989. A sample of psychology students and faculty were examined one week and a sample of medical students 4 months after the earthquake. The peritraumatic dissociative+ phenomena that were assessed involved alterations in cognition, memory, and time perception as well as depersonalization and derealization. Alterations in cognition included confusion, hypervigilance, exaggerated startle responses, difficulty with new information, and narrowing of attention as well as a sense of timelessness, detailed memory of the adverse event (in Cardeña and Spiegel's study an earthquake), and lack of interest in activities. The involved peritraumatic phenomena address alterations in the quality and quantity of mental contents, and certainly need not be manifestations of a dissociation of the personality. Grouping the wide variety of peritraumatic phenomena under the label of 'dissociation' is therefore problematic (see Chapters 12–14 for a deeper discussion).

(Note once again that I write dissociation+ when this term stands for such a wide variety of phenomena.)

Peritraumatic dissociative+ phenomena can emerge both during and immediately after a confrontation with an adverse event, and they can remain active for some individuals (Carlson, Dalenberg, & McDade-Montez, 2012). For example, individuals with accident-related PTSD had more dissociative+ symptoms than those who did not develop PTSD subsequent to the accident they experienced and the severe physical injuries they implied (Baranyi et al., 2010). In a retrospective study, delayed recall of CSA was associated with peritraumatic sensorimotor dissociation and the severity of this abuse (Nijenhuis, Van Engen, Kusters, & Van der Hart, 2001). As discussed in the previous chapter, individuals exposed to major threat can also engage in tonic immobility, a type of mammalian defense that is strongly associated with PTSD symptoms, an unfavorable PTSD treatment prognosis, and complex dissociative disorders.

Dissociative symptoms can appear in the proximity of the involved injurious events in young children. As measured with the Child Dissociative Checklist (CDC; Putnam, Helmers, & Trickett, 1993), most of whose items seem to address manifestations of a dissociation of the personality, abused and maltreated preschool-aged children had more dissociative symptoms than children who had not met these adversities (Macfie, Cicchetti, & Toth, 2001a, 2001b). Dissociative symptoms in these children were associated with maltreatment severity and chronicity, multiple subtypes of maltreatment – sexual abuse, physical abuse, neglect, severity, and chronicity were all implicated – and internalizing and externalizing symptomatology.

In fact, many studies, including prospective and clinical studies, have found a statistically significant and robust relationship between peritraumatic dissociation+ and later posttraumatic stress (for reviews, see Breh, & Seidler, 2007; Lensvelt-Mulders et al., 2008; Van der Hart, Van Ochten, Van Son, Steele, & Lensvelt-Mulders, 2008; see Sugar & Ford, 2012, for a retrospective study with psychiatrically impaired youth). However, in several studies peritraumatic dissociation+ did not prospectively predict PTSD symptoms beyond mental health problems assessed soon after the 'traumatic event' (e.g., Van der Velden et al., 2006; Wittmann, Moergeli, & Schnyder, 2006). Why these inconsistencies?

One reason could be that research into peritraumatic dissociation+ to date has involved several methodological differences and shortcomings with respect to study design, sample characteristics, measurement instruments, and control for moderating or mediating variables (Lensvelt-Mulders et al., 2008). In addition, peritraumatic dissociation+ is inconsistently conceptualized and defined across different studies. Thus, there is a call for a more precise definition of the concept of 'peritraumatic dissociation' and more sophisticated study of different kinds of altered consciousness (Bryant, 2007; Lensvelt-Mulders et al., 2008). As indicated before, phenomena (or some of the phenomena) collected under the heading of peritraumatic dissociation+ do not or not necessarily pertain to an emerging dissociation of the survivor's personality. They may rather pertain to detachment phenomena such as an altered sense of time, out of body experiences, derealization, depersonalization, feeling disconnected from one's body, and feeling confused or disoriented. There are some indications that the Peritraumatic Dissociative Experiences Questionnaire (PDEQ, Marmar et al., 1994), the scale that is often used to evaluate the severity of peritraumatic dissociation, may include two factors (Brooks et al., 2009). These are (1) alterations in awareness and (2) distortions in perception of the self and the world. The latter perceptual distortion may mediate the relationship of peritraumatic panic and PTSD (panic → depersonalization/derealization → PTSD; Bryant et al., 2011).

Another problem concerns the reliability of retrospective subjective assessment of peritraumatic dissociation+ over time. For example, the consistency of this assessment was lower in individuals with PTSD than in individuals who did not develop PTSD or who overcame their PTSD (David, Akerib, Gaston, & Brunet, 2010). It is conceivable that this lower test-retest consistency relates in part to the existence of different dissociative parts of the personality in this disorder: Different dissociative parts may have different recollections of the peritraumatic reactions, so that the results of a measurement will be dependent on the part of the personality that completed the items of a questionnaire.

Other Peritraumatic Risk Factors

Peritraumatic physiological arousal (Gutner et al., 2010) and peritraumatic distress also statistically predict PTSD. However, like peritraumatic dissociation+, the correlation of peritraumatic distress and PTSD tends to decline as time elapses between the adverse, potentially traumatizing event and the assessment of PTSD (Thomas, Saumier, & Brunet, 2012). This suggests that factors other than peritraumatic dissociation+ and peritraumatic distress may lead to the development of PTSD as time progresses. One of these is the mental avoidance of emotional experiences (sometimes also referred to as 'dissociation,' rather than as an action that may elicit or maintain a dissociation of the personality). Efforts to suppress, control, and avoid unwanted emotions, sensations, thoughts, and memories might lead to mental and behavioral difficulties (Hayes, Wilson, Gilford, Follette, & Strosahl, 1996; Marx & Sloan, 2002; Nijenhuis et al., 2002b; Van der Hart et al., 2006). A prospective study of undergraduates who experienced a campus shooting found that peritraumatic dissociation+ and emotional avoidance had unique influences as risk factors for PTSD following this potentially traumatizing event (Kumpula et al., 2011).

Biological Risk Factors for Trauma-Related Disorders

Researchers are beginning to find biological risk factors for trauma-related disorders as well. For example, long-lasting alterations in the hypothalamic-pituitary-adrenal (HPA) axis may increase vulnerability to disease, including PTSD and other mood and anxiety disorders. Genetic association studies also indicate that these alterations may be partly mediated by gene-environment interactions involving particular polymorphisms within two key genes (i.e., CRHR1 and FKBP5) (Gillespie, Phifer, Bradley, & Ressler, 2009). The findings suggest that these two genes regulate HPA axis function in conjunction with exposure to interpersonal adverse events in childhood. Gillespie et al. also reported mounting evidence from animal studies that increased activity of the amygdala-HPA axis induced by experimental manipulation of the amygdala mimics several of the physiological and behavioral symptoms of stress-related psychiatric illness in humans. Interactions between the developing amygdala and HPA axis may be associated with critical periods for emotional learning, which is modulated by developmental support and maternal care. Gillespie et al. hypothesized that

> high levels of early life trauma lead to disease through the developmental interaction of genetic variants with neural circuits that regulate emotion, together mediating risk and resilience in adults (p. 984).

Conclusion

Several features influence the probability that an individual develops a trauma-related disorder, including a mixture of biopsychosocial factors. Exposure to a 'traumatic event' or a 'trauma' in the sense of an event is necessary but insufficient. The use of the terms 'traumatic event,' 'traumatizing event,' and 'trauma' in the sense of an event irrespective of the presence or absence of pathological consequences of the involved event for the exposed individual(s) must therefore be rejected. Whether or not a particular adverse event causes a trauma-related disorder depends on a constellation of preceding, accompanying, and subsequent intrapersonal features and interpersonal causes.

Adverse Childhood Events, Dissociative Symptoms, and Dissociation of the Personality

Fryers and Brugha (2013) did not include dissociative disorders in their otherwise excellent review of precursors of adult psychopathology. Such an exclusion in epidemiological studies is not at all exceptional. As Sar (2011a) poignantly explained,

> [g]eneral psychiatric assessment instruments do not cover DSM-IV dissociative disorders. Many large-scale epidemiological studies led to biased results due to this deficit in their methodology. Nevertheless, screening studies using diagnostic tools designed to assess dissociative disorders yielded lifetime prevalence rates around 10% in clinical populations and in the community. Special populations such as psychiatric emergency ward applicants, drug addicts, and women in prostitution demonstrated the highest rates. Data derived from epidemiological studies also support clinical findings about the relationship between childhood adverse experiences and dissociative disorders. Thus, dissociative disorders constitute a hidden and neglected public health problem. Better and early recognition of dissociative disorders would increase awareness about childhood traumata in the community and support prevention of them alongside their clinical consequences.

This absence begs the question why dissociative disorders are so often ignored in psychiatry? A partial answer is that the old idea that traumatic neurosis and hysteria are generally due to simulation is still alive (for a more complete answer, see Chapter 20). In fact, the past two decades have witnessed fierce confrontations between those who consider dissociative disorders to be authentic trauma-related conditions and that remembering childhood traumatization following a period of apparent (but not real) oblivion may happen; and those who believe dissociative disorders are simulated conditions involving false memories of traumatization (Bremner, 2010; Coons, 2005; Fraser, 2005; Giesbrecht, Lynn, Lilienfeld, & Merckelbach, 2010; Gleaves, 1996; Loewenstein, 2007; Piper & Merskey, 2005; Sar, 2005). The so-called 'sociocognitive model of DID' more specifically reflects the idea that DID is due to negative endogenetic causes such as suggestibility, fantasy proneness, and attention seeking, and to exogenetic factors such as suggestive therapies and media influences (Giesbrecht et al., 2008; Giesbrecht, Merckelbach, Kater, & Sluis, 2007; Lilienfeld et al., 1999; Piper & Merskey, 1994a, 1994b; Spanos, 1994). Remembering childhood abuse and neglect after a delay is similarly explained (Spanos, 1996). These 'delayed memories' would not be recollections of real traumatization but pseudomemories suggested by therapists, books, or the media, or some other self-suggested phenomena.

The discussion between clinicians and scientists who adhere to the trauma-related view and those who are committed to the suggestion/fantasy model persists to this day. It repeats in many regards the controversy from the 19th and early 20th century regarding the nature of traumatic neurosis and hysteria. Provided they are grounded in solid and sound theoretical reflections, research and careful clinical observations may finally settle the issues at stake. These data will be detailed in Chapter 15, but some findings can already be listed here. In a literature review, Dalenberg et al. (2012) found that

- the relationship between adverse events and dissociative+ symptoms is consistent and moderate in strength;
- this association remains significant when objective measures of the adversities are used;
- dissociative+ symptoms and disorders tend to emerge during or following adverse events, and they tend to lessen with trauma-related treatment;
- the correlation between dissociative+ symptoms and adverse event exposure remains statistically significant following a correction for the influence of fantasy proneness;
- dissociation is not reliably associated with suggestibility or fantasy proneness. For example, women with major DID are not high fantasy prone (Nijenhuis & Reinders, 2012; Schlumpf et al., 2013).
- the prediction of the fantasy model that recovered memories of traumatic experiences are more inaccurate than narrative autobiographical memories does not hold. The review by Dalenberg et al. (2012) demonstrates in fact that dissociation+ is positively related to a history of trauma memory recovery and negatively related to narrative cohesion. All in all, there is no support for the idea that the association between dissociation and adverse events is due to fantasy proneness or confabulated memories of traumatizing events.

Furthermore, every controlled study that tested TSDP-based hypothesized biopsychosocial differences between ANP and EP in DID has found them (Hermans, Nijenhuis, Van Honk, Huntjens, & Van der Hart, 2006; Reinders et al., 2003, 2006; Schlumpf et al., 2013, 2014). These studies also documented that high and low fantasy-prone mentally healthy individuals, actors, and members of the general population were unable to simulate these two prototypical dissociative parts of the personality. Presented and discussed in more detail in Chapters 16–18, the findings are at full odds with the hypotheses that dissociative parts are caused by suggestion, suggestibility, fantasy, fantasy proneness, or motivated role-playing.

Further, there is no empirical evidence that ignoring or rejecting dissociative parts of the personality is in any way therapeutic, and that patients with complex dissociative disorders have a suboptimal response to standard exposure-based therapy for PTSD as well as high levels of attrition from treatment (Brand, Lanius, Vermetten, Loewenstein, & Spiegel, 2012; Brand, Loewenstein, & Spiegel, 2014). Emerging scientific evidence demonstrates that a phase-oriented integration-focused approach to treatment is generally helpful to them (Brand, Classen, McNary, & Zaveri, 2009; Brand & Stadnik, 2013; Brand et al., 2012; Brand et al., 2014; Myrick et al., 2012; Myrick, Brand, & Putnam, 2013). With this treatment patients with minor and major DID attained decreased symptoms of dissociation+, depression, PTSD, distress, and suicidality (Brand & Stadnik, 2009). Young adults generally improve faster than older adults (Myrick et al., 2012), as do those with less initial dissociative+ symptoms (Brand & Stadnik, 2013), fewer current stressors, and less revictimization (Myrick et al., 2013). These findings are fully consonant with consistent three decades of clinical observations (Van der Hart et al., 2006).

Dissociative+ Symptoms and Childhood Maltreatment, Abuse, and Neglect

There is accumulating evidence from retrospective as well as prospective, longitudinal studies that dissociative+ symptoms are related to childhood maltreatment, abuse, and neglect. The association has been found for children (Macfie et al., 2001a, 2001b; Manzano-Mojica, Martinez-Taboas, Sayers-Montalvo, Cabiya, & Alicea-Rodriguez, 2012; Silberg, 2000), adolescents (Diseth, 2006), and adults (Boon & Draijer, 1993b; Dell, 2006b; Dutra et al., 2009; Nijenhuis, Spinhoven, Van Dyck, Van der Hart, & Vanderlinden, 1998; Ogawa et al., 1997; Ross & Ness, 2010; Somer & Dell, 2005; Trickett et al., 2011). The populations that have been examined include the general population, students, traumatized individuals, as well as patients with complex dissociative disorders (e.g., Boon & Draijer, 1993a; Chu, Frey, Ganzel, & Matthews, 1999; Dell, 2006b; Nijenhuis et al., 1998b; Lewis, Yeager, Swica, Pincus, & Lewis, 1997; Ross & Ness, 2010). Depersonalization disorders has also been associated with childhood interpersonal traumatization, particularly emotional maltreatment (Simeon, 2004).

Cognitive-Emotional Dissociative+ Symptoms in PTSD and More Complex Dissociative Disorders

Leaders in the field agree that re-experiencing traumatic memories – a core feature of PTSD – constitutes a dissociative symptom (Carlson et al., 2012). They also recognize that patients with PTSD have a range of other pertinent cognitive-emotional dissociative+ symptoms. For example, reviewing the literature, Carlson et al. (2012) concluded that there is a considerable to strong association between PTSD symptoms and dissociative+ symptoms as measured by the Dissociative Experiences Scale (DES, Bernstein & Putnam, 1986) and the Structured Clinical Interview for DSM-IV Dissociative Disorders (SCID-D; Steinberg, 2000; e.g., Bremner, Steinberg, Southwick, Johnson, & Charney, 1993). The DES evaluates the severity of manifestations of a dissociation of the personality as well as symptoms of lowering of the level and field of consciousness that need not relate to a dissociation of the personality. The association between PTSD symptoms and DES and SCID-D scores was upheld when the dissociative symptoms of behavioral re-experiencing of traumatic memories and gaps in memory were excluded from the calculations (Carlson & Dalenberg, 2009).

PTSD patients also report symptoms that are not mentioned in the description of PTSD in DSM-IV but that can certainly point to a dissociation of the individual's personality. For example, many veterans as well as civilians with PTSD hear voices (Andrew, Gray, & Snowden, 2008; Anketell et al., 2010; Brewin & Patel, 2010). Whereas this phenomenon has frequently been understood as a psychotic symptom, these voices can involve the voices of dissociative parts of the personality (e.g., Longden, Madill, & Waterman, 2012; Van der Hart et al., 2006). Hearing voices in PTSD according to Anketell et al. (2010) and Brewin and Patel (2010) was related to other dissociative+ reactions, did not occur in veterans and civilians without PTSD, and had the characteristics of pseudohallucinations.

According to Brewin and Patel (2010), these results point to the dissociative nature of PTSD. This view is also consistent with the fact that beliefs about voices, dissociation of identity and body, and interpersonal impact were central superordinate themes associated with hearing voices in PTSD (Anketell, Dorahy, & Curran, 2011). Patients had no control over the voices, experienced them as ego-dystonic, and felt isolated and ashamed because of their presence.

Whereas PTSD is generally associated with moderate cognitive-emotional dissociative+ symptoms as assessed with self-report instruments (Amdur & Liberzon, 1996; Nejad & Farahati, 2007), patients with a complex form of PTSD have more severe cognitive-emotional dissociative+ symptoms than patients with simple PTSD (Boroske-Leiner, Hofmann, & Sack, 2008; Zucker et al., 2006). Patients with minor DID have marked cognitive-emotional dissociative+ symptoms (Boon & Draijer, 1993b; Nijenhuis et al., 1999), and in major DID these symptoms are extreme (Boon & Draijer, 1993a; Frischholz et al., 1990; Nijenhuis et al., 1999). The documented progression of cognitive-emotional dissociative+ symptoms from simple PTSD to complex PTSD to minor and major DID support the clinical observations that the complexity of the dissociation of the personality increases with the complexity of the trauma-related disorder. This relationship is predicted by and supportive of TSDP.

Cognitive-Emotional Dissociative+ Symptoms, Childhood Traumatization, and Several Other Features

There are also consistent relationships between dissociative+ symptoms, adverse events in childhood, and several other features. These features include unresolved attachment status (Bailey, Moran, & Pederson, 2007; Lyons-Ruth, Dutra, Schuder, & Bianchi, 2006), violence (Moskowitz, 2004), antisocial personality disorder (Semiz, Basoglu, Ebrinc, & Cetin, 2007), and proneness to experience hallucinations (Varese, Barkus, & Bentall, 2011). The relationship between cognitive-emotional dissociative+ symptoms and childhood adverse events was also found in young mothers (Marysko et al., 2010). Maternal psychopathology has a serious impact on child development, particularly in the first year of life. The findings of this prospective study are therefore of immediate relevance for the detection and assistance of at-risk mother-infant dyads.

Suicide. Suicide, suicidal ideation, and suicide attempts are risks that are particularly associated with cognitive-emotional dissociative+ symptoms. Whereas dissociative disorders are often overlooked in studies of suicide and suicidality, there is evidence that they may be a significant or even very strong predictor of multiple suicide attempter status (Akyuz et al., 2005; Foote, Smolin, Neft, & Lipschitz, 2008; Sar et al., 2007a). Patients with dissociative disorders frequently engage in suicide attempts as well as in self-mutilation without having suicidal thoughts. Both actions are associated with childhood abuse and neglect (Jacobson & Gould, 2007; Sar et al., 2007a; Ozturk & Sar 2008; Zoroglu et al., 2003). DSM-5 states that over 70% of outpatients with DID have attempted to commit suicide, that multiple attempts are common in this population, and that many engage in other self-injurious behaviors.

Substance Abuse and Self-Mutilation. In female college students cognitive-emotional dissociative+ symptoms mediated the relationships between CSA and and both drug and alcohol abuse (Rodriguez-Srednicki, 2001). In this study the dissociative+ symptoms also explained significant variability when added to the regressions of risky sex and suicidality. Severe cognitive-emotional dissociative+ symptoms involved a major risk for self-mutilation in a large sample of adolescents, both before and after adjustment for several possible confounding factors (Tolmunen et al., 2008). In fact, many patients with serious cognitive-emotional dissociative+ symptoms and complex dissociative disorders engage in self-mutilation such as cutting, burning, and banging body parts.

Sensorimotor Dissociative Symptoms in PTSD and More Complex Dissociative Disorders

Sensorimotor dissociative symptoms include negative phenomena such as analgesia, various kinds of anesthesia as well as difficulty in moving the body or a particular body part, and paralysis of the body or some part thereof (Nijenhuis, 2004). They also encompass positive symptoms such as intruding body sensations and movements. The severity of these symptoms can be evaluated with the SDQ-20 (Nijenhuis et al., 1996)[4]. The phenomena belong to the major symptoms of hysteria that Janet (1901/1977, 1907) described at the beginning of the previous century (see also Nijenhuis, 2004, 2009). Oppenheim reported their presence in patients with traumatic neurosis, Rivers observed them in traumatized World War I veterans, and Kretschmer (1923) associated these phenomena with hysteria. There has nonetheless been, and continues to exist, a tendency to exclude sensorimotor dissociative symptoms from the domain of dissociative phenomena. For example, they are categorized in DSM-IV and DSM-5 as conversion symptoms. This practice is at odds with the strong conceptual and empirical evidence that sensorimotor dissociative symptoms are characteristic of patients with dissociative disorders.

Table 6.1 lists the severity of sensorimotor dissociative symptoms for a wide range of diagnoses. The findings match the hypothesis that the severity of sensorimotor dissociative disorders relates to the severity of the dissociation of the personality. Roughly speaking, major DID is associated with mean SDQ-20 scores between 50 and 60, suggesting severe sensorimotor dissociative symptoms. Minor DID in turn is associated with mean scores between 40 and 50, indicating marked sensorimotor dissociation. Mean scores between 30 and 40, representing a significant degree of sensorimotor dissociative symptoms, have been documented in patients with PTSD, conversion disorder (DSM-IV, APA, 1994)/dissociative disorders of movement and sensation (ICD-10, WHO, 1992), including pseudoepilepsy (labeled dissociative convulsions in ICD-10), and patients with eating disorders, particularly those who report traumatization. Patients with other mental disorders tend to have scores below 30, as do individuals in the general population.

Considering that the cutoff in the screening for DSM-IV dissociative disorders is > 28 (Nijenhuis, 2009; Nijenhuis et al., 1997b, 1998c), it is noteworthy that the mean SDQ-20 of patients with PTSD was 38.7 (Amaral do Espirito-Santo & Pio-Abreu, 2007) and 35 (Müller et al., 2010). The findings suggest that PTSD patients have as many sensorimotor dissociative symptoms as Oppenheim's patients with traumatic neurosis had (see my approximations in Chapter 3), but that they have less severe and extensive sensorimotor dissociative symptoms than patients with complex dissociative disorders, particularly those with minor or major DID. The findings are consistent with TSDP's hypothesis that

4 Because the items of the SDQ-20 were specifically construed to measure sensorimotor manifestations of dissociation of the personality, no + symbol is added to the terms 'sensorimotor dissociative symptoms' and 'sensorimotor dissociation.' However, it clearly cannot be excluded that in some cases a particular sensorimotor phenomenon does not pertain to a dissociation of the personality.

Table 6.1. Sensorimotor dissociative symptoms in different diagnostic categories.

		SDQ-20	
		M	*SD*
Dissociative disorders			
DID	Nijenhuis et al., 1996	51.8	12.6
	Nijenhuis et al., 1998b	57.3	14.9
	Sar et al., 2000	58.7	17.9
DDNOS + a few with depersonalization disorder	Nijenhuis et al., 1996	43.8	7.1
DDNOS	Nijenhuis et al., 1998b	44.6	11.9
	Sar et al., 2000	46.3	16.2
Mixed group of dissociative disorders, including depersonalization disorder and DDNOS	Espirito-Santo & Pio-Abreu, 2007	39.3	12.0
Spirit possession disorder	Van Duijl et al., 2010	39.4	7.4
Depersonalization disorder	Simeon et al., 2008	28.2	7.6
Sensorimotor dissociative disorders			
Mixed sensorimotor dissociative disorders	Roelofs et al., 2002a	30.5	8.5
	Nijenhuis et al., 1999	31.9	9.4
Pseudoepilepsy	Kuyk et al., 1999	29.8	7.5
	Lawton et al., 2008	39.0	21.9
Conversion disorder	Sar et al., 2004	81.6% of sample: $M > 35$	
	Espirito-Santo & Pio-Abreu, 2007	39.8	14.1
Somatoform and somatic disorders			
Somatoform pain disorder			
Chronic headache	Yücel et al., 2002	32.6	10.4
Chronic low back pain		30.6	10.9
Women with chronic pelvic pain	Nijenhuis et al., 2003	25.7	9.3
Female orgasmic and sexual pain disorders	Farina et al., 2011	31.0	22–45
Temporal lobe epilepsy	Kuyk et al., 1999	24.3	6.8
Nontemporal lobe epilepsy		25.6	7.3
Epilepsy	Lawton et al., 2008	29.0	17.0
Other DSM-IV axis I diagnoses			
PTSD	Espirito-Santo & Pio-Abreu, 2007	38.7	11.7
	Müller et al., 2010	35.0	14.7
Borderline personality disorder	Korzekwa et al., 2009	28.0	6.5
Schizophrenia	Sar et al., 2000	27.1	9.5
Eating disorders	Nijenhuis et al., 1999	27.7	8.8
Mixed types			
Anorexia nervosa, restrictive	Waller et al., 2003	27.0	7.6
Anorexia nervosa, binge purge		38.2	14.8
Bulimia nervosa		32.6	–

		SDQ-20	
		M	*SD*
Anxiety disorders	Sar et al., 2000	26.8	6.4
Anxiety disorders and depression	Espirito-Santo & Pio-Abreu, 2007	29.2	6.7
Affective disorders	Roelofs et al., 2002a	23.0	3.8
Major depressive episode	Sar et al., 2000	28.7	8.3
Bipolar mood disorder	Nijenhuis et al., 1999	21.6	1.9
	Sar et al., 2000	22.7	3.5
Mixed psychiatric disorders, particularly anxiety disorder and major depressive episode	Nijenhuis et al., 1996	23.5	4.0
	Nijenhuis et al., 1999	22.9	3.9
Nonclinical groups			
Adults from Turkey	Sar et al., 2000	27.4	8.2
Adults from Uganda	Van Duijl et al., 2001	27.0	4.7
Adults from Finland, low SDQ-20, low DES	Maaranen et al., 2005b	20.8	1.3
low SDQ-20, high DES		21.9	1.8
high SDQ-20, low DES		28.2	3.0
high SDQ-20, high DES		34.5	9.4
Adults	Nähring & Nijenhuis, 2005	23.2	5.0
Students from The Netherlands		24.4	4.4
Students from Italy	Farina et al., 2011	23.0	5.5

there is a dimension of severity of sensorimotor dissociative symptoms and a related dimension of severity of personality dissociation. TSDP postulates that the dissociation of the personality is severe in major DID, marked in most cases of minor DID, moderate in spirit possession disorder, complex PTSD, and complex dissociative disorders of movement and sensation, and significant in simple PTSD and simple sensorimotor dissociative disorders. The theory also postulates that dissociation of the personality is absent to insignificant in patients with other mental disorders and in mentally healthy individuals.

Sensorimotor Dissociative Symptoms and Cognitive-Emotional Dissociative+ Symptoms. TSDP holds that sensorimotor and cognitive emotional dissociative+ symptoms are strongly associated phenomena. This link has indeed been found in different populations, including the general population (Farina, Mozzotti, Pasquini, Nijenhuis, & Di Giannantonio, 2011b; Näring & Nijenhuis, 2005), patients with DSM-IV dissociative disorders and ICD-10 dissociative disorders of movement and sensation (for a review, see Nijenhuis, 2009), adolescent psychiatric inpatients (Soukup, Papezova, Kubena, & Mikolajova, 2010), and patients with orgasmic and sexual pain disorders (Farina, Mozzotti, Pasquini, & Manzione, 2011a). In the study of Farina et al. (2011b), the correlation between scores on the DES (cognitive-emotional dissociative+ symptoms) and the SDQ-20 (sensorimotor dissociative symptoms) was particularly strong for individuals with high DES scores.

Severe dissociative symptoms are associated with ill health. For example, in a general population sample, Maaranen et al. (2005a) found that individuals with high cognitive-emotional dissociative+ symptoms and sensorimotor dissociative symptoms had more depressive symptoms and suicidal ideation, while receiving inadequate social support. Their working ability was reduced, and their financial situation and general health were poor.

Sensorimotor Dissociative Symptoms, Stress-Related Psychopathology, and Adverse Events

Major sensorimotor dissociative symptoms such as analgesia, anesthesia, motor stiffening (freezing), and paralysis (tonic immobility) are all components of mammalian defensive reactions to physical threat and threat to life. Re-enactments of traumatic memories also tend to include sensorimotor dissociative symptoms. The presence of these symptoms might therefore relate to adverse, stressful events.

Consistent with this TSDP-based hypothesis, sensorimotor dissociative symptoms were associated with stress-related psychopathology (i.e., anxiety, depression, symptoms of traumatic stress, alexithymia) in nonpsychiatric and nonclinical young adults (Bob, Selesova, Raboch, & Kukla, 2013), as well as in clinical groups (Nijenhuis, 2004). They are also associated with reported and documented interpersonal adversities in childhood. Sensorimotor dissociative symptoms were particularly associated with threat to the body and life itself in every study with the SDQ-20, a questionnaire that includes many items that address analgesia, anesthesia of various kinds, motor inhibitions, and paralysis (Nijenhuis et al., 1996; for a review, Nijenhuis, 2009; see also Chapter 16).

The samples in which links between sensorimotor dissociative symptoms and adverse events were found include general population samples (Näring & Nijenhuis, 2005), as well as patients with DSM-IV dissociative disorders (for a review, see Nijenhuis, 2009), possession disorder (Van Duijl et al., 2010), and fibromyalgia syndrome (Bohn, Bernardy, Wolf, & Hauser, 2013). The correlation between these symptoms and adverse events was not mediated by absorption (Näring & Nijenhuis, 2005). Nor does the association seem to be attributable to cultural beliefs, because it was also found in Uganda, a country in which there is no cultural belief in an association between dissociative symptoms and adverse events (Van Duijl et al., 2010).

The association of sensorimotor dissociative symptoms and adverse events has also been documented for patients with DSM-IV conversion disorders. These individuals had considerable sensorimotor and cognitive-emotional dissociative+ symptoms, and they reported more childhood physical, sexual, and emotional abuse as well as emotional neglect than matched controls (Ozcetin et al., 2009; Sar, Akyuz, Dogan, & Ozturk, 2009). Sar et al. (2009) more specifically found that a lifetime diagnosis of dissociative disorder, major depression, and childhood physical abuse predicted the presence of sensorimotor symptoms in patients with DSM-IV conversion disorder.

Ozcetin et al. (2009) concluded that DSM-IV conversion disorder is better categorized as a dissociative disorder, but this view failed to affect DSM-5. For example, psychogenic nonepileptic seizure disorder continues to be referred to as a conversion disorder in DSM-5. However, in the ICD-10 it is classified as a dissociative disorder of movement and sensation. The condition is associated with significant sensorimotor dissociative symptoms (see above) and cognitive-emotional dissociative+ symptoms as well as with childhood emotional neglect and emotional abuse (Proenca, Castro, Jorge, & Marchetti, 2011), and physical abuse (Spinhoven et al., 2004). Consistent with this, psychogenic nonepileptic seizure disorder involved cognitive-emotional dissociative+ symptoms in patients presenting with DSM-IV conversion disorder, somatization, or undifferentiated somatoform disorder, DSM-IV dissociative disorder not otherwise specified, example 1 (DDNOS-1), and PTSD (Marchetti, Kurcgant, Gallucci Neto, Von Bismark, & Fiore, 2009).

Powerful evidence for a causal relation between childhood traumatization and sensorimotor dissociative symptoms comes from a prospective longitudinal study by Diseth (2006), who examined three groups of patients with congenital anomalies: adolescents with anorectal anomalies, adolescents with Hirschsprung disease, and hospitalized controls. The parents of the children with anorectal abnormalities had been obliged to perform anal dilation during the first four years of the child's life. This painful and invasive medical treatment procedure was correlated with the frequency and severity of persisting dissociative symptomatology. It was the only significant predictor of SDQ-20 and Adolescent-DES scores, and one of two significant predictors of DES scores. As Diseth (p. 233) concluded,

> [t]his 'experiment of nature' permitted a specific and unique opportunity to examine the impact of early traumatic exposure on child development in the absence of parental malevolence, and on later dissociative outcome in adolescence and adulthood.

The association between adverse events and sensorimotor dissociative symptoms could be nonlinear. As displayed in Figure 6.4, only psychiatric outpatients who reported more than four different types of such events had significantly higher scores for sensorimotor dissociation. Maaranen et al. (2004) similarly found a strong, graded relationship between an increasing number of adverse childhood experiences and high sensorimotor dissociative symptoms in a general population sample. The findings are in line with the idea that, up to a point, individuals can cope with adversities that happen to them, but too much is just too much. As the Great War demonstrated, every individual has a breaking point.

Participants reporting four or more than four different Criterion A events had significantly higher SDQ-20 scores than the other groups (Nijenhuis et al., 2002; range of possible SDQ-20 scores 20–100). As noted above, the SDQ-20 cutoff value in the screening for DSM-IV dissociative disorders is > 28 (Nijenhuis, 2009; Nijenhuis et al., 1997b, 1998c).

Sensorimotor Dissociation and 'Conversion' in DSM-5

DSM-5 (APA, 2013, p. 291) states that dissociative disorders are "characterized by a disruption of and/or discontinuity in the normal integration of consciousness, memory, identity, emotion, perception, body representation, motor control, and behavior." However, the text on the dissociative disorders almost exclusively addresses cognitive-emotional dissociative+ symptoms. It does not discuss loss of motor control, nor does it state the empirically documented fact that dissociative disorders also involve a disruption or lack of integration of sensations. Phenomena such as intruding "dissociated actions" and "feeling like one's body or actions is not one's own" are mentioned (p. 292), but are linked to depersonalization.

Like DSM-IV, its successor basically continues to regard sensorimotor dissociative symptoms/disorders as conversion symptoms/disorders, ignoring the fact that sensorimotor dissociative symptoms are a core feature of complex dissociative disorders. For example, the system misinforms that "non-epileptic seizures and other conversion symptoms are prominent in some presentations of DID, especially in some non-Western settings" (p. 293). The alleged restrictions ("some presentations of DID," and the emphasis on "non-Western settings") would probably have surprised if not shocked Briquet, Janet, and other 19th-century experts on hysteria who regarded sensorimotor dissociative symptoms as *major* symptoms of hysteria. Contemporary research findings confirm these 19th-century observations that negative and positive sensorimotor dissociative symptoms are prominent in hysteria/dissociative disorders. For example, the SDQ-20 performs equally well as the DES and the Multidimensional Inventory of Dissociation (MID; Dell, 2006b; Somer & Dell, 2005) in the screening for DSM-IV dissociative disorders (Müller et al., 2013). It is unclear why the authors of DSM-5 ignored the science of sensorimotor dissociation.

Sensorimotor dissociative disorders according to ICD-10 are classified as conversion disorder in DSM-5. According to the DSM-5 guidelines, individuals who meet the criteria for a DSM-5 dissociative disorder and DSM-5 conversion disorder are to receive both diagnoses. All that is said regarding dissociative symptoms in the text on conversion disorder is that "[c]onversion disorder is often associated with dissociative symptoms such as depersonalization, derealization, and dissociative amnesia, particularly at symptom onset or during attacks" (APA, 2013, p. 320). The DSM-5 is silent why there is a close association of 'conversion disorder' and 'dissociative symptoms,' what the causes of this association are, and in what sense 'conversion symptoms' and 'dissociative symptoms' might be different. The authors of the DSM-5 seem committed to the view that there *are* real differences between the two concepts – or else the statement that "[d]issociative symptoms are common in individuals with conversion disorder" (p. 321) is clearly tautological. However, they leave it to the reader to guess what these differences would be.

Sensorimotor dissociative symptoms thus remain strongly underrecognized or underemphasized in DSM-5. The bias also applies to contemporary psychiatry more generally. For example, many studies on dissociative disorders do not include an assessment of sensorimotor dissociative symptoms.

Hysteria from 1980: DSM-III, DSM-IV, and DSM-5

Together with the appearance of PTSDs in 1980, DSM-III introduced several dissociative disorders, including multiple personality disorder, which would eventually be renamed dissociative identity disorder in DSM-IV (APA, 1994). The disorders were not new but emerged from previous DSM formulations that included dissociative psychoneurotic reaction (DSM-I, APA, 1952), hysterical neurosis, dissociative type, and depersonalization neurosis (DSM-II, APA, 1968). These terms clearly indicated that the contemporary dissociative disorders root in the 19th-century category of hysteria.

DSM-5, on the other hand, includes several dissociative disorders:

Dissociative Identity Disorder (DID)

DID is defined as a disruption of identity that is characterized by two or more distinct personality states.

Comment

This description is clearly underinclusive, because DID involves far more than a disruption of identity. Apart from marked discontinuity in sense of self and agency, there are major related alterations in affect, behavior, consciousness, memory, perception, cognition, and sensorimotor functioning. Dissociative parts of the personality also involve their own biopsychosocial features (see Chapters 16–18). They are not 'distinct' because they overlap (see Chapter 13), and a dissociative part of the personality typically does not encompass a single 'state,' but sets of different biopsychosocial states (see Chapter 13).

The comorbidity of DID includes DSM-5 conversion disorder, commented on below.

Dissociative Amnesia (DA)

As a disorder DA involves a subjective inability to recall important autobiographical experiences and knowledge.

Comment

The amnesia commonly pertains to mental contents that would ordinarily be remembered, though it may also encompass skills. The deficit commonly pertains to or at least includes experiences and knowledge of a traumatic or stressful nature. The lost memories are not 'gone' from the patients' mind, rather the organization is now such that one or more dissociative parts of the personality do not recall explicit and/or implicit memories (e.g., due to avoidance) that are available to one or more other dissociative parts. DA can often be overcome with suitable psychotherapy. It may be difficult to decide exactly how likely it is that an individual with DA has in fact a more complex dissociative disorder. Which diagnosis applies may only become clear in the course of treatment.

The DSM-5 mentions that many individuals with DA have symptoms that meet the criteria for a comorbid somatic symptom or related disorder (and vice versa), including somatic symptom disorder and conversion disorder. For comments regarding conversion disorder, see below.

Depersonalization/Derealization Disorder (D/DD)

Patients with D/DD are characterized by a more or less complete and enduring feeling of unreality or detachment from, or unfamiliarity with, the person they are. For example, they may feel that they have no self, are like a robot, feel no feelings, and have thoughts that are not their own. This lack of personification thus includes a lack of agency and a lack of ownership. Patients with this disorder can also have more or less extensive and intensive episodes in which they feel detached from that the world, or feel that the world – be it individuals, objects, surroundings, and events – is unreal.

Comment

What sets D/DD apart from the other dissociative disorders is that it does not necessarily include a dissociation of the personality. However, and as applies to DA, it cannot always be said *a priori* and with any confidence whether or not a patient with this disorder has an ANP-EP structure. One patient's severe depersonalization disorder – she had no derealization symptoms – remained untouched by her and my conjoint psychotherapeutic efforts to change her debilitating condition. Only after 4 years did a child-like EP make herself known. As this part – with the identity of a 5-year-old girl – the patient was fixed in a traumatic childhood. The 'girl' had experienced pervasive emotional neglect by her egoistic and cold mother, and had become stuck in a singular rape by her otherwise non-abusive father. ANP knew the emotional neglect, but displayed dissociative amnesia about the rape. With the integration of the recalled sexual abuse, the patient's depersonalization disorder rapidly and permanently lifted.

Other Specified Dissociative Disorders

Individuals with dissociative disorders that do not meet the full criteria for "one of the disorders in the dissociative disorders diagnostic class" (APA, 2013, p. 306) must be diagnosed as 'other specified dissociative disorders.' DSM-5 lists several examples. They involve "chronic and recurrent syndromes of mixed dissociative symptoms," "identity disturbance due to prolonged and intensive coercive persuasion," "acute dissociative reactions to stressful events," and "dissociative trance." The chronic and recurrent syndromes of mixed dissociative symptoms – a mouthful indeed! – include "identity disturbances associated with less-than-marked discontinuities in sense of self and agency, or alterations of identity or episodes of possession in an individual who reports no dissociative amnesia" (p. 306).

Comment

The section in DSM-5 on these different dissociative disorders replaces the DSM-IV section on dissociative disorders not otherwise specified (DDNOS), which were also merely indicated in the form of examples. Many Western clinicians note that they diagnose lesser forms of DID (minor DID) more often than full-blown (major) DID. Patients with this disorder, who were sometimes referred to as 'DDNOS Type 1,' share many features with DID patients. However, their dissociative symptoms are marked rather than severe (Boon & Draijer, 1993a; Coons, 1992; Nijenhuis et al., 1996, 1999; Ross et al., 1992; Ross, Duffy, & Ellason, 2002; Ross & Ellason, 2005; Sar et al., 2007b; Van der Hart et al., 2006). Clinical observations show that the dissociation of personality is less profound in these individuals. They tend to have fewer dissociative parts, and ANP aside these parts tend to be less evolved.

The remark in DSM-5 that 'chronic and recurrent syndromes of mixed dissociative symptoms' do not involve symptoms of dissociative amnesia is an overstatement. Although (major) DID is certainly associated with more dissociative amnesia symptoms, DSM-IV 'DDNOS Type 1' can also include symptoms of dissociative amnesia (e.g., Dell, 2009a; Hornstein & Putnam, 1992; Silberg, 1998; Vanderlinden, 1993). Dell's (2009a) excellent chapter on 'partial multiple personality disorder' culminated in a solid proposal to remove lesser cases of DID from the DSM-IV DDNOS category. The terms he suggested for DSM-5 were 'complex dissociative disorder I' as an alternative term for DID, and 'complex dissociative disorder II' as a diagnosis that captures DSM-IV DDNOS Type 1. While the terms 'I' and 'II' sound perhaps a little too technical, I fully concur with the idea.

The DSM-5 statement regarding dissociative amnesia could also partly relate to my impression that European clinicians have a higher threshold for diagnosing DID than at least some North American colleagues. For most European colleagues, DID is strictly reserved for individuals whose dissociative amnesia is severe and who fully and recurrently alternate (i.e., 'switch') between their different dissociative parts.

Even if the term is dissatisfactory, the phrase 'chronic and recurrent syndromes of mixed dissociative symptoms' seems to apply when, in terms of TSDP, ANP largely dominates consciousness and behavior, but is recurrently influenced by one or more voices, sensations, emotions, thoughts, memories, and motor actions of one or more EPs (Van der Hart et al., 2006). However, some alternation between the different dissociative parts may occur, and these different Janetian 'subsystems of ideas and functions' may not be in touch with each other, at least not in all instances. This could explain why these patients can also have substantial symptoms of dissociative amnesia. Like patients with DID, patients with 'chronic and recurrent syndromes of mixed dissociative symptoms' have substantial and similar comorbidity (Brand et al., 2009b). In summary, it can thus be said that in general 'chronic and recurrent syndromes of mixed dissociative symptoms' and DID are prototypes on a continuum of severity of dissociative pathology.

The prevalence of 'chronic and recurrent syndromes of mixed dissociative symptoms' may be clinically masked and somewhat obscured in scientific studies, because, according to the DSM-IV rules, a case of 'DDNOS Type 1' can be made only when the patient does not meet the criteria for one of the *other* dissociative disorders (Ross et al., 2002). Nonetheless, the diagnosis had the highest prevalence of all DSM-IV dissociative disorders in most studies (Dell, 2009a; Dell & O'Neil, 2009; see below). It was disappointing that an important proposal for the dissociative disorders in DSM-5 did not include a suggestion for a specific and fitting name for the condition (Spiegel et al., 2011). An NOS category is not the place to put the prime member of a diagnostic family (DSM-IV), and the term 'chronic and recurrent syndromes of mixed dissociative symptoms' (DSM-5) is imprecise. For example, other dissociative disorders such as PTSD and DID also involve chronic and recurrent mixed dissociative symptoms. The term further raises the question how the intended syndromes would be different from each other.

A simple and straightforward solution of these various problems is the recognition of two dissociative disorders that include different degrees of severity with respect to negative and positive cognitive-emotional and sensorimotor dissociative symptoms: minor DID involving marked dissociative symptoms, and major DID comprising severe dissociative symptoms. According to TSDP, major DID prototypically involves more than one ANP and more than one EP. At least some EPs are quite elaborate and emancipated, and some EPs may include some ANP-like features. Minor DID prototypically involves one ANP and more than one EP. While one or more EPs can dominate consciousness and take behavioral control for some time in minor DID, this happens less often and less extensively than in major DID. The division of the personality in minor DID is, however, more complex than that in more simple dissociative disorders such as PTSD and simple sensorimotor dissociative disorders. These disorders prototypically involve one major ANP and one EP. Minor DID and major DID are the terms I have already applied in this book, and I will continue to use them.

The 'acute dissociative reactions to stressful events' pertain to conditions that typically last less than 1 month, and sometimes only a few hours or days. They are characterized by a constriction of consciousness, depersonalization, derealization, perceptual disturbances such as time slowing and macropsia[5], microamnesias, transient stupor, and/or alterations in sensorimotor functioning such as analgesia and paralysis. The implication is that acute stress reactions involving positive dissociative symptoms must be diagnosed as

5 Perceiving objects within an affected section of the visual field as larger than normal, causing the individual to feel smaller than he or she actually is.

'acute stress disorder' (ASD). Apart from negative dissociative symptoms, ASD involves positive dissociative symptoms such as flashbacks (APA, 2013, p. 281). Whereas ASD thus includes a wider spectrum of dissociative symptoms, ASD, in contrast to 'acute dissociative reactions to stressful events,' is not classified as a dissociative disorder, but as a trauma- and stressor-related disorder. Sometimes it can be hard to get DSM-5's logic.

Another example of the inconsistencies in DSM-5 is that the text on the 'acute dissociative reactions to stressful events' (APA, 2013, p. 307) describes alterations in "sensory-motor functioning (e.g., analgesia, paralysis)" as dissociative. Had the system been consistent, the text should either have stated that the disorder includes conversion symptoms, or it should have discarded the terms 'conversion symptoms' and 'conversion disorders' altogether and exchanged these for 'sensorimotor dissociative symptoms/disorders.' The latter option might also have lead to a satisfactory presentation of the documented existence of sensorimotor dissociative symptoms in minor and major DID.

Prevalence of DSM-IV Dissociative Disorders[6]

Dissociative disorders are common in both general population samples and psychiatric samples. The lack of dissociative disorders sections in general psychiatric screening instruments has resulted in the omission of dissociative disorders in many large-scale epidemiologic studies.

General Population

Approximately 3% of the general population have pathological degrees of dissociative symptoms. The lifetime prevalence of dissociative disorders among women in a general urban Turkish community was 18.3%, with 1.1% having major DID. In a study of an Ethiopian rural community, the prevalence of dissociative disorders was 6.3%, so that these disorders were as prevalent as mood disorders (6.2%), somatoform disorders (5.9%), and anxiety disorders (5.7%). A similar prevalence of ICD-10 dissociative disorders (7.3%) was reported for a sample of psychiatric patients from Saudi Arabia.

Psychiatric Samples

The reported prevalence of DSM-IV-TR dissociative disorders in psychiatric samples from various European and North American samples was between 5% and 17%. Dissociative disorders are commonly diagnosed in both inpatient and outpatient settings in India (Chaturvedi, Desai, & Shaligram, 2009). Dissociative motor disorder (43.3% outpatients, 37.7% inpatients), followed by dissociative convulsions (23% outpatients, 27.8%

6 For (additional) references, see Van der Hart & Nijenhuis, 2008.

inpatients) were the most common dissociative disorders. DID was rarely diagnosed in contrast to possession states. Future research should examine to what degree individuals with these possession states meet the criteria for major or minor DID (see also Chapter 15).

Dissociative disorders were exceptionally prevalent in a Turkish psychiatric emergency ward. This also applied to adolescents referred to a university psychiatric outpatient clinic (Sar, Onder, Kilicaslan, Zoroglu, & Alyanak, 2014). Almost half of the sample had a dissociative disorder; 16.4% had major DID and 28.8% minor DID.

Major DID

The prevalence of major DID in community samples was between 0.4% and 1.5%, and between 1% and 6% in psychiatric samples.

Minor DID

Minor DID is more common than major DID. For example, in a North American community sample the prevalence within the past year of depersonalization disorder was 0.8%, DA 1.8%, major DID 1.5%, and minor DID 4.4%. The lifetime prevalence of minor DID among women in a Turkish community was 8.3%. However, some cases of minor DID may have involved other examples of DSM-IV DDNOS.

Comorbidity

Complex dissociative disorders entail major comorbidity that mostly includes personality disorders and PTSD. Major commonalities regarding major DID, minor DID, and PTSD suggests that these disorders are closely related (see Chapters 18–19).

Misdiagnosis

Dissociative disorders often go unrecognized in general clinical practice. For example, the majority of a substantial sample of Northern Irish clinicians failed to diagnose DID in a clear-cut case. In China, DID is practically unknown. This does not mean that the disorder does not exist in China. For example, among 98 patients in a Chinese mental healthcare center, many of whom had been previously diagnosed as cases of schizophrenia, 28% had a readily assessable dissociative disorder (Yu et al., 2010).

Conversion Disorder

While DSM-IV and DSM-5 conversion disorder are like the dissociative disorders that DSM-IV and DSM-5 recognize were rooted in 19th-century hysteria, DSM-IV and DSM-5 do not regard conversion disorder as a dissociative disorder. As previously mentioned, the name and the description of the disorder as well as its separate classification from dissociative disorders suggest a Freudian rather than a Janetian conceptualization and understanding of a set of sensorimotor symptoms that, according to 19th-century insights, belonged to the major symptoms of hysteria. One may conveniently say that DSM-IV and DSM-5 split the mind and the body by "dissociating" the sensorimotor and cognitive-emotional symptoms of hysteria, and by splitting hysteria into (cognitive-emotional) dissociative disorders and sensorimotor dissociative disorders under the label of conversion disorder.

Chapter 7

The Capricious Historical Understanding of Traumatic Melancholia and Hysteria: Part I. Psychological Considerations

> *A frog in a well cannot conceive of the ocean.*
> Zhuang Zi

> *Whatever is encountered must be valued in one way or another – like, dislike, ignore – and acted on some way or another – attraction, rejection, neutrality. This basic assessment is inseparable from the way in which the coupling event encounters a functioning perceptuo-motor unit and it gives rise to an* intention *(I am tempted to say "desire"), that unique quality of living cognition.*
> Francisco Varela, 1991, p. 97

La donna è mobile (Woman is fickle) sings the cynical Duke of Mantua in *Rigoletto*. Guiseppe Verdi composed the opera in 1851, only a few years before the first empirical study of hysteria saw the light of day (Briquet, 1859). The irony of this aria is that the playboy Duke himself is *mobile* (i.e., volatile, inconstant). The limited historical excursions in Chapters 1 to 6 were intended to illustrate that the clinical and scientific understanding of melancholia and hysteria from ancient Greek times to modern times has been as changeable as the purported fickleness of the hysterical woman, and the observed inconstancy of patients with trauma-related disorders more generally. Table 7.1 and Table 7.2 summarize this recurrent variability.

Trauma: A Natural Phenomenon or A Cultural Invention?

The idea that adverse environmental events can mentally injure individuals has been present across the ages. Young's (1997) claim that trauma is a culture-bound phenomenon that emerged in the 19th century therefore impresses as an overstatement. Traumatization rather seems to involve natural laws that operate in part irrespective of the survivors' conscious intentions, thoughts, and cultural environment. The history of traumatic melancholia and hysteria also indicates that traumatization as well as the interpretations of the

Table 7.1. The mobility of professional ideas regarding (traumatic) hysteria and melancholia until 1950: The most characteristic features of each position.

	Two diagnostic compartments		Etiological roots		Nature of etiology		Prime etiological locus		
Authors/subjects	Hysteria	(Traumatic) melancholia	Exogenesis	Endogenesis	Adverse events	Personal features	Body: Biological Causation	Mind: Mental Causation	Sex
Ancient Greeks and Romans		melancholia	+		+		no body-mind distinction		m/f
Ancient Greeks and Romans	hysterical ailments			+			no body-mind distinction, yet focus on a biological, materialistic explanation: disorders related to the uterus		f
Plutarch (46–120)			+		severe danger			fear	
Guibert (1055–1124)		melancholia	+		demons			fear	
Sir Pierre			+		attack magical bear	felt guilt		fear	
Petrarch		acedia		+		felt mental weakness	battle between bodily needs	and mental ability to control them	
Middle Ages	hysteria		+		possession by the devil	witches	the devil works on the body	and the soul	f
Johnson and Wier, 16th century	hysteria			+			functional disorder of the whole body, including the brain		f
Lepois, 17th century	hysteria			+			disorder of the body and the mind; symptoms come "from the head"		m/f
Plater/Burton16th and 17th century	hysteria	melancholia; Burton: hysteria and hypochondria are forms of melancholia	+		sudden imminent danger; dose dependent		spleen emits vapors in hypochondria	fear	m/f
Willis, 17th century	hysteria; explosive animal spirits	melancholia; nonexplosive animal spirits		+			disorder of the nervous system		m/f

	Two diagnostic compartments		Etiological roots		Nature of etiology		Prime etiological locus		
Authors/subjects	Hysteria	(Traumatic) melancholia	Exogenesis	Endogenesis	Adverse events	Personal features	Body: Biological Causation	Mind: Mental Causation	Sex
Sydenham, 17th century	hysteria		+		tensions and stresses within the culture		animal spirits link body and mind; foremost an emotional disorder		m/f
17th and 18th century		mal de corozon; nostalgia; *Heimweh*; Da Costa's syndrome; neurasthenia		+		moral and emotional weakness cowardice, homesickness		emotional condition or disorder	m
Cheyne, 18th century	hysteria			+		extreme sensibility		extreme sensibility	m/f
19th century, Erichsen c.s.		railway spine	+ before 1875	+ from 1875 exogenesis and endogenesis	railway accidents		before 1875: physical damage such as concussion of the spine	from 1875: a role for psychological causation	m/f
19th century, Page c.s.	symptoms of railway spine and hysteria closely match	railway spine	+	+	railway accidents			fear	m/f
19th century, many authors		railway spine		+	railway accidents	wish to receive a pension		wish fulfillment	m/f
Briquet, 1859	hysteria		+	+	parental maltreatment of children, maltreatment of women by spouse, relational problems, and other incidents that trigger strong emotional reactions	impressionability, affective sensibility	the described events affect the part of the brain that is involved in emotions	strong emotional reactions to sad or adverse life events	m/f

	Two diagnostic compartments		Etiological roots		Nature of etiology		Prime etiological locus		
Authors/subjects	Hysteria	(Traumatic) melancholia	Exogenesis	Endogenesis	Adverse events	Personal features	Body: Biological Causation	Mind: Mental Causation	Sex
Charcot, from 1889	traumatic hysteria (grand hysteria would be different)		+	+	accidents as agents provocateurs	constitutional predilection to nervous degeneration	nervous degeneration	dissociation of fixed ideas	m/f
Janet, from 1889	hysteria		+	+	terrifying events including abuse; dose-dependent effects	innate and event-related low integrative capacity; hysteria involves a mental insufficiency to integrate experiences	to be found physiological modifications "accompany and provoke this cerebral insufficiency" (1907, p. 528). Janet did not regard body and mind as different substances; body does not cause mind and mind does not cause body	dissociation of the personality	m/f
Oppenheim, from 1884		traumatic neurosis	+	+	accidents, war	there is no predisposition to traumatic neurosis	emphasis on accident-induced pathology of the nervous system	included an etiological role of psychological factors	m/f
Many German psychiatrists at the turn of the 19th to the 20th century	hysteria			+		mental weakness, work-shyness, financial gain, will to sickness, cowardice, simulation, etc.		mental and moral weakness in the context of accidents and war	m
Breuer & Freud	hysteria, conversion hysteria, defense hysteria		+	+	sexual abuse	infantile sexuality	biology of infantile sexuality	repression, hypnoid states	f

	Two diagnostic compartments		Etiological roots		Nature of etiology		Prime etiological locus		
Authors/subjects	Hysteria	(Traumatic) melancholia	Exogenesis	Endogenesis	Adverse events	Personal features	Body: Biological Causation	Mind: Mental Causation	Sex
Freud	hysteria			+		wish-fulfillment, fantasy		deferred suggestion	f
Freud		anxiety neurosis	+	+	war	self-destructive tendencies	contrast between Eros and death drive		m
Ferenczi	hysteria		+	+	sexual abuse	infantile sexuality, identification with the aggressor		dissociation of the personality	m/f
Kretschmer	hysteria		+		bodily threat	instinctive defensive reaction patterns	dissociation between higher and lower motivations (will): lower motivations in trauma involve hyponoic conditions		m/f
Rivers		traumatic neurasthenia	+	+	+	shock, strain, illness and fatigue lower the individual's integrative and controlling forces	lack of integration of different, conflicting instincts, that is, of instinctive physical defense, and instinctive interests of daily life; conscious repression		m/f
Rivers	hysteria		+		adverse events and suggestion	suppression	unconscious suppression of the danger instinct and substitution of instinctive defensive reaction by immobilization as one particular kind of defense		m/f
Myers		shell-shock	+		war	lowering of the integrative capacity		dissociation of the personality	m
Kardiner		traumatic neurosis	+		war		physioneurosis		m

Table 7.2. The mobility of professional ideas regarding (traumatic) hysteria and melancholia from 1950: the most characteristic features of each position.

	Two diagnostic compartments		Etiological roots		Nature of etiology		Prime etiological locus		
Authors/subjects	Hysteria	(Traumatic) melancholia	Exogenesis	Endogenesis	Adverse events	Personal features	Body: Biological Causation	Mind: Mental Causation	Sex
Kluft, Putnam, Coons	dissociative disorders		+	+	commonly related to traumatizing events, but this exposure may not be a sufficient cause			disruption and/or discontinuity	m/f
DSM-III DSM-IV		PTSD ASD	+	+	DSM-III version based on war trauma; DSM-IV A 1 Criterion limited to bodily threat of self or observed others	A2 Criterion: individuals must have responded to an A1 Criterion event with extreme fear, helplessness, or terror.	growing emphasis on biological etiological factors	fear, helplessness, horror	m/f
Marmar		PTSD ASD	+	+	potentially traumatizing events			peritraumatic dissociation+	m/f
DSM-IV	dissociative disorders		+	+	may be related to life threatening, traumatic, stressful, or overwhelming life events	dissociative amnesia and DID could be due to high suggestibility and suggestion		disruption of integrated functions of consciousness, memory, identity, or perception of the environment	m/f

	Two diagnostic compartments		Etiological roots		Nature of etiology		Prime etiological locus		
Authors/subjects	Hysteria	(Traumatic) melancholia	Exogenesis	Endogenesis	Adverse events	Personal features	Body: Biological Causation	Mind: Mental Causation	Sex
DSM-5	dissociative disorders; intentionally placed next to, but are not part of, the trauma- and stressor-related disorders, reflecting the close relationship between these disorders	trauma- and stressor-related disorders, including dissociative subtype of PTSD	+	+	dissociative disorders are frequently found in the aftermath of trauma; interpersonal physical and sexual abuse is associated with an increased risk of DID; prevalence of childhood abuse and neglect in Western samples is 90%	DSM-IV A2 criterion for ASD and PTSD was dropped, as was the statement that dissociative amnesia and DID could be due to high suggestibility and suggestion	"certain genotypes may be either provocative or increase risk of PTSD after exposure to traumatic events" (APA, 2013, p. 277)	disruption of integrated functions of consciousness, memory, identity, emotion, perception, body representation, motor control, and behavior	m/f; female sex is a risk factor for ASD and PTSD

phenomena of trauma-related symptoms and disorders are subject to the sociocultural and historical context in which they occur. These contexts include the state of clinical and scientific knowledge, and the biases of the holders of this knowledge.

The history of trauma also testifies that personal, professional, and societal interests strongly affect the degree to which the injurious effects of accidents, war, abuse, and neglect are recognized, acknowledged, and realized. It reveals that ignoring the existence and adversity of particular events and their sequelae is a far easier action than knowing and realizing these facts. However, whatever form it takes, ignorance cannot control the brute realities and human fragility in the end. These realities and this fragility do and will persist and resurface when suppressed. Sooner or later, like any neglected or ill-treated wound, the consequences of horrific events will be felt and smelled.

Trauma: Exogenesis, Endogenesis, or Both?

The clinical and scientific understanding of hysteria, melancholia, and descendant disorders has recurrently alternated between exogenic (i.e., the disorder is exclusively or primarily caused by factors external to the individual), endogenetic (i.e., the disorder comes exclusively or mainly from within), and mixed exogenetic and endogenetic explanations.

Exogenesis

Although the insight that severe accidents and war experiences can be mentally injurious has been around since ancient Greek times, its recognition and acceptance in psychiatry and society more generally came late – and far from easy or naturally. The clinical, scientific, and societal identification of the existence, prevalence, and detrimental effects of interpersonal violence in the form of sexual abuse and harassment as well as physical maltreatment and emotional abuse has been even more vexing. For example, some 19th-century physicians and psychologists recognized and demonstrated the existence and impact on mental health of these in part less visible events. Other professionals chose to ignore, deny, or misperceive (e.g., held onto the idea that the child had seduced the perpetrator) the facts.

Psychiatry has a very poor track record regarding an appreciation of the consequences of severe emotional neglect and emotional unavailability of primary caregivers, something that in some regards extends to this day. For example, according to the authors of DSM-5, emotional neglect by and the emotional unavailability of primary caretakers cannot be a prime causal factor in PTSD. However, the system does include reactive attachment disorder, whose only known risk factor is "serious social neglect" (APA, 2013, p. 269). The diagnosis can only be applied in children younger than 5 years, because it is "unclear whether reactive attachment disorder occurs in older children, and, if so, how it differs from its presentation in young children" (p. 267). Apart from reactive attachment disorder, DSM-5 does not include a single trauma- and stressor-related disorder that captures the impact of serious and chronic emotional neglect and other grave forms of emotional unavailability of primary caretakers. The diagnosis of adjustment disorder does not provide a suitable escape because severe and chronic emotional neglect is not a circumstance of life to which an individual should, as it were, 'adjust.'

Harlow and his collaborators (e.g., Harlow & Suomi, 1971) showed the world decades ago what these life circumstances do to infant rhesus monkeys. It is now known that there are important commonalities between neglected children and these poor monkeys. Without love, or as Bowlby put it, 'attachment bonds' between child and primary caretakers, they do not thrive, but rather grow up to be disturbed individuals (Suomi, Van der Horst, & Van der Veer, 2008; Vicedo, 2010, 2012). Bowlby's major contributions (e.g., Bowlby, 1980) were not at all readily accepted. Whereas his emphasis on the unique importance of the mother-child bond may have been an overstatement, Harlow's and Bowlby's work has been a major impetus and inspiration for subsequent work on attachment by Mary Ainsworth (e.g., 1979), Mary Main (Hesse & Main, 2006; Main & Morgan, 1996), Karlen Lyons-Ruth (2008; Lyons-Ruth, Dutra, Schuder, & Bianchi, 2006) and many others. In the wake of their studies, clinicians and scientists are currently starting to develop a far sharper eye and a much better feel for the detrimental biopsychosocial effects of emotional neglect and the emotional unavailability of primary caretakers.

There is now a substantial literature on the crucial links between disrupted attachment and interpersonal childhood traumatization in the form of adverse caretaker acts of omission and commission. Studies particularly point to associations between interpersonal childhood adversity, disorganized attachment, and dissociative symptoms and structures. Bowlby, in fact, observed the existence of different disconnected 'selves' in individuals who had suffered essential emotional losses. He referred to these selves as segregated "Principle Systems of behaviour, thought, feeling and memory" (Bowlby, 1980, p. 347). His descriptions of his patient Geraldine and Miss B. are highly suggestive of the presence of a major ANP and a minor, yet influential, occasionally intruding EP:

> On the one hand is a system, the one governing her everyday life, that takes for granted that she [Miss B as ANP] has neither mother nor, perhaps, any other attachment figure and that she therefore has no option but to fend for herself. On the other is a system, largely deactivated and with only marginal access to consciousness [i.e., to the system that governs daily life], that is organized on the assumption that her mother is still accessible and that, somehow, she can either be recovered in this world or else joined in the next. The latter system [Miss B as EP], to which it seems likely all her attachment desires, feelings and personal memories belong, provided only fragmentary evidence of its existence. Yet it was not completely inert. Not only did it [EP] influence all Miss B's [ANP] day and night dreams but from time to time it influenced also her behaviour; and it did so in ways that made her appear crazy to observers ignorant of its premises.

Whereas Bowlby (1980) applied the term 'segregated,' the lengthy quote shows that the two different principle systems that in TSDP are called ANP and EP were not segregated (fragmented or split), but rather divided. EP with its striking "intensity of feeling" (p. 348) recurrently intruded ANP. Another observation is that, in contrast to Bowlby's curious choice of terms, the EP is not unconscious but conscious. EP is also endowed with

> ... all those cognitive and affective elements that qualify it to be regarded as mental, namely desire, thought, feeling, and memory. From time to time, also, when it takes control of behaviour, the segregated system shows itself to be organised with reference to persons and objects in the environment that it is capable of framing plans and executing them, albeit in rather clumsy and ineffective ways. A main reason for this inefficiency, it is postulated, is that the system, being largely deactivated (by means of the defensive exclusion of virtually any sensory inflow that might activate it), is denied access to consciousness with the many benefits that brings. (Bowlby, 1980, pp. 347–348)

Bowlby (1980) in fact corrects himself on p. 348: "Thus, within a single personality, there were two Principle Systems, organized on opposite premises, yet both of them active and conscious." Geraldine and Miss B are highly reminiscent of Janet's patient Irène, who also encompassed, next to an ANP, an EP who continued to take care of her mother – who had in fact already died (Janet, 1904; Van der Hart & Friedman, 1989). There are also some parallels with Norman, the main character of Hitchcock's *Psycho*[1].

Hard-won gains in recognition of external causes of trauma were recurrently lost over time only to be recaptured later. In light of this alternating pattern, there is no guarantee that the current increase in the realization of childhood traumatization (e.g., Agirton et al., 2009; Denton, Newton, & Vandeven, 2011; Radford et al., 2011; Svevo-Cianci, Hart, & Rubinson, 2010; Taylor, Baldwin, & Spencer, 2008) and other kinds of traumatization is here to stay. The recognition, acknowledgment, and realization of the high prevalence of childhood adverse events in its different forms (e.g., sexual abuse by the clergy, organized forms of sexual violation of children) will probably remain an ongoing struggle. It is far easier to ignore than to face adverse realities and their consequences.

Endogenesis

The history of melancholia and hysteria illustrates that the disorders have sometimes been seen as endogenetic conditions rather than as disorders that are causally related to or strongly influenced by an adverse environment. The purported endogenous features typically pertained and continue to pertain to negative personal characteristics.

---

1 The movie was based on the novel *Psycho* by Peter Bloch, who in turn was inspired by the sad case of Ed Gein. Mr. Gein was emotionally abused by his mother, and developed a love-hate relationship with her. Unable to overcome her death, he isolated himself and started to enact his mother in far-fetched ways. He was convicted for murdering two women and spent the rest of his life in mental institutions.

A number of authors emphasized endogenetic explanations of melancholia and hysteria so much that they almost forgot about the influence of the environment. For example, following his rejection of the exogenetic seduction theory, Freud (1905/1958; 1933/1960) started to focus ever more on his patients' ideas and seemed far less concerned with the social and material world in which they had been raised and perhaps still lived. He eventually became convinced that reports of traumatic experiences by women with hysteria mostly concerned wish-fulfilling fantasies. Faced with internal conflicts, they would consciously or unconsciously construct traumatic experiences. Even in cases of documented adverse events, Freud and many of his followers were mainly concerned with the intrapsychic dynamics of the traumatized individual. It was this isolation of the individual from his or her environment that bothered Ferenczi (1929, 1932, 1933) so much. Ferenczi thus urged psychoanalysts to consider the harmful effects of caretaker violence against children more, but following Freud's lead, most psychoanalysts completely ignored Ferenczi's work on childhood adverse events for decades. Many World War I psychiatrists also took a one-sided endogenic explanatory route by claiming that soldiers who broke down had a weak mental and moral will. Still, individuals are "thrown in a world" as phenomenologists assert (Heidegger, 1986), and this world can bring both joy and sorrow.

The critique of the rather exclusive endogenetic perspectives is not just that individuals are affected by the world in which they live. As mentioned before, a deeper philosophical insight is that no one – no brain, no body, and no mind-*could* exist in an environmental vacuum, just as objects and events do not exist separately from the individuals who experience and know them. I detail these crucial ideas in Chapters 8 and 10.

Mixed Exogenetic and Endogenetic Explanations of Trauma

Mixed explanations became en vogue from the second half of the 19th century. Briquet (1859) conceded that adverse events can cause melancholia and hysteria in combination with high impressionability. Charcot (1889) proposed a link between these kinds of events that work as *agents provocateurs* and degeneration or constitutional nervousness. Janet (e.g., 1889, 1901/1977, 1907) and Myers (1940) agreed that adverse events tend to cause a division of the personality when an individual's integrative capacity is (too) low. This position clearly did not involve blaming the survivor.

Most contemporary models of PTSD and complex dissociative disorders involve mixed endogenetic and exogenetic interpretations. For example, research on PTSD suggests that the disorder relates to a variety of endogenetic and exogenetic factors. In consonance with Janet (1907), Kluft (1985) proposed a four-factor model of complex dissociative disorders that includes a genetic tendency toward dissociation of the personality, chronic traumatization starting in early childhood, and lack of emotional and social support. However, the results of the few studies of a genetic endowment for dissociative phenomena are inconsistent (Becker-Blease et al., 2004; Jang Paris, Zweig-Frank, & Livesley, 1998; Lochner et al., 2007; Savitz et al., 2008; Waller, Putnam, & Carlson, 1996). This inconsistency could in part relate to the inconsistent ways in which the concept of 'dissociation' is defined (see Chapters 13 and 14). The 19th-century idea that a developmental, stress-induced, or otherwise existing low integrative capacity constitutes a risk factor for trauma-related disorders including dissociative disorders continues to be seen as an important causal factor (e.g., Becker-Blease et al., 2004; Van der Hart et al., 2006).

Some individuals may thus be more *vulnerable* to adverse events than others. It was recently suggested that some individuals are highly *sensitive* (Moskowitz, 2014). This sensitivity can constitute a splendid feature when one's life is benign, but may predispose to psychopathological reactions when one's world turns a very grim face. This emergent idea revisits the classic 18th-century English and 19th-century French ideas that hysteria is sensitivity gone awry (see Chapter 2).

Another revived historical idea involves a contemporary variety of a particular mix of endogenic and exogenic causes, that is, the idea that dissociative symptoms and disorders are due to the patient's fantasy proneness and suggestibility (endogenesis) in combination with suggestive, illness-inducing or illness-reinforcing actions of other therapists and the media (exogenesis). These thoughts have been influential, but individual views and facts can be opposite (see Chapter 15). An attempt by some proponents of the so-called sociocognitive model of DID to erase DID as a mental disorder in DSM-5 failed.

A Harsh World and the General Problem of Realization

Why has it been so hard to recognize and acknowledge wartime and civilian traumatization? Why has the sexual abuse of women been denied for so long? And why have childhood abuse, maltreatment, and neglect by relatives and professional caretakers been mostly overlooked, ignored, or forgotten throughout the ages rather than seen, acknowledged, and attended to by patients, perpetrators, involved families, and institutions (e.g., the clergy, child welfare institutions, institutions for the care of mentally handicapped children, sporting clubs, and others), psychiatry, and society alike? For example, why did a large, relatively recent literature on incest taboos for the major part address only sexual play of same-age children and sexual relations of consenting related adults (Korbin, 1977, 1987)? Why have gains in recognition and understanding of childhood and other kinds of traumatization been lost again and again?

The heart of the matter may be that ignoring, downplaying, or denying the existence, prevalence, and impact of severe interpersonal violence, particularly childhood abuse, maltreatment, and neglect, turn out to be far easier and subjectively more appealing actions than *realizing* these dreadful societal facts (see Chapter 20). Indeed, what would remain of the glory of war, a comfortable professional career in psychiatry, and the cherished privacy of the family domain if one would not just know, but realize what drama this public glory and private comfort entail for numerous individuals (Van der Hart et al., 2006)?

Knowing means perceiving the facts. Realization involves acting on known facts. More than knowing, realization involves taking responsible action to prevent, limit, and hopefully heal the harm that trauma creates (Van der Hart et al., 2006). But taking action can be demanding, difficult, and scary. A particularly difficult action is realizing the extent and degree of childhood traumatization by caretakers. It is not just a major hurdle for the traumatized, but also for perpetrators, involved families, psychiatry, and society at large. For example, the deep realization of the prevalence and impact of intrafamilial child abuse and neglect cannot but have serious implications for the general position of caretakers regarding their children. The societally condoned privacy of family life in the end serves the interests of the abusive and the neglectful family members, and it physically and mentally imprisons affected children. While modern societies demand education and certification for every other job, they act as if every adult will be a good parent, just by nature. Of course, everyone knows this is a dramatic misconception, but how many realize it to the fullest degree? Democracy is based on the principle that power is checked, but what checks exist regarding parental and familial power over their children?

The realization of childhood traumatization requires societies to deeply reconsider exceedingly complex matters. How can children be raised in a safe and stimulating environment? How can the rights of children be installed, honored, and checked? What rights and obligations should parents and other caretakers have – or not have? How can parents and families be raised to be better caretakers and educators? How can harmed children be helped so that they do not pass on the horrors that happened to them to future generations? At the very least, this realization implies setting up an infrastructure to detect, report, record, and analyze child abuse and neglect. Whereas this infrastructure exists to a degree in some 'advanced' societies, in Third World countries it is often underdeveloped or nonexistent.

Professional and Societal Thought as an Exogenetic Influence on Trauma

Professional and societal views of mental disorders can, within limits, influence the disorders as such. They can affect the way in which afflicted individuals perceive and present themselves, the way in which they are seen and treated by other people including professionals, as well as the way the disturbances progress. For example, how likely is it that traumatized patients who hear angry and commanding voices will talk about these experiences if the clinicians they meet believe – contrary to the facts (Longden et al., 2011) – that hearing voices is a specific marker of psychosis? How was Augustine to feel that Charcot, the man who invented the concept of 'traumatic hysteria,' did not address her traumatization? How will patients with a complex dissociative disorder feel, think, and act when professionals assert that dissociative parts are manifestations of the devil, extreme sensibility, figments of their imagination, or the confused ideas of their psychotherapists? And who would not become angry sooner or later if professionals interpret alternations between different dissociative parts as efforts to split the therapeutic team, whereas it is the team that is split regarding the very existence and nature of DID? How will severely emotionally neglected and emotionally abused individuals respond when they read that, according to some professionals, war trauma is a true catastrophe, and that there is a trend to overextend the concept of 'civilian traumatization'? How will they feel when they hear that, according to the DSM-IV and DSM-5, only threats to one's *physical* integrity are a potential cause of PTSD? What about threats to one's *mental* existence? As the Dutch psychologist Kouwer (1963, 1970) observed, individuals tend to react to professional statements regarding their alleged psychological characteristics, which may thereby confirm (e.g., enact) or counter these claims. Patients can fulfill and/or defeat psychiatrists' and psychologists' prophecies and predictions.

Professional thought and conduct have been and will always be influenced by clinical and scientific views that were or are not supported by solid and consistent empirical evidence. Professionals have thus not been, and will probably never be, immune to strongly and recurrently voiced opinions that alleged traumatized veterans are in fact just looking for a pension, lazy, or deficient effeminate men, or that patients with DID are just faking it. For example, particularly in the 1980s and 1990s many colleagues were convinced that minor and major DID were self-suggested or iatrogenic conditions. They did not seem concerned that these ideas were not scientifically tested in studies of minor and major DID. Many professionals seem to have felt or still feel that their truth is so evident that they need not be scrutinized. To this day, scientists engaged or intending to engage in neuroimaging studies of DID tend to meet a rather hostile or condescending climate regarding the disorder in universities. It is hard to get started anyway, since it is very difficult even to get the studies funded. Pharmaceutical industries are not interested, because patients with complex dissociative disorders do not favorably respond to known medication (although some medications may dampen some of the symptoms). Many other financiers seem prejudiced to believing that these disorders are not real to start off with.

The empirical facts are at odds with these nonscientific positions. For example, there is a major disbalance between the impact of and the evidence for the sociocognitive model of hysteria (i.e., DID). Here are some examples of documented facts that are incongruent with this model and that will be detailed more in later chapters (Chapters 15–19):

- Patients with DID are not particularly prone to engage in fantasies (Dalenberg et al., 2012; Nijenhuis & Reinders, 2012; Schlumpf et al., 2013, 2014);
- Low and high fantasy-prone, mentally healthy women as well as female actors, all of whom were instructed, motivated, and trained to simulate ANP and EP in women with DID, were unable to do so in reaction times studies (Hermans et al., 2006; Schlumpf et al., 2013) and psychophysiological and neuroimaging studies (Reinders et al., 2012; Schlumpf et al., 2013, 2014; see Chapter 17 and 18);
- Longitudinal, prospective studies of children who experienced severe interpersonal adversity and who display disorganized attachment revealed solid relations between these events and this attachment style and dissociative symptoms many years later (Dutra et al., 2009; Ogawa et al., 1997; Trickett et al., 2011);

- Disorganized attachment is a serious risk of PTSD (Currier, Holland, & Allen, 2012) and is associated with parental disconnected behavior (Out, Bakermans-Kranenburg, & Van IJzendoorn, 2009), childhood traumatization/maltreatment (Cyr et al., 2010; Joubert, Webster, & Hackett, 2012), and socio-economic risks (Cyr et al., 2010). Disorganized attachment is a major feature of many patients with minor and major DID (Van der Hart et al., 2006);
- Some clinicians and scientists believe that delayed memories of childhood traumatization involve a figment of the patient's imagination, commonly caused by self-suggestion or hetero-suggestion. However, delayed trauma memories can be accurate and are generally no less accurate than permanently available memories of traumatization (Dalenberg, 2006). False allegations of child sexual abuse occur, but are outnumbered by true allegations (e.g., Ingemann-Hansen, Brink, Sabroe, Sorensen, & Charles, 2008);
- Some physicians were convinced that rape of an infant is technically impossible, and that reports of such abuse must therefore be false. Gruesome contemporary videos prove them wrong, alas. For example, in 2013 a man was convicted for sexually abusing more than 80 young children in a daycare center and in other settings in Amsterdam. He admitted that the abuse included oral and vaginal rape of babies. One lesson to draw from this case is that one should avoid believing that particular forms of abuse and neglect must be false just because they are extreme or considered unlikely. However, despite the availability of huge child pornographic internet material – child pornography is reported to be one of the fastest growing multibillion internet industries with content that is getting worse (Internet Watch Foundation, 2008) – there are a substantial number of people who do not believe or realize that most serious and systematic group-wise chronic traumatization of children exists or that it is extensive. One prejudiced *a priori* physical judgment is that patients who report such horrors must be fantasizing or responding to suggestions by the media and therapists. Whereas some patients may be confused and some therapists may have provided undue suggestions of such abuse, how likely is it that chronic traumatization of a child is performed only by a single perpetrator and not by groups of perpetrators? How can one *a priori* exclude the existence of systematic groupwise chronic childhood traumatization in a world in which any other known criminal act performed by an individual (e.g., theft, forgery, physical maltreatment, murder, cannibalism, cutting individuals to pieces) is also committed by groups, some of which are well organized? Why would systematic groupwise sexual, physical, and emotional abuse of children be an exception? The sad fact is that it is not at all an exception, given the legal evidence for the existence of organized sex crimes against children (e.g., Bernstein, 2003; Marquis, 2001; Tagliabue, 2005; BBC, 2001), involving increasingly severe abuse (Ruethling, 2006);
- As indicated in Chapter 6 and discussed more in Chapter 15, phase-oriented treatment of complex dissociative disorders does not induce or amplify dissociative symptoms. Emerging clinical and scientific evidence shows rather that this treatment effectively reduces symptoms and improves the quality of life.

Professionals must be open to the question of how their professional and societal opinions and behaviors affect the disorder they are trying to describe and comprehend. Such openness is not always present. For example, clinicians and scientists who adhere to the sociocognitive model of DID – and/or other 'would-be' trauma-related disorders – do not seem to realize that, by the very model they proclaim, their own communications regarding the disorders also constitute sociocognitive suggestions. Moreover, mental disorders do not exist in an environmental vacuum, but are an intrinsic component of a historical organism(s)-environment system. In this sense, *any* mental disorder is socioaffective, sociocognitive, sociobehavioral, and culture-dependent. University professors who tell patients and the public that a so-called trauma-related disorder is not due to traumatization but to laziness, a weak will, a desire for a pension or social attention, suggestibility, fantasy-proneness, suggestion, or fantasy (or the like) provide suggestions. And to the extent that their ideas are not grounded in careful studies of the population they address, these ideas concern personal and professional fantasies rather than scientific facts.

Professional communications are bound to affect patients, clinicians, scientists, and the general public in one way or another. The effects will be particularly powerful when scientific judgments or professional opinions in general are seen as major 'providers of truth,' and when there is a personal, professional, or societal *will*, a deep *desire* to *believe* in the alleged truths. In the case of trauma, this interest may be mental avoidance by the patient ("I do not need to deal with traumatic memories; I was not abused"), by professionals ("No need to burden my professional life with matters of child abuse and neglect"), or by society ("There's no serious societal problem of childhood traumatization"). The motivation may also be economic ("No need to finance expensive treatment") or emotional ("There are no such things as conscious dissociative parts, our 'I' is not frail and not subject to division").

These interests are and were present at all times. For example, if the railway companies were to blame for serious railway accidents, and if these accidents physically or mentally injured a number of passengers, then the companies could be held responsible for these consequences. If soldiers can become traumatized because of the horrors of war rather than because of a dubious wish to receive a pension, then any state going to war can be held financially and morally responsible rather than the veterans and their alleged weak morals. And if childhood abuse and neglect are predominant causes of an affected individual's mental disorder, then the question must be raised as to who pays for the implied mental and economic damages. The victim? The perpetrator? The family, the professional, the institution (e.g., the family physician, the Church), or even the state and the social environment that knew (or could have detected without a lot of trouble) what happened to the child but did not interfere?

The recognition and acknowledgment of the existence of adverse events and the impact they can have are bound to be proportional to the interests to ignore or otherwise reject their reality. This particularly, but not solely, applies to childhood traumatization in its different forms (e.g., sexual abuse by the clergy, organized forms of sexual violation of children). The pattern of knowing and not knowing trauma (Laub & Auerhahn, 1993) at the professional and societal levels in fact more or less parallels the recurrent intrusion and mental avoidance of traumatic memories in patients as well as the shifting dominance of Myers' 'emotional and apparently normal (parts of the) personality.' From an ANP-like position, trauma tends to be ignored, denied, downplayed, or simply forgotten. Like controlling EPs that blame fragile EPs for being weak, unduly vulnerable, or seductive, there is a trend for controlling perpetrators, families, professionals and societies to blame or even punish traumatized individuals in similar ways. For example, in March 2012 Afghan raped women were put in prison. These and related parallels in the functioning of traumatized individuals and their social environments constitute the theme of Chapter 20.

Hysteria: A Women's Affair?

Professional capriciousness in the history of traumatic melancholia and hysteria also pertains to gender. For a long time it was beyond dispute that hysteria constitutes a female condition. Whereas physicians and psychologists such as Sydenham, Cheyne, Charcot, Janet, and Kretschmer clearly saw and communicated that men might also be affected, the idea that hysteria is strange to men continued to dominate professional and societal thought. One way of dealing with the discordant observations was to claim that hysterical men were simply effeminate. Myers' solution was to rename hysteria in World War I to veterans shell-shock.

Amid professional and cultural biases regarding gender, melancholia and hysteria in children were rarely considered. Burton's observation that children might develop melancholia and Briquet's findings regarding juvenile hysteria belong to the exceptions to the rule that for a long time children with these disorders did not attract professional interest. In fact, to this day the study of dissociation of the personality in children receives scarce attention (Diseth, 2005; Putnam, 1997; Silberg, 1998, 2000). One consequence of this is that to date little is known how this organization of the personality evolves under the influence of adverse events in early or later childhood.

Hysteria: A Matter of Negative Character Features?

Hysteria and patients with this condition have often been misunderstood and rejected throughout its tumultuous history. Many different interpretations of the disorder have been offered across the ages, including physical, metaphysical, psychological, social (e.g., sociocognitive), and cultural. Many afflicted individuals have been punished for their symptoms. For example, in the Middle Ages they were seen as witches, patients with hysteria might be tortured or burnt, later soldiers with hysteria would be looking for a pension and were seen as cowards or effeminate men. In our times, patients with hysteria may be disbelieved, ridiculed, misdiagnosed, given loads of medication for years that are not very helpful to them, they may be offered ineffective forms of psychotherapy or withheld effective treatment altogether.

Hysteria and Traumatic Melancholia: Two of a Kind?

There are consistent indications that the disorders conveniently gathered here under the labels traumatic melancholia and hysteria involved at least very similar symptoms (e.g., analgesia, anesthesia, paralyses and other movement disorders, amnesia, emotional numbing, flashbacks, nightmares, hypervigilance, dissociation of the personality). This commonality also applies to their contemporary descendants, that is, ASD/PTSD and complex dissociative disorders. The intimate correspondence lead Page and Charcot to state that traumatic melancholia/neurosis and hysteria basically constitute a single disorder – a position that does not deny that there are different degrees of severity within an essentially single disorder. Among others Oppenheim and Myers resisted Page and Charcot's logical conclusion. Part of the resistance was the stubborn but unfounded idea that hysteria is largely a women's affair. Another obstacle to the unification of traumatic melancholia and hysteria was the thought that hysteria is not a real disorder, but rather a condition precipitated by negative personal characteristics.

The book is not closed on the idea that ASD and PTSD involve a dissociation of the personality as a whole system in at least two, insufficiently integrated subsystems or parts, each with their own at least rudimentary subjective models of self and world (Dorahy & Van der Hart, 2014; Nijenhuis, 2012; Nijenhuis & Van der Hart, 2011a, 2011b; Van der Hart et al., 2006; Ross, in press). There is growing empirical evidence that PTSD and trauma-related dissociative disorders are intimately related conditions (Dorahy & Van der Hart, 2014; Nijenhuis, 2014b; see Chapter 18). The documented parallels pertain to brain structure, brain functioning, mental symptoms, including dissociative symptoms and other correlates, as well as treatment requirements. For example, PTSD includes (dissociative) symptoms that are typically manifestations of a dissociation of the personality, and these symptoms are positively associated with the severity of PTSD. As detailed and discussed in Chapters 17 to 19, gray and white matter abnormalities in PTSD and DID are in many regards very similar, and hyperaroused re-experiencing of traumatizing events in PTSD and DID is associated with common subjective, physiological, and neurophysiological features. The correspondence also holds for nonarousal or hypoarousal in response to reminders of traumatic experiences in these disorders. The closely matching biopsychosocial reactions to perceived threat cues strongly support the contention that these disorders are in principle one of a kind, that the complexity of this disorder increases from (simple) PTSD to complex PTSD and minor DID, and that this complexity reaches its summit in major DID. Although the complex dissociative disorders were not included in the DSM-5 chapter on trauma- and stressor-related disorders, the DSM-5 states that these two groups of disorders are closely related. This statement reflects an important, unmistaken rapprochement between traumatic melancholia and hysteria.

A resolution of the discussion regarding the view that PTSD involves a relatively simple dissociative disorder requires additional empirical evidence that patients with PTSD have contrasting biopsychosocial features over time. These shifts should be characterized by significant, consistent, and recurrent alternations of the patients' sense of who they are, what other people and the world more generally is like, and how they relate to themselves, these others, and this world. That is, they should pertain to alternations of the different kinds of person perspectives. In terms of TSDP, prototypical cases of PTSD involve one major ANP and one far less evolved fragile EP. As ANP, they aim to function in daily life and mentally avoid traumatic memories. As fragile EP, they are caught in these memories, living a nonintegrated horrific past, place, and identity. It is for further study to examine if aggression in PTSD relates to a more or less rudimentary controlling EP.

Clinicians and some researchers have consistently observed and reported these contrasting biopsychosocial features within traumatized individuals in the past 150 years (e.g., Janet, 1907; Myers, 1940; Van der Hart et al., 2006; Wang et al., 1996). Despite these findings, the psychobiological study of PTSD was initially based on the assumptions that the patients' psychobiological responses to trauma reminders are consistent over time, and that each patient has quite similar hyperarousal reactions to these cues. As discussed in Chapters 5 and 6, it is an encouraging development that some researchers have started to acknowledge that these assumptions are false (Lanius et al., 2010, 2012). A technical problem of PTSD research is that it remains difficult to elicit the otherwise naturally occurring biopsychosocial shifts (e.g., shifts from hyperaroused [re]activity to nonaroused or hypoaroused [re]activity) in controlled experimental settings. One solution would be to study naturally occurring intrapersonal shifts of several PTSD patients over time by using continuous or at least frequently repeated measurements per patient over a period of time. The value of this multiple case approach has already been demonstrated in psychoneuroimmunological research (Schubert, 2011).

Would it perhaps be the existence of the alternating different 'selves' within traumatized individuals that is impeding the recognition of ASD and PTSD as dissociative disorders? Would it be too threatening to realize the fragility of our cherished 'I?' Is distinguishing between a hyperarousal subtype of PTSD and a dissociative subtype of PTSD – where dissociation merely describes a couple of negative symptoms – safer than acknowledging a 'self behind ourself,' as Emily Dickinson put it? The resistance could perhaps relate to Von Uexküll's (1994, p. 32) assertion that: "We'd rather deny our own liveliness and the liveliness of nature than engage in a relationship that may be painful. The less we are able to bear illnesses, the more we feel a need to distort reality." In any case, trauma-related dissociation of the personality challenges the idea that we are born with a self, or better, with *one* self, and that this unitary self is given. Indeed, as several authors have observed, studied, and demonstrated, patients with PTSD, like patients with a complex dissociative disorder, encompass more than one "I, me, myself," more than one first-person, quasi-second-person, second-person, and third-person perspective.

One might counter that Buddhism has maintained for thousands of years that the 'self' is a conception, and that everyone has multiple 'I's. These objections are not persuasive. There is a major difference between a voluntary journey toward loosening our customary sense of self through meditation, and the involuntary violence-based or attachment disruption-based emergence of additional 'I's, some of which are certainly not the kind of guests one would choose to have. It is true that no one is a perfect unity. Everyone has different moods and can have difficulty reconciling conflicting motivations. However, this suboptimal integration is different from being divided in different self-aware subsystems that deeply fear or hate each other, leading to major and unrelenting struggles for control. Mentally healthy individuals, patients with mental disorders that do not qualify as dissociative, and patients with 'ego-states' are certainly not perfectly integrated, but they can personify their different moods, conflicts, or 'ego-states.' Dissociative parts of the personality resist this personification because of unilateral or reciprocal fear, shame, contempt, or hate. To clarify this issue of 'self' and "our self behind ourself," the origins of the 'sense of self' and the different 'senses of self' in dissociative disorders are examined in Chapter 12.

A Phobia of Hysteria in Psychiatry and Psychology?

Would it be too far fetched to say that there exists a phobia of minor and major DID in psychiatry and psychology, just as there has been and perhaps to a degree still is a phobia of childhood traumatization? Here are some facts. Minor and major DID remain understudied to this day and are often misrepresented. For example, the firm statement in ICD-10 (WHO, 1992) that multiple personality disorder (i.e., DID) is rare, conflicts with the facts. Complex dissociative disorders are in fact relatively common in general and clinical populations, and there is no evidence that they constitute a local Western phenomenon. The estimated prevalence of major DID is 0.5%–1.5% in the general population, whereas the estimated prevalence of schizophrenia, another severe mental disorder, is 4.0 per 1000 individuals in the general population (Saha, Chant, Welham, & McGrath, 2005). Politics are sometimes reflected in numbers. This may be seen in Google and PubMed: Entering 'dissociative disorders' in Google yielded 2,620,000 hits and 'dissociative identity disorder' 1,570,000 hits (December 20, 2013). Entering schizophrenia gave 7,550,000 hits. PubMed, a search system for scientific articles, generated for the term 'dissociative disorders' 3,808 studies, and for 'dissociative identity disorder' 338 articles. 'Schizophrenia,' however, gave 106,547 articles, 'anxiety disorders' 75,439, and 'major depression' 48,279. Combined with the term 'neuroimaging,' the numbers were 78 for the term 'dissociative disorders,' 10 for 'dissociative identity disorder,' 3,524 for 'schizophrenia,' 1,213 for 'major depression,' and 987 for 'anxiety disorders.' Politics sometimes becomes clearer in graphs, hence Graph 7.1. The numbers are totally out of balance with the estimated prevalence rates of these different disorders in psychiatry: schizophrenia 1% (Van Dongen & Boomsma, 2013), DID 1%-6%, major depression 7.2% (Luppa et al., 2011), anxiety disorders 7.3% (Baxter, Scott, Vos, & Whiteford, 2012), and dissociative disorders 10% (excluding sensorimotor dissociative disorders). The numbers for minor DID are even lower, despite the fact that this disorder is associated with the highest prevalence of all dissociative disorders.

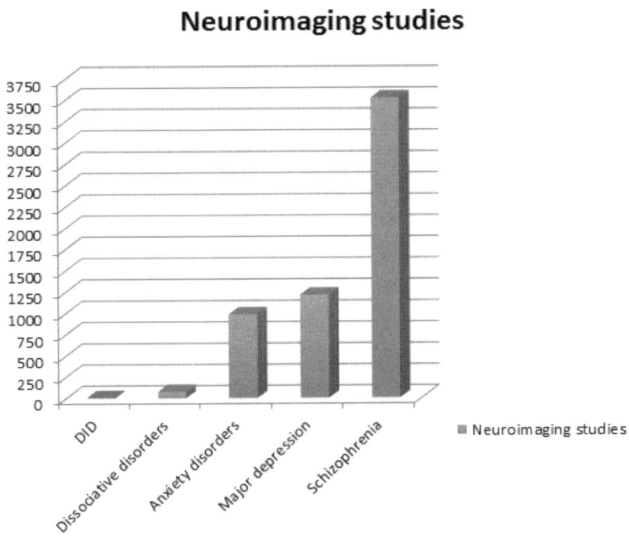

Figure 7.1. Numbers of neuroimaging studies of different mental disorders as reported in PubMed.

The level of expertise in the domains of psychiatry, psychology, and psychotherapy regarding the characteristics, origins, assessment and treatment of minor and major DID is wanting (e.g., Dorahy, Lewis, & Mulholland, 2005). Many patients with complex dissociative disorders report that the clinicians they met in their psychiatric careers did not understand or wish to understand their disorder. They were often given inaccurate diagnoses. However, there have been important changes for the better. Expert-based treatment guidelines (International Society for the Study of Dissociation et al., 2005; International Society for the Study of Trauma and Dissociation, 2011) are available. Many clinicians have become aware that they need more knowledge and skills to properly assess and treat patients with complex dissociative disorders. For example, they may start to notice dissociative phenomena in some of their patients during EMDR treatment and develop a need to comprehend and treat these symptoms better. Conferences, workshops, and courses on dissociative disorders are well attended and are drawing a widening audience. With this education and training, clinicians, and their patients notice that they become more effective in their diagnostic and therapeutic work with the conditions. However, participants in courses struggle with the confusing ways in which the concepts of trauma and dissociation are defined in the literature. They also have difficulty grasping the logic of the distinctions made between PTSD, conversion disorder, dissociative disorder, and psychosis in the DSM as well as understanding the differences and commonalities between dissociative parts and 'ego-states.' Conceptual clarity is not just the philosopher's and theoretician's need.

Chapter 8

The Capricious Historical Understanding of Traumatic Melancholia and Hysteria: Part II. Philosophical Considerations

> *... in any functional sense organism and environment are inseparable and form only one unitary system.*
> Timo Järvilehto (1998, p. 321)

Across the ages, many have attempted to explain trauma in terms of matter (the body/brain) or of the mind. Whereas in many epochs the dominant third-person understanding was that the melancholia and hysteria constitute physical diseases, there have also been times in which the mind was seen as the source and realm of these disorders. Few have tried to understand the pathology that belongs to the 'melancholia-line' and 'hysteria-line' in holistic terms. Sydenham as well as Janet were among the exceptional authors who contended that hysteria involves the *whole* person, that is, the whole human organism.

The recurrent historical vacillation of professional ideas regarding traumatic melancholia and hysteria thus includes alternating explanations in terms of physical or mental causation. These two different perspectives were not specific to the understanding of these disorders, but pertained rather to different ways in which the human mind attempts to understand itself in general. The desire to gain knowledge and wisdom in this regard was not easily fulfilled. The problem of understanding matter and mind is in fact an ongoing quest and struggle. It is so complicated that other desires may emerge: "Can't we keep things simple?" – "Can't we leave the matter alone?" – "Isn't this just food for philosophers?" The answer is a threefold "no." Too much is at stake to travel these evasive roads. The point is that answers to the riddle of physical and mental causation strongly influence one's perspective on the advancement of the science and clinical practice of human experience and behavior. They affect the projects of studying, understanding, and treating trauma per implication.

Philosophical Materialism: You Are a Body with a Brain

Philosophical materialism or physicalism[1] includes the assumption that mental disorders essentially involve physical abnormalities. The idea is that the sensorimotor, cognitive, emotional, and/or behavioral symptoms of the disorder under investigation can and must, at least in principle, be fully understood in physical terms. Matter would be all that, well, matters. In this philosophically materialistic or physicalistic persuasion, the causal formula is this:

matter → causes → mind

Materialistic explanations of melancholia and hysteria and their derivates have typically focused on a particular physical structure (e.g., the womb, the spine, the brain, a part of the brain) or on (neuro)physiology (e.g., an overabundance of black bile, a lack of nervous energy, a particular genotype). They have attempted to explain the mental and other abnormalities on the basis of the structural or functional abnormality of this particular physical subsystem. The explanations commonly include the idea that one physical abnormality causes another:

material conditions → cause → structural or functional physical abnormalities → mental abnormalities

For example, some scientists hypothesize that adverse events – understood as material environmental conditions – can cause a small hippocampal volume. This structural physical feature would then constitute a risk factor for PTSD, which they also understand in physicalistic terms.

There is presently a tremendous interest in the brain. A significant part of the will to explore and understand the brain is the desire to better comprehend consciousness and self-consciousness. This atmosphere also breeds a growing interest in the neurobiology of PTSD. Will the study of the brain as the object of investigation advance the understanding of trauma? It surely will. Will it also provide a deeper insight in the subjectivity of traumatization? In some regards, yes, but certainly not in all regards. The issue is that materialists have been and continue to be confronted with explicatory problems. Some of these are so serious that it would be wise to have a modest outlook on the explanatory reach of materialism in psychology.

An empirical problem in the history of physicalistic and physical explanations of trauma was that the belief in some kind of somatic cause of melancholia and hysteria has

1 Physicalism is the ontological monistic philosophical assumption that there is "nothing over and above" the physical, or that everything supervenes on the physical. In this view, any mental disorder is essentially a physical disorder. Philosophical dualists (see below) may judge that some mental disorders or components of mental disorders are due to physical abnormalities, and that other disorders or components of these disorders are caused by mental factors.

repeatedly been upended by the absence of the purported physical abnormalities. The uterus of hysterical women was *not* dry and did *not* wander; the spine of individuals with railway spine might *not* be shaken. In 1889, Oppenheim recanted his previous claim that physical lesions lie at the core of traumatic neurosis. The condition of traumatized soldiers was not satisfactorily explained solely by physical shocks due to shelling. Contemporary examples are that many (Karl et al., 2006), but not all, patients with PTSD have small hippocampal volume (Chalavi, 2013; Chalavi et al., 2014; Chen & Shi, 2011), and that small hippocampal volume may not be specific to trauma-related disorders. Studies suggest that this deviation may also show in individuals who experienced adverse events, but who did not develop PTSD or some other trauma-related disorder (Woon, Sood, & Hedges, 2010). Also, a reduction rather than a stress-induced increase in adrenal glucocorticoid levels in patients with PTSD is puzzling, and the abnormality is not a consistent feature of the disorder (Fink, 2011).

These empirical problems might merely reflect the current imperfect state of the physical sciences, some materialists hope. For example, they may concede that negative findings of brain abnormalities were (or still are) due to a lack of knowledge and absence of sophisticated instruments to examine the brain. They trust that increasing insights into the structure and functioning of the brain will *eventually* reveal the causes of trauma-related disorder, other mental disorders, and human experience and behavior more generally. The scientific examination of the brain in relation to matters of consciousness and self-consciousness is obviously a most important enterprise. An increasing number of studies show that the brain of individuals with trauma-related disorders includes structural and functional abnormalities, and there is every reason to expect that this development will continue. It is thus easy to see how the study of the brain contributes to an understanding of minds that feel safe and sound as well as of scared and troubled minds that have been injured by an adverse life.

However, can materialism provide a *complete* scientific account of consciousness? Will it ever obtain a full explanation of the subjective experience of becoming and being traumatized? Will it ever explain the personal meaning of adverse events? Or could there be principled reasons that restrict the reach of empirical brain studies in these regards? Suppose that some future day particular invariant structural and functional brain abnormalities are found in individuals with trauma-related (or any other mental) disorders. Then, what do third-person, disengaged scientific assessments say about the patients' primary consciousness?

From the 18th century onward, several philosophers have felt that there are limits to what a science of the brain can elucidate (e.g., Leibniz, 1714; Kant, 1781/1998; Schopenhauer, 1818/1844/1958; Huxley & Youmans, 1868). They have wondered whether consciousness can be completely explained in terms of neural events occurring within the brain. As Huxley (1868) mused, "how it is that any thing so remarkable as a state of consciousness comes about as the result of irritating nervous tissue, is just as unaccountable as the appearance of the Djin when Aladdin rubbed his lamp?" More recently, David Chalmers (1996) proposed a distinction between the 'easy' and the 'hard' problems of consciousness. Easy problems are those that can be solved by specifying a certain brain mechanism that is involved in a particular function of consciousness, such as the ability to attend to something or to report mental states. The hard problem of consciousness lies in explaining how and why we have '*qualia*' or *phenomenal experiences*. That is, how and why are we conscious, do we have experiences, do we have feelings, and do we comprise a sense of selfhood? Chalmers disputes that the phenomenal consciousness can be explained mechanistically, and he is not the only one who takes this position.

It is possible to study what brain activity (changes in neural structure and activity, synaptic changes, neurotransmitters, gene-expression) coincides with the execution of particular mental actions (perceiving, thinking, conceiving, reasoning) and their contents such as a particular perception, thought, or conception, or particular relationships between different conceptions. However, such brain-mind correlations do not explain phenomenal experience (Block, 1998), our first-perspective, and they do not tell the complete story of our second-person perspective (knowing others is referred to as the problem of other minds [Fuchs & DeJaeger, 2010]; see below). Brain structures and brain activity do not show us *what, how,* and *why* an individual was experiencing. Neural facts do not and cannot speak for themselves in this regard. A particular pattern of brain activity does not show what being a subject is like, what it is like to be traumatized, what it means to have abusive and neglectful parents, how and why neglected and abused children continue to return to their perpetrators, how re-experiencing traumatizing events feels, what the phenomenal self and world are like when one re-enacts traumatic experiences, what it is like to be recurrently intruded on by deeply hurt and brutal controlling voices, or to have more than a singular sense of selfhood. Materialists, thus, should not cry victory, should not claim they have explained phenomenal experience, when they discover that a particular neural fact coincides (i.e., correlates or parallels) with a certain mental fact. How, then, can philosophical materialists come to terms with the type of consciousness – consciousness is a mongrel term – that can be described as the *phenomenal mind*?

Philosophical Dualism: You Are Two

Some materialists are philosophical dualists. They purport that matter and mind involve different substances (substance dualists) or different properties (property dualists).

Dualism has been around since Ancient Greek philosophy. For example, Plato held that physical bodies are imperfect copies, metaphorical shadows of the distinct immaterial and eternal Forms that make the world possible and intelligible. We are able to grasp our world and ourselves because our intellect has an affinity with these Forms or Ideas. This affinity is in fact so strong that our soul wants to escape the bodily prison in which it is incarcerated during our earthly lifetime, so that it can return to the realm of the immaterial Forms from which it came once the body has deceased. This reunion is not an easy endeavor, and it may take several reincarnations before it is accomplished.

Major problems of Plato's philosophy are that it does not explain why and how a particular soul becomes *linked* with a particular body. Dualism poses a mind-body and a body-mind problem:

matter (body, brain) ← ? → mind

Aristotle, Plato's longtime student, did not believe that eternal Forms exist independently from their instances. In his philosophy, forms are the natures and properties of things, and these exist embodied in those things. Yet he concurred with Plato that there exists an immaterial soul that returns home after the individual's bodily death. Immortal and eternal, our soul includes a divine, essential element that links us to God. And it is thanks to this divine inspiration that we can understand ourselves and the world we inhabit.

Although Aristotle is often seen as a materialist, this understanding is flawed. According to Bos' reinterpretation (1998, 2003), Aristotle believed that the psyché or soul is the immaterial, leading principle of a special 'natural body' (*sôma physikon*) that potentially possesses life. The soul uses this fine-material body as an instrument (*organon*) for the formation, vitalization, and motion of the visible coarse-material body. He called this *sôma physikon pneuma* (warm air) in higher animals and 'vital heat' in lower animals and plants. Aristotle defined the soul as 'the first entelechy of the natural body,' that is, as the form that leads the development of a living creature from the beginning to its end (*telos* means goal). As *pneuma* mediates between the immaterial soul and the visible body, it becomes the vehicle of desire (*orexis*): An indissoluble unity with the soul, it constitutes the prime mover of all vital activity. According to Bos' reinterpretation, Aristotle's philosophy was thus clearly dualistic.

The idea that *pneuma* includes a divine element was also held by the Stoics, who believed that the human *pneuma* is a part of the general *pneuma*, which in turn is the soul of God. Aristotle comprehended the general *pneuma* as the mysterious 'unmoved mover.' Traces of Aristotle's ideas regarding *pneuma* may be found in Descartes' philosophy. As mentioned before, Descartes (1641) proposed that matter (extendedness, the body and matter more generally) and mind (thought and consciousness more generally) constitute different substances. This dualism suggests that there can be objects without subjects, and subjects without objects. It also entails the idea that mind and matter are ruled by their own laws. These contentions led his contemporaries Princess Elisabeth of Bohemia and Spinoza to ask how *res cogitans* (mind) and *res extensa* (matter) as two essentially different substances can at all affect each other? How can mind cause matter (mental causation), and matter cause mind (physical causation) if they are indeed different substances? In an attempt to solve the problem, Descartes stated that the mind interacts with the body through the pineal gland, and that this gland controls the flow of animal spirits around the brain and body. Had the animal spirits in Aristotle's days been portrayed as weightless, invisible entities to mediate the functioning of the body, for Descartes they were fluids of some kind that flowed through hollow nerves. Since the pineal gland and fluids are material entities, Descartes' brilliant mind did not solve the vexing issue. Aristotle's 'fine-material' pneuma fails to explain the bridge between mind and matter for the same reason: One cannot propose a material substance to link the immaterial and the material. Consistent with a remedy he applied to himself, Descartes wrote the Princess on June 28, 1643[2]:

> what teaches us how to conceive the soul's union with the body is ·the ordinary course of life and conversation and ·not meditating or studying things that exercise the imagination. … [W]hat belongs to the soul's union with the body is a very dark affair when it comes from the intellect (whether alone or aided by the imagination), but it is very bright when the senses have a hand in it. … [E]veryone always experiences within himself without philosophizing – simply·by knowing that he is a single person who has both body and thought whose natures are such that this thought can move the body and can sense what happens to the body.

The continuing respectful correspondence between the two demonstrates that Descartes' suggestion to simply live her life and to stop contemplating the mind-matter problem, or at least to restrain the urge to engage in the philosophy of mind, failed to silence the Princess' will to question and understand. Spinoza's remedy was to propose a monistic alternative (see below).

History shows that Descartes' idea was most enticing – despite its profound riddles. Traces of it can still be found in terms such as 'psychophysiology,' 'psychosomatic,' and 'conversion disorder.' Conversion in psychiatry refers to the idea that mental conflicts can be transformed into physical symptoms. But, the materialist asks, can mental conflicts at all exist in the absence of a living brain? And if that is not possible, as the materialist concedes, then how can a mental conflict *not* in essence be a matter of matter? The unimpressed dualist counters that the materialist cannot actually show how matter becomes mind. Different strands of philosophical dualism are thus up and running (e.g., Chalmers, 1996), for the most part because materialism fails to come to terms with phenomenal consciousness.

Engaged in life, most mentally healthy individuals are not troubled by the question of how matter and mind get integrated, because they are generally coordinated and integrated in their lived experience. They are not troubled by the riddles of the philosophy of mind. (Wittgenstein, 1953, once said that philosophical problems are like an illness that must be cured.) However, many traumatized individuals experience that their mind and body are far from coordinated and integrated, and that different dissociative parts of their personality tend to experience different degrees of coordination and integration of their mind and body. Mind-body integration, we see, is not given. Whereas dissociative disorders offer an excellent opportunity to study the topics of coordination and integration, it seems that most scientists overlook that promise. Patients with dissociative disorders are rare guests in research centers.

---

2 Bennett, the translator, added that "[s]mall ·dots· enclose material that has been added, but can be read as though it were part of the original text. Occasional ·bullets, and also indenting of passages that are not quotations, are meant as aids to grasping the structure of a sentence or a thought."

Philosophical Identity Theory: Matter Is More Equal than Mind

If materialists wish to avoid the problems of dualism, they may choose the camp of the identity theorists. Identity philosophers and scientists assume that brain activity and mental activity are one and the same thing:

matter = mind

Still, many identity theorists have a lopsided interest in the brain and seem to feel that explanations of human experience and behavior cast in terms of particular neural activity patterns are more 'scientific,' more 'objective' than a systematic observation of an individual expressing an emotion or a thought, or doing something. This position is reminiscent of the major maxim in George Orwell's *Animal Farm* that "all animals are equal but some animals are more equal than others." Many neurobiologists have a tendency to regard subjectivity, sometimes rather disdainfully addressed as "mere subjectivity," as a queer and unreliable bedfellow. Still, whether or not they recognize or acknowledge it, subjectivity is the foundation on which their whole professional enterprise rests – and to which they must and always will return.

As the history of trauma reveals, many clinicians and scientists have nearly ignored, neglected, or mistrusted the subjective experiences of traumatized individuals. This mistrust – caused in part or at least strengthened by the troubles of introspection – certainly was and is not specific to professionals who adhere to some form of philosophical identity theory. But, one may ask, isn't there also reason to 'mistrust matter' in that physicists have no coherent idea to date of what matter essentially is or could be (Montero, 2009; Robinson, 2009)? And, as Järvilehto (2004, #37) holds, whatever matter is, it is dependent on knowing subjects and the measurement devices they invent and use:

> As a matter of fact, the "hunt for elementary parts of the matter" is a hunt which will never end. The more ingenious systems of measurement are created the more elementary particles will be found. Matter is infinite and shows always new properties and aspects when new measuring devices are developed.

Indeed, according to quantum theory, the properties of some aspects of matter are created by our measurement. It applies to *any* observation and measurement, says Järvilehto, that the observed object and the observer join in the organism-environment system they constitute together.

Reductive Physicalism: You Are Your Brain

Still other materialists reduce philosophical monism to philosophical materialism, also described as reductive physicalism. Thus, some authors reduce the whole person to components of his or her brain and thereby attempt to eliminate the mind as a phenomenon of investigation. As Joseph LeDoux (2002, p. 324) conceded, "[Y]ou are your synapses. They are who you are." Crick (1994, p. 3) similarly proclaimed, "You're nothing but a pack of neurons." It is the general hope of reductive physicalists that a deep future physical understanding of the brain implies an explanation of mental phenomena such as consciousness and self-consciousness. In this light, trauma would be neurons and synapses gone awry:

> matter (neurons, synapses) → cause and (eventually) fully explain → consciousness

These scientists and philosophers trust that the problem of the how, why, and what of phenomenal experience will somehow dissolve along the way. However, this hope is an illusion, phenomenologists say. No physical fact about an individual (animal, person) can individuate what that individual feels, believes, wants, remembers, or dreams (Graham, Horgan, & Tienson, 2009). Kant (1781/1998; 1786/1970) was the first to take this position (see also Northoff, 2012): "The only thinking subject whose inner sense one can investigate is oneself" and, still more troublesome, "even the observation itself alters and distorts the state of the object observed" (1786, p. 471).

The Brain as a Headtop: You Are a Machine

Reductive physicalists portray us as a complex machine. In this light, it is not coincidental that authors of many contemporary papers on psychology speak of 'mechanisms,' and that cybernetic/information processing metaphors have become very popular. As Bitbol (2002, p. 21) remarked,

> [i]t is not unusual today to hear somebody saying, e.g.: "My brain is processing the information" instead of "I am thinking hard," or "My circuits are overloaded" instead of "I am unable to figure out what to do in these complex circumstances," or "Your neurons are working overtime" instead of "You are mentally exhausted," etc.

As if we have some direct or complete insight into the workings of our brain! This type of thinking also appears in the trauma field. For example, the working of Eye Movement Desensitization and Reprocessing (EMDR) is explained in terms of physiological information processing (Shapiro & Maxfield, 2002). These authors' model of Adaptive Information Processing suggests that the brain of traumatized individuals has not managed to create adaptive links between the representation of the traumatic experience and stored representations of previous experiences. EMDR is a method that purports to stimulate the brain to forge these connections. This reprocessing heals the brain and per implication the mind. AIP thus seems to involve philosophical materialism. The problem is that this philosophy does not tell how matter generates mind.

The general contemporary understanding of the term 'information' is that objects and situations are given and have a predetermined meaning. Computers work in the way they are programmed to work; they do not make meaning, they get told what to do with what. But are we fancy computers? A few phenomena have a preset meaning for us from birth in the sense that we know how to respond to them. No learning is needed in these cases. In the jargon of classical or Pavlovian conditioning, given a required organismic state (e.g., being hungry, being wide awake), we react to 'unconditioned stimuli' with particular given 'unconditioned responses.'[3] For example, we do not need to learn to squint our eyes in reaction to bright light, salivate in reaction to the sight and smell of food, drink from mother's breast when thirsty, or freeze when threatened. We do not need to learn to become scared when we hear a loud tone of voice or to withdraw from something that hurts. Confronted with these kinds of simple phenomena, we activate emotional action or will systems that evolution has brought forward, and guided by them we more or less effectively find a way to (re)act.

However, more generally and in contrast to machines, we must learn to distinguish, to perceive objects, and to assign meaning to most phenomena (Hutto, 2010). As applies to most 'stimuli,' 'information' does not exist independently from organisms for whom something has meaning (Merleau-Ponty, 1945). A perception or conception always involves someone's perception, someone's idea. What thus exist are organisms that *generate* information. The major part of our world is not given – it is not precoded. Little constitutes a stimulus or informs in and of itself. Rather, we must generate perceptions and conceptions: We must make meaning. We cannot fall back on a programmer who has done or who will do the job for us. We are not computers fed by input and producing output. In most cases, we must *work* before anything becomes a stimulus or informative for us (Hutto, 2010; Krueger, 2010; Merleau-Ponty, 1945; Schopenhauer, 1958; Spinoza, 1996; Varela, 1996).

This work is in fact what the original Latin verb *informare* indicates. It means 'to give form' or 'to form an idea of.' It is this original understanding of *informare* as an action that is lost if it is assumed that objects and situations in and of themselves entail information, that is, in and of themselves inform us. But this is how the term 'information' is commonly used today. It has come to stand for something that has a certain pregiven meaning, as 'input' that, transported from cell to cell, is 'processed' by the brain; as something that becomes 'encoded' and 'stored,' that can later be 'retrieved,' and that leads to 'output.'

---

3 As I discuss in more detail later, it is an oversimplification to say that there are fixed links between unconditioned stimuli and unconditioned responses (e.g., Panksepp & Biven, 2012). The point is that a particular unconditioned stimulus can very well elicit different unconditioned responses. For example, depending on the individual's perception and evaluation of the context in which the unconditioned stimulus appears, he or she may engage in flight, freeze, or still some another mammalian defensive reaction. Unconditioned stimuli, thus, may activate an action system such as the mammalian defense system rather than a singular unconditioned defensive response. This feature may in part explain why a traumatized individual can show different, albeit related reactions to reminders of events that were traumatizing for them at different points in time.

'Trauma' in this perspective would be an independently existing event occurring in an independently existing world that constitutes the input into someone's brain. This position reflects naïve realism, the view that objects have an observer-independent existence with properties that we can perceive as they really are. This information is processed by the brain and reappears on the outside as reported experiences and observable behaviors (e.g., as symptoms):

isolated adverse event → constitutes input and mechanically causes → processing errors of the brain as a machine → symptomatic experiences and behaviors as output

A major problem with trauma would be that the event becomes encoded and stored in maladaptive 'representations' of reality. These maladaptive 'representations' become 're-activated' by potent reminders of trauma, that is, particular 'conditioned stimuli' (CS). These previously neutral stimuli automatically, that is, mechanically, retrieve the 'representations of the trauma' once these stimuli have become associated with the unconditioned stimuli (US):

CS → reactivate stored representations of traumatic experiences, US → conditioned reaction

Pavlov's work and ideas on classical conditioning are important and helpful. A complication in trauma is that different dissociative parts of the personality can have different reactions to a particular stimulus – and very different reactions at that. For example, a patient with a complex dissociative disorder consistently panicked when she heard a siren or a similar high-pitched tone. As ANP, she did not understand why she became so fearful, but as a young EP, these tones reminded her of her angry mother entering her bedroom through a squeaking door and being hit so hard against her ears by her mother that they had started to squeak. As this EP she had learned a referential relationship between high-pitched tones (CS) and physical abuse (US), so that they started to squeak again when the patient heard a siren. As ANP, she mentally avoided these traumatic memories, as well as the involved EP.

There are major problems of representationalism (Braude, 1995, 1997; Bursen, 1978; Edelman & Tononi, 2000; Heil, 1978, 2011; Hutto & Myin, 2013; Northoff, 2003) that will be addressed later. Suffice it to say here that autobiographical memory is not an inner library filled with books that contain traces (i.e., representations) of things past. However, if the mind does not include representations, they cannot be 'reprocessed.' Apart from this, it is also unclear what this 'reprocessing' would precisely entail. What connections are the 'right' and the 'wrong' connections? How is the brain to know this?

Strong Eliminativism: You Are Not

Still other philosophical materialists attempt to eliminate the problem of primary consciousness by declaring it a nonissue. Their dissolution is to regard consciousness and self-consciousness as epiphenomena or by-products, that is, as inert, coincidental, and irrelevant phenomena (Caston, 1997; Huxley [1893/2011] talked about 'collateral products'). They would be causal dead-ends.

However, this attempt to solve the problem of consciousness creates several riddles. One problem is that epiphenomenalism is counterintuitive because what could be more real than raw feelings motivating us to act? Don't we cry because we are in some kind of pain? Don't traumatized individuals suffer because the adversities that happened to them hurt?

A second problem of epiphenomenalism is the question why evolution would have generated sensations, affects, perceptions, thoughts, beliefs, fantasies, memories, as well as the feeling and idea of being someone if they were mere epiphenomena? Why would they have survived to this day, and why would consciousness and self-consciousness play such a major role in lived experience? If the brain causes behavior irrespective of consciousness, then why should brain states include conscious states at all? Why would unconscious life not suffice if epiphenomenalism were true? Why would people feel that traumatizing events hurt if the pain did not serving any real function? Nature would be playing traumatized individuals a very dirty trick if their suffering were basically useless.

A third conundrum of epiphenomenalism is the problem of other minds. How can I relate to other people and these people's experiences? How could I do that if not by reference to my own consciousness, that is, by extrapolating my personal experiences to that of other individuals who seem so similar to me? My mirror neurons might do the job, but would these devices also affect my behavior if I were a zombie, an automaton devoid of consciousness? Is it really true that consciousness does not matter?

Behaviorism: You Are a Black Box

During the heyday of behaviorism, the problem of consciousness and self-consciousness was in reaction to the failure of Wundt's introspectionism also erased from the scientific agenda. Trying to establish an objective psychology, psychologists tried to surpass the elusive mind that was methodologically better treated as a black box. Their job was to study relationships between observables (observable by the scientists' mind, that is . . .), between input into and output from the black box:

> stimuli as input → . . . ? . . . → observable behaviors (responses) as output

In this context, Watson (1913, 1930) and like-minded psychologists believed that human and other animal behavior was completely shaped and controlled by reward and punishment. As Watson (1930, p. 82) famously declared,

> [g]ive me a dozen healthy infants, well-formed, and my own specified world to bring them up in and I'll guarantee to take any one at random and train him to become any type of specialist I might select – doctor, lawyer, artist, merchant-chief and, yes, even beggar-man and thief, regardless of his talents, penchants, tendencies, abilities, vocations, and race of his ancestors. I

> am going beyond my facts and I admit it, but so have the advocates of the contrary and they have been doing it for many thousands of years.

Behaviorism, which was to become a dominant persuasion for years, relied on the assumption that there are universal rules of learning. Behaviorists believed that these rules apply irrespective of the kind of stimuli (input) and responses (output) the subject is learning about. This idea has become known as the 'equipotentiality principle' of general process learning theory. Other assumptions were that the laws of learning apply to man and other animals alike, and that these laws can be detected in strict laboratory experiments such as rats pressing levers or pigeons responding with key pecking to obtain rewards or avoid punishment. What was found for the stimuli and responses in these artificial settings would also apply to relationships between stimuli and responses in the organism's natural niches.

Evolutionary Perspectives: You Are Another Mammal

Each of the assumptions of this 'radical behaviorism' has since been challenged (e.g., Domjan, 2012). For example, scratching and yawning are not subject to reinforcement (Thorndike, 1911). Behaviorists chose to ignore this troublesome finding for five decades, but eventually became confronted with ever more findings suggesting limits to learning. Racoons would rather rub coins against each other than put them in a slot to obtain food rewards; pigs would root the coins on the ground (Breland & Breland, 1961). As Keller and Marian Breland put it, the animals displayed a drift from unnatural, experimentally reinforced responses toward instinctual responses. Having observed and experimented with thousands of animals over 14 years, they concluded that "the behavior of any species cannot be adequately understood, predicted, or controlled without knowledge of its instinctive patterns, evolutionary history, and ecological niche" (1961, p. 684).

The work of Garcia and his colleagues on taste aversion (Garcia, Kimeldorf, & Koelling, 1955; Garcia, Lasiter, Bermudez-Rattoni, & Deems, 1985) also demonstrated that several classic assumptions about classical conditioning were false. In taste aversion learning, the time gap between the taste of the food as the conditioned stimulus and getting and being sick as the unconditioned stimuli can be very long, the aversion to a food can be learned in one trial, and this learning resists unlearning. Garcia's work also challenged the equipotentiality assumption, because it appeared that food aversion is highly selective. For example, rats that had drank saccharin-flavored water in a red-lighted cage, and that were then exposed to a dose of radiation that turned them sick, later avoided saccharin-flavored water but not the red light. Also, when rats got shocked after tasting saccharin-flavored water, they subsequently avoided the place where they were shocked but continued to drink the water. These results and conclusions were met with skepticism, mostly because they did not fit the assumptions of behaviorism. But Garcia's (1981) rejoinders were convincing.

More discrepancies from the standard ideas of behaviorism had already been found and reported. Thus, Lorenz (1937) and Tinbergen (1951, 1953) suggested that animals do not enter the world *tabula rasa*, but in fact are endowed with species-typical behaviors. In the same vein, Bolles (1970) found that rats have difficulty learning to press a lever to avoid an electrical shock, but quickly learn to avoid the shock by freezing, jumping out of a box, or running in a wheel. Freezing, jumping and running are innate, that is, natural defensive behaviors of rats, but pressing a lever is not. Similarly, pigeons find it easy to learn to peck to obtain food – pecking is natural action for pigeons with an appetite – but they have difficulty learning to avoid an electrical shock by pecking. Pecking is not a part of pigeons' evolutionary derived natural defensive repertoire. Social ethological studies demonstrated the existence of evolutionary derived, natural behaviors in animals that live in groups. These sociobiological behaviors include detecting predator/prey, communicating alarm signals, other defensive actions such as freeze and flight, but also territorial defense. They also encompass competing for status such as staring (many animals fear being stared at; Kalin, Shelton, & Takahashi, 1991) and threat displays. The weaker individuals may be wise to appease by showing submission postures, which often include the showing of vulnerable body parts, and infantile behaviors in the form of cowering, whining, crying, begging, and nervous laughter. These defensive actions are functional in that they may avoid predator attack. Certain prosocial behaviors (e.g., play and grooming as well as other ways of comforting each other by contact) are also innate, as are many procreative actions (e.g., finding a sexual partner, courtship, mating, raising offspring).

Had traditional learning research frequently treated organisms as unorganized bundles of reflexes and random responses, in a *behavior systems approach*, an organism includes a set of organized and interrelated regulatory systems that precede, support, and constrain learning (Timberlake, 1993; Timberlake & Lucas, 1989):

behavior systems → constraint, support → reactivity to events

Consistent with this view, animals do not respond to aversive, threatening stimuli with single responses, but with qualitatively different behavioral and physiological states that are tuned to optimizing survival chances in successive stages of imminence (Bolles, 1970; Bolles & Fanselow, 1980; Fanselow & Lester, 1988). These states are mutually inhibitive, and there is evidence suggesting that the various defensive subsystems (e.g., affiliative behaviors, freezing, aggression) are mediated by different neurochemical systems (Kalin & Shelton, 1989).

As mentioned in Chapter 4, Panksepp (1998; Panksepp & Biven, 2012) similarly proposes that mammals are mediated by evolutionary-derived action systems. He added the important element that these action systems involve raw affective feelings. These subjective experiences are all but epiphenomena: They are essential features of these systems because they provide the individual with an experienced motive to approach particular subjects, objects, and situations – and to avoid or escape from others. With Panksepp, thus, subjectivity not only re-entered psychology, including neuroscience, but consciousness and self-consciousness received a pivotal place in the study and understanding of mammalian behavior:

emotional action systems → mediate and imply → phenomenal experience and behavior

His studies demonstrate that raw affective feelings do not depend on the higher reaches of the mammalian brain, as is often but erroneously thought. For example, even decorticated animals work hard to get particular feelings such as feeling excited and pleasures involved in play or those that are provided by particular drugs, as well as avoid aversive feelings such as threat-related fear. They engage in frantic action to achieve these feelings. Emotional action systems (e.g., seeking, play, lust, and fear) involve basic urges. There is the deep will to do all of these things. Hence I refer to these systems as *will systems*.

Because the possibilities of studying brain stem and emotional brain functioning in humans are limited, Panksepp and Biven (2012; also: Panksepp, 1998) propose a triangulation of studies of brain, mind, and behavior. More specifically, they advocate research focusing on an understanding of (1) the mammalian brain, (2) the instinctual emotional behaviors of other animals, and (3) the subjective states of the human mind. In light of the failure of introspectionism, a crucial concern of this scheme is *how to assess subjective states.* In the case of trauma, the issue is how to assess the traumatized individuals' states of mind, and in the case of dissociation of the personality it is how to assess the mental states of the different dissociative parts and the effects these states have on the mental states of other dissociative parts. I revisit these questions below.

Philosophical Idealism: You Are Your Dream

In contrast to philosophical materialists, philosophical idealists assume that, in some sense, the physical world is itself mental. One version of the position that the world is itself mental is that "the physical world exists only as a complex feature of experience; it exists only 'in the minds of' those who do or might experience it" (Robinson, 2009, p. 190). Schopenhauer concurred with Kant in this regard by saying that "[t]he world is my idea." Philosophers such as Leibniz and Hegel proposed a different idealism, which involved the idea that "the physical world itself is a mind, or consists of minds" (Robinson, 2009, p. 190).

Transcendental Idealism: You, a Dance of Mind and Matter

Transcendental idealism does not hold that our ideas are not *empirically* real. Following Kant, Schopenhauer's transcendental[4] argument is rather that "... all *object*, and hence

4 In Kant's theory of knowledge, the term 'transcendental' pertains to the conditions of possibility of knowledge. He thus explored how objects are possible *a priori* and called knowledge *transcendental* if it is not knowledge of objects, but knowledge of how we can possibly know objects before we experience them.

the empirically real in general, is conditioned by the subject in a twofold manner. In the first place, it is conditioned *materially*, or as *object* in general, since an objective existence is conceivable only in the face of a subject and as the idea of this subject." Indeed, as remarked above, we are not the passive recipients of a world – the world does not automatically 'present' itself to us, and we do not 're-present' the world that could exist independently from us. We rather perceive and conceive of the world and everything in it *in our particular way, from a particular perspective,* and *with a particular interest* (Varela, Thompson, & Rosch, 1993). In the words of Hilary Putnam (1981, p. 52),

> 'Objects' do not exist independently of conceptual schemes. *We* cut up the world into objects when we introduce one or another scheme of description. Since objects *and* the signs alike are *internal* to the scheme of description, it is possible to say what matches what.

The second way in which the object is according to Schopenhauer (1958, Vol. II, p. 8; italics in the original text) conditioned by the subject is that:

> . . . the whole of the material world with its bodies in space, extended and, by means of time, having causal relations with one another, and everything attached to this – all this is not something existing *independently* of our mind, but something that has its fundamental presuppositions in our brain-functions, *by means of* which and *in* which alone is such an objective order of things possible. For space, time, and causality, on which all those real and objective events rest, are themselves nothing more than functions of the brain . . .

We are then a dance of mind and matter, an ongoing *pas de deux* of subject and object. Subject and object are intrinsic parts of one whole that only become separated by the intellect, as Schopenhauer put it (1958, Vol. II, p. 17–18). Still, whatever our ideas may be, the will that precedes any cognition is the force that sets and keeps us in motion, both behaviorally and intellectually.

A basic but often overlooked or ignored feature of materialism[5] is that the whole venture hangs on the thin thread of consciousness, as Schopenhauer (1844/1958) realized. Materialism exists in virtue of conscious individuals who engage in the *game* of science (Wittgenstein, 1953). The study of the brain and the understanding of its methods and findings *presupposes* consciousness. Schopenhauer (1958, Vol. II, p. 13) therefore emphasized that "[i]t is just as true that the knower is a product of matter as that matter is a mere idea of the knower; but it is also one-sided. For materialism is the philosophy of the subject who forgets to take account of himself."

5 However, see below for some brief remarks on the intrinsic relationship between some properties of matter and the observer.

The Irreducibility of Consciousness: You Are

A crucial characteristic of consciousness is that it is irreducible to something else, said Francisco Varela (1996; see also Bilodeau, 1996; Bitbol, 2008; Hut & Shepard, 1998; and see below). It is existentially primary (Bitbol, 2008). This is why Schopenhauer described his philosophy as *transcendental* idealism. The irreducibility of consciousness implies that any attempt at accounting for consciousness by way of the law-like network of relations posited by a materialistic or cognitive science that remains limited to the third-person perspective is bound to fail (Bitbol, 2008). Because it is impossible to reduce conscious experience as a whole to structure (i.e., to a networks of relations) – to turn the absolute into something relational – brain features are unable to explain the subjective or private quality of consciousness. Materialism cannot explain why a feeling would *feel* a particular way, and what it is like to be an 'I.' Even the most advanced and fancy picture of brain activity cannot tell whatever the owner of the brain was feeling, perceiving, thinking, or willing – or why. No matter how worthwhile neuroscience, including the neuroscience of trauma, may be, of necessity it remains an incomplete science.

The Intentionality of Consciousness: You Are About Something

Consciousness has a Janus-face. It is not only absolute, it is also about something beyond itself. Being conscious means being conscious *of* something. This intentionality presents another riddle for the materialist, in that matter does not show the 'aboutness' of consciousness in and of itself.

Mind-Brain Correlates and the Problem of Physical Causation of Mind

Furthermore, how should brain studies tell us how consciousness and self-consciousness arise out of matter (e.g., neurons, groups of neurons) if all materialists find and, indeed, *can find* are *correlates* between experience and physical features? There have certainly been advances regarding an understanding of the brain structures and the neurochemicals required for particular states of mind. However, there is ongoing controversy regarding the level of organization (e.g., some subcellular or cellular level, the level of particular neural networks such as the brainstem, the emotional brain or the neocortical reaches) at which that generation happens (Damasio, 1994, 1999; Panksepp & Biven, 2012; Rolls, 1999). But these are the easy problems. With respect to the hard problem of consciousness, no one to date has even the faintest clue how matter would generate qualia, that is, phenomenal consciousness. There is not even an answer to this question if Varela and like-minded authors are right that consciousness is irreducible to anything else.

Autoepistemic Limitation: Deep Inside, You Are a Stranger to Yourself

As the history of philosophy, psychology, psychiatry, and neuroscience shows, including the history of traumatic melancholia and hysteria, it is ever so tempting to regard subjects and objects in isolation of each other, or, more generally, to conceive of the mind, the brain, the body, and the environment as isolated entities. The temptation seems partly due to the fact that our brain does not have a communicable idea of its own states. As a result, we do not have insight into the workings of our brain as a vehicle or apparatus of our mental states, that is, of our mental contents. Insofar as we are conscious of our mental states, we experience our brain states as mental states. We have sensations, emotional feelings, ideas of self (i.e., our 'I,' 'me,' 'myself,' 'mine'), as well as ideas of 'objects,' 'events,' 'other people,' etc., but our brain does not divulge to us *how* it generates these phenomena. We know *that* something is the case, but we do not know *how* we know that. We experience that we have an 'I,' but we have no clue whatsoever where our 'I' comes from. The Ancient Greek aphorism 'Know thyself' sounds wise, but overlooks our principled cognitive limits. Our autoepistemic limitation (McGinn, 1999; Metzinger, 2003; Northoff, 2003; Schopenhauer, 1958; Spinoza, 1677/1996) leads us into believing that our mind, including our 'I,' could exist by itself. This belief is *the myth of the given*, Hurley (1998) said. It seems to us that our sensations, feelings, and 'I' are given, rather than generated by our brain (in intrinsic relation to our body and the environment in which we live; see below).

Knowing that we do not know where our consciousness, our wills and affections stem from, was already described by Chuang Tzu who lived from approximately 369 to 286 BC (Watson, 1968, pp. 37–38):

> Joy, anger, grief, delight, worry, regret, fickleness, inflexibility, modesty, willfulness, candor, insolence – music from empty holes, mushrooms springing up in dampness, day and night replacing each other before us, and no one knows where they sprout from. Let it be! Let it be! [It is enough that] morning and evening we have them, and they are the means by which we live. Without them we would not exist; without us they would have nothing to take hold of. This comes close to the matter. But I do not know what makes them the way they are. It would seem as though they have some True Master, and yet I find no trace of him. He can act – that is certain. Yet I cannot see his form. He has identity but no form.

Schopenhauer (1958, Vol. II, p. 259) similarly held that

> ... insofar as the brain *knows*, it is not *itself* known, but it is the *knower*, the subject of all knowledge ... On the other hand, what knows, what *has that idea*, is the brain; yet this brain does not know itself, but becomes conscious of itself only as the intellect, in other words as *knower* and thus only subjectively.

Because of autoepistemic limitation, it is easy to confuse the question of what *is* (ontology) with the question of what is *known* (epistemology). For example, Descartes (1641) grounded his proposal that matter (extendedness) and mind (thought) constitute different ontological substances on his knowing "I think, therefore I am." Solipsistic subjective idealism, which entails the idea that the human mind involves an independent, internal world, also seems to be grounded in the oversight of autoepistemic limitation. Like philosophical dualism, this type of idealism overlooks that the brain and body are underlying epistemic vehicles for the constitution and generation of mental states (Merleau-Ponty, 1962). Believing that our mind could exist by itself in ontological regard is an epistemic illusion (Northoff, 2003). Hence, subjective idealism and substance dualism seem to be false.

Philosophical materialism is not a viable alternative because our subjectivity precludes us from studying consciousness in psychology and neuroscience – and by implication, trauma – in a pure, 'objective' fashion. All objectivity depends on a conscious individual, just as a subject is only a subject insofar as he or she has an object, and that object is (or in any case includes) matter.

Stuck in a Nasty Dilemma?

To reiterate, the core of the matter (sic) may be that reductive physicalists and identity theorists who focus on the brain more than on the mind overlook or ignore the fact that brain science itself is dependent on experiencing and knowing subjects, that is, on subjectivity; and that the knower remains unknown. It may thus very well be an illusion to think that physical phenomena can fully describe and explain conscious and self-consciousness (e.g., Schopenhauer, 1958, 2007; Varela et al., 1993).

Idealists insist that our intellectual understanding of matter can only be our *human* understanding. We cannot form any conception of how "a mind-independent world might be independently of the categories which are plainly modes of understanding or interpretation, rather than the properties of the world in its own right" (Robinson, 2009, p. 204). Human understanding is of necessity an understanding in terms of space, time, and causality. As Kant detailed in *Critique of Pure Reason* (1781/1998), we can only think in terms of these concepts because this is how we are built. Objective (i.e., subject-independent) knowledge is nonexistent; anything known exists in virtue of a knower. The thing in itself remains hidden, or rather the thought that there is a thing in itself is another human thought.

From an idealistic standpoint regarding mental disorders, whatever physical features these conditions may have, they are to be analyzed in terms of the laws of the mind. However, "overrating the fact that third-person accounts are produced by (communities of) sentient subjects located in a network of natural and social links, usually means indulging in skepticism, relativism, or subjective idealism," as warns the philosopher Michel Bitbol (2002, p. 182).

Are we thus stuck in a dilemma with two problematic horns: materialism and subjective idealism? Or is there a solution? Is there a different way to describe, study, and comprehend human experience, knowledge, and behavior, and by implication is there any different way to address trauma?

Spinoza's Philosophical Monism: You Are One

The idea that mental disorders, and hence trauma, can be deeply understood only in terms of abnormal physical structures and/or functions, or the conjecture that they can only be understood in mental terms may both be misguided. Philosophical monism does not necessitate a physicalistic and mechanistic, *or* idealistic path. To avoid the problems of philosophical materialism/physicalism and philosophical dualism or Descartes' error, as the neurologist Antonio Damasio (1994) called it, one may with Spinoza (1677/1996) metaphysically assume that matter and mind concern different attributes of one substance. In his words (Part II, prop. 7), "... the thinking substance [the mind] and the extended substance [the body] are one and the same substance, which is now comprehended under this attribute [i.e., as mental states], and now under that [i.e., as body, including brain states]." This singularly existing substance, Spinoza stated in his *Ethics*, can be referred to as God or Nature[6]. He believed that Nature has many other attributes, but that these may remain beyond human understanding, presently or absolutely. In this light it is interesting to know that attempts to integrate quantum mechanics and relativity theory, to develop a "theory of everything," have led mathematical physicists to design theories that encompass up to eleven different dimensions (i.e., M-theory, string theories; Greene, 1999, 2004), far more than the three spatial dimensions and the dimension of time that we experience and know.

Spinoza's monism fosters the integrative study of the mental, the brain, and the rest of the human body, existing in historical and personal time, and embedded in an outer world. These components are intrinsically related phenomena, not each other's causes. Individuals and their environment, thus subject and object, cannot be isolated from each other *in principle.* The world as we know it, is dependent on us. Without us as experiencing and knowing individuals, that world would not exist: An object only exists in someone's consciousness. But it is also true that without objects, no subject could exist. There can be no subject without an object, "no knower without something different from this that is known" (Schopenhauer, 1958, Vol. II, p. 202). Subject (mind) and object (matter) are ontologically co-constitutive (i.e., the one cannot exist without the other, the one constitutes the other) and functionally co-dependent (i.e., the one cannot function without the other).

6 Spinoza realized that the *Ethics* would not be acceptable to the clergy of his time. It might even cost him his life. For example, he identified God and Nature, and denied an Act of Creation. In fact, Spinoza thought along evolutionary lines and can be considered as a predecessor of Darwin. He rejected the idea that God was or could be interested in the concerns and fate of individual beings. In his view, God was not a third substance, as Descartes had it. Excommunicated by the Jewish community and Church from 1656, and given the Church's banning of his anonymously published *Theologico-Political Treatise* (1670), Spinoza concealed his magnum opus in his writing desk until his dying day in 1677. Immediately after the *Ethics* was published, the book was denounced as atheistic. Although it remained banned for two centuries, it nevertheless became influential. It is now seen as a classic of modern philosophy.

If Spinoza was right, there may be a way out of the lopsidedness of materialism in which the knower has vanished from consideration, as well as an escape from the asymmetry of subjective idealism in which the object, a real world disappears, as if life were a mere dream. The question might also be framed like this: Might it be possible to *connect* and *coordinate* the first-person, quasi-second-person, second-person, and third-person perspective?

A good start to this endeavor is the realization that "the human mind does not know the human body itself, nor does it know that the body exists, except through the ideas of affections by which the body is affected" (Spinoza, 1996, Part II, propositions 19–29). Consciousness starts with sensing, and subsequently perceiving and conceiving of the living body when the body is affected by some cause. Cognition is grounded in experience; cognition does not cause experience (Schopenhauer would agree: The will becomes a motive for the intellect; the will precedes the intellect). As Spinoza continues in proposition 26, objects ("external bodies") appear for us when they affect our body, and when we, as a whole organism, notice that affection:

> The human mind does not perceive any external body as actually existing, except through the ideas of the affections of its own body. Demonstration: If the human body is not affected by an external body in any way, then the idea of the human body, that is the human mind, is also not affected in any way by the idea of the existence of that body, in other words, it does not perceive the existence of that external body in any way.

Consciousness thus begins with ideas of affections of the body. In this conscious awareness, the subject (i.e., the conscious organism) and the object (i.e., the thing that the subject perceives) become linked but also differentiated ("I am not the thing that affects me"). Bridging the first-person and third-person perspective may take the second-person perspective. There is no substitute for individuals working together, for the realization that you are because of other 'you's:'

> To man ... there is nothing more useful than man. Man, I say, can wish for nothing more helpful to the preservation of his being than that all should so agree in all things that the minds and bodies of all should compose, as it were, one mind and one body; that all should strive together, as far as they can, to preserve their being, and that all, together, should seek for themselves the common advantage to all. [Spinoza, 1677/1996, p. 125–126]

Interpersonal traumatization, of course, is the utter antonym of these words of wisdom.

Phenomenology: You Live

In consonance with Schopenhauer, phenomenologists such as Husserl point out that *the third-person perspective presupposes the first-person perspective*, and that materialists overlook or ignore this important fact. In this spirit, and as remarked before, Varela (1996, p. 334) holds that "[t]he phenomenological approach starts from the irreducible nature of conscious experience. Lived experience is where we start from and where all must link back to, like a guiding thread." Bitbol (2002) is not any less clear. Like Schopenhauer before him, and with reference to Husserl (1970), he argues (2008, p. 56) that scientists who believe in and look for objectively existing invariants in nature tend to forget themselves in the act:

> Now, the problem is that the very success of this procedure of extracting invariants yields a sort of amnesia. The creators of objective knowledge become so impressed by its efficacy that they tend to forget or to minimize that conscious experience is its starting point and its permanent requirement. They tend to forget or to minimize the long historical process by which contents of experience have been carefully selected, differentiated, and impoverished, so as to discard their personal or parochial components and to distillate their universal fraction as a structure. They finally turn the whole procedure upside down, by claiming that experience can be explained by one of its structural residues. Husserl severely criticized this forgetfulness and this inversion of priorities, that he saw as the major cause of what he called the "crisis" of modern science (Husserl, 1970). According to him, it is in principle absurd to think that one can account for subjective conscious experience by way of certain objects of science, since objectivity has sprung precisely from what he calls the 'life-world' of conscious experience.

As Husserl wrote in his uncompleted last book (Husserl, 1970, p. 265),

> The idea of an ontology of the world, the idea of an objective universal science of the world, having behind it a universal a priori according to which every possible world is knowable *more geometrico*[7] ... is nonsense.... Nature can be thought as a definite manifold, and we can take this idea as a basis hypothetically. But insofar as the world is a world of knowledge, a world of consciousness, a world with human beings, such an idea is absurd for it to an unsurpassable degree.

He and other phenomenologists thus set out to examine the first-person perspective, not by distancing oneself from experience, as introspectionism prescribed, but by promoting intimacy with lived experience.

Neurophenomenology: Finding You in a Dance of Subject and Object

According to Varela, the dilemma of materialism and subjective idealism can be overcome, albeit not by finding a "theoretical fix or extra ingredient nature" (1996, p. 41) to account for how consciousness emerges from matter and brain, but by finding meaningful bridges between mind and matter as two irreducible phenomenal domains. In the words of Bitbol (2002, p. 221):

> His [i.e., Varela's] specific suggestion consisted in complementing the set of standard practices of science with disciplined attention, and connecting the first-person outcome of this attention with neurobiological invariants. Such sophisticated practices clearly have a disclosing aptitude

7 Geometrical proof.

> (through their phenomenological "descriptive" component), but they also focus on shaping experience (1) by the phenomenological "reduction" they rely on, and (2) by the neurophenomenological feedback loop they institute. Far from generating objectivist shortsightedness, the motto "just develop the scientific inquiry" here partakes of a larger project in which subjectivity is recognized both as an ubiquitous background and a dialectical partner.

As Bitbol (2008) emphasizes, there is every reason to return to where we come from, to the most primitive 'given,' to the 'world as I found it' (Bitbol, 2008; Wittgenstein, 1953). This world is neither an external universe nor a purely internal world. It an inextricably united experience-of-a-world. It is out of this world that the poles of the duality of subject and object are differentiated (Petitmengin, 2007). Varela (1996, p. 41) thus wrote:

> I take lived, first-hand experience as a proper *field of phenomena*, irreducible to anything else. ... no theoretical fix or 'extra' ingredient in nature ... can possibly bridge this gap [between first-hand experience and third-person perspectives on experience]. Instead, this field of phenomena requires a proper, rigorous method and pragmatics for its exploration and analysis. The orientation for such method is inspired from the style of inquiry of phenomenology in order to constitute a widening research community and a research programme. This research programme seeks articulations by mutual constraints between the field of phenomena revealed by experience and the correlative field of phenomena established by the cognitive sciences. I have called this point of view *neurophenomenology*.

The neurophenomenological method is not an attempt to absorb contents of experience or phenomenological reports into the structural and relational network of objective science (Bitbol, 2008). Neurophenomenologists neither eliminate nor reduce these contents and reports, nor do they state that the mind and the brain are identical. Their aim rather is to embed phenomenal experiences within a broader relational network of which the law-like structure of the objective domain is only a small part. In this embedment science and experience constrain and modify each other as in a *dance*.

Whereas experience is of necessity someone's experience, it is not private. Individuals are not solipsistic creatures thrown in a pregiven, subject-independent world. As phenomenologists realize, human experience is rooted in a phenomenal corporeal and social world (Varela, 1996). Consciousness is about the body and other embodied minds. In this sense, the brain can be seen as an organ for relationships (Fuchs, 2010).

The Trinity of the Brain, the Body, and the Environment: You Are Embrained, Embodied, and Embedded

A living brain cannot and does not exist in isolation from a living body and an environment, a living body cannot and does not exist in isolation from a living brain and an environment, and an environment only exists for a living brain/body because there is no observer-independent environment. As Northoff (2003) suggests, there exist *intrinsic re-*

lationships between the brain, the body, and the environment in ontological regard. He refers to the intrinsic relationship between brain and body as embodiment, whereas the terms embeddedness or embedment capture the existence of the intrinsic relationship between brain/body and environment. Embodiment means that the brain is intrinsically integrated within the body (e.g., Gallagher, 2005; Lakoff & Johnson, 1999; Varela et al., 1993).

Embodiment

Enactivism is the view that consciousness and cognition are phenomena that emerge through our recurrent patterns of world-engaged perception and (motor) action (Fuchs & DeJaeger, 2010; Krueger, 2010; Thompson, 2007). In this perspective, thinking is grounded in, but does not cause, motor action (as cognitivists claim). Rather, cognitive acts and structures – including the cognitive capacities at the root of our social interactions – are grounded in ongoing embodied patterns of environmental interaction. When individuals interact, they enact a world of meaning, they make sense together by coordinating their movements. For example, they attune to each other and often repair misattunement. They may imitate each other and resonate, just as they can engage in rhythmic covariation of gestures, facial or vocal expressions, tone of voice, direction of gaze (Fuchs & DeJaeger, 2010; Merleau-Ponty, 1945). Going in and out of synchrony, they make meaning together.

Our sensorimotor experiences are, thus, the ancestors of our ideas, that is, of our perceptions and conceptions: Spinoza's unfathomable insight. These bodily experiences and physical movement are through and through affect laden, they are fully will, and constitute the root of our ideas: Spinoza's brilliant view and Schopenhauer's no less profound understanding. And Wittgenstein (1953, p. 178) concluded: "The human body is the best picture of the human soul."

Our embodiment is also crucial with respect to the symbols we have developed as a species, that is, to our language (Wittgenstein, 1953). As Järvilehto's (2004, #15) concedes,

> Those parts of the universe which became objects of language were primarily those that were needed by the human being in the framework of the structure of the body. Therefore, the perceived (conscious) structure of the world reflects more the structure of the human body, as far as it may form a system with specific parts of the world, than any independent structure of the world. The implicate order of the universe (cf. Bohm, 1980) is the implicate order of the human body as a constituent of an organism-environment system.

Lakoff and Johnson (1999) similarly postulated that our words are largely shaped by our bodily experiences and body features (see also next chapter). Our language is closely grounded in and connected with our body as well as with the limitations of human understanding.

Embedment

The brain/body unity is intrinsically integrated, that is, it is embedded within the environment. Whereas there exists only an environment – objects, events – because there is an experiencing and knowing embodied and embrained individual, the brain, as the necessary vehicle for mental contents[8], is also dependent on the environment with respect to these contents.

We evolve in a world, but how that world is depends on us. How we come to understand the things of that world, others, and ourselves is determined by our will as well as how we grasp and respond to that will. As anyone knows, babies and young children desire to drink and sleep, seek to evade physical pain, and most of all have an urge to be safe with and seen by others. In the words of Krueger (2010, pp. 66–70),

> ... fundamental *affective* structures ... scaffold basic forms of social understanding, support the emergence of sensorimotor skills enabling this basic understanding, and ... motivate our most fundamental sense of self. [Hence,] ... why not speak of our earliest intersubjective engagements as involving a kind of affect-laden, but nonconceptual (i.e., nonrepresentational) understanding? ... even our earliest interactions are bathed in feeling – that is, exquisitely tuned *feeling-relations* that attune us to others in fundamental ways, and which provide the inter-corporeal scaffolding both supporting and motivating the growth of our capacities and competencies for social engagement, as well as the development of our sense of self.

Based on Tronick, Als, Adamson, Wise, and Brazelton's (1998) exceptionally important studies of early mother-child interactions, Krueger (2010, p. 70) concludes, that "... the self arises within a sympathetic context of *sharing*, that is, an affective ethos of bodily relatedness that confers phenomenally new (i.e., enriched) experiences of the world-as-shared" (see also Lees-Grossman, 2010). How children feel and think about themselves depends largely on how they are received, how they are treated and seen by their caretakers, the ones to whom they desire and need to attach, the ones with whom they interact. The straightforward implication is that when this interaction is badly and recurrently hurting, children will develop very different ideas of themselves, other individuals, and things than when they are welcomed, loved, and inspired to thrive. Understanding and

8 The idea that advanced mental contents such as differentiated thoughts crucially depend on an intact and functioning neocortex is challenged by analyses of personal and other individuals' near-death experiences (Alexander, 2012). Neurosurgeon Eben Alexander's personal near-death experience was caused by a rare and severe form of bacterial (*Escherichia coli*) meningitis. Having survived a week of coma, he reported experiences during the time of his coma that neither involved a common sense of self, nor a sense of time and space. These and similar reports could indicate that some form of consciousness involving perceptions, feelings, and thoughts might not dependent on a functional neocortex. Alexander suggested that the implications of these reports for an understanding of consciousness and the function of the human brain could be far-reaching. For example, the brain may not generate consciousness but could be some sort of receiver. Who knows? The matter will not be further considered here.

assisting individuals who have been neglected, maltreated, and abused by others thus requires a meticulous analysis of the patterns of physical and affective exchanges among the victim, the perpetrator(s), and other insiders – of their joint sense-making.

Because environment and brain are necessary conditions for each other, they are bilaterally dependent (Northoff, 2003). They also determine each other, which also applies to the relationship between the body and the environment. Individuals as whole organisms adapt to their environment and can creatively change this environment by selecting particular actions to achieve their actual goals. Indeed, not even bacteria leave the world as they found it (Laland & Brown, 2006). Organisms in part create their niches. They affect their ecosystems and their evolutionary path. Organisms and environments are inseparable partners. Organisms adapt to and alter their environments, and altered environments select organisms. In this context, individuals at the brain level select particular dynamic patterns, and at the brain/body level they engage in particular patterns of motor actions that match and mold the environment.

Conversely, the particular environment in which an individual is embedded influences the dynamic brain states and motor actions that will be selected (Northoff, 2003). For example, the smell of food activates our action system of energy management when we have an appetite. Threat to physical integrity awakens the action system of defense, so that we startle, freeze, flee, fight, or play dead. However, what smells foster eating and what conditions present a 'threat' is species-specific. Homo sapiens despises particular smells that signal a copious meal for particular insects, but does not flee from birds that have insects for dinner.

The idea of embedment sharply contrasts with the understanding of the brain, the body, and the environment as isolated, albeit correlated or interacting, phenomena. The ideas that an environment and events as changes in the environment can exist separately from an experiencing and knowing individual are examples of such isolation. Embedment is incompatible with the idea that the brain, the body, and the environment can be understood in terms of ontological properties. For example, it suggests that the brain cannot be understood in terms of properties that exist in isolation of the person's body and his or her material and social environment. The domain of ontology consists in *ontological relations.*

The point is that the brain, the body, and the environment not just continuously influence and change each other, but that they mutually constitute and determine each other and are bilaterally dependent. Co-occurrent, co-constitutive, and co-dependent, they are intrinsically coupled (Van Gelder, 1995), and this coupling is dynamic, selective, adaptive, and creative. As Järvilehto (2004, #6) put it,

> [s]ubjectivity, thus, is not an "inner" property of the organism, but rather a point of view, a perspective, or a description of the asymmetry of the organism-environment system in action. Also, this means that subjective experience is not in the idealistic or solipsistic sense absolutely subjective, but it can be studied and, to some extent, shared by other people. Thus, in this framework the subject-object dichotomy, for example, is abolished, because the subject and the object are aspects of the same system. The subject is the system in action, and the object is the result of this action.

In sum, what exist are *dynamic configurations of the brain, the body, and the environment.* These intrinsic configurations are self-organized, ever-changing, and flexible forms of selective-adaptive coupling between the brain, the body, and the environment (Thompson, 2007; Varela, 1996; Von Uexküll, 1994). An organism and its environment are not interacting but otherwise independent systems, but rather are *intrinsically and dynamically related.* Formulating his theory of the organism-environment system, Järvilehto (1998, p. 321) summarized this fundamental insight as follows:

> The theory of the organism-environment system starts with the proposition that in any functional sense organism and environment are inseparable and form only one unitary system. The organism cannot exist without the environment and the environment has descriptive properties only if it is connected to the organism. Although for practical purposes we do separate organism and environment, this common-sense starting point leads in psychological theory to problems which cannot be solved. Therefore, separation of organism and environment cannot be the basis of any scientific explanation of human behavior. The theory leads to a reinterpretation of basic problems in many fields of inquiry and makes possible the definition of mental phenomena without their reduction either to neural or biological activity or to separate mental functions. According to the theory, mental activity is activity of the whole organism-environment system, and the traditional psychological concepts describe only different aspects of organisation of this system. Therefore, mental activity cannot be separated from the nervous system, but the nervous system is only one part of the organism – environment system.

The intrinsic relationships between the embrained, embodied, and embedded individual as a whole biopsychosocial organism are also characterized by this system's biological, psychological, and social phylogenetic and ontogenetic history. For example, current brain-body-environment relationships will be influenced by prior and anticipated experiences, past social relations, and the individual's developmental biopsychosocial phase.

In sum, an individual organism and his or her environment do not reciprocally interact, but constitute a phylogenetically and ontogenetically evolved organism-environment system. Conceptualizing, defining, studying, and treating trauma, particularly interpersonal trauma, must therefore be done at the level of *this* system.

Scientific and Clinical Dancing with the Traumatized

Whatever else the past and evolving history of professional interest and evaluation of childhood and other kinds of traumatization may show, it reveals the involvement of subjectivity, selectivity, and politics in the 'objective and scientific' third-person perspective. Contrary to the portrayal of science as an 'objective' endeavor, scientists are not detached observers who gather empirical data and check these findings against falsifiable hypotheses derived from a theory (Depraz et al., 2002; Lakoff & Johnson, 1999; Varela, 1996). The reality of science is very different in that subjective judgment is not at all a stranger to this domain: Scientists are all too human, their subjectivity – and social mediation more generally – are an inherent part of science (Depraz et al., 2002). The third-person perspective involves first persons living in a world of second-person relationships. They are anything but impersonal machines. Their subjectivity and social mediation, among others, have manifested and continue to manifest in the problems of recognition, acknowledgment, and understanding of mentally injurious events, in the subjectivity of clinicians,' scientists,' and society's understanding and appreciation of events that can cause or contribute to an individual's psychopathology, as well as in the particular difficulty to realize the extent and impact of chronic childhood traumatization.

Enactive Trauma Science

The lessons of history can be cast in terms of several recommendations for a future science of trauma. A major lesson from philosophy is that the derivates of traumatic melancholia and hysteria should not be studied from an exclusive or predominant third-person perspective. It should be recognized and realized more that physical judgments in the third-person perspective depend on the first-person, quasi-second-person, and second-person perspectives. The third-person perspective must therefore be complemented and guided by the meticulous inclusion of, and an empathic attunement to, the patients' and scientists' own first-person, quasi-second-person, and second-person perspectives. For example, to comprehend what a particular pattern of neural activity means, scientists need to know and appreciate what the subject was willing, feeling, and thinking during and around the actual measurements. This understanding is to be grounded in a combined third-person perspective clinical or experimental observation, intimate self-observation (the studied individual), and dialogue between the participating parties (cf. Engel, 1997). The realization of this methodological stance among other things fosters a rethinking of the method of groupwise comparisons, in which important potential differences within individuals over time are missed and differences between individuals are 'partialed out' – and hence may remain undetected. Time-series studies of individual cases may constitute an alternative or supplementary methodology to capture this changeability over time (Schubert, 2011).

One obvious difficulty lies in assessing the first-person, quasi-second-person, and second-person perspectives of both the patients and the scientists, i.e., the ways in which they perceive and conceive of themselves and of their world – of which they are a part – as adequately as possible. A minimal, elementary form of intersubjective consent will not do. The criteria of intersubjective understanding rather must be amplified to refine the stability and sharpness of subjective experience (Bitbol, 2008). Given traumatized individuals' mental disorder, the perspectives involved may not be sufficiently available to them, as in fact is also the case with many mentally healthy individuals. Not many people are naturally born mentalizers, and adverse life events may have compromised the ability to mentalize. Varela (1996) therefore recommended that subjects be trained to become more intimate with their own perspectives. Individuals can achieve this aim in meditation

(Lutz, Greishar, Rawlings, Ricard, & Davidson, 2004; Wallace, 2000) or in dialogue with second persons (Depraz, Varela, & Vermersch, 2003; Petitmengin, 2007). Since traumatized individuals particularly learn to become more intimate with themselves in trauma-focused psychotherapy, it is important to include the patient's therapist in the scientific exploration of trauma and dissociation (be it neuroscientific or otherwise). To speak with Spinoza (1677/1996, p. 155, italics in original),

> [a]ll our strivings, *or* desires, follow from the necessity of our nature in such a way that they can be understood either through it alone, as through their proximate cause, or insofar as we are a part of Nature, which cannot be conceived adequately through itself without other individuals.

An obvious prerequisite is that the patient feels deeply understood by the therapist. If this approach is to work, the patient should not follow the therapist's ideas. Rather, the aim is for the therapist to assist the patient in becoming maximally intimate with his or her own experiences prior to and during the scientific measurements. To this end, patients who have survived their horrific social environment by adapting themselves to the actual or subjectively presumed demands of perpetrators and their accomplices must be trained to become more faithful to their own desires. Bitbol (2008) suggests that a combination of first- and third-person modes by biofeedback may also expand the basis of possible intersubjective consensus beyond recognition.

The existence of different (prototypes of) dissociative parts of the personality constitutes a major complication of this work. Whereas these parts belong to one organism, it is also true that they engage in their own set of person-perspectives as well as the associated behavioral, physiological, and neural characteristics. Research of these disorders must thus examine these different dissociative subsystems and their dynamic relationships with each other. For example, some dissociative parts may have a lack of abnormal heart rate reactions to trauma reminders (i.e., neither hyperreactivity nor hyporeactivity), some may become hyperaroused, and still other parts may become hypoaroused. To know if a lack of arousal is associated with, say, an ANP, a controlling EP, or a fragile EP engaging in playing dead, the researcher must be thoroughly aware of the type of dissociative part of concern and his or her phenomenal and behavioral characteristics. To understand the part, the researcher needs to become particularly acquainted with this part's will, affects, thoughts, and behaviors.

One technical problem lies in the difficulty in activating these different parts in a controlled setting. It must also be realized that the ecological validity of controlled settings in experimental research cannot be taken for granted. Common life may be very different from lab life. This implies that the ecological validity of the experimental research needs to be *demonstrated.* Researchers may alternatively choose a setting that matches common life circumstances more. For example, they may aim to measure biopsychosocial changes of interest while the patient engages in common life.

Another concern is that scientists must examine, recognize, acknowledge, and integrate their own first-person, quasi-second-person, and second-person perspectives. The historical excursions in the first chapters of this book illustrated how common it is that the researchers' own beliefs, biases, and personal and professional interests interfere with the ideal of 'objective, impartial' research. There is little reason to trust that this standard is currently realized better than in times past. Engaging in the science of human experience and behavior thus becomes an inclusive and integrated act that is as demanding as it is necessary. Philosophy and history teach us that ignoring or excluding these various phenomenal experiences and phenomenal judgments does not provide an 'objective' view of the world and its inhabitants. The scientific challenge is thus to recognize, acknowledge, coordinate, and integrate the patients' and the scientists' own person perspectives.

This task becomes even more complex when the patient's personality includes more than one set of person-perspectives. This situation arises, for example, when the injury that adverse life has brought is a division of patient's personality. Researchers always need to examine themselves whether they are willing to accept that an individual's personality can become divided in two or more conscious and self-conscious subsystems. Currently, few scientists seem to realize this can be the case. This situation has certainly compromised the understanding and appreciation of this dissociation to date: As mentioned before, research into dissociative disorders is extremely unpopular.

However, the history of science demonstrates that the *a priori* assumptions of scientists regarding what can and cannot be the case have frequently been overruled by later findings. As the French philosopher Gaston Bachelard (1884–1962) put it, "the characteristic of scientific progress is our knowing that we did not know." One task of epistemology, he felt, is to find and examine scientists' mental patterns that entail obstacles to knowledge. Epistemological obstacles to research of dissociative disorders are as common as fierce.

Struggling with a Professional Dissociation

The conceptual and classificatory separation of traumatic melancholia and hysteria extends to this day. It also includes a kind of dissociation with regards to professional societies, journals, and conferences. The core interest of the International and the European Society of Traumatic Stress Studies (ISTSS, ESTSS) is ASD and PTSD. These societies are not concerned much with the dissociative disorders, the core business of International Society for the Study of Trauma and Dissociation (ISST-D) and the European Society of Trauma and Dissociation (ESTD). The ISTSS and ESTSS are associated with the *Journal of Traumatic Stress* and the *European Journal of Psychotraumatology*, respectively. The ISST-D has intimate ties with the *Journal of Trauma and Dissociation*. Focusing on the study of ASD and PTSD, the ISTSS and ESTSS can, broadly speaking, be seen as lending weight to the 'traumatic melancholia-line,' whereas the ISST-D and ESTD emphasize the study of dissociative disorders (DSM-5/ICD-10), thus representing the '(traumatic) hysteria-line.'

To the extent that the supporters of the classification of ASD and PTSD as a trauma and stress-related disorder in DSM-5 address dissociative symptoms, they tend to disregard or dispute positive dissociative symptoms. For them, dissociation basically pertains to negative symptoms such as absent-mindedness, depersonalization, and derealization. As discussed above, these phenomena involve alterations in consciousness that may but need not relate to a division of personality. Lanius et al.'s (2010, 2012) dissociative subtype of PTSD may have the political asset that clinicians and scientists who specialize in ASD and PTSD become more acquainted with the theme of dissociation. However, it remains to be seen whether that development will at some point include the acceptance and understanding of positive dissociative symptoms and, more generally, of dissociation as a division of the personality involving negative and positive dissociative symptoms that can be of cognitive-emotional or sensorimotor type.

Enactive Trauma Therapy

In my view, what goes for science, goes for clinical practice as well. As detailed in the third part of the current trilogy, psychotherapy best involves the therapist's effort to attune to the patient's first-person, quasi-second-person, second person, and, if applicable, third-person perspective, in order to grasp and share the patient's will-guided lived experience and ideas. This work also takes clinicians' ongoing appreciation of their own person perspectives and includes a recognition, acknowledgment, and navigation of their 'countertransferential' reactions to the patient. If successful, this attunement, grasping, sharing, and coping generates a solid working relationship, a consensual mutual second-person perspective that opens the door to therapeutic stimulation, to helping the patient move toward change: "Nothing can agree more with the nature of any thing than other individuals of the same species" (Spinoza, 1677/1996, p. 156). The steps indicated are not linear but constitute ongoing and recurrent advances in a helix to healing. This project is more than, and different from, friendship, because it is connected and coordinated with the therapist's multiple person-perspectives that include, apart from his or her other person-perspectives, his or her third-person perspective on psychopathology and psychotherapy. The treatment of dissociative disorders is clearly complicated by the interest of attuning to, grasping, sharing, and changing the lived experience of each dissociative part, with their will as a central concern. This demanding work is not a goal in itself, but constitutes a prerequisite on the way to the (re)integration and coordination of the patient's whole personality. I call the whole enterprise 'therapeutic dancing with the patient.'

Conclusion

Blind to his own mobility, the Duke of Mantua in Verdi's Rigoletto broadcasts that women are fickle. Traumatized individuals are inconstant and divided in certain regards, but so is the historical and contemporary professional and societal appreciation, understanding and treatment of those who have become injured by adverse life. The conceptualization and classification of traumatic melancholia and hysteria as well as the philosophical assumptions regarding the nature of these disorders have continuously and profoundly shifted, and will continue to shift over time. This inconstancy, that also pertains to the very concepts of trauma and dissociation, has been and will be significantly affected by the subjectivity of the alleged "objective" third-person stance. Just as the Duke would also better take a good look in the mirror, clinicians and scientists would better face this reality.

In the awareness of this subjectivity and temporality, and in the interest of developing maximally clear and specific conceptualizations, the next three chapters (9–11) address the concept of 'trauma.' Chapter 12, the opening chapter of Volume II, addresses consciousness and self-consciousness in dissociative disorders. This work will support the definition of dissociation in trauma in Chapter 13.

Chapter 9

The Concept of Trauma and Derivate Concepts: Symbols and Meaning

Where can I find a man who has forgotten words so I can have a word with him?
Chuang Tzu

Mephistopheles: *On the whole, to words stick fast!*
Through the safest gate you'll pass
To the Temple of Certainty.
Student: *Yet surely words must have a sense.*
Mephistopheles: *Why, yes! But don't torment yourself with worry,*
Where sense fails it's only necessary
To supply a word, and change the tense.
With words fine arguments can be weighted,
With words whole Systems can be created,
With words, the mind does its conceiving,
No word suffers a jot from thieving.
Johann Wolfgang von Goethe, *Faust*[1]

Sequence

First there was sitting
and then there was chair,
in that sequence of language.
As simple as that.
Jan Glas (2012, p. 175)

1 The original German text is in some regards more powerful. **Schüler:** *Doch ein Begriff muß bey dem Worte seyn.* **Mephistopheles:** *Schon gut! Nur muß man sich nicht allzu ängstlich quälen; Denn eben wo Begriffe fehlen, Da stellt ein Wort zur rechten Zeit sich ein. Mit Worten läßt sich trefflich streiten, Mit Worten ein System bereiten, An Worte läßt sich trefflich glauben, Von einem Wort läßt sich kein Jota rauben.*

There is a lack of clarity regarding the concept of 'trauma' and the derivative concepts of traumatic experiences, traumatic events, traumatizing memories, and traumatizing events. These terms are used in a confusing variety of ways in both the clinical and scientific literature and discourse, and indeed they often remain undefined. To be useful, however, clinical and scientific concepts need a clear definition and sufficient constraints. As Schopenhauer (2007, p. 1) reminded us

> [t]he divine Plato and the marvellous Kant unite their mighty voices in recommending a rule, to serve as the method of all philosophizing as well as of all other science. Two laws, they tell us: The law of *homogeneity*, and the law of *specification*, should be equally observed, neither to the disadvantage of the other. The law of *homogeneity* directs us to collect things together into kind, by observing their resemblances and correspondences, to collect kinds again into species, species into genera, and so on, till at last we come to the highest all-comprehensive conception. [...] the law of *specification* [...] requires [...] that we should clearly distinguish one from another the different genera collected under one comprehensive conception.

But what principle, what criterion defines what "things" do and do not belong together? What constraints shall be used? According to Lakoff and Johnson (1999, p. 553), it has been and still is often assumed that there exists "the objective world." The "objective world," it is believed, "has a unique category structure independent of the minds, bodies, or brains of human beings" and includes "universal reason that characterizes the rational structure of the world." The universal reason would use "universal concepts that characterize the objective categories of the world." These concepts and this "universal reason" exist "independent of the minds, bodies, and brains of human beings." According to this view of the world, a persuasion known as philosophical realism, human reason is the capacity of the human mind to use some portion of universal reason and the instrument that allows this use is the human brain. Since a human body other than the brain as a part of the whole body would not be required, human reason is disembodied.

This view of the world and human beings as a part of that world is probably false, as I discussed shortly in the previous chapters. In the current context, it is important to realize that Wittgenstein (1953) abandoned the idea of the existence of given, natural categories. The world can be parsed in millions of ways, none of which is *a priori* better than the others. He thus replaced the classic idea of natural categories by the insight that any distinction and categorization is man-made *according to some (necessarily human) point of view, principle, or interest*, hence artificial. For example, we may categorize phenomena that, in our human view and only in that perspective, belong to a particular 'family' or think in terms of 'prototypes' (Rosch, 1977). Lakoff and Johnson (1980) proposed that we create general cognitive structures that are intimately related to our embodiment. We thus have kinesthetic image schemas that stem from bodily experiences, such as the 'container' schema (as in the mind as container), the 'part-whole' schema (as in dissociative parts of the personality as a whole system), and the 'source-path-goal' schema (as in will-action-goal fulfillment). There are no pregiven categories but categorization is certainly an important and fundamental cognitive activity. Creating well-defined and well-constrained clinical and scientific concepts that allow for homogeneous as well as specific categorization according to a particular point of view, principle, or interest remains important as ever.

The objective of this chapter and the next is to gain clarity regarding the concept of 'trauma' and its derivates, and to define them on this basis while seeking to apply the laws of homogeneity and specification. To this end, I extend the discussion of some philosophical issues that were introduced before. In the current and next chapter, questions that are raised and considered include

- 'Is trauma an event or a feature of an individual?'
- 'What is an event?'
- 'Is there a causal relationship between an event- and trauma-related pathology?
- 'In what way are events and pathology experienced and known?

Chapter 11 offers distinctions between and definitions of the concepts of trauma, traumatic experience, traumatic event, traumatic memory, as well as potentially traumatizing and actually traumatizing events.

Icons, Indexes, and Symbols

Considering that clinical and scientific terms are experiences and ideas cast in words, it may be helpful to start the present chapter with a look at what, according to biological anthropologist Terrence Deacon (1997, p. 21), constitutes a crucial difference between human beings and other species on the planet: our unparalleled cognitive ability, our ability to use symbols. He wrote:

> We think differently from all other creatures on earth, and we can share those thoughts with one another in ways that no other species even approaches. In comparison, the rest of our biology is almost incidental. Hundreds of millions of years of evolution have produced hundreds of thousands of species with brains, and tens of thousands with complex behavioral, perceptual, and learning abilities. Only one of these has ever wondered about its place in the world, because only one evolved the ability to do so.

Figure 9.1 captures the basic idea.

Language

Apart from the will and environment we share with other creatures, we generate a world of symbols, a linguistic domain "full of abstractions, impossibilities, and paradoxes" (Deacon, 1997, p. 22). We can make up and think about what is not here, what may never be, or what has never been. We imagine experiences, tell ourselves and each other stories

Figure 9.1. The differentiation of will.

about our present, past, and future, and are influenced by them. This socially shared, virtual world is intimately related to human language, to a world perceived, conceived, and cast in words by us and for our purposes.

We are a symbolic species[2]. Words, woven in strings that make sense to us, are symbols that refer to real or imaginary objects, events, and relationships. The advantages of this evolutionary invention are huge. With its help, we can not just efficiently communicate, but free ourselves from the tangible; we develop new horizons, grasp and modulate what is and has been, and can, at least in principle, better predict what will happen. Our capacity for symbolic reference allows us to look at things in a different light, make meaning, construct theories, regulate our affects and those of others, guide our and other individuals' ongoing actions and plan new ones. Because of this palette of functions language has an important place in trauma and trauma therapy.

Symbol and Meaning

Human language and many symbols more generally are also tricky. Words are signs or symbols that refer to something beyond themselves. That is, their referents are not intrinsic to them. For example, there is nothing in the word 'trauma' that is intrinsically related to the referent of this written or spoken word. The user must link words or other symbols

2 Some apes have, usually following many learning trials, learned to grasp some simple symbolic referents (e.g., Deacon, 1997; Savage-Rumbaugh & Lewin, 1994; Tomasello, 1999).

and their referents, and use this link in a particular way (Heil, 2011), just as the receiver must interpret what words as symbolic referents stand for and what they mean in a particular context. Our models of the world must be *made* to represent (Braude, 2006). Because representations are not given, and because no one does the representing for us, *we* are the ones who must create a link between what we take to be a representation and what it in our view represents. Meaning, thus, commonly takes four 'players': The individual who uses symbols in a certain way, the individual who interprets these symbols, the symbols themselves (e.g., words), and their referents.

In the view of representationalism, the philosophical doctrine that underlies much of contemporary psychology, our mind involves representations (*representanda*) of 'things' that exist in the 'objective world' and of relations between the different things that we represent (*representata*). The words and sentences we can have in our minds – more generally, our thoughts, our perceptions and memories, including memories of traumatic experiences, and our concepts – all would be mental representations of something else, and that something is a part of some presumed 'objective reality.' Representing would be possible because there are classical, given categories as well as singly necessary and jointly sufficient conditions for category membership. There would be 'universal reason.' However, as mentioned above, there are in fact no natural (i.e., given) categories and essences such as 'game,' 'redness,' 'chair,' or 'traumatizing event' (Wittgenstein, 1953). We know foremost thanks to Darwin's theory of evolution that Plato's eternal ideas – given categories such as the idea of man as a species – do not exist. This means that perception and reason cannot be guided or governed by eternally existing, objective ideas (e.g., Edelman, 1992), that there are no fixed and determinate relationships between representations and whatever it is that representations actually represent. This constitutes a grave problem for representationalism, and several other most serious concerns have been raised against this philosophical perspective as well (Braude, 1997, 2002, 2006; Bursen, 1978; Edelman, 1992; Malcolm, 1977; Putnam, 1988). Some of these will be addressed later.

The categories we use such as 'red,' 'chair,' or 'traumatizing event' are often enough fuzzy in that their boundaries are uncertain. Some items impress (some of) us as being 'more red' than other items, and we cannot draw a sharp line between items that are, say, more red than orange or more orange than red (apart from this, colors do not exist beyond those creatures that are constructed such that they perceive color). Similarly, we may feel that a particular kind of event is a more central member of the category of 'traumatizing events' than another event. However, there is no 'essence of traumatization.' It is us humans who categorize phenomena using guidelines such as family resemblance, centrality, prototypicality (Rosch, 1977; Wittgenstein, 1953), or sensorimotor-based metaphors (Lakoff & Johnson, 1999; see below). We can take the world to ourselves in many different ways, and how we take it depends on a host of variables that include the sensed and perceived state of our brain and body as well as our history, current interests, and environment.

The gap between words as such (or other symbols) and their referents as well as the different usage of a particular symbol by different users or by the same user at different points in time implies the obvious risk of misunderstanding and miscommunication. The 19th-century North American philosopher Charles Peirce (1978) called the required interpretative actions 'interpretants.' Thus, as perceivers we must recognize that a symbol (or another sign) refers to something beyond itself, but we may not succeed in grasping the intended reference. For example, we may misinterpret the way in which the speaker or writer uses a particular word, phrase, or sentence, just as speakers or writers may use symbols whose referents are not or not fully clear to themselves. We take phenomena such as words to ourselves (see Chapter 4). We place the meaning we assign to them 'before' us, in part by bringing the different words together in a way that makes sense to us. We per-ceive and we con-ceive. 'Per' means 'before,' 'con' means 'together,' and, as noted before, '-ceive' relates to Latin verb *capere* that captures the action of taking something to oneself.

What Is Special About Words?

Peirce discovered that interpretants can be more or less complex as well as of different kinds. What is special about words and sentences as symbolic referents? A first guess may be that words *bring mental images to mind*. True, following associative learning, a word may have that effect, but so can nonverbal signs.

Would the distinctive feature of words perhaps be the fact that the relationship between a word and its referent is *arbitrary*? Whereas this relationship is indeed arbitrary in most cases, arbitrariness can also apply to the relationship between a discriminative cue (e.g., a flashing light), an action (e.g., pressing a lever), and a subsequent cue or reinforcer (e.g., food delivery) in a Skinnerian operant conditioning experiment. The relationships between the flashing light, lever pressing, and food delivery are arbitrary because prior to the associative learning, the flashing light did not have a special meaning for the involved animal, and because the discriminative cue might have been a ringing bell, or whatever other stimulus.

The relationship between a classically conditioned stimulus and an unconditioned stimulus can also be arbitrary. For example, salivation is a normal, unlearned (unconditioned) response to smelling or seeing food – provided the organism has an appetite – but it does not naturally occur when a buzzer is rung. However, when Pavlov rang a buzzer (or let a metronome tick) and briefly thereafter presented his dogs food a couple of times, they also started to salivate when he rang the buzzer (or let a metronome run), but did not present the food (Pavlov, 1957). In his terminology, the sound of the buzzer had become a conditioned stimuli, and the release of saliva a conditioned response.

Less well-known is that something similar happened when his experimental dogs had almost drowned during the terrible flooding of the Neva in St. Petersburg on September 23, 1924. When a couple of days after this life-threatening event a small stream of water was allowed to trickle noiselessly into a particular dog's room and form a pool on the floor, the animal jumped up quickly, and gazed restlessly at the pool, tried to get off the stand (on which it was mounted), breathed heavily, denied food, and did not salivate anymore to food-signaling conditioned stimuli (Pavlov, 1927). Together with the appearance of these sympathetically mediated conditioned defensive reactions (hypervigilance, flight), the conditioned reactions to food-signaling stimuli were inhibited. It thus appears that the dog had learned to regard the pool of water as a signal of life-threatening masses of water. Numerous later experiments have shown that after a few pairings of a threatening, unconditioned stimulus with a formerly neutral stimulus (within in critical time-constraint), animals as well as humans will experience a state of conditioned fear and display defensive behavioral reactions when only the previously neutral cue is presented (Fendt & Fanselow, 1999). Thus, survivors can learn to respond with fear, flight, and other mammalian emotions and defensive reactions to previously more or less neutral salient stimuli that preceded the start of abuse or some other adverse event by a brief and critical margin of time. Again, because the relationship between the conditioned stimulus and the unconditioned aversive stimulus is arbitrary, arbitrariness of signal and referent is not specific for words.

Transmission of signs between individuals is not specific for words and sentences either. Thus, when one patient on the ward of a mental hospital relives a traumatic experience, he or she may utter nonverbal sounds that may signal acute danger in the ears and eyes of other traumatized patients – which may therefore trigger traumatic memories in them as well.

What, then, is specific to words and sentences, that is, to human language? According to Deacon (1997), the answer lies in *our symbolic competence*. Words tend to elicit other words in individuals who understand the word, and who have a command of the language to which the word belongs. Signs and referents can be related in a variety of ways, as Peirce (1978) recognized. He distinguished, among others, icons, indexes, and symbols.

Icons

An icon involves a similarity between a sign and its referent. For example, a drawing of a traumatic experience or anything else involves in a material sense nothing else than paper and graphite, ink, or paint. However, the drawing is an icon of something else when it, in the eye of the beholder, stands for its referent in some crucial regards, so that the symbol practically *becomes* the referent. Iconic reference is thus grounded in a lack of distinction of the sign and the referent. Traumatic memories are not indexes or symbols of a lived traumatic experience, but rather involve icons. Survivors who relive a reactivated traumatic memory do not or at least insufficiently distinguish the 'there and then and past me' of the traumatic past, and the actual 'here and now and present me.' Rather, for them, the past *is* the present, or is in any case far too near and real (Janet, 1919/1925, 1928; Van der Hart et al., 2006; Van der Kolk & Van der Hart, 1989). They do not relate a story of what happened to them, but tend to relive it, and when they re-enact the past, they become the one they were at the time, and lose their present identity (see Chapter 4).

Indexes

Indexes involve a physical or temporal link between sign and referent. An index and its referent are correlated and contiguous (i.e., near in space or time). A particular after-shave can refer to a perpetrator for a survivor when this perfume was characteristic of that individual, that is, when the perfume was strongly correlated with the presence of the perpetrator. In learning theoretical terms, this index constitutes a classically conditioned *referential* stimulus that in common clinical discourse is known as a 'trigger.'

There are different kinds of conditioned stimuli or triggers. Some *signal* what is going to happen. This type of classical conditioning, known as Pavlovian or signal learning, is largely based on contiguity. Thus, when a parent tends to become particularly abusive when annoyed, the maltreated child will soon learn that the perpetrator's shift from being happy, interested, or occupied to being irritated signals that bad things are about to happen. Based on this kind of contiguity, a cue that previously did not have a special meaning for the survivor – in the example, the mood shift – can become an index for imminent abuse.

Other species can also learn iconic and indexical relationships, and these relationships are not specific for symbolic reference. Whereas words can serve as icons or indexes, such as when a dog responds to the spoken command 'sit!,' this does not mean that the animal has in fact understood the word in a symbolic sense. *Understanding symbolic referents requires the ability to grasp higher-order relationships.* This ability pertains to discovering an implicit pattern in the relationships between several indexical connections. To detect this pattern, the involved previously learned indexical associations must be seen in a new perspective in which they become reorganized with respect to one another (Deacon, 1997). For example, a survivor who has learned a host of indexical relationships between particular (conditioned) stimuli and impending abuse by a particular perpetrator may rather suddenly stop responding to these cues with fear, other emotions, and defensive action, when he or she *realizes* for the first time that the abuser is dead. Although a perpetrator may have been dead for years, the survivor may not have realized this fact as some dissociative parts of his or her personality. In this case, the survivor does not have to modify the association between every single index of impending abuse and actual abuse, but can grasp all at once that the whole class of these associations does not apply anymore because of a major contextual shift: the abuser's death. Getting this higher-order combinational pattern among indexes, 'seeing' this 'logical group,' saves a lot of troubles and work, as well as a lot of mnemonic capacity.

Symbols

Language is a system of symbolic referents. Symbols do not just refer to things in the world, if a particular object or word is used that fashion, but they also refer to each other. Symbols are part of a system that includes other symbols. As Deacon (1997, p. 100) puts it,

> [b]ecause symbolic reference is inherently systemic, there can be no symbolization without systematic relationships. Thus, syntactic structure is an integral feature of symbolic reference, not something added and separate. It is the higher-order combinatorial logic, grammar, that maintains and regulates symbolic reference.

However, the combinational logic among different symbols is not given. We must *discover* it. For example, we must 'see' that 'apples,' 'potatoes,' and 'sausages' are all items of 'solid food,' and different from 'water,' 'orange juice,' and 'beer,' which are items of 'fluid food.' While most animals are not able to develop this 'insight' and even the higher apes can hardly reach it, children will 'get' it once they have sufficiently matured. Some chimps and bonobo's can learn to 'see' such relationships between symbols and referents, but it commonly takes a lot of training. (An exception to this rule is the chimp Kanzi.) Grasping higher-order relationships among indexical relationships is thus unique to humans.

A core problem of traumatization is that traumatized individuals are in several crucial regards lead by iconic and indexical relationships more than by higher-order symbolic relationships. They struggle with most confusing phenomena that they notice within themselves and in their environment. With respect to trauma-related signals or referents, they have not been able to refer to these interoceptions and exteroceptions in a symbolic fashion, but are caught in iconic and indexical referents. Their bodies, so to speak, *ache*, are anesthetic, or sometimes even seem to have a mind of their own. They may hear intruding voices and in any case suffer panic attacks and flashbacks by day, and they cannot get seem to get rid of their haunting dreams by night. Their intimate relationships may run amok. Some may not be able to resist the temptation to numb themselves with alcohol or drugs, or to find rest in death. Many struggle to focus on concerns of daily life and may even appear 'normal' at those times. However, at other times, they are fixated in a horrific past that won't leave them. In these circumstances, the past is the present, and they become their former selves again. For these individuals, this past is not cast in words and sentences. They have yet to put the involved experiences in words, or rather in the form of a recital. An organized, coordinated and integrated set of symbols, this recital is a story told.

Symbol and Meaning

Clinicians and scientists who work with traumatized individuals can be confused if not overwhelmed by the complexity of their symptoms. To get a better hold of them, they use a set of technical symbols that organize otherwise perplexing phenomena. These symbols/terms and the systematic relationships among them are not given, but they must invent, most carefully formulate, and accurately interpret them. I mentioned above that we do not function the way computers do. Computers operate on ('process') predefined symbols ('information') in predefined ways (according to a set of syntactical rules). Computers do not define what constitutes 'information' for them nor what they are to do with it and how – that's the role of programmers and users. We do not have the luxury of inner homunculi to do the programming for us when it comes to finding meaning. Neurons, hormones, electrochemical signals, brain structures, neural networks, and the brain as a whole do a lot of beautiful things, but they do not and cannot find meaning. Only we as whole individuals can accomplish it. We do not live in a precoded world that provides us with 'information' that we then 'process' (Bursen, 1978; Järvilehto, 1999; Merleau-Ponty, 1962). Whereas computers do not have problems of semantics, we humans must assign meaning, invent what stands for or refers to what, and decide or grasp how different symbols relate to each other. And the less clear the referent of a signifier or symbol (i.e., words, terms, concepts) is, the less clear the relationships between different signifiers (models, theories) are, the more confused we will be.

Words as Proposals for Action

Words are social and involve consciousness. According to Järvilehto (2000, 2004), consciousness was created by individuals whose actions had to be combined for the achievement of common results. This social joining was possible through communication, and this communication later developed into language. For example, as Järvilehto illustrates, the word ship indicates and communicates the possibility to go overseas. In this sense, a word is basically a proposal for common action, something originally concrete, which later takes on abstract meanings for those who grasp it.

Language and the Body

The insight that abstract knowledge stems from experience and perception was fully clear to Schopenhauer (1958, Vol. II, p. 71–72):

> It has been shown that concepts borrow their material from knowledge of perception, and that therefore the whole structure of our world of thought rests on the world of perceptions. It must therefore be possible for us to go back from every concept, even if through intermediate stages, to the perceptions from which it has itself been directly drawn, or from which have been drawn the concepts of which it is in turn an abstraction. . . . Therefore these perceptions furnish us with the real content of all our thinking, and wherever they are missing we have had in our heads not concepts, but mere words. . . . The innermost kernel of every genuine and actual piece of knowledge is a perception; every new truth is also the fruit of such a perception. All original thinking is done in pictures or images; the imagination is therefore so necessary an instrument of thinking . . .

Before him, Spinoza had already asserted that consciousness, hence also abstract thought, starts with concrete perceptions, that is, with perceptions of the body (see Chapter 8). Going back in time even further, according to Thomas Aquino, Aristotle more generally conceded that "[t]here is nothing in the intellect that was not previously in sense-perception" (Copleston, 1955). Kant (1998) also agreed that no knowledge stems solely from pure reason.

Lakoff and Johnson (1999) similarly postulated that our words are not due to 'disembodied human reason' as inspired by our modest access to 'universal reason.' Rather, our language is largely shaped by our bodily experiences and bodily features as well as by the limits of human understanding. Our concepts are *embodied*. They are first of all grounded in and crucially shaped by our perceptual and motor systems to support our functioning in daily life (e.g., the experience that we can move over water in a boat). Since we can project beyond our basic-level experiences, we can use our sensorimotor experiences as a basis for more abstract concepts in terms of conceptual metaphors (e.g., "we're in this boat together"; "this ship has two captains") and prototypes (e.g., a prototypical ship, sailing boat, or canoe). The first sentence of Dutch poet Jan Glas' poem *Sequence* – a motto of this chapter – goes like this: "First there was sitting and then there was chair in the sequence of language." Before we invented words, our species engaged in sensorimotor action. To quote Goethe (1808/1959), "In the beginning was the deed."

In this sensorimotoric light, the concept of 'mental trauma' is a metaphorical derivate of the experience or perception that an object or person has inflicted a physical wound onto "some body." Similarly, the concept of 'mental traumatization' involves the conceptual metaphor that the movement of an object (e.g., a crashing car) or of someone (e.g., physical abuse) can injure someone's *mind*.

Symbol and Referent

How efficient language as a means of reference is depends on the clarity with which a symbol, a word, or a term points to something else, that is, to a different symbol or to a 'thing in the world.' It is not always clear what the referent of a word is, because it may mean different things in different contexts, and users may not be very clear about the way in which they intend the symbol. For example, the term 'trauma' currently stands for a physical event, a physical wound, a stressful but not mentally injurious event, a stressful but not mentally injurious experience, a mentally injurious experience, or the mental wound as such. The term 'traumatic memory' is also used in a variety of ways: Sometimes it refers to a recital, to a narrated autobiographical version of a terrible experience, but it can also denote a sensorimotor, highly emotionally charged iconic version of an overwhelming experience. The term can refer to an event that can cause or has caused a mental injury. However, it can also stand for an event that may, but need not, cause or have caused a mental injury. In this case it is unclear what the referent of the term 'traumatic' is and how this adverb relates to the noun 'trauma' and to the verb 'traumatize.' In fact, because of the presently capricious use of the terms 'trauma,' 'traumatic,' 'traumatizing,' 'traumatize,' it is hard to detect what their systematic relationships actually are. *Detecting a higher-order combinational logic of a set of terms is difficult, sometimes outright impossible, if the intended referent or referents of these terms are not or insufficiently specified.* Words and other symbols are social tools that work well only when their meaning is clear to their users. This particularly applies to social domains, where precision is mandatory. Science as well as good clinical practice are just such fields.

The language of the Smurfs, the heroes of the comic, is a funny example of the troubles that emerge when the referents of the words are unclear. Smurfs are blue creatures created by the Belgian cartoonist Peyo, a pen name of Pierre Culliford. They speak in smurf language, which is characterized by the recurrent use of the word 'smurf' and its derivatives such as 'smurfette.' The problem of smurf words is that they can have a multitude of meanings. In fact, the Smurfs replace so many nouns, verbs, and adverbs with smurf words that their conversations are barely understandable without contextual cues that hint at the referents of these terms. Thus, when a Smurf says "Let's go smurfing," his or her audience can only guess what the mannekin wishes to express by considering the contextual features.

Imagine what would happen if pilots would speak smurf words; notice, too, the confusion that plagues the trauma field where terms like 'trauma' and 'dissociation' can mean so very many different things. Scientists and clinicians must avoid using smurf-like terms or using originally clear terms in smurf-like ways. However, this is far easier said than done, in part because language is a dynamic system. Although the original meaning and referents of a technical term can be clear at one point in time, over time other authors than the original ones who proposed and defined it may start to use the symbol in a different way, so that it starts to refer to some other phenomena. These shifts in meaning would not pose a major problem if scientists and clinicians (1) would agree on the (new) referent(s) of the symbol and on the relationships of the symbol to other symbols and to nonsymbolic referents, (2) would at the same time agree to abandon the former referents and relationships that do not apply anymore, and (3) would find and accept some new term for the old term. When these criteria are not met, the risk of a smurf-like language becomes very real indeed. This danger has already turned into a fact with respect to the terms 'trauma' and 'dissociation' and their derivates. A related concern is that few scientists and clinicians seem really concerned.

Trauma as 'Traumatic Events': Overinclusiveness and Underinclusiveness

The Merriam-Webster dictionary gives three different formulations for the term 'trauma.' Consistent with the original meaning of the term, in medicine trauma denotes a serious physical injury: 'An injury (as a wound) to living tissue caused by an external agent.' Its second meaning reads 'A disordered psychic or behavioral state resulting from severe mental or emotional stress or physical injury,' and thus denotes a mental wound or injury. The distinction between the first meaning (physical wound) and the second meaning (mental wound) is not sharp when a physical injury is associated with a mental effect and when a mental injury also has a physical description (see below). The third referent of trauma is 'an emotional upset.' It reflects a societal trend to regard even minor 'mental scratches' as traumas. Actor Jamie Lee Curtis must have had such mild distress rather than a disorder in mind when she said "People get real comfortable with their features. Nobody gets comfortable with their hair. Hair trauma. It's the universal thing . . ." The problem of this extremely liberal use of the term 'trauma' is that it becomes unclear what the authors or speakers have in mind when they use it: a minor scratch, a considerable wound, or a form of serious pathology?

The involved lack of specificity is only one conceptual problem regarding the term 'trauma.' Another, but previously mentioned concern is that there is a current trend to use the terms 'trauma' and 'traumatic events' as synonyms (e.g., APA, 2013; Briere & Spinazzola, 2009). This practice evidently confuses the injury and the event that caused it (or that in any case was an important cause among other causes of the injury). Sometimes both formulations are used interchangeably. For example, on p. 13 of their chapter Ford and Courtois (2009) define 'complex psychological trauma' as a condition that results from exposure to severe stressors, but two pages later they 'refer to the stressor event(s) as psychological or psychic trauma, the traumatic stressor, or complex trauma.'

Still another problem is that both terms are often not or not clearly distinguished from the concepts of 'adverse' or 'stressful events.' To create a distinct category of 'traumatic events,' one must define how 'adverse or stressful events' are different from 'traumatic events.' When this distinction is not made – and often it is not – the lower bound of the category remains uncertain. There is currently a trend to describe ever more kinds of adverse events as traumas, for example, divorce, chronic or terminal illness, loss of employment, death in the family, accidents or injuries, substance abuse in the family, challenging life transitions, witnessing violence, motor vehicle accidents, assaults, and sexual abuse – whether or not exposed individuals develop a form of pathology in the proximity of and close relation to these events. This practice does not honor the law of specificity and hence implies an overinclusive category of events that count as 'a trauma' or as 'traumatic.' Whereas the category is sensitive with regards to events that are adverse for those who are exposed to them or for many individuals who witness or hear about them, it is not specific by including events that both do and do not cause subsequent psychopathology. This major lack of specificity should be of concern to scientists and clinicians alike. If one wants to define trauma in terms of external agents or forces at all – and there are serious reasons to refrain from this temptation, as I will discuss shortly – one must in any case constrain the concept – or else even 'hair troubles' and other common stressors will be counted as 'traumas.'

To meet the problem of overinclusiveness, constraints on the concepts of 'trauma' and 'traumatic event' – also described as 'traumatic stress' – have been proposed. For example, and to refresh what was already stated in Chapter 6, the DSM-5 A criterion for PTSD is limited to directly experienced or witnessed actual or threatened death, serious injury, or sexual violence. However, events that do not involve actual or perceived threat to the integrity of the body (minus the brain) such as emotional neglect and abuse can also harm the survivor's brain and mind (e.g., Choi, Jeong, Rohan, Polcari, & Teicher, 2009; Draijer & Langeland, 1999; Tomoda et al., 2010). This empirical fact also applies to attachment disruptions in early childhood (e.g., Dutra et al., 2009), particularly when these disruptions include caretaker betrayal (Brown & Freyd, 2008), and observed threat to the psychological and psychosocial well-being of significant others (Motta, 2008). Moreover, chronic childhood traumatization typically involves particular constellations of sexual abuse, physical and emotional maltreatment, and emotional neglect. There is increasing evidence that this type of traumatization can harm the mind and the brain. For example, it is associated with feelings of intense fear, rage, betrayal, shame, and resignation (Ford & Courtois, 2009; Freyd, De Prince, & Gleaves, 2007; Van der Kolk, 2005). Chronic childhood traumatization often implies threats to a child's physical and mental integrity committed by the parents or other primary caretakers, which implies a major risk of attachment disorders (see Chapter 6). There is also increasing evidence that chronic childhood traumatization involves a serious risk of functional and structural brain damage (Anda et al., 2006; Bremner & Vermetten, 2001; Van der Kolk, 2003; see Chapters 17–19), as well as 'somatic diseases' such as autoimmune diseases (Dube et al., 2009), chronic pulmonary heart disease (Anda et al., 2008), and ischemic heart disease (Dong et al., 2004). The DSM-5 A Criterion and similar definitions are thus *overly specific*. To avoid the problem of underinclusiveness, any definition of the term 'traumatic event' must therefore consider threat to the physical, psychological, and psychosocial integrity of the survivor and significant others that can lead to serious biopsychosocial problems.

Trauma as Injury

A next conceptual and definitional problem is that referring to trauma as an 'event' conflicts with its original meaning. The term trauma essentially means, that is, stands for, 'wound,' 'injury,' or 'shock.' Thus, Eulenburg (1878) had the psychological impact of adverse or otherwise stressful events in mind when he introduced the term 'psychic trauma' – not these events as such. In this spirit it makes sense to reserve the concept of trauma for the negative *impact* of particular events rather than for a particular class of events. A profound reason to resist defining trauma in terms of external agents or forces is that the same external agent or force can have very different health-related effects for different exposed individuals. As discussed above, an adverse event does not invariably injure those who take part in it. Some develop a considerable or severe physical or mental injury, immediately ('peritraumatic' effects) or after a delay ('posttraumatic' effects), others a mere 'mental scratch.' Still others show resilience (Mancini & Bonnano, 2008; Fryers & Brugha, 2013).

The idea that particular external agents or forces per se can cause an injury of some kind does not empirically hold up. Exposure to such agents is obviously necessary, albeit insufficient for injuries to emerge (Fryers & Brugha, 2013; Yang et al., 2013). It also takes other factors. These include personal attributes such as developmental phase, sex, and intelligence as well as contextual variables such as social support (Brewin et al., 2000). In this light, the conceptualization and definition of particular agents or forces as traumas or traumatic stressors must be rejected.

What is the injury that some types of events may inflict? Apart from the core symptoms of ASD and PTSD, these disorders can encompass other features and the risk of comorbidity is very high. The symptoms include fear, anger, depression, shame, disgust, substance abuse, self-depreciation, sexual problems, suicidality, self-mutilation, eating problems, sleep problems, attachment disruptions, dissociative phenomena, psychosis, relational problems, academic and occupational achievement, and several physical illnesses. As discussed in Chapter 6, some authors have proposed developmental trauma disorder a new diagnostic category to subsume many of these pathological features associated with chronic childhood traumatization (Van der Kolk & d'Andrea, 2010). Proposals for ICD-11 include the diagnosis complex PTSD. However, childhood traumatization is also associated with complex dissociative disorders and severe mental illness (Dalenberg et al., 2012; Friedman et al., 2011; Mauritz, Goossens, Draijer, & Van Achterberg, 2013). In fact, many mental disorders are related to adverse events, but some more strongly than others (Fryers & Brugha, 2013).

The broad array of trauma-related signs, symptoms, and disorders raises the question whether trauma entails a palette of quite different, only loosely pathological phenomena; or whether there is perhaps some structure, some unity in this diversity that can be of help to organizing our world and our actions. According to TSDP, the essential problem in all trauma-related disorders is the inability to integrate traumatic experiences in the framework of one's personality, an integration that includes realization. Whereas it makes sense to understand trauma in the sense of injury, these wounds obviously relate to environmental events. To define concepts such as 'traumatic event' and 'traumatizing event,' one must therefore first define the concept 'event' and consider the causal relationships between subjects and objects or, more specifically, the relationships between mind, brain, body, and environment.

Chapter 10

The Concept of Event: Ontological, Causal, and Epistemological Considerations

> *. . . nothing is more difficult than to express learned ideas so that every one must understand them.*
> Arthur Schopenhauer

Defining the term 'event' in both ontological and epistemological regards is a complex enterprise. Ontologically, one must ask 'What *is* an event? Epistemologically, the question is 'How can and do we *know* an event?'

Ontology and Causality

Event as an Isolated, External State of Affairs

In the spirit of the idea that there is an 'objective world' involving 'universal reason,' 'events' (e.g., hurricanes) are often understood as occurrences that exist in principle independent of knowing subjects. Although they are seen as ontologically isolated, it is thought that they can affect experiencing and knowing individuals:

event → affects → organism

In this perspective, a 'trauma' is an external event – or a constellation of events – that in principle exists in isolation of an organism, which is, however, affected by it in one way or another:

traumas as events in the outer world → can cause → physical or mental disruptions

Many books and articles on trauma including the DSM-5 A criterion seem to follow this understanding. However, as discussed above, this view entails serious problems. An empirical problem in the definition of 'trauma as an isolated causal event' is that it does not injure *everyone* who lives or observes it. A conceptual trouble lies in the fact that the term 'trauma' cannot stand for an event as well as for an injury. Given the original meaning of the term, it is therefore better to reserve the term for a particular injury, and to replace the term 'trauma in the sense of an event' with the term 'adverse event.' If one wishes to include a reference to 'trauma as an injury,' the phrase 'potentially traumatizing event' can be used as a synonym for adverse event:

adverse event/potentially traumatizing event → can cause → a trauma

When the involved event has caused a trauma, the event becomes a 'traumatic event' for the involved individual:

traumatic event → has caused → a trauma

Four Kinds of Causes

The move to reconceptualize 'trauma' and 'traumatic event' as 'adverse' or 'potentially traumatizing events' constitutes an empirical and conceptual improvement. However, it does not remedy another nasty problem pertaining to the presumed linear causal relationship between an isolated adverse event and the injury that may follow.

Aristotle proposed that there are four different kinds of causes (e.g., Falcon, 2008; Northoff, 2003). The *material cause* of a 'thing' (this might be an organism) involves the kind of 'stuff' that thing (e.g., molecules, cells, muscles, organs, bones) is made of. Its *efficient cause* is the force(s) that bring it into being. Efficient cause describes a simple physical and linear cause → effect relationship. *Formal cause* determines why a particular thing is one sort of thing rather than another thing. Finally, the concept of 'final cause' pertains to the goal toward which a thing aims.

With the development of Newtonian mechanics and modern materialistic science, only the concept of efficient cause in the sense of physical causation became regarded as acceptable and fundamental (Juarrero, 1999). The concepts of final cause and formal cause became disregarded, if not banned. According to philosophical materialism,

matter → causes chances in → matter

Combining material and efficient causation, the idea became that

an isolated, material event → linearly causes changes in → a material organism

Because a mechanistic, materialistic worldview allows only for efficient and material causes, science started to focus on parts of the whole rather than on the whole phenomenon under consideration. This tendency is quite alive, perhaps even dominant, today. Thus, psychology studies mechanisms as parts of a whole in the hope that the whole will become understood once its composing parts have been adequately analyzed:

a part → linearly and efficiently causes → a disturbance of the whole organism

This approach, however, easily leads to the study of ever smaller particles, as physics clearly demonstrate. The motto becomes 'small is beautiful.' Focusing on parts of wholes more than on wholes can also easily lead to mereological errors, that is, flaws of part-whole relationships (Bennett & Hacker, 2003). To illustrate, and as indicated in Chapter 8, we are not the sum of our synapses – we are not even our whole brain. Synapses can never fully tell or explain what we feel, desire, think, or do, and an isolated brain won't either. Materialism cannot (adequately) explain consciousness.

In a mechanistic worldview, injuries are caused by adverse events:

isolated adverse event → mechanically and efficiently causes → injury

Physically, it might be a blow to the head, and mentally it could be a metaphorical blow to the mind such as betrayal. Philosophical realists concede that adverse isolated events might, like any event, constitute a collection of stimuli existing in the objectively existing, subject-independent outer world to which an organism reacts and of which the individual is a part. They hold that "the world is objectively real, you are part of this objectivity, and we as scientists can study and grasp the world in an objective fashion because there is universal reason and because we have access to this universal reason":

a third person can physically judge that: an isolated adverse event as a collection of objectively existing stimuli → affects → subject

Object and Subject

The deep problem of this view is that an event *would not exist* if it were isolated from an experiencing and knowing subject. As Kant (1998) and Schopenhauer (1818/1844/1958) emphasized, the world is our idea (Chapter 8). However, Schopenhauer added that without matter, without an embrained body and an embodied brain, there would be no subject. There is no subject without an object, and no object without a subject. Without an experiencing and knowing subject, that is, without a mind, there is no matter. However, without matter, no mind could exist. The mind requires a living brain, and the living brain could not exist without a living body, just as a living body needs a living brain. The brain, the body, and the environment occur together, and they constitute and depend on each other (Gallagher, 2005; Lakoff & Johnson, 1999; Northoff, 2003; Varela et al., 1993):

subject ← *co-occurrence* → object
subject ← *co-constitution* → object
subject ← *co-dependency* → object

As introduced in Chapter 8, ontologically there are *intrinsic relationships* between the brain, body, and the environment, as Northoff (2003) in tandem with Schopenhauer philosophizes. To repeat, the embodied and embrained subject necessarily exists in an environment, whereas that environment would not exist, if there were no conscious subject. There is ontological embedment of the brain, the body, and the environment:

brain ← intrinsically related → (rest of the) body,

This results in:

embodied brain ← intrinsically related → embrained (rest of the) body

Because the brain and (rest of the) body cannot exist in a void, and because there cannot be an environment in isolation of experiencing and knowing individuals:

brain/body ← intrinsically related → environment

What we have are *dynamic configurations* of the brain, the body, and the environment (Northoff, 2003). The brain, the body, and the environment are not correlates among independent variables, but are *intrinsically related*. That is, they exist and change in virtue of each other, everywhere and at any time. Mental and behavioral states are such dynamic configurations.

Realizing ontological embedment can be seen as a move in philosophy and psychology from absolutism to relativism. It is a turn from thinking of subject and object as ontologically isolated phenomena with their own 'absolute' ontological *properties* to an understanding of subjects and objects in terms of ontological *relationships*. Thinking in terms of ontological relationships (i.e., intrinsic relationships of the brain, the body, and the environment) and actions, rather than ontological properties (i.e., regarding the brain, the body, and the environment as ontologically isolated phenomena, each with its own properties) involves a paradigm shift (Järvilehto, 2004; Northoff, 2003). Making this shift involves the challenge to grasp *the relativity of the brain, the body, and the environment*: What used to be comprehended in terms of absolute properties becomes understood in terms of relativity and subject-object dependency. The move is not unlike the paradigmatic shift in physics from Newton's theory of mechanics to Einstein's theories of general and special relativity where all motion is relative and where space and time are also relative to each other.

So moving from Newtonian psychology to *relativity psychology* is as mandatory for the future of psychology as it may have been for advancements in physics. As Järvilehto (2004, #50) asserts,

> [f]or Newtonian physics a psychology based on Newtonian concepts of man and his environment as moving bodies was good enough. With relativity physics this connection disappeared, and probably many difficulties a physicist encounters nowadays is due to the fact that he uses Newtonian psychology when trying to understand the universe with the help of relativity principles.

The assumption of the existence of isolated events is characteristic of philosophical realism (i.e., the idea that there exists a subject-independent 'real world') and empiricism (i.e., the idea that one can objectively observe this objectively existing world). The assumption of the existence of a mind in isolation of the brain, the body, and the environment characterizes (solipsistic/subjective) idealism, that is, the idea that the world is a subjective idea. The notion of intrinsic relationships between the brain, the body, and the environment that manifest in dynamic configurations is incompatible with these philosophies and sciences built on them. Hence, the principles of ontological embodiment, embrainment, and embedment call for a science and clinical practice that embrace the principles of ontological relativity, of dynamic configurations of the brain, the body, and the environment – and of embedded events as observable and to be effectuated changes within the environment as their context (e.g., Northoff, 2003; Varela, 1996).

Dynamic Causation

The idea is thus that the brain, the body, and the environment arise together, reciprocally depend on each other and mutually determine each other ontologically speaking. They *necessarily* occur together and constitute each other at all times. Because of this co-occurrence, co-dependency, and co-constitution, the brain, the body, and the environment are not each other's isolated efficient causes (Northoff, 2003). Because events crucially co-depend on us as experiencing and knowing individuals (Kant, 1998; Schopenhauer, 1958), and because consciousness is irreducible to anything else, events cannot be the simple physical and linear causes of our feelings, thoughts, and behaviors. In the case of intrinsically related phenomena, efficient cause and effect are inseparable. *In the domain of embodiment, embrainment and embedment, there is no room for isolated material and efficient causes.*

The fact that cause and effect are inseparable in the case of co-occurrence and co-constitution does not imply that there is no causation at all. Rather than efficient causality, embodiment, embrainment, and embedment predominantly imply *dynamic causation*, that is, ongoing mutual determination and reciprocal causal relationships between the brain, the body, and the environment. As Northoff (2003) in tandem with Schopenhauer (1958) insists, *dynamic configurations of the brain, the body, and the environment are compatible with formal and final causation.*

Final Causes

Final causes have often been associated with the idea that the development of an individual (i.e., ontogeny) or a species (i.e., phylogeny) follows a predesigned path. Since Darwin's days, many feel that this idea does not hold. The concept of 'final cause,' however, can be fruitfully limited to the idea that evolution has brought forward functions (e.g., eating, sleeping, forms of procreation along with lust, defense), and that these phylogenetically evolved functions are basically linked to emotional action systems or, as I also sometimes call them, *will systems*. Any will has an object: What we want is some particular effect, and to that end we act. We move toward what we want to have, and we attempt to evade what we fear and despise. Whatever material and efficient causes may explain, they are silent regarding the existence and forms of the will.

A final cause is thus a goal toward which an organism aims. It is this type of cause that integrates the organism's brain and body, and environment. As whole organisms, we adapt to the environment we find, and we change it if that is what we want and can in fact achieve. Survival is adaptation as well as niche construction (Flynn, Laland, Kendal, & Kendal, 2013; Odling-Smee, Erwin, Palkovacs, Feldman, & Laland, 2013; see Chapter 8). Our environment adapts to and changes us, and we adapt to and change our environment. Moreover, in the act and within limits, we change ourselves. We are dynamic will and action. Striving to get what we phenomenally experience and judge as attractive and trying to evade or get rid of what we phenomenally experience and judge as adverse, we select and engage in fitting actions that imply our the brain, the body, and the environment.

As discussed in Chapter 4, like Spinoza, Schopenhauer (1958) emphasized the major power of our basic will, our essential desires, urges, or motivations. In his view, our different wills are evolutionary differentiations or a primordial, singular will. They cannot be resisted – or only with immense difficulty. We love what we love, and hate what we hate. We strive to get the things we fancy, and urge to evade or destroy the things we detest. For example, we cannot postpone our will to sleep on end, and we find it most difficult to refrain from defending ourselves under severe threat or resisting the natural desire to have sex, drink fluids, and eat for extended periods of time. It is very hard not to be a slave of one's wills: There is always something we want to have, avoid, enjoy, or do. And whatever it is that we strive for, it shapes what we feel, think, remember, and imagine. In a word, will precedes our ideas and our conceptions (*Vorstellungen*). Will also precedes our conscious intentions: We cannot will to have a particular will, and cannot 'unwill' what we want. We can put ourselves to work, but we do not have the power to will ourselves to work. We can will ourselves to achieve something (e.g., "I want to eat, sleep, play, defend"), but we cannot force ourselves to have an ambition. We cannot will to have an appetite or repulsion of some sort. We are will, and that's about it.

Our various wills exist in the framework of emotional action or will systems that organize our mental and behavioral life, our sensations, feelings, emotions, perceptions, conceptions, thoughts, and motor actions. For example, mediated by the action or will system of attachment, we seek protection by a caretaker in situations that we perceive as calling for this form of protection. Mediated by the will system for physical defense, we are oriented toward the goal of maintaining our physical integrity when, under the influence of this will system, we perceive threat to the integrity of our body. These and other will systems thus bias us as whole systems toward generating and synthesizing particular sensations, perceptions, emotions, conceptions, thoughts and memories, and toward the effectuation of particular goals through action.

As Northoff (2003) puts it, goals are about observable and to-be effectuated events in the environment. 'Observable events' pertain to embodied and embedded sensory perception. 'To-be effectuated events' involves embodied and embedded goal-directed mental and motor action. And because goals involve will, and hence affect, goal-orientation involves sensorimotor and affective integration. This integration cannot be captured in terms of linear and physical cause-effect relationships. Affects, sensations, and perceptions are not the linear and physical cause of motor actions, and goal-directed motor actions are not the linear and physical cause of affects, sensations, and perceptions. Affects, sensations, perceptions, thoughts, memories, and goal-directed motor actions rather have an ongoing effect on each other (Hurley, 1998). Moreover, as stated in Chapter 8, physical activity such as patterns of brain activity reveal neither what the owner and agent of that activity was sensing and doing, nor *why*. Hence, sensorimotor integration, more complex forms of integration, and goal-orientation (e.g., the urge, will, or aim to attach and defend, to explore, to play) cannot be explained in terms of physical (material) causation either. *Integration and goal-orientation rather involve final causes.*

Final Causes of Dissociative Parts of the Personality

Personality is a system guided by will. This also applies to a dissociated personality. No matter how dissociated an individual's personality may be, it is still one whole system. Individuals whose personality is not dissociated may struggle with ambivalences or rather polyvalences, or even with different ego-states, that is, states that are not well integrated but that still resort under the flag of one overarching conception of self. However, the different wills of patients with a dissociated personality are distributed over various dissociative parts each with his or her own sense of who he or she is, what the world is like, and how he or she relates to that world. Polyvalences are not personalized by one overarching identity, but each dissociative part stands for his or her own will. Polyvalences in dissociative patients, then, manifest themselves as struggles among dissociative parts guided by incompatible or outright opposite wills.

Mediated by different action or will systems, the different parts exert one or more different functions. As a prototypical ANP, traumatized individuals strive to fulfill functions that relate to daily life. For example, as ANP they may want to sleep, eat, drink, be loved, take care of their children, or work. They commonly also try to avoid traumatic memories associated with fragile EP, as well as to evade the aggression and control of controlling EP. As a prototypical fragile EP, traumatized individuals want to defend themselves in one or more ways such as flight, freeze, tend and befriend, warding off, or tonic immobility. These parts may also be primarily mediated by the urge to attach. Prototypical controlling EPs strive to control other dissociative parts and other individuals (often including therapists). In this sense they do not wish to be associated with fragile EPs and ANPs – which they tend to regard as 'sissies.' The will of these different dissociative parts of the traumatized individual's personality strongly influences what they tend to sense, perceive, feel, think, remember, or imagine as well as the meaning they give to their conceptions. *Their will precedes their conceptions.* Like integrated individuals, dissociative parts inescapably have their particular desires, and they can just as much not will themselves to have other desires and urges than the ones they have – and that guide their functioning.

The will of dissociative parts becomes more differentiated the more they contact, accept, and learn to cooperate with each other. This development reaches its summit when they eventually fuse, that is, become completely united. A fusion between formerly dissociated parts implies a coupling of the different will systems that were previously distributed over the involved dissociative parts. In this phase the patient learns to deal with polyvalences or inner conflicts that characterize common life and that pertain to contradictions among different wills, now under the umbrella of being one 'I.'

Formal Causes

Formal causes describe what makes a particular 'thing' one sort of 'thing' and not another sort of 'thing.' And they describe the kind of organization of the 'thing.' As noted before, we thus do not simply respond to physical 'stimuli' and, unlike computers, do not 'process' 'information' understood as discrete, encapsulated, symbolic, and predefined, thus context-independent and context-isolated instructional codes. Rather, we are enactive complex systems that find or generate meaning in a dynamic and self-organizing fashion (Edelman & Tononi, 2000; Thompson, 2007). We *act*[1], that is, we engage in action, both mentally and behaviorally. We feel, wish, perceive, conceive, decide, remember, and behaviorally do 'things.'

And we perceive more than we see, more than our rods and cones could possibly tell us. One way this has been empirically documented is the discovery that there are neurons that respond to events involving behavioral significance, but not to stimuli without such significance (e.g., Sakagami & Niki, 1994). Meaning-sensitive neurons are even found in the primary visual cortex, a brain structure involved in an early phase of visual percept development (Pasternak, Bisley, & Calkins, 2003). We 'take in' the world in goal-oriented action, we conceive rather than 'represent' an 'objectively existing' world.

Formal Causes of Dissociative Parts of the Personality

Dissociative parts of the personality are self-organizing and meaning-making subsystems of the personality as a whole system (see Figure 9.1). According to TSDP, the dissociative organization of the personality in trauma is not a random or coincidental phenomenon. The theory rather holds that this dissociation is evolutionarily prepared. We do not come into this world as *tabula rasas*, but are shaped by the evolutionary history of our species.

1 The Dutch and German equivalent of the verb 'to act' is *handelen* and *handeln*, respectively. The words for action are *handeling/Handlung* (or *Aktion*). These are very apt terms, because they refer to hands, to the body, and because *mentale handelingen/mentale Handlungen* (mental actions), as they are now known, are intimately related to physical actions at the brain level (e.g., Jeannerod, 1997). These links evolve very early in life (e.g., Gallagher, 2005; Sommerville, Woodward, & Needham, 2005).

The phylogenesis that is most relevant to trauma is our encompassing different wills, and that it is far easier to synthesize bodily and emotional feelings, thoughts, memories and behaviors *within* will systems than *between* different will systems. Still, some will systems can quite smoothly complement each other. For example, Panksepp's 'seek' (exploration) system goes rather well together with action systems like lust, play, caregiving, and energy management (Panksepp, 1998; Panksepp & Biven, 2013). Each of these systems is about approaching and attaining desirable objects and other subjects. It is much more challenging to synthesize opposite will systems. However, as discussed before, it is exceptionally difficult to synthesize or coordinate the will to attach to a father and mother (approach) and the will to defend against them when they are abusive (avoidance, escape). The will to move toward these important subjects contradicts the will to evade them as dangerous, hurting objects. (In defense, the other is an object more than a subject.) This could well be the reason that abused and emotionally neglected children are prone to develop disorganized attachment. However, it is doubtful that the involved attachment patterns are 'disorganized.' According to TSDP, these patterns rather involve shifts between different wills and will systems regarding primary caretakers (Van der Hart et al., 2006). In this sense there is a certain organization in the apparent disorganization.

Interdependency of Aristotle's Four Causes: Dynamic Causation

Dynamic self-organizing and meaning-making systems like the brain, a personality as a whole system, or dissociative parts of that whole system, are compatible with final and formal causes. In the case of isolated efficient causes, cause and effect can be determined and separated. This determination and separation is not possible in the case of final and formal causes, because in these types of causality cause and effect are reciprocally connected and mutually determine each other.

Individuals as whole embodied and embedded biopsychosocial systems as well as dissociative subsystems of the personality are associated with all four causes. These systems and subsystems involve an aim (final causality), an organization (formal causality), material (material causality) and forces (efficient causality). The members of the causal quartet are interdependent and complement each other (Northoff, 2003). For example, an aim cannot be realized without an organization, just as an organization is impossible without an aim. To use Aristotle's classic example, a house is built for a reason (final causality) and according to a concept or plan involving a particular structure (formal causality). The structure is realized from suitable material components (material causality) that are connected (efficient causality) according to a plan (formal causality).

As dynamic, self-organizing systems we are oriented toward observable events that we, guided by our particular goals (final causes), try to influence. Being goal-oriented, the brain/body system integrates itself within the environment because its aims pertain to (or at least include) the environment in which it is embedded. The goals of a system can be realized only by a particular organization of that system, that is, by particular dynamic configurations of the brain, the body, and the environment. These organizations depend on goals. Without goals and without forces that couple the components of the organization, nothing could be organized. With regard to the brain, the efficient cause of a dynamic configuration, of a mental and behavioral state, includes "the force of the neural mechanisms by means of which different parts of the brain are specifically related to each other with the ultimate realization of self-organization and dynamic pattern formation" (Northoff, 2003, p. 291). The neural mechanisms involved couple different parts of the brain like nails, bolt, nuts, glue, and cement (efficient causes) couple bricks, wooden and iron pillars, tiles, and pipes that together yield a structure (formal cause) in which one can stay warm and dry, cook a meal, take care of bodily functions, and sleep (final causes). Some houses are big and in some cases they serve the owners' desire to impress friends and neighbors – another final cause.

Our goals are neither singular nor constant. We shift from one goal to the next, or we struggle to coordinate two or more goals that occupy us at the same time. Hence, we shift between different dynamic configurations of the brain, the body, and the environment. We can also experience conflicts between different dynamic configurations that exist in parallel. Guided by different wills, they may be hard to coordinate and integrate. As a result, the organization can become rigid or disorganized, in part because the forces that should keep the structure intact become overstrained (bolts may break, cement may crack).

Survival is Our Primary Aim

We thrive when we can cope with the challenges we encounter, and feel great when we master them. Challenges are not absolute, but relative to our will and to our ability to deal with them, that is, relative to the four causes. The environment can be at odds with our aim to keep our physical and mental integrity intact. The aims of survival and coping with or even mastering embedded environments may fail under these circumstances. Our final causes can become frustrated ("I cannot protect myself") or become conflicted ("I strive to attach to my parents, and strive to defend myself against them"). In this context, the organization of our personality as a whole dynamic system (a formal cause) becomes jeopardized. It may crack as happens in dissociative disorders or even obliterate, as is characteristic of psychosis. The forces that should be connecting the elements of the structure falter (disruption of efficient causes). For example and in physical terms, flooded with excessive stress hormones, the various parts of the brain can become disconnected. The material brain structures may change – some become smaller, others bigger (disruption of material causes).

The TSDP harbors the idea that the structure of our personality can 'crack' under massive threat, which does not mean that it completely disintegrates. When the structure becomes less cohesive, there need not be excessive disorganization (as may characterize psychosis[2]), but the personality may still become (re)organized at a simpler level. In this context, 'simpler' stands for a lower degree of integration of the personality as a whole system, thus a lower degree of systemic complexity. The idea is that the whole system may become organized in simpler subsystems that are insufficiently connected with each other when it becomes too difficult to coordinate and integrate different wills, hence different will systems. For example, someone who suffers a major loss and cannot accept it may feel: "I want my loved one to stay with me" as well as "I must go on with my life." This may result in a dissociation of two Bowlbian principle systems, each of which is simpler than a coordinated and integrated personality as a whole system would be.

Children who are chronically abused and emotionally neglected by their parents or other primary caretakers live a more complicated life. They tend to feel: "I must defend and be on guard at all times" and "I want to be safe with my parents" and "I want to be loved by them" and "I need to go to school" and "I want to play" – and much more. Encompassing various incompatible wills, their personality may become divided into several insufficiently coordinated and integrated subsystems, each guided by their own will. This grave organizational disconnectivity becomes associated with profound and recurrent shifts between different wills, particularly shifts between investment in the interests of daily life, defense, and control. It also tends to imply less adaptive and creative neural connectivity, and more structural brain damage.

These subsystems of the personality are of course what in TSDP are called dissociative parts of the personality with ANP, fragile EP, and controlling EP as the main prototypes (see Figure 10.1). Each dissociative part is a dynamic self-organizing system within the confines of a wider personality system (formal causation). Each is oriented toward its own basic motivations and functions (will, final causation). Each involves its own kind of psychophysiological and neural forces (efficient causality), as well as environmental forces (material and efficient causation), and each is tied to the brain and the rest of the body (material causation).

These very different but interdependent causes of the various dissociative parts of an individual's personality relate to the different sets of dynamic configurations of the brain, the (rest of the) body, and the environment they generate (see Figure 10.2). This set is commonly far more extensive for ANP than for fragile EP and controlling EP. However, the degree of elaboration and emancipation of EPs and ANPs can be quite variable. Some EPs engage in a very limited number of dynamic configurations, whereas others can encompass far more mental and behavioral states. Some are unable to take full executive control, whereas others can take control, but only for a very limited stretch of time. Still other EPs can – and will – recurrently take full control. Many ANPs are elaborate, but as happens in DID, some may only generate a rather restricted set of dynamic configurations

2 The concept of 'psychosis' obviously needs to be better defined, a difficult task that is postponed until Volume III. Volume II (Chapters 12 and 21), however, do include some remarks on dissociative psychosis.

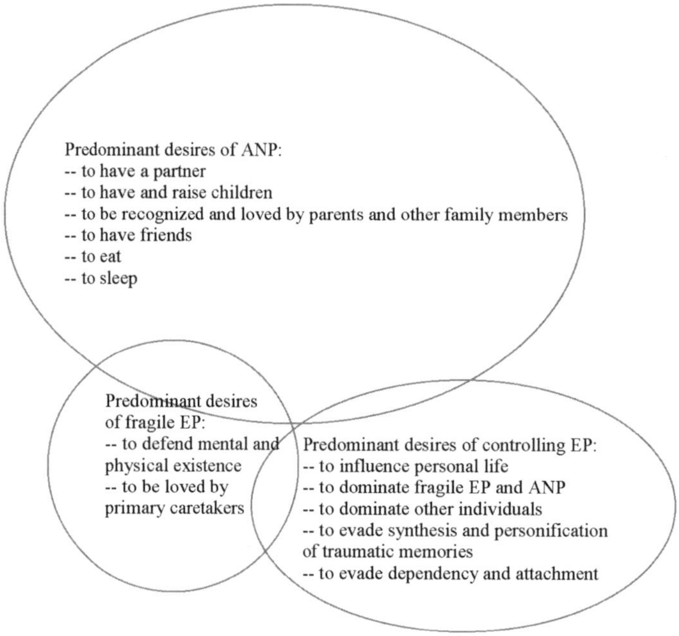

Figure 10.1. Distribution of different wills (final causation) in a hypothetical dissociated personality involving one ANP, one fragile EP, and one controlling EP (formal causation).

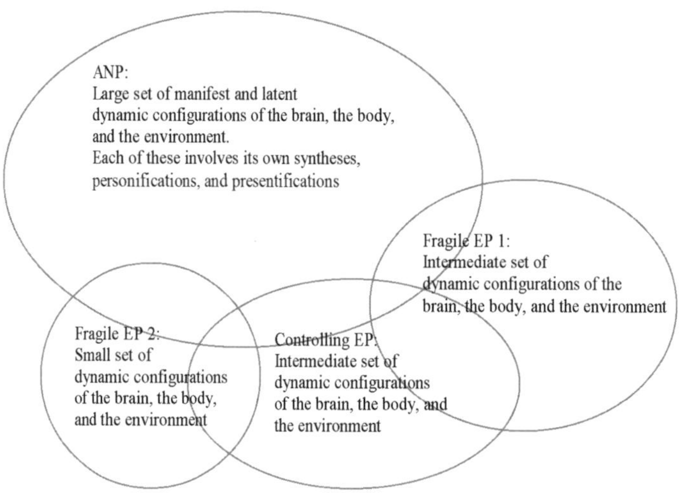

Figure 10.2. Different sets of manifest and latent dynamic configurations of the brain, the body, and the environment in a hypothetical dissociated personality involving one ANP, two fragile EPs, and one controlling EP.

of the brain, the body, and the environment. For example, the only concerns of one ANP in a patient with DID were to take care of her child, to leave other jobs to other ANPs, and to evade fragile and controlling EPs as much as possible.

The figures illustrate that, according to TSDP and consistent with Janet (1907), Hart (1926), and McDougall (1926), the different dissociative subsystems of the personality to some degree overlap. Whereas some actions and contents are specific to a particular dissociative part, dissociative parts also tend to share certain actions, hence 'contents.' For example, an ANP, a fragile EP, and a controlling EP may all be able to walk, talk, and speak the same language. However, each part may also have his or her own way of walking and talking. Dissociation of the personality is not simply a cake cut into pieces.

Embedded Events and Dynamic Causality in Trauma

One implication of embedment and the interdependency of the four causes is that it cannot be said that particular '(objectively existing) events' are the efficient cause of the biopsychosocial pathology of the injury that trauma is. The idea that objectively existing events are the efficient cause of PTSD or some other kind of pathology is untenable. The terms 'trauma,' 'traumatic event,' and 'traumatizing event' are on very shaky ground if the noun 'trauma' and the adjectives 'traumatic' and 'traumatizing' are taken to denote efficient causality – and if the noun 'event' stands for an isolated environmental occurrence, that is, for an event that, in principle, could exist independent of individuals who experience or know it.

Whether an embedded event is traumatic or traumatizing cannot be said *a priori*, at least not with certainty. This assessment can only be made *de post facto*. What can be said *a priori* from a third-person perspective is that some embedded events are more likely to be injurious than others. To say that an embedded event has been traumatizing means that it has been an important dynamic causal factor with respect to the ensuing biopsychosocial injury. The statement does not imply, however, that the event is the *only* causal factor. Events are not occurrences that exist in isolation of historical and situated individuals. Rather, events are always embedded; they are relative, not absolute. The probability that an injury ensues thus depends on the context. This context is complex because it includes the context of the historical and developing embodied and embrained individual, previous adverse embedded events, social support in the aftermath of the event(s) (or the lack thereof), the subject's developmental phase and the stage of his or her brain maturation, the individual's genetic make-up, including sex, and still more.

Where Does Embedment Leave the Mind?

While we may feel that our mind could exist separately from our brain/body, this ontological belief involves an epistemic illusion caused by our autoepistemic limitation. Whereas it may be assumed that there is no mind without a brain, the mind does not in fact equal the brain. And although we tend to experience that our mind is in our head, no one has actually found the mind in the brain. Then where is our mind? According to Alva Noë (2009, p. xiii),

> [h]uman experience is a dance that unfolds in the world and with others. You are not your brain. We are not locked up in a prison of our own ideas and sensations. The phenomenon of consciousness, like that of life itself, is a world-involving dynamic process. We are already at home in the environment. We are out of our heads.

The mind does not reside in the brain, but it does exist, regarded under the Spinoza's attribute of matter, in particular dynamic configurations of the brain, the body, and the environment (Noë, 2009; Northoff, 2003). To speak with Noë (2009, p. 24), "[c]onsciousness isn't something that happens inside us: It is something that we do, actively, in our dynamic interaction with the world around us." Consciousness, hence the attribute mind, pertains to *action*, and first of all to social action (Järvilehto, 2000b, 2004). More than anything else, the human world is a social world.

The Mind of Dissociative Parts of the Personality

The implication of these deliberations is that the mind of dissociative parts exists as action. This action involves the generation of particular dynamic configurations of intrinsically related brain, bodily, and environmental states and the implied contents of these states. Their mind is not their brain, because, like a largely integrated personality, dissociative parts could not exist as mere brain. The mind of dissociative parts is more than a particular set of brain-body states, because without an environment to which these states are intrinsically related, they could not exist at all. Dissociative parts are world-engaged. Whatever they are aware of, it depends on their actions as an insufficiently integrated part of a whole organism-environment system. How they sense, perceive, feel, and think about themselves and the world they live all depends on their action. And it is this action that provides the feeling and idea of what is and what happens. The events they experience and know are not isolated from them. They are relative to their ongoing action.

The Concepts of 'Event' and 'Trauma': Epistemic Considerations

There are several reasons why events codepend on us as experiencing and knowing subjects. One major reason is that everything that exists for us exists in our awareness. Without that awareness, events would not take place. When we experience, perceive, and conceive of the world and ourselves as a part of the world, we take the environment and ourselves (as the organism each of us is) to ourselves (as the conscious and self-conscious individual each of us is), and we take them to be true insofar as we do not regard our perceptions to be illusions or delusions. The deep implication is that the question of what exists – the problem of ontology – eventually becomes identical to the question of what we can experience and know – the problem of epistemology. As noted before, what exists exists through subject and object. Schopenhauer (1958, Vol. I., p. 273) thus asserted that "[t]his actual world of what is knowable, in which we are and which is in us, remains both the material and the limit of our consideration." Subject and object are not given, but appear as the ideas of a subject. Impersonal ideas, views from 'nowhere,' do not exist. Whatever is experienced and known is tied to an environmentally embedded, living subject.

Events – constellations of subjects and objects – are thus not given either. Subject and object are co-occurrent, co-constitutive, and co-dependent. Events – and by implication adverse or traumatic events – can therefore not be defined as occurrences that exists in isolation of an experiencing and knowing individual (see also Chapters 8 and 9). There is no world 'in itself,' either subjectively or objectively (Merleau-Ponty, 1945/1962). Plato's intuition that there are eternal ideas whose shadows we can perceive does not hold. This also applies to the Kantian metaphor of a 'thing in itself' as distinct of that particular 'thing for me.' What exists is what someone (i.e., a living organism) experiences and knows. What can exist is what someone can experience and know in principle. This is the world of actual and possible phenomena. This is the world as ideas (Kant, 1998; Schopenhauer, 1958, Vol. II, pp. 17–18).

Events: Contents, Boundaries, and Meaning

The second, closely related way in which an event is dependent on us is that its *content* (what is the event about? what feelings, thoughts, and behavioral actions does it include? who is involved?), *boundaries* (when does the event start and end? what belongs to the event as it proceeds and what not?), and *meaning* are not given either but also depend on us as experiencing and knowing subjects. For example, whereas scientists, clinicians, or other observers can conceptualize categories of events such as emotional neglect, physical maltreatment, and sexual abuse from a third-person perspective, they cannot define the meaning of these events in isolation of and for individuals who live them.

Contents and Boundaries

When we are awake or dream, we are consciously aware of some-'thing.' Even when our level of consciousness is low, there is still something we are consciously aware of. When we are consciously aware of nothing, we are unconscious (e.g., as in dreamless sleep). Our phenomenal contents do not spontaneously erupt in us. Rather, we must *do* something to have feelings, thoughts, or fantasies. Mental action and mental content are two sides of a coin. No content without action, and no action without content. To see a sight, we must engage in the action of seeing, to have a sensation we must sense, and our memories imply the act of remembering. Any act of seeing, feeling, or remembering implies a sight, a feeling, and a memory, respectively. As Spinoza (1677, Axioma 3, p. 32) asserted,

> [t]here are no modes of thinking[3], such as love, desire, or whatever is designated by the word affects of the mind, unless there is in the same individual the idea of the thing loved, desired, and the like. But there can be an idea, even though there is no other mode of thinking.

3 The term 'thinking' has a broad meaning in Spinoza's work. It is not restricted to cognition, but includes, as the quote demonstrates, "affects of the mind."

To have a coherent and cohesive experience, more action is needed than an isolated act of seeing, or feeling, or remembering, etc. As mentioned before, this takes several integrative actions (see Chapters 2 and 4). A component of our dynamic self-organization is that we, to speak with Kant and Janet, must *synthesize* what we sense, feel, see, hear, smell, taste, think, remember, and do. A synthesis in which the various elements are intimately linked and coordinated, this unity only becomes *our* synthesis when we *personify* it. And our personalized synthesis becomes embedded in our life history only when we also *presentify* it. In this action, we bring the past and future to the present, but such that we experience and know that the past is past, that the anticipated future may become a reality, and that what has been and will be are less real than what presently is. As a result of these different integrative actions, we experience and know events as environmental changes that exist in the context of other events. Some of these other events happened in the past, others happen presently, and still others are anticipated. What happens now relates for us to what was and will be – not automatically, but because of our integrative actions. It is because of these conjoint integrative actions that events exist – exist for us – and become spatio-temporally defined and embedded.

Epistemically, we thus do not experience, perceive, conceive, and react to isolated stimuli or to a collection of isolated stimuli. We rather experience and know events as organized whole structures – and only as changes in the environment as the respective context: What happens, happens in a world, and that world is never the same thereafter. *Panta rhei* Heraclitus taught. Within limits we can distinguish different elements of an event, but we experience and know them as elements of an event in which they are embedded.

Integration Implies Differentiation

The integrative actions of synthesis, personification and presentification should not be confused with brewing English stew. The various ingredients must be brought together, yes, but in principle they should also be distinguishable – even when distinguishing between them can sometimes be a challenge, as in tasting the different tones of a delicate French or Italian wine. For example, whereas we must couple what we feel, see, hear, and do, we must also distinguish between a sensation, a sight, a sound, and a movement, or else we would experience synesthesias. We should also bind but differentiate the experience and the agent and owner of the synthesis, or else our 'I' and our experience would be indistinguishable. We should also be able to differentiate between our own desires, urges, experiences, thoughts, and movements, and those of others, or else there will be confusion regarding the actual agent and owner of an experience, thought, memory, or movement. Adequate synthesis and personification, therefore, involve differentiation as much as binding or coupling of the elements that together constitute an experience, thought, etc. Differentiation in time is inherent in presentification, or else we could only guess whether something has happened, is presently happening, or will probably happen.

Without differentiated synthesis, personification, and presentification, we would not even know events. All we would experience would be a blur.

To the extent that individuals are consciously aware of their mental contents, they can communicate them, both to themselves and to others. However, knowing embedded events does not mean that individuals are necessarily conscious of this embedment and its implied relativity. Large parts of the mind operate in a way that remains unknown to its owner. For example, we do not have access to the way in which our mind synthesizes what we see, hear, feel, etc. We can reflect *that* we synthesize, but we do not know *how* we do it. We know we use a host of grammatical rules as we talk and write, but many people have no clue what grammatical rules they apply. Perhaps only exceedingly clever linguists know them all. Apart from these unconscious actions, our mind also operates preconsciously.

The implication is that we neither fully know what we are doing, nor do we fully know how we do what we know we do. However, there are some indirect ways to demonstrate and access unconscious or preconscious mental actions and implied states. For example, scientists can use subliminal exposure to cues to explore preconscious reactions to these signals. Chapter 18 gives some examples of this research with regard to trauma-related cues, and describes how different prototypes of dissociative parts can have different reactions to identical, subliminally presented cues. Scientists get to know more than the individuals they study know. But as detailed in the previous chapter, there is also a lot that they cannot tell from their third-person perspective. No matter how much they know about the brain, third-person knowledge of the brain will never tell them what it is like to have a particular experience or to have experiences in general. To reiterate, consciousness is irreducible to something else, including the brain (Varela, 1996).

In sum, an event, and more specifically, its content, boundaries, and meaning, are dependent on the individual who experiences and knows it, and experiencing and knowing an event depends on integrative actions: synthesis, personification, and presentification. Integrative action also encompasses the action of realization. This action involves experiencing and knowing how real the experienced and known event is, and what consequences it will and must have. What happened long ago and what may happen in a distant future should generally be less real than what is happening right now. Fantasies (i.e., ideas of what might be) should be generally experienced as less real than what actually happens or is very likely to happen. And what is real according to common sense (e.g., that someone has a body and that that person is in a shop), must be experienced as real, or else symptoms of depersonalization ("It is as if I do not really exist") and derealization follow ("It occurs to me that the shop I'm in is not real; it looks very hazy. Am I dreaming?").

Meaning

In the large majority of cases, events do not have a given, precoded meaning for us. Rather, we unconsciously, preconsciously, or consciously assign meaning to experienced, perceived, and conceived changes in the environment. As remarked before, there are a number of 'unconditioned stimuli' – that is, stimuli as elements of embedded events – that have gained a prefixed meaning in evolution. 'Meaning' stands in this case for a particular evaluation (pleasurable, aversive, or dangerous) and typical associated 'unconditioned' reaction (approach, avoidance). However, in most cases, we must assign meaning to changes in the environment as we evolve:

subject ← experiences, knows, and assigns meaning to → embedded events

Events are thus phenomenally experienced and known as bounded and spatiotemporally embedded. The meaning they have for the individual who directly experiences or witnesses them will be co-dependent on the context of the current environment, as well as on the embedded events that preceded and that are anticipated to follow the current one. However, this contextualization, the meaning an event will have for the involved individual, depends on the degree to which that persons synthesizes, personifies, presentifies, and realizes what happened.

In this light embedded adverse events cannot be seen as changes (within the environment as the context of these events) that have a preset meaning. These events probably include 'unconditioned stimuli,' but these stimuli are not isolated phenomena. They are elements of embedded events, and individual evaluate embedded events, not isolated stimuli. For example, intense pain inflicted by a dentist is different from intense pain due to sexual abuse. Another illustration is that intense pain in the context of sexual abuse by a caretaker is bound to be different from intense pain in the context of sexual abuse by a stranger followed up by recognition and emotional support from a loving and trusted caretaker. And sexual abuse in childhood is different from sexual abuse in adulthood following a safe childhood, a related development of high integrative capacity, and sound maturation of the brain.

Integrative Limitations of Dissociative Parts

The integrative actions of traumatized individuals are deficient. This deficiency manifests itself, among others, in dissociative symptoms. Each dissociative part of a traumatized individual's personality is conscious, that is, it synthesizes, personifies, presentifies, and realizes 'some things' but not 'other things.' The 'things' they integrate – these contents of consciousness – generally pertain to embedded events. These contents are bounded and have a particular meaning for the involved dissociative part.

However, each dissociative part also fails to integrate at least some crucial embedded events. For example, ANPs and controlling EPs commonly do not or insufficiently integrate traumatizing events in which fragile EPs are stuck. As fragile EPs they may not or not know sufficiently that the traumatic experiences are over, in which case their presentification falters. ANPs may not sufficiently synthesize bodily sensations and emotional

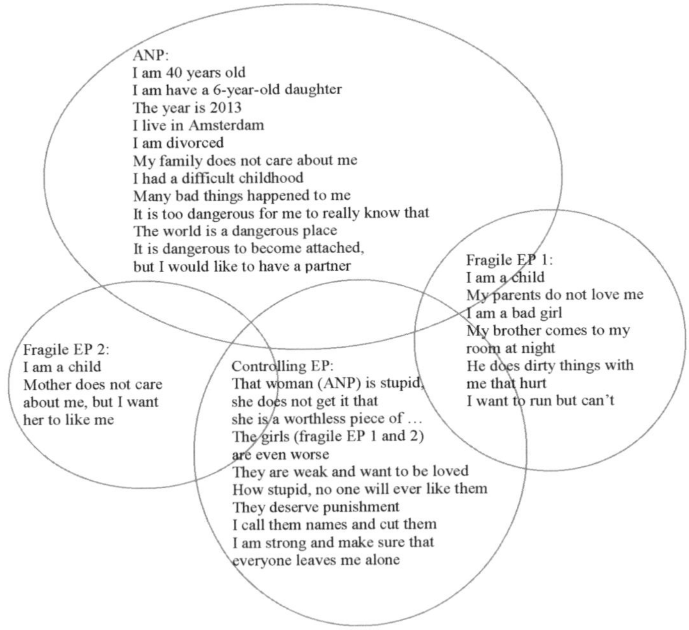

Figure 10.3. Different ways of experiencing and knowing themselves and the world in a hypothetical dissociated personality involving one ANP, two fragile EPs, and one controlling EP.

feelings, except when they are intruded on by fragile EPs who do synthesize the awful sensations that ANPs are unable or unwilling to synthesize. It can also happen that ANPs know the traumatic experiences, but have difficulty realizing their meaning. A main effect of a lack of synthesis, personification, and presentification is that the different dissociative parts have their own ideas of self, world, and self-in-the-world (see Figure 10.3).

The general point in trauma is thus that each dissociative part integrates some things, but not nearly all. For example:

> ANP → integrates → embedded event A and B, but not – or insufficiently – embedded event C (e.g., a traumatic event)

and

> fragile EP → synthesizes and personifies → embedded event C, but not – or insufficiently – embedded event A (e.g., a situation at work)

When ANP does not integrate embedded event C, the traumatized individual does not or insufficiently integrate the traumatic past that therefore continues to exist as a 'parasite' in the mind, as Charcot put it. In this context, fragile EP remains overly isolated from ANP.

Still, dissociative parts are commonly not fully 'split' in that, for example,

> ANP and fragile EP → integrate → embedded event B

Figure 10.4 depicts this epistemic constellation of embedded events.

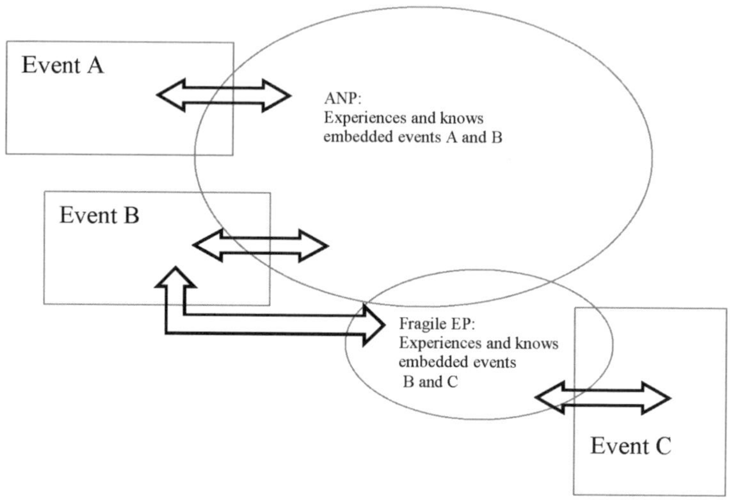

Figure 10.4. Different ways of experiencing and knowing embedded events in a hypothetical dissociated personality involving one ANP and one fragile EP.

The consequence is that this personality is and remains dissociated until the involved ANP and fragile EP can and do engage in the same integrative actions:

ANP and fragile EP → integrate → embedded events A, B, and C

This joint integrative action implies that embedded event C becomes embedded in a new way. For example, fragile EP's previous dynamic configuration with respect to C involved a sensorimotor and highly affectively charged present experience: "A horrible thing happens (synthesis), it happens to me (personification), and it's happening now (deficient presentification)." With the integrative action, this previously iconic experience version may take on a new form. It may become an emerging, clearer, and more distinct idea like: "A horrible thing happened to me when I was 6 years old. For a long time, ANP did not want to feel and know this, and abandoned me. Now she (i.e., ANP) has also felt (i.e., synthesized) what it was like, and that it also happened to her (i.e., personification). She now stays with me more, so that I start to feel that the bad thing happened in the past (i.e., emergent presentification for EP)."

Epistemology and Dynamic Configurations of the Brain, the Body, and the Environment: Epistemic Pluralism

There is epistemic pluralism, since embedded events can be known from different person perspectives (Northoff, 2003; Varela, 1996).

The First-Person Perspective

To refresh and extend what was stated in Chapter 5, the first-person perspective concerns subjective, phenomenal experience: our 'raw' or prereflective sensations and other feelings that are experienced as subjective, private, and internal. It includes our body as our spatial center and our 'I' as the center of our existence.

In other words, the first-person perspective pertains to the subjective feeling of being someone with a point of view, that is, of being an acting and experiencing self with a subjectively experienced outward perspective on one's perceived environment, and a subjectively experienced inward perspective regarding oneself (Metzinger, 2003). This someone involves our 'I' or our 'self.' The first-person perspective thus subserves living present events (Northoff, 2003) and, as it were, answers the question: What it is like to be an 'I,' to be a subject, to have experiences, to be an agent, and to have a personal point of view? For example, it entails what it is like to see redness, to enjoy music, to be curious, scared, horrified, in pain, or disgusted.

Our 'I' is not given, and it cannot exist by itself, but is dependent on ongoing action of an embrained, embodied, and embedded conscious organism. Our 'I' thus involves a 'phenomenal self-model,' says philosopher Thomas Metzinger (2003), or in my terms[4], a phenomenal (i.e., subjectively experienced) idea or conception of self. The phenomenal conception of self is dynamic because it is continuously generated and adapted by a part[5] of an individual as a whole awake or dreaming organism (Metzinger, 2003; Metzinger's theory will be detailed in Chapter 12).

How this idea or conception is generated by this 'part' of us remains hidden because the brain/body does not reveal how it generates its own states, including our 'I,' our phenomenal idea of self. As discussed above, because of this autoepistemic limitation, we experience our self as well as our phenomenal experiences in general as something given. It occurs to us that we simply 'have' our sensations, other perceptions, feelings, and a self. Unable to peep inside ourselves and discover how we as living organisms generate these phenomena, we are tempted to believe that the mind could exist by itself. We *can contemplate* that consciousness and self-consciousness are not givens, but concern the mental contents we generate as organisms in action. However, we *cannot experience* that our 'I' and the feelings, perceptions, etc., are continuously generated conceptions.

The Quasi-Second-Person Perspective

As was also discussed in Chapter 5, we do not have only phenomenal experiences, but can detect, recognize, and compare our different phenomenal-qualitative states (Chalmers,

---

4 The reason for substituting the term 'model' for the term 'conception' or 'idea' as a synonym of 'conception' is given in Chapter 12.

5 It should be clear that the term 'part' as used in this sentence does not stand for 'dissociative part of the personality.'

1996) – and thus judge our phenomenal experiences. Whereas the first-person perspective is all about intrasubjective experience, the quasi-second-person perspective is a form of intrasubjective communication. It serves the development of a 'relation of mineness' (Metzinger, 2003), that is, the phenomenal relationship between an experiencing individual and this individual's *phenomenal judgment* regarding himself or herself, resulting in 'I – me, myself, mine' relationships. For example, in the quasi-second-person perspective, we can say "I feel and know this is my body," "The idea was mine," and "I am ashamed of myself."

The quasi-second-person perspective involves a slightly more reflective idea of self than the phenomenal experience of self in the first-person perspective. In the first-person perspective, personification, i.e., the mental action of owning experience, and the mental action of experiencing and owning agency, is prereflective. In the quasi-second-person perspective, personification involves at least a little reflection. For example, it can involve phenomenal judgments like "I feel my hand," or "I am angry at myself." The judgments in the quasi-second-person judgments include phenomenal judgments of *ownership* (e.g., "my body hurts") and of *agency* (e.g., "I squeeze my hands"). In other words, our phenomenal idea of self is a bit more explicit and reflective in our quasi-second-person perspective than it is in our first-person perspective.

The Second-Person Perspective

In Chapter 5 I said that the second-person perspective comprises 'I-You' relationships. It denotes the phenomenal relationship between our 'I' and the 'I' of another person, the 'Thou' (Buber, 1983) and concerns a *phenomenal judgment* grounded in the first-person and quasi-second-person perspectives. For example, one might phenomenally experience and judge that "I am glad to meet you, and you seem to be happy to meet me as well," or "Although we share the same mood, we are different individuals."

Access to someone else's *phenomenal experience* exists, but only indirectly. This involves actions such as empathy, joint perspective taking, and imitation. These actions include the activity of particular brain structures and functions, e.g., mirror neurons (e.g., Rizzolatti & Sinigaglia, 2007) and canonical neurons (Pineda, 2008) that mediate our phenomenal sense of being in mental touch with another individual.

The Third-Person Perspective

Whereas the quasi-second-person and second-person perspective concern *phenomenal judgment*, in the third-person perspective the judgment is physical (Northoff, 2003). In this epistemic perspective, there is an 'I' who judges what this 'I' knows is a subject or object with particular physical features. For example, we regard a chair, book, car, or glass of wine as objects – as 'things' – each with their own physical features such as a particular volume, shape, texture, and color. Neuroscientists study the brain and its workings as physical objects in the third-person perspective, as do clinicians when they assess and analyze their patients' mental disorders (to the extent that clinician phenomenally empathically relate to their patients, they engage in a second-person perspective).

Epistemic Dependency and the Third-Person Perspective

As was detailed above, many individuals, among them scientists and clinicians, seem subject to the illusion that there is an objective truth, and that they have access to this truth, particularly when they adhere to a stringent, scientific third-person perspective. However, I have emphasized that it should not be overlooked, ignored, or otherwise denied that, without experiencing and knowing subjects, there are no subjects and objects – and no events. The realization of this ontological subject-object co-constitution, co-dependency, and co-occurrence effectively destroys our hope that our physical judgment could tell us how things 'really are.' Whatever we know and can know, it will be the 'thing for me,' not the 'thing in itself.' In fact, there is no 'thing in itself.' All that exists is necessarily co-dependent on someone's idea of what exists. We should therefore not overlook, ignore, or deny the 'I' in the third-person 'I-object' relationship (see Chapter 8). Knowing the world is the (ad)venture of an experiencing and knowing organism. Isolated from the other person perspectives, there is no, and indeed cannot be a, third-person perspective. Any view is always someone's view. There is no absolute truth. We cannot do like the Baron Von Münchhausen, who managed to lift both himself and his horse out of a swamp by pulling on to the tail of his wig. We cannot escape our human condition.

The third-person perspective exists in virtue of a physically judging individual, and being an individual implies first-person phenomenal experience as well as quasi-second-person phenomenal judgment. Being someone means having desires, feelings, preferences, aversions, and interests. All of these and still other all-too-human features influence our physical judgment. We are not devices that operate in a mechanical fashion, which, given energy and instructions like computers, process information.

The third-person perspective also implies the second-person perspective. Very rare exceptions aside, all individuals have been raised and live in a social domain. Without this social background and context, we would not even be capable of a sophisticated third-person physical judgment. We are 'I's' who love and hate – and anything in between. We have our likes and dislikes, desires, attractions, and repulsions. Our 'I's' relate phenomenally to our 'me, myself, mine' and to other individuals. We want to have and keep what we feel belongs to us. We like or reject ourselves and others, seek the recognition or admiration of other individuals, trust or mistrust them. How could phenomenal experience and phenomenal judgment *not* affect our physical judgment? There is no escape from subjectivity. The idea of pure objectivity is a fable.

For example, science is a social enterprise that has meaning only in a wider existential and societal frame. Scientists too have been raised and live in a world. That historical and present 'life-world' (Husserl, 1970) is social. Most work in teams, all operate in a scientific community, and all have sociopolitical interests that cannot but affect their physical judgment. Psychiatry, psychology, and psychotherapy are social per definition. To be effective, psychotherapists must empathically attune to their patients. However, clinicians may have personal interests, problems, and deficiencies that may cause them to misjudge their patients in certain regards.

The history of trauma is replete with illustrations of phenomenal experience and judgment coloring third-person scientific, physical judgment. Some of these were briefly described in the first chapters of this book. Like anyone else, scientists and clinicians have feelings about themselves, other individuals (such as their colleagues) as well as the object of their scientific or clinical interest. The themes of trauma and dissociation elicit strong personal feelings and opinions that are not necessarily supported or influenced by empirical facts. For example, some clinicians say: "I have never seen a case of DID. I am a good diagnostician, and I surely cannot have overlooked this disorder. DID must be a fad." Some scientists who have not studied a single case of major or minor DID and who otherwise adhere to rigorous scientific principles nonetheless feel entitled to voice strong opinions regarding patients with complex dissociative disorders as well as their psychotherapists, even if their views are not supported by any scientific evidence or have since been falsified by controlled studies. Some editors and reviewers of scientific journals have accepted articles on DID which are not based on the study of individuals with the disorder of concern. One may wonder whether they would also accept articles that voice strong opinions regarding some other severe mental disorder which are not supported by research of the population of concern. For example, what editor or reviewer would accept papers on schizophrenia which make strong claims about the essence of this disorder not based on studies of schizophrenic patients? There seems to be something special about complex dissociative disorders that precipitates the peculiar treatment these disorders receive from a substantial number of scientists and clinicians. What this 'something' might be is addressed in Chapter 20.

Epistemic Dependency and the Quasi-Second-Person and Second-Person Perspective

The first-person perspective can exist without our quasi-second-person perspective and second-person perspective. However, like the third-person perspective, the quasi-second-person and second-person perspective depend on the first-person perspective. This dependency exists because phenomenal judgment presupposes phenomenal experience. Without phenomenal experience, nothing can be phenomenally judged. Phenomenal experience is the object of phenomenal judgment.

The mental content of the quasi-second-person and second-person perspective can influence the mental content of the first-person perspective. In other words, phenomenal experience can be affected by phenomenal judgment. Although affect and basic will (phenomenal experience) precedes cognition (i.e., judgment), cognition can influence affect to a degree. For example and as was discussed above, the way in which traumatized individuals recall highly adverse events depends in part on their phenomenal judgment of their phenomenal experiences. Thus, a later adverse event may give the original adverse event a much more threatening meaning (Davey, 1989; Ehlers & Clark, 2000). This principle is illustrated by the raped woman who developed PTSD after hearing that the rapist had killed another woman he had raped before her (Kilpatrick et al., 1989).

Loss and Substitution of Person Perspectives

We can lose our person perspectives and/or substitute one type of person perspective for another. For example, loss of consciousness clearly involves the loss of all person perspectives. Lowering of the level of consciousness diminishes mental contents. It also negatively affects the quality of phenomenal experience, phenomenal judgment, and physical judgment. We may lose our focus and become absent-minded. Our experiences and perceptions may become cloudy, confused, or unreal – as happens in depersonalization, bodily and affective numbing, and derealization. Our field of consciousness typically shrinks and widens over time and situations. This phenomenon is as common as shifts in the quality of consciousness. However, the attentional field may become too small or may include items that are irrelevant to our present objectives and the implied person perspectives. It is often good to focus, but our field of consciousness has become unduly small if we do not sense and perceive what is necessary to be up and running in whatever person perspective or combination of these perspectives.

Loss and Substitution of the First-Person and Quasi-Second-Person Perspective

The more we fail to synthesize bodily and affective feelings or personify our syntheses, the more we lose our first-person perspective. The phenomenal losses involved manifest themselves in negative symptoms such as loss or reduction of consciousness, derealization, depersonalization, analgesia, anesthesia, and amnesia. These negative symptoms are negative dissociative symptoms when something one or more dissociative parts do not synthesize and personify is synthesized by one or more *other* dissociative parts. For example, amnesia qualifies as dissociative amnesia when an individual does not recollect an experience as ANP – but does remember it as a fragile EP. Individuals who do not recollect particular episodes and who do not encompass dissociative parts do not have dissociative amnesia. They have simply forgotten them.

Loss of the quasi-second-person perspective does not necessarily imply the loss of the first-person perspective. For example, some individuals do not (or insufficiently) phenomenally judge themselves when something terrible happens to them. This implies that they do not (or insufficiently) realize at the time, or during and following re-enactments that "this is (was) happening to me" or that a particular action is (was) theirs. However, they do feel that something terrible is happening or has happened, and they act on impulse. Their 'I' is up, but their 'I – me, mine, myself' relationship is down.

Traumatized individuals may also lose the quasi-second-person perspective and substitute it for a second-person perspective by ascribing their own mental and behavioral actions and contents to others. For example, they may project their feelings to someone else, and say "I am not angry, you are," or they may claim that the other person has particular ideas that are in fact their own.

Dissociation of the personality also involves a particular confusion of the quasi-second-person and second-person perspective. This happens when dissociative parts of the personality judge that particular mental and behavioral states of other dissociative parts do not belong to them as well. For example, they may say that "she [a different dissociative part] is weak, but I am tough." Dissociative parts may not engage in a social relationship with other parts, but still know and relate to them. In this case, they are substituting the first-person and quasi-second-person perspective for a third-person perspective in which they perceive other dissociative parts not only as 'not me,' but physically judge them as if they were mere objects.

An excellent example of loss of the quasi-second-person perspective and how this point of view is exchanged for a third-person view was given by the physician, neurologist, and writer Oliver Sacks (1984). One bad day, he went for a firm walk. Alone, high up in the mountains, he enjoyed the landscape. But then joy turned into dread when a bull chased him. Dr. Sacks managed to save himself from the beast's fury, but fell while doing so. His leg was terribly hurt (first-person synthesis). As he examined his extremity, he automatically shifted from a first-person and quasi-second-person perspective to a third-person medical perspective. The leg became numb (lack of synthesis in the first-person perspective), and indeed ceased to be *his* leg at all (lack of personification of the extremity). The analgesia and anesthesia reflect a loss of the first-person perspective (experiencing the hurting) and the quasi-second-person perspective regarding his leg. His leg became *a* leg, a mere object. Engaged in the third-person perspective, Dr. Sacks physically judged that the leg was broken, and he realized there was more than just a leg to fix. It would soon be dark, and his chances to survive the deep nightly frost would be minimal. So he dragged 'the endangered body' down the mountain. He lost his phenomenal leg, but saved his life.

The leg recovered beautifully in the physical sense, but Dr. Sacks was shocked that he was in fact unable to use it in any way. He failed to reinstall the lost first-person experience and quasi-second-person personification of his leg. Apparently stuck in his third-person medical perspective, there was no "I can move my leg" (lack of phenomenal agency) or the realization that "the recovered leg is my leg" (lack of phenomenal ownership). The shock that the leg had "moved itself" (lack of agency, deficient ownership) during a night at the hospital was even more unnerving to him. The leg had technically healed, but not its owner, who had to be trained to repossess the extremity. He had to synthesize and personify it anew.

Loss and Substitution of the Second-Person Perspective

Loss of the second-person perspective may, among other things, occur when we are seriously threatened by someone else and start to perceive the other person as a dangerous object. We then transform our second-person perspective with regard to this individual into a third-person relationship. The 'I-You' relationships becomes an 'I-object' relationship.

Some perpetrators also seem to make this shift. For example, a mother may engage in a second-person perspective of her daughter at times, but typically loses this outlook and substitutes it for an emotionally distant third-person perspective when she abuses her child or neglects her child's needs. Her daughter then becomes more of an object to her, a *thing* to be used for her (i.e., the mother's) personal needs. This perspective reflects an 'I-object' relationship, a third-person perspective. Indeed, perpetrators typically do not empathize with the ones they hurt.

Lina, a patient with DID reported that when her father abused her sexually in brutal ways, she was a mere physical object of his lust and aggression. Once a horrific episode was over, he felt bad about his actions. In tears he excused himself and promised her that "it would never happen again," though 'never again' lasted only a day or two. Lina's descriptions of her father's presentations strongly suggested that he was recurrently alternating between a second-person phenomenal judgment and a third-person physical judgment of her. Her father's shame and excuses may also have been a way for him to ensure that Lina would not tell her mother or other people what her father had done to her. This was at least the view that she developed in a later stage of her successful treatment (she eventually completely overcame her DID). If her interpretation depicts the facts best, her father regarded Lina as a thing he wished to possess and control. During the abuse, he stole her body, and after it, he took her words.

Individuals who have been abused and neglected by other individuals may start to perceive them as dangerous objects when the perpetration sets in. They may also alternate between a second-person ("she is my mother") and third-person perspective ("she is a hurting block of ice"), or have a second-person view as one or more dissociative parts ("my mother is ok"), and a third-person outlook as one or more other dissociative parts ("she's not my mother, she is a disaster"). For example, a chronically abused and neglected child as one of her dissociative parts may phenomenally experience and judge: "I need you, but you scare me" or "You say I'm bad; you must be right, because you are my mother. You punish [i.e., abuse] me, and only bad girls get punished." As a different dissociative part, she may physically judge that "the woman is a monster."

In their dealings with fragile EPs and ANPs, controlling EPs may imitate the perpetrator's third-person physical judgment of their victims. This provides them with a sense of control and power, it may mask that they in fact do care about the other parts, and it hides that they are fragile themselves. In silence, controlling EPs may feel: "Where would we be if I were to show and realize my fragility? I must be tough, I must stay in charge, that's the only thing that counts."

Loss and Substitution of the Third-Person Perspective

The third-person perspective gets lost and becomes substituted for a second-person perspective when an inanimate object is seen as a subject. In the movie *Cast Away*, Tom Hanks is the sole survivor of an airplane crash and is stranded at an uninhabited island. Feeling lonely, he draws a face on a ball, names it 'Wilson,' and starts talking to his friend. He is devastated when he loses Wilson in a storm as he escapes the island on a self-built raft. A patient with minor DID similarly started to experience kettles and pots as her best friends when her mother recurrently locked her in a cellar for a day and a night or longer.

Symptoms and Abnormal Person Perspectives

Many symptoms reflect abnormal person perspectives. Table 10.1 gives an overview.

Table 10.1. Some examples of abnormal person perspectives involving nondissociative and dissociative symptoms.

	Nondissociative: The symptom and abnormal person perspectives apply to the whole individual.	Dissociative: The symptom and abnormal person perspectives apply to one or more, but not all, dissociative parts.
Depersonalization	Abnormal first-person and quasi-second-person perspective. For example, "I act like a robot." "I'm not in touch with myself."	Abnormal first-person and quasi-second-person perspective for one or more dissociative parts. For example, as an ANP the patient doubts: "Do I really exist?" As an EP, he or she does not experience this uncertainty: "Of course I'm here!"
Derealization	Abnormal second-person and third-person perspective. For example, "Everything looks so unreal."	One dissociative part may say, "You and this room look foggy to me, I hardly recognize you, is it you?" Other dissociative parts of the individual perceive the room and the person present as real.
Amnesia	The whole individual has forgotten a particular episode in all person perspectives. For example, "I do not recall what happened that day" or "I forgot what I was supposed to do today."	One dissociative part does not recall a particular condition, episode, or assignment in any person perspective, whereas another dissociative part remembers. For example, one part does not know that the individual is pregnant, whereas another is highly aware of it and knows how the pregnancy occurred. One dissociative part may know that not she but another dissociative part is pregnant. This is a confusion of the first-person/quasi-second-person perspective and the second-person perspective.

	Nondissociative: The symptom and abnormal person perspectives apply to the whole individual.	Dissociative: The symptom and abnormal person perspectives apply to one or more, but not all, dissociative parts.
Anesthesia (kinesthetic, visual, auditory, gustatory, olfactory, genital, and other proprioceptual anesthesia)	Loss of the first-person and quasi-second-person perspective. For example, "During the marathon, at some point I did not feel my legs and feet running." An individual with major depression may say, "My body is numb, it's more like a thing than my body."	Loss of the first-person and quasi-second-person perspective for one dissociative part, but not for another dissociative part. For example, one dissociative part says, "I do not feel (a part of) the body" or "This arm is not mine, I do not feel it." Another dissociative part, however, experiences that "my body is hurting."
Motor inhibitions	Loss of the first-person and quasi-second-person perspective. For example, "I cannot move (a part of) the body" (e.g., as the result of a drug).	Loss of the first-person perspective for a particular dissociative part. For example, "I cannot move my arm" or loss of the first-person and quasi-second-person perspective, as in "I cannot move the leg." However, another dissociative part may feel that "it's too dangerous to move my body."
Intrusions	Lack or loss of the quasi-second-person perspective. For example, "I hear voices in my head."	Loss of the first-person and quasi-second-person perspective for one dissociative part with regard to voices. For example, "I hear voices speaking to me." The voices are the voices of different dissociative parts that address the dissociative part that hears their utterances: "I talk to him, but he does not listen and understand." The first dissociative part thus substitutes the first-person and quasi-second-person perspective for a second-person perspective ("That other part talks to me"), or third-person perspective ("There's a lot of noise in my head").

Intentionality

When we are conscious, we are conscious of something. Every mental act has a mental content, and this content pertains to a perceived and conceived 'object.' Every perception, belief, desire, etc., has an object that it is about: the perceived, the believed, the wanted (see http://en.wikipedia.org/wiki/Intentionality). This 'aboutness' is what the philosophical term 'intentionality' entails. It stems from the Latin *intendere*, which once referred to drawing a bow and aiming at a target. As Thompson (2007) holds, in phenomenology consciousness is seen as intentional by 'aiming toward' something beyond itself.

The intentional object can pertain to an object that is perceived to exist internally or externally. An internal intentional object could be a sensation or a thought, and an external one a physical object, a person, or a situation (that actually includes a perceived constellation of objects). Interoception and exteroception are combined in what Metzinger (2003) calls the 'phenomenal model of the intentionality relation,' that is, the individual's idea of the relationship of his or her 'I' and the intended objects as he or she perceives them. Whereas, ontologically speaking, we are *of* the world rather than *in* the world, the integration of these two phenomenal conceptions (i.e., 'I' and 'object of my consciousness') subjectively situates us *in* the world, *in* the environment as we perceive it.

It is better to use the term 'idea' than the term 'model.' In the phrase 'phenomenal model of the intentionality relation,' the term 'model' concerns a representation or a copy of something else. But what we perceive and conceive is not a representation, copy, or model of something else. There is no 'original version' of the intentionality relation that could be represented, copied, or modeled. As discussed before, there is no thing in itself. There is nothing that exists beyond a living creature's consciousness. All there is is what exists according to an experiencing and knowing organism. For this reason, I use the term 'phenomenal conception' or 'idea of the intentionality relation' (see also Chapter 12).

Another terminological matter is that, given intrinsic links between subject and object, the terms 'subjective' and 'objective reality' or 'external' and 'internal world' can strictly speaking no longer be used. The subjective world and objective world are ontologically identical, as are the external and internal world. However, there are differences between phenomena that are experienced or understood as internal and those that are experienced and known as external: the phenomenal internal world and the phenomenal external world. In this sense, there is a difference between ontology and epistemology.

Person Perspectives and Traumatic Experiences/Memories

The quasi-second-person and the second-person perspective are epistemic intermediates between phenomenal experience in the first-person perspective and physical judgment in the third-person perspective. In the first-person perspective, we are experientially and spatially centered in our body – provided we, for example, do not experience out of body phenomena or sensory anesthesia, as can happen in trauma. In the quasi-second-person perspective, we are also centered in our body, but since we phenomenally judge our phenomenal experience, we are linked with, but also at some distance from, our mental and bodily state. In the quasi-second-person perspective, our phenomenal conception of the intentionality relationship is somewhat more explicit and reflective. We do not just experience, say, pain, but also know that touching some objects hurts, and analogously that touching other objects feels pleasant. For example, in the quasi-second-person perspective we can compare and reflect on the effects of touching hot, warm, and cold objects.

The epistemic bridge between phenomenal experience in the first-person perspective and phenomenal judgment in the quasi-second-person perspective can help us to modulate our emotional experiences. In Spinoza's impressive words (Part V, proposition 3): "An affect which is a passion, ceases to be a passion as soon as we form a clear and distinct idea of it." "Passion" can be understood as intense emotional experience in the first-person perspective. "Clear and distinct idea" pertains to phenomenal judgment and symbolization of phenomenal experience in the quasi-second-person perspective, which modulates the intensity of phenomenal experience in the first-person perspective.

Traumatic memories (defined in Chapter 11) can be understood as passions in the first-person perspective which can be modulated, altered, and integrated in the quasi-second-person perspective. This perspective is needed for personification and certainly for presentification. Combined, these two actions allow the traumatized individual to realize that "the bad things happened (past tense, presentification) to me (quasi-second-person perspective) in that old house (determination of space) when I was a child (determination of time). I now realize how I suffered (synthesis in first-person perspective), but also feel (synthesis in first-person perspective) that it's all over now (presentification of the traumatic past)." Raising the ability and motivation to engage in these integrative actions are major means to achieving the major therapeutic goal of changing sensorimotor, affective traumatic memories (passions) in symbolized autobiographical memories, that is, in narratives involving clear and distinct ideas of *what* happened, *where* it happened, and to *whom*.

In particular following chronic childhood traumatization, traumatized individuals need a relationship with one or more significant and trusted others to engage in these most difficult actions – and to complete them. To be helpful, these others (such as psychotherapists) should not, or at least not only, judge the survivor in an 'objective' fashion, that is, engage in a physical judgment that characterizes the third-person perspective. Rather, they must also phenomenally judge the survivor in the second-person perspective. This phenomenal judgment involves attuning to the survivor's phenomenal world ("pacing"). Pacing is grounded in empathy and joint perspective taking, and implies the phenomenally judging individual's phenomenal experience, hence his or her first-person perspective. At the biological level, second-person perspective relates to mirroring neuron activity and activating the ventral vagal system, which allows for interpersonal affect regulation (Porges, 2007; see Chapter 16).

Epistemic Dependency in Trauma

Trauma-related disorders include and share profoundly shifting dynamic configurations of the brain, the body, and the environment as well as implied epistemic perspectives. A main and common feature of trauma is that these different configurations and epistemic perspectives are insufficiently integrated in the individual's personality. Each dissociative part of the personality is characterized by its own dynamic configurations and epistemic perspectives. In other words, each part encompasses its own set of actual and possible mental and behavioral states. These states involve particular syntheses, personifications, and presentifications, some of which are unique to each dissociative part. An understanding and repair of this dissociative organization of the individual's personality thus requires an understanding of each dissociative part's dynamic configurations of the brain, the body, and the environment and implied epistemic perspectives as well as an understanding of the dynamic relationships among the different dissociative parts. In this sense, it is the whole organism-environment system that is the basic unit of analysis (Järvilehto, 1998a, 1998b, 1999, 2000a, 2000b, 2000c).

As any embedded event, adverse events constitute changes in the actual and historical environment as their context that an individual or dissociative part of an individual senses, perceives, and conceives, and effectuates (Northoff, 2003). The subject who lives them may phenomenally experience and phenomenally judge that a particular change is or was adverse or traumatic. A physical judgment in the third-person perspective does not suffice, because it depends on phenomenal experience and phenomenal judgment. An embedded event is therefore neither adverse nor traumatic just because the DSM-5, scientists, or clinicians say so from a third-person perspective. What scientific and clinical observations can estimate is *how statistically likely* it is that particular kind of embedded event will injure a particular individual. That is, these observations can approximate the statistical probability that a particular event will be a traumatizing biopsychosocial factor in the context of other causal ('risk') factors. Scientists and clinicians can also physically judge whether a particular past event has injured, that is, traumatized, an exposed individual by assessing the symptoms and disorders known to be causally related to particular potentially traumatizing (embedded) events.

Individuals will generally phenomenally experience and judge on their own whether and to what degree events are adverse. When these events, in combination with other causal factors, do cause an injury, that is, a trauma, they have, according to a third-person physical judgment, been traumatizing. When individuals have phenomenally experienced the event as injurious, the adverse event therefore entailed for them a traumatic experience. In the quasi-second-person, they can phenomenally judge that the adverse events constituted a traumatic event. Someone who empathizes with the involved individual can also phenomenally judge and agree that the experience and event were traumatic for that person.

Embedded Events as Action-Dependent Epistemic Units: A Summary

Dynamic configurations of the brain, the body, and the environment constitute the ontological presupposition for the epistemic possibility of events and environments. As discussed before, the environment is not isolated from us as human beings who experience and know this environment. Rather, we are an intrinsic part of the environment to which we are epistemically coupled. In this sense the environment is embedded. In this sense, we are not *in* the world, but are *of* the world as we experience and know it. The implication is that we only experience and know events in the framework of an embedded environment as their context. Embedded events, thus, are not facts – as facts can be isolated from a context – but depend on changes in the environment as their context that we sense, perceive, and conceive.

Our mental and behavioral states are about embedded events and concern meaning. Each of these states is due to synthetic action, that is, the action of synthesizing (Kant, 1781/1998; Janet, 1889) embodied and embedded bodily and emotional feelings and perceptions (i.e., observable events). This synthetic action commonly includes goal-directed mental and motor actions (i.e., to-be-effectuated events). Each mental and behavioral state thus comprises sensorimotor and motorsensory integration (Hurley, 1998; Northoff, 2003).

Our goal-oriented sensorimotor and motorsensory syntheses also tend to include our sense and conception or idea of self. This personification is not given, but depends on two particular actions. One action is the phenomenal conception of a self, and the other action is the integration of a goal-oriented sensorimotor/motorsensory synthesis and this phenomenal sense and conception of self. When we personify a synthesis, we will prereflectively experience in a first-person perspective, and a bit more reflectively know in a quasi-second-person perspective, that the goal-oriented synthesis *concerns us*.

We act on observable events to exert a particular effect, to achieve a particular goal. Our sensorimotor and cognitive actions are thus guided by something beyond themselves. This 'something' involves our will to effectuate events within the environment. What kind of sensorimotor and motorsensory synthesis we generate at a particular time and in a particular situation depends on one or more our current desires. These final causes may pertain to reflective goals (e.g., the desire to own a particular watch), but much more essentially concern basic desires. These are evolutionary derived prereflective desires (urges, strivings) to survive, procreate, explore, eat, sleep, play, attach, defend, etc. For example, being exposed to adverse events, our will concerns the deep will to survive by defending ourselves in one way or another.

Will is experienced in the first-person perspective and precedes phenomenal judgment in the quasi-second-person and second-person perspective, as well as physical judgment in the third-person perspective. Because will as a basic force precedes cognition in the sense of reflective consciousness, the meaning of an embedded event is strongly influenced by will.

The meaning of an embedded event is relative. We do not phenomenally experience and judge a particular event and our implied mental and behavioral state or states in isolation of other events, but we rather distinguish the event and implied states from billions of other possible events and states (Edelman & Tononi, 2000). What we experience and notice are changes in the environment. For example, we phenomenally judge that a particular current event/state is dangerous, dreadful, disgusting, etc., and as such differs from prior or anticipated other events/states that we phenomenally judge to be less dangerous, more joyful, etc. In this sense, we also distinguish between our present goal-orientation(s) and our past and future goal-orientations. Embedded events are about just these changes.

Distinguishing between our past, present, and future goal-orientation is the mental action of presentification (Janet, 1928a; 1935; Van der Hart et al., 2006). Presentification involves

> our creation of the present moment from a synthesis of personified experiences stretched over time and situations, from the past, the present, and the projected future. Ultimately, presentification is our construction of the context and meaning of the present moment within our personal history. (Van der Hart et al., 2006, p. 157)

The intrinsic relationship between the present embrained and embodied individual as a whole biopsychosocial system and the present environment is thus co-dependent on, co-constituted by, and co-occurrent with this individual's biological, psychological, and social spatiotemporal context. This context includes components such as the individual's prior and anticipated (i.e., simulated) experiences, past social relations, and developmental biopsychosocial phase. In short, we are organism-environment systems, living a life in which subject and object are relative to each other. This is the heart of relativity psychology.

Conclusions

Ontology

Anything that is exists by virtue of intrinsic and dynamic configurations of the brain, the body, and the environment. Thus, 'stressful,' 'adverse,' 'traumatic,' and 'traumatizing' events do not exist in ontological isolation from us; rather, we are ontologically embedded in these configurations. And we do not exist in a philosophical idealistic void, but are intrinsically embedded in a material and social environment.

Causality

There are no 'objective' events that are the efficient, linear cause of the way we feel, think, dream, and act. Embodied and embedded, we are associated with interdependent final, formal, material, and efficient causes. Among these, final causes play a major role, because we are meaning-making, self-organizing dynamic systems that strive to realize our will. We can silence our will for a while by satisfying our present desires and urges, and we may even control them a bit. But our pluriform will returns ever and again, and it inescapably and strongly influences our entire life.

Any conceptualization of traumatic events as isolated objects that operate as the efficient cause of a subject's disorder is thus inconsistent with the existence of intrinsic ontological relationships between subject and object. Given dynamic causation, there can be no objectively existing A criterion or other events that linearly, mechanically, and efficiently 'cause' mental disorders such as PTSD or more complex dissociative disorders. By the same token, individuals with these disorders are not the efficient cause of events, because events are not mere conceptions. They do not only exist, so to speak, between the ears.

Intrinsically and dynamically related, adverse events and the environmental context in which they occur as well as the phylogenetically prepared and ontogenetically developing individual cause and mold each other. What exist are intrinsic ontological relationships between conscious subjects (brain, body) and embedded adverse events. These embedded adverse events involve changes in the actual and historical environment as their context that a subject can observe (i.e., sense, perceive, conceive), and effectuate (Northoff, 2003).

This results in particular dynamic configurations of the brain, the body, and the environment which entail 'resilience,' 'pathology' – or anything in between.

To say in third-person perspective that an embedded event has been 'traumatizing' means that it constituted an important dynamic causal factor with respect to the biopsychosocial (see below) injury that evolved. The statement does not imply that the involved event was the only causal factor. For example, the probability that an injury ensues also depends on contextual embedded events such as previous adverse embedded events, lack of social support in the aftermath of the event(s), the subject's age and stage of brain maturation, and his or her genetic make-up.

Epistemology

Distinct dynamic configurations of the brain, the body, and the environment account for pluriform and interrelated epistemic abilities and inabilities. The first-person, quasi-second-person, second-person, and third-person perspective are such configurations that determine what we can experience and know.

In the first-person, quasi-second-person, and second-person perspective – and guided by basic desires – we experience, perceive, conceive, and act on observable and to-be-effectuated events. The first-person perspective is essentially about synthesis and the prereflective phenomenal conceptions of oneself, the world, and intentional relations of self and world.

In the quasi-second-person perspective, these conceptions become a bit more reflective. Personification and presentification also become more explicit and can reach a 'higher' degree of abstraction in this person perspective.

In the second-person perspective, we situate ourselves socially. The reflection in the quasi-second-person and second-person perspective involves phenomenal judgment.

In third-person perspective, we engage in physical judgments. Physical judgment is subjective as well, because it entails an 'I' (subject) – 'object' relationship. If this subject-dependency is overlooked or ignored, we tend to have the idea that there is an objective world we can access and assess. However, this idea is an epistemic and ontological illusion.

Throughout these different epistemic perspectives, there are many different degrees of synthesis, personification, and presentification (cf. Van der Hart et al., 2006). In trauma, these actions are compromised. In Chapter 12, I go into more detail about how the dissociative parts of the personality involve their own first-person, quasi-second-person, second-person, and third-person perspective, that these features relate to these subsystems' problems with synthesis, personification, and presentification (Van der Hart et al., 2006). I thereby use the insights of the current chapter in the next chapter to determine what concepts are needed to capture the phenomena of trauma, and how to define them.

Chapter 11

Trauma and Derivative Concepts: Definitions

> *If names be not correct, language is not in accordance with the truth of things. If language be not in accordance with the truth of things, affairs cannot be carried on to success.*
> Confucius

Using the ontological, epistemological, and empirical considerations outlined in Chapter 9 and Chapter 10, in the present chapter I want to distinguish, link, and define several concepts that together capture one conceptual and metaphorical 'trauma domain.' This domain includes the concepts of 'traumatic experience,' 'traumatic event,' 'traumatic memory,' 'memory of traumatic experiences/events,' 'potentially and actually traumatizing events,' and 'trauma.'

General Ontological Considerations

Ontologically speaking, all of the concepts to be defined pertain to embedment, to particular dynamic configurations of the brain, the body, and the environment. Because any experience and event is relative to other experiences and events, these concepts do not address facts that can be isolated from a context. Rather, they depend on changes in the environment as their context.

Different mental states can be distinguished from each other, because the present dynamic configuration involves a transition from a previous dynamic configuration and will be followed by a transition to a subsequent one (Northoff, 2003). For example, traumatic experiences involve survivors' dynamic configurations of their mental and behavioral state or set of related states that differ from their previous and subsequent dynamic configurations (e.g., their mental state of feeling calm and safe).

General Epistemological Considerations

Transitions between different mental and behavioral states and the implied dynamic figurations of the brain, the body, and the environment can be

- phenomenally experienced in the first-person perspective,
- phenomenally judged (detected, known, personified, distinguished, compared) in the quasi-second-person perspective,
- phenomenally judged in the second-person perspective, and
- physically observed in the third-person perspective.

Traumatic Experience

Experiences that are phenomenally overwhelming and injurious constitute the category of 'traumatic experiences.'

Phenomenological and Epistemic Considerations

Phenomenal experience is tied to the first-person perspective, and involves phenomenal-qualitative properties, commonly described as *qualia*. Qualia concern 'what it is like' to have particular experiences, for example, what it is like to be glad, angry, afraid, ashamed, or overwhelmed.

Qualia

Qualia pertain to combinations of bodily and emotional feelings that lie at the heart of human consciousness. The pivotal role of bodily feelings for consciousness and self-consciousness was clearly recognized by Spinoza. In his *Ethics* (1677), he stated that "[w]e feel that a certain body is affected in many ways" (Axioma 4, p. 32). This body concerns our body, he specified in *De Nagelate Schriften van B.d.S.* (1677), the Dutch translation of the *Opera Posthuma,* which includes *Ethics*.

Experiencing the affections of our body is the cornerstone of self-consciousness, because "[t]he human mind does not know itself, except insofar as it perceives the ideas of these affections of the body" (1677, Proposition 19, p. 47). Spinoza defined an idea as "a concept of the mind which the mind forms because it is a thinking thing" (Definition 3, p. 32). He thus held that our body is affected – and that we can conceive these affections. In this mental act, we become consciously aware of our body: "The object of the idea constituting the human mind is the body, or a certain mode of extension which actually exists, and nothing else" (Proposition 13, p. 39). And it is through our body that we can become consciously aware of external bodies: "The human mind does not perceive any external body as actually existing, except through the ideas of the affections of its own body" (Proposition 26, p. 50).

Thus, without feelings there is no consciousness. Consciousness is primarily experiencing bodily feelings that emerge when the body is affected by affections. This does not mean that we must reflect in order to have these feelings; rather, they are prereflective or precognitive, private, individual, and intrasubjective – and they are fundamental to emotions (Panksepp, 1998). Phenomenal experience, thus, precedes phenomenal judgment.

We become more reflectively aware of our bodily and emotional feelings in the quasi-second-person perspective. In this person perspective we relate ourselves to these feelings, Phenomenally judging that our phenomenal feelings are *our* feelings, they become personalized: "I have bodily feelings, they are my feelings; I have a body, and my body is affected by affections."

Given this private, intrasubjective nature, feelings are not directly accessible by others. Still, emotions are in part social, because they involve outwardly directed and publicly observable actions and vegetative functions (Damasio, 1999). They are therefore, at least in part, open to the second-person and third-person perspective.

Traumatic Experience: A Particular Quale

I propose to reserve the term 'traumatic experience' for the *quale of becoming or being overwhelmed and injured*. 'Being overwhelmed' is a metaphor derived from the physical experience of being physically engulfed, as if by a wave, of becoming submerged, of going under water. Being overwhelmed by experiences thus means being completely and decisively defeated, of being deeply affected in mind and emotion. 'Becoming or being injured' is a related metaphor that pertains to the feeling that phenomenal events (affections) are causing or have caused a phenomenal 'wound.' When experiences are phenomenally experienced and judged as painful, threatening, disgusting, etc., but still 'manageable,' these experiences are not phenomenally experienced and judged as 'traumatic.' No matter how demanding and awful the experiences may be, they are 'challenging,' 'adverse,' or 'highly stressful,' but not 'traumatic.'

Individuals can feel physically and emotionally numbed during one or more episodes of a traumatic/traumatizing event (described and defined below). For example, this sort of anesthesia is implied in tonic immobility (i.e., playing dead). Feeling numb as such does not fit the category of traumatic experience, because it does not involve the quale of being overwhelmed. However, for some individuals the experience of losing or having lost bodily and emotional feelings for a period of time can be phenomenally overwhelming and hence traumatic.

Traumatic experience can be associated with the diminution or loss of mental and behavioral functions. For example, survivors may experience difficulty seeing, hearing, or concentrating as the drama unfolds. They may also lose their ability for phenomenal judgment in the quasi-second-person and second-person perspective, and their ability for physical judgment in the third-person perspective in some respects and degrees. When these diminutions or losses phenomenally overwhelm them, the experience constitutes a traumatic experience.

Traumatic Experience and Phenomenal Self

In most cases, a traumatic experience includes the synthesis of a phenomenal conception of self, however rudimentary this idea may be. Individuals who undergo the experience commonly generate an 'I' who is the subject of the experience and who has a point of view. Some individuals report that they lost any coherent idea of self during such horrific events, which was the most frightening aspect. One patient experienced her (conception of) self shattered in a multitude of disconnected and discoordinated pieces when her father forced a loaded gun in her vagina during her childhood[1].

It can happen that individuals do not integrate the phenomenal conceptions of self, world, and self-of-the-world which they generate during such an experience and their previous and subsequent phenomenal conceptions of self, world, and self-of-the-world. Their personality does not become divided when the nonintegrated phenomenal conceptions of self, world, and self-of-the-world cease to exist when the experience is over. In this case, the individuals involved do not form a lasting autobiographical memory of the episode. They forget what happened and what they did. For example, they may have been drunk or drugged. (I have disregarded implicit memory in the example.)

This type of explicit amnesia, this kind of forgetting, is very unlikely to happen with respect to excessively adverse events. The evolution of our species would not have carried us very far if we were to commonly forget what (kind of) events pose a most serious threat to our mental and physical integrity. However, recollecting extremely adverse events and integrating these recollections are two different things. When individuals do not integrate the phenomenal conceptions of themselves, the world, and their self-of-the-world that they generated during a traumatic experience into their pretraumatic and posttraumatic life (and occasionally re-enact these conceptions), their personality constitutes a dissociative structure. The nonintegrated phenomenal conceptions of self, world, and self-of-the-world involved qualify as an EP. The existence of the EP implies that the individuals' posttraumatic personality also encompasses an ANP. The dissociation of their personality lasts until they integrate the ANP and EP, and all that belongs to these subsystems, particularly the traumatic memories that EP 'contained,' or rather, occasionally re-enacted.

As stated above, more than one EP and one ANP may evolve in the context of one or more adverse events, particularly chronic childhood abuse and neglect. When chronic adverse events start early in life, the child may not have had or may not get a chance to become a reasonably integrated personality. Developing an integrated phenomenal self is a developmental achievement. This explains in part why the formation of a complex dis-

1 As shared by the patient during a videotaped sensorimotor psychotherapy session with Pat Ogden.

sociation of the personality is far more likely in the context of early onset of adverse life, than in the context of adversity happening to an adult whose pretraumatic personality constituted a rather coherent and cohesive structure.

Traumatic Experience and Intentionality

Traumatic experience does not exist in an environmental void, but is intentional. That is, survivors relate their phenomenal experience to their perceived and conceived environment. In other words, the traumatic experience comprises a synthesis of their current phenomenal conception of self ('I, me, mine, myself') and their current phenomenal conception of the intentionality relation ('I as related to [a part of] my environment'). The term 'traumatic experience' captures the integration of survivors' actual, interoceptive 'I' and their actual, exteroceptive phenomenal world. The traumatic experience pertains to their personal feelings of being overwhelmed and getting injured by their conception of what happens to them.

Traumatic Experience and Physical Judgment

Physically observed and judged in the third-person perspective, the difference between traumatic experiences and adverse, highly stressful experiences is that the latter (but not the former) are associated with (largely) adequate synthesis, personification, and presentification (see below). An adverse experience is clearly awful, but it does not involve a lack of coordination and integration of the experience into the individual's personality. Traumatic experiences, however, do not become integrated in the individual's personality, do not, or insufficiently, become symbolized once the experience is over, and continue to exist as traumatic memories (defined below).

Causal Considerations Regarding Traumatic Experience

The transitions of dynamic configurations of the brain, the body, and the environment with respect to traumatic experience involve all four Aristotelian causes.

Final Cause

Traumatic experience involves a synthesis, a particular phenomenal integration of observable and to-be-effectuated events in the environment. Mediated by will as a basic force and goal-orientation, the synthesis includes a perception of danger and terror, related feelings and emotions, and goal-oriented behaviors. This involves the will to survive, to defend one's body and life by means of actions such as tend and befriend, flight, freeze, fight, or tonic immobility. It can also concern the urge to cry for a protective caretaker (attachment cry).

The urges to defend and find caretaker protection serve as the final causes of the dynamic configuration that the traumatic experience is in ontological regard. In other words, the individual's will to survive threat causes a particular dynamic configuration of his or her the brain, the body, and the environment. This will causes the dynamics of his or her feelings, perceptions, conceptions, and behavioral actions: There is a danger, and that danger must be dealt with. This does not imply that the involved synthesis is in fact adequate. For example, the attempt at flight or other forms of mammalian defense may be more or less disorganized (and fail).

Formal Cause

The formal cause of a traumatic experience relates to an organizational or structural division of personality as a whole system. The major characteristic of this organization is the dissociation of the personality in two or more dynamic self-organizing subsystems (Nijenhuis & Den Boer, 2009; Van der Hart et al., 2006). Each of these includes a phenomenal conception of self, an 'I,' world, and self-of-the-world, however rudimentary and prereflective (i.e., precognitive) the involved conceptions may be (see Chapters 12 and 13). This dissociation relates to a lack of integration of traumatic experience in the personality as a whole biopsychosocial system. It more specifically involves a particular lack of adequate synthesis, personification, and presentification.

In trauma, the basic division of the personality is between two dissociative subsystems or parts, fragile EP and ANP. Mediated by action systems for defense and/or attachment, as fragile EP the patient is phenomenally immersed in the traumatic/traumatizing event (defined below). Mediated by action systems for daily life, as ANP the patient does not, or only insufficiently, integrate the traumatic experience as it unfolds or in the posttraumatic stage for the duration of the trauma-related disorder. When ANP attempts to go on with life without integrating the traumatic experience and the implied fragile EP, this EP remains phenomenally fixated in the traumatic experience.

A division of a fragile EP may occur during a traumatic experience. For example, whereas one fragile EP might feel, and thus synthesize the bodily and emotional components of the experience, a different fragile EP might only see and hear what happens, and thus synthesize only particular visual and auditory perceptions. Phenomenally, this 'observing' EP can be out of the body.

When the traumatic experience has passed, the survivor can overcome his or her division of personality by integrating the traumatic experience and the different dissociative parts that have evolved. The traumatic experience is resolved and becomes an integrated autobiographical memory of an experience that occurred but is no longer traumatic. However, when the dissociative subsystems mentally avoid each other due to a lack of integrative capacity, motivation, and lack of integrative support from trusted other individuals, such integration fails to occur. In this context and with recurrent traumatic experiences, rudimentary EPs may become more elaborate. They can 'emancipate' themselves (Van der Hart et al., 2006). When EPs emancipate themselves, they integrate additional traumatic experiences and possibly some nontraumatic experiences as well.

Most dissociative parts also intrude on each other's domains. For example, ANP may phenomenally experience dissociative flashbacks that 'stem from' a fragile EP, whether or not ANP knows this. When ANP does not 'use' these intrusions to recognize and accept the fragile EP – and help this dissociative part by integrating its traumatic experiences – the fragile EP may feel rejected by ANP. This may reinforce EP's feelings and ideas of worthlessness and that life is essentially misery.

For brevity's sake, the above discussion does not include controlling EPs, but let it be understood that these prototypical EPs can be major components of the survivor's personality structure, particularly following chronic interpersonal abuse and neglect. Controlling EPs are primarily mediated by the social dominance action system.

Efficient and Material Causes

Traumatic experience cannot be adequately understood in terms of isolated efficient and material causes. The existence of dynamic ontological relations between the brain, the body, and the environment precludes an explanation of trauma in terms of an isolated material and/or social cause (i.e., an isolated material and/or social event) and effect (i.e., an isolated mind/brain). It also bars an account in terms of an isolated efficient cause (e.g., a physical cause such as the release of stress hormones or the formation of particular neuronal states) and effect (e.g., phenomenal mental states). Causation is dynamic, circular, and pluriform. According to Northoff (2003, pp. 293–294), "[f]inal and formal causes serve as a guide for material and efficient causes, which, in turn, provide realization and implementation of the former. Material and efficient causes may therefore be regarded as intermediate causes since they depart from and return to final and formal causes."

Definition of Traumatic Experience

Ontologically speaking, traumatic experience involves a particular dynamic configuration of the brain, the body, and the environment – i.e., an embedded mental and behavioral state or a cohesive set of closely related states – that differs from previous and subsequent nontraumatic dynamic configurations.

Phenomenally speaking, traumatic experience concerns a felt injury. The injury involves overwhelming bodily and emotional feelings with respect to an injurious phenomenal world (i.e., traumatic/traumatizing events, defined below).

Epistemically speaking, traumatic experience is essentially tied to the first-person perspective. It involves a current prereflective phenomenal conception of self, an 'I' (however rudimentary) centered in actual bodily and emotional feelings. Traumatized individuals synthesize this 'I' with their current phenomenal here and now, that is, their prereflective phenomenal conception of the actual environment and their relationship to this world.

Causally speaking, traumatic experience is associated with dynamic causation. The final cause of traumatic experience is the will to defend and find safety. Its formal cause is a division of the personality, with at least one EP immersed in overwhelming bodily feelings and emotional reactions, and at least one ANP remaining at an experiential and epistemic distance from one or more EPs and the traumatic experience of these parts. However, EP may also be mediated by tonic immobility, which implies features such as a degree of analgesia, anesthesia, emotional numbing, bodily paralysis, depersonalization, and derealization. Different dissociative parts have different phenomenal experiences during and following traumatic/traumatizing events. For example, different EPs can synthesize different feelings. ANP may not be activated during the event, so that this dissociative part does not participate in the traumatic experience. When ANP is activated, this part does not or insufficiently synthesize, personify, and presentify the experience. For example, ANP may be 'out-of-the-body' during the event or feel depersonalized and emotionally detached. This lack of integration involves a lack of synthesis, personification, and presentification with respect to the involved EPs and their experiences. The dynamic causation of a traumatic experience includes material causes (e.g., neurons) and efficient causes (e.g., massive release of norepinephrine and occurrence of environmental forces) as intermediate causes.

Traumatic (Embedded) Event

Phenomenological and Epistemic Considerations

The concept of 'traumatic event' pertains to individuals' phenomenal judgment of their traumatic experience(s). Since the phenomenal judgment of bodily and emotional feelings is crucial in this regard, traumatized individuals can phenomenally judge their traumatic experiences only directly as the dissociative part or parts of them that synthesized these feelings. As these parts, they can, in the quasi-second perspective, phenomenally detect, recognize, and know that a particular experience has been overwhelming, and they can compare the judgment with their phenomenal judgment of other experiences. This direct comparative phenomenal judgment yields the conception of a traumatic event: "Unlike other experiences, this terrible event overwhelmed and wounded me."

Phenomenal Judgment, Personification, and Presentification

Personification as well as integration and temporal segregation of past, present, and future events, that is, presentification, are epistemic conditions for the possibility of adequate, direct phenomenal judgment (Chalmers, 1996; Northoff, 2003). Dissociative parts involved in traumatic experiences will phenomenally judge that the traumatic experience has happened to them, although some may insufficiently personalize it. For example, the mental state someone engaged in tonic immobility may not allow adequate personalization. Dissociative parts not experientially involved in traumatic experiences such as ANPs may judge that they do not pertain to them. ANPs may know about the experiences, but knowing about these experiences does not necessarily imply personifying and realizing them. They may phenomenally (mis)judge that the events happen or happened to somebody else.

Like any event traumatic events are in principle phenomenally judged in terms of space, time, and causality. Thus, the dissociative part or parts of a survivor which phenomenally experience the event or events also phenomenally judge that the events happen in a particular place and time, and that they involve cause and effect relationships. Traumatic events also commonly involve meaning, because they pertain to observable and to-be-effectuated events within the environment. For example, when an individual as a particular EP experiences and judges that the traumatic event is happening in the 'here and now,' he or she may phenomenally judge: "He wants to get me, I must run," or "This is so disgusting, how can I stop it?"

The dissociative part or parts of individuals which phenomenally experience a traumatic event commonly phenomenally judge that the traumatic experiences and events they re-enact constitute *actual* traumatic experiences and events. Re-enacting these experiences and events, they may phenomenally judge that they are presently in a traumatizing, rather than in a safe environment (misjudgment of space), and that the traumatic event is happening right now (misjudgment of time). They may also believe that the traumatic event happens because they are "bad and deserve punishment," or that uttering anger regarding a perpetrator might provoke this individual and cause more abuse, rather than realizing that the perpetrator has long died or cannot hear their words when they talk to their therapist or some other trusted individual.

Phenomenal misjudgment of space, time, and causality of dissociative parts are not limited to these re-enactments. For example, many fragile EPs do not appreciate that traumatic experiences are different from preceding and later nontraumatic experiences. They do not grasp that time matches past the traumatic experiences, and that these experiences are in fact over. Their misjudgment also pertains to their own and others' identity. EPs phenomenally misjudge that they are still the ones they were when the traumatic events happened, and that other dissociative parts and other individuals including the perpetrators have not grown older. Phenomenally they are caught in a horror that does not age, for them life is a ongoing struggle to survive traumatic events.

Traumatic Events in the Second-Person Perspective of Observing Dissociative Parts

To repeat, some dissociative parts judge that one or more adverse events in fact did not happen to them. This misjudgment can ensue when they have not synthesized and personified these events or the components of these events. However, they may still know about them. They may phenomenally judge that one or more other dissociative parts were exposed to these events, and that these events were traumatic for these parts. This judgment is possible when they relate to the involved dissociative parts in a second-person perspective. For example, the judging dissociative part might empathically say, "I am sorry for him." However, their second-person perspective and phenomenal judgment may also be dismissive. For example, an ANP might assert, "I want her (i.e., a fragile EP) to leave me alone." A controlling EP may phenomenally judge that the involved fragile EP is despicably weak, and tell her "I loathe you." The possibility of engagement in a third-person physical judgment regarding hurt EPs is discussed below.

Traumatic Events in the Second-Person Perspective of Observing Individuals

Family members, partners, friends, psychotherapists, or still other persons may also phenomenally judge that particular events were traumatic for an individual, provided they relate to this individual in a second-person perspective. Engagement in this empathic relationship may stress or even overwhelm the observer. For example, overly empathic therapists risk burnout, compassion fatigue, or secondary traumatization. Therapists may also overidentify with the interests of fragile EPs and in this context ignore or downplay the will of ANPs and controlling EPs. When this happens, therapists have practically become a part of their patient's dissociative system and traumatic life, rather than a guide toward an integrative solution to s or her dissociative disorder.

In the extreme case, an engaged observer may start to phenomenally experience, and perhaps even phenomenally (mis)judge, what actually happened to a survivor or what happened to the observer. For example, in the course of his treatment it turned out that a patient's recurrently intruding traumatic memories did not pertain to his life but to that of his grandfather (Van der Hart & Van der Velden, 1995, p. 430). The grandfather had shared his traumatic experiences with the patient when he was only a young boy. Deeply touched by his beloved grandfather's suffering, the patient took these experiences so strongly into himself that he later relived them as if they were his own personal experiences.

Traumatic Events: Beyond the Reach of the Third-Person Perspective

When dissociative parts or individuals engage a third-person perspective of the dissociative part or whole individual they are observing, they may physically judge that the event was *traumatizing* for the involved dissociative part or individual.

The third-person perspective characterizes ANPs and at least some controlling EPs. The more the judging dissociative parts engage in this epistemic perspective, the less they will know the event as a traumatic event – and the more they will perceive it as a phenomenally distant occasion. For example, Rita regarded the motor vehicle accident that happened to her when she was three years old as a distant phenomenal and physical event. It was still slightly phenomenal for her as ANP, because she vaguely recalled it as a personal event, but she more essentially related to the accident as a mere physical and inconsequential event that was of no concern to her anymore. However, for the three-year-old fragile EP that Rita's personality also encompassed, the accident constituted a recurrent traumatic event.

Clinicians and scientists who attempt to analyze or study individuals 'objectively' also take the third-person perspective. Engaging in this perspective, they may physically judge that a particular event has traumatized an individual who experienced it. They may assess symptoms, disorders, abnormal brain structures, and abnormal patterns of brain activity. These are all material and efficient causes.

There are several downsides to a third-person judgment that is presumed to be 'purely objective,' i.e., purely physical. Perfectly objective observers cannot empathically understand what the traumatic experience was really like, and thus they cannot phenomenally assess whether the event was in fact *traumatic* for the involved person or dissociative part. They are also unable to grasp the meaning the adverse event had for the individual involved. Another individual's ability to empathize and sympathize with an individual's traumatic experience, and to grasp its meaning for this person, depends on his or her ability and willingness to engage in the second-person perspective.

The most serious trouble of 'perfect objectivity' is that it is an *illusion*. We are not machines. Our third-person perspective is possible only because of the existence of our first-person perspective. Phenomenal experience and judgment always precede physical judgment. Furthermore, we are not tabula rasas. We have interests. We are under the spell of a will that affects our physical judgment, for better or for worse. We can modulate and coordinate our will to a degree, but we cannot annihilate it.

For example, professional role prescriptions cannot prevent that professionals engage in an affective second-person perspective on the traumatized individuals they study. Some professionals empathize with them. Others fear, despise, or otherwise reject them, for example, because traumatized individuals confront them with human fragility in a harsh world – two realities that some would rather keep at bay. Third-persons may also have personal problems or features that manifest in their first-person and quasi-second-person perspectives, that obscure or distort their phenomenal judgment in the second-person perspective and their physical judgment in third-person perspective. These problems are a common cause of countertransferential reactions regarding traumatized individuals.

Enriching Physical Judgment with an Explicit Phenomenal Judgment

Dissociative parts that physically judge an event to have been traumatizing for particular other dissociative parts can in principle enrich their view with the phenomenal judgment that the event was traumatic for those part(s). This deepening occurs when they also engage in a second-person, empathic relationship with the judged parts. This enrichment is actually a common, explicit treatment goal, however hard it may be for the involved dissociative parts to overcome their fear, disgust, or hate of the parts they may judge so mercilessly.

A next step may be the substitution of the second-person perspective for the first-person and quasi-second-person perspectives. With this additional step, previously uninvolved dissociative parts will assume the experience of the traumatic event. This integrative action involves a synthesis and personification of the experience. The traumatic event, then, becomes a personal traumatic experience.

Observers may also shift from the third-person perspective to the second-person perspective. This shift involves a move from an observational stance to an experiential relationship. For example, scientists who tried to be 'objective' regarding patients with complex dissociative disorders in their studies may become more affectively involved when they get to know their 'observational objects' more as deeply hurt individuals. This shift may also happen to clinicians who initially believed that DID is factitious, when they get to know afflicted individuals and their disorder better.

Causal Considerations

Traumatic events are associated with dynamic causation. That is, the transition of dynamic configurations of the brain, the body, and the environment which are associated with shifts from nontraumatic to traumatic events involves all four Aristotelian causes.

Final Cause

Like traumatic experiences, traumatic events essentially include a goal-orientation in relation to changes in the embedded environment. Hence, traumatic events are about meaning and do not pertain to isolated stimuli.

Formal Cause

The difference between an aversive or highly stressful event and traumatic event is that the first (but not the latter) is associated with (largely) adequate synthesis, personification, and presentification by the individual as a whole system. The term 'traumatic event' stands for the phenomenal judgment in quasi-second-person perspective and second-person perspective that a particular event was injurious. This judgment is typically associated with a particular organization of the personality of the individual who experienced the event. This organization is the formal cause of a traumatic event. It involves a dissociation of the personality in one or more ANPs and EPs. In chronic traumatization, particularly when it started in early childhood, the division is commonly between one or more prototypical ANPs, fragile EPs, and controlling EPs. The different dissociative parts that have evolved will judge the dissociation-eliciting event differently. For example, some, but not all, parts may regard it as a traumatic event and/or as a personal event (see above).

The dissociation of the personality is adaptive when the individual is unable to integrate the traumatic experience/event. The division is maladaptive when he or she maintains the dissociation of the personality despite sufficient ability and opportunity to integrate the traumatic events and the different dissociative parts.

Failure to integrate a traumatic event in the personality of the phenomenally judging individual is clearly adequate when the involved individual did not actually have the traumatic experience. Having empathy with a survivor or a surviving dissociative part is proper. Symbiosis is not.

Material and Efficient Causes

The phenomenal judgment of events as something traumatic requires material and efficient causes, such as a brain and brain states as well as a body and physiological states. These causes must not be understood in a classical sense of isolated causes leading to isolated effects. Material and efficient causes rather constitute intermediates in a framework of dynamic and circular causality that crucially involves formal and final causality.

Definition

Ontologically speaking, a traumatic event is embedded, because it involves a particular dynamic configuration of the brain, the body, and the environment.

Epistemically speaking, a traumatic event concerns the phenomenal judgment of a traumatic phenomenal experience, thus it pertains to meaning. In the quasi-second-person perspective, this judgment involves intrasubjective communication, i.e., the detection, recognition, and personification of a traumatic experience as a phenomenal-qualitative state, and the comparison of this state and other states. Traumatized individuals or dissociative parts thereof thus know a traumatic event to be a combination of particular changes in their embedded brain, body, and environment. This knowledge appears to them as a mental state, because the human brain does not tell its owner how it forms its own brain states. In the second-person perspective, the phenomenal judgment involves intersubjective communication. This communication can be between different dissociative parts or between different individuals.

Traumatic events are associated with dynamic causation. The final cause of a traumatic event is the phenomenally judged goal(s) to which the survivor's actions are oriented with respect to his or her perceptions of changes in the environment. Different parts tend to have their own final cause(s). The formal cause of a traumatic event is a dissociative self-organization of personality. The dynamic causation of a traumatic event includes material and efficient causes (e.g., stress hormones, environmental stimuli) as intermediate causes.

Different dissociative parts with phenomenal access to traumatic experiences tend to phenomenally judge these experiences in their own way. Dissociative parts without phenomenal access to these experiences are not in a position to engage in this phenomenal judgment. At best, they can physically observe and judge a traumatizing event (discussed and defined below) in third-person perspective.

Traumatic Memory

Phenomenological and Epistemic Considerations

Reactivated traumatic memories are re-enactments that involve reconceptions of past experiences and events. Traumatized individuals (i.e., the dissociative parts of them) who re-enact a traumatic memory in the form of active mammalian defensive reactions or attachment re-experience it in highly aroused sensorimotor and often highly emotionally charged behavioral ways. Their field of consciousness is small. Fixated on a past goal-orientation that they phenomenally experience and judge as an urgent present goal-orientation, they say to themselves "I am in danger, I must defend myself." When they spot the threat and hide, run, freeze, fight, or cry for help, they are generally highly emotional. Dissociative parts that re-enact a degree of tonic immobility become more or less paralyzed and hypoaroused. The quality of consciousness diminishes, which then manifests itself in symptoms of depersonalization, derealization, anesthesia as well as absent-mindedness and other losses of concentration. Some people apparently lose consciousness altogether, as happens in a dissociative stupor.

A particular type of traumatic memory is traumatic relational re-enactment. In relational re-enactment a traumatized individual relates to another person as if he or she were or were like a perpetrator. The traumatized individual may, but need not consciously, be aware of this transference. Moreover, conscious awareness of the phenomenon does not necessarily end it. Affect generally precedes cognition, so that the will to prevent further relational harm may dramatically outweigh the traumatized individual's understanding that the other person, say, his or her psychotherapist, has no intentions to hurt him or her whatsoever. A further relational complication is that each dissociative part can entertain his or her own kind of traumatic relational re-enactment. These different transferences entail complications for the therapeutic endeavor as well as for the relations that the different dissociative parts have with each other. For example, one EP may feel attached to the therapist, another EP may despise him or her, and the ANP may stay at a comfortable emotional and physical distance.

Traumatic Memory and EP

Tied to one or more EPs, traumatic memories are not or insufficiently integrated in the personality. Different EPs may have synthesized and personified different components of the traumatic experience. For example, one EP may have synthesized the fear it involved, a different EP the rage. Or one EP has synthesized one episode of a traumatic event, another EP has 'absorbed' a different episode of the complete event. Different involved EPs therefore tend to reconceive and re-enact the traumatic experience and event in their own way.

Traumatic Memory and ANP

As ANP, traumatized individuals are focused on the present, and have not or insufficiently integrated (synthesized, personified, presentified) the traumatic past. Unless intruded on by re-enacting EPs, ANPs do not or insufficiently recollect the nonintegrated traumatic experience and event in the first-person and quasi-second-person perspective. They may physically judge the traumatic memory in the third-person perspective (e.g., describe the event in a nonpersonal, factual way), or phenomenally judge it from a rather distant second-person perspective involving a more or less far reaching lack of synthesis and personification (e.g., describe it with some feelings, but talk about the event as if it has happened to someone else).

An EP's re-enactment can be more or less complete. When an EP intrudes on an ANP, the ANP may more or less fully re-enact the traumatic experience and event along with the EP. When the ANP becomes hyperaroused or hypoaroused, it may not manage to integrate the traumatic memory. The ANP may also stop integrating the traumatic memory when particularly difficult episodes and feelings come into focus. An ANP's highway to this avoidance is lowering the level of consciousness – or even losing consciousness altogether. For example, the involved individual may faint, have a pseudoepileptic attack, or switch from ANP to some EP.

ANPs may also be amnestic for the traumatic event. In this case, they do not engage in any person-perspective regarding the event. This lack does not preclude the possibility that they are occasionally influenced by EPs in some regards. For example, an ANP may be intruded on by an EP's physical pain, yet remain unaware that this intrusion in fact stems from the involved EP and one or more traumatic memories associated with this EP. In this case, ANP experiences the pain, but does not understand its source and meaning.

Traumatic Memories and Autobiographical Memories of Traumatic Experiences/Events

There are major distinctions between traumatic memories and integrated, autobiographical memories of traumatic experiences and events.

Autobiographical memories of traumatic experiences/events are primarily phenomenal judgments and involve the quasi-second-person perspective ("I remember my painful past"). In functional regard, this remembrance involves a linkage between two final causes, i.e., the past and the present goal-orientation (cf. Northoff, 2003). When survivors recollect a traumatic experience/event as an autobiographical memory, they phenomenally take the past to the present with the understanding that the present is more real than the past. In this ideal case, they have synthesized, personified, and presentified the traumatic past, so that they can subsequently 're-collect' it as a part of their personal history.

Engaging in this reconception, they simulate a past goal-orientation and compare this orientation to their present goal-orientation. This comparison includes a comparison between past and actual feelings and emotions.

As narratives – as stories told – memories of a traumatic past involve *symbolic referents* (words – capture – experiences, events; Deacon, 1997). Through symbolization the traumatic past becomes condensed, more voluntarily recalled and socially shared, and thereby less emotional and less physical. The less traumatized individuals can disentangle the horrific past and the safer present, the more this past takes to the form of *icons*, as sensorimotor and emotional re-enactments, rather than of symbols (Peirce, 1978).

Integration of Traumatic Memories

How iconic the recollection of a traumatic past becomes depends on the extent to which the traumatic memories are integrated into the personality, and thereby changed. The more they become integrated, the less physical and emotionally intense they become. With difficult integrative actions, icons become symbols, which means that traumatic memories become autobiographical memories of traumatic experiences and events.

To paraphrase Spinoza, a traumatic memory, which is a passion (i.e., an intense inadequate affect), ceases to be passion when a traumatized individual has developed a clear and distinct conception of what happened to him or her and can put the experience and event in a narrative form, that is, in verbal symbols. This symbolization, Janet taught, involves the survivor's realization (1) about what the traumatic experience was like (synthesis), (2) that the traumatic experience happened in the past, (3) that it had consequences for his or her later existence, thus that this past is embedded in the present and future (presentification), and (4) that it happened to him or her personally (personification).

When traumatized individuals have fully integrated their traumatic memories, they commonly still recognize the past feelings in the quasi-second-person perspective. They may also continue to be in subjective contact with their former goal-orientation in the first-person perspective, but this goal-orientation is no longer experienced in an immediate and total sense (Northoff, 2003). They also know that they are reflectively oriented toward a past goal-orientation that is different from the present goal-orientation when they remember the traumatic past and occasionally share it with other individuals.

The past goal-orientation may still have some qualitative features, but it is not an immediate phenomenal experience anymore. It resembles telling or retelling a sad story (Janet, 1928a; Van der Kolk & Van der Hart, 1991; Van der Hart et al., 2006). Autobiographical memories of traumatic experiences are thus primarily narratives regarding recognized former observations and goal-orientations. They are condensed, adapted to an audience, and hence social, and they can be interrupted and resumed at will.

Definition

Ontologically, traumatic memories involve a particular dynamic configuration of the brain, the body, and the environment. *Phenomenally* in the first-person perspective, and *epistemically* in the quasi-second-person perspective, traumatic memories involve confusion between past and present observed and to-be-effectuated events within the environment. The confusion is that there are no, or in any case far too little, experienced and known distinctions between the phenomenal past and present. Because of a lack of integration of the traumatic past, this past remains too phenomenally real and remains too iconic when reactivated. In this context, the actual present does not become phenomenally real enough for the EP who holds (or EPs who hold) the involved memory. ANPs tend to lose their phenomenal orientation to the actual present during massive intrusions in at least some crucial regards; otherwise they would appreciate far better that they are actually safe.

Traumatic memories are associated with dynamic causation. Material causation (e.g., an intact brain and [rest of the] body) and efficient causality (e.g., neurophysiological and other physiological reactions) serve as intermediate goals. The dissociation of the personality in dissociative parts that do and do not remember the traumatic past in part or in full constitutes the formal cause of traumatic memories. The phrase 'to-be-effectuated events' captures the final cause or goal-orientation that characterize the involved memories.

Traumatic memories cannot be experienced in the third-person perspective. However, as observable emotions and associated behaviors, they are open to physical judgment. Observers have only indirect access to traumatized individual's traumatic memories. In the empathic second-person perspective, they can come closer in this regard, and feel along more with the re-enacting survivor.

Traumatizing (Embedded) Event

Ontological Considerations

Whether or not an embedded event will be, is, or has been traumatizing for a particular individual cannot be determined in isolation of that individual and cannot be determined a priori. This is because what exists are dynamic configurations of the brain, the body, and the environment, and because it is the individual who phenomenally experiences (first-person perspective) and phenomenally judges (quasi-second-person perspective; and some dissociative parts of the personality in second-person perspective) the event. Without phenomenal experience and judgment, events, and hence traumatic/traumatizing events, would not exist.

Epistemological Considerations

The terms 'potentially' and 'actually traumatizing event' pertain to physical judgment in third-person perspective. The term 'traumatizing' involves the physical judgment that a particular embedded event has injured the individual in a biopsychosocial sense. This physical judgment eventually relies on the phenomenal experience and phenomenal judgment of observers, without which a physically judging person could not know or understand human mental and behavioral life in any way.

Empirical Considerations

Some embedded events are statistically, and hence empirically, more likely than other embedded events to be traumatizing. As would be expected from the idea that what exists are dynamic configurations of the brain, the body, and the environment, research demonstrates that the relative probability of an event being traumatizing depends on a number of the brain-, body-, and environment-related factors. These factors include developmental age, physical condition, intelligence, sex, and intensity as well as duration of adverse stimulation. In general, extreme threats to the integrity of the body and to biopsychosocial life constitute environmental components of dynamic configurations of the brain, the body, and the environment that entail a high risk of being traumatizing.

Definition

Ontologically, a traumatizing event, like any embedded event, involves a particular dynamic configuration of the brain, the body, and the environment. *Epistemically*, the term 'traumatizing event' pertains to the third-person perspective, thus to the physical judgment that a particular event may cause (potentially traumatizing or adverse event) or has caused (actually traumatizing event), in a dynamic sense, a biopsychosocial injury described as a trauma. The essence of this injury is a lack of integration of the phenomenal experience and phenomenal event in the survivor's personality.

Trauma

Ontological and Epistemological Considerations

Ontologically, trauma involves a particular dynamic configuration of the brain, the body, and the environment. *Epistemically*, trauma reflects a biopsychosocial injury that can be phenomenally experienced in the first-person perspective, phenomenally judged in the quasi-second-person and second-person perspective, and physically judged in the third-person perspective.

In the first-person perspective, trauma is the phenomenal experience of being injured (e.g., experiencing trauma-related symptoms such as experiencing flashbacks, nightmares, emotional and physical numbing, hearing voices of dissociative parts that imitate perpetrators). In the quasi-second-person and second-person perspective, trauma reflects the phenomenal judgment of being injured (e.g., detecting and recognizing in a phenomenal sense that a nightmare pertains to a traumatic event). In the third-person perspective, trauma constitutes the physical observation and judgment that an individual has developed biopsychosocial pathology in intimate relationships with a prior adverse event that is therefore physically judged to be an actually traumatizing event.

Causal Considerations

According to physical observation and interpretation, trauma involves a biopsychosocial injury related to a particular dynamic and historical configuration of brain body, and environment. While the injury can involve a wide variety of biological, psychological, and psychosocial phenomena, its formal cause is a lack of integration of particular experiences/events. This lack of integration manifests itself as a particular dissociation of personality. The different dissociative parts that have evolved include their own final causes (e.g., the will to survive, attach, procreate, etc.), formal causes (i.e., each dissociative part has its own biopsychosocial organization) and efficient causes (e.g., neurophysiological reactions). They also include their own person perspectives.

Trauma involves dynamic causation and thus cannot be reduced to material and efficient causality. Material and efficient causation have a mediating role in the context of dynamic causation, which more essentially includes final and formal causes. For example, smaller hippocampal volume may be a material cause of memory problems, but this structural brain feature in itself does not determine what a traumatized individual does not recall as ANP, but does recall as EP.

Empirical Considerations

The odds that a trauma ensues is dependent on the current and past dynamic configurations of the involved individual's brain, body, and environment. Subject (brain/body)-related risk factors include biological and psychological features such as the individual's genetic makeup, age and developmental phase, sex, intelligence as well as the phenomenal experience *and judgment of his or her prior life. Because the human mind requires interpersonal relations to exist and evolve, trauma is as much psychosocial as it is biological and psychological.*

Object (environment)-related risk factors (which are necessarily dependent on an experiencing and knowing subject, since there is no object without an experiencing and knowing subject) include features such as the kind, intensity, and duration of environmental stimulation as well as the relationship between the exposed individual and the perpetrator. The wider environmental context must also be considered, such as affective support after the event, and the kind of relations with other individuals more generally. There is ample evidence that each of these factors can affect the probability that a particular embedded event inflicts pathology (Lanius, Vermetten, & Pain, 2010), that is, pathology that would not have emerged had the event under the given co-constitutive, co-dependent, and co-occurrent subjective and objective circumstances, not happened.

Definition

Ontologically, trauma involves particular intrinsic relationships of the brain, the body, and the environment. *Epistemically*, in the first-person perspective, trauma reflects the phenomenal experience of biopsychosocial injuries that relate to traumatic events. In the quasi-second-person and second-person perspective, trauma entails phenomenal judgments related to the traumatic experiences, and in the third-person perspective, trauma reflects physically observed biopsychosocial pathology.

According to the third-person perspective, there is a dimension of complexity of trauma-related disorders. This complexity can be expressed in terms of complexity of the dissociation of the personality (Van der Hart et al., 2006). Trauma cannot be fully understood in terms of material and efficient causes, but rather requires analysis of dynamic causation, which crucially includes final and formal causes.

Conclusions

Adverse, Traumatic, and Traumatizing Events

The present understanding and definition of trauma and derivative concepts is incompatible with the view that the brain, the body, and the environment are independent, albeit correlated phenomena. Hence, the current understanding and definitions are also incompatible with the view that traumatic and traumatizing events can exist and can be defined in isolation of experiencing and knowing individuals. Contra DSM-5 and similar views, motor vehicle accidents, assaults, rapes, etc., cannot be defined as traumas or traumatic events in isolation of subjects who experience these adversities. These kinds of events rather involve *potentially traumatic or adverse events* in the quasi-second-person and second-person perspective, and *potentially traumatizing or adverse events* in the third-person perspective. Whether or not these potentialities become actualities can only be determined de post facto. Life must be lived before it can be judged.

Dissociation of the Personality in Trauma

The current definition of trauma fits the definition of dissociation in trauma that is offered and defended in Chapters 12 and 13. A condensed version of this definition reads as follows: Dissociation in trauma involves a division of the personality as a whole organism-environment system into two or more conscious and self-conscious subsystems or dissociative parts during or following traumatic/traumatizing events. This division is a *core feature of trauma*. Theoretically, individuals who synthesize, personify, and presentify adverse, potentially traumatizing experiences and events they are confronted with do not get injured. Practically speaking, the full integration and realization of traumatic experiences and memories heals trauma-related pathology.

Nonintegrated experiences and memories do not exist in a void but are always someone's traumatic experiences and memories. This 'someone' involves one or more conscious or self-conscious subsystems fixated in the traumatic memories (i.e., EP). Traumatized individuals (try to) keep these 'someone(s)' at bay as the one or ones who strive to cope with daily life (i.e., ANP).

Dissociation and Trauma

It makes no sense to contend that trauma 'causes' dissociation, or that trauma (as one independent variable) is 'associated with' dissociation (as another independent variable). What can be said from the third-person perspective is that exposure to adverse, potentially traumatizing events is a *risk factor* for dissociation. This is almost the same as saying that living adverse events is a risk factor for trauma. Still, dissociation in trauma and trauma are not the same thing – they are not synonyms. Dissociation in trauma involves a particular division of personality, whereas trauma pertains to the complete gamut of biopsychosocial phenomena that make up traumatic experiences, traumatic events, and traumatizing events.

Treatment

Ontologically, the resolution of trauma requires a new, much more integrated dynamic configuration of the brain, the body, and the environment. That is, it involves a resolution of the formal and final causes of trauma. The resolution of the formal causes of trauma takes the (re)integration of the dissociated personality. Overcoming the final causes of trauma takes the coordination of different and often opposite wills. This achievement depends on the resolution of major conflicts between the different desires, and on balancing or overcoming contrary goal-orientations such as distancing and approaching abusive and neglectful caretakers. *Epistemically*, the resolution of the formal and final causes of trauma requires changes in the way that the different dissociative parts phenomenally experience and judge the traumatic memories. How much work these therapeutic objectives entail depends on the survivors' brain, body, and environment. For example, it makes all the difference whether they continue to be traumatized, have physiologically and psychologically matured, received adequate social support, and have developed a reason and right to live that the perpetrators did not grant them.

When traumatic memories are integrated, they turn from sensorimotor and often strongly emotionally charged iconic experiences into recitals or narratives, that is, into symbolic, autobiographical memories. With this conversion and integration, there is no point in keeping dissociative parts apart, so that they can in principle (re)integrate, spontaneously, or with therapeutic assistance.

Volume II

The Concept and Facts of Dissociation in Trauma

Chapter 12[1]

Consciousness and Self-Consciousness in Dissociative Disorders

> *There is nothing worse than a sharp image of a fuzzy concept.*
> Ansel Adams, photographer

According to the DSM-5 (APA, 2013, p. 292), DID is characterized by a "disruption of identity" in the sense that individuals with this disorder encompass "distinct personality states, which may be described in some cultures as an experience of possession." The text clarifies, that

> [t]he disruption in identity involves marked discontinuity in sense of self and sense of agency, accompanied by related alterations in affect, behavior, consciousness, memory, perception, cognition and/or sensory-motor functioning. These signs and symptoms may be observed by others or reported by the individual.

The DSM-5 also refers to the involved personality states as "alternate identities," and mentions that in

> many possession form cases of dissociative identity disorder, and in a small proportion of non-possession-form cases, manifestations of alternate identities are highly overt. Most individuals with non-possession-form dissociative identity disorder do not display their discontinuity of identity for long periods of time.

The degree to which alternate identities present themselves overtly partly depends on culture (e.g., in some cultures possession-form-presentations are more acceptable than in others). The discontinuities in identity and memory an individual experiences may not observable by others. One cause for a covert presentation is that some individuals with DID attempt to hide the alternations. Another circumstance is that alternate identities need not necessarily take full executive control in order to have an effect. They can remain

1 Chapter 12 is an expanded and revised version of Nijenhuis, E. R. S. (2012). Consciousness and self-consciousness in dissociative disorders. In V. Sinason (Ed.), *Trauma, dissociation, and multiplicity: Working on identity and selves* (pp. 111–154). London: Routledge.

backstage and influence the overt alternate identity, which experiences these pressures as intrusions. For example, the dominant alternate identity hears the voices of other alternate identities or is intruded on by their bodily and emotional feelings, thoughts, and movements. These intrusions do not imply that the dominant alternate identity in fact recognizes that they stem from other alternate identities. A lack of recognition of the existence of alternate identities is one ground that the individual's dominant alternate identity does not necessarily recognize that he or she is an alternate identity himself or herself.

Alternate identities that remain covert to observers can obviously be identified only indirectly. Observers may notice that the dominant alternate identity gets somehow disturbed at some point, but they have no direct access to its cause. DSM-5 lists two indicators: sudden alterations or discontinuities in sense of self and agency, and recurrent dissociative amnesias described as "[r]ecurrent gaps in the recall of everyday events, important personal information, and/or traumatic events that are inconsistent with ordinary forgetting." When the diagnosis is certain, phenomena such as sudden interruptions of speech, tense facial expressions, tendencies to shake the head or cover the ears, and difficulty hearing what other individuals say can be indications that the dominant alternate identity is affected by alternate identities that exert influences from behind the scenes.

Terminology

DSM-5 does not define the term 'distinct personality state' or the term 'alternate identity,' which is used as a synonym. The classificatory system also does not elucidate the component terms 'distinct,' 'personality state,' 'alternate,' 'identity,' and 'self' (as in the phrase 'sense of self'). This terminological ambiguity is remarkable given the essential role of these states/identities in DID. To bring more terminological clarity, there is a need for a conceptual analysis of the structures dissociated from each other in DID.

Distinct

The term 'distinct' means that two or more phenomena are distinguishable from each other. These phenomena need not be different in all regards, but there must be one or more features that set them clearly apart. This formulation leads to the question in what crucial ways the dissociative structures are different from each other.

Dissociative Personality State

A state is a mode or condition of being. Spinoza defined mode as "the affections of a substance, *or* that which is in another through which it is also conceived" (Spinoza, Definition 5, p. 1). Merriam Webster similarly says that mode is "a manifestation, form, or arrangement of being; *specifically*: a particular form or manifestation of an underlying substance" (6a) and "a particular functioning arrangement or condition" (6b). Spinoza's and Merriam Webster's definitions of mode both include the term 'substance,' which Spinoza (1677, Definition 4, p. 1) defined as "what is in itself and is conceived through itself, that is, that whose concept does not require the concept of another thing, from which it must be formed." And what is in itself, or cause of itself is "that whose essence involves existence, *or*, that whose nature cannot be conceived except as existing" (Spinoza, 1677, Definition 1, p 1). A substance is thus what exists, or rather what is taken to exist and what cannot be reduced to anything else. A dissociative personality state is thus an affection of an underlying substance.

More Than a State

Although dissociative personality states are unduly stable or rigid in many important regards, these organizations are also changeable in other regards, particularly when they are quite elaborate. For example, they commonly encompass and alternate between different moods, desires, and thoughts, and they can learn. Because in the large majority of cases dissociative personality states entail more than one state, the term 'personality *state*' is not acceptable and must be replaced by a different term (see below).

Alternate Identity

It is a bit strange and awkward to say that a dissociative personality state is an identity. Individuals and dissociative parts of their personality are not mere identities. They are rather living organisms with particular characteristics that they can identify themselves with and/or that other individuals ascribe to them. The underlying substance of an alternate identity is not an identity, but a (part of a) living organism.

The term 'alternate identity' is also unacceptable if it is supposed to mean that an individual with DID encompasses a (healthy?) identity and one or more alternate identities. The existence of one alternate identity implies the existence of two alternates. The duality 'normal personality' and 'dissociative personality' that is sometimes used in the literature is by the same logic also unacceptable. Individuals with DID are 'dividuals' who encompass two or more abnormal ways of being rather than one normal, and one or more abnormal conditions.

Dissociative Personality State: More than Mental

States are affections of a substance. So what substance 'underlies' dissociative personality states? The term 'alternate identity' seems to suggest they are mental. The emphasis on the mental in DSM-5 is also suggested by statements such as "[d]issociative symptoms can potentially disrupt every area of psychological functioning" (p. 291). However, the text also communicates that individuals with DID can experience "intermittent functional neurological symptoms" (p. 292). In the DSM-5, these phenomena are understood as symptoms of conversion disorder (functional neurological symptom disorder); they are not described and classified as dissociative symptoms/disorders. The distinction between conversion and dissociation in the DSM-5 is problematic. For example, it is unclear why dissociative symptoms/disorders such as dissociative amnesia are not seen as functional neurological phenomena? The distinction between psychological and neurological functioning also suggests that the DSM-5 adheres to philosophical dualism (i.e., the idea that nature encompasses two different substances), so that it is subject to all profound criticisms that have been raised against the idea that body and mind constitute different substances.

In Spinoza's philosophical monism body and mind are two attributes of nature as the singularly existing substance that probably includes many more attributes unknown to us. Accepting this philosophical persuasion, the term '(alternate) identity' would better be exchanged for a term that refers to the body as much as to the mind. The term 'personality' can be understood and used in this fashion. Furthermore, and also in the light of the conceptual, empirical, and clinical arguments presented in Volume I, the term 'conversion' is better replaced by the term 'sensorimotor dissociative symptoms/disorders.'

Personality

Allport (1961) defined personality as "the dynamic organization within the individual of those psychophysical systems that determine his characteristic behavior and thought." Limitations of this definition are that this organization also comprises an individual's characteristic perceptions, sensations, and affects, and that the intended psychophysical systems also mediate that person's interpersonal behavior. The systems are thus more than psychophysiological in nature. They are also social.

Personality as a Biopsychosocial Organization

The awkward term 'biopsychosocial' indicates that personality can be described and analyzed biologically, psychologically, and psychosocially. These different perspectives address different attributes of a single, whole, natural system, so that one discipline does not fully describe and explain the phenomena being studied by the other disciplines. For example, neuroscience shows that structures such as the amygdala tend to be activated when we feel anxious, and that this feeling goes along with the presence of high levels of noradrenaline. However, these findings do not allow the conclusion that we are afraid *because* our amygdala fires or *because* there is a lot of noradrenaline circulating. Biological, psychological, and psychosocial phenomena are not the dynamic causes of each other. The firing of the amygdala may be one among several efficient causes of fear, and the presence of noradrenaline may be one of several material causes, but these material and efficient causes do not fully explain fear. To comprehend fear, it is even more important to know final and formal causes, and these causes cannot be derived from the living brain. They require an analysis of the individual's consciousness and behavior – and most of all their will.

Personality: Environmentally Embedded

Allport's definition includes another limitation: It does not communicate that an individual's personality is intrinsically embedded in, and continuously influenced by, the individual's environment. As detailed in Volume I, the brain, the body, and the environment are intrinsically related. The personality is not environmentally isolated, and the individual's characteristic actions are co-constituted by and co-dependent on his or her past, current, and anticipated environment. As a more or less integrated composition of different biopsychosocial systems, the integrated personality is an overarching environmentally embedded biopsychosocial system that in turn exists only as a component of an organism-environment system.

Personality: A Dynamic Organization

In mental health, personality is a dynamic organization because it is open to change through experience, other kinds of learning, development, and maturation. Yet personality is often understood as some *intra*personal property. Once evolved, an individual's personality would, accordingly, be largely stable and more permanent than the different 'me's' this organization may involve. Yet, the view that we 'have' a personality inside that causes us to act in stable ways does not fit the principle of embedment. An environmentally embedded personality is a component of a relational matrix. Whereas the concept of 'personality' captures an individual's predisposition to (re)act in particular ways, these relatively fixed action patterns do not exist in isolation and can be altered by the material and social environment in which that individual has evolved, presently lives, and will live in the future.

For example, some previously unremarkable individuals may rise to challenging occasions (such as war) in unpredictable ways. Rats of a breed that is extraverted by nature may become introverted for the rest of their lives upon exposure to extremely aversive conditions (Cools & Ellenbroek, 2002). Similar dramatic personality alterations can occur to individuals who have become severely and chronically traumatized (Herman, 1997; Van der Kolk et al., 1996). Following chronic traumatizing events previously well-functioning individuals may develop disorders that encompass 'injuries' such as difficulty to regulate affect, including fear, anger, shame, and disgust, suicidal and other self-destructive actions, attachment disruptions, mood swings, and still more. Previously outgoing and self-respecting individuals may become withdrawn and beset by self-depreciation following chronic traumatization.

In sum, our personality is an embedded biopsychosocial system that entails the intrinsic dynamic relationships of the brain, the body, and the environment. An individual's personality can thus, among others, change in relation to environmental conditions, which certainly include continual adversities. *Trauma is an injury of the personality.*

Personality Defined

In view of these various remarks, I propose to define personality as follows:

> A living individual's personality is a particular organization of assorted dynamic systems that can be more or less integrated among each other. It comprises biological, psychological, and psychosocial attributes of a singular substance. An intrinsic component of the individual as a living organism-environment system that is historical and ever evolving (within limits), an individual's personality is an important, albeit incomplete, cause of his or her characteristic mental and behavioral actions. The particular organization of an individual's personality constitutes its formal cause, and the conjoint wills it encompasses constitute its final causes. The material and efficient causes an individual's personality entails serve as its intermediate causes.

The Dissociative Personality: Too Stable

The term 'dissociative personality' is sometimes used to capture dissociative *parts* of the personality. However, an individual, no matter how dissociated he or she may be, cannot have more than one personality when the term 'personality' is defined as the whole biopsychosocial system that makes up an individual. It is therefore better to speak of *dissociative parts of the* (individual's singular) *personality*.

The personality is environmentally embedded, as are the dissociative parts of the personality, per implication as well as phenomenally because dissociative parts include the perceptions and conceptions of a world they are a component of. An essential problem of the dissociative personality as a whole environmentally embedded system and the dissociative parts its entails is that they are insufficiently affected by changed conditions, some of which are environmental. That is, the dissociative personality is overly closed to adaptive and creative change through new experiences – and in at least some important regards through new environmental and personal contexts (e.g., living in a different social context, maturation).

In line with this formulation, it can be said that the personality of individuals with a dissociative disorder encompasses two or more insufficiently integrated embodied and environmentally embedded components or subsystems. Each of these embedded dissociative subsystems or parts of the personality (less formal and more briefly: dissociative parts) can and in most cases will involve (far) more than one state.

In sum, the personality of mentally healthy individuals constitutes a relatively permanent but nonetheless dynamic organization, because it is open to change, for example, through experience and maturation (within limits). The dissociative personality as a whole system and the involved dissociative subsystems or parts thereof are, though to a degree and in some regards still dynamic, unduly stable (Van der Hart et al., 2006). That is, the system as a whole and the dissociative parts it includes are overly closed to adaptive and creative[2] change through new experiences as well as new environmental and personal contexts (e.g., living in a different social context, maturation). They learn too little as they proceed.

The Individual

Logic has it that dissociative parts are, well, dissociated from each other. In dissociation there is thus not an individual and one or more dissociative parts, but rather, as the A Criterion for DID states, there is in DID "a disruption of identity characterized by two or more distinct personality states" that are dissociated from each other. While the A Criterion is clear in this regard, the DSM-5 also uses the term 'individual' when the text seems to pertain to an alternate identity that is frequently dominant. This is confusing. The individual is always the whole organism, no matter how dissociated that person may be. In dissociation, one encompasses at least two dissociative parts that may be smaller (often an EP) or larger (often an ANP) structures, and none of these parts completely comprises the patient as an individual (individuum). Each dissociative part is a part of a whole, hence a 'dividual' or a 'dividuum.'

The individual (ANP plus EP) and the ANP are thus clearly not synonyms. For example, it is not 'the individual' who attempts to hide dysfunction, as the DSM-5 suggests, but one or more ANPs who try to appear as normal as possible. This is precisely what the term 'apparently normal part of the personality' expresses.

Sense of Self

To bring more clarity to the vague phrase 'sense of self,' we need to define the term 'self.' This is a complicated task, if only because this term is used in innumerable ways. Still, this cannot be put aside if it is true that dissociative parts have their own 'sense of self,' and that it is this feature that essentially distinguishes dissociative parts from other insufficiently integrated subsystems of the personality. Having long contemplated the issue, I have indeed come to the conclusion that the existence of their own person perspectives – with their own first-person perspective as the core – is the constraint that sets dissocia-

2 Individuals do not just try to adapt, but also tend to change the world as they find it. More than adaptive, they can also be very *creative*.

tive parts apart from, say, conflicts between contrary desires (i.e., common 'ambivalences' [the term means 'both valences'] or 'polyvalences') and insufficiently integrated 'ego-states.'

'Self' can be used as a substitute for 'individual organism.' For example, studying "the many social selves of insects," Queller and Strassmann (2002) state that "[f]or evolutionary biologists, the self is the individual, the unit that is coherently selected to nourish itself, to protect itself, and especially to reproduce itself" (p. 311).

However, 'self' is commonly used in many other ways. Self is sometimes portrayed as a homunculus (the Latin word for 'little man'). This practice involves a pseudoexplanation, because it leads to an illegitimate regress in which each homunculus is explained by introducing another one. The term 'self' may also serve as a synonym of 'identity,' in which context the term 'dissociative self' is no improvement over the term 'dissociative identity.'

Self and Other

In social psychology, the term 'self' stands for an individual's lifelong ongoing and subjective construction. This construction is strongly influenced by other individuals, foremost those who play a significant role in the person's life. For example, according to Georg Herbert Mead (1925), founder of symbolic interactionism, individuals become a self and learn empathy when they relate to another individuals. Within this framework, they put themselves in the role of the other: "It is just because the individual finds himself taking the attitudes of the other who are involved in his conduct that he becomes an object for himself" (Mead, 1925, p. 268). A lot of children's play and games are thus about learning to assume the role of the other.

We organize our actions by considering how others treat us and how they will probably respond to our actions. The involved others may be present in an interaction but we can also take the role of the 'generalized other.' This happens, for example, when we defend our 'rights,' such as the right to protect our property and our life. Taking the role of the other does not involve complete imitation of someone else's actions but taking this role to a degree that enables us to act and to react socially. We defend ourselves only when we realize that someone is about to attack us; we can play only when we grasp the different roles of the diverse participants in the play; and we can attach ourselves only when we can assume the role of the significant caretaker. There is no victim without a perpetrator, no playmate without another playmate, no child without a mother.

This role-taking often focuses on 'gestures,' on the part of an action or an attitude of one individual which serves as the stimulus to other individuals to carry out their part of the whole interaction. Gestures generally belong to the beginning stages of an action, such as a slight modulation in the tone of voice, facial expression, or breathing rhythm, a shift in body position, and particular words that announce of accompany the physical action. Words of a language in our command are symbols that arouse reactions in us. According to symbolic interactionism, we are symbolic creatures, consciously searching for meaning. Thus as we speak we share ideas with each other, and of course we can talk to ourselves. By talking to ourselves, we can assume the role of an acquaintance, engaging in a second-person perspective. For example, children tend to speak aloud to themselves and engage in a dialogue with their parents as well as other caretakers. They thereby learn to own their rules and ideas as well as to regulate their conduct and emotions (Piaget, 1959; Vygotsky, 1934/1986). By the time we reach school, this private speech, which serves no social function, becomes buried in us. Nevertheless, sometimes we can revert to this mode when we are struggling with a difficult task. Some EPs use private speech quite a lot, and ANPs may also use it when they find themselves in challenging circumstances.

Our roles are not of our own invention. Rather, they have their roots in our specific social and (sub)cultural world. The world can assign roles. For example, parents may especially love one daughter and abuse and neglect the other. How these two girls evaluate themselves and what roles they tend to play in the rest of their life is strongly influenced by these different appraisals. As Goethe wrote,

> Der Mensch erkennt sich nur im Menschen, nur
> Das Leben lehret jedem was er sei
>
> [Only in man does man know himself;
> life alone teaches each one what he is.]

According to Charles Horton Cooley (1902, see p. 179–185), social referencing often takes the form of imagining how one's self, understood as any idea the individual appropriates, appears in someone else's mind. The 'looking glass self,' as he called it, encompasses the imagination of our appearance to the other person, the imagination of that person's judgment of our appearance as well as some sort of self-feeling:

> Each to each a looking-glass
> Reflects the other that doth pass. (Cooley, 1902)

We shape ourselves based on the way in which other people perceive and treat us and thereby confirm these perceptions. Self-images are influenced by other-images and reinforce them. In trauma, the negative images perpetrating and neglectful significant others have of a child (e.g., "you're good for nothing") may thus become the vicious core of the child's self-image, which the child will subsequently enact. The self-fulfilling prophecy is clear.

As we further mature, we also start to converse with the 'generalized other.' This action allows us to attain levels of abstract thinking and impersonality that involves our cherished 'objectivity' – our third-person perspective. Selves thus arise when organisms develop the ability to take the role of the other, and when selves emerge, so do minds.

While the ability to engage in role-taking is in Mead's view dependent on particular features of the brain, "the structure of the central nervous system is too minute to enable us to show the corresponding changes in the paths of the brain" (1925, p. 267). But mind is not located in the brain:

> As long as consciousness is regarded as a sort of spiritual stuff out of which are fashioned sensations and affections and images and ideas or significances, a mind as a locus of these entities is an almost necessary assumption, but when these contents have returned to things, the necessity of quarters for this furniture has disappeared also. (Mead, 1925, p. 57)

This view on mind was already presented in Volume I. Consciousness and self-consciousness do not 'sit' in the brain but evolve when there are intrinsic relationships between a particular structural and functional organization of the brain, the body, and the environment.

Our self is thus strongly shaped by our roles in life and by important life events. Abused and neglected children, adolescents, and adults have received and may also have assumed roles of victims (fragile EP) but also tend to resist these roles by acting as if nothing is wrong – or at least by trying to act as if they were not in fact deeply wounded (ANP), or by acting as if they are almost omnipotent (controlling EP). *These features mark the trinity of trauma: ignorance, fragility, and control.*

At first sight, it seems an attractive option to say that dissociative parts are parts of the self. However, this view entails several problems. One issue is that, being a social construction, self (in Mead's sense) is quite malleable. In this light, it seems less appropriate to refer to the whole system as 'the self,' and to dissociative parts as 'parts of this self.' Better would be a term for the whole that expresses stability plus changeability.

A perhaps more substantial concern is that, while the term (dissociative) 'self' suggests consciousness and self-consciousness, dissociative parts involve more than a conscious self. ANP and EP (Reinders et al., 2003, 2006, 2012) certainly have, albeit not exclusively, different biopsychosocial reactions to cues that they are consciously aware of. These different types of dissociative parts also had various psychophysiological and neural reactions to facial expressions presented ever so briefly, which they were not consciously aware of (Hermans et al., 2006; Schlumpf et al., 2013; see Chapter 18). The fact that ANP and EP have different subconscious reactions demonstrates that different prototypes of dissociative parts include more than differences in the domain of consciousness and self-consciousness. The term 'dissociative self' does not capture this wider range of unconscious, preconscious, conscious, and self-conscious systems that an individual is if the term 'self' is taken to reflect (self-)consciousness.

In social psychology, the term 'self' generally refers to what I have called the quasi-second-person perspective, the epistemological perspective that involves phenomenal judgment of prereflective phenomenal experience. It generates 'I-me,' 'I-myself,' and 'I-mine' relationships, that is, relationships between immediate preflective feelings, sensations, other perceptions, thoughts, memories, and behavioral actions, and their agent and owner. In this sense we have different social selves, or as James (1910) put it, "social me's or selves." James (1890, chapter 10), in fact, recognized several 'selves as known' that together make up the 'empirical me' or 'empirical self':

> The Empirical Self of each of us is all that he is tempted to call by the name of *me*. But it is clear that between what a man calls *me* and what he simply calls *mine* the line is difficult to draw. We feel and act about certain things that are ours very much as we feel and act about ourselves. Our fame, our children, the work of our hands, may be as dear to us as our bodies are, and arouse the same feelings and the same acts of reprisal if attacked. And our bodies themselves, are they simply ours, or are they *us*? Certainly men have been ready to disown their very bodies and to regard them as mere vestures, or even as prisons of clay from which they should some day be glad to escape.

The three constituents of the empirical self are the material, social, and spiritual self. The core of the material self is the body, though it also encompasses what may be called our extended body: our clothes, immediate family (e.g., when they are insulted, "our anger flashes forth as readily as if we stood in their place" [James, 1890/2007, p. 292]), home, and other personal belongings. The spiritual self does not pertain to our passing states of consciousness. It rather addresses our mental faculties and dispositions taken concretely as an object of our personal reflection. As the spiritual self, we have an intimate relationship to our thoughts, sensations, feelings, and decisions. We own, we personify them in the quasi-second-person perspective.

The social self captures our social roles. In this sense, James (1890/2007, p. 294) asserted,

> *a man has as many social selves as there are individuals who recognize him* and carry an image of him in their mind . . . But as the individuals who carry the images fall naturally into classes, we may practically say that he has as many social selves as there are distinct *groups* of persons about whose opinion he cares. He generally shows a different side of himself to each of these different groups . . . From this there results what practically is a division of the man into selves; and this may be a discordant splitting, as where one is afraid to let one set of his acquaintances know him as he is elsewhere; or it may be a perfectly harmonious division of labor, as where one tender to his children is stern to the soldiers or prisoners under his command.

Authors who propose a basic multiplicity of mind such as James seem to have the empirical self, foremost the social self, in mind. The empirical self pertains to the self as known, and this self is not one. To be sure, there can be conflicts between these different known selves. To quote James (1890/2007, pp. 309–310) once again,

> [w]ith most objects of desire, physical nature restricts our choice to but one of many represented goods, and even so it is here. I am often confronted by the necessity of standing by one of my empirical selves and relinquishing the rest. Not that I would not, if I could, be both handsome and fat and well dressed, and a great athlete, and make a million a year, be a wit, a *bon-vivant*, and a lady-killer as well as a philosopher, a philanthropist, statesman, warrior, and African explorer as well as a 'tone-poet' and saint. But the thing is simply impossible. The millionaire's work would run counter to the saint's; the *bon-vivant* and the philanthropist

> would trip each other up; the philosopher and the lady-killer could not well keep house in the same tenement of clay. Such different characters may conceivably at the outset of life be alike *possible* to a man. But to make any one of them actual, the rest must more or less be suppressed. So the seeker of his truest, strongest, deepest self must review the list carefully, and pick out the one on which to stake his salvation. All other selves thereupon become unreal, but the fortunes of this self are real. Its failures are real failures, its triumphs real triumphs, carrying shame and gladness with them. This is as strong an example as there is of that selective industry of the mind on which I insisted some pages back (p. 284 ff.). Our thought, incessantly deciding, among many things of a kind, which ones for it shall be realities, here chooses one of many possible selves or characters, and forthwith reckons it no shame to fail in any of those not adopted expressly as its own.

The Elusive 'I'

We do not only encompass 'me's.' We also experience and know ourselves as the one who feels, knows, and acts, that is, as the agent. This is, James holds, the self as knower, and it is this self that is never complete for as long as we live. Whereas our empirical me fluctuates almost as much as the river that is never identical to itself across time, the self as knower is much more stable. Beyond all empirical me's, beyond all phenomenal judgments in quasi-second-person perspective, there is a sense of a core that remains unwavering. The 'I' that engages in the quasi-second-person perspective knows the empirical me's and can therefore not itself be the aggregate of personified feelings, thoughts, memories, and conducts. But then, who or what is this 'I,' the one who engages in mental and behavioral actions? To repeat, it makes no sense to say this is 'the self.' As a provisional solution to the classic riddle of philosophy and psychology, James (1890/2007, p. 401) asserted that

> [i]f the passing thought be the directly verifiable existent which no school has hitherto doubted it to be, then that thought is itself the thinker, and psychology need not look beyond.

Even if the thought is itself the thinker, we are still left with that ever-present 'I.' Wherever we go and whatever we do while awake or dreaming, our 'I' follows us like our own shadow. What is more, within the confines of our phenomenal perspectives, we have no clue where our 'I' comes from. Like our perception of our body and a world around us, to us it is simply 'there.'

This omnipresence does not imply that this 'I' can exist only in the singular form, and that dissociation can pertain only to a division of the empirical self, of the self as known. On the contrary, in dissociation it is the 'I' that multiplies. This fact obliges us to take a closer look at the elusive 'I,' our first-person perspective, and the multiplication of the 'I' in dissociation. These issues constitute the theme of the remainder of the chapter.

To summarize, the whole that can become divided into parts cannot be adequately described in terms of a division of self. The whole and its parts are particular biopsychosocial organizations that are not satisfactorily captured by the common use of the concept of 'self,' which pertains to self as a social creation. The whole can indeed become distributed in different 'me's,' but the presence of different me's is a ubiquitous phenomenon. The specific feature of dissociation is that the whole encompasses different 'I's,' each with its own set of 'me's' that can be more or less elaborate. This division of the first-person perspective is anything but the norm, although it may be more common than many tend to know or believe.

Self and Personality

Self and personality are different constructs. Self or rather the colony of selves is an ongoing, mostly subjective creation that is heavily influenced by images of others and their feedback, and something that shifts with changes in roles and settings. Whereas self has a strong social flavor, personality is primarily seen as a set of rather stable predispositions to act and react in particular ways. A child's personality is influenced by his or her life experiences, but once evolved, it would seem to be relatively steady. Whether this is indeed the case can be assessed in the third-person perspective by studying the individual's actions across time.

Following Janet's original concept of 'dissociation' and our efforts to revive this understanding (Van der Hart et al., 2006), dissociation involves a division of personality, not a division among different selves, although each dissociative part can include one or more phenomenal selves. Each of these parts includes its own first-person perspective, its own *phenomenal self*, its own 'I.' So, what is the phenomenal self, what is this 'I'?

The Person Perspectives of Dissociative Parts of the Personality

One way in which the maladaptive stability in DID manifests itself is in the fixed belief of dissociative parts that they are or have their own 'self.' For example, as one of her dissociative parts, Jenny told her therapist: "I am me, *just me*, Dorien. I want to be myself, and do not want the others around [i.e., Jenny's other dissociative parts]. *They* are the problem, not me. Please, send them away!" But most of the other dissociative parts that Jenny encompassed were as convinced of their subjective existence and were as strongly attached to their 'I' as Dorien was. They were not at all willing to be "sent away." Dorien, Jenny, and all other dissociative parts each had their own ideas of the body, the world, and their place in the world. Thus, Dorien was convinced that she had her own body, that she was 14 years old, living with her parents, and that she was being physically, sexually, and emotionally abused on a daily basis.

Dorien and Jenny's other dissociative parts were not a whim, since they had been around for over two decades. Yet, following extensive and intensive psychotherapy, Dorien ceased to exist, once and for all, within a period of no more than 10 minutes. This happened during a session in which she had agreed to 'fuse' (i.e., completely integrate) with Anna, a different dissociative part of Jenny. Anna, who had not been any less invested in her 'I' than Dorien, also vanished from existence in this integrative action, in any case as Anna. Along with the fusion, a new dissociative part emerged that, after some time, would refer to herself as Eva and that had her own idea of the body, the world, and her relationship to this world.

These perplexing phenomena raise the primary questions of the current chapter. What and who were Jenny, Dorien, Anna and Eva? What were their 'I's,' and in this sense, their phenomenal 'selves?' Where did these phenomenal 'selves' come from? And where did they go to when they fused? How could these dissociative parts be so convinced of their personal existence and be so attached to their selves for such a long time – but then disappear forever as two separate parts in a brief span of time? And how can a new 'self' be subsequently generated within minutes? The quick dissolution of dissociative parts of the personality during fusion (which commonly becomes possible only after major preparatory therapeutic work) and the appearance of a new dissociative part strongly suggest that dissociative phenomenal 'selves' and their accompanying ideas of the body, the environment, and relations among self and world involve *conceptions.* It thus seems worthwhile to examine the problem of dissociative phenomenal selves in the light of a constructivist theory of consciousness and self-consciousness (Metzinger, 2003). As I see it, Metzinger's theory has several strengths and weaknesses. The reason for contrasting some of Metzinger's views and my take on the issues is to detail some of the problems of philosophical materialism as well as the representational and information-processing models of mind, and to present some alternatives to these ideas, which are presently so much en vogue.

A closely related theme is that dissociative parts of the personality also present in other dissociative disorders than major DID, including simple and complex PTSD, and, of course, minor DID. If it is assumed that each dissociative part is endowed with at least a minimal degree of consciousness and self-consciousness, what constitutes such a minimal degree? One may also ask whether there are natural boundaries of dissociative parts of the personality? Or, in case such natural boundaries do not exist, how can dissociative parts of the personality be usefully differentiated from other kinds of insufficiently integrated subsystems of the personality? For example, what would be the difference(s) between dissociative disorders and ego-dystonic phobias or schizophrenia? Patients with ego-dystonic phobias know that their fear and avoidance regarding particular stimuli are unfounded, yet this awareness fails to inhibit their phobic reactions. Patients with schizophrenia commonly hear voices and experience that particular emotions and motor actions are "made" in them. Do such symptoms involve influences from one or more dissociative parts of their personality, and, if so, would this imply that ego-dystonic phobias and schizophrenia are dissociative disorders?

A third question pertains to consciousness more generally. Many contemporary clinicians and scientists believe that the narrowing and lowering of consciousness belongs to the domain of dissociative phenomena. It was emphasized in Volume I that this conceptualization does not follow Janet's original definition of dissociation (Janet, 1907). He delimited dissociation to a lack of integration among two or more subsystems of the personality and dissociative symptoms to manifestations of this structural division of personality. We have revived this perspective (Van der Hart et al., 2004, 2006; also see the condensed description on the theory of structural dissociation of the personality [TSDP] in Volume I). When exploring what abnormal forms of consciousness are conceptually *specific* to patients with dissociative disorders, hence dissociative, I use Metzinger's (2003) eleven constraints on consciousness, one of which involves a first-person perspective – and then add a twelfth.

The Mereological Fallacy

The first issue to address in examining these kinds of questions is the best level at which to study dissociative 'selves.' It is a widespread philosophical assumption that goals and actions guided by explicit goal conceptions should be analyzed at the level of the whole system constituting a living human being (Metzinger, 2003). Living human beings have goals and execute actions – not their brains or some other functional modules of them. The same argument seems applicable to personality as a whole dynamic, biopsychosocial system.

Ascribing psychological predicates to functional parts of a whole system involves a mereological[3] fallacy (Bennett & Hacker, 2003). It is neither false nor true to ascribe psychological predicates to parts of a system such as the brain, but it makes no sense. As Wittgenstein (1953, entry 281) insisted: "It comes to this: Only of a human being and what resembles (behaves like) a living human being can one say: It has sensations; it sees; hears; is deaf; is conscious or unconscious." The issue that Wittgenstein addresses may in fact not only apply to "human beings, and what resembles (behaves like) human beings," but to all living systems that include mental features.

Cartesians engage in a mereological error by distinguishing between a body and a mind, and by ascribing thoughts, feelings, beliefs, fantasies, and other psychological predicates to the mind rather than to a living human being or that person's personality as an embodied functional entity. But the mind is not a kind of thing that has such faculties. Mind rather is a term that denotes a range of human powers, the exercise of these powers, and a range of characteristic human character traits. As Jonas (1966, p. 1) asserted, there may in fact exist a strong continuity of the mental and the biological, of mind and life: " [...] the organic even in its lowest forms prefigures mind, and [...] the mind, even on its highest reaches remains part of the organic." This continuity may start with the cell that can be regarded as the most basic autonomous dynamic system (Thompson, 2007).

3 Mereology is the logic of part-whole relations.

Although many contemporary neuroscientists repudiate Descartes' body-mind dualism, they too often assign features to parts of a whole that are characteristics of the whole rather than of the parts. These scientists first exchange the body-mind divide for a separation of the body and brain, and subsequently ascribe psychological attributes to the brain. In their view, it is the brain or parts thereof that perceive, experience, think, guess and decide rather than the individual as a whole system. But "[t]he brain is not a logically appropriate subject for psychological predicates" (Bennett & Hacker, 2003, p. 72). These predicates are inherent features or functions of the whole biopsychosocial system that constitutes an individual.

Still, the idea that goals and actions mediated by these goals must necessarily be analyzed at the level of the whole system does not empirically hold in all cases (Metzinger, 2003). The philosophical intuition that underlies the assumption is empirically incorrect, because the whole system can encompass two or more subsystems, each of which has its own goals (i.e., final causes) and to that end engages in explicit goal-directed action. Among other things, this applies to mental disorders involving subsystems of the personality that are insufficiently integrated in a functional sense[4]. Considering the degree of relative autonomy and goal-directedness of many dissociative parts in dissociative disorders, it is mereologically correct to maintain that a full understanding of this mental disorder must include an analysis of these functionally divided parts. This analysis encompasses an examination of the subjectively experienced 'selves' of these parts as well as their intentional relation to objects, situations, and other subjects. It makes sense to say that a dissociative part of a patient decides, thinks, or feels something provided it is realized that (1) this part is a subsystem of a higher-order system that constitutes the patient's personality, which in turn is an intrinsic part of an organism-environment system, (2) this dissociative subsystem is not totally separated from other dissociative parts of his or her personality, (3) a full understanding of dissociative parts involves an analysis of their mutual relations, and (4) a full understanding of the patient requires a structural and functional analysis of his or her personality as a whole embedded biopsychosocial system.

Metzinger's Self-Model Theory of Subjectivity[5] and Critique

The analysis of the development and existence of self-consciousness in dissociative parts of the personality can start with an exploration of Metzinger's theoretical reflections on the origin and nature of self in mentally healthy individuals briefly mentioned already in Chapters 5 and 10. Whereas some of his ideas strike me as important and useful, I am

4 Although these disorders are basically functional disorders, they also involve structural brain abnormalities. See Chapter 19.

5 Metzinger hardly refers to his inspirational sources. Some of the concepts he proposes or discusses can also be found in the work of predecessors, such as the phenomenologists Husserl, Heidegger, and Merleau-Ponty. His theory is also grounded in neuroscience.

also critical of some of his proposals in the light of the philosophical complexities indicated in Volume I. As I present Metzinger's analyses and concepts, I want to address these criticisms and propose some alternative formulations. At the end of the current chapter, I offer a table that summarizes the commonalities and differences between Metzinger's theory and my own understanding of subjectivity and objectivity.

As integrated personalities, we believe we are or have a self, that we are strongly attached to it, and we believe our self remains with us whether awake or dreaming. However, Metzinger (2003) contends that there is no such 'thing' as a self, and he certainly was not the first to claim this (Varela et al., 1993). Our self is not a *thing*, not an independent entity or substance that could live by itself, not an unchanging center or invariant set of intrinsic properties, and not a unique and indivisible unity. The self would rather be a phenomenal mental *model* of ourselves as a whole system that we, as the whole system we are, continuously generate and adapt:

> Nobody ever *was* or *had* a self. All that ever existed were conscious self-models that could not be recognized as models. The phenomenal self is not a thing but a process – and the subjective experience of *being someone* emerges if a conscious information processing system operates under a transparent self-model. (Metzinger, 2003, p. 1)

The phenomenal self entails our conscious subjective experience and the idea of our being someone, of being a bodily, emotional, cognitive, acting subject. What we often naively call our 'self' is just this phenomenal self, i.e., the content of our self-consciousness as given in our experience. A result of evolution, the phenomenal self is "a wonderfully efficient two-way window that allows an organism to conceive of itself *as a whole*, and thereby to causally interact with its inner and outer environment in an entirely new, integrated, and intelligent manner" (Metzinger, 2003, p. 1). Conscious awareness additionally encompasses a phenomenal world that appears to a phenomenal self in conscious experience. The phenomenal self and its implied subjectivity emerge when a particular subsystem of us develops a theoretical and, as Metzinger suggests, empirical[6] entity, something he describes as the *phenomenal self-model* (PSM).

The PSM, says Metzinger, captures our whole system for us, that is, the whole organism that we are. Our PSM becomes situated in and linked with a phenomenal world when we (that is, a subsystem of us as a whole biopsychosocial system) also develop a *phenomenal model of the intentionality relation* (PMIR). A PMIR concerns a model of how we and an 'object' are linked during a certain episode. For example, an individual may say, "I am someone who is reading this book," "I am someone who understands the content of this sentence," or "I am someone who is not worthy of attention." The essence of this consciously experienced conception is the specific intentionality relationship of the complete

6 Empirical entities are entities that we can find. According to Metzinger, the phenomenal self-model can be found as particular neural correlates. For a critique of this position, see Chapter 8 as well as the remainder of the present chapter.

system as captured in a PSM ("I") and an object (in the examples, "the book," "the sentence," and "attention"). The 'object' of a PMIR can involve physical objects existing in the environment ("book"), personal experiences (thoughts, feelings, behaviors, etc., an example being a "sentence" one has heard or read), other individuals and other individuals' mental and motor actions (e.g., "attention").

There is an intimate relationship between a PSM and a PMIR, because the content of consciousness never involves just an object, but always a *relationship* between a self-conscious system and an object. Thanks to these models, there is, phenomenologically speaking, the experience of a self in the act of perceiving, knowing, feeling, thinking, doing, wanting, and relating to other people (Metzinger, 2006). The ongoing and principled connectivity between the PSM and PMIR culminates in a lived, embodied first-person perspective.

Whatever we cannot integrate in a PSM or appropriate under a PMIR escapes our volitional control. For example, in alien hand syndrome (Marchetti & Della Sala, 1998), a neurological condition, the patients are consciously aware of movements exerted by the nondominant hand that displays a will of its own. Patients neither experience a desire to move this hand nor do they experience agency of the initiation and execution of the hand's goal-directed movements. In one case, the patient's nondominant hand seized nearby objects, pulled and picked at her clothes, and even grasped at her throat as she was sleeping (Banks et al., 1989). In the alien hand syndrome, the patients' hand movements are goal-directed, but beyond their volitional control. Neither the goal of the movement nor experienced agency are part of their PSM and PMIR.

The alien hand seems to be driven by visually perceived objects in the immediate environment, that is, by the *affordances* of the object (Gibson, 1977, 1979). Affordances of the object involve the actions that individuals can in principle perform regarding the object. The automatic actions of the alien hand point to the function of our conscious first-person perspective: The stronger and more stable our conscious first-person perspective, the lesser the degree to which our actions are primarily driven by affordances.

Mental Representation

Metzinger's theory is a representational theory of consciousness and self-consciousness. Mental representation is commonly understood as a process by which some biosystems generate a functionally internal version of parts of reality. The object of representation or *representandum* can involve an external fact, such as a source of food or an enemy, and an internal fact, such as one's current blood sugar level. It can also pertain to properties, relations (e.g., the distance to a goal), and classes (e.g., events that generate pain). According to Metzinger, a part of particular biosystems can represent the system as a whole system, thus the individual's personality as a whole with all its internal, relational, and public properties.

Metzinger lists four basic features of mental and phenomenal representation. First, he holds mental representation to be *functional* because it rests on a transient and continuous change in the functional properties of the system. Second, he regards the *representatum*, i.e., the mental state or process that functions as the placeholder for the representandum, to be a theoretical fiction. The fiction is that a representatum is not a kind of thing, but a mental vehicle, a time slice of an ongoing representational *process.* The representatum thus continuously changes as the representational action proceeds. Insight into this fact should keep us from turning processes into things, from reifying the experiential content of a continuous representational action. For example, rather than like a book stored in the library of our life history, a memory is an action, a mental vehicle that implies a particular mental or behavioral content. In order to have a memory, we must engage in the act of remembering; to have a feeling, we must feel; and to have an idea of self, we must conceive of a self. Thus, when we are asleep and not dreaming, our self does not exist. But when we are awake, the system that we are resumes the modeling of self and world, so that we experience "I awaken." Third, Metzinger contends that the representatum supervenes on internally realized functional, neurological properties, so that, in this sense, a theoretical distinction can be made between mental content (i.e., the representatum) and mental vehicle (i.e., the representational process)[7]. In Metzinger's view, phenomenal content is thus an abstract property of contemporaneous physiological processes. And fourth, phenomenality is a property of a certain class of mental representata, which encompasses the representata that the individual is or can become *consciously aware* of. Mental representata more generally include representata that the individual is not or in principle cannot be consciously aware of. For example, a traumatic memory that is phenomenal for a patient as EP need not be phenomenal for the individual as ANP. And no one can consciously be aware of *all* actions that are involved in walking, talking, remembering, etc.

Some Problems of Representational Theories

The idea that we model a self, a world, and a self-in-the-world implies the idea that there is in fact a self, a world, and a self-in-the-world that can get modeled, and that these are not models themselves. To qualify as representanda that are not models of some other thing, the representanda should involve an objectively existing 'reality' (an 'I,' a world, other subjects, situations, events, objects, etc.). Indeed, one of Metzinger's 'background assumptions' is that there is a reality that exists independently from experiencing and

7 More generally, mental content and mental vehicle cannot be separated. Mental content and mental vehicle are two strongly interrelated aspects of one and the same phenomenon. They in fact constitute two sides of a coin: Each mental vehicle has mental content, and each mental content requires a mental vehicle. For example, a thought depends on the, in Metzinger's terms, process of thinking, and a bodily feeling on the process of sensing that feeling. Below, I will exchange the term 'process' for the term 'action' and also explain why.

knowing subjects. What that reality might be remains inconceivable for us, but Metzinger assumes that our representata are minimal models that serve survival:

> What we see and hear, or what we feel and smell and taste, is only a small fraction of what actually exists out there. Our conscious model of reality is a low-dimensional projection of the inconceivably richer physical reality surrounding us and sustaining us. Our sensory organs are limited: They evolved for reasons of survival, not for depicting the enormous wealth and richness of reality in all its unfathomable depth. Therefore, the ongoing process of conscious experience is not so much an image of reality as a tunnel *through* reality. (Metzinger, 2009, p. 6, original emphasis)

The first sentence of this quote is reminiscent of Spinoza's metaphysics. Spinoza postulated that nature consists of infinite attributes, and that matter and mind are the only two attributes of nature we can experience and know. The idea that nature consists of infinite attributes might be our best guess. As Schopenhauer taught, anything that exists exists for an experiencing and knowing organism. Any reality is someone's reality, hence someone's idea. This implies that Spinoza's infinity of natural attributes, Kant's 'thing in itself,' and Metzinger's "inconceivably richer physical reality" do not escape the human world of ideas. They are beautiful conceptions, but conceptions they are.

Metzinger's idea that we travel "through reality" presupposes the existence of a world that *objectively exists*, that is, an observer-independent world. However, is it not the philosopher's task to examine ontological background assumptions, rather than to postulate them? A major question is how can we experience and know that this reality exists.

We may *believe* that there is a reality apart from experiencing and knowing beings, but a belief is a conception, not a demonstrated metaphysical truth. A belief is intentional in the sense that it is about something that constitutes, so to speak, the belief's content. In other words, intentionality concerns three conceptions. It is (1) a conceived relationship between (2) a conception of who one is and (3) what this 'I' believes, which is another conception. However, Metzinger says that a subject generates (#i) a phenomenal model of an intentionality relation between (#ii) himself or herself (the modeled 'I') and an objectively existing object. But Metzinger does not, and I fear cannot, explain how we can have some sort of contact with the objectively existing world. To explain intentionality in this way, one would need to lift oneself above the limitations of one's experiential and epistemic abilities – and who could do that?

Metzinger (2003, p. 53) states that "[r]epresentata are those simulata whose function *for* the system consists in depicting states of affairs in the *real* world with a sufficient degree of temporal precision." But how can we know how well a model of the real world models this real world? In order to know that, we must already know this presumed real world. Furthermore, as Harman (2011, p. 30) comments: "It is in no way clear how such a thing could even be possible, given the absolute nature of autoepistemic closure." As discussed below, autoepistemic closure stands for the fact that we cannot know how our brain models the world. Whatever a representandum would be, it is of necessity an idea, a conception

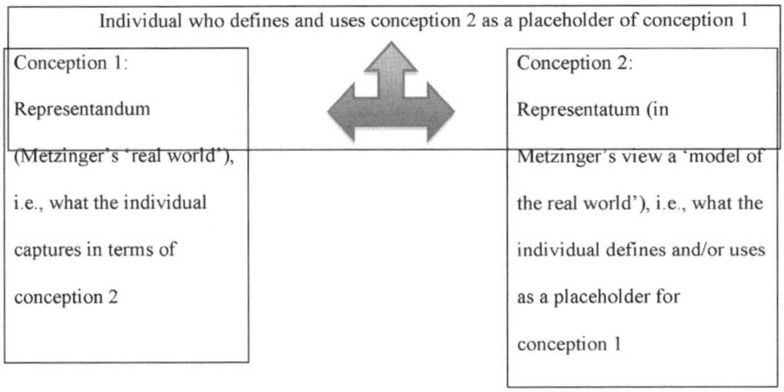

Figure 12.1 Representandum and representatum: two interconnected conceptions.

as such. We cannot elevate ourselves beyond our phenomenal and conceptual life. There is only *a 'thing' for us* or for any other experiencing and knowing organism when we or some other organism experience and conceive some 'thing.' Subject and object are co-occurrent, co-constitutive, and co-dependent. Subjects generate conceptions, not in an idealistic void, but in intrinsic relation with something that the involved subjects can experience and know. But what and how that experience and knowledge will be is dependent on the involved experiencing and knowing subjects.

There is no view from nowhere, as it were, no absolutely existing representandum, no absolute 'reality.' If this statement holds, it implies that we cannot say that we *model* a self, a world, and a self of this world. The idea of modeling presupposes that there is something to model from. But we cannot know that 'something'; we cannot know the representanda such as what our PSM and PMIR are models of. We cannot say anything about a 'self in itself,' about an 'intentionality relation in itself,' and about an 'objective world.' But if we cannot know the representandum – i.e., what we are modeling – we cannot know that we *model*, that we *represent*, and *what* we represent. The idea of the existence of a representandum is a conception in itself. If this is true, then a self-model (a particular representatum) is a model of a model, rather than a self-model of an objectively existing self (see Figure 12.1). The 'modeling' Metzinger has in mind thus implies a *regressio ad infinitum*, because there is no representandum that is not a model itself. Hence, there is 'no self in itself' that can be modeled, and there is no 'thing in itself,' no objective world.

Ontology and epistemology thus effectively boil down to the same thing: What exists is what is or can be experienced and known to exist. We can *conceive* of an 'I,' a 'world' (other 'I's,' 'objects,' 'situations,' 'events,' 'shapes,' 'temperatures,' etc.) and an intentionality relationship between our 'I' and that 'world,' but we cannot refer to the existence of anything we cannot know. The presumed existence of a particular representandum (e.g., a self, a world) is another conception.

Given the indicated problems of the idea that we represent or model an objectively existing world, the terms 'representation' and 'model' must be rejected and are better replaced by the term 'conception' or its synonym 'idea.' The terms 'conception' and 'idea' capture Spinoza's and Kant's notion that whatever we experience and know, and whatever we can experience and know, is made possible and is limited by our perceptual and conceptual powers. We can only feel, perceive, think, and speak about what we (can) experience and know. I therefore use the terms *phenomenal conception of self* (PCS) and *phenomenal conception of the intentionality relation* (PCIR). Synonyms are *phenomenal idea of self* and *phenomenal idea of the intentionality relation*. When the terms 'representandum' and 'representatum' or 'representation' are occasionally used in the remainder of this chapter (which is inescapable in a presentation of Metzinger's ideas), let it be clear that I understand and intend them as ideas or conceptions of a living embodied and environmentally embedded organism – not as reflections of some objectively existing 'reality.'

In this sense, intentionality involves a (#i) conceived relationship between (#ii) an experiencing and knowing individual whose 'I' involves a phenomenal conception of self, and this individual's (#iii) idea or conception of an object. I avoid the term 'construction' because that term might suggest a philosophical idealism in which our 'I' and whatever this 'I' experiences and knows are mere constructions, mere dreams. However, this idealism must be rejected given the co-occurrence, co-constitution, and co-dependency of subject and object, of an individual and his or her environment.

Problems with the Term 'Physiological Process'

Metzinger asserts that representation is a physiological process. Phenomenal content would thus be an abstract property of contemporaneous physiological processes that we cannot introspect. We are epistemically closed in this regard: Our brain engages in these processes, but it does not tell us how (or why).

The involved physiological processes are the mental vehicles necessary to having mental contents. Metzinger is thus a philosophical materialist who feels that the mental can be 'naturalized,' that is, reduced to the physical. In his view, there is the physical and the mental, and the mental supervenes on the physical[8]. But how the brain would generate our experiences – from beauty and love to ugliness and hate as well as both our superficial and our deep thoughts – is a question Metzinger does not answer. In fact, he admits that neuroscience has not even minimally enlightened us about how matter would make mind.

The term 'process' has become popular in the current cybernetic era. It clearly makes sense to say that there are physical and mechanical processes in nature (e.g., tides, erosion,

8 As Harman (2011) put it: "But Metzinger does not hold that *every* layer of reality is dependent in turn on sub-layers inaccessible to it. There is indeed a privileged layer in his model of the mind, and not surprisingly it is a *physical* layer. He admits that for him it is a 'background assumption' that 'what the system consciously experiences locally supervenes on its physical properties with nomological necessity.' ... Or as he puts it in greater detail: 'phenomenal representation' is ... completely determined by the spatially internal and synchronous properties of the respective organism, because they supervene on a critical subset of these states. If all properties of my central nervous system are fixed, the contents of my subjective experience are fixed as well ..."

seasons, information processing machines). For example, it can be said that a machine is constructed to engage in particular processes (e.g., adding figures, storing a text). However, it can be doubted whether the mental can be completely reduced to the physical and physiological, whether mental vehicles are best understood as physiological processes.

Capturing the generation of a phenomenal self and world as physiological processes masks the fact that these organisms can be understood only in terms of dynamic causality, with formal and final causes as its core. Material and efficient causes can be described in terms of physiological processes, but they are intermediate causes, as was detailed above. They do not explain our experience, thought, and behavior. Matter cannot explain itself. Philosophical materialism and materialistic neuroscience do not explain consciousness, but rather *presuppose* it. To understand what the brain, brain processes, and the study of the brain are about one must be a willful and conscious subject.

Materialistic data (e.g., particular patterns of neural activity) do not show and cannot explain that we and other living creatures are conscious, what it is like to be conscious, and that we strive to achieve particular goals. But anyone experiences and knows that we engage in actions to get what we want and to avoid what we don't want. We are will. And observers cannot understand human experience and behavior if they remain ignorant of what individuals experience and aim to get or seek to avoid. In this light, it is better to avoid third-person perspective terms such as 'processes' and 'mechanisms' and exchange them for terms such as 'actions' and 'will' or 'goal-orientation.'

In conclusion and contra Metzinger's philosophical materialism, human experience, thought, and behavior cannot be completely reduced to physical and physiological processes. The idea of intrinsic relationships between the brain, the body, and the environment certainly entails the idea that phenomenal content is in part dependent on physiological processes. It also includes the realization that these processes are insufficient to explain human experience, thought, and behavior. Given dynamic causality, it seems therefore better to say that we engage in biopsychosocial actions, and that some of these are associated with consciousness.

Problems of Information Processing Theories

I discussed in Volume I that it is problematic to say that living organisms 'process information.' No information exists independent from the perceiving agent (Merleau-Ponty, 1945). As Thompson (2007, pp. 51–52) emphasizes, "... information is context-dependent and agent-relative; it belongs to the coupling of a system and its environment. What counts as information, is determined by the history, structure, and needs of the system acting in its environment." An individual must thus consciously or unconsciously decide what shall *count as* information. This determination involves meaning making, an essential issue often overlooked or ignored in information-processing theories.

The idea that we are 'headtops' (i.e., that we are our brain and that our brain is an information-processing device) hides that in many regards the world does not have a preset meaning for us. Whereas organisms like humans are evolutionary prepared to respond to a few particular cues in particular ways (e.g., we are prone to respond to 'unconditioned stimuli' with 'unconditioned reactions'), we are foremost epigenetic: We have our genetic make-up, but whether or not our genes become expressed co-depends on our environment. Thus, in the large majority of cases we must make meaning. We enact ourselves, our world, and ourselves as phenomenally situated in and, ontologically, as being a part of this world.

Rather than comprehending phenomena such as thinking, perceiving, sensing, and behaving in terms of information processing, it is more adequate to say that a thought is the fruit of the act of thinking, that a perception is tied to the act of perceiving, that a bodily feeling is the result of the action of sensing the body and creating a body image, and that a memory is the counterpart of the act of remembering. Phenomenal conceptions of self, world, and self-in-the-world or rather self-of-the-world are not abstract processes but mental contents that are intrinsically related to the actions of conceiving a self, a world, and a self in or of that world. With Spinoza (1677), an idea is a 'concept of the mind which the mind forms because it is a thinking thing' and 'concept seems to express an action of the mind' (p. 32).

The Problem of Presumed Isomorphy

A major problem of many representational theories is the claim that there exists some kind of isomorphy between the representandum and the representatum (Braude, 1979, 1997). Isomorphist theories assume a conservation of at least some structural similarity between the two. However, there need not be any such isomorphy at all. It is important to realize that one thing or process must be *made to* represent another thing or process. For example, there is nothing isomorphic between the word 'angry' and the actual mood it represents, between my memory of a sunset and the actual sunset I remember, and between our representation of ourselves and ourselves as a whole system.

Metzinger (2003) recognizes the problem of isomorphist theories of representation. He seeks to resolve it by replacing a two-way relationship between representatum (image) and representandum (object) for a three-way relationship between the image, the object, and the representing system as a whole. In this configuration, there need not be any isomorphy of the representatum and representandum. What counts is how the representing system *uses* or *defines* the relationship between the two. Anything can represent anything, if so used by the whole system in a certain context (Braude, 1997). For example, a sailor may move a bun over a table to show how he navigated his sailing ship across a stormy sea. The bun stands for the ship, the table is the sea, and his vigorous movements indicate the storm and its effects on the ship that he tried to control.

Cast in terms of conceiving ourselves and our world, it is the way in which we define and use our conceptions that makes a difference. The bun comes to mean a ship, because the sailor uses the bun in this fashion, and because his audience understands that it was not the actual bun that sailed the ocean. Meaning is made.

How the whole system represents the representandum often depends on the history, goals, and action tendencies of that whole system. Our conceptions are not given; rather our will and nature more generally as well as our culture, social group, and life experiences guide how we tend to conceive our selves, our world, and our relationships with that world. A traumatized individual thus has very different conceptions of self, world, and people in that world than a person who was raised in a loving family. By the same token, different dissociative parts of the personality have different conceptions of themselves as well as their physical and social environment including other dissociative parts, and their relationship to the environment as they conceive it.

Representata (Conceptions) as Tools

Metzinger contends that representata exert a function *for* the whole system, that they are *tools* to achieve certain goals, for example, goals that have been or still are of importance in an evolutionary or social context. In this teleofunctional[9] perspective, the representational process is being optimized toward a functional optimization of behavioral patterns of the whole system – that is of its *viability* – and not toward the perfectioning of a structure-preserving kind of representation. Indeed, what counts is not how accurate our conceptions are, but how well they help us to keep our heads up, how well they allow us to navigate the world in which we have been 'thrown,' and in which we do not find meaning, but must largely make it. In this sense, we are rather an inherent component *of* the world as we conceive it than situated *in* the world.

Metzinger contends that one essential function of the conceptual action is to emulate[10] objects, subjects, and relationships between them, so that the whole system can effectively work with them. The emulation includes creating an illusion of the transtemporal identity of the conceptions, at least within episodic limits. For example, our 'I' changes continuously. Although we may know this, we nonetheless experience our 'I' as something constant. We cannot transcend this illusion of constancy from our first-person perspective, because the conceptual action hides its own temporality. That is, we can analyze that generating conceptions requires time, and that we therefore constantly and inescapably lag behind what we conceive. From a theoretical, third-person point of view, we may appreciate or believe that our conceptions involve a virtual domain, i.e., a domain of *possible* realities, but we cannot

9 Telos is Greek for goal, end, purpose.

10 To emulate means to strive to equal or excel, particularly but not necessarily by means of imitation by an emulator. In computer science, an emulator is hardware or software that permits programs written for one computer to be run on another computer (Merriam-Webster). The use of the term emulation in this chapter does not communicate that human beings operate as computers.

experience that we live at a principled distance from 'reality,' that is, from that which we conceive. This implies that our PCS and PCIRs involve possible rather than absolute realities, but that we nonetheless experience them as given. The illusory experience stems from the fact that we do not have phenomenal insight into the actions that generate our conceptions of reality. Our brain does not reveal to us how it works, how it contributes to the conceptions of an 'I,' world, and self-of-the-world.' As Metzinger formulates it, these actions are absolutely *transparent* for us in the sense that we cannot 'see' that we engage in these mental actions. We 'look through' our execution of these actions so that we are fooled to believe that the contents that these action imply are given.

We are commonly not consciously aware of (mis)taking a possible reality for an actual reality. This confusion, known as the *reification of the phenomenal*, is adaptive because it gives us a reference point. Metzinger refers to this reference point as the 'world zero.' The world zero allows us to take our present experience for real rather than for a conception or simulation. This evaluation, which from the third-person perspective is naïve and mistaken, helps us to distinguish the actual and the possible (e.g., plans for the future; memories), reality and appearance, factuality and counterfactuality.

We are systems that constantly simulate possible realities (Leopold & Logothetis, 1999). Out of all simulated realities, we select one that subsequently becomes a reality for us. According to Metzinger, representata are those simulata whose function for the system consists in conceiving of states of affairs in the real internal and external world with a sufficient degree of temporal precision: The representatum is the selected simulatum that constitutes for us, subjectively, the *actual* state of affairs in the real inner and outer world.

But remember that ideas of what 'the real inner and outer world' are constitute individuals' conceptions. A simulation is "something that is made to look, feel, or behave like something else" (Merriam Webster). As detailed above, we do not and cannot experience and know a representation of the objectively existing 'real world.' The idea of representing an objectively existing 'real world' is ontologically empty. We conceive of things, and in mental health our conceptions of our self, our world, and our self-of-this-world are both adaptive and creative.

This does not mean that sometimes we do not engage in simulation of possible realities. *Mental simulation* involves the conception of possible or counterfactual situations such as those that occur in dreams and hallucinations. Whereas mental simulations do not involve conscious awareness, *phenomenal simulations* are conscious. For example, we consciously explore possible worlds in planning and in predicting the probable future.

Just as adaptive or viable[11] mental simulation, phenomenal simulation serves survival interests. It is of crucial importance for organisms to have a set of *values* that tell them

11 The term adaptation masks the fact that healthy organisms not only adapt themselves to their environment, but also shape or create their environment. Thompson (2007) therefore proposes exchanging the term 'adaptation' for the term 'viability.' I apply the term adaptation in the sense of (promoting) viability, but also use the terms viability and creativity.

what possible worlds are safe and attractive – or dangerous and aversive. Endowed with such values, they can compare future-oriented simulata ("what will happen if . . ." [possible worlds]) and conceptions that they regard as the actual reality, and that constitute the world zero ("that which is Now;" "the real world").

Another way in which phenomenal conception serves as a tool relates to introspection. Mental states we introspect are phenomenal states. They are mental states we consciously experience. Introspection is the internal conception of active mental conceptions. Hence, introspection involves metaconception: In introspection, already active mental conceptions are conceived for a second time. These metaconceptions are *functionally internal* states in the sense that their intentional mental content can be made globally available to us. More specifically, they can be made globally available for our attention, cognition, and voluntary control of motor actions within a window of presence, within a phenomenal Now, discussed below, that we have realized.

As explained above, individuals and their environment are intrinsically related. They are not two isolated entities, that is, units that exist or could exist in themselves. The individual and the environment do not interact, but stand and fall together. In sum, conscious, phenomenal experience involves a phenomenal self, a phenomenal material and social world, and an intrinsic relationship between this phenomenal self and these phenomenal worlds.

The Phenomenal Conception of Self (PCS)

The PCS includes three components described by Metzinger (2003) as self-representation, self-simulation, and self-presentation.

Self-Representation

A special phenomenal representatum emerges when a part of a whole system generates a representatum of that whole system. This representatum involves the phenomenal subject in the first-person perspective. Metzinger (2003) describes this representatum as the phenomenal self that we create in an ongoing three-way representational action (representandum – representatum – representing subject). He asserts that a phenomenal self is a representatum of the whole system that a part of the whole system develops for the system as a whole. This part of the whole system represents the selection of properties of the system as a whole it can phenomenally access. As any representatum, this representatum is not a thing, but a mental content that is implied in a particular mental action. Apart from occasional interruptions such as dreamless sleep and temporary complete loss of consciousness, this action goes on throughout life.

Given the problems of representationalism, I would like to rephrase Metzinger's statements as follows:

Dreaming and awake individuals create in ongoing embodied and environmentally embedded actions a conception of who they are. This self-conceiving action gives them their first-person perspective, their 'I.'

According to Metzinger (2003), we require the first-person perspective for the phenomenal experience of being someone, for the control of our actions, for becoming the object of our own attention, and for cognitive self-reference. This perspectivalness is also needed for creating a link between ourselves as a phenomenal subject and the phenomenal world. When this link exists, we can appreciate that we are acting and experiencing subjects of the world as we experience and know it. The PCS and PCIR we create are therefore intimately linked conceptions that allow us to experience and know that we exist in a world. In order to live in and be part of a material world, we need the subjective experience of having a(n untranscendable) self, of having a consciously experienced first-person perspective. We also need it for the experience of living in a world with other subjects, hence for our social existence.

Self-Simulation

Self-representation, or as I prefer, self-conception involves a special case of self-simulation. Self-simulation as in fantasy and dreaming is opaque, because the system is consciously aware of creating possible worlds when it is engaged in actions such as fantasy, dreaming, and planning. In self-conception, the system also generates a possibility – a possible self. However, conceiving of a self is a transparent action (see section 7 below). That is, the system is not consciously aware of the fact that the self is not a given but a conception, that is, a possible self. Metzinger (2003) points out that this confusion is functionally adaptive in that the system can treat the current self-conception as a reference point. It helps the system to distinguish between the current self-conception (phenomenally experienced as immediately given in the mode of naïve realism) and possible self-conceptions (as in memory and in planning).

Self-Presentation

Like Spinoza (1677) and Damasio (1999), Metzinger (2003) proposes that a primitive, prereflective form of phenomenal self-consciousness constitutes the origin of our first-person perspective. This pertains to the feeling of being in contact with ourselves; it is a "subjectively immediate and fundamental form of nonconceptual self-knowledge preceding any higher forms of *cognitive* self-consciousness" (2003, p. 158). Because this awareness of the presence and current state of the body is immediate and nonconceptual, Metzinger suggests that it does not involve a self-representatum but a self-*presentatum*. Self-presentations are seldom available for categorical perception, concept formation, and autobiographical memory, because in his view they are nonconceptual. However, self-presentations are available for inward-directed attention, so they serve as an excellent reference base. Bodily self-consciousness is, in fact, our most important *source of invariance*, both phenomenologically and functionally. It entails nonconceptual knowledge about the presence and current state of our own body. That is, it involves *nonreflected, immediate experience.* Self-presentation also provides centeredness, an *inner* world and an inward perspective. Commonly centered in bodily self-consciousness, self-presentation creates a consciously available divide between self and world.

Metzinger thus contends that presentata are nonconceptual. I agree they do not qualify as explicit conceptions, that is, as conceptions we can reflect on. However, conceptions can also be implicit. Our qualia, our presentata, are still ways in which we conceive ourselves, our world, and our relationship to this world. They are not simply given, not merely 'presented,' but rather involve the particular ways in which we perceive and conceive of ourselves and the world (as explained before, constructions with "-ceive" stem from the Latin verb capere, which means to take, more specifically, to take something to oneself). For example, 'pain' is not a given. Whether or not we experience 'pain' and how we experience 'pain' depends on us as living organisms, even if we do not have direct access to our relevant conceptual actions. Some dissociative parts are more or less analgesic; they may not experience pain when they cut or burn themselves. Some dissociative parts do experience pain, but in fact appreciate the feeling because it is better than feeling nothing; or it is deemed 'good' because they feel that it serves them right. However, other dissociative parts may be hyperesthetic, or feel that they do not deserve pain.

These examples illustrate that presentata may involve or include the phenomenal experiential contents that relate to implicit conceptual actions. We experience presentata as given, but they may relate to preconscious conceptual action. It might thus be helpful to distinguish between *phenomenal presentata* or *implicit conceptions* (phenomenal experiences or presentata such as pain, warmth, beauty, minimally different shades of red) and *explicit conceptions* (e.g., ideas, fantasies, thoughts, plans).

Metzinger (2003) emphasizes that having a subjective, centralized point of view, i.e., a phenomenal self entertaining a particular perspective (we generally experience ourselves as the center of our world), is intimately tied to *embodiment* because our sensory and motor systems are "physically integrated within the body of a single organism" (p. 161). This embodied perspectivalness is crucially linked to internally generated, elementary bioregulatory processes, such as the beating of the heart and breathing. Together with the sensory and motor systems, these processes create a global region of maximal stability and invariance because, in standard cases, the *body is always more or less present, and can therefore serve as a much-needed stable point of reference.*

At higher levels of mental action, the conceptual space centered by a phenomenal self can enable the attribution of psychological properties to the system itself. That is, at these levels, we can attribute psychological properties to ourselves. These higher-level mental actions require a metaconceptual ability that is a precursor to our reflective subjectivity and social cognition.

An integrated PCS thus encompasses integrated phenomenally transparent and opaque self-conceptions. These conceptions involve self-simulational actions and the phenomenal contents these actions generate: our subjectively experienced bodily and emotional feelings, thoughts and fantasies, autobiographical memories, and plans for the future. These different components of the PCS are integrated by the mental actions of synthesis, personification, and presentification. In synthesis, we integrate various phenomenal components of experience such as what we see, hear, feel, and do. Personification is the ability of a part of the whole system that we are to make our syntheses and actions our own, to take our experiences and actions to ourselves. This personification stimulates us (i.e., the whole embodied and environmentally embedded system that we are) to take responsibility for engaging in particular mental or behavioral actions. For example, when we personify our current bodily and emotional feelings, we may express that we are tired and want to take a rest, or that we made a mistake and wish to correct it. Personification generates such motivations. It also generates the property of mineness in the quasi-second-person perspective. Mineness exists in kinds and degrees. For example, the sense of agency ("I did it") differs from the sense of ownership ("It happened to me").

In sum, the basic function of a normal PCS (i.e., a PCS in mental health) is to make system-related experience and knowledge globally available to the entire system. The whole system is the biopsychosocial organism that an individual is. The subsystem of the individual that generates a PCS implicitly and explicitly conceives of the whole system's mental and behavioral actions and their results, and emulates the abstract properties of this system's functioning. Following the background assumption of teleofunctionalism, it engages in this mental and phenomenal simulation as well as this emulation *for itself* as a whole system. In ongoing experiential and conceptual action, the PCS-generating subsystem of the whole individual regards the target system as subject and object at the same time. The degree to which the PCS is conscious depends on the degree to which it satisfies the constraints for conscious content, as discussed below.

A Catalogue of Consciousness and Multiple PCSs and PCIRs in DID

It is time to examine to what extent dissociative parts of the personality in patients with DID and other dissociative disorders include their own PCSs and PCIRs. Considering that self-consciousness is a special type of consciousness, any analysis of self-consciousness and consciousness in mentally healthy individuals and in dissociative parts in dissociative disorders must be embedded in an analysis of consciousness. Consciousness, hence phenomenal experience and knowledge, exists in many different forms, intensities, and degrees of internal complexity. These differences can be expressed in terms of Metzinger's (2003) very useful preliminary catalogue of constraints on consciousness. The degree to which these constraints are fulfilled indicates whether a certain mental state may also be a conscious, phenomenal state. The catalogue is intended to serve as a set of provisional but workable tools. The primary level of description is the first-person perspective, though Metzinger has extended this level with several other levels of description such as the functional, computational, and neurobiological level. The present focus lies on the first-person perspective, albeit without specification, sometimes a few other levels of description are briefly considered as well. Each of the constraints are first discussed and applied to dissociative parts of the personality in patients with dissociative disorders, although far from exhaustively.

1. Global Availability

From a phenomenological perspective, the concept of 'global availability' involves the notion that the contents of states of consciousness never stand alone but are found and integrated *in a single world*. This world commonly is a highly integrated conception. It consists of many connected but differentiated components that are unified in a whole. A conceived world, in this sense, involves a highest-order situational context in which the phenomenal contents of more or less distinctive conscious states are embedded.

All systems operating with globally available conceptions are systems that experience themselves as living in a world, provided a number of other constraints on consciousness, discussed below, are also met. Global availability is one of the few *necessary* conditions in ascribing phenomenality to conceptions currently operating within a whole system.

The contents of states of consciousness can be globally available in a variety of ways. A somewhat crude classification is that they can be globally available for guided attention, cognitive reference, and control of behavioral action. For example, we can deliberately attend to the content of our consciousness, say, focus on an object, on its color or shape, or on a subject and that person's behavior. In at least some cases, we can form thoughts about these contents, say, think about a subject, form a concept about a certain class of subjects, or talk about these features and concepts. We may also be able to use these contents, say the shape of an object, to control our behavior, for example, to sit down on the thing, or to sort a variety of things into coherent groups. Global availability of mental contents is thus an adaptive tool.

Because the intentional content of phenomenal conceptions is globally available for further action such as attention, memory, concept formation, planning and motor simulations, phenomenal states increase the flexibility of the behavioral profile of the system as a whole. The more experience and knowledge are phenomenal, the higher the flexibility and context sensitivity with which the system can react to environmental challenges. From a teleological perspective, the features of global availability are of particular importance for goal-directed actions in which adaptation does not exclusively depend on speed – as in defensive reflexes – but also on volitional control, planning, and thought.

As mentioned above, some phenomenal contents do not involve explicit conceptions, but constitute phenomenal presentata[12]. As indicated, phenomenal presentata are simple stimulus-correlated interoceptive system states that are *globally available for our guided attention and behavioral action control*, but not for explicit cognition. That is, we cannot further subjectively differentiate or penetrate our phenomenal presentata by reflection. Phenomenal presentata include, for example, sounds, smells, pleasant sensations or pain, and perceiving fine shades of colors. We can attend to these phenomenal states and use them to guide our behaviors, but we cannot cognitively categorize or cognitively integrate them in the form of a perceptual memory. For example, we can attend to and distinguish delicate shades of red from each other, but we cannot not conceptualize these subtly different shades when we do not actually perceive them. The same would apply to minor nuances of sounds, smells, and temperature. Presentational content is unable to stand by itself. It always is integrated in some relation, in a higher-order whole. For example, as a phenomenal presentatum, pain is always experienced as localized in some body part.

Phylogenetically, phenomenal presentational content is probably one of the most ancient forms of conscious content. It is functionally most reliable. Being an ultrafast action, we cannot trace how we react to the stimuli that elicit the presentation. In this sense, phenomenal presentational content is fully 'transparent.' That is, we cannot introspectively access our perceptual act. For example, we have bodily feelings, but are unable to look inside ourselves to adjudge how we generate these feelings.

An important function of presentational content is to 'flag the present.' As subjectively instant sensory experience, this phenomenal content helps us to prevent confusion between what (we assume that) actually exists and what we simulate (e.g., remember, plan).

Global Availability in Dissociative Parts of the Personality. No matter how simple and limited content of consciousness of a dissociative part may be at times, it is commonly an inherent component of that part's conception of the world. For example, Ingrid, a dissociative part a patient with major DID, felt extremely threatened when a picture of a man with an angry facial expression was moved in the direction of her face in the context of experimental research. At this point, she had the experience of leaving her body and floating above it. Despite her out-of-body experience, Ingrid integrated these diverse experiences in a quite limited conception of the world: She saw her body below as well as how "the man" threatened it. She also bound but differentiated a number of other components of her experience, such as her fear and her perception of the picture of the man. For example, she appreciated that her body and the picture were two different things. However, while subjectively floating above her body, her physical feelings and control over her behavioral actions were not globally available to her. With her eyes averted from the threat cues, staring into nothingness, she was physically passive just as she had reacted as this part upon being sexually and physically abused. Ingrid later reported that her body had

12 Metzinger (2003, pp. 63–86) proposes that the concept of phenomenal presentation – involving the simplest forms of phenomenal content – replaces that used to be called qualia.

been paralyzed during the exposure to the picture and the first minutes after this experimental test. It also appeared that she was unable to recall what had happened when the picture had been held within 70 cm from her face. Her level of consciousness had apparently been so low at this time that she had not formed a memory of the event, in any case not a phenomenal (i.e., explicit) memory.

Disintegration of the focal content of consciousness may also happen, which implies the loss of the single, coherent conception of the world. For example, some dissociative parts report that their world (and their feeling of being someone; see section 6) disintegrated into many disconnected bits and pieces when they were extremely threatened and abused. As mentioned in Volume I, this happened to a 6-year-old girl when her father forced a loaded gun into her vagina and told her how eager he was to fire the weapon. As a dissociative part of her told the therapist many decades later, she (her PCS) and her world (her PCIRs regarding the abuser and the environment more generally) had been shattered during the most horrible moments of the abuse. The loss of a coherent conception of the world and her phenomenal self was exceptionally frightening.

Dissociative parts sometimes experience presentata where they, for adaptive reasons, actually would better experience and know explicit conceptions. This happens, for example, when they re-experience traumatizing events. As remarked before, dissociative parts that are fixated on these events do not remember them as autobiographical, narrative memories, that is, as simulations of the past; rather, traumatic memories are phenomenal presentata. They involve iconic, involuntary, mostly nonverbal sensorimotor and in many cases highly affectively charged experiences that are insufficiently condensed in time (Janet, 1928a; Van der Hart, Bolt, & Van der Kolk, 2005; Van der Kolk & Van der Hart, 1989; see Chapter 11, where it is also detailed that some traumatic memories do not involve hyperarousal but hypoarousal). For example, dissociative parts may feel pain in some body parts, smell particular body odors, feel that someone touches or hits them. These presentata subjectively 'flag the present' for them. For such parts, the dread happens or happens again, here and now. As phenomenal presentata, traumatic experiences are globally available for the patient's attention and, within narrow limits, for the control of some behavioral actions, particularly defensive actions. For example, a patient who re-experiences a traumatizing childhood event may hide behind a couch as she did when the event happened.

To the degree that traumatic memories involve phenomenal presentata, they are commonly unavailable for cognitive control. Dissociative parts who contain such memories therefore have very little cognitive control over them. When patients, as one or more of their dissociative parts, manage to symbolize traumatic memories (e.g., in treatment), these phenomenal presentata become phenomenal conceptions. With this significant shift from immediate experience to – a degree of – reflective symbolization, traumatized individuals gain the ability to attend to these memories deliberately, to think about, comprehend, and categorize them, to assign them their place in the history of their life, and to use them for behavioral action control in a far more flexible way (e.g., they can now refrain from acting out the memory). This achievement obviously enhances the patient's capacity for adaptation.

2. A Phenomenal Now

Whatever we experience, we experience it *now*. This now is not some formal now or a now shared among different individuals, but rather constitutes our subjectively experienced present. It is our *phenomenal now* (Metzinger, 2003). The phenomenal now generally encompasses a couple of seconds, and it may be displaced in objective time. For example, a dissociative part in an adult patient may be convinced that "now" is a moment in 1986, rather than a couple of seconds in the actual, intersubjective present.

Whatever an individual knows follows phenomenal experience because meaning making takes time. This implies that our phenomenal now is a specious present (James, 1890) or a remembered present (Edelman & Tononi, 2000). It entails a 'window of simultaneity' or 'window of presence' in which we commonly integrate different, but physiologically not completely synchronous, mental actions such as our sensations, perceptions, emotions, and memories (cf. Janet, 1935; Van der Hart et al., 2006). To create the phenomenal now at the level of mental content, the conceiving system must exclude conceptions of the timeframes of the actual different mental vehicles that are involved in the current mental content. For example, the different time slots for mental actions of generating sensations, emotions, and memories should not become a part of our phenomenal content, or else our phenomenal now would dissolve.

Considering that, from the third-person perspective, there is neither now, past, or future, the phenomenal experience of time is a simulation. Phenomenal mental content is thus a simulation existing in a globally available phenomenal world and a phenomenal now.

Window of Presence in Dissociative Parts of the Personality. Clinical observations suggest that all dissociative parts of the personality experience that they live in a present, and that all naively believe that their sense of the present – their phenomenal now – equals the actual now. As these parts, patients with dissociative disorders can be confused in a double sense. First, they do not experience that their phenomenal now is a simulation, as is true for all of us. (I already discussed that this simulation is adaptive.) But, second, the phenomenal now of dissociative parts can be confused in a pathological sense. For example, the phenomenal now of some dissociative parts may, in fact, pertain to a remote past. They may believe it is 1970 or any other past time. Sometimes their phenomenal now shifts, say, from 1968 to 1972, and from that year to 1981. Other dissociative parts may not be able to state the year in which they subjectively live and refer to their experienced present in the context of sentences such as "I must go to class in a minute." Dissociative parts that exert functions in daily life (e.g., those who take care of children, who explore the environment, or who engage in a sport) are commonly far better oriented to the actual present than dissociative parts that are fixed in traumatic memories. Some dissociative parts may at times have a weak phenomenal now (Van der Hart et al., 2006). For example, they may just drowse on a couch for hours with very little sense of time.

3. Situatedness and Global Coherence

Global availability (see 1) is a functional reading of a more general constraint, which holds that we subjectively always live in a world – that we are phenomenally situated beings. In other words, phenomenal experience involves situated actions. It is a phenomenal being-in-the-world ("I live in a world") or phenomenal being-of-the-world ("I am my world"). We are situated because we preconsciously bind our individual phenomenal experiences into a global situational context, into the context of a single world that is presented in the mode of naïve realism. Naïve realism entails that we (or a part of us) take our conceptions of the world that we generate for *the* world: "The world is how I see, hear, and feel it" ("Don't tell me there is no mountain over there!").

Although the phenomenal conception of the world we entertain is commonly highly differentiated, it is also coherent at any given moment. It constitutes a whole, not a sum of parts. We thus integrate our phenomenal content into a highest-order conceptual structure that can be described as 'our world.' In order to continuously embed new phenomenal contents into the global conception of this world, the system we are requires the integrative ability to bind and differentiate figure and ground, to identity a figure from its background, as well as to link and distinguish many different modalities (e.g., what we hear, see, feel, do) on many different levels of granularity[13].

Situatedness and Global Coherence in Dissociative Parts of the Personality. Consciousness is being-in-the-world or being-of-the-world (e.g., Gallagher & Zahavi, 2008). Just like mentally healthy individuals, dissociative parts of the personality commonly experience that they are situated. This means that they live and act in a single world that they experience as real. Each dissociative part thus experiences and conceives of its own subjective and singular world, and situates its experiences and actions in that world. We can call this conceived world as their phenomenal conception of reality. This conception may not be explicit, which means that dissociative parts do not necessarily have explicit concepts such as 'world,' 'reality,' 'past,' or 'future.' For example, no explicit concepts are needed to experience color or temperature.

The conceptions of the dissociative parts of the world may be quite curtailed, incomplete, anachronistic, and more or less hallucinatory. However, in most cases these conceptions nonetheless constitute a highest-order coherent whole for these parts, and this whole constitutes the context for their lower-order phenomenal contents. Consistent with Metzinger's theory (2003), dissociative parts thus usually integrate their present experiences into the framework of their more general conception of the world.

However, dissociative parts may temporarily lose their sense of situatedness as well as the coherence of their conception of the world. As discussed in section 1, this can happen

13 Granularity is a measure of the size of the components, or descriptions of components, that make up a system (www.en.wikipedia.org).

when they are extremely anxious or when they are excessively absent-minded. Loss of situatedness and global coherence does not imply that these parts lose consciousness completely; a dissociative part that experiences and conceives of the world in lose bits and pieces is still conscious of these fragments, and a part that loses the feeling and knowledge that its experiences are tied to a particular situation (e.g., a part that experiences "I do not know where I am and what really happens") can still be consciously aware of some unbound or undifferentiated perceptions.

More generally, patients with dissociative disorders lack global coherence, in the sense that each of their dissociative parts phenomenally experiences and conceives of its own world. Their phenomenal experience and conception of a particular situation can be quite dissimilar, and they embed their different conceptions in their different phenomenal worlds. For example, a patient can feel as one dissociative part that the environment is safe, whereas the same patient as another part believes to be endangered. These different phenomenal worlds may alternate with the successive reactivation of these different parts, or they may coexist in a parallel fashion when two or more dissociative parts are activated in parallel (Van der Hart et al., 2006).

Just as for mentally healthy individuals, for dissociative parts the perceived and conceived world – the world zero – is for them *the* world. To the degree that different parts communicate with each other, they can be, and often are, in conflict with each other over how the world *really* is. They may disagree about how the world currently is, how it has been, and how it will be. If only because their different conceptions of the world are transparent, different dissociative parts commonly find it hard to understand that different parts have dissimilar ideas of the world. They do not easily grasp these disparate ideas of other dissociative parts – if at all. This fact strongly contributes to the maintenance of the dissociation of the personality.

4. Convolved Holism

Different phenomenal wholes do not tend to coexist as isolated entities, but rather commonly appear as flexible, convolved, or nested patterns. These multilayered experiential gestalts are organized in mereological hierarchies, that is, in lower-order wholes that belong to a higher-order whole. Phenomenal wholes include phenomena such as experienced, perceived, and conceived objects (e.g., a synthesis of perceived form, color, and texture), sensory wholes (e.g., a synthesis of what we see, feel, hear, and smell), complex scenes and situations (e.g., a synthesis of two successive events), and a phenomenal self in-the-act-of-knowing (cf. Damasio, 1999). Because of the convolved holistic nature of consciousness, we can bind (i.e., link) but also differentiate such different phenomenal lower-order wholes into higher-order structures.

To constitute a presence, phenomenal wholes have to be integrated within a phenomenal now. As noted above, we do not have the faintest idea about how we continuously and automatically integrate phenomenal parts into phenomenal wholes, because the involved integrative mental actions occur at a preattentive and preconceptual level of meaning making. These actions are transparent. That is, we engage in them, but we do not have phenomenal access to them (see section 7). However, we can access our conscious thoughts: They are opaque for us. This implies that "to experience a world is different than to think a world" (Metzinger, 2003, p. 145).

Whereas conscious experience constitutes a whole, it is not an undifferentiated mass. For example, we live in brief moments of time through a wide range of different conscious states. A major advantage of convolved holism, of well differentiated but nested mental and phenomenal contents, is that the contents of individual conceptions can be recurrently updated in a fast, flexible, and context-sensitive manner. But what guides these integrative actions?

I already remarked that mental and phenomenal simulation serves survival interests, and that adaptive functioning requires values that define what is safe and attractive – or dangerous and adverse. These values guide what we tend to perceive, feel, think, and do, and they strongly influence what meaning we assign to external and internal stimuli (Corr & McNaughton, 2012; Gonen, Admon, Podlipsky, & Hendler, 2012; Lang & Bradley, 2009; Panksepp, 1998; Panksepp & Biven, 2012). As Hurley (1998; see also Gibbs, 2005) maintained, perception, cognition, and motor actions are not 'vertically' distinct general modules of mind, as the classical view on brain organization has it. This classical perspective constitutes a linear input-output model suggesting that we first perceive a stimulus or situation, then develop thoughts and plans, and finally engage in motor actions. However, this sequential model does not work, because adaptive functioning requires recurrent feedback loops among perceptions, affects, thoughts, and motor actions, and because general modules do not provide the specific values needed to guide our functioning. Hurley alternatively asserted that perception, affect, cognition, and motor action are organized in integrative 'horizontal' modules, in which these different mental and motor actions are tightly interconnected in recurrent feedback and feedforward loops. As has become clear in artificial intelligence and psychobiology, these modules must include *values* or else they will not work.

Spinoza's desires, Schopenhauer's will, and Panksepp's basic motivations (see Volume 1) constitute essential values. They do not exist in a biopsychosocial void, but each constitutes an essential component of a particular action system. These action of will systems include attachment, play, exploration, social engagement, reproduction, and mammalian defense with subsystems such as flight, freeze, flight, and tonic immobility. For example, the action system of attachment tells us to connect to certain individuals, and the will system of mammalian defense tells us what objects and individuals we would better avoid. Horizontal modules within action systems provide specific action-organizing values. Thus, the action system or constellation of action systems and the implied horizontal modules activated at a given moment strongly influence what we likely perceive, feel in a bodily and emotionally sense, think, want, fantasize, and do, and how these various mental and motor actions get integrated.[14]

Recent research suggests that personality can be understood as a certain constellation of will systems (e.g., Davis & Panksepp, 2011; Nijenhuis & Den Boer, 2009). In mental health, the various action systems for functioning in daily life (approaching attractive cues) and functioning under threat and attack (avoiding and escaping from aversive cues) are integrated into a whole that constitutes the individual's personality. This integration allows for links and flexible shifts among various action systems or modules within will systems.

In sum, values (i.e., basic desires, wills, motivations) organize action systems as well as horizontal modules within action systems, and the mentally healthy personality as a whole system involves an integration a set of different action systems. This integration allows for flexible, adaptive functioning in a changeable internal and external milieu. Values, will systems, and the healthy personality as an integration of multiple action systems and the implied values strongly support the capacity for convolved holism of the individual as a whole system.

Convolved Holism in Dissociative Parts of the Personality. Like integrated individuals, dissociative parts of the personality generally do not experience isolated objects, subjects, or scenes, but integrated, nested wholes. However, the experiential and cognitive domains of dissociative parts, i.e., the range of their integrated mental and physical states, tend to be more limited and sometimes far more limited in scope, restricting their degree of convolved holism. The consequence of this restriction is that dissociative parts, and the dissociative patient as a whole, cannot embed nonintegrated mental and behavioral actions and contents in a quick, flexible, and context-sensitive manner in the whole of their other experiences.

According to TSDP, dissociative parts are primarily mediated by one action system or a few action systems and their implied values. The action system or limited constellation of action systems that a particular dissociative part activates at a given moment strongly

14 Action systems can be understood as dynamic, nonlinear systems with emergent properties (see Hurley & Noë, 2003; Thompson, 2007). Values can be seen as *attractors* that organize these dynamic systems. An attractor of a dynamical system is a set (i.e., a collection of distinct objects) toward which a variable evolves over time within the dictates of that system. There are different types of attractors such as fixed point, limit cycles, and strange attractors. For example, a fixed point attractor is the point where a weight that hangs at the end of a cord will be and will return due to gravity after it has been moved by some other force than gravity. The seasons involve a limit cycle attractor, with recurrent shifting average temperatures from winter, to spring, to summer, and to autumn. Attractors that have a fractal structure are called strange attractors. The values of action system attract these dynamical systems in quite particular directions. For example, the 'sets' (i.e., the mental and behavioral actions and their implied contents) of the flight system are so to speak drawn toward detecting dangerous objects, fear, and flight, and that of social engagement are so to speak attracted toward interacting with trusted others.

influences what that dissociative part perceives, feels in a bodily and emotionally sense, thinks, wants, fantasizes, and does. In this light, the range of objects, subjects, and scenes that dissociative parts of the personality emulate, and the wider whole or wholes in which they embed their mental and behavioral contents (hence their capacity for convolved holism), are limited by the action systems or constellation of action systems that mediate them.

Humpty Dumpty

From a philosophical point of view, the personality can become divided in an endless number of ways in the context of traumatization. A closely related issue is that the particular way in which a personality has become divided does not necessarily say anything about the way in which the previously integrated personality was organized (assuming it was integrated in the first place). Believing otherwise would mean succumbing to the mistaken premise of *compositional reversibility*, also described as the 'Humpty Dumpty fallacy' (Braude, 1995). This fallacy involves the idea that the structure of the pre-existing personality can be inferred from the organization of the subsequent dissociative personality. However, "[j]ust because something is now in pieces, it does not follow that those pieces correspond to permanent or previously existing natural elements or divisions of that thing" (Braude, 1995, p. 139). According to TSDP, some kinds of divisions of the personality in traumatization are nonetheless *more probable* than other divisions. For example, the development of an ANP that aims to navigate daily life and an EP that engages in mammalian defenses during or following adverse intrafamilial adversity is more probable than the development of random dissociative parts, say, one dissociative part that likes sports and binges and freezes a lot, and another dissociative part that is fond of pancakes and that also engages in flight at the perception of threat. The different will systems and the contrasting values they can imply regarding subjects (e.g., abusive and emotionally neglectful parents) and objects (e.g., a knife as a weapon and as a utensil) are in TSDP thought to constitute naturally existing potential fault lines within the evolving personality.

Limited degrees of convolved holism can manifest as cognitive-emotional and sensorimotor dissociative symptoms (Nijenhuis, 2004). Dissociative symptoms that flow from a dissociation of the personality relate to a limited degree of convolved holism, because they reflect a lack of integration (synthesis, personification, presentification) of particular presentata and explicit conceptions into the personality at large. For example, amnesia becomes a cognitive-emotional dissociative symptom when the patient does not recall something as one part, say an ANP, but does recall it as another part, say, an EP. Along the same line of reasoning, analgesia is a sensorimotor dissociative symptom when one dissociative part does not feel pain in a particular part of the body, whereas another dissociative part does suffer this pain.

5. Dynamicity

Phenomenal states hardly ever involve static or highly stable mental contents, but rather generally include elements such as (flow of) time, duration, change, and agency. They are involved in ongoing motion, and they are dynamic: "Our conscious life emerges from integrated psychological moments, which, however, are themselves integrated into the flow of subjective time" (Metzinger, 2003, p. 151). This dynamicity is not given, but results from a physically and mentally acting individual who is an affective, attentional, cognitive, and volitional agent. From a teleological point of view, phenomenal dynamicity makes dynamical properties of our behavioral space or ecological niche available for a multitude of actions at the same time. It provides us with temporal knowledge that helps us to adapt to a changeable interoceptive and exteroceptive world.

Our experiences of duration and change are superimposed on our phenomenal now, on the present as we experience it. This superposition involves the mental action of *presentification*, the action of bringing our past and future to our phenomenal now, to our present, while realizing that the past and the future are linked to the present, but that the present is the most real. Assigning the highest degree of reality to the phenomenal now is adaptive because we can only act in the present.

Whereas a PCS is in constant flux, most individuals experience that they remain the same person despite the ongoing shifts. According to Metzinger (2003), it is the invariance of bodily self-awareness through proprioceptive and kinesthetic feedback of agency and of autobiographical memory which constitutes the conscious experience of an enduring self that is stable across time and changing situations.

Dynamicity in Dissociative Parts of the Personality. Dynamicity is deficient in patients with dissociative disorders. The lack manifests itself in compromised autobiographical memory, planning, ideals, meaning making, and integration among action systems. For example, dissociative parts may fail to phenomenally experience and conceive of change, or to conceive of change only in a limited sense. It may occur to them that every hour and every day are the same. When hypoaroused, they can experience that hours pass by in a void. Some dissociative parts lack all sense of time and have to be educated in treatment about the characteristics of time.

The phenomenology of dissociative patients confirms Metzinger's hypothesis (2003) that dynamicity is not a necessary feature of consciousness. The limited dynamicity that many dissociative patients display does not imply a complete loss of consciousness, but an attenuation thereof. The degree of dynamicity can be particularly limited in EPs. Fixated on a traumatic past they experience as the present, these parts' mental contents are abnormally and maladaptively invariant. Their lack of dynamicity also affects their subjective sense of age and time. One child EP of a patient with minor DID told her therapist: "You have grown older this week, because you have been around for many hours, but not me. I have not been around much, thus I hardly grow older." Dynamicity is also limited in most ANPs, albeit less severely in most cases (Van der Hart et al., 2006).

Whereas many dissociative parts integrate at least some significant experiences across time and situations, none integrates them all. Adaptive and creative dynamicity and presentification are in fact major problems for all dissociative parts. For example, ANPs typically do not integrate one or more traumatic memories, and EPs commonly do not integrate a host of autobiographical memories, the actual present, and adaptive simulations of the future. The PCS of many EPs of adults with a dissociative disorder involves a child-like or adolescent identity, which shows that these dissociative parts do not integrate the aging body and large parts of the patient's life history. ANPs may also lack autobiographical memories that do not pertain to traumatic experiences, and some only simulate a future in a very limited sense. Most ANPs, thus, also develop a limited degree of dynamicity.

Most dissociative parts have the experience and conception that they remain the same 'person' across time, even when they in fact change to a degree. However, they notice change more the more they synthesize, personify, and presentify. For example, previously bodily and emotionally anesthetic dissociative parts start to feel shifts in their feelings. EPs who start to presentify more begin to experience and appreciate how the actual present is different from the present as they previously conceived of it. They thereby extend their autobiographical memory. Similarly, as ANPs who integrate traumatic memories, the past becomes sadder, but more differentiated. With an increase of personification, dissociative parts develop a richer sense of agency and mineness, that is, a stronger and more elaborate quasi-second-person perspective.

For example, as an ANP focused on work, a patient with DID sincerely believed that she did not have a child. However, as another dissociative part, she recalled frequent rapes by her stepfather in her teens, getting pregnant when she was 15 years old, giving birth to a daughter when she had barely turned 16, and 20 years of caretaking too well. The ANP experienced a profound subjective and objective change when she integrated this other part's traumatic memories and memories of motherhood. This integration happened in a psychotherapeutic session more than 20 years after the birth of her daughter. It instantly and immensely affected her interactions with her daughter for the better.

6. Perspectivalness

I have already detailed how, according to Metzinger (2003), the PCS offers a first-person perspective, i.e., the phenomenal experience of being someone, and how this PCS encompasses phenomenal self-presentata and more explicit phenomenal self-conceptions.

Perspectivalness in Dissociative Parts of the Personality.

– *Self-Presentata:* Dissociative parts with a first-person perspective lie at the phenomenal center of their phenomenal world when they minimally experience some basic bodily

feelings. In this case, they experience a phenomenal self. Many dissociative parts have strong, explicit bodily feelings and generally own (i.e., personify) these sensations. In this case, they couple the synthesis of bodily feelings in the first-person perspective and personification in the quasi-second-person perspective. The latter perspective involves a phenomenal judgment (see Volume I, Chapters 5, 6, 10, 11), thus at least a minimal degree of reflection and hence an at least minimal explicit phenomenal conception of the feelings involved. For example, when they experience and own pain, they can say "My body hurts." In close relationship with the personified bodily feelings, they experience and know that they are the phenomenal center of their phenomenal world.
Some dissociative parts, however, have (a degree of) bodily anesthesia or analgesia regarding the whole body or particular body parts. As one part with severe sensory and emotional anesthesia wondered, "Do I really exist? Am I a dream?" The fact that this particular dissociative part referred to herself as "I" suggests that she had a PCS, however faint. She generated a PCS, but lacked a *centralized* point of view as she felt that she was floating "everywhere." With this degree of bodily anesthesia and similar sensorimotor dissociative symptoms (Nijenhuis, 2004), sensing the body as a stable point of reference is severely weakened, and together with it, the PCS. These clinical observations are consistent with Spinoza's and Metzinger's hypothesis that self-consciousness primarily entails bodily awareness, thus in a synthesis of bodily feelings framed in a PCS. Therefore, it can be said: few or no body sensations, little or no phenomenal self.

- *Self-Conceptions:* The PCS of a dissociative part is in some cases very limited. For example, it may encompass merely the conception of being 4 years old, scared, dirty, and bad. In other cases the PCS is far richer. For some ANPs, it can even be highly differentiated and coherent. Thus, some ANPs have a differentiated conception of the one they are, involving among other things a refined sense of age, skills, expertise, preferences, and existence across time and space. But even in these cases, the PCS of the dissociative parts of an individual with DID patient is less complete and complex than the PCS that person is bound to have as a fully integrated personality.
- *Self-Simulata:* Like the PCS of mentally healthy individuals, the PCS of dissociative parts denote a *possible* reality that they subjectively experience as *the* reality. And as in the mentally healthy, this confusion is adaptive because the dissociative part can use the current PCS as a point of reference. This reference base is needed for the ability to distinguish between the current conception of self (phenomenally experienced as immediately given in the mode of naive realism) and other possible conceptions of self (that the patient generates when remembering an experience, making plans, or fantasizing).

7. Transparency

Individuals do not necessarily have introspective epistemic access to their mental actions that generate their phenomenal states, i.e., know them through introspection. Lack of this introspective access is known as autoepistemic limitation, a limitation to knowledge of how mental states are generated (Northoff, 2003), or, somewhat counterintuitively, transparency (McGinn, 1989; Metzinger, 2003). As discussed before, the idea of 'transparency' is that we often 'look through' (i.e., are unaware of) the fact that our experiences result from earlier mental actions. In many cases we do not have introspective access to the medium (i.e., a component of the whole system that we are) that generates our experiences, and we are only phenomenally aware of the results of this medium's activity.

To the degree that we lack this access, we experience our sensory experiences and phenomenal conceptions of the world as *given, real, and undoubtedly existing* (see Metzinger, 2003, p. 167). That is, transparency entails functioning in the mode of naïve realism. Functioning in this mode is most useful, however, because it allows us to make a phenomenal distinction between (phenomenal) reality and (phenomenal) appearance. It allows us to engage in actions such as planning and fantasy, because we can distinguish between phenomenal facts, perceived and conceived in the mode of naive realism (e.g., "There is a mountain in front of me"), and generated possible worlds (e.g., "I can imagine a mountain in the Netherlands").

To give another example, we can distinguish between "I see my friend walking my way" and the plan "I will meet my friend tomorrow." The first statement means something like "There is no doubt in my mind that the person I see is my friend; he and my perception of him are real" (naïve realism: The world is they way I see it). The second utterance stands for "I am consciously aware of my plan to visit my friend tomorrow. I know I have planned this visit, and I realize that some other thing may happen that will prevent me from putting my plan in action" (the position of simulating a possible future: The world may become the way it expect it to become). But mountains in the Netherlands? It would take another ice age for the country to become known as the Highlands.

Metzinger (2003) suggests that for any phenomenal state, the degree of phenomenal transparency is inversely proportional to the introspective degree of attentional availability of earlier processing (or, as I prefer, *action*) stages. There are, thus, degrees of transparency and opacity. For example, we can sometimes, perhaps with considerable mental effort, appreciate that we are engaging in a projection as a psychological defense, rather than in an objective assessment of someone else's actions or intentions. More generally, our conscious thoughts are more or less opaque.

Transparency in the Dissociative Parts of the Personality. Transparency is present in all dissociative parts, that, as was provisionally suggested above, have a degree of consciousness and that entertain a PCS, however minimal this conception may be. This clinical observation fits Metzinger's self-model theory of subjectivity (2003), which proposes that transparency is one of three minimal constraints on consciousness. The other two minimal constraints are global availability of mental contents within a phenomenal now.

Although some dissociative parts find it subjectively difficult to tell facts from fantasies, many parts do not doubt the reality of most of their phenomenal conceptions. Because the conception of different dissociative parts can be quite different from each other, there are frequent conflicts among them regarding the question of what is real as well as conflicts between these dissociative parts and individuals (e.g., spouses, therapists) who challenge their phenomenal conceptions of self and world. The conceptual character of the dissociative parts' phenomenal conceptions of self, world, and self-in/of-the-world becomes particularly evident when these ideas are at odds with the facts, when two or more dissociative parts fuse into a new subsystem of the patient's personality, or when all dissociative parts blend into one whole system. The conceptual nature of dissociative parts' PCS is commonly quite clear from a third-person perspective. For example, as Anna, a girl of 7 years, a male patient with minor DID was convinced he was living with his abusive and neglectful parents, and that he was about to be abused again. As Robert, the patient appreciated he was a 40-year-old man who was living on his own and who was not being abused anymore. Observers obviously saw an adult male body, not a 7-year-old female body when Anna was activated, even if Anna talked and behaved like a youg girl.

The conceptual character of PCSs of dissociative parts is also demonstrated by the sudden disappearance of these conceptions and the rather sudden appearance of a new PCS when two or more dissociative parts have fused. However, it may take a lot of integrative therapeutic work before such fusion can take place. This work includes making opaque the transparent aspects of the PCS of dissociative parts that can in principle be made opaque. For example, the therapist helped Robert realize that the 7-year-old part of him – i.e., of him as a complete individual – believed she was a girl, and that she was seen as a girl by himself as ANP, because "girls get raped, not boys." By holding on to this idea, as ANP Robert believed that he had not been sexually abused.

The loss of homogeneous phenomenal presentata and explicit conceptions (see section 10) may involve a limitation of transparency in dissociative parts. This loss happened to the patient who was introduced in section 1 of this chapter. She experienced that her world and her self had shattered into many bits and pieces when she was exposed to extreme sexual abuse that included a serious threat to her life. In these cases, dissociative patients may experience that components of presentata and explicit conceptions become disconnected. This phenomenon could reflect a certain degree of opacity regarding mental actions that are normally transparent.

8. 'Offline' Activation

Functioning in the mode of naïve realism strongly depends on embodiment, sensorimotor action, and a phenomenal now. These features define the phenomenal present for us as a whole system: We sense and move in the experienced reality of the here and now.

Nonintended phenomenal simulations (e.g., spontaneous dreams and fantasies) and intended phenomenal simulations (e.g., deliberate planning of actions) are less dependent on actual sensorimotor input. They involve conceptions of the past or the imagined future that can include a degree of sensorimotor imagination (Weber, Wermter, & Elshaw, 2006). By means of our 'offline' simulations of the past, which are usually more opaque than transparent, our historicity becomes cognitively available. Autobiographical memory appears: "I now remember what happened to me. I know that what I am currently experiencing is a memory." In intended simulations, we conceive of ourselves as agents who generate phenomenologically opaque mental conceptions. For example, in planning we develop an opaque conception of a possible world and a possible self: "I imagine (think, picture, believe) that I can do the job in this manner." This kind of simulation of a possibility allows us to reflect on ourselves, so that we can regard ourselves as historical persons.

'Offline' simulations thus enable self-simulations (e.g., "how will I act best?") as well as simulations of other agents (e.g., "what would he do?"), which support social cognition. To the extent that these predictions are accurate, they obviously greatly enhance adaptive and creative behavior. They promote adaptive and creative behavioral actions in the short run (as in sensorimotor loops) and in the long run (as in long-term planning and in simulations of the behavior patterns of other people; Gallese, 2007). Generally speaking, beings that can engage in offline simulation are intelligent systems.

'Offline' Activation in the Dissociative Parts of the Personality. Dissociative patients often confuse 'online' and 'offline' simulations. For example, as EP they recurrently take traumatic memories that are 'offline' simulations pertaining to the past for online, present experiences. Normative autobiographical memories are largely opaque, 'offline' conceptions of the past which go along with a capacity for self-reflection ("I remember that I wrote the letter, and I am consciously aware that I remember that I wrote the letter"). In contrast, traumatic memories are subjectively experienced as if they were 'online' presentations and conceptions ("It hurts, he is dangerous, I run"). They usually do not include self-reflective actions. In other words, what for all adaptive and creative purposes should be an 'offline' conception of the past is experienced by the survivor as an online current event.

Patients with DID sometimes remember emotionally charged nontraumatizing events with significant sensorimotor components as well (Van der Hart, Bolt, & Van der Kolk, 2005), hence as a mixture of phenomenal presentata and phenomenal conceptions. Furthermore, these patients may believe that 'offline' simulations of the future (e.g., "I imagine how I hit him") have, so to speak, online consequences (e.g., "I am bad because I would like him to be dead; I deserve punishment"). The failure to distinguish between 'offline' simulations and 'online' presentata and conceptions seriously limits the individual's capacity for adaptive and creative action.

9. Intensity

Phenomenal presentations such as pain and perceptions of shades of a color or shifts in temperature vary along a dimension of intensity. From a teleofunctional, evolutionary perspective, it is clearly adaptive to experience the intensity of stimuli. For example, we would better feel how painful a particular stimulus is. Phenomenal presentation of intensity is functional in that it generates a motivation to act ("this is really hurting, I must see a doctor").

Intensity in the Dissociative Parts of the Personality. Some dissociative parts experience a loss of intensity of interoceptive or exteroceptive stimuli and consequently underreact to these stimuli. For example, analgesia and bodily and emotional anesthesia are distinctive sensorimotor and cognitive-emotional symptoms in dissociative disorders, because they are experienced by some dissociative parts, but not by others (Nijenhuis, 2004). When the intensity of phenomenal presentata and conceptions is low, it may seem to the patient that their phenomenal contents are not very real – or not at all real – so that they may not act when action is needed. For example, one dissociative part completely neglected serious physical wounds. Depersonalization symptoms in dissociative parts also relate to a lack of experienced intensity of interoceptive stimuli, and dissociative parts may only vaguely appreciate that their own or other dissociative parts' autobiographical memories pertain to real historical events. Dissociative parts with symptoms of derealization insufficiently assess the reality of external events. In other words, some stimuli and events are *not real enough* for them (Van der Hart et al., 2006). Dissociative patients may also experience that phenomenal presentata and conceptions are exceptionally intense. One type of mental state or series of mental states in which this intensity evidences is re-experiencing and re-enacting traumatizing events. These experiences are *too real* for them (Van der Hart et al., 2006).

There is a subtle difference between the intensity of stimuli and events and the assignment of the degree of reality of presentata and more explicit conceptions. Phenomenal simulations can be intense, but this does not necessarily imply that they are also experienced as *real* (Janet, 1919/1925, 1928, 1932). For example, an intensely experienced thriller or theatrical drama does not imply loss of the realization that the portrayed events are simulations. Stimuli and events that are not particularly physically intense such as a murmuring internal voice can become very real for some dissociative part when the voice whispers: "I will kill you if you talk about this." To highlight the difference between the phenomenal intensity and phenomenal reality of stimuli/events, I would therefore like add a constraint regarding the phenomenal reality of experiences to Metzinger's list (see section 12).

10. Homogeneity or Ultrasmoothness of Simple Content

Homogeneity also pertains only to phenomenal presentations. It denotes the internal, structureless density of, say, the color of an object. We do not perceive bits and pieces of color, nor "perceptual grains," but objects that are colored in a homogeneous way. The fundamental features of our sensory perceptions of the world and of ourselves are that they appear to us as ultrasmooth, grainless, and simple. Without these features, we could penetrate earlier stages of mental action, which would dissolve our phenomenal conception of the world and of ourselves. We should have homogeneous perceptions, not images of their elements and ways in which our perceptions are composed.

Homogeneity in Dissociative parts of the Personality. Clinical observations suggest that dissociative parts generally experience phenomenal presentata in a homogeneous way. However, the holistic character of presentations – and with it their homogeneity – may be lost to a degree for these parts in extreme situations. For example, previously simple and smooth phenomenal presentata can become complex and fragmented for an exceptionally frightened dissociative part. When this happens, the phenomenal world becomes a set of disconnected elements.

11. Adaptivity

Conscious experience, a phenomenal self, and the first-person perspective were acquired during millions of years of biopsychosocial evolution. We can experience our evolutionary background in terms of our phenomenal emotional states. Our experienced emotions are about "the logic of survival" (Damasio, 1999, p. 54; Spinoza, 1677), because they involve a phenomenal "affective tone" that provides us with the adaptive value of a certain situation, action, or person. Phenomenal emotions concern the biological or social *value* of a state of affairs for the organism as a whole, and they make this value globally available for the flexible control of behavioral action, for cognition, for memory, and for attention. Whereas emotions involve *embodied conceptions of goals*, they are more than 'mere' conceptions. Metzinger (2003) suggests that, as emotional conscious states developed in evolution, they actually must have *possessed* functional survival value. Indeed, without will, without desires, and without urges to achieve something, life basically ends.

Consciousness can more generally be seen as a virtual organ for the generation of adaptive and creative behavior. It is a device for motor control and sensorimotor integration. As answers to evolutionary challenges, phenomenal presentata and conceptions can also be seen as transient virtual organs. They are 'good' presentata and conceptions if and only if they successfully and reliably meet those challenges.

Adaptivity in Dissociative Parts of the Personality. As discussed before, action systems and the values that are their essence (will, desires) are major organizers of attention, cognition, and behavioral action. They guide what is to be integrated and ignored, and what is to be pursued. From this perspective, dissociative parts are subsystems of the personality, and their mental and phenomenal contents are best seen as an organism's efforts at adaptation under conditions of limited integrative capacity (Nijenhuis et al., 2002; Van der Hart et al., 2006).

Many authors regard dissociation as a mental defense, but this overlooks or disregards that there is nothing defensive about positive dissociative symptoms. For example, hearing crying, screaming, and aggressive voices that come and go as they seem to please, intruding feelings of pain, being dirty or sexually touched by someone, and re-experiencing of traumatic memories are very disturbing experiences. Negative dissociative symptoms may support adaption, however, when the integrative capacity is low. Thus, chronically abused and neglected children may be able to cope better with daily life when they develop one or more ANPs. As ANP, they tend to be less consciously aware of traumatic memories and associated emotions and sensations, less aware of the facts that they are basically living with adults who engage in criminal acts against them, and that they must continue to live with these individuals for years to come. They may be aware of these facts to a degree, but this type of knowing does not imply that they also *realize* them.

The high price survivors pay for their mental avoidance of what is real is that they become fixated on these memories as one or more EPs, up until the very day they integrate these memories and implied EPs as one or more ANPs. Reactivated by conditioned inner or outer stimuli, the traumatic memories of EPs can intrude on the phenomenal domain of ANPs. When ANPs do not integrate the memories of EPs (that is, mental actions and implied contents of EPs), that is, when they do not nest them in the totality of his or her autobiographical memories, EPs will remain fixated in these sensorimotor and often highly emotionally charged actions. Consequently, these traumatic memories will intrude on the domain of the involved ANPs time and again. When ANPs and EPs remain dissociated from each other, traumatized individuals as a whole remain stuck in their lack of flexible, fast, and context-dependent control regarding nonintegrated mental actions. These actions particularly, but not exclusively, pertain to traumatic memories.

Ongoing dissociation with its implied lack of convolved holism, personification, and presentification thus constitutes a major adaptive problem if traumatized individuals are in fact to be able to integrate previously dissociated mental contents/actions. Deficient convolved holism strongly restricts their control over traumatic memories and leaves classically conditioned trauma-related reactions that do not fit their present life unaltered. And worse, their functions such as attention, emotion, cognition, and motor action eventually become deficient in a much broader sense. In this important sense, dissociation does not constitute a mental defense at all.

12. Degrees of Reality

The world zero and transparency are tools for understanding how we do not recognize phenomenal conceptions as simulations, and how we generate a reference base for what we regard as our present, past, and future – and what we feel is real. Proposing a hierarchy of degrees of reality, Janet (1919/1925, 1928, 1932; see also Van der Hart et al., 2006) asserted that in order to adapt we must experience that the present is generally more real than the recent past and immediate future, and that the recent past and immediate future are more real than the distant past and future. Our 'ideal self' – the phenomenal simulation of our future phenomenal self – should be quite real, but not as real as the present self, in order to motivate us to press on. And our 'ideal' self should not be too distant either, as otherwise we would be without hope that we can ever realize the ideal. Dreams, vague ideas, and thoughts should be even less real to us than the distant past and future. Janet's hierarchy is a useful, albeit perhaps overly fixed set of principles that may actually be more flexible (Van der Hart et al., 2006). For example, how real something should be for us is also context-dependent. Sometimes it is more adaptive to focus more on the probable consequences of our actions or that of others than on the reality of the present.

Degrees of Reality in Dissociative Parts of the Personality. Many dissociative parts of the personality misjudge the degree of reality of their phenomenal presentations and conceptions. As EP, they tend to experience their conceptions of the past as too real, so that these become their phenomenal present. In this context, they experience and regard the factual (third-person) present as unreal or even as nonexistent. Dissociative patients tend to experience reality as a kind of dream when they function as an EP who engages in tonic immobility in response to actual or perceived danger. These EPs are quite absent-minded and anesthetic. As a depersonalized ANP, traumatized individuals may not experience the present as very real, which manifest in symptoms of derealization. Depressed ANPs may not see any near or distant future for them and may lack ideals. ANPs who function reasonably well commonly assess the reality of the present and the future quite adequately, though for them the past and particularly the traumatic past can be insufficiently real. Nonrealization is a core symptom in patients with dissociative disorders (Van der Hart et al., 2006).

Minimal Constraints on Consciousness and an Overview of Constraints on Consciousness

According to Metzinger (2003), our mental contents are also phenomenal contents when they are (1) globally available for our guided attention, cognition, and/or behavioral control ("There is a world"), and (2) appear in a window presence ("That world is now") (3) in a transparent fashion ("This is simply how it is": There is no possibility to introspect the ongoing mental actions that generate this world and this now). When the constraint of convolved holism is added, we can segment scenes and experience complex situations. Dynamicity adds the dimensions of duration and change, so that our phenomenal contents can become organized in a framework of the present, the past, and the future. With the introduction of the sixth constraint of perspectivalness, our phenomenal content involves a point of view. When we start to conceive ourselves, we develop a first-person perspective that is integrated into our dynamic phenomenal states. Memory, planning, and self-conception are special, inward-directed phenomenal conceptions. They emerge with constraint eight that concerns 'offline' activation.

Minimal Constraints for Consciousness and DID

Through TSDP, dissociative parts in DID involve dynamic biopsychosocial subsystems of an overarching environmentally embedded dynamic system that is the patient's personality. In light of Metzinger's analysis of consciousness, I submit that these subsystems are also *phenomenal subsystems of the personality*, because they – some exceptions such as profound loss of consciousness in dissociative convulsions (WHO, 1992) aside – fulfill the three minimal constraints of consciousness: They involve transparent PCIRs in the context of a global and usually coherent conception of the world – however limited this conception may be – and they embed these PCIRs in a phenomenal now.

As illustrated with some case examples, dissociative parts can have problems regarding any of the other constraints on consciousness. They may not have, or temporarily lose, one or more of these qualities. However, what always characterizes awake or dreaming dissociative parts is their own PCS, their own first-person perspective. With few exceptions, these parts are convinced that they exist. They experience that they are *someone*, that they are a subject.

But the more the different dissociative parts start to share experiences, sensations, emotions, cognitions, memories, skills, and other motor actions, the more their phenomenal conception of self, world, and self-of-the-world become similar. When two or more dissociative parts fuse, that is, fully integrate, they lose their different and separate PCSs and PCIRs. Metzinger's theory suggests that this implies the disappearance of their former PCSs, and the transparent appearance of a new PCS with associated PCIRs. Clinical observations are consistent with this hypothesis. After a while, newly created dissociative parts or the patient's fully fused personality find it commonly quite difficult to recall what their previous subjective existence was like. Their actual PCS and associated PCIRs seems far more real to them than the phenomenal conceptions of self, world, and self-of-the-world of the dissociative parts from which they evolved. The new conceptions encompass many elements of these older versions, but often many new elements as well. Theoretically, these new elements appear because a fusion of the nonlinear dynamic systems that make up dissociative parts in the third-person perspective generates more than the sum of the properties of the previously dissociated parts of the personality.

Multiple PCSs and PCIRs in Other Dissociative Disorders than DID

According to TSDP, the existence of two or more dissociative subsystems of the personality that are aware of themselves and their *Umwelt*,[15] however rudimentary some of these subsystems and their PCS and PCIRs may be, constitutes an essential property of *all* dissociative disorders. Individuals with depersonalization disorder who do not encompass dissociative parts remain the exception. However, the category does include PTSD and sensorimotor dissociative disorders.

Mental contents become phenomenal contents for a dissociative part when they are included into the PCS and PCIRs of the part. Dissociative parts can then attend to particular mental contents, think about them, and use them for volitional behavioral action control. Thus, the more limited a dissociative part's phenomenal conceptions of self and world are, the less attentional, cognitive, and volitional control the involved part will have, and the more that part is directed by affordances and conditioned stimuli. The part's actions are then generally impulsive and reflex-like. Elaboration of the PCS and PCIRs of the different dissociative parts is therefore an explicit and major treatment goal. To this end, therapists ground their treatment in the analysis of the functioning of the different ANPs and EPs, of these parts' functioning regarding each other, and of the functioning of the personality as a whole system.

The cardinal feature of patients with dissociative disorders is that they involve multiple first-, quasi-second-, second-, and third-person perspectives. They encompass at least two dissociative parts, each of which generates a PCS and a set of associated PCIRs, however simple these dissociative conceptions may be in some cases. This definition implies that ego-dystonic phobias and the like do not involve dissociative parts of the personality inasmuch as the patient includes only one PCS. That is, although the subsystem of the personality that causes an ego-dystonic phobia is not fully integrated into the personality at large, it does not encompass its own PCS. Such patients still will say that *they* are afraid (e.g., "I [the patient's singular PCS] → fear and avoid → heights, although I know my phobia is a bit silly"). A phobia is a component of a dissociative disorder, when the phobia is ego-syntonic for one or more dissociative parts, and ego-dystonic for one or more other dissociative parts. One or more dissociative parts may also be afraid of something, whereas one or more other dissociative parts do not share the phobia.

A different view is that dissociative parts of the personality do not necessarily involve consciousness and self-consciousness (Brown, 2006; Holmes et al., 2005). In the current terminology, they would not encompass their own PCS and PCIRs. Dissociation, in Brown's and Holmes' perspective, involves a compartmentalization of higher-order and lower-order information processing systems. All dissociative symptoms result from a loss of normal high-level attentional, conscious control over low-level processing systems that do not necessarily involve conscious awareness and self-awareness.

Brown's and Holmes' view is problematic because it does not define the minimal constraints on the concept of 'dissociative parts of the personality.' Human individuals in-

15 This concept stems from Von Uexküll (Agamben, 2004). The *Umwelt* entails the environment as perceived by an organism given its build, maturation, and development. We can say that the totality of someone's PCIR constitutes his or her *Umwelt*. Dissociative parts include their own *Umwelt*.

clude many low-level 'processing systems' (molecules, neurons, neural organs, neural groups, etc.) that may not operate in fully integrative ways. In other words, Brown and Holmes do not clarify how dissociative, compartmentalized processing systems of a dissociative nature differ from other kinds of more or less compartmentalized systems. For example, they do not provide a criterion that can be used to say why subsystems mediating ego-dystonic phobias and complex tics as in the syndrome of Gilles de la Tourette would or would not be dissociative parts of the personality.

Multiple perspectivalness, i.e., the existence of two or more different PCSs within one individual, can serve as a *useful* criterion for delimiting the category of dissociative parts of the personality and thereby the category of dissociative disorders as well. By acknowledging that all categorizations are man-made and hence artificial (Wittgenstein, 1953), I insist that nonintegrated subsystems of the personality with and without their own person perspectives involve different properties that are of theoretical, scientific, and clinical interest. For example, it is of clinical importance to realize that it is possible to communicate with dissociative parts *because* they generate their own PCS and associated PCIRs, even when these dissociative parts are rather rudimentary. A thorough understanding of the PCS and PCIRs of dissociative parts of the personality helps the clinician to empathize, accept, understand, and influence the different parts – and to assist them in becoming more empathic, more accepting, and more understanding of each other. These are the pivotal ingredients to attaining cooperation among the dissociative parts as well as their eventual fusion.

Psychosis

In the 19th century individuals with a dissociative disorder with profound psychotic symptoms were seen as cases of hysterical psychosis. Most psychiatrists ceased using the diagnosis that encompassed a vast amount of posttraumatic psychopathology in the early 20th century (Van der Hart, Witztum, & Friedman, 1993). The decline of hysterical psychosis as a disorder was due in part to the idea that it would not have an organic base (Babinsky, 1901, 1909; Witztum & Van der Hart, 2008). This position clearly reflects Cartesian thinking regarding the matter-mind problem, with an emphasis on philosophical dualism. The abandonment of hysterical psychosis as a diagnosis was also related to Bleuler's introduction of the term 'schizophrenia' (Bleuler, 1911/1950) and his claim that hysterical psychosis involved schizophrenia in a personality that was premorbidly hysterical (Witztum & Van der Hart, 2008). By correcting the absence of a precise description of the disorder, Hollender and Hirsch (1964) formulated that hysterical psychosis involves a form of ego disruption marked by a sudden and dramatic onset temporally related to an event or circumstance that profoundly upset the involved individual. As they detailed, its symptoms include "hallucinations, delusions, depersonalization and grossly unusual behavior. Thought disorders, when they do occur, are usually sharply circumscribed and very transient. Affectivity, if altered, is changed in the direction of volatility and not flatness" (Hollender & Hirsch, 1964, p. 1066).

DSM-II (APA, 1968) did not reintroduce hysterical psychosis, but rather encompassed brief reactive psychosis as a new diagnosis. The term 'reactive' expressed the view that the disorder – like hysterical psychosis – evolves as a response to major stress. The index of DSM-III (1980) included the term 'hysterical psychosis' in reference to brief reactive psychosis and factitious disorder with psychological symptoms. DSM-5 (APA, 2013) contains brief psychotic disorder, which applies when an individual has at least one of the following three symptoms: delusions, hallucinations, and disorganized speech. He or she can also have grossly disorganized or catatonic behavior. The symptoms must have lasted at least one day but less than one month, with eventual full return to premorbid functioning. Further, the symptoms should not be better explained by major depressive or bipolar disorder with psychotic features or some other psychotic disorder such as schizophrenia and catatonia, and they should not be attributable to the physiological effects of a substance. The condition can, but need not, occur in response to one or more marked stressors. Problems of brief reactive psychosis and brief psychotic disorder are that they do not need to be brief (i.e., the symptoms may last longer than one month), that no reference is made to a possible dissociative nature of the psychosis and the implied 'ego-disruption' that the 19th-century psychiatry as well as Hollender and Hirsch (1964) and others (e.g., Prinquet, 1977) had emphasized, and that the differential diagnosis does not include (other) dissociative disorders. Moreover, Pitta and Blay (1997) concluded that the operational criteria for DSM-III-R brief reactive psychosis, and DSM-IV and ICD-10 brief or acute psychotic disorder, bore little resemblance to the concept of 'hysterical psychosis' (see Witztum & Van der Hart, 2008).

Trying to correct the limitations of brief reactive psychosis, Van der Hart, Witztum, and Friedman (1993) reintroduced hysterical psychosis as reactive dissociative psychosis. Although their proposal did not lead to a general recognition of reactive dissociative psychosis or its introduction into modern classificatory systems, the start of the 21st century did witness renewed interest in the relationships between adverse events, dissociation, and psychosis (e.g., Moskowitz, Schäfer, & Dorahy, 2008). Recent empirical and clinical findings are considered in Volume III. Here I only wish to comment on the concept of 'psychosis' with respect to dissociation of the personality.

The key features that define the psychotic disorders listed in DSM-5 comprise delusions, hallucinations, disorganized thinking (formal thought disorder), grossly disorganized or abnormal motor behavior including catatonia, and negative symptoms. Delusions are "fixed beliefs that are not amenable to change in the light of conflicting evidence" (APA, 2013, p. 87). Hallucinations involve "perception-like experiences that occur without an external stimulus" (p. 87). They are "vivid and clear," escape voluntary control, and "may occur in any sensory modality" (p. 87). Formal thought disorder pertains to derailment of thoughts and loose associations. It also shows in incoherent speech, also known as "word salad." Catatonia involves a marked decrease in reactivity to the environment, which can present in a variety of ways including mutism and stupor. Finally, negative symptoms comprise diminished emotional expression, avolition, alogia (diminished speech output), anhedonia, and asociality.

Psychosis is often loosely seen as a mental condition characterized by phenomenal experiences, phenomenal judgments, and behaviors that do not fit 'objective reality.' For example, the speech and the goal, if any, of physical movements of affected individuals may seem to be almost or completely beyond common or clinical understanding. The behaviors range from "childlike 'silliness' to unpredictable agitation" and may apply to "any form of goal-directed behavior, leading to difficulties in performing activities of daily living" (APA, 2013, p. 88). One problem of this characterization is that it is not always easy to decide what constitutes 'objective reality.' Even mentally healthy individuals frequently contest each other's takes on 'reality.' As pointed out before, any phenomenal judgment (in quasi-second and second-person perspective) and physical judgment (in third-person perspective) of what is and is not real is a particular conception of reality. There is no absolute, given reality. What counts as 'real' and how 'real' something is is relative to someone's phenomenal and physical judgment. Reality is a broad notion, and there are no clear boundaries between what is phenomenally and physically 'real' and what is not. This problem was discussed at length in Volume I, and as detailed in the present chapter, the degree of reality constitutes a constraint on the concept of 'consciousness.'

Applied to the theme of psychosis, one may ask whether Anja, a 43-year-old woman, was out of touch with 'objective reality' when she went at a snail's pace, taking tiny steps, feet turned inward, slowly orienting herself with hazy yet wide-open eyes, murmuring with a child-like voice "red . . ., red . . ., all red . . .," and doing and saying nothing else (see Van der Hart et al., 2006, p. 121)? Were her words and behaviors meaningless or just beyond someone else's understanding? Was she stuck in a first-person perspective, in a solipsistic world, or would she still be able to engage in a meaningful second-person perspective? Upon my return from a brief leave, a psychiatric nurse of a clinical unit where Anja had landed 2 weeks previously, brought Anja to the outpatient unit of the psychiatric hospital where I worked. The nurse told me that her apparent psychotic disorder had started suddenly. It had caused her physician to request clinical admission, and it had remained unaltered since. Since Anja was in treatment with me for minor DID that evolved in the context of chronic childhood traumatization, I knew her well. I also knew she had experienced several psychotic episodes before, but had not met her so far during one of these states. The psychotic periods had previously lasted *months* until they spontaneously remitted for unknown reasons to resurface after a shorter or longer delay. The attending clinicians had consistently diagnosed a psychotic disorder, but had overlooked her minor DID. The neuroleptics they prescribed had helped, yet no one had any idea whether there was meaning to her psychotic presentation, let alone what that meaning might be.

As I describe in more detail in Volume III, I managed to enter into contact with Anja. My approach started with consistent and minute empathic attunement to whatever posture and movement she displayed as well as to any single word she uttered. In this sense, and under intentional withholding of any reference to my perceptions of reality, we agreed that her world and she as a part of that world were the way she experienced and conceived them. Following and extending this path with sincere curiosity about her experiences, behavioral actions, and final causes, I gradually saw that Anja phenomenally experienced and judged that she was a 3-year-old girl (PCS) who had been anally raped by a neighbor a short while ago in a black car. Shocked by the rape and by the blood in her pants (a set of extremely significant PCIRs), all she saw as the involved EP was "red." Her peculiar way of walking was due to the intense anal pain she had experienced. It also mirrored the gait of her handicapped grandfather, another man who had recurrently abused her sexually in her childhood. Meticulous attunement to the PCS and PCIRs the EP presented was helpful in revealing the trauma-related nature, contents, context, and meaning of the psychotic episode. And, in accord with Spinoza's psychology, the psychotic "passion" ceased to be a passion once we succeeded to turn it in a "clear and distinct idea," in a narrative that Anja synthesized, personified, and presentified.

In terms of the presented constraints on consciousness, the EP saying that "all is red" met several constraints on consciousness. However restricted, her mental contents were globally available for her guided attention, cognitive reference, and control of her behavioral actions (global availability). She perceived the redness, the pain, etc., as present events (phenomenal now). She lived in a very small but terrible world, and experienced and perceived that world as a whole (situatedness and global coherence). She encompassed her own first-person perspective (perspectivalness), but neither appreciated that her self was a phenomenal conception, nor did she knew how she had generated this conception in ongoing mental action (transparency). The redness she perceived was very intense (intensity) and extremely homogeneous (homogeneity). After some therapeutic work, it appeared that the redness, pain, and physical movements were lower-order elements of a higher-order whole, even if this whole was very limited in scope (convolved holism). This convolved whole was not static but dynamic, as it encompassed various phases of a traumatizing event which were associated with somewhat different biopsychosocial states (dynamicity). A core problem was that other dissociative parts of 'the whole Anja' (Anja as ANP plus her various other EPs) had not integrated the experience (lack of convolved holism, lack of synthesis and presentification, lack of dynamicity) as a personal experience and memory, just as the 3-year-old EP had not integrated and realized the rest of Anja's existence (multiple perspectivalness, lack of personification and presentification).

In the course of Anja's treatment with me – it took a total of 70 sessions to achieve full and lasting recovery from her minor DID and psychotic episodes – it became apparent that her previous psychotic episodes had concerned re-enactments of particular traumatic experiences by one or more EPs as well. For example, as several childlike EPs she had been obsessed by and intensely afraid of men in black suits during one of these episodes. The terrifying fear had, despite appearances, not been a mere delusion, because her sexually and emotionally abusive grandfather had habitually worn black suits. These other EPs met the same constraints on consciousness as the one that was fixed in a red world.

All EPs assigned paramount reality to their phenomenal experiences and perceptions that in the third-person perspective were re-enactments of the past rather than actual occurrences. In contrast, they poorly perceived their actual material and social environment as it existed in a third-person physical assessment of it, and they did not phenomenally judge that what they noticed of it was very real. Whereas their past was far too real for them, the third-person present was not nearly real enough. They were thus confused about what constituted 'online' and 'offline' conceptions of reality from the third-person perspective. Whereas 'offline' simulations such as fantasies of mentally healthy individuals are commonly opaque, they were transparent for the involved EPs. That is, because they were lacking in self-reflection and reached only a low degree of convolved holism and dynamicity (because the EPs included only a very limited portion of the patient's life and history), they were not consciously aware of the third-person fact that they were engaging in simulations of their past. In this context the rest of Anja's existence and history were nonexistent or insufficiently real to them.

The judgment whether Anja was in touch or out of touch with reality as the involved EPs depends on one's person-perspective and the implied types of judgment. From their first-person, quasi-second-person, and second-person perspectives and the implied phenomenal experiences and judgments, the involved EPs would certainly have resisted the idea that they were confused about reality and that their actions were not goal-directed. A third-person physical judgment that they were caught in mere delusions, hallucinations, disturbed thinking, and grossly disorganized motor behavior would also be partly disputed by those who phenomenally judge from an empathic second-person perspective and/or physically judge from a third-person perspective that the patient re-enacted one or more components of her traumatic memories.

What constitutes hallucinations and delusions in a third-person physical psychiatric or common judgment may thus be real in the phenomenal experience and judgment of the involved dissociative part. This phenomenal reality, this domain of particular presentata and conceptions, does not match the physical judgment of present reality by third persons, but it may relate to a past third-person reality. Whereas a hallucination constitutes a sensory perception in the absence of existing external stimulation, it may concern a re-enactment of a former physical traumatizing or other reality. In this sense a hallucination need not consist of a more or less extensive lack of contact with physical reality. It can also be a sensory and emotional perception of a past reality that is phenomally experienced and judged as a present event rather than as a simulation of that past, that is, as an autobiographical memory. Third persons should be aware that they can only reach a solid conclusion regarding a possible correspondence of past and present phenomenal and physical realities when they get to know the *context* of the isolated or fragmented presentata and conceptions. This context may, but clearly need not, involve traumatizing events.

A related but more general problem encountered in defining psychosis as being seriously out of touch with 'objective reality' is that *any* dissociative part of the personality includes phenomenal presentata and conceptions that are at odds with a third-person judgment of reality. For example, all EPs, including those in PTSD, are fixed in a traumatic past that they phenomenally experience and judge as the present, and they all phenomenally conceive of their self, world, and self-of-the-world in ways that are in a least some major regards at odds with the third-person views of reality. Thus, clinicians physically judge that an EP is not actually, say, a 10-year-old boy, but in fact a dissociative part of a mature woman. Many ANPs also have misconceptions of 'objective reality' which are hard to change, even when confronted with contrary third-person facts. To honor DSM-5 definition of delusions as fixed beliefs that are not amenable to change in the light of conflicting evidence, clinicians would have to physically judge that the involved dissociative parts, and hence the patient at large, are psychotic. However, most clinicians resist drawing this conclusion in order to avoid the uncomfortable implication that basically *any* individual with a dissociative disorder is necessarily psychotic.

This issue raises the question 'how psychotic' an individual with a dissociative disorder must be in order to be deemed psychotic? When is a sensation, an image, or some other perception a hallucination? When is a conception a delusion? The technical and practical problem is that the lower boundary of the concepts of 'psychosis' and 'psychotic features' remains unclear. This ambiguity may and indeed does cause overdiagnosis of psychotic disorders such as schizophrenia. For example, auditory hallucinations can very well involve one dissociative part hearing the voice of another dissociative part. Since these 'voices' tend to say things that relate to their phenomenal reality which have roots in a third-person physical reality, they do not utter complete nonsense. An ANP may at times hear the voices of a crying fragile EP, a fragile EP shouting "Stop!" in an effort to protect herself, a controlling EP commanding a fragile EP or ANP (e.g., "Shut up, don't trust anyone!"), or a controlling EP telling a fragile EP that she is "a dirty little brat." Different EPs may also hear each other, and EPs may hear ANPs speak. EPs can also have visual (e.g., images of blood, someone haunting them), tactile (e.g., "Someone touches me" [abusive sexual touch]), and kinesthetic sensory presentata and associated conceptions that, in the eye of an observer, do not seem to relate to outer events (e.g., "I feel a big thing moving in my body up to my throat" [rape]). Each of these can intrude on ANPs and other EPs. Intruding EPs generally know how the involved phenomena fit their wider phenomenal world. They tend to meet the criteria of convolved holism and dynamicity in some limited sense. The same patterns may apply to gustatory perceptions (e.g., "There is a salty taste in my mouth" [sperm in mouth]) and olfactory sensations (e.g., "There is an awful smell, it makes me sick" [a perpetrator's aftershave]). Such sensory presentata and conceptions, which may also involve physical and emotional pain, from the third-person perspective may be seen as hallucinations. However, they tend to be real experiences and events in the first-person and quasi-second-person perspective, a fact that can be phenomenally and empathically appreciated in the second-person perspective. What is true for positive symptoms such as the phenomena noted above can also be true for negative symptoms. For example, in some cases catatonia in the form of stupor concerns a fragile EP engaging in defensive freezing or tonic immobility, rather than constituting a negative symptom of schizophrenia. Each of these sensorimotor phenomena may relate to components of traumatizing events that the involved dissociative part of the personality (re-)experiences and (re-)conceives, and that have not been integrated and realized by the patient as a whole organism-environment system. As indicated in square brackets, all of the examples presented both above and below involved clinically observed components of traumatic memories in which fragile EPs were fixed as well as actions of controlling, perpetrator imitating EPs. The involved ANPs were not aware of the origin of the phenomena and their context before they got into close(r) contact with the involved EPs.

Like dissociative hallucinations, dissociative delusions tend to involve simulations of past realities which one or more dissociative parts of the personality phenomenally judge as the phenomenal now. For example, EPs may believe and communicate the following: "There are men chasing me [groupwise abuse by men]"; "There are men with big mouths who want to eat me" [indoctrination by a group of men, loudly commanding the patient when she was a teenager to hurt younger children]; "People haunt me" [past and present intrusive actions of family members]; "This woman is not my mother" [a claim by an EP who cannot live with the fact that her mother abused, neglected, and maltreated her]; "They will throw me in a deep well where no one will ever find me if I don't obey" [perpetrators who scared the patient as a child, so that she would stop resisting their instructions to maltreat other children]; "I am a bad dirty girl" [repeated accusations by the patient's abusive father that she imitated]; "we do the right thing" [perpetrators belying the patient that abusing children is justified]. Still another trauma-related thought that may appear as a delusion from the third-person perspective in the absence of knowledge or appreciation of the context of the idea was that being comforted was extremely dangerous [Father who had "comforted" the patient when she had been crying following physical maltreatment by her mother. His "comforting" had started with stroking and had ended in rape]. Some controlling EPs utter grandiose ideas that often contain reflections of ideas that perpetrators cherished, which these EPs assume in order to gain a sense of control hiding their fragility and powerlessness.

Apart from such positive dissociative symptoms, which clinicians may or may not be inclined to classify as psychotic symptoms, there are also negative dissociative symptoms that third persons may interpret as psychotic symptoms. For example and as already noted above, a particular individual's presumed negative symptoms of schizophrenia or some other psychotic disorder embraced by DSM-5 may actually involve negative dissociative symptoms (e.g., an emotionally numb and depersonalized ANP, a fragile EP engaging in tonic immobility; a fragile EP who is too scared to speak; a despondent, depressed, and anhedonic ANP; a suicidal, avolitional EP who shows no interest in social contact). There are also psychotic phenomena that do not characterize dissociative disorders. These include thought broadcasting, speaking or writing word salad, persistent formal thought disorder, and confused thinking that cannot be contextualized and in part for that reason remains incomprehensible for second and third persons. Further, dissociative psychotic symptoms are, as applied to Anja, generally not remedied by neuroleptics.

In conclusion, the lower boundary of the concept of 'psychosis' is unclear, and phenomena the DSM-5 defines as key features of psychotic disorders can be dissociative in nature. It would therefore be a mistake to physically judge from a third-person perspective that key DSM-5 features of the psychotic disorders embraced by this classificatory system can be symptoms only of these disorders. In fact, the symptom can also be a manifestation of a dissociative disorder, and the category of dissociative disorders clearly includes dissociative psychosis, even if DSM-5 does not acknowledge it. According to the present delimitation of the concept of a 'dissociative part,' apparent or real psychotic phenomena are dissociative when they characterize one or more subsystems of the personality that generate their own (i.e., nonshared) PCS and PCIRs, and that do not characterize one or more other dissociative parts. Clinicians should therefore carefully consider whether an apparent case of schizophrenia, bipolar mood disorder, or some other 'nondissociative' psychosis might actually be a case of dissociative psychosis or some other dissociative disorder. For this reason and given the frequent misdiagnosis of complex dissociative disorders, DSM-6 and ICD-11 should include dissociative disorder as a differential diagnosis. In order to delimit the concept of 'dissociative psychosis' and to distinguish between dissociative psychosis and other dissociative disorders, the following can be said, in major agreement with Van der Hart et al. (2006):

1. Like any dissociative disorder, dissociative psychosis involves one or more insufficiently integrated conscious and self-conscious subsystems of the personality.
2. In contrast to dissociative parts of the personality that are better not categorized as psychotic, psychotic dissociative parts involve EPs that dominate consciousness and behavior for an extended and uninterrupted period of time (e.g., several days, weeks, or months).
3. These EPs assign a high degree of reality to their commonly quite restricted experiences, sensations, perceptions, and thoughts, which they maintain despite conflicting third-person perspective evidence.
4. Their phenomenal experiences and judgments meet the following constraints on consciousness: global availability, phenomenal now, situatedness and global coherence, little convolved holism and dynamicity, transparency, and perspectivalness.
5. Their sensorimotor, cognitive-emotional and behavioral functioning commonly relates to traumatizing events and powerful reminders of such events.
6. In this sense and from a third-person clinical perspective, the involved EP or EPs tend to involve regressions to some former time and place, and a former sense of personal identity (i.e., to a former PCS and set of PCIRs). The regressions can even pertain to early childhood.
7. The individual's dissociative psychotic condition exists as a component of a constellation of other dissociative symptoms.
8. In some cases, dissociative psychotic episodes can last several months, although their duration is usually shorter.
9. Dissociative psychotic episodes can be recurrent.
10. Other dissociative disorders can, but need not, include dissociative psychosis.

11. The symptoms are not better explained by another mental and behavioral disorder, are not due to the direct effects of a substance or medication, and are not due to a neurological condition or other disorder or disease, or to fatigue or hypnogogic or hypnopompic states.
12. The symptoms are of sufficient severity to produce significant impairment in personal, family, social, educational, occupational, or other important areas of functioning.
13. As a rule, the condition does not favorably respond to neuroleptics.

Alterations in Consciousness in Dissociative Disorders, Other Mental Disorders, and Mental Health

Global availability, a phenomenal now, and transparency aside, individuals who do not have a dissociative disorder or any other mental or neurological disorder can fail to meet one or more constraints on consciousness. For example, anyone of us may sometimes experience that our phenomenal presentata and more explicit conceptions are not very real, appear less intense than they normally do, or do not fit our idea of the world so well. We can also experience shifts in the flow of time (time may seem to speed up or slow down), we may have difficulty remembering certain experiences, and we can feel less centered or present at times.

Many phenomena described in the literature as dissociative in fact entail such *common alterations in consciousness* rather than specific phenomena that flow from a dissociation of the personality (Van der Hart et al., 2004). Common alterations in consciousness include changes with respect to situatedness and global coherence, convolved holism, dynamicity, intensity, adaptivity and degree of reality of mental contents. In statistical terms, these phenomena are *sensitive but not specific* to dissociative disorders. The involved alterations are certainly more extreme in individuals with dissociative disorders than in mentally healthy individuals, but they can also present in individuals with other mental disorders. For example, individuals with major depression tend to have a rather low level of consciousness, and the field of consciousness of individuals with obsessive-compulsive disorders and phobias is unduly focused on particular feared objects and efforts to avoid perceived risks. It is therefore confusing and imprecise to conceptualize common alterations in consciousness as dissociative symptoms.

Mentally healthy individuals and psychiatric patients who do not have a dissociative disorder do not generate multiple PCSs and associated PCIRs. Thus, it is dissociation of the personality – i.e., the existence of more than one PCS and associated different PCIRs as well as the symptomatic manifestations of this organization of personality – that is *specific* to dissociative disorders. There are two known exceptions to this rule: individuals who develop temporary multiple perspectivalness following hypnotic suggestions, and particular mediums who may encompass more than one PCS, but who do not have a dissociative disorder.

Table 12.1. Different alterations in consciousness in mental health, dissociative disorders, and other mental disorders.

	Mental health	Dissociative disorders including dissociative psychosis	Other mental disorders (i.e., disorders that do not involve a dissociative division of the personality)
1. *Global availability*	Intact, but the availability for attention, cognition, and motor control can decrease, as sometimes happens in absorption, lowering of the level of consciousness, and restricting the field of consciousness.	Intact, but the availability for attention, cognition, and motor control is often limited (e.g., due to a low level of consciousness, such as in tonic immobility and implied anesthesias), and it can be exceptionally restricted for EPs.	Intact, but the availability for attention, cognition, and motor control can be pathologically limited. Examples include low intensity of consciousness in major depression, derealization not associated with the existence of dissociative parts, and restricted manifest and latent PCIRs in phobias unrelated to the existence of dissociative parts.
2. *Phenomenal now*	Intact.	Intact, but EPs' phenomenal now typically involves the third-person past. ANPs may become reoriented to the traumatic past when intruded on by traumatic memories in which EPs are fixed. ANPs may then temporarily lose the third-person present.	Vague sense of the present as in major depression. In several mental disorders the patient is focused on the past or future more than the present. For example, individuals with anxiety disorders concentrate on the future they fear and on past situations in which they were exceptionally scared.
3. *Situatedness and global coherence*	Intact.	Dissociative parts may not be sufficiently aware of the complex situation they are in. This applies more to EPs than to ANPs, but certainly also applies to ANP.	Severely depressed or psychotic patients may be poorly aware of the actual situation they are in (i.e., as perceived in third-person perspective).
4. *Convolved holism*	Intact, but the field of consciousness, that is, the set of manifest PCIRs changes constantly.	Commonly intact in the sense that the experiences of dissociative parts are embedded in their conception of the situation they are in. However, the field of consciousness of dissociative parts is not just changeable, but also permanently and unduly restricted. Each dissociative part has a set of manifest and latent PCIRs, although this collection is underinclusive. The different dissociative parts have their own PCS and associated set of manifest and latent PCIRs, none of which includes them all. Thus, each dissociative part has an unduly restricted PCS and associated set of PCIRs.	Commonly intact, but the field of consciousness, that is, the individual's set of latent and manifest PCIRs, may be unduly restricted.

	Mental health	Dissociative disorders including dissociative psychosis	Other mental disorders (i.e., disorders that do not involve a dissociative division of the personality)
5. *Dynamicity*	The sense of duration and change shifts, but the phenomenal now is always linked with a sense of duration and change, i.e., with the past and the future.	Presentification is deficient: EPs live in the third-person past that they experience and know as the present; ANPs have insufficiently integrated the third-person past; as judged in third-person perspective, EPs and often ANPs as well do not generate an adequate (i.e., adaptive and creative) idea of the future.	Lack of an (adaptive) idea of the future in major depression, often also a limited idea of the past; strong maladaptive negative anticipations in anxiety disorders. Many patients with mental disorders of some kind can have a weak recollection of their childhood.
6. *Perspectivalness*	Singular.	Multiple (i.e., more than one 'I').	Singular. Some patients with mental disorders encompass 'ego-states,' though the patient still recognizes these as own states. When a patient with psychotic symptoms includes different PCSs and associated PCIRs, he or she has a dissociative disorder that may be dissociative psychosis or some other dissociative disorder. A constellation of negative and positive symptoms (intrusions) is the rule in dissociative disorders. Further study must settle the question whether voices (e.g., as found in schizophrenia) that, no matter what a sensitive clinician attempts to achieve in this regard, are or seem unable to enter a second-person perspective, constitute dissociative parts. My provisional third-person physical judgment and second-person phenomenal judgment are that these voices do not meet the criteria of a dissociative part. In any case, the differential diagnosis of psychoses such as schizophrenia and bipolar mood disorder includes dissociative psychosis or a different dissociative disorder. This differential diagnostic work, however, is rarely performed in modern psychiatry, leading to many false-negative cases of dissociative disorder. Correction of this practice is urgent

	Mental health	Dissociative disorders including dissociative psychosis	Other mental disorders (i.e., disorders that do not involve a dissociative division of the personality)
7. *Transparency (regarding PCS!PCS)*	Intact.	Intact. A possible exception may be a state of extreme fear in which the patient's PCS temporarily disintegrates into a phenomenal multitude of disconnected bits and pieces. This mental state may involve partial access to mental states preceding the formation of a minimally coherent and cohesive PCS.	Intact.
8. *'Online' and 'offline' activation*	'Online' and 'offline' activation are commonly distinguished from each other.	Sometimes confusion of 'offline' and 'online' activation. For example, EPs may sometimes confuse fantasy and 'third-person' reality. EPs typically confuse the actual (i.e., according to third-person physical judgment) present and past.	Confusion of 'offline' and 'online' activation in psychosis. Compromised 'offline' activation such as a certain inability to foresee the future and recollect the distant past in major depression.
9. *Intensity*	Changeable.	Changeable. Phenomenal contents can be too strong (e.g., intense sensory perceptions and emotions during a re-enactment of a traumatic memory) or too weak (e.g., depersonalization, emotional numbing, derealization).	Changeable. Phenomenal contents can be too strong as in anxiety disorders and some forms of nondissociative psychosis – or too weak, as in major depression and nondissociative psychotic conditions dominated by negative symptoms.
10. *Homogeneity*	Intact.	Disintegration of homogeneity may occur in EPs (e.g., as in the exceptional state described in #7 of this table).	Fragmentation possible with extreme anxiety.
11. *Adaptivity*	Adaptive.	Dissociation of the personality is (only) adaptive given insufficient integrative capacity. For example, chronically abused and neglected children may function better when they develop one or more ANPs. Nonadaptive when the individual would in principle be able to integrate his or her dissociative parts and dissociated traumatic memories. Dissociation of the personality can, given insufficient integrative capacity, be adaptive for ANPs, but it is not adaptive at the level of EPs.	Abnormal and maladaptive forms of consciousness can be present such as derealization in nondissociative psychosis and nondissociative major depression.

	Mental health	Dissociative disorders including dissociative psychosis	Other mental disorders (i.e., disorders that do not involve a dissociative division of the personality)
12. *Degree of reality*	Commonly intact, although anyone can temporarily misconceive the reality of situations ("Did I really win this competition?"), thoughts (i.e., disregarding the accuracy of certain ideas), and feelings (i.e., disregarding accurate intuitive feelings).	ANPs usually assess third-person reality better than EPs, but there tend to be profound limitations in all dissociative parts. Because ANP individuals may not realize their painful past, it remains insufficiently real. For hyperaroused EPs this past may constitute the present, in which sense the past is too real. Hypoaroused EPs also tend to be fixed in the third-person past that they phenomenally experience and judge to be the present. However, they do not tend to experience this phenomenal present as very real.	Particular situations are conceived as 'too real' in pathological but nondissociative acute anxiety states, phobias, and psychoses, or as 'not real enough,' as in derealization and major depression.

Table 12.1 offers some examples of normal and pathological alterations in consciousness. It shows that only multiple perspectivalness is specific to dissociative disorders.

Summary and Discussion

'Personality' and 'self' are different concepts. Our personality constitutes a living and ever-evolving embrained, embodied, and environmentally embedded system. This organism-environment system can become chronically divided. Dissociative parts are manifestations of this division. Whereas it can be said that nature comprises perfect integration, human beings fall profoundly short of this excellence. Everyone struggles at times with contrary wills and opposing desires. In individuals with a nondissociative mental disorder, a particular interest has become overly dominant, whereas other desires remain unfulfilled. For example, in phobias, the will of the action system of defense (avoidance of and escape from some perceived danger, such as having panic attacks in shops) rules to the expense of the desires of the will system of exploration (e.g., exploring new fashions). In insomnia, urges associated with the action system of energy management (sleep, rest) remain frustrated, and in major depression desires associated with the actions systems of social engagement, exploration, and play wither. Ego states include their own desires and goals, but these states are still states that their owner recognizes and accepts as his or her own. In other words, individuals encompassing different ego-states still personify these at a metalevel of identity, or, technically speaking, within the framework of one phenomenal metaconception of self (i.e., "I know and accept that I am my different ego-states"). An individual's overarching personification of the different mental and phenomenal states they comprise does not exist in dissociative disorders. These disorders involve a division of the personality into subsystems, each of which crucially involves its own phenomenal conceptions of self, world, and self-of-the-world. The existence of this division sets dissociative disorders apart from mental health and all other mental disorders.

Dissociative parts have evolved most strongly in patients with major DID, but they also exist in several other dissociative disorders, including minor DID, sensorimotor dissociative disorders, complex PTSD, simple PTSD, and dissociative psychosis. However, EPs may be rudimentary. These EPs encompass relatively few actions and implied contents. Some EPs in major DID can also be rudimentary.

Whereas the presence of two or more dissociative parts constitutes the best criterion for the existence of a dissociative disorder, this organization of the personality – the disorder's formal cause – may not always be instantly accessible, and it is certainly not instantly accessible in full when the dissociation of the personality is complex. The assessment of a dissociative disorder in this particular case therefore involves prolonged and careful diagnostic work. Dissociative patients are bound to present symptoms that point to the existence of dissociative parts. These symptoms are the ground for a provisional assessment of a dissociative disorder. However, two or more dissociative parts need to be discovered before a definitive diagnosis can be made.

Dissociative symptoms must be distinguished from other phenomena that also involve alterations in consciousness. These other alterations in consciousness are sensitive, but not specific, to dissociative disorders, hence they are conceptually, clinically, and scientifically best distinguished from phenomena that are expressions of the existence of a dissociation of the personality. Restriction of the field of consciousness as well as 'upward' shifts (i.e., experiencing a feeling, thought, physical action, or situation as exceptionally intense and real) and 'downward' swings (i.e., experiencing a feeling, thought, physical action, or situation as unreal) of the intensity, homogeneity, situatedness, dynamicity, and experienced degree of reality (i.e, 'consciousness') are also ubiquitous in mentally healthy individuals, patients with other mental disorders, and patients with a neurological disorder. These phenomena do not point to the presence or absence of a dissociative disorder. Technically, the involved alterations with respect to the various constraints of consciousness are sensitive, but not specific to, dissociative disorders.

In the context of traumatization, dissociation thus entails a division of personality – i.e., of the dynamic, biopsychosocial system as a whole, which determines an individual's characteristic mental and motor actions – in two or more dynamic, albeit unduly stable subsystems. Each of these subsystems generates its own, however rudimentary, phenomenal conceptions of self, world, and relationship between self and world. Phenomenologically, such a lack of integration of personality manifests itself in dissociative symptoms that can be categorized as negative (functional losses such as amnesia and paralysis) or positive (intrusions such as flashbacks or voices), and cognitive-emotional (symptoms such as amnesia, hearing voices) or sensorimotor (symptoms such as anesthesia or tics). In the next chapter, I complete this definition of dissociation with some more components and further elucidate it.

Many clinical implications can be derived from these insights and formulations. For example, only when mental contents become phenomenal contents can dissociative parts attend to them, think about them, and use them for the conscious control of their actions. This control of attention, cognition, and motor action are exerted by fractions of the system as a whole that generate the involved PCSs and PCIRs. The PCSs and PCIRs of the different dissociative parts are often not mutually exclusive, because there is usually mental and phenomenal overlap among their conceptions of self, world, and self-of-the-world. This often implies that the involved dissociative parts have at least some epistemic access to each other. When this phenomenal access does exist, as one dissociative part individuals know that they are dissociated from another dissociative part. The mental and phenomenal overlap among the dissociative parts increases during successful treatment; the mental and phenomenal differences eventually disappear altogether: They fuse. The fusion of dissociative parts thus implies the generation of new conceptions of self, world, and self-of-the-world. The new PCS and PCIRs partially include formerly dissociated experiences and conceptions (e.g., particular memories), but exclude others (e.g., the conceptions of being a child, of living in 1980 or thereabout, of living with deceased parents, of being caught in an eternally traumatizing life).

The study of neurological disorders provides major insights into the neural functioning of healthy individuals. The biopsychosocial study of consciousness and self-consciousness in dissociative disorders can similarly greatly enhance our understanding of normal consciousness and self-consciousness. If only for this reason it is remarkable that so very little effort has been invested to date in discovering the biopsychosocial features of dissociative disorders. This curious phenomenon demands some explanation (see Chapter 20).

The current theoretical reflections suggest many empirically testable hypotheses. For example, using neuroimaging techniques, the TSDP-derived hypothesis could be tested that at least some of the patient's PCIRs are ANP-dependent and EP-dependent, and that this dependency implies ANP-dependent and EP-dependent patterns of physiological and neural activity. One test would be to instruct separately activated ANPs and fragile EPs to mentally and physically rest. TSDP predicts that these different prototypes of dissociative parts will activate neural patterns involved in self-consciousness, and that fragile EPs will be associated with more activation of brain structures involved in sensorimotor and affective actions. Actors who simulate ANPs and EPs would have different neural activation patterns, more specifically patterns associated with role playing. Healthy controls would have still other patterns of neural activity, because they are neither dissociative nor playing a role. This research has actually been performed (Schlumpf et al., 2013, 2014). Its results are discussed in Chapter 18, along with other TSDP-based biopsychosocial hypotheses (see Chapters 16–19). These include a test of the hypothesis that there are also differences between ANPs and fragile EPs with regard to stimuli that provoke mental but not phenomenal reactions, that is, stimuli perceived by these dissociative parts preconsciously (Schlumpf et al., 2013). Another TSDP-based hypothesis is that the neural activity for ANP will be different when this dissociative part listens to a recording of (1) ANP's self-spoken self-description, (2) an EP's self-spoken self-description, or (3) an acquaintance's self-spoken self-description. Such differences would also exist when the individual listens as an EP to this part's self-description, ANP's self-description, and an acquaintance's self-description. These different reactions of ANP, or if that is the case EP would not exist for controls who are instructed to imitate ANP and EP to the best of their abilities. At the time of writing of these lines, this research is in preparation.

Metzinger's theory (2003) has met with positive and critical reactions from other philosophers (Gallagher, 2005; Ghin, 2005; Himma, 2005; Legrand, 2005; Livet, 2005, Weisberg, 2005; Zahavi, 2005; Metzinger's rejoinders: 2006a-g). As I have pointed out, I am critical of some of his proposals myself. However, some frequent misunderstandings regarding the theory should be prevented or corrected. One misunderstanding is that Metzinger thinks that the self is an illusion. I don't think this is what he has in mind. The illusion, he says, is that the self is a thing or a substance rather than a recurrent presentational and representational process – or as I would say, a conceptual action. Another mistaken belief regarding the theory is that PCSs and PCIRs are senseless because they are simulations. The critique is that distinguishing between reality and appearance is impossible if everything that exists consists of appearances. In this chapter I have described how, according to Metzinger (2003), we take particular simulations for reality and how some simulations work better than others. To reiterate, chronically abused and neglected children may be unable to integrate their exceptionally difficult life into one coherent experience and conception of self and world. It can be adaptive in these circumstances to generate one or more ANPs and one or more EPs. These children may fare better in certain regards when they simulate as ANP(s) that they are not also EP(s). The accuracy of this statement can, among others, be derived from clinical experiences with adult patients with a dissociative disorder who were severely abused as children. Attempts to expose them as ANP to the conceptions of self (PCS) and world (the characteristic set of PCIRs) of one or more EPs while ANP's integrative capacity is still low commonly result in serious decompensations (suicide attempts, self-mutilation, panic reactions, etc.). The rationale of a phase-oriented treatment of trauma and dissociation is to gradually increase patients' integrative capacity (Van der Hart et al., 2006), so that they can overcome their dissociation of the personality in the steps they can manage. This development generates simulations of self, world, and self-of-the-world which are more viable and livable than the simulations of the previously dissociative parts of the personality, provided sufficient integrative capacity and an *Umwelt* that has changed for the better.

Metzinger's theory (2003) is a representational theory, and there is serious philosophical critique regarding representational theories (e.g., Bursen, 1978). Further analysis is needed to examine whether the critique is resolved when the traditional two-way relationship between representandum and representatum is substituted for a three-way relationship with the representing system as the third player. In the current chapter I have proposed to replace the terms and concepts of 'representa-

Table 12.2. Commonalities and differences between Metzinger's self-theory of subjectivity and the theory of structural dissociation of the personality.

	Metzinger	TSDP
Our self is not a *thing*, not an independent entity, or a substance that could live by itself, not an unchanging center or invariant set of intrinsic properties, and not a unique and indivisible unity:	+	+
Self can become divided, in which case, an organism can involve more than one 'self':	An individual can encompass more than one phenomenal self-model (PSM).	An individual can encompass more than one phenomenal conception of self (PCS).
Being someone depends on ongoing:	Physiological processes.	Actions of an individual as an an organism-environment system that comprises the brain, the body, and the environment as three intrinsically related components. Matter and mind are two attributes of a singular substance. They are not each other's causes.
Consciousness and self-consciousness:	Can be fully naturalized, that is, reduced to physiological processes.	Mind and matter constitute two attributes of one substance called 'nature.' It is worthwhile and possible to study these different attributes in relation to each other. Mind and matter cannot be directly related to each other, though indirect linkage is feasible. This study starts and ends with lived experience that can therefore not be reduced to matter. Consciousness is primary, any study of consciousness and self-consciousness depends on conscious and self-conscious subjects with a desire, a will to perform this work. Its results can only be understood by conscious and self-conscious subjects, and only make sense to them.
A self is:	A model or representation.	A conception of a conscious organism-environment system.
The world:	Objectively exists and can be accessed in the form of a set of phenomenal models of the intentionality relationship (PMIRs).	Is a conception (or rather, a collection of conceptions) of an experiencing and knowing organism. There is an environment, there are objects, but objects are conditioned by the subject, just as the subject is conditioned by objects.
Subject and object:	Self is a model, and there is an objectively existing world.	Are co-occurrent, co-constitutive, and co-dependent.
Phenomenal intentionality relationship (PMIR):	Subject can access (i.e., know) 'objective reality' in the form of PMIRs.	Subjects, objects, and intentionality relations of subject and object are all phenomenal conceptions (PCSs and PCIRs).S Subject and object are relative to each other.

	Metzinger	TSDP
Global availability:	+	+
Minimal consciousness is grounded in global availability:	+	+
in the phenomenal now:	+	+
and in transparency:	+	+
in situatedness:	+	+
in convolved holism:	+	+
in dynamicity:	+	+
in perspectivalness:	+	+
Offline/Online:	+	'Offline' and 'online' are misleading metaphors because any assessment of 'reality' involves a conception. It may be alternatively said that some phenomenal conceptions correspond more with third-person 'facts' than others do.
Intensity:	+	+
Homogeneity:	+	+
Adaptation:	+	Human beings adapt and create. They find and change their *Umwelt*. Also, adaptation means adjustment to a conceived world, and that conception includes a degree of creativity.
Degrees of reality:	Assumption of the existence of a real world which can be assessed in the form of PMIRs.	Any reality is a conception, but some conceptions are more adaptive and more creative than others. For example, believing one is haunted by ghosts is generally less adaptive than believing that ghosts do not exist.

tion'/'model' by 'idea' or 'conception,' those of 'information' by 'meaning,' and that of 'process' by 'goal-directed action.' These substitutions are motivated by the attempt to avoid suggesting that (1) an objective reality exists that is 'represented' or 'modeled,' that (2) 'information' exists that is given (i.e., informative and meaningful in and of itself), and that (3) 'processes' exist that run in a mechanical fashion and that (iv) can be fully studied in terms of material and efficient causality. Table 12.2 provides an overview of the commonalities and differences between TSDP and Metzinger's self-model theory of subjectivity.

In closing the chapter, let me reiterate some conclusions of Volume I. Metzinger (2003) claims that the PCS supervenes on functional, neurological properties, and that it can therefore can be empirically found. But how can we assess that a particular pattern of neural activity involves an individual's actual PCS and PCIR? This assessment requires an examination of the particular relationship (and type of relationship) of this neural activity and these individuals' first-person, quasi-second-person, second-person, and third-person perspectives. The trouble is that neuroscientists cannot know what a particular pattern of brain activity is about if they are aware of only this neurophysiological activity, that is, if they do not also know the subjective experiences of being someone with a point of view who relates to himself or herself, other individuals, and objects. They must know all these things about the subjects (i.e., the individuals) and the objects (the patterns of neural activity) they study. Moreover, if neuroscientists were 'objective information processors,' if they were 'objective research machines,' they would not have even the slightest idea what consciousness and self-consciousness are – and they would have no clue about what is like to be an experiencing and knowing individual. Without neuroscientists' consciousness, self-consciousness, and will to explore, their discipline would and indeed could not exist. 'Objective' neuroscience or any other science and clinical practice hang on the thread of our principled subjectivity and the life world this subjectivity entails (Husserl, 1970; Varela, 1996). Like all other sciences and science-based practices, they emerge from lived experience and only carry meanings of this shared lived experience. To our individual and joint lived experience, they must – and will – return.

Chapter 13

Dissociation in Trauma: A New Definition and Comparison with Previous Formulations[1]

It is better . . . to speak of dissociation of the personality.
William McDougall (1926, p. 234)

Despite the controversy regarding the psychobiological construct of dissociation, efforts to formulate a more precise definition of dissociation are rare. As indicated above, some definitions of dissociation are so broad that a host of common psychobiological phenomena would qualify as dissociative. Overly narrow conceptualizations of dissociation, on the other hand, exclude certain phenomena that originally, and perhaps for good reasons, were regarded as dissociative. A common lack of conceptual distinctions between dissociation as process, organization, deficit, psychological defense, and symptomatic only adds to the current confusion. This chapter proposes and elucidates a definition of dissociation within the context of traumatization, in short, *dissociation in trauma*, whether acute or chronic. Second, it compares this formulation with several other definitions of the construct and highlights how the new definition overcomes the flaws of the previous ones.

The Problem

As discussed in Chapter 2, in the 19th century dissociation was the essential feature of a class of mental disorders called hysteria. The construct was foremost developed by Pierre Janet (1889, 1907, 1911), who defined dissociation as a lack of integration among two or more different "systems of ideas and functions that constitute personality" (Janet, 1907,

1 This chapter represents a partially revised version of Nijenhuis, E. R. S., & Van der Hart, O. (2011). Dissociation in trauma: A new definition and comparison with previous formulations. *Journal of Trauma and Dissociation, 12*, 416–445.

p. 332). Janet proposed that this deficit was caused by a lowering or limitation of integrative capacity, leading to an inability to integrate experiences, to develop an awareness of reality as is, to accept it, and then to reflectively and creatively adapt to it. He suggested that the lack of integrative capacity can be related to a genetic component, to severe illness and fatigue, and particularly to experiencing adverse, potentially traumatizing events. Janet also noted that dissociation of the personality manifests itself in dissociative symptoms, including those at a sensorimotor level (e.g., bodily anesthesia) (see Nijenhuis, 2004; Van der Hart & Dorahy, 2009; Van der Hart & Friedman, 1989). Dissociation (of the personality) and the symptoms of hysteria (i.e., of this organization of personality) were thus two clearly different, albeit closely related, constructs, pertaining to different logical levels.

Since the 1980s, however, many often contradictory conceptualizations of dissociation have been proposed. These conceptual revisions generally were simultaneously overinclusive and underinclusive compared to the original idea. The notion of dissociation of the personality often was lost, somatoform manifestations of dissociation were commonly seen as conversion or somatization symptoms, and positive symptoms of dissociation such as intrusions of traumatic memories were generally excluded from the domain of dissociative symptoms and recategorized as posttraumatic stress symptoms. Moreover, in contemporary psychology and psychiatry, the term 'dissociation' pertains at least to (1) symptoms, (2) a presumed cause of symptoms, including a presumed function such as psychological defense (cf., Cardeña, 1994), and (3) normal and pathological alterations in consciousness, including hypnosis. It often remained unclear which of these possible uses was intended, and in most empirical and clinical studies the term in fact went undefined (see Van der Hart et al., 2004, for a critique). A review of 53 empirical studies on the relationship between peritraumatic dissociation+ and posttraumatic stress did not bring forward even a single definition of dissociation (Van der Hart et al., 2008).

My colleagues and I suggested a return to the original 19th-century understanding that dissociation involves a lack of integration of the personality, manifesting in the existence of two or more insufficiently integrated, that is, dissociative, subsystems or parts of the personality. We referred to this phenomenon as a *structural dissociation of the personality* (e.g., Nijenhuis et al., 2002; Van der Hart et al., 2004, 2006). We also contended that the domain of dissociative symptoms consists of specific manifestations of these dissociative parts, and that other alterations in consciousness such as retraction and lowering of consciousness do not per se belong to this realm (Steele, Dorahy, Van der Hart, & Nijenhuis, 2009; Van der Hart et al., 2004, 2006). Furthermore, we asserted that all dissociative subsystems of the personality involve at least a rudimentary sense of self (Van der Hart et al., 2006). In this book, dissociation pertains to a dissociation of the personality and dissociative symptoms to the manifestations of this organization. It is important to distinguish this understanding of dissociation from the presently rather common use of the term, which includes a mixture of this dissociation of the personality and its symptoms and/or alterations in quality and quantity of phenomenal mental contents. I continue to write dissociation+ to capture this practice.

The Proposed Definition

The definition, which is not self-evident, reads as follows:

> Dissociation in trauma entails a division of an individual's personality, that is, of the dynamic, biopsychosocial system as a whole, which determines his or her characteristic mental and behavioral actions. This division of personality constitutes a core feature of trauma. It evolves when the individual lacks the capacity to integrate adverse experiences in part or in full, can support adaptation in this context, but commonly also implies adaptive limitations. The division involves two or more insufficiently integrated, dynamic but excessively stable subsystems. These subsystems exert functions and can encompass any number of different mental and behavioral actions and implied states. These subsystems and states can be latent, and activated in a sequence or in parallel. Each dissociative subsystem, that is, dissociative part of the personality, includes at least its own, at a minimum rudimentary, first-person perspective. Dissociative subsystems also commonly have their own at least rudimentary quasi-second-person, second-person, and third-person perspectives. As each dissociative part, the individual can interact with other dissociative parts and other individuals, at least in principle. Dissociative parts maintain particular biopsychosocial boundaries that keep them divided, but in principle they can also dissolve them. The experiential and epistemic access of one dissociative part to the experiential and epistemic contents of another dissociative part can be more or less elaborate and reciprocal. Phenomenologically, this division of the personality manifests itself in dissociative symptoms that can be categorized as negative (functional losses such as amnesia and paralysis) or positive (intrusions such as flashbacks or voices), and cognitive-emotional (symptoms such as amnesia, hearing voices) or sensorimotor (symptoms such as anesthesia or tics).

Elucidation

Each term or phrase of this definition is in need of elucidation.

Dissociation in Trauma

As discussed and defined in Volume I, a trauma is a biopsychosocial injury that evolves in relation to a variety of coupled psychological, biological, social, and other environmental factors. These biopsychosocial factors include limitations to the exposed individual's integrative capacity, revealed, for example, in dissociative reactions, affect dysregulation, and persistent avoidance of traumatic memories. Environmental factors include characteristics of present and prior adverse, potentially traumatizing events, caretaker dysfunction and unavailability, and lack of social support to integrate adverse experiences (e.g., Brewin et al., 2000; Ozer et al., 2003). Longitudinal and prospective studies found a relationship between exposure to adverse events, including poor early childhood care and sensorimotor and cognitive-emotional dissociative symptoms, and alterations in quality and quantity of phenomenal mental contents (Diseth, 2006; Dutra et al., 2009; Ogawa et al., 1997; Trickett et al., 2011). The term 'dissociation in trauma' thus denotes the division of an individual's personality that can evolve during or following exposure to adverse, potentially traumatizing events in combination with several other factors.

I reiterate that studies of the relationship between adverse event exposure and dissociation+ are troubled by including symptoms that, in our view, are not inherently dissociative in nature (e.g., lowering the quality of phenomenal mental contents) and by excluding symptoms that are in fact dissociative (e.g., sensorimotor dissociative symptoms) and two major symptom clusters of PTSD, that is, numbing and intrusion (e.g., re-experiencing traumatizing events) (Nijenhuis, 2014; Van der Hart et al., 2006).

Division

Dissociation involves a division of personality rather than a separation, because dissociative parts of the personality are not fully separated from each other. They are not like pieces of a broken vase. Rather, each dissociative part of the personality involves a particular organized set of manifest and latent mental and behavioral actions, not some metaphorical pieces of a thing called mind. These sets are functional. For example, one dissociative part may care for a daughter or run a shop and another part may defend the integrity of the body when there is real or perceived threat. However, in some cases, the actions of one part involve unsuccessful *attempts* to exert one or more functions. The functions or particular desires/urges of a dissociative part constitute their final cause, just as the collection of the individual's different and often contrary desires constitutes the final cause of the individual as a whole organism-environment system.

The Corporation Metaphor

Different dissociative parts can engage in the same actions (e.g., both can run), and two or more different parts can be activated in parallel. A corporation encompassing several departments and temporary projects might serve as an apt metaphor for dissociation. Each division or department (dissociative part) of the corporation (the traumatized individual) exerts one or more functions, has a main goal to pursue, and includes several employees (actions). Particular employees, but not all employees, can be associated with more than one department (dissociative parts share actions and have unique actions), and the different departments and their employees can participate in one or more temporary projects that may run across different departments (two or more different dissociative parts may temporarily cooperate in particular circumstances). The corporation we have in mind is a special once, as it lacks a central management, but is organized by the interactions among the various departments and the employees. There is thus no hierarchically highest-level dissociative part that guides all lower-level parts. This organization that can be described and understood in terms of nonlinear dynamic systems theory as applied to human functioning. The corporation-metaphor reflects that, no matter how dissociated and different parts of the personality may be, they are still linked and together constitute a whole system (cf. Braude, 1995; Van der Hart et al., 2006).

Personality

The concept of 'personality' was defined in Chapter 12. This definition highlights that personality includes perception and emotion, that perception, emotion, and thought involve mental actions, including decision making, and that behavior involves combined mental and motor action. Personality constitutes a whole system that has an ongoing tendency toward integration, i.e., binding and differentiation of different components of experiences (e.g., perceptions, emotions, thoughts) as well as different experiences across time (Edelman & Tononi, 2000; Van der Hart et al., 2006). In dissociation in trauma, personality as a system includes two or more insufficiently integrated subsystems. This is the formal cause of the disorder.

Consciousness Cannot Be Divided

The term 'dissociation of consciousness,' a common expression in the literature, must be rejected because normal cognition does not involve a compound of elements of consciousness capable of independent existence (cf. McDougall, 1926).

In fact, 'consciousness' is a problematic notion because the term can have many different meanings (Natsoulas, 1983). There is not a single, paradigmatic theory of consciousness to date, and no systematic and comprehensive catalogue of phenomena belongs to the domain of consciousness and requires explanation (Metzinger, 2003). Consciousness "may turn out to be a *cluster concept*, that is, a theoretical entity only possessing overlapping characteristics" (Metzinger, 2003, p. 107). However, it is clear that some mental and behavioral actions encompass subjective experience. Subjectively experienced, that is, phenomenal, mental contents exist in many different forms, intensities, and degrees of internal complexity (Metzinger, 2003; see Chapter 12).

Some dissociative parts may be rudimentary by encompassing only few mental and motor actions involving a very limited range of phenomenal experiences. However, other parts engage in many mental and motor actions that are associated with phenomenal experiences. Therefore, these parts have a far richer subjective life, that is, are more elaborated.

Biopsychosocial

This term conveys that personality is an organization defined by a constellation of interacting biological, psychological, and social factors (for a review in the context of dissociation, see Nijenhuis & Den Boer, 2009). It also communicates the philosophical position that body and mind do not involve different substances or things, but that mind is based on an integrative structural and functional organization of the brain and body (Edelman, 1992; Janet, 1889) of an environmentally embedded individual. As explained in Volume I, brain, body, mind, and environment exist only in relation to each other, that is, they are ontologically intrinsically related (Northoff, 2003). Mind is a broader concept than consciousness, because not all mental actions imply mental contents that are also phenomenal contents: Many mental contents are not subjectively experienced. Many actions of the mind actions are autoepistemically closed[2].

Division as a Core Feature of Trauma

The division of personality is a key element in trauma because, once survivors have overcome this division, they have largely overcome their traumatization (see below and Van der Hart et al., 2006).

Insufficiently Integrated

The division of the personality in trauma relates to limitations of an individual's integrative capacity, which may in part be related to genetic factors (Xie et al., 2009). Given these limitations, and a lack of social support to compensate for them, such a division may enhance an individual's chance to survive. Consistent with this idea, some experimental studies found directed forgetting effects regarding explicit memory between different dissociative parts (Elzinga, Phaf, Ardon, & Van Dyck, 2003). This lack of integration among dissociative parts, however, usually comes at a price: Like one or more other dissociative parts, most of these individuals are bound to re-experience the traumatizing events (e.g.,

2 Autoepistemic closure is not specific to particular mental actions. To quote Harman (2011): "For if it is true that humans have no access to the subpersonal components at work in their brain cells, it is equally true that neurons and peptides have no causal access to the twirling of quarks and electrons in their own tiniest, innermost physical recesses. Metzinger's theory of 'autoepistemic closure' could have been a bold theory about how *every* level of entity is cut off from the structure of its own composition. Instead, he simply gives us yet another philosophy containing the same two basic characters as ever: physical stuff in direct contact with all of its neighboring physical stuff, and a phenomenal sentient sphere cut off from everything. Worse yet, he does not even leave these two in an equal relationship, but dissolves the second into the first, failing to consider that to be generated by something does not always mean to be ontologically dependent upon it."

in recurrent nightmares and flashbacks) at some point in their life – or they will develop other symptoms of mental disorder.

Dissociation Involves a Particular Organization of the Personality.

Dissociation of the personality involves the capacity to organize or reorganize the personality into two or more dissociative parts of the personality. The maintenance of dissociation relates to the ability to keep two or more parts of the personality and the associated actions and phenomenal mental contents relatively divided from each other. In this context, dissociative parts can assume more and more diverse actions and phenomenal mental contents, a trend known as the *elaboration of dissociative parts* (Van der Hart et al., 2006).

Dynamic but Excessively Stable

Personality and dissociative parts of the personality constitute a dynamic system and dynamic subsystems, respectively. Thus, most dissociative parts engage in different mental and behavioral actions across time and contexts. The interactions among different dissociative parts are not totally fixed, and the biopsychosocial features of dissociative parts may shift with their order of appearance (Putnam, 1988).

However, dissociative parts are also excessively stable in at least some crucial regards, involving a lack of systemic complexity (Edelman & Tononi, 2000). Adaptation requires systemic complexity, that is, the ability of a (sub)system to develop new actions that fit changed inner and outer conditions as well as the ability to continue previously developed, effective actions when conditions remain unchanged. Living systems that are too stable do not adjust their actions to altered circumstances. As overly stable (sub)systems, dissociative parts often engage in fixed actions that may have worked previously but that do not fit transformed conditions (Nijenhuis et al., 2002; Van der Hart et al., 2006).

These Subsystems Exert Functions

We and others have suggested that dissociation in trauma involves different prototypes of dissociative parts (e.g., Liotti, 1999; Nijenhuis et al., 2002; Nijenhuis & Den Boer, 2009; Van der Hart et al., 2006) that are mediated by one or more evolutionarily derived action (sub)systems or emotional operating systems (Panksepp, 1998). In previous chapters, I related 'function' to 'will' and similar terms such as 'desire' and 'urge.'

Action Systems as Will Systems

Many human mental and behavioral actions constitute manifestations of innate, but experience-dependent and in many cases maturation-dependent action systems (Nijenhuis & Den Boer, 2009; Panksepp, 1998). Being evolution-based, and considered under the attribute of matter, these systems are founded in the subcortical neural systems that human beings share with many other creatures, and that have become linked with higher cortical functions (Panksepp, 1998). Some of these higher functions are specific to humans. For example, from approximately 9 to 12 months, infants start to understand that others make choices in their perception and other actions, and that these choices are guided by desired outcomes, that is, goals, a faculty unavailable to primates (Tomasello, 1999). This also applies to the human ability to extend action tendencies in time and space (Panksepp, 1998). The major action systems are defense, attachment of offspring to parents, parental attachment to and care for offspring, procreation, sociability (also described as intersubjectivity), energy management, exploration, and play. Action systems involve particular *values* that define for an individual what is safe and attractive, or dangerous and adverse. The values of will systems guide what an individual is likely to perceive, feel, think, and do.

Two Major Types of Dissociative Parts

ANPs are predominantly mediated by action systems for functioning in daily life. For instance, an ANP strongly influenced by the action system of energy management will look for food and eat it (one subsystem) or prepare for sleep (another subsystem). Fragile EPs are primarily mediated by the defense will system regarding threats to the integrity of the body and/or the action system for attachment cry, that is, crying for attachment upon loss of an essential caregiver. The core values of the physical defense action system are avoiding or escaping from aversive stimuli, and the core value of the action system for attachment cry is attracting protection. In chronic traumatization by parents or other close relatives or caretakers, there is often also at least one controlling EP. Controlling EPs are primarily mediated by the will to have an influence on oneself, other individuals, and one's environment more generally. This will could well relate to an emotional will system for social dominance (Toronchuk & Ellis, 2012). In the framework of the will having at least some power, they are prone to imitate, to enact perpetrators.

Action systems affect the meaning that a particular stimulus may have. Thus, a patient's evaluation of her abusive parent and her actions regarding this parent depend on the will system that is dominant at a given moment. For example, as an ANP dominated by the action system of attachment, she thinks well of the involved parent and tends to approach him or her – the parent is "good"; but as an EP dominated by the action system of mammalian defense, she is afraid, and hides or runs – the parent is "bad." As a controlling EP, she is bound to express that the fragile EP(s), the ANP(s), and often the therapist as well are "weak" and "despicable."

Overlapping Abilities and Traits in Dissociative Parts

As mentioned in the corporation metaphor, different parts can, to some degree, involve the same abilities and traits (Braude 1995; Dorahy & Huntjens, 2007) and thus can within limits engage in the same kind of mental and behavioral actions. For example, several different dissociative parts may both be able to walk, talk, or be afraid of loud voices.

These Subsystems Encompass Any Number of Different Mental and Behavioral Actions and Implied States

Although dissociative subsystems are often described as 'dissociative states' (see below), almost all dissociative subsystems encompass a *constellation* of mental and behavioral states rather than a singular state. Some dissociative parts encompass far more states than others.

These Subsystems and States Can Be Latent or Activated in Sequence or in Parallel

Dissociative subsystems and particular states of these subsystems can be latent or activated. At times only one dissociative part is activated, which is sooner or later followed up by a different subsystem. We called this phenomenon *sequential dissociation* (Van der Hart et al., 2006), commonly also known as 'switching.' In parallel dissociation (Van der Hart et al., 2006), two or more dissociative subsystems are simultaneously activated, which implies the co-occurrence of at least two different mental or behavioral states. The phenomenon has also been described as *co-presence.*

Each Subsystem Includes at Least its Own, Rudimentary First-Person Perspective

Anyone's personality includes some subsystems that are not fully integrated. For example, all people sometimes experience conflicts between thinking and feeling, or between different roles in life, and everyone knows ambivalences. Furthermore, not all neurological subsystems are fully in tune, and some operate more or less independently from each other. This lack of psychological and biological integration applies in particular to individuals with mental disorders.

Looking for constraints for the construct of dissociation, I (Nijenhuis, 2012; see Chapter 12) proposed to delimit the category to dissociative subsystems that entail their own first-person perspective. This perspective, detailed in Chapter 12, pertains to the phenomenal feeling of being someone with a point of view, that is, of being an acting and experiencing self with a subjectively experienced outward perspective on one's perceived world, and an inward perspective regarding oneself (Metzinger, 2003).

As an example, if we apply this constraint, then an ego-dystonic phobia counts as a dissociative disorder when there is at least one ANP and EP. In this case, ANP knows that the phobic fear and avoidance fear are unfounded, EP perceives the phobic stimuli as most threatening, and ANP's experience and behavior are influenced by EP, but ANP is not or insufficiently under the influence of ANP. When the patient does not include two or more dissociative subsystems endowed with a first-person perspective, but only a singular first-person perspective, the disorder would not qualify as a dissociative disorder but as a (non-dissociative) anxiety disorder (e.g., agoraphobia).

Patients with DID encompass more or less evolved ANPs and EPs with their own first-person perspective. Patients with minor DID and patients with complex PTSD also have such parts, usually one strongly evolved ANP as well as more than one, albeit less evolved EPs, but all with their own first-person perspective. The personality of patients with simple PTSD tends to include one strongly evolved ANP and one quite limited EP. No matter how rudimentary this latter subsystem may be, it tends to have its own first-person perspective and thereby qualifies as a dissociative part of the PTSD patient's personality.

Dissociative parts of the personality are conscious subsystems, because they meet at least the minimal constraints for consciousness which apply to any conscious system, that is, situatedness, phenomenal now, and transparency (Metzinger, 2003; Chapter 12). These constraints help us to decide whether a certain mental state is also a consciously experienced one, that is, a *phenomenal* state. Dissociative parts usually include more than one phenomenal state.

Dissociative Parts that Meet the Three Minimal Constraints

Dissociative parts that meet only the three minimal constraints (situatedness, phenomenal now, and transparency) experience one unified world as given and as frozen in an eternal now. Very few dissociative parts of the personality meet only these three minimal constraints for consciousness at times. Then they are consciously aware of a world (i.e., of some objects and/or subjects) that they experience as undoubtedly existing and given, but they lack a sense or idea of *who* they are or even *that* they are someone, and they lack a firm sense of past and future. At these times, these dissociative parts are thus extremely depersonalized and disoriented in real time. They do not experience themselves as agents of actions or owners of experiences, and they do not have a sense of personal continuity or identity (i.e., the feeling that they are the same as the one they were before). For example, one dissociative part said she was "no one."

We include these dissociative subsystems in the category of dissociative parts because they generate at least some phenomenal sense and conception of self once their mental level of functioning increases. This may, for example, happen when they become less fearful. For example, "no one" soon developed a limited PCS with a set of PCIRs when she became more engaged in therapy.

The First-Person Perspective

Most dissociative parts in fact meet more than the three minimal constraints for consciousness, because they continuously generate a first-person perspective, however rudimentary this perspective may be, when they are dreaming or awake (Nijenhuis, 2012; see Chapter 12). A first-person perspective arises when individuals (or dissociative parts of an individual) who meet the three minimal constraints for consciousness also meet several other constraints for consciousness (Metzinger, 2003). These additional constraints are (1) integrating components of objects, whole objects, subjects, or scenes into larger wholes, so that each separate phenomenal experience fits a wider experiential frame; (2) experiencing flow and directedness of time (i.e., experiencing that time flows from the past to the future) as well as experiencing duration and change; and (3) having a point of view, a perspective. Regarding the second constraint, it must be noted that some EPs encompass only a very limited range of experiences, and that their experience of duration and change is therefore also quite restricted. But even these dissociative parts are consciously aware that the initial moments of an experience are different from later moments of that same experience.

We develop a point of view – the fourth constraint for consciousness – when we transparently generate within ourselves the subjective experience of *being someone* who is related to our phenomenal conception of reality, that is, to objects, other subjects, or to the individual we are (Metzinger, 2003). We would cease to experience that we are or have a self if we had introspective epistemic access to the fact that we construct our self in the framework of intrinsic relationships of the brain, the body, and the environment. This conscious introspection would lead to an infinite regress that would disrupt any adaptive sense and idea of self. The point is that full epistemic access to the fact that our self is a conception would involve another self that would have that access, but then that other self would also experience and know that our phenomenal self is a conception, and so on. Hence, it is highly adaptive that we (i.e., the whole organism-environment system that we are) generate our 'I,' 'myself,' 'me' in a transparent way. As detailed in Chapter 12, self is then a phenomenal conception that a part of the whole system that we generate for us as the whole system (Metzinger, 2003). Our phenomenal self-conception thus depends on our ongoing mental action.

To have a first-person perspective, we must integrate our PCS with our PCIRs in a specific way. This pertains to the fact that consciousness is intentional. That is, it is 'about' something beyond itself (Thompson, 2007). Every phenomenal perception, feeling, belief, desire, etc., has an object that it is about: the perceived, the felt, the believed, the wanted. We are always conscious *of* something. A first-person perspective thus involves a phenomenal self that is intentionally related to something else, for example, "I (PCS) perceive a book (an intentional object)," "I believe in God," "I am a woman," or "I am afraid."

Self-Consciousness, Other-Consciousness, and Object-Consciousness

Apart from the exceptions mentioned above, dissociative parts, like integrated individuals, also believe they have or are a self, and they also have a first-person perspective. This was a major theme of the previous chapter. For example, they say or have the feeling that they exist, they perceive an external world and embed their experiences in this world, they distinguish themselves from that perceived world, and they intentionally relate their phenomenal self to other phenomenal mental contents. Thus, they might say, "I am a child."

Practically all dissociative parts also have a quasi-second-person perspective. For example, referring to one hand of their body they experience and appreciate that "this hand is mine," and referring to some action that involved this hand they experience and know that "It was me who did it." However, they may also conspicuously lack this perspective. This happens when they do not synthesize, and hence phenomenally experience, a part of the body or even the whole body" ("I don't feel it") or do not personify it ("This is not my hand"). In this context, dissociative parts can take the body for a thing and thus may engage in a third-person perspective regarding their own body. Similar confusions can happen with respect to thoughts, memories, and other mental contents. For example, as ANP, a patient may phenomenally experience and judge that sometimes thoughts are "made" inside her, and that these thoughts are not hers. Dissociative parts may also judge that not they, but someone else (e.g., a different dissociative part) engaged in a particular action. Dissociative parts may thus confuse the quasi-second- and second-person perspective. When they do not know who engaged in the action, or even that there is a dissociative part who engages in the action, they tend to physically judge the thought, image, or movement, that is, to conceive of them in a third-person perspective.

Many dissociative parts, like integrated individuals, furthermore have a second-person perspective regarding other individuals (e.g., "I fear that man") as well as regarding other dissociative parts (e.g., "I hate the weak one; "I feel sorry for that little boy who had such hard times"). Thus, in dissociative disorders what should be a quasi-second-person perspective (e.g., "I find it hard to accept I was so vulnerable as a child") becomes phenomenally a second-person perspective ("I am not that weak child, I am tough"). The phenomenal self-conception of dissociative parts and the first-person perspective and included second-person perspective of these parts are neither given nor fixed, and require ongoing mental action under the transparency constraint.

PCSs and PCIRs can strongly differ in terms of complexity and richness in different individuals (Metzinger, 2003). These dimensions also apply to dissociative parts. The contents of some dissociative part's various person perspectives and implied presentata and conceptions are rather simple and limited. In other parts, these are more complex and full, and still other dissociative parts have a most differentiated and rich or most elaborate set of mental and behavioral contents. Furthermore, the degree diverges to which the first-person, quasi-second-person, second-person, and third-person perspectives of the different dissociative parts are dissimilar.

Understanding that the different person perspectives involve an individual's conceptions helps to appreciate that divisions of personality entail the appearance of two or more linked phenomenal selves and worlds. This understanding also explains why full (re)integration of conscious and self-conscious dissociative parts implies the rapid (re)appearance of a singular set of person perspectives, the swift disappearance of the different person perspectives that were associated with the now fully integrated dissociative parts of the personality as well as the dissolution of the second-person and third-person person perspectives that these previously existing parts had regarding other dissociative parts.

More and Less Rudimentary Person Perspectives

The generation of more than one first-person, quasi-second-person, second-person, and third-person perspective is not an all-or-nothing phenomenon. The phenomenal conceptions of self, world, and intentional relationships of the phenomenal self to phenomenal conceptions of objects and subjects can entail many different levels and degrees of mental action and related levels and degrees of mental content. The precise description of these different qualities (e.g., the level of the mental actions and contents involved in the generation of a first-person perspective) and quantities (the number of different, though related mental actions and contents involved in this generation) is an important and complicated task. The constraints on consciousness presented in the previous chapter can be useful in this regard. Their refinement is helpful for distinguishing among more and less rudimentary person perspectives.

Biopsychosocial Features

The biopsychosocial features of these dissociative parts can be scientifically studied by successively activating them in an experimental context. Chapters 16–18 details and discusses several neuroimaging studies in which biopsychosocial hypotheses derived from TSDP were put to the test.

Dissociative Parts Maintain Biopsychosocial Boundaries That Keep Them Divided, but That They Can in Principle Dissolve

Different parts maintain boundaries that keep them divided (Braude, 1995; Putnam, 1997). These boundaries depend on the mental actions of these parts, and these actions are open to change, at least in principle, so that the boundaries can become more permeable or even disappear altogether. According to TSDP, the boundaries among dissociative parts relate to phobias of traumatic memories, to phobias that these parts have regarding each other as well as to dissociative part-dependent phobias such as affect phobia in an ANP (Van der Hart et al., 2006).

Permeable Boundaries

Dissociative parts can access or intrude on each others' domains to some degree. This permeability can be two-sided, for example, two different parts may know each another, or one-sided, for example, one part (A) may know that another part (B) exists, but B may not be aware of A's existence. Or A may experience what B feels or does, whereas the reverse does not apply.

Dissociative Symptoms

For conceptual clarity, it is important to distinguish between dissociation as a particular organization of personality and the symptoms that stem from this organization, that is, dissociative symptoms.

Phenomenological Distinction

The distinction between negative and positive symptoms, discussed below, is based on appearance, not on a principle. There is no vital difference between dissociative symptoms that manifest 'in the body' and those that manifest 'in-the-mind.' The difference is only phenomenological, hence the expressions 'sensorimotor' and 'cognitive-emotional dissociative symptoms.'

Negative Dissociative Symptoms

Negative dissociative symptoms refer to apparent losses, for example, of memory, motor control, skills, and somatosensory awareness. Negative cognitive-emotional dissociative symptoms include, among others, dissociative amnesia and dissociative loss of affect and will. Negative sensorimotor dissociative symptoms involve, among others, dissociative analgesia, anesthesia, and loss of motor control, such as dissociative aphonia. Within this negativity, some phenomena seem to be lacking that should be present. But the loss is not absolute: For a negative symptom to be dissociative, whatever experience of function is missing for one dissociative part should be available to another dissociative part (Janet, 1911; Nijenhuis, 2004; Van der Hart et al., 2006).

Positive Dissociative Symptoms

Positive dissociative symptoms involve ideas, reactions, behaviors, and functions of one dissociative part that intermittently intrudes on one or more other dissociative parts. The symptoms, among others, include dissociative flashbacks and partial or full re-experiencing of traumatizing events as well as intruding voices, thoughts, movements, and emotional or physical feelings, including pain, that stem from other dissociative parts. Such intrusions are very common in dissociative disorders and tend to be phenomenally very disturbing (Dell, 2006).

In sum, in order to resolve current conceptual confusion, the term dissociation in the context of traumatization is best limited to a division of the personality into at least two dissociative parts that generate (or can generate) at the very least a rudimentary first-person perspective. As a consequence, the category of dissociative symptoms is best limited to the manifestations of these dissociative parts.

Limitations of Other Definitions of Dissociation in Trauma

The literature contains a host of other definitions of the concept of 'dissociation in trauma.' (Several of these definitions also pertain to dissociation in other contexts such as hypnosis and mediumship. This will be briefly addressed in the discussion.) An examination of a sample of other definitions of dissociation in trauma shows that each of them is wanting in some regard. We can start with a definition that, in its simplicity, involves a common misunderstanding in the field (Cardeña, 1994; DePrince & Freyd, 2007; Steele et al., 2009; Van der Hart et al., 2006).

Dissociation as Narrowed Consciousness

Some authors conceptualize dissociation as "narrowed consciousness" (e.g., Hovens, 2007, p. 98). However, dissociative parts and many dissociative symptoms such as hearing voices and other intrusions cannot be satisfactorily described or explained in terms of narrowed consciousness. Furthermore, these authors failed to define or operationalize the construct of consciousness, so that it remains unclear *what* exactly would be "narrowed." As detailed in Chapter 12, there are at least 12 different constraints on consciousness, each of which can involve its own kind of psychopathology. Any claim that dissociation involves abnormal consciousness must therefore specify the term 'consciousness' and must detail what particular constraint or constraints on consciousness are intended.

Also, the definition does not state how "narrowed consciousness" differs from attention. Attention by definition involves sustained phenomenal perception of a *selection* of stimuli or events (i.e., PCIRs) that a particular individual in principle could phenomenally perceive. Furthermore, excessive and maladaptive selective perception is a major feature of many mental disorders (see Table 12.1). It would be curious to consider such a ubiquitous phenomenon as the essential feature of one particular group of mental disorders, that is, dissociative disorders, while the existence of dissociative parts and its symptomatic consequences are overlooked or ignored.

Dissociation as Alterations in the Quantity and Quality of Consciousness

Patients with dissociative disorders generally experience a wide range of alterations in consciousness, that is, different degrees and forms of being awake (cf. Natsoulas, 1983). For example, they may be disoriented in time or not centered in their body. They may misperceive the intensity of stimuli, engage in maladaptive images or trance-states (i.e., altered states of consciousness rendering a subject hypersuggestible (Udolf, 1981)), and confuse what is intersubjectively real, less real, or not real at all (Van der Hart et al., 2006). Several authors consider these and other alterations in consciousness, described as absorption, altered time sense, spaciness, daydreaming, imaginative involvement, trance-like behavior, derealization, and certain hallucinations to be 'normal dissociative' phenomena (e.g., Bernstein & Putnam, 1986; Butler, 2004). These phenomena are thus conceptualized as residing on a continuum, with 'normal dissociation' at one end and 'pathological dissociation' (i.e., symptoms that typically manifest from a division of the personality, such as identity alteration and dissociative amnesia) at the other end.

There are at least three major problems of this view. First, none of the alterations in consciousness that are listed as 'normal dissociation' necessarily derives from a dissociative organization of the personality; these alterations therefore belong to a different conceptual category. Grouping symptoms that do and that do not specifically involve manifestations of dissociative parts of the personality together generates an overgeneral category. The dissociative symptoms as defined in this chapter are specific to mental disorders that involve a division of the personality such as minor and major DID as well as simple (minor) and complex (major) PTSD (for a description of these mental disorders, see Van der Hart et al., 2006; Van der Hart & Nijenhuis, 2008). Other alterations in consciousness such as abnormal low intensity of PCS and PCIRs and undue narrow phenomenal perception (i.e., underinclusive and maladaptive PCS and PCIRs) are *sensitive for but not specific to* this group of mental disorders. Second, listing these kinds of 'alterations of consciousness' as instances of '*normal* dissociation' is inconsistent with the acknowledged fact that these phenomena can reach *pathological* proportions (Van der Hart et al., 2004).

Third, the fact that manifestations of dissociation of the personality correlate positively with measures of absorption, imaginative involvement, and other manifestations of 'normal dissociation' has been used to argue that these kinds of altered consciousness belong to the domain of dissociative symptoms (Dalenberg & Paulson, 2009). However, manifestations of a dissociation of personality also moderately to strongly correlate with several other kinds of psychopathology, and high correlations between phenomena do not logically imply that these phenomena belong to the same class. For example, the very strong correlation between eyesight and hearing does not imply that there is no major difference between these faculties. Dalenberg and Paulson also feel that excluding the phenomena of 'normal dissociation' from the domain of dissociation would lead clinicians to overlook these 'symptoms.' However, clinical and scientific progress is often enhanced and not hampered by theoretical and empirical distinctions.

It is important to make a careful distinction between dissociation of personality and its symptoms versus other forms of 'altered consciousness.' Eve Carlson (2014), one of the two authors of the DES, a widely used self-report instrument that evaluates the severity of cognitive-emotional dissociative symptoms and that includes items addressing absorption and imaginative involvement, now agrees that phenomena pertaining to absorption and imaginative involvement are better removed from the domain of dissociation. We also need to make clear the distinctions between different kinds of alterations in consciousness that do not specifically relate to the existence of dissociative parts of the personality (Steele et al., 2009; Van der Hart et al., 2006; Nijenhuis, 2012). For example, there are differences between a voluntary limitation of one's current set of manifest PCIRs, (i.e., voluntary concentration) and involuntary restrictions of this set, as happens when we are unwillingly preoccupied with some matters. These restrictions can be adaptive such as when we are concentrated on our tasks during working hours. They may also be maladaptive. For example, patients with an obsessive-compulsive disorder excessively focus on a small number of thoughts and exteroceptive stimuli that they experience and regard are dangerous. Further, considerably limited PCSs and sets of PCIRs, and low intensity of PCSs and PCIRs as in absorption, absent-mindedness, sleepiness, drunkenness, and uncritical acceptance of ideas are very different phenomena. Whereas these limitations and low intensities can be (cor)related, they are certainly not identical phenomena.

Disruption in Usually Integrated Functions

DSM-5 (p. 291) states that dissociative disorders are "characterized by a disruption of and/or discontinuity in the normal integration of consciousness, memory, identity, emotion, perception, body representation, motor control, and behavior." Reading this formulation, one would expect that sensorimotor dissociative symptoms and disorders would be recognized in this classificatory system. As detailed in Chapter 6, DSM-5 continues to regard these symptoms and disorders as conversion symptoms and disorders. One might perhaps think that 'conversion' and 'dissociation' are synonyms. If the difference were only terminological, this should have been clearly stated. In fact, the authors of the DSM-5 seem committed to the view that there *are* real differences between the two concepts, or else the statement that "[d]issociative symptoms are common in individuals with conversion disorder" (p. 321) is clearly tautological. The confusion lingers because the text does not explain what these presumed differences would be.

Coexistence of Separate Mental Systems

One of the definitions that Cardeña (1994) proposed is to see dissociation "as the coexistence of separate mental systems that should be integrated in the person's consciousness, memory, or identity" (p. 19). This definition adequately includes the notion of dissociative systems rather than dissociative states. However, Cardeña's definition lacks the notion of personality as a whole biopsychosocial system. As detailed more in Chapters 16–18, dissociative parts of the personality are not just insufficiently integrated "mental systems." They also constitute different biological or (neuro)physiological systems. Furthermore, Cardeña's definition lacks constraints on the concept of 'dissociative systems,' and it seems to overemphasize the separateness of these dissociative systems. Dissociative subsystems are commonly not *that* separate (see also Chapter 15).

Detachment and Compartmentalization

Cardeña (1994), Holmes et al. (2005), and Brown (2006) joined other critics in stating that the dissociation concept has been overextended to encompass almost any alteration in consciousness. Cardeña (1994) suggested that dissociation should not be applied to ordinary instances of less-than-full engagement with one's surroundings, experiences, and actions, and should be restricted to "qualitative departures from one's ordinary modes of experiencing, wherein an unusual disconnection or disengagement from the self and/or the surroundings occurs as a central aspect of experience" (p. 23). Following Cardeña, Holmes, Brown and colleagues proposed a model of dissociation that includes two distinct categories of 'dissociative' phenomena labeled 'detachment,' and 'compartmentalization.'

Detachment

Holmes et al. (2005) defined detachment as "an altered state of consciousness characterized by a sense of separation (or "detachment") from aspects of everyday experience" (p. 5). Brown (2006) listed different detachment phenomena such as the individual's emotional experience (as in emotional numbing), sense of self (as in some depersonalization phenomena), body (as in out-of-body phenomena), or the world around (as in derealization). He furthermore referred to phenomenological descriptions such as "being spaced out," "disconnected," "unreal," or "in a dream," a sense of being an outside observer of one's body, and perceptions of the outside world as flat, lifeless, and "strange," as noted by a number of previous authors. In the terms of Chapter 12, detachment can stand for problems regarding global coherence, situatedness, perceptual intensity, distinctions between what is 'online' and 'offline,' and assessment of the degree of reality of perceptions. Such experiences are commonly – but certainly not exclusively – experienced during, or immediately after, potentially traumatizing events, and have been subsumed under the label of 'peritraumatic dissociation' (e.g., Marmar, Weiss, & Metzler, 1998; see for a critique Van der Hart et al., 2008; see Chapter 6). Indeed, Brown (2006) added that many individuals report mild and transient detachment experiences during periods of fatigue, intoxication, or stress. It must also be remembered that many mental disorders include problems regarding global coherence, situatedness, perceptual intensity, distinctions between what is 'online' and 'offline' as well as regarding assessment of the degree of reality of perceptions. Detachment phenomena can thus be arranged on a continuum of increased distress and disability, ranging from mild and nonpathological experiences of detachment to extremely disabling symptoms, such as those seen in depersonalization disorder. Comments on this view follow below.

Compartmentalization

The second category Holmes et al. (2005) and Brown (2006) distinguished is called 'compartmentalization,' a term introduced by Spiegel and Cardeña (1991; see also Cardeña, 1994). These authors referred to dissociation "as involving at least momentarily unbridgeable compartmentalization of experiences" (p. 367). Following these authors, Holmes et al. (2005) defined compartmentalization as follows: (1) The phenomenon involves a deficit in the ability to deliberately control processes or actions that would normally be amenable to such control; (2) the deficit cannot be overcome by an act of will; (3) the deficit is reversible, at least in principle; and (4) it can be shown that the apparently disrupted functions are operating normally and continue to influence cognition and emotion, and action.

Comments

Holmes et al.'s (2005) and Brown's (2006) distinction between phenomena of detachment and compartmentalization is important. However, it is confusing and unnecessary to include conceptually and empirically different phenomena under one generic label (i.e., dissociation). Also, the term 'compartmentalization' is not the best label to refer to a division of personality because it suggests less permeable boundaries among dissociative parts of the personality than those found in clinical practice and experimental research, and than Cardeña, Spiegel, and Holmes et al. actually seem to have in mind.

Holmes et al.'s (2005) and Brown's (2006) four criteria of compartmentalization above are in line with but in part different from the definition of dissociation that Van der Hart and I (2011; Chapter 13) proposed. A problem of Holmes et al.'s and Brown's criteria is that they miss the constraints that enable clinicians and scientists to distinguish dissociative subsystems of the personality in dissociative disorders from other insufficiently integrated subsystems of the personality. As mentioned above, insufficient integration of the personality is a most general feature of psychopathology. It has long been recognized that any psychopathological "... symptom is the expression of disorganization of a certain integration level of a functional system ..." (Farina, Ceccarelli, & Di Giannantonio, 2005, p. 289).

According to Brown (2006), compartmentalization can pertain to a lack of integration between two cognitive structures, the primary attentional system (PAS) and the secondary attentional system (SAS), but it can also occur solely within the SAS. For our purposes, suffice it to say that PAS does not involve self-consciousness, whereas SAS does.

In Brown's (2006) view, DID involves compartmentalization within the SAS, and it implies the existence of two or more compartments that include their own sense and idea of self. Less complex dissociative disorders would involve a lack of integration between the PAS and SAS (Brown, 2006). Patients with these disorders would therefore entertain a *singular* first-person, quasi-second-person, second-person, and third-person perspective. However, patients with dissociative disorders that are less complex than major DID can also include two or more different conscious and self-conscious dissociative parts (e.g., APA, 1994; Boon & Draijer, 1993a; Dell, 2009a; Steinberg, 1995; Van der Hart et al., 2000, 2006).

Thus, Holmes and Brown's "compartmentalization of processes" is overly general, and Brown's distinction between compartments with self-awareness (i.e., compartmentalization within SAS) and between one compartment with (SAS) and one without self-awareness (PAS) does not seem to hold in many cases. Spiegel and Cardeña's (1991) phrase "compartmentalization of experiences" is more specific and closer to our definition, because experiences imply consciousness and usually self-consciousness as well. Exceptions aside, an experience is generally *someone's* experience. As a rule, experience includes a PCS. It should be reiterated, however, that more is compartmentalized than experiences. For example, ANP and EP involve their own sets of explicit PCIRs, and they have different biopsychosocial profiles.

A final problem of the distinction between 'detachment' and 'compartmentalization' is that some alterations in consciousness do not fit this dichotomy very well. For example, the simple twofold categorization does not seem to accommodate the undue focus on a very limited number of perceptions (i.e., limited PCSs and restricted sets of manifest and latent PCIRs; limited global coherence and situatedness) that is not caused by mental detachment. Similarly, it does not capture confusions between fantasies and hallucinations, on the one hand, and generally shared perceptions of 'reality' in second and third-person perspective on the other. Such distinctions require a fine-grained catalogue of constraints on consciousness like the one presented in the previous chapter.

Dell's Five Kinds of Dissociation

Trying to come to terms with the elusive concept of 'dissociation,' Dell (2009b) pinpointed a set of different phenomena and mental disorders that would be dissociative, that is, 'dissociation-potentiated repression,' 'intrusions from dissociated structures,' 'evolution-prepared dissociation,' 'depersonalization disorder,' 'type II normal dissociation,' and 'conversion disorder.' The distinction between these different phenomena and disorders is important because each requires recognition and study. However, can they be meaningfully clustered in one category?

In Dell's (2009b) view, *all* dissociative experiences involve "unexpected, involuntary intrusions into one's conscious functioning" (p. 806). These intrusions are caused by a failure to keep mental and behavioral actions and their implied contents out of conscious awareness. It is hard to see why negative symptoms such as dissociative amnesia and depersonalization as well as successfully repressed mental contents would be intrusions or automatisms (i.e., positive symptoms). In fact, negative dissociative symptoms are the *reverse* of positive dissociative symptoms (e.g., intrusions) and they usually go together (Janet, 1911; Nijenhuis, 2004; Van der Hart et al., 2006). The statement that all dissociative experiences involve intrusions into one's conscious functioning has two problems. The first is that intruding dissociative parts are conscious and self-conscious subsystems; it is therefore unclear what the phrase "one's conscious functioning" actually means. In dissociation, there is no single conscious subsystem (i.e., a singular PCS associated with a particular set of PCIRs), but two or more. A closely related problem is that, in dissociation, there is no mental or behavioral content that is kept out of awareness since what one dissociative part keeps out of awareness is still experienced and known by one or more other dissociative parts.

Dissociation-Potentiated Repression. It is also hard to see why dissociation-potentiated repression (whether or not repression exists is not under discussion here) would be dissociation. *Repression*, described by Dell as "a motivated mental effort to escape discomfort by pushing uncomfortable realities out of conscious awareness" (Dell, 2009, p. 808) is potentiated by a "high level of dissociative ability." This statement pushes the conceptual and definitional problem back to defining dissociative ability, which Dell does not do. In our view, dissociative ability involves an individual's ability to divide the personality in two or more insufficiently integrated, hence dissociated parts, each with, at a minimum, his or her own first-person perspective. Repression can be understood in terms of mental avoidance. Individuals who repress particular consciously or unconsciously feared mental contents keep these contents in a latent state, so that they do not become part of *any* person's perspective. In other words, they engage in one kind of action (mental avoidance) and do not engage in another action (recollecting the feared contents). If they are successful in this avoidance, they manage to leave these recollections in some kind of dynamic unconscious condition. In this light, it seems apt to say that repression requires an ability for repression, and dissociation requires a dissociative ability.

However, Dell (2009b) states that routine repression "may be transformed by the mechanism of dissociation into a full-blown splitting-off" (p. 808). This would happen when the individual is motivated to repress uncomfortable realities (a *sine qua non* for repression to occur) and has a high dissociative ability. Assuming that repression exists, it makes sense to say that, in individuals with a high ability for repression but a low ability for dissociation, painful realities vanish from their singular person perspectives when their repression is successful. It also makes sense to say that, in individuals with sufficient dissociative ability, at least one dissociative part mentally avoids becoming (fully) consciously aware of the painful knowledge and experiences associated with at least one other dissociative part. But what is hard to understand is that an ability for dissociation would potentiate repression. We have suggested that many dissociative parts try to mentally avoid becoming consciously aware of each other (particularly each other's experiences and cognitions) but *realize* each other's existence in at least some regard. This mental avoidance can involve different actions described in Chapter 12 such as actions that cause a reduction of the field of consciousness (e.g., excessive focusing on work and turning attention away from voices), more specifically actions that cause reduced global coherence, situatedness, and convolved holism (e.g., feared memories may become fragmented and isolated), or low intensity of mental contents (e.g., feared memories become vague or distant). Mental avoidance may also come in the form of undue engagement in 'offline' activation (e.g., engagement in trance-like and dream-like states), or avoidance of realization (e.g., assigning a low degree of reality to feared memories or feared perceptions as in derealization). Behavioral avoidance of feared mental contents includes self-mutilation generating endogenous opioids, and substance (ab)use (Van der Hart et al., 2006).

Intrusions from Dissociated Structures. Dell (2009b) believes that dissociation-potentiated repression produces dissociated structures, that is, structures we refer to as dissociative subsystems or dissociative parts of the personality. In his view, dissociated structures hold unaccepted or disowned aspects of life, the self, and significant others. There are several conceptual problems with this proposal. One problem was described above and concerns the question why an ability for dissociation – rather than an ability for repression – would potentiate repression rather than a division of personality.

A second concern is that Dell (2009b) limits dissociative structures to what we have called EPs. His statement that "[d]issociated structures are experienced by the person as operating with considerable autonomy" (p. 808) details that a dissociative individual is an experiencing, consciously aware person *plus* one or more dissociated structures. But in a divided system, insufficiently integrated structures are, of logical necessity, *all* dissociative parts of that whole system. Consistent with this, research has documented that these "persons," which other authors have referred to as "normal consciousness," are not biopsychosocially "normal" at all (see Chapters 15–18): Their normality is only apparent, hence our term 'apparently normal part of the personality' (ANP). It must also be realized that ANPs can intrude on EPs as well as on other ANPs when they have evolved, much as EPs can intrude on ANPs or other EPs.

A third concern is the idea that the person (i.e., as an ANP) pushes unwanted realities out of conscious awareness. This idea is confusing because EP includes at least his or her own first-person perspective. Thus, in dissociation nothing is removed from conscious awareness; rather, there is a division of two or more different dissociative parts, each with, at a minimum, his or her own first-person perspective.

A final concern is that Dell (2009b), while acknowledging that ANP does not accept and integrate EP's first-person perspective, seems to overlook the fact that the same goes for EPs vis-à-vis ANP(s) and other EPs. For example, a controlling EP of a patient who is a physician said "I'm no doctor. I wanna have fun, not patients. It's her (i.e., ANP's) thing, not mine!" In Dell's Freudian vocabulary, EPs thus "push" subjectively unacceptable realities out of their conscious awareness as much as ANPs. Each dissociative part tries to avoid actions that would result in knowing and experiencing, that is, integrating other dissociative parts completely or in at least some crucial regards.

Evolution-Prepared Dissociation. Dell (2009b) claims that what he calls evolution-prepared dissociation does not pertain to repression but to suppression, a term he leaves undefined. This proposed kind of dissociation pertains to immediate suppression of fear and other emotions, altered information processing, and immediate execution of nonreflective actions that facilitate survival and that, Dell claims, instantly end once the danger is past.

It is certainly true that tonic immobility (death feigning, playing dead) is associated with, among others, limited experienced negative affect, a low intensity, and often also low degree of phenomenal reality of mental contents, and that some EPs engage in this animal defensive reaction pattern when feeling threatened. But why would tonic immobility in itself be a kind of dissociation? Some EPs engage in tonic immobility when confronted with real or perceived threat, but tonic immobility in itself is an animal defensive response including, among others, low intensity of PCS and PCIRs, which can happen in individuals whose personality does not encompass dissociative parts.

As remarked above, a low-intensity (self-)consciousness is a different phenomenon than the existence of two or more dissociative parts of the personality and is therefore better not described as a dissociative phenomenon. If there is no dissociation of the personality, there is no (other) dissociative part that has a different reaction to the situation. In this case, the anesthesia that tonic immobility often implies constitutes a lack of synthesis that is not dependent on there being one or more dissociative parts. As argued before, including any lack of synthesis in the domain of dissociation generates a huge category. This category would include *any* limitation of PCSs and PCIRs.

Another problem of Dell's (2009b) position is that the involved animal defensive reactions sometimes persist when the danger is past. These reactions, whether in EPs or in nondissociative individuals, do not immediately end when the danger is past, but can linger for some time or even become fixed for years through classical conditioning.

The concepts of repression and suppression are used and defined in psychiatry and psychology in various ways. Although they are sometimes used as synonyms, repression is often seen as an unconscious mental action and suppression as a conscious one. It is very doubtful whether animal defensive reactions such as tonic immobility involve suppression (i.e., conscious mental avoidance) of emotional and physical feelings, and whether mental avoidance among dissociative parts (Dell's dissociation-potentiated repression) need be an *unconscious* mental action. Clinically, it is evident that dissociative parts (also) engage in *conscious* mental action to avoid or escape each other.

Depersonalization Disorder. This disorder concerns chronic phenomenal (emotional and bodily) detachment from self and sometimes also from the world. As discussed above, phenomenal detachment is a different phenomenon than dissociation of the personality and to avoid confusion is better not referred to as a form of dissociation. Depersonalization disorder can but need not involve dissociative parts. If the presence of a previously latent or hidden dissociative part is detected, in the present understanding the condition from then on qualifies as a dissociative disorder with at least two dissociative parts: the patient as he or she originally presented (ANP) and a newly found part, commonly an EP.

Type II Normal Dissociation and Conversion Disorder. Type II normal dissociation is believed to involve voluntary, positively valued automatisms that can be achieved only by individuals with a special dissociative ability. Dell (2009b) includes in this category (1) evolutionary-prepared, survival-oriented dissociation, (2) hypnotic performance, (3) psychologically healthy forms of possession, (4) creative automatisms, and (5) transcendent experiences. However, including a wide variety of different phenomena in the domain of dissociation is not helpful.

By defining conversion symptoms as unconscious self-hypnotic negations of physical or mental functions, Dell (2009b) regards conversion disorder as a separate form of dissociation and more specifically as the pathological form of Type II normal dissociation. This position raises many concerns. For example, it is unclear why the pathological form of Type II normal dissociation would be conversion disorder, if only because Type II normal dissociation pertains to an indistinct class of phenomena. It is also unclear why DSM-IV and DSM-5 dissociative disorders in Dell's view would not also be a pathological form of Type II normal dissociation. Still another concern is that conversion symptoms may not involve *unconscious* causes. For example, an EP may consciously decide to move the body in a certain way; the ANP may not understand why her leg kicks, but the kicking EP surely knows.

Many authors continue to use the terms 'conversion symptoms' and 'conversion disorders' uncritically despite major theoretical, conceptual, and empirical objections that have been raised against this terminology (e.g., Brown, Cardeña, Nijenhuis, Sar, & Van der Hart, 2007; Nijenhuis, 2004; Van der Hart et al., 2006; Chapter 6). Many authors have described and documented the dissociative nature of these symptoms and disorders (e.g., Brown et al., 2007; Janet, 1907; McDougall, 1926; Nijenhuis, 2004; Van der Hart et al., 2000). In empirical studies, for example, very high correlations between cognitive-emotional and sensorimotor dissociative symptoms were found among different diagnostic groups, and sensorimotor dissociative symptoms are highly statistically predictive of minor and major DID. Thus, our definition of dissociation in trauma describes dissociative symptoms that manifest in positive and negative sensorimotor dissociative symptoms.

Discussion and Conclusions

The value of scientific and clinical concepts lies in their combined sensitivity and specificity. To that end the concept and definition of dissociation should not be so broad that a huge group of psychopathological symptoms would count as dissociative. Nor should they be so narrow that phenomena best understood as dissociative would not be included in the category.

Strengths of the Proposed Conceptualization and Definition of Dissociation in Trauma

There are two crucial differences between our definition of dissociation in trauma and other definitions of the concept. One difference lies in constraint that dissociation pertains to a division of personality, and that, immediately related to this, dissociative symptoms are manifestations of the existence of two or more dissociative parts of the personality. The other difference involves the constraint that activated dissociative parts of the personality engage in actions that, among other things, generate their own unique conscious conceptions of self and world, and self-of-the-world (i.e., their own PCS and set of latent and manifest PCIRs). This consciousness of self-of-the-world constitutes the first-person perspective of dissociative parts. Most dissociative parts also entertain a perspective regarding themselves and other individuals, that is, a quasi-second-person and second-person perspective, respectively. Apart from these phenomenal experiences and phenomenal judgments, they tend to have a perspective regarding objects that they physically judge. This involves their third-person perspective.

In our view, conceptualizing and thus defining dissociation in this way has major assets. One advantage is that it involves clear distinctions between dissociation as an organization of personality, dissociation as defense, dissociation as pathology, and dissociative symptoms, both cognitive-emotional and sensorimotor as well as negative and positive. These distinctions can guide clinical practice and empirical research as well as more generally the discussion regarding dissociation in the literature. Furthermore, clear distinctions between dissociative symptoms and other 'alterations in consciousness' (e.g., changes in global coherence, situatedness, convolved holism, intensity, 'offline' and 'online' activation, and degree of reality) guide a better understanding of each of these related but different phenomena and their causes and correlates.

A second advantage of our conceptualization and definition of dissociation is that it involves a clear delimitation of the category of nonintegrated or incompletely integrated subsystems within the personality that count as dissociative parts of the personality. Constraining the category of dissociative parts to subsystems capable of actions that generate consciousness and self-consciousness provides much needed specificity of the concept of 'dissociation,' and, in its wake, equally needed constraints on the symptoms that count as dissociative symptoms.

Dissociation in Hypnosis and Mediumship

Our definition of dissociation pertains to a division of the personality in the context of trauma. We are aware that this division may also occur in hypnosis and mediumship, that several other definitions of dissociation also address these other contexts, and that there are some indications that dissociation in these other contexts is also best understood as a division of personality. For example, Hilgard's (1970) well-known 'hidden observer,' found in some highly hypnotizable subjects, would seem to involve a dissociative part of the personality that is endowed with consciousness and self-consciousness. However, the phenomenon is disputed (e.g., Kihlstrom, 1998 & Lynn, 1998). Mediumship may involve conscious and self-conscious dissociative parts of the personality (Braude, 1995), but dissociation in mediums is in several regards different from dissociation in DID (Moreira-Almeida, Neto, & Cardeña, 2008). The possible involvement of dissociative parts of the personality in hypnosis and in dissociative parts in mediumship needs to be examined in more detail before a conclusive general definition of dissociation can be formulated.

This chapter focused solely on dissociation in trauma. As difficult as the definition of a construct can be, this is necessary for theoretical advancements, classification, the formulation of clear and effective approaches to treatment, the development of sophisticated measurement instruments as well as the design and interpretation of scientific studies. The definition of dissociation in trauma and dissociation in other contexts is no exception.

Chapter 14

Criticisms of the Proposed Definition and Rejoinder[1]

When one [i.e., an individual as a whole personality] doesn't notice something, doesn't make some associations with it, this is not dissociation. It is a suppression of work, of synthesis.
Pierre Janet (1927/2007, p. 375)

I am not bound to please thee with my answer.
William Shakespeare

Jennifer Freyd, the esteemed editor of the *Journal of Trauma and Dissociation* in which Van der Hart and I published our definition of dissociation in trauma, invited several equally esteemed colleagues to comment on the article. She in turn granted us space for a rejoinder. The comments – available at www.enijenhuis.nl under 'downloads for members' – are briefly stated and the authors who voiced them are added in parentheses. The references to their reactions are included in the reference list and can be identified by the author names, the year 2011, and the journal name.

A Rejoinder

We are most thankful for our esteemed colleagues' reviews of our proposal for a definition of dissociation in trauma, and for their critical comments and compliments. We gratefully acknowledge that many discussants are in agreement with us that the definition of dissociation needs more specificity – we just disagree about the degree and kind of specificity. We also appreciate the editors' generous invitation to respond.

1 The present chapter is an elaborated version of Nijenhuis, E. R. S., & Van der Hart, O. (2011b). Defining dissociation in trauma. *Journal of Trauma & Dissociation, 12*, 469–473.

According to One or Several Reviewers, Our Definition ...

... involves artificial distinctions (Butler)

Any conceptualization, distinction, or categorization is human-made, according to some point of view, principle, or interest. Thus, indeed, our conceptualization of dissociation involves artificial distinctions, as do *all* conceptualizations.

... involves one feature of an entire elephant (Bowman, 2011; Butler, 2011; Cardeña, 2011; Dell, 2011; Kirmayer, 2011)

Bowman's (2011) metaphor presupposes that lowering and retraction of consciousness, and dissociation of the personality are different features of one 'animal' (i.e., dissociation), rather than features of different species. But on what grounds does one decide that they are features of *that* one 'animal' rather than characteristics of two different 'animals?'

With Brown (2006) and Holmes et al. (2005) we believe that the phenomena of 'compartmentalization' and 'detachment' constitute features of more than one 'animal.' One concern pertains to *convergent validity*. For example, while there are moderate correlations between these features, absorption correlates less with manifestations of dissociation of personality than different manifestations of divided personality correlate with each other. Also, extreme dissociation of personality is *not* associated with high fantasy proneness. Alterations in consciousness can exist without any division of personality, and extremely lowered and retracted consciousness does not imply division of personality. These and related research findings suggest that dissociation of personality and other alterations in consciousness constitute different empirical domains, though these domains may be correlated in some ways.

We are particularly concerned about the *discriminant validity* of liberal definitions of dissociation. Positive correlations (or 'family relations;' Kirmayer, 2011) between 'dissociation-like' phenomena (Dell, 2011) can co-exist with *major* conceptual and empirical differences between them (e.g., men and women share many features, but are conceptually and empirically also crucially different). Thus, dissociation of personality and detachment (e.g., absorption and fantasy (which, by the way, may constitute two different domains) include different correlates, which supports the conceptual distinctions between them. For example, sensorimotor dissociative symptoms (a manifestation of dissociation of personality) are correlated among students and in the general population with reported traumatization beyond their association with absorption (see Chapter 16). This indicates that sensorimotor dissociative symptoms are more strongly associated with traumatization. Also, fantasy proneness is not or hardly correlated with hippocampal and parahippocampal volume, whereas complexity of dissociation of personality, sensorimotor dissociative symptoms, symptoms of posttraumatic stress, and reported traumatization are strongly correlated with these volumes (Ehling, Nijenhuis, & Krikke, 2007, see Chapter 19). Furthermore, women with DID are hardly more fantasy-prone than mentally healthy women, and less fantasy-prone than borderline personality disorder patients (Nijenhuis & Reinders, 2012).

Butler (2011) suggests 'normative' and 'pathological' dissociative phenomena are related at the process level. With Janet (1907, 1927) and Brown, we disagree with the idea that division of personality and 'normative dissociation' (absorption, fantasy, daydreaming) involve similar mental and behavioral actions. Dissociative parts of the personality include different kinds of neural and psychophysiological organizations and reactions that are not evident in 'normative dissociative' phenomena. Thus, highly fantasy-prone healthy controls who were instructed and motivated to simulate DID had very different biological reactions to reminders of threatening experiences than DID patients (see Chapters 17–18). However, we applaud Butler's suggestion to extend the study of the (different) actions involved in dissociation of personality and 'normative dissociation.'

Putting a division of personality ('compartmentalization') and absorption, and still other alterations in consciousness ('detachment') into one category for pragmatic reasons (Brown) does not particularly stimulate further clarification and distinctions that would be important to science and treatment.

... is overly constrained (Bowman, 2011; Butler, 2011; Cardeña, 2011; Dell, 2011; Kirmayer, 2011)

Whether or not our definition is overly constrained depends on the outcomes of empirical research and clinical experience. With Brown (2006) and Holmes et al. (2005), we feel that empirical data to date support our distinctions. We also believe that the definition is clinically and scientifically most useful. For example, individuals who fantasize about having dissociative parts (false positives) and those who actually encompass such parts (true positives) require very different treatments – and must and can be distinguished in research (see Chapter 15).

... is circular (Cardeña, 2011; Dell, 2011), absolutistic, and dogmatic (Dell, 2011), and not empirically founded (Bowman, 2011)

In our view, we have defined a particular domain of phenomena and distinguished them from other phenomena, in order to study the convergent and discriminative validity of the demarcated domain and its mediating actions ('processes'). The heuristics are open to empirical confirmation and falsification, and our definition and theory allow us to explore whether or not the dissociation of personality involves its own signs/symptoms, dimensions of complexity, actions, and correlates.

Our definition and theory are not truths carved in stone. In our view, the prime function of clinical and scientific conceptualizations and definitions is not to represent the world – this should be clear from Volume I and Chapter 12 – but to serve as tools that inspire clinical practice and research. The definition and theory proposed suggest statistical, subjective, physiological, and neurophysiological differences between phenomena of dissociation of personality and other phenomena (some of which are correlated). For example, whereas a division of personality involves a *multiplication* of an individual's PCS and set of latent and manifest PCIRs, absorption involves the *suspension* of self-awareness and awareness (cf. Butler, 2006). Treatment implications are detailed in Volume III of this series.

Several hypotheses have already been derived from our dissociation definition and theory. The findings to date are quite supportive, but further research is needed. Several neuroimaging studies included patients with dissociative disorders, PTSD, false-positive cases of DID, and actors who are instructed to imagine/fantasize and enact ANP and EP (see Chapters 17–18). This work demonstrated that these different dissociative parts and different groups engage in different actions (Butler). Other studies using a similar methodology are in progress. Also, our definition is consonant with Brown's (2006) and Holmes et al.'s (2005) conceptual and empirical work on distinctions between 'compartmentalization' and 'detachment.'

... divides what Janet united (Bowman, 2011)

As the opening quote of this chapter indicates, Janet (1907) did not, as Bowman suggests, unite "dissociative retraction" – he never used this expression – and dissociation of personality, but *distinguished* between dissociation and retraction of the field of consciousness.

... involves Janetian theory, not neuroscience and attachment theory (Bowman, 2011)

Our definition and dissociation theory are biopsychosocial, as this book amply demonstrates. The theory seriously considers attachment disruptions (Van der Hart et al., 2006; this book) and neuroscientific findings, and offers neuroscientific hypotheses (Chapters 16–19). Also, the understanding of dissociation as a division of personality was not only Janet's idea. It was the *general* 19th- and early 20th-century view.

... is tied to the theory of structural dissociation (Dell, 2011)

While TSDP is consistent with the definition, the relationship is not bilateral. Even if TSDP were misguided in full or in part, this would not necessarily discredit the proposed definition of dissociation.

... only applies to complex dissociative disorders (Bowman, 2011; Brown, 2011) and not to PTSD (Dell, 2011)

We have proposed that simple trauma-related disorders, including PTSD, also involve dissociative parts with different conceptions of self, world, and self-of-the-world. As detailed in Volume I, for example, during re-enactments, PTSD patients reconceive a former 'I' and 'here and now,' which they mistake for the actual 'I' and 'here and now.' In this regard, they are living on 'trauma time.' These models remain unintegrated with the phenomenal conceptions generated in current daily life, as shown in recurrent re-enactments of traumatic experiences without resolution, recurrent avoidance of traumatic reminders, and recurrent hypervigilance. Consistent with DSM-IV and DSM-5 descriptions of dissociative flashbacks episodes (how are these different from other flashbacks, we wonder?), and new empirical findings that PTSD, DID, and DDNOS are related syndromes (e.g., Rodewald, Wilhelm-Gössling, Emrich, Reddemann, & Gast, 2011; see also Chapter 15), we contend that the re-enactment of traumatic memories is a dissociative phenomenon, and that PTSD constitutes a dissociative disorder of a lesser degree. As Bowman (2006) has shown, pseudoepilepsy also involves a dissociative disorder.

... complicates matters by linking dissociation to trauma (Cardeña, 2011)

We agree that dissociation (of personality) also occurs in other contexts (e.g., Cardeña, 2011; Kirmayer, 2011), and requires a clear definition. The concept of 'trauma' was defined more precisely in Volume I of the present series than could be done in the original article. The current book also details why in our view dissociation in trauma is the essence of trauma.

Conclusion

In conclusion, we maintain that our proposed definition of dissociation in trauma is conceptually clear and adequately sensitive and specific – as well as theoretically, clinically, and scientifically useful. We appreciate all the constructive feedback and look forward to further discussions and collaborations with our colleagues regarding these complex phenomena and concepts that unite our professional interests.

Chapter 15

Trauma Models Versus Sociocognitive and Fantasy Models of Major DID

The truth is a snare: You cannot have it, without being caught. You cannot have the truth in such a way that you catch it, but only in such a way that it catches you.
Søren Kierkegaard (Heiberg & Kuhr, 1909)

There is an ongoing controversy regarding the existence, nature, and causes of major DID and dissociative symptoms and disorders more generally (Bremner, 2010; Coons, 2005; Fraser, 2005; Giesbrecht et al., 2008; Gleaves, 1996; Piper & Merskey, 2004a, 2004b, 2005; Sar, 2005). One view is that the involved phenomena are often trauma-related (e.g., Dell & O'Neil, 2009; Kluft 1984a, 1985, 1987; Putnam 1989, 1997; Ross, 1997; Van der Hart et al., 2006). Another view is that they are due to suggestion, suggestibility, fantasy and fantasy proneness, and motivated role-playing.

TSDP and Dynamic Causation

The idea furthered by the present book is that an individual's dissociation of the personality is the result of dynamic causation, that is, a constellation of material, efficient, formal, and final causation. Dynamic causation works within the confines of the organism-environment system. Exceptions such as mediumship aside, adverse events are a necessary efficient cause of an individual's dissociation of personality. Material causes (i.e., 'environmental-, brain-, and body-stuff') and other efficient causes such as particular (neuro)physiological reactions are obviously also involved. When a dissociative part of a traumatized female develops a male identity, that is an efficient cause as well. It is important to reiterate that efficient and material causes are intermediate and hence insufficient causes. For example, stress hormones operate as material and efficient causes – they involve a kind of matter, and they operate on other forms of matter – but to what degree an individual as a whole organism releases stress hormones is not defined by these hormones themselves. Similarly, the fantasy of an emotionally abused and neglected girl that she must be a bad, worthless child is in itself and on its own incapable of generating a particular dissociation of the personality. A dissociation of the personality into one or more ANPs and one or more EPs is a formal cause of a dissociative disorder, and this organization as well as involved material and efficient causes (e.g., the existence and release of stress hormones, particular conceptions) are insufficient to explain the traumatized individuals feelings, thoughts, behaviors, and physiological as well as neurophysiological features. All are eventually determined by two essential final causes: the individual's will to survive adversity and his or her will to live daily life. Life wants to be lived. These two final causes are exceptionally hard to integrate in the case of interpersonal abuse and neglect by caretakers. There is the deep need to attach to these caretakers and the no less profound need to defend against them. These contrary desires are not dependent on conscious deliberations. They are what essentially comprises any human being: will. And it is this will that drives the organism-environment system. There is a child that wants to live his or her life, one or more perpetrators who want to use the child for their ill purposes, and a pluriform society. This society has basic interests of its own. The sad truth about childhood abuse and neglect is that generally speaking societies have mostly tried to control the problem of childhood traumatization by ignoring or denying its existence, leaving the fragile yet developing and maturing child to his or her own devices. In the framework of this organism-environment system dissociation of the personality evolves and is maintained.

In this conceptualization, adverse events do not exist separate from, but are co-dependent on an experiencing and knowing individual. Events are not 'things out there.' Subject (brain and body) and object (material and social environment) depend and constitute each other, and they occur together at all times. Without a subject, there is no object (e.g., an adverse event), and the subject does not and cannot exist in a vacuum. We are not even living entities 'in' a world, but an intrinsic component of the world as we experience and conceive it. We co-constitute our world and ourselves as a part of this world with every heartbeat and every split second of a dream or waking life.

Because of this co-dependency and co-constitution, any adverse event is necessarily someone's conception. This conception is not a mere idea, nor is it a fantasy, a dream, an hallucination, or some other 'offline' mental content when it is co-dependent on and co-constituted by an environment in an intimate and direct fashion. In a dream one may manage to lift up a truck unaided, but lifting up a truck unaided in waking life remains a dream. Thus, something adverse that happens in the world is necessarily something that happens to and for a person. But it is not just the subject's idea: It is also dependent on the object, on the material environment, and on the social environment in which the subject is embedded.

If and to what degree a particular embedded event becomes traumatizing depends on a collection of material causes (e.g., structural brain features), efficient causes (e.g., functional brain features), formal causes (e.g., prior and current organization of the personality as a whole biopsychosocial system embedded in a wider organism-environment system), and final causes (will, desires). Only in the context of this dynamic causation can an adverse event or will be injurious to the individual who lives it.

Another reservation is that an individual's recollection or denial of the occurrence of one or more traumatizing events need not be completely or even partly accurate. Since any conception is a particular conception of reality and not an absolute truth, the term 'accurate' means that the conception fits the embedded environment. That is, a conception is accurate when it is in accordance with the wider empirically conceived world. Fantasies are conceptions that are not or not yet in accordance with the present empirical world. The phenomenal feeling or phenomenal idea that one can fly unaided is not in accordance with the empirical and physical world. The first-person fantasy that one could fly to the moon with a rocket was once generally seen as an idiot's dream. But some dreams eventually come true. They become a fact, that is, real in the third-person perspective. Other dreams remain what they are. Whereas dreams and facts are different phenomena, dreams can be very valuable. Dissociative parts include conceptions regarding who they are, what the world is like, and who they are of this world. These conceptions include phenomenal realities that do not fit physical realities. For example, in the first and quasi-second-person perspective, an ANP or controlling EP may feel that she was not raped by her father for years, or that he meant no harm or felt guilty, whereas in an empirically founded third-person perspective these ideas constitute fantasies. The phenomenal features of dissociative parts thus depend to a degree on the generation and maintenance of phenomenal conceptions that do not necessarily correspond with third-person views. The conceptions are tied to creative mental actions that include imagination and fantasy. What keeps the fantasies of ANPs and controlling EPs going is that they serve a purpose – they have a final goal. Without the particular fantasies that dissociative parts or traumatized individuals more generally cherish, life might have been utterly impossible for them. In my view, it is in part due to this context that particular traumatic memories may include distortions of what constitutes 'reality' in third-person perspective. These distortions can be negative in the sense that they do not include particular third-person facts (e.g., some ANP and controlling EP deny it, but they were traumatized as much as the fragile EP). The distortions can also be positive, for example, when a phenomenal idea involves the hallucination that something exists that in fact does not exist in the third-person perspective. An abused boy's phenomenal judgment but not the third-person fact may be that "mommy feels guilty because of what she did to me." Negative and positive distortions of third-person facts often exist in combination with each other. For example, the boy may believe that his mother feels guilty that she abused him sexually (positive), and he may also feel that the abuse was not so bad after all (negative). Some traumatized individuals fantasize a traumatic experience to cover up an even worse reality. For example, it is at least conceivable that a severely emotionally neglected individual makes up a story of physical maltreatment to mask the deeper pain of the emotional neglect.

'Offline' conceptions are not exclusive to individuals with DID but are common in many mental disorders. For example, individuals with a psychosis can have hallucinations or paranoid ideas, and individuals with obsessive-compulsive disorders may believe that it is dangerous to touch particular objects, whereas these ideas – these phenomenal conceptions – do not empirically hold in the third-person perspective.

'Offline' conceptions are not even exclusive to individuals with mental disorders but can apply to anyone. For example, and without being blasphemous, it can be and often has been said that the idea that there is a God, or that there is a God who is more sympathetic to one's own all too human interests than to other people's or other living creatures' interests, are metaphysical beliefs. They qualify as fantasies because there is no way of proving their truth – and because they are contradictory: An almighty God cannot favor particular individuals or peoples, and this God cannot favor human beings over dogs, bacteria, or stones, as Spinoza (1677) pointed out ages ago. To give another example, a scientist's idea that DID is the result of suggestion, suggestibility, and fantasy might in fact be a fantasy itself.

As applies to any form of human existence and to any mental or physical disorder, dissociation of the personality and traumatization are subject to sociocultural influences, which are inescapable because anyone is an intrinsic element of an organism-environment system. Any conscious being exists as an intrinsically related trinity of the brain, the body, and the environment, and the human environment is material and social.

Sociocognitive and Fantasy Models of Dissociation/Dissociative Disorders

Using the present terms, some authors reject the ideas that adverse events and an individual's biopsychosocial reactions to these embedded events can be an efficient cause of (minor and major) DID, that a dissociation of the personality exists as formal cause of DID, and that the will to survive these events constitutes the final cause of DID. In their view, DID is primarily, if not completely, due to suggestibility and suggestion, fantasy proneness and fantasy, and motivated role-playing (Giesbrecht et al., 2008; Merckelbach, à Campo, Hardy, & Giesbrecht, 2005; Merckelbach, Devilly, & Rassin, 2002; Merckelbach, Rassin, & Muris, 2000; Piper & Merskey, 2004a, 2004b, 2005; Rassin, Merckelbach, & Spaan, 2001).

Fantasy proneness stands for a deep and profound involvement in fantasy and imagination (e.g., Lynn & Rhue, 1988; Wilson & Barber, 1983). According to these fantasy/suggestion models, the traumatizing events that DID patients report are typically pseudo-memories (Loftus & Ketcham, 1994; McNally, 2003b), thus, 'offline' phenomenal contents. Dissociative phenomena as well as dissociative parts of the personality would be artefacts induced by providing role suggestions to highly suggestible and fantasy-prone individuals (Giesbrecht & Merckelbach, 2006; Giesbrecht et al., 2007; Lilienfeld et al., 1999; Merckelbach et al., 2000; Rassin et al., 2001; Spanos, 1994, 1996). The dissociation of the personality would thus also be a mere 'offline' idea.

In this sense, Giesbrecht, Lynn, Lilienfeld, and Merckelbach (2010, p. 10) assert that "dissociation is related to self-reported but not objective trauma." It is also claimed that the correlation between dissociative symptoms and reported adverse events involves a positive reporting bias (Merckelbach, Muris, Horselenberg, & Stougie, 2000), suggestibility, and fantasy proneness (Merckelbach, Horselenberg, & Schmidt, 2002). For these reasons, the association between dissociative symptoms and disorders and adverse events would be low. Giesbrecht et al. (2007) also advanced the idea that dissociative symptoms can be a sign of mild neurological impairment. They do not explain what exactly causes this impairment that supposedly operates as the material and/or efficient cause of these dissociative symptoms, hence of DID.

History Repeats Itself

The clash between these different explanations repeats 19th-century and early 20th-century debates on grand and traumatic hysteria, and traumatic neurosis in several regards. In these former times, some clinicians also felt that these disorders were not authentic or were not related to adverse events (see Volume I). For example, Seeligmüller (1890) asserted that traumatized soldiers were driven by imaginative desires (*Begehrungsvorstellungen*). Bonhoeffer (1911) believed they had a will to sickness. Freud (1905/1958; 1933/1960) rejected his own original idea that intrafamilial sexual abuse of children might have a major causal role in hysteria, and therefore rejected Ferenczi's and Janet's insights to the contrary. Memories of such abuse, Freud (1905/1958; 1933/1960) claimed are fantasies driven by the involved individual's sexual desires. Some physicians reflexively held that certain kinds of adverse events could technically not have happened, such as abusive sexual penetration of a three-year-old girl. Reports of such atrocities thus had to be lies, confused ideas, and/or pseudomemories. History was to prove these phenomenal judgments, which were presented as if they involved established third-person physical facts, as very wrong.

The Sociocognitive Model of DID

The core of the sociocognitive model of DID is that psychotherapists who 'believe in' DID suggest that the individual has DID (Spanos, 1994, 1996). The model also includes the idea that individuals may convince themselves that they have DID, and that they are (also) inspired in this regard by other 'suggestive' sociocultural influences such as the media, the church, and other individuals with mental disorders. The fantasy model of DID embraces these ideas and adds that high-fantasy-prone individuals are at particular risk of engaging in suggested roles. As Spanos (1996, p. 239) asserted, suggestible individuals can develop full-blown DID in response to minor directions:

> The rules for enacting the [DID] role [. . .] are as follows. (1) Behave as if you are two (or more) separate people who inhabit the same body. (2) Act as if the you I have been addressing thus far is one of those people and as if the you I have been talking to is unaware of the other coinhabitants. (3) When I provide a signal for contacting another coinhabitant, act as though you are another person. To the extent that patients behave in terms of these rules, the "classic"

> symptoms [of DID] follow by implication and do not have to be taught through direct instruction or further suggestion.

To ensure a fruitful discussion regarding the existence and nature of complex dissociative disorders, it is important to stick to the basic rules of science. Any theory or model is welcome, as long as its hypotheses are scientifically and clinically testable and tested. Hypotheses are predictions and in some ways can actually be seen as bets (Hofstee, 1980). The explanation of a phenomenon or set of phenomena that fits the scientific and clinical findings best leads the pack until it is outperformed by an even better understanding. To win the bet, one must obviously study individuals with the disorder(s) one is trying to comprehend. To win the scientific bet regarding DID, for example, one must primarily study afflicted individuals, as is generally conceded (e.g., Giesbrecht et al., 2008).

A Comparison of the Empirical Evidence for Sociocognitive and Fantasy Models of Dissociative Symptoms and Disorders

After reviewing the evidence for trauma-related and fantasy models of dissociative phenomena, Dalenberg et al. (2012, p. 550) concluded that

> [in] keeping with the trauma model, the relationship between trauma and dissociation was consistent and moderate in strength, and remained significant when objective measures of trauma were used. Dissociation was temporally related to trauma and trauma treatment, and was predictive of trauma history when fantasy proneness was controlled. Dissociation was not reliably associated with suggestibility, nor was there evidence for the fantasy model prediction of greater inaccuracy of recovered memory. Instead, dissociation was positively related to a history of trauma memory recovery and negatively related to the more general measures of narrative cohesion. Research also supports the trauma theory of dissociation as a regulatory response to fear or other extreme emotion with measurable biological correlates. We conclude, on the basis of evidence related to these 8 predictions, that there is strong empirical support for the hypothesis that trauma causes dissociation, and that dissociation remains related to trauma history when fantasy proneness is controlled. We find little support for the hypothesis that the dissociation-trauma relationship is due to fantasy proneness or confabulated memories of trauma.

To the best of my knowledge there is no evidence to date showing that suggestion and suggestibility, and fantasy and fantasy proneness can cause DID. A PubMed search entering the keyword 'dissociative identity disorder' in combination with the keywords 'suggestion,' or 'suggestibility,' or 'fantasy proneness,' or 'fantasy' did not turn up a single study that demonstrated or examined a causal relationship between these features (i.e., efficient causes) and major or minor DID. The majority of studies on dissociation and suggestion, suggestibility, fantasy, and fantasy proneness pertain to nonclinical samples, and these commonly involved students.

The Dissociation and Trauma Constructs

Before examining the empirical status of trauma and fantasy models of dissociation and DID in some detail, I would like to repeat that Dalenberg et al.'s (2012) and many other authors' definitions of trauma and dissociation differ from mine. They use the term 'trauma' as a synonym of adverse events that may or may not have wounded the exposed individuals. In my view trauma better stands for a biopsychosocial injury that can emerge in the framework of particular intrinsic relationships between the brain, the body, and the environment, that is, the organism-environment system (see Volume I).

To reiterate, in the discussion on the existence, nature, and correlates of dissociation, the term can be a placeholder for one, some, or all of these different concepts and phenomena: (1) shifts in the phenomenally experienced or judged intensity of mental contents, (2) shifts in the phenomenally experienced or judged reality of mental contents, (3) alterations in the number of phenomena that an individual phenomenally conceives at a time, (4) avoidance of feared, shameful, or despised mental contents, (5) dissociation/division of the personality, (6) negative symptoms that may or may not relate to a division of the personality, and (7) cognitive-emotional dissociative symptoms that do relate to this division. Dissociation may further pertain to (8) sensorimotor dissociative symptoms, but these phenomena are often overlooked or ignored. Sensorimotor dissociative symptoms/disorders are often described as conversion symptoms/disorders. Dissociation can also capture (9) particular positive dissociative symptoms such as re-enactments of traumatic memories. However, various other positive dissociative symptoms may be ignored, not consistently considered, or not seen as dissociative. The combined overinclusiveness and underinclusiveness of the referents of the term 'dissociation' is most confusing and obscures the discussion. What is more, authors commonly do not detail which concept or phenomenon they have in mind when they use the term 'dissociation.'

As discussed above, alterations in the intensity of phenomenal mental contents, the attentional field, and the phenomenally experienced and phenomenally judged reality of mental contents are ubiquitous phenomena. However, in some individuals they can reach pathological proportions. Dissociation of the personality is far less common and in most cases involves a pathological phenomenon. Perhaps with the exception of some hypnotic subjects and some paranormal media, mentally healthy individuals do not encompass more than one set of first-person, quasi-second-person, second-person, and third-person perspectives. Individuals whose mental disorder does not belong to the spectrum of disorders that constituted the 19th-century category of hysteria do not encompass multiple and nonintegrated first-person and related other-person perspectives either. It is therefore important to distinguish between manifestations of a dissociation of the personality and alterations of the quality and quantity of phenomenal mental contents that can, but need not, be related to a dissociation of the personality. They are different concepts with their own biopsychosocial correlates.

In many studies on dissociation, the construct is operationalized as the score on self-report instruments. Commonly used scales such as the DES address cognitive-emotional manifestations of the existence of a dissociation of the personality. They also include items addressing shifts in the quality and quantity of phenomenal contents, but do not or at least not systematically assess sensorimotor dissociative symptoms. The items of the SDQ-20 specifically address the latter phenomena. Remember that, to distinguish between (1) manifestations of a dissociation of the personality and (2) alterations in the quality and quantity of phenomenal contents that do not necessarily relate to this division, I use the terms 'cognitive-emotional' and 'sensorimotor dissociative symptoms' to capture the first set of phenomena (#1). I use dissociation+ when a mixture of the first (#1) and the second (#2) set of phenomena is present or seems to be intended, or perhaps even only the second set (#2). In many cases, the term 'dissociation' pertains to cognitive-emotional dissociative symptoms if it pertains to manifestations of a dissociation of the personality at all. When sensorimotor dissociative symptoms/disorders are specifically intended, I use these terms. When authors used the term 'dissociation' to denote a form of mental avoidance, I write mental avoidance. A more fine-grained distinction is between mental and phenomenal avoidance: Mental avoidance stands for unconscious or preconscious avoidance of mental contents or in any case avoidance of mental contents that are not necessarily phenomenal. The term 'phenomenal avoidance' captures consciously experienced and/or intended avoidance of mental contents. Where authors apply the term 'trauma' or 'traumatic event' for an event that may or may not have been traumatizing (i.e., biopsychosocially injurious), I exchange these for the term 'adverse event' or its synonym 'potentially traumatizing event' when a third-person physical judgment is involved. When a phenomenal judgment is intended, I apply the term 'traumatic event.' This terminology follows the definitions given in Chapter 11.

Dissociation+ and Adverse Events

Hypothesis of Sociocognitive and Fantasy Models of Complex Dissociative Disorders (SC- & F-Models of Dissociation)

Dissociative+ symptoms are not associated with one or more adverse events (but see below).

Hypothesis of Trauma-Models (T-models of Dissociation)

One or more adverse events tend to be an important although insufficient cause of dissociation+ and complex dissociative disorders.

Hypothesis of TSDP

Adverse events tend to be a frequent and important but insufficient efficient cause of dissociative disorders and the implied symptoms of the implied division of the personality. The category of dissociative disorders includes ASD, PTSD, and sensorimotor dissociative disorders. Depersonalization disorder is theoretically excluded from this category in so far as the disorder does not involve a dissociation of the personality. Dissociation of the personality is due to dynamic causation, that is, a constellation of efficient, material, formal, and final causes.

Dalenberg et al. (2012) included 38 studies that passed their selection criteria. They found an overall weighted estimate of the correlation between reported adverse events and dissociation+ of $r = .32$. The effect sizes were moderate. Dissociation+ was measured with various instruments. They included the DES, the adolescent version of the DES (ADES; Armstrong, Putnam, Carlson, Libero, & Smith, 1997), and the Child Dissociative Checklist (CDC; Putnam, Helmers, & Trickett, 1993). To illustrate, Collin-Vézina and Hébert (2005) found a relationship between CDC scores and sexual abuse among 134 abused children who had been evaluated in a hospital and their matched controls. The effect size of the association was large. Sexual victimization significantly increased the odds of presenting with a clinical level of dissociation+ by eightfold and PTSD symptoms by fourfold. In controlled studies of dissociative disorders (Duffy, 2000; Foote, Smolin, Kaplan, Legatt, & Lipschitz, 2006; Ross & Ness, 2010; Sar et al., 2007a), the mean weighted correlation of DES scores and reported sexual and physical abuse were $r = .52$ and $r = .54$, respectively (Dalenberg et al., 2012).

Retrospective Studies

Practically all retrospective studies have found a consistent and strong association between complex dissociative disorders and reported adverse events (e.g., Duffy, 2000; Foote et al., 2006; Nijenhuis et al., 1998b; Ross & Ness, 2010; Sar et al., 2007a, 2007b). The association also exists for dissociation+ and documented adverse events (Coons, 1994; Coons & Milstein, 1986; Chu et al., 1999; Diseth, 2006; Hornstein & Putnam, 1992; Lewis, Yeager, Swica, Pincus, & Lewis, 1997).

Prospective, Longitudinal Studies

Dissociation+ was related with documented adverse events in prospective longitudinal studies as well (Lyons-Ruth et al., 2006; Ogawa et al., 1997; Trickett, Noll, Reiffman, & Putnam, 2001; Trickett et al., 2011). Disorganized attachment in early childhood, which in our view involves dissociative attachment (Van der Hart et al., 2006) as well as observed lack of parental responsiveness in infancy statistically predicted dissociation+ in late adolescence and early adulthood (Dutra et al., 2009; Ogawa et al., 1997). Childhood verbal abuse was the only type of adverse event that added to the statistical prediction of dissociation+ provided by lack of parental responsiveness in infancy in Dutra et al.'s study.

The relationship between dissociation+ and adverse events should be weaker for reported than for documented adverse events if the hypothesis is to hold that dissociation+ and reported adverse events are both largely due to fantasy and fantasy proneness. However, the correlation does not wane. The association between dissociation+ and self-reported adverse events and dissociation+ and more objective assessed adverse events is of a similar magnitude (Dalenberg et al., 2012).

When evaluating the results of the impact of chronic childhood abuse and neglect, it is important to keep in mind that adverse events such as sexual abuse, physical maltreatment, emotional neglect, including lack of parental responsiveness to the child's needs, often come in clusters. Because these events are bound to affect each other and together constitute the child's world, it is rather artificial to calculate the correlations between each of these kinds of events and their psychopathological consequences. In this context, it is also of note that a child's disorganized attachment does not come out of thin air, but may be a consequence of the child's and the parents' organism-environment system. Statistical distinctions among some variables do not necessarily reflect the totality of the real world.

Decline of Dissociative+ Symptoms over Time

Carlson et al. (submitted, cited in Dalenberg et al., 2011) tracked adults who experienced severe injury themselves or severe injury to a loved one. The assessed dissociation+ symptoms dissipated over time. This finding is predicted by T-models of dissociation+. For example, according to TSDP, dissociation involves a lack of integration. The problem ensues when individuals are unable to synthesize, personify, and presentify one or more adverse experiences. These therefore comprise for them a traumatic experience. This dissociation is generally associated with a reduction in mental efficiency that can manifest in a lowering of the quality and a reduction of the quantity of phenomenal mental contents. However, when the traumatizing event or events are over, stress levels generally decrease, so that traumatized individuals are in a better position to engage in the required integrative actions. Caring significant others may assist them in this regard. Empathic support raises the integrative capacity of traumatized individuals. Where a public event is concerned, there is also a degree of societal pressure to acknowledge the events' reality and to integrate the painful experiences and facts.

The observed temporal decrease of dissociative+ phenomena fits the idea that exposed individuals who were exposed to adverse/traumatizing events tend to integrate traumatic memories posttraumatically. As in many other studies, dissociation+ and PTSD symptoms assessed in real time were strongly correlated in Carlson et al.'s study. This association obviously fits T-models of dissociation+ including TSDP, but it is hard to reconcile with the idea that dissociation is fantasy-based. This also applies to the relationship between documented adverse events, disorganized/dissociative attachment in childhood and dissociative+ symptoms many years later.

Social Support

Consistent with the prediction of T-models of dissociation, social support in the aftermath of an adverse/traumatizing event is associated with fewer or reduced dissociative+ symptoms, including PTSD symptoms, and lack of social support is a risk factor for PTSD (Brewin et al., 2000; Dimitry, 2013). For example, in a retrospective study of adults who had experienced a parent with cancer during their childhood or adolescence, there was a negative relationship between the severity of their current PTSD symptoms and their satisfaction with social support (Wong, Looney, Michaels, Palesh, & Koopman, 2006). A prospective study documented that the persistence of PTSD at 1 year after a traffic accident was related to lower social support and limitations in work and in social life (Yasan, Guzel, Tamam, & Ozkan, 2009). Youths who experienced accidental injury and who lived in cohesive families had less dissociative symptoms at 6 weeks than those who lived in less cohesive families (Nugent, Sledjeski, Christopher, & Delahanty, 2011). Individuals from a general population sample with high cognitive-emotional dissociative+ symptoms and sensorimotor dissociative symptoms experienced more inadequate social support than those with fewer symptoms (Maaranen et al., 2005b). Social support after the World Trade Center disaster had a powerful ameliorating influence on PTSD symptoms (Simeon, Greenberg, Nelson, Schmeidler, & Hollander, 2005). Lesser improvement in posttraumatic stress symptoms over the first year was significantly related to less social support and greater comorbid dissociation+ in this prospective study.

Adequate social support does not necessarily prevent dissociation of the personality. Having a close relationship with a parent, a sibling, an extraparental adult, or a friend did not have a mediating influence on the severity of dissociative+ symptoms in female psychiatric inpatients who had been sexually abused in childhood (Zlotnick et al., 1995). Their dissociative+ symptoms were also associated with childhood physical neglect, and witnessed sexual abuse or physical maltreatment. Andrews, Brewin, and Rose (2003) similarly found more negative effects of a lack of social support than positive influences of social support in women who had experienced an assault.

Betrayal

Consistent with the definition of adverse/potentially traumatizing events presented in Chapter 11, there are more things that can be adverse and traumatizing than just perceived life threats. Betrayal trauma theory (Freyd, 1996), for example, holds that events involving profound social betrayal can be injurious, and that interpersonal relationships play a crucial factor in recovery (Freyd & Birrell, 2013). This theory emphasizes the importance of the kind and quality of social relationships in comprehending the effects of adversities and their influences on healing. Supportive evidence comes from various sources. DePrince (2001) found that self-reported instances of betrayal predicted various measures of cognitive dissociation+, sensorimotor dissociative symptoms (SDQ-5), and PTSD withdrawal scores higher than fear in a study with college students. The number of times caregiver abuse occurred predicted DES and SDQ-5 scores more than noncaregiver abuse. Betrayal was similarly associated with posttraumatic stress symptoms following interpersonal and severe relational violations in a different study with college students (Kelley, Weathers, Mason, & Pruneau, 2012). In still another study with college students, greater adverse event exposure was related to more symptoms of depression, dissociation+, and PTSD (Martin, Cromer, DePrince, & Freyd, 2013). Adverse events involving high betrayal contributed most to the prediction of these various but related symptoms. Similar findings were reported by Goldsmith, Freyd, and DePrince (2012).

Hypothesis TSDP

Sensorimotor dissociative symptoms are associated with reported and documented adverse events, but these events are not their singular cause.

Dalenberg et al. (2012) did not include studies of a possible relation between sensorimotor dissociative symptoms and reported and documented adverse events in their review. However, there is increasing evidence for such an association. Table 15.1 extends the findings presented in Chapter 6. In the studies a variety of different instruments was used to evaluate reported potentially traumatizing events, such as the Traumatic Experiences Checklist (TEC; Nijenhuis, Van der Hart, & Kruger, 2002) and the Childhood Trauma Questionnaire (CTQ; Bernstein et al., 2003).

The table also includes Diseth's (2006) longitudinal follow-up study on the mental consequences of a harsh, painful, and recurrent medical procedure that had to be applied by the child's parents during the first four years of the child's life. The participants were enrolled in the study in their adolescence. At this point in time (T1), they completed several questionnaires, including the ADES. Then, 10 years later (T2), they completed, among others, the SDQ-20 and DES. The medical procedure was associated with the ADES at T1, and the SDQ-20 and DES at T2.

Reviewing the literature on sensorimotor dissociative disorders, Brown and Lewis-Fernandez (2011) stated that the prevalence of potentially traumatizing events is disproportionally high among individuals with conversion/pseudoneurological symptoms, that is, sensorimotor dissociative symptoms. This conclusion corresponds with the findings summarized in Table 15.1.

In sum, studies involving a variety of populations and methodologies have consistently documented associations between (1) reported and documented adverse events and (2) cognitive-emotional and sensorimotor dissociative symptoms as well as alterations in the quality and quantity of phenomenal mental contents. Correlations between ASD and PTSD symptoms, which according to TSDP essentially include dissociative symptoms, and adverse events are obviously present, because these events are a criterion for the diagnosis.

Table 15.1. Sensorimotor dissociative symptoms and reported traumatization in a variety of populations.

Study	Sample	*n*	SDQ-20 × adverse events		DES × adverse events	
			r	*p*	*r*	*p*
Näring & Nijenhuis, 2005	General population	147	.20*	< .05	.10*	*ns*
Näring & Nijenhuis, 2005	Students	73	.27*	< .01	.32*	< .001
Maaranen et al., 2004	General population	1739: 742 men, 997 women	Men: normal versus high SDQ-20 scores: poor relationship with parents, unhappy childhood home, physical punishment; women: normal versus high SDQ-20 scores: unhappy childhood home, hard parenting, physical punishment, domestic violence, alcohol abuse at childhood home; men and women: strong relationship with physical punishment			
Bob et al., 2013	Young adults, general population	250	.55"	< .0001		
Brown et al., 2010	Students; high and low on SDQ-20	124	Students high on SDQ-20 had higher TAA*** scores:			
Nijenhuis et al., 2002	General psychiatric patients	155	.57	< .0001	.43	< .0001
Waller et al., 2000	General psychiatric patients	72	.32	< .01	.27	< .05
El-Hage et al., 2002	General psychiatric patients	140	.41	< .0001		
Nijenhuis et al., 2003	Women with chronic pelvic pain	52	.69	< .0001	.44	< .001
Näring, Van Lankveld, & Geenen, 2007	Patients with fibromyalgia syndrome (FMS) and rheumatoid arthritis (RA)	28/51 FMS RA	.45 .48 .26	< .001 < .01 *ns*		
Bohn et al., 2013	fibromyalgia syndrome	117	SDQ-20 × emotional abuse sexual abuse emotional neglect physical neglect		SDQ-20 .32 .18 .23 .24	 < .001 < .05 < .01 < .01
Waller et al., 2003	Eating disorders		SDQ-20		DES	
	Nonclinical controls	75	.35	< .01	.13	*ns*
	Restrictive anorexia nervosa	21	.40	< .01	.22	*ns*
	Binge-purge anorexia nervosa	40	.32	< .05	.25	*ns*
	Bulimia nervosa	70	.09	ns	.06	*ns*
Müller-Pfeiffer et al., 2010	General psychiatric inpatients and outpatients, including 39 patients with dissociative disorders	225	.46	< .001	.52	< .001
Nijenhuis et al., 1998b	Dissociative disorders vs. psychiatric controls	47/43	.40	< .0001		

Study	Sample	n	SDQ-20 × adverse events		DES × adverse events	
			r	p	r	p
Van Duyl et al., 2010	Spirit possession disorder vs. mentally healthy controls	112/73	.65	< .0001	.61	< .0001
Simeon et al., 2008	Depersonalization disorder vs. healthy controls	54/47	.25	*ns*		
Roelofs et al., 2002b	Somatoform dissociative disorders vs. affective disorders	54/50	more childhood trauma in somatoform disorders (67.9% correct classification)			
Spinhoven et al., 2004	Patients with chronic pelvic pain, nonepileptic seizures, and two samples of patients (102 and 54) with predominantly motor or sensory types of conversion disorder	52/61/ 102/54	physical abuse predicted level of somatoform dissociation over and above level of psychopathology			
Diseth, 2006	Longitudinal study; adolescents with anorectal abnormalities, Hirschsprung disease, and hospitalized controls; 10-year follow-up	14/ 14/ 14	Anal dilatation, an invasive medical treatment procedure related to inborn anorectal abnormalities, had to be performed daily by the parents during the first four years of the child's life. The procedure was correlated with the frequency and severity of persistent dissociative symptomatology (SDQ-20: $r = .39$, $p < .05$). It was the only significant predictor of SDQ-20 and ADES scores, and one of two significant predictors of DES scores.			

*Correlations adjusted for absorption, **correlation with the Trauma Symptom Checklist, TSC-40 (Briere, 1996), ***Trauma Assessment for Adults (Resnick et al., 1993).

Peritraumatic Dissociation+

Hypothesis SC- and F-Models

Peritraumatic dissociation+ does not constitute a risk factor for complex dissociative disorders, although engagement in fantasy may be a means to cope with adverse events (see next section).

Hypothesis of T-Models

Peritraumatic dissociation+ is a risk factor for trauma-related disorders.

Hypothesis of TSDP

Adverse events can be an efficient cause of a dissociation of the personality during or immediately following the event in a context of other causes. Given dynamic causation, maintenance or strengthening of this division is co-dependent on other causes as well.

As indicated in Chapter 6, many studies have suggested that experiencing adverse events can elicit peritraumatic dissociative+ reactions. However, it is insufficiently clear what the concept of 'peritraumatic dissociation' precisely encompasses. Candidates include absorption, emotional numbing, a lack of integrative capacity, and symptoms of a dissociation of the personality – or a mixture of these very different but probably related and in any case not mutually exclusive features. A sharper definition of the concept of 'peritraumatic dissociation' should detail what the involved symptoms are symptoms of, and the formulation should also place solid constraints on the concept. Based on this work, T-models would be able to develop more precise hypotheses as to why the involved peritraumatic phenomena would predict the emergence of an enduring dissociation of the personality.

According to TSDP, the concept of 'peritraumatic dissociation' stands for (manifestations of) an emergent division of the personality during or shortly after an adverse event. This division, which constitutes the formal cause of all trauma-related disorders, occurs when the individual is unable to integrate the adverse event. In the context of dynamic intrinsic relationships of the brain, the body, and the environment, this integrative inability constitutes the subject-pole of trauma. An adverse event becomes a traumatic event in the second-person perspective and a traumatizing event in the third-person perspective when this dissociation occurs with at least one ANP and at least one EP. Prior indicators of limited intrapersonal and interpersonal integrative capacity (e.g., PTSD in relation to a previous traumatizing event, developmental phase, dissociative attachment, loneliness, emotional neglect) can therefore constitute important pretraumatic efficient and formal causes for a trauma-related disorder. Posttraumatic efficient causes or risks include lack of social support as well as mental avoidance of traumatic memories and the associated EPs by the ANPs. To overcome their symptoms and the disorder itself, traumatized individuals must integrate these memories and the various person perspectives associated with these memories. Such integration constitutes the major aim of treatment. To achieve this goal following chronic abuse, maltreatment, emotional neglect, and attachment disruptions, it is often necessary to develop a trusting relationship with one or more therapists as well as with at least a few significant others in daily life. Trust in a significant other increases the individual's integrative capacity (cf. thoughts on Porges' [1995, 2001, 2003, 2007, 2009] polyvagal theory are presented in Chapter 16).

To the degree that the SC- and F-models of dissociation do not include the hypothesis that adverse events can be an efficient cause of dissociative disorders (see below), they have difficulty explaining (1) the emergence of cognitive-emotional and sensorimotor dissociative reactions during or following an adverse event, (2) the enduring dissociation of the personality, (3) pathological alterations in the quality and quantity of phenomenal contents, (4) still other symptoms such as depressive mood, anger, shame, phobias of cues related to the reported traumatizing events, PTSD symptoms, self-destructive behaviors, including substance abuse, self-mutilation and suicidality, sexual problems, and relational difficulties, (5), the influence of emotional neglect and other forms of betrayal on dissociative symptoms, and (6) the remission of these various symptoms and the dissociation of the personality following the integration of traumatic memories and the various dissociative parts of the personality. These models also do not explain why (vii) factual prior adverse events increase the likelihood that an individual should develop peritraumatic dissociative+ symptoms. However, if these models consistently included the hypothesis that adverse events can prompt the traumatized child to engage in fantasy in order to evade the terrifying and neglectful world, and that fantasy plays a contributing role in the emergence and maintenance of a dissociation of the personality, these models share some common ground with TSDP and other T-models of dissociation+ (see next section).

Dissociation+ as Fantasy and Absorption

Hypothesis SC- & F-Models

Dissociation+ is caused by fantasy proneness and absorption.

Hypothesis T-Models

Dissociation+ is associated with absorption. Dissociative parts of the personality are in part fantasy related.

Hypothesis TSDP

Absorption and a certain degree of imagery are sensitive but not specific to dissociative disorders.

On a fantasy model of dissociation+, dissociation+ as well as the association between dissociation+ and reported adverse events are basically explained by fantasy and fantasy proneness (see Dalenberg et al., 2012). However, things are not that straightforward. The constructors of fantasy proneness questionnaires have also recognized that fantasy can be a means to cope with adverse life events (Merckelbach et al., 2001; Wilson & Barber, 1983). For example, Merckelbach et al. (2001, p. 988) stated that for some individuals "a profound fantasy life may have become a means to cope with or escape from negative experiences." In agreement with this hypothesis, compared to low fantasy-prone individuals, higher fantasy-prone individuals reported "greater frequency and severity of physical punishment, greater use of fantasy to block the pain of punishment, more thoughts of revenge toward the person who punished them, greater loneliness, and a preference for punishing their own children less severely" (Rhue & Lynn, 1987, p. 121). High fantasy-prone individuals also reported more severe and more frequent childhood punishment (Wilson & Barber, 1983). More than a decade earlier, Josephine Hilgard (1970) had proposed two pathways to high hypnotizability: imaginative involvement in fantasy and mental avoidance of the consequences of parental abuse and neglect.

Given the acknowledgment that fantasy can be a strategy to cope with adverse events, and given the above findings, it is not clear why proponents of SC- and F-models of dissociation do not regard negative symptoms of dissociation+ in DID as a way to cope with adverse events. For the same reason it is equally unclear why particular positive dissociative symptoms (i.e., intruding traumatic memories associated with EP, other features of EP) in their view would not be an indication that ANP's coping fails at times. The more general unclarity of SC- and F-models of dissociation is that they do not detail exactly when dissociation+ would be associated with adverse events and when dissociation+ would not relate to these kinds of events but be purely fantasy-based.

Trauma-related views prominently include the idea that patients with DID or a different trauma-related disorder may engage in fantasy to cope with or escape from a lived adverse world. A study with DID patients provided supportive evidence for this hypothesis (Nijenhuis & Reinders, 2012; see below). According to TSDP, fantasy is not limited to ANPs, but also pertains to controlling EPs. For example, these parts may fantasize that they were not abused, neglected, or hurt, and that fragile EPs are to blame for the abuse and neglect. Absorption-like phenomena such as spacing out can mark ANP who engage in emotional avoidance of traumatic memories and EPs. It can also be a feature of EPs who engage in tonic immobility.

In a study with nonclinical 3- to 4-year-old children, dissociation as measured with the CDC (Putnam, Helmers, & Trickett, 1993) was associated with parent report of fears, problem behaviors, and nightmares (Carlson, Tahiroglu, & Taylor, 2008). According to the authors, CDC scores may reflect some degree of difficulty in children's lives. However, children who engaged in role-play, in particular when this role-play involved imaginary companions, had higher scores on the CDC than other children. Their role-play was not related to fears or problem behaviors. Fantasy-based high CDC scores thus may indicate absorption in role-play and do not necessarily indicate mental problems, and children with dissociative symptoms are not necessarily excellent fantasizers.

Other sources similarly indicate that fantasy proneness is closely related to absorption (Dalenberg et al., 2012; Geraerts, Merckelbach, Jelicic, Smeets, & Van Heerden, 2006, p. 1143; Merckelbach, Horselenberg, & Muris, 2001; Platt, Lacey, Iobst, & Finkelman, 1998; Wilson & Barber, 1983). It is of note that the authors of the DES purposively included absorption items in the scale (Bernstein & Putnam, 1986), as did the authors of fantasy-proneness scales (Merckelbach et al., 2001; Wilson & Barber, 1983). When – in contrast to my position – absorption is also seen as dissociation, then trauma-related and sociocognitive/fantasy models of dissociation+ both predict a positive correlation between dissociation+ and fantasy proneness/absorption.

TSDP predicts that absorption may reach pathological proportions in complex dissociative disorders. As described above, absorption and detachment can be features of avoidant and numb ANPs and of hypoaroused EPs engaging in tonic immobility. Highly selective attention marks many hyperaroused EPs who are fixated on trauma-related cues as well as ANPs that excessively focus on a tasks of daily life in an effort to phenomenally and behaviorally avoid trauma-related cues. TSDP additionally postulates that absorption can reach pathological proportions in other mental disorders as well. Pathological degrees of absorption and other pathological alterations in the quality and quantity of phenomenal contents are in this view sensitive for dissociative disorders and several other mental disorders alike. Findings that fit these hypotheses are that absorption as measured by the absorption subscale of the DES was prominent among patients with a dissociative disorder, but that absorption was also high up among those with a different mental disorder (Leavitt, 2001). Patients with high absorption scores from either diagnostic class had more psychopathology across a broad range of symptoms.

These results complement those of several other studies. For example, absorption and imaginative involvement were more strongly related with severe psychopathology (Allen & Coyne, 1995) and general distress (Allen Coyne, & Console, 1996) than were depersonalization and dissociative amnesia. Allen, Coyne, and Console (1997) performed a factor analysis of the DES, and found two dimensions of dissociative detachment: detachment from one's own action and detachment from the self and the environment. In a sample of female inpatients with severe trauma-related disorders each detachment dimension was strongly related to scores for thought disorder and schizotypical personality disorder. Allen et al. (2002) also documented that absorption was more strongly correlated with severe psychopathology than with amnesia and depersonalization.

In sum, absorption and imaginative involvement are correlated with reported adverse events, and they are sensitive but not specific to dissociative disorders. Associated with general psychopathology, absorption and imaginative involvement characterize psychiatric populations more generally. There is thus not only a conceptual difference between absorption/imaginative involvement and dissociative symptoms, the distinction is also empirical: Only dissociative disorders, including ASD and PTSD, involve a particular dissociation of the personality, which manifests itself in dissociative cognitive-emotional and sensorimotor dissociative symptoms.

Dissociation+, Fantasy Proneness, and Reported Adverse Events

Hypotheses SC- and F-Models

Dissociation+ is due to fantasy proneness, particularly in DID, and adverse events reported by high fantasy-prone individuals are generally fantasy-based pseudomemories.

Hypothesis T-Models and TSDP

Dissociation+ relates to reported adverse events over and above the influence of fantasy/absorption.

Additional Hypotheses TSDP

Individuals with DID are not abnormally fantasy prone. As ANPs and controlling EPs, they tend to use fantasy as one of their means to avoid and escape from traumatic memories in which they are fixed as fragile EPs. ANPs may fantasize that the traumatization did not occur, that it was not so bad after all, or that it does not pertain to them. Controlling EPs commonly fantasize that they are powerful, and that they were not traumatized or affected. Fragile EPs may use fantasy to lessen the impact of the traumatization in their own way (e.g., a fragile EP who is rejected and abandoned by her mother may believe than her mother is looking for her; an EP who recalls sadistic abuse believes that her father did not mean to hurt her).

Reported adverse events, fantasy proneness, and dissociation+ in students and the general population. Fantasy proneness is associated with suggestibility (Braffman & Kirsch, 1999; Levin & Spei, 2004; Merckelbach et al., 2001; Poulsen & Matthews, 2003; Rassin et al., 2001; Silva & Kirsch, 1992). Thus, fantasy-prone individuals may be open to suggestions with respect to dissociative+ phenomena and a history of adverse events. In consonance with this possibility, dissociative+ phenomena were correlated with fantasy proneness, heightened suggestibility, and susceptibility to pseudomemories among university students (Levin & Spei, 2004; Merckelbach, Muris, & Rassin, 1999; Merckelbach & Muris, 2001; Rauschenberger & Lynn, 1995; Silva & Kirsch, 1992). Compared to university students with average scores for fantasy proneness, high fantasy-prone students reported more dissociative+ phenomena (Rauschenberger & Lynn, 1995).

However, the idea that fantasy and suggestibility are efficient causes of dissociative phenomena is problematic. One concern is that correlations do not imply efficient causation. The tendency to engage in fantasies might be a consequence rather than an efficient cause of adverse events. As noted above, some fantasizers use fantasy as a mental defense (e.g., Rhue & Lynn, 1987). The final cause is not to fantasize traumatic events, but to keep their heads up in daily life by dreaming a better or in any case a less dreadful world. Whereas for some individuals fantasy is a means to navigate a harsh world, most individuals use it for other reasons. Fantasy-proneness can be associated with significant psychopathology, though most fantasy-prone individuals are well adjusted (Barrett, 1992, 1996; Rhue & Lynn, 1987; Wilson & Barber, 1983). They love to fantasize and spend a lot of time in a vivid secret imaginary world, but they do not imagine or report adverse events (Barrett, 1992, 1996). The final cause of their frequent and deep engagement in fantasy is the will to play. In short, fantasy mediated by the will systems of play and defense involves very different final causes.

SC- and F-models also have a hard time explaining why patients with minor and major DID would engage in fantasy as much as these models suggest they do. If the idea is that playing a DID role is worthwhile because it gains attention (e.g., Spanos, 1994), then clinicians and scientists who adhere to this hypothesis should systematically test this hypothesis. But no such study has been undertaken to date. In fact, the evidence points in the reverse direction. As Gleaves (1996, p. 45) summarized,

> [i]n most mental health settings, patients diagnosed as having DID or who present symptoms of DID appear to experience especially hostile treatment. When these patients are hospitalized with a diagnosis of DID, staff (sometimes including unit directors) often tell them that they are lying or faking, their diagnosis is incorrect, or even that their therapists are crazy . . . Patients with DID are often told that they are actually psychotic or borderline, and in many hospital settings the terms multiple and borderline are used as if they are synonymous . . . [There are] numerous examples of the type of extreme and nonprofessional skepticism that patients and therapists receive regarding the diagnosis.

There is evidence that false-positive cases can evolve in a clinical setting (Draijer & Boon, 1999), but false positives are not true positives. Since the symptoms, dissociative parts, re-enactments of traumatic experiences, and traumatic memories of DID patients are often met with rejection, disdain, misdiagnosis, and misunderstanding in psychiatry (and in the world in general), it is unclear why they would fantasize these symptoms, parts, experiences, and alleged pseudomemories? What could be the final cause of DID and its manifestations if having or talking about one's 'DID' is clinically, scientifically, and socially punished? A "suggestive therapist" would certainly not be the only efficient (and sufficient) influence, and the responsible therapist will foster integration, not dissociation. The sad fact is that many patients with DID meet with rejection in both psychiatry and society. They therefore often *suffer*. In fact, most *hide* their condition as much as possible. Overt presentation of dissociative parts and dissociative symptoms is the exception. There is substantial comorbidity of dissociative disorders, other DSM-IV axis I disorders, and DSM-IV personality disorders in the general population and in clinical samples (Boon & Draijer, 1993b; Dell, 1998; Ellason, Ross, & Fuchs, 1995; Fink, 1991; Lipsanen et al., 2004; Sar, Akyuz et al., 2004; Scevola et al., 2013; Yargic, Sar, Tutkun, & Alyanak, 1998). However, the prevalence of histrionic personality disorder among patients with major DID is low (Boon & Draijer, 1993b; Fink, 1991), and it is similar to the prevalence of this personality disorder in patients with other mental disorders.

SC- and F-models of DID also have difficulty explaining DID in individuals who have not been exposed to therapists (who 'believe in' and 'suggest' DID), who have not had access to media reports on DID, and who showed the signs and symptoms of the disorder before DID was a topic in psychiatry of society more generally. It is thus a pertinent challenge for SC-and F-models of DID to explain the efficient and final causes of fantasizing dissociative symptoms and playing the role of a DID patient. The efficient and final causes that SC- and F-models postulate do not seem to apply.

Another concern with the idea that fantasy efficiently causes dissociation is that dissociation in studies on dissociation and fantasy proneness included phenomena that do not necessarily point to a dissociation of the personality. Given a correlation between fantasy proneness and absorption, a possible association between fantasy proneness and dissociation might be foremost mediated by alterations in the quality and quantity of phenomenal consciousness – and not by a dissociation of the personality.

Moreover, dissociation+ relates to reported adverse events over and above the influence of fantasy proneness (Merckelbach et al., 2002; Pekala, Angelini, & Kumar, 2001; Pekala et al., 1999–2000; Thomson, Keehn, & Gumpel, 2009) and absorption (Näring & Nijenhuis, 2005). These findings support trauma-related models of dissociation and are inconsistent with the SC- and F-models. The point is that the latter models imply a lower correlation between dissociation+ and documented adverse events and reported adverse events after controlling for fantasy proneness and absorption. For example, we documented that the range of reported potentially traumatizing events was more restricted among students than in a general population sample (Näring & Nijenhuis, 2005). After partialing out absorption as a measure of (one kind of) suggestibility/imaginary involvement, the relationship between reported potential traumatization and DES scores diminished substantially in both samples. However, the magnitude of the correlation with sensorimotor dissociative symptoms as measured with the SDQ-20 remained significant for student and members of the general population alike (see Table 17.1). This difference could be due to the fact that the SDQ-20 was specifically designed to evaluate the severity of a dissociation of the personality, and that the DES also includes items assessing several alterations in the quality and quantity of phenomenal contents that do not necessarily relate to a trauma-related dissociation of the personality.

We concluded that findings regarding correlations between reported adverse events and dissociation+ in students can be generalized to the general population only with caution. The study also indicates that while DES and SDQ-20 scores are correlated – a consistent finding in studies of different populations – they may in part have different correlates or different magnitudes of shared correlates. Studies on dissociation should therefore consistently include cognitive-emotional as well as sensorimotor dissociative symptoms.

Fantasy Proneness and Dissociation+ in Clinical Samples

Findings regarding a possible link between dissociative+ phenomena and fantasy proneness in clinical samples are inconsistent. In one study of schizophrenia, borderline personality disorder and major depressive disorder, dissociative+ symptoms and fantasy proneness were moderately correlated phenomena ($r = 0.55$; Merckelbach et al., 2005). However, these disorders, perhaps with the exception of some cases of borderline personality disorder, do not involve a dissociation of the personality. In this context it is of note that patients with borderline personality disorder did not have high scores for sensorimotor dissociative symptoms (SDQ-20: $M = 28.0$; $SD = 6.8$; Korzekwa et al., 2009). This finding is consistent with the idea that the personality of individuals with borderline personality disorder who do not also have a dissociative disorder is not divided in two or more dissociative parts, each with their own conceptions of self, world, and self-of-the-world.

Studying patients with somatoform disorders, Van der Boom, Van den Hout, and Huntjens (2010) found modest correlations between fantasy proneness and DES scores ($r = 0.23$) as well as SDQ-20 scores ($r = 0.27$). The mediating influence of fantasy proneness on the correlations between DES and SDQ-20 scores, and reported adverse events ($r = 0.27$) and $r = 0.28$, respectively) was negligible. This finding lead Van der Boom et al. to conclude that the mediating role of fantasy proneness on the association of dissociative+ symptoms and reported adverse events may be an artefact of student samples.

Are DID Patients Excellent Fantasizers?

On the hypothesis that DID is due foremost to high fantasy proneness, patients with this disorder should be extremely gifted fantasizers, and they should be able to use their purported skills to consciously, intentionally, and purposively create dissociative parts. If this capacity constitutes a risk for developing pseudomemories of traumatizing events, DID patients should also engage in such confabulations rather than try to avoid these 'memories.'

The severity of an individual's tendency to engage in fantasy (i.e., fantasy proneness) can be estimated by the Creative Experiences Questionnaire (CEQ; Merckelbach et al., 2001). Huntjens et al. (2006) reported that female patients (n = 22) with major DID had higher CEQ scores than mentally healthy controls and nonclinical DID simulators. However, their score of $M = 9.2$ ($SD = 4.4$) was very similar to the mean for female college students. We examined fantasy proneness in a sample of 42 carefully diagnosed cases of major DID, and explored the contents of these patients' fantasies as well as their subjective motives (i.e., their final causes) to engage in fantasies (Nijenhuis & Reinders, 2012). The sample consisted of women who were in an assessment phase upon their referral to an outpatient trauma clinic, who were in outpatient treatment, who participated in research projects, or who had come in for a second opinion regarding their diagnosis.

Their CEQ score ($M = 9.83$, $SD = 5.25$) was very similar to the CEQ score of DID patients in Huntjens et al. (2006). It was lower than the mean CEQ score of amateur actors and actresses, regular visitors of exhibitions about paranormal issues, and fantasy role players, i.e., people who spend a great deal of their free time to re-enact great historical events (Merckelbach et al., 2001). These groups had means of 10.8 ($SD = 3.9$), 11.1 ($SD = 4.4$), and 13.2 ($SD = 4.4$), respectively. The mean score of undergraduate university students was 8.3 ($SD = 3.9$). The DID patients also had lower CEQ scores than patients with borderline personality disorder ($M = 11.8$, $SD = 5.1$; Merckelbach et al., 2005), a disorder that is not seen as caused by or primarily related to fantasy proneness. Furthermore, the mean CEQ score for the women with DID was not much higher than that for patients with schizophrenia ($M = 8.4$, $SD = 4.4$), and quite comparable to the level of fantasy proneness in a sample of female high school students, university students, and university employees ($M = 9.2$, $SD = 4.4$; Merckelbach et al., 2001). Figure 15.1 presents an overview of the results.

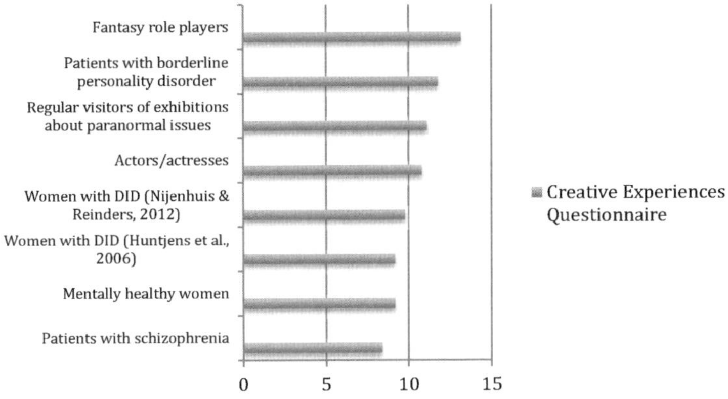

Figure 15.1. Fantasy proneness in different diagnostic groups.

Presenting these data we added that

> [c]onsidering the CEQ scores of patients with DID, it must be noted that some items of the instrument measure common dissociative symptoms in DID, such as 'feeling controlled by something or someone outside myself' and out of body experiences. One CEQ item inquires about having felt alone as a child. In fact, many DID patients report that they felt alone as a child in the context of emotional neglect and secretive traumatization. Endorsement of this item may thus be fact-based rather than fantasy-based. Still other items may measure post-traumatic stress symptoms. For example, item 16 can pertain to the reactivation of traumatic memories and item 18 to the reactivation of these memories following confrontation with conditioned trauma-stimuli. The CEQ scores of DID patients were artificially inflated in our sample because of these particular items (Nijenhuis & Reinders, 2012).

Fantasies of Women with Major DID: Content and Subjective Function

The typical fantasies of the women with major DID that we studied concerned living in a better, less neglectful, and less abusive personal world. All patients used their fantasies to cope with ongoing and recalled traumatization. Some reported imagining that the neglect and abuse were not real or that they were not touched by it. None reported fantasizing about traumatic incidents or voluntary engagement in thinking about these events. However, some had strong, albeit mistaken ideas that particular (alleged) perpetrators were still alive, that (alleged) perpetrators might be entering the therapy room anytime, that these individuals always know where they (i.e., the patients) are, etc. Whereas patients with DID may have difficulty telling fact from fiction in some regards, this difficulty does not necessarily pertain to all dissociative parts. For example, as EP but not as ANP may they believe that deceased perpetrators are about to get them, again and again.

In conclusion, women with DID are not abnormally fantasy prone. In fact, they are comparable to normal women in this regard. They generally try to avoid their traumatic memories as much as possible rather than fantasize traumatic events.

Dissociative+ Symptoms and Suggestibility

Proponents of SC- and F-models are concerned that dissociative+ phenomena and traumatic memories of patients with dissociative disorders are due to suggestion and suggestibility. For example, Giesbrecht et al. (2008) believe that patients with dissociative disorders are at serious risk of overreporting adverse events in response to self-report questionnaires of interviews that address such events. However, Dalenberg et al. (2012, p. 14) counter that "[i]t seems ill advised and potentially harmful to discourage patients from reporting trauma exposure due to fears of high rates of false report without strong evidence for this hypothesis." Their review of suggestibility studies shows that there is no convincing evidence for a close and consistent relationship between dissociation+ and suggestibility.

There are different kinds of suggestibility, such as individuals' tendency to respond to hypnotic suggestions or their tendency to yield to social pressure or misleading questions that a nonautobiographical or autobiographical event happened that in fact did not happen. Still other types of suggestibility are tendencies to misjudge the source of a real or alleged memory, and to inflate imagined or real (childhood) memories.

Hypnotizability. Responsiveness to hypnotic suggestions is one type of suggestibility. It is often hard to say what correlations between scores for 'hypnotizability' and 'dissociation' actually mean (Dell, 2009b). Current instruments to evaluate 'hypnotizability' may measure more than one feature, and the same concern applies to instruments measuring 'dissociation.'

Hypnotizability and Dissociation+. With these reservations in mind, correlations between dissociative+ phenomena and hypnotic performance were low to modest among adults (e.g., Silva & Kirsch, 1992). A more recent study found that the correlation between these two variables in general population samples is weak (Dienes et al., 2009). High dissociation+ (i.e., high DES) scores correlated with high scores on a scale that measures phenomenological experiences of deep trance. However, some college students with high DES scores had low hypnotizability scores as well as low scores for deep trance phenomena (Kumar, Marcano, & Pekala, 1996). High dissociation+, thus, does not necessarily imply high hypnotizability.

High hypnotizability, in turn, does not imply dissociation+ either. For example, in a sample of mentally disturbed children between the ages of 8 and 15, hypnotic and nonhypnotic suggestibility were positively correlated with fantasy proneness, but imaginative suggestibility and hypnotizability were not associated with dissociative behaviors that the parents observed and reported (Poulsen & Matthews, 2003). Also, some highly hypnotizable nonclinical adults have far higher scores for dissociation+ than others (Terhune, Cardeña, & Lindgren, 2010).

7 = Differences Among High Hypnotizable Individuals. Another issue to consider is that there is a remarkable heterogeneity among highly hypnotizable individuals (Dell, 2009; McConkey, Glisky, & Kihlstrom, 1989). Barrett (1992, 1996) distinguished between two groups: high fantasizers and high dissociators. Fantasizers easily passed standardized hypnotic suggestions without a preceding hypnotic induction, swiftly attained a deep hypnotic trance, and engaged in vivid and phenomenally realistic imagery. Upon waking from a hypnotic trance, they were calm and quickly reoriented themselves to reality. The fantasizers also frequently engaged in fantasy during their waking life. High dissociators did not readily enter a trance state, and did not experience their fantasies as completely realistic. These individuals also had difficulty remembering parts of their experiences during imagery and trance. Half of them did not recall the contents of their trance experience. Waking from the induced trance, dissociators blinked their eyes and appeared confused. During trance and daydreaming, they went blank rather than engaging in rich fantasies. This group reported childhood adverse events that had happened to them and that they recalled themselves, or that others had told them about. Some had a history of multiple burns and fractures for which their parents gave unlikely explanations. Many had recurring nightmares and a lack of memories before the age of 7 or 8. Their blank spells involved a flight into numbness and an effort to forget adverse events.

Hypnotizability and Dissociative Disorders. Some, but certainly not all, individuals with a dissociative disorder have elevated levels of hypnotizability. For example, studying sexually abused girls aged 6 to 15 years and matched controls, Putnam, Helmers, Horowitz, and Trickett (1995) found weak correlations between hypnotizability and clinical dissociation. There were no significant differences in hypnotizability between abused girls and controls, but abused girls had higher scores on a measure of clinical dissociation (i.e., the CDC), initially as well as on 1-year retest. Highly hypnotizable abused girls were significantly more dissociative than less hypnotizable girls, and girls who had been abused by multiple perpetrators and who had also been physically abused had higher levels of clinical dissociation. A small subgroup was high in both hypnotizability and dissociativity. The involved girls had been abused by multiple perpetrators, and their abuse had been of earlier onset. Individuals with hypnotic talents may thus have practiced and perfected their skills during and in the aftermath of chronic abuse and neglect to evade horrible bodily and emotional feelings, trauma memories, and associated dissociative parts.

A finding that could fit these hypotheses is that patients with DID were more hypnotizable than those with a different dissociative disorder (i.e., depersonalization disorder, dissociative amnesia) and nondiagnosed mentally healthy controls in one study (Dale, Berg, Elden, Odegard, & Holte, 2009). One limitation of this study is that the DID sample size was small. Whereas individuals with pseudoepilepsy – i.e., an ICD-10 dissociative disorder of movement and sensation – did not have high scores for hypnotizability (Goldstein, Drew, Mellers, Mitchell-O'Malley, & Oakley, 2000), patients with conversion disorder were more responsive to hypnotic suggestions than control patients (Roelofs et al.,

2002a). In the latter study there was also a positive correlation between hypnotizability and the number of conversion symptoms (i.e., sensorimotor dissociative symptoms). However, a review suggests that, although individuals with sensorimotor dissociative disorders tend to be more susceptible to hypnotic suggestions, very few of them are highly suggestible (Brown & Lewis-Fernandez, 2011).

In light of these findings, it cannot be concluded that dissociative symptoms and disorders are or even can be generally induced by hypnotic or hypnotic-like suggestions.

Hypnotizability in ASD and PTSD. Individuals with ASD had higher hypnotizability scores than those who had subclinical ASD or who did not develop ASD (Bryant, Guthrie, & Moulds, 2001). PTSD patients were also more hypnotizable than controls (e.g., Keuroghlian, Butler, Neri, & Spiegel, 2010). For example, Vietnam veterans with PTSD had higher scores for hypnotizability than patients with different other mental disorders and a control sample (Spiegel, Hunt, & Dondershine, 1988). Since hypnotizability was assessed after the adverse event, these kinds of studies do not allow the conclusion that high hypnotizability is a risk factor for ASD evolving into PTSD. To examine posttraumatic temporal relationships, Yard, DuHamel, and Galynker (2008) assessed hypnotizability at intake and after a brief treatment program. Whereas hypnotizability scores were generally stable over time, two thirds of participants with ASD responded differently at intake and after a brief treatment program. Increased hypnotizability scores at the second assessment were correlated with elevated PTSD avoidance scores. This association may indicate that some patients with PTSD use their hypnotic talent to avoid traumatic memories, which inhibits the integration of these memories and the associated EP(s).

Proponents of the SC- and F-models of dissociation and DID fear that highly hypnotizable individuals are prone to develop pseudomemories in response to suggestions. This concern may be unjustified in that highly hypnotizable and low hypnotizable simulating subjects were equally likely (47.83% and 64.29%, respectively) to report pseudomemories when tested for pseudomemories after instructions to awaken from the induced hypnotic trance (Lynn, Rhue, Myers, & Weekes, 1994). It has further been reported that hypnotizability and childhood adverse events are not significantly associated phenomena (Nash & Lynn, 1986; Nash, Lynn, & Givens, 1984). It thus seems that only some chronically traumatized are highly hypnotizable, and that high hypnotizability is not required for the development of a trauma-related dissociation of the personality.

Conclusion. In conclusion, dissociation+ and hypnotic suggestibility are weakly related constructs. Individuals with high scores for dissociation+ or with a complex dissociative disorder are not necessarily highly hypnotizable. Because individuals with ASD or PTSD may also be more susceptible to hypnotic suggestion, one must wonder why DID would be due to suggestion and would not, like ASD and PTSD, be a trauma-related condition. Whereas hypnotic suggestibility does not seem to be the efficient cause of dissociative+ phenomena and dissociative disorders, individuals with hypnotic talents may use and develop their disposition to cope with adverse events that have traumatized them. The tendency to use this talent might be proportional to the severity of these events and the lack of other ways of coping with these occurrences such as receiving and accepting social support.

Event Suggestibility

Dissociation+ is not consistently associated with nonautobiographical event suggestibility, and the estimated effect size over studies is very small (Dalenberg et al., 2012; Gudjonsson, 2003; Horselenberg et al., 2000). Moreover, individuals with delayed recall of traumatic memories did not commonly yield to an interrogator's pressure to accept a suggested nonautobiographical event as a personal memory. They had in fact *lower* scores on interrogator suggestibility than a comparison group of psychiatric patients who did not recall sexual abuse (Leavitt, 1997). The latter patients were also more at risk for altering memories to suggestive prompts.

As reviewed by Dalenberg et al. (2012), average weighted effect sizes regarding an association between dissociation+ and suggestibility are very small. Future studies would therefore better examine interactions between these two parameters and other variables such as acquiescence to false statements in relation to demand characteristics of the study and executive dysfunction.

Source Monitoring

There is no convincing evidence that source monitoring errors are strongly or uniquely associated with dissociation+. In these studies, individuals must commonly distinguish between competing sources of an alleged memory. For example, their task is to decide whether the 'memory' came from a picture they saw or a story they heard. Participants may also be instructed to read a list of words that are all related to a particular overarching category (e.g., 'dream' and 'nap' as related to the category of sleep-related words). They must thereafter decide whether they read a word that belongs to the same category, but that they in fact were not given to read (e.g., doze). It is studied to what degree participants err.

Individuals who had lived through documented adverse events generated more false recalls than nonexposed individuals (Zoellner, Foa, Brigidi, & Przeworski, 2000). The error rate seemed to be due to adverse events exposure, because it was the same for individuals with or without PTSD. However, this is not a consistent finding. For example, war-traumatized individuals with PTSD were more susceptible to memory errors than individuals who were also exposed to war, but who did not have PTSD (Brennen, Dybdahl, & Kapidzi, 2007). Regardless of whether false recall in these studies was attributable to PTSD or to adverse event exposure, it is clear that the participants had been exposed to real adverse events, and that their memory errors were not related to fabricated events (cf. Dalenberg et al., 2012). Memory errors in source-monitoring studies, thus, do not allow the conclusion that the participants fabricated memories of adverse events. These errors rather pertain to some to be identified effect of adverse event exposure and/or to the presence of a trauma-related disorder such as affective stimulus generalization. Moreover, the false memory effect has not been found in all studies. For example, in a study by Hauschildt, Peters, Jelinek, and Moritz (2011), the PTSD group neither generated higher rates of false memories nor expressed more confidence in errors. They rather showed inferior memory sensitivity. In still another study, false memories were related to depression, not to adverse event expose or PTSD (Jelinek, Hottenrott, Randjbar, Peters, & Moritz, 2009). According to TSDP, the presence, degree, and kind of memory errors might be in part related to the presence of an ANP or EP during the different phases of the experiment.

Imagination Inflation

The findings of these studies are inconclusive, and will therefore not be discussed here.

Overall Findings

In a review of the literature, Dalenberg et al. (2012) found an average weighted effect size between dissociation+ and various measures of suggestibility of 1%–3% of the variance. This very low figure does not match the strong claims of SC- and F-models of dissociation. Dalenberg et al. also warn that a differentiation must be made between false memories and acquiescence. They are also right in pointing out that the performance of traumatized individuals on suggestibility tests may be influenced by factors such as fear-based deference or distrust of authority. To reiterate, these kinds of influences may be different for different types of dissociative parts of the personality.

Delayed Memories of Lived Adverse Events

Hypothesis SC- and F-Models

Delayed memories of lived adverse events are generally pseudomemories or false memories.

Hypothesis T-Models

Delayed memories of lived adverse events are not more or less reliable than continuously available recollections of such events.

Hypothesis TSDP

The availability of a recollection of a lived adverse event depends in part on the activation of a traumatic memory-avoidant dissociative part of the personality (e.g., an ANP) and a dissociative part that is fixed in this memory (i.e., a fragile EP).

The evidence to date suggests that there are no differences regarding the accuracy of continuous and delayed memories of childhood adverse events (Geraerts et al., 2007; Dalenberg, 1996; Williams, 1995). This conclusion has been reached in studies with abused and nonabused, clinical and nonclinical participants as well as in experimental studies (Dalenberg, 2006).

Individuals who had spontaneously recalled abuse after a substantial delay were better at suppressing thoughts in an experimental setting than individuals who had never forgotten the abuse they lived (Geraerts, McNally, Jelicic, Merckelbach, & Raymaekers, 2008). They also had less rebounds of their thoughts they had been instructed to suppress. Whereas correlations do not prove causation, the findings are consistent with the idea that delayed recall might be related to an ability to suppress painful memories.

Sociocultural Influences

Hypotheses SC- and F-Models

DID is caused by sociocognitive- and sociocultural factors.

Hypothesis T-Models

DID is in some regards influenced by sociocognitive- and sociocultural factors.

Hypotheses TSDP

DID is in some regards influenced by sociocognitive- and sociocultural factors, but the disorder is not dynamically caused by them.

As applies to any mental disorder, some features of authentic dissociative disorders are influenced by sociocultural factors (Van der Hart et al., 2006). This does not mean that these factors satisfactorily explain these complex conditions (Gleaves, 1996). For example, if severe dissociative disorders were sociocultural phenomena, DID patients from different cultures should have very different presentations. There is no evidence for this hypothesis. To illustrate, Chinese patients with DID are characterized by the same dissociative and other symptoms as North American and European patients with the disorder (Ross, 2011; Ross et al., 2008; Yu et al., 2010). As Xiao et al. (2006) wrote,

> [p]athological dissociation can be detected readily among psychiatric outpatients in China but is much less common in the general population. Pathological dissociation is more frequent in more traumatized subsamples of the Chinese population. The findings are not consistent with the sociocognitive, contamination, or iatrogenic models of dissociative identity disorder

Chaturvedi et al. (2009) examined patterns of dissociative disorders among inpatients and outpatients attending a psychiatric hospital in India between 1999 and 2008. A total of

893 patients had been diagnosed with dissociative disorder. Dissociative motor disorder (43.3% outpatients, 37.7% inpatients) was the most common diagnosis, followed by dissociative convulsions (23% outpatients, 27.8% inpatients). Major DID was rarely diagnosed, but possession states were common. The DSM-5 (APA, 2013, p. 292) states that DID involves a "[d]isruption of identity characterized by two or more distinct personality states which may be described in some cultures as an experience of possession." Whereas possession states can relate to DID, these states may also be more benign part of spiritual practice.

Indeed, to the extent that spiritist mediums include possession states, it is important to mention that there are differences between Brazilian mediums and North American patients with DID (Moreira-Almeida et al., 2008). The mediums had better social adjustment, lower prevalence of mental disorders, lower use of mental health services, no use of antipsychotics, and lower prevalence of histories of physical or sexual childhood abuse sleepwalking, secondary features of DID, and symptoms of borderline personality. There are thus important differences between spirits that visit largely healthy individuals and dissociative parts of the personality that relate to adverse life events.

The association between dissociative+ symptoms and adverse events holds for different cultures. For example, the total score for the Korean version of the Childhood Trauma Questionnaire correlated with the DES-Taxon score among 163 nonpsychotic outpatients (Kim, Park, Yang, & Oh, 2011). Van Duijl, Cardeña and De Jong (2005) reported that dissociative amnesia and depersonalization are generally recognized and seen as the result of traumatic experiences, and are regarded as useful categories in Uganda. Dissociative fugue is comprehended as spirit possession and is related to other conditions such as alcoholic fugues and dementia in this country. Local healers interpreted DID as a possession trance disorder. Whereas some characteristics of the DSM-IV dissociative disorders are understood differently in Uganda – e.g., dissociative symptoms are commonly related to influences from deceased ancestors – the psychopathological features are not. The correlation of cognitive-emotional and sensorimotor dissociative symptoms in Ugandan patients with possession disorder and healthy controls was as high as in studies from Western countries (Van Duijl et al., 2010). The correlation of these symptoms and reported adverse events was also very strong, even though Uganda possession disorder (i.e., DID) is not understood as a trauma-related disorder in Uganda.

There is an extensive body of empirical data from Turkey showing that major and minor DID and sensorimotor dissociative disorders involve very similar dissociative symptoms as individuals with these disorders from Western countries (e.g., Sar et al., 2006, 2007a, 2007b; Tezcan et al., 2003; Yargic et al., 1998; Zoroglu, Sar, Tuzun, Tutkun, & Savas, 2002). These disorders were associated with reported adverse events, and dissociative+symptoms were strongly linked with sensorimotor dissociative symptoms.

Van Ommeren et al. (2001a, 2001b) documented the existence of dissociative disorders as well as an association of these disorders and adverse events in Bhutan. Compared with nontortured refugees, tortured refugees were more likely to report 12-month ICD-10

PTSD, persistent somatoform pain disorder, dissociative amnesia, and sensorimotor dissociative disorders. In terms of Western psychiatric constructs, refugees with medically unexplained symptoms had somatoform symptoms of both acute anxiety and dissociation. Some 60% of these individuals reported visual hallucinations, and 28% had auditory hallucinatory experiences. Case status was statistically predicted by recent loss, early loss, childhood trauma, and heart rate frequency.

Reviewing the literature, Brown and Lewis-Fernandez (2011) concluded that ICD-10 dissociative stupor/convulsions (psychogenic nonepileptic seizures and loss of consciousness) and dissociative motor symptoms are the most common sensorimotor dissociative disorders across cultures. These disorders are often associated with adverse events, and there are also cultural similarities regarding comorbidity and other features. These include female preponderance, demographic profiles associated with psychiatric and personality disturbance as well as psychosocial complaints. These commonalities do not fit the idea that sensorimotor dissociative disorders are efficiently caused by suggestion and suggestibility.

In this context, it can also be remarked that, at the time of the development of the SDQ-20, it was not generally known, described, or acknowledged that sensorimotor dissociative symptoms are very characteristic of dissociative disorders (Nijenhuis et al., 1996, 1999). By the 1980s and 1990s the findings of elaborate 19th-century clinical studies on sensorimotor dissociative symptoms had generally become covered under a thick layer of dust. How could patients with dissociative disorders have known that they 'should' have analgesia, various anesthesias, stiffening and paralysis of (parts of) their body, or difficulty to speak? How could they have fantasized these symptoms? And how could therapists have suggested these symptoms? In my own case, how could I have suggested these symptoms to the first DID patients I met in the early 1980s when I did not know anything about cognitive-emotional and sensorimotor dissociative symptoms or, for that matter, traumatization? And if analgesia were not an authentic phenomenon but a mere fantasy, how could patients with dissociative disorders have baffled physicians with respect to their ability to endure painful medical procedures without the use of anesthetics?

In conclusion, there is substantial evidence that dissociative disorders around the globe involve very similar presentations and correlates, including actual and reported adverse events. DID may present as possession states, but these states may also be a part of spiritual practice.

False Positives

It is possible to fake some of the subjective features of DID (Brand, McNary, Loewenstein, Kolos, & Barr, 2006). False-positive cases of DID do exist, but there are differences between individuals with false and authentic DID (Draijer & Boon, 1999). Some individuals imitate authentic cases, but their presentation nonetheless differs from authentic cases. For example, false-positive cases tend to present their 'DID' eagerly and give textbook examples of dissociative amnesia and other dissociative phenomena. Some false-positive cases are in part due to inadequate treatment. Careful adherence to the guidelines for the assessment and treatment of DID and solid training in these disciplines are therefore mandatory. It should be obvious that the existence of false-positive cases does not allow the conclusion that authentic DID does not exist.

Adherence to these guidelines is also important with respect to the physical (i.e., third-person) judgment of the validity of recollected adverse events. Clinicians should not reflexively believe or reject these in the absence of proof. As applies to any crucial continuous or delayed memory, they should rather examine the memory from a variety of perspectives in close collaboration with the patient. The patient must eventually decide if or to what degree the memory reflects real events. In Volume III of this series, I describe how therapists can responsibly react to reported memories of traumatic events.

Dissociation+, Elapse of Time, and Treatment

Hypotheses SC-and F-Models

Dissociative+ symptoms increase over time as a result of the development of fantasized dissociative parts of the personality and associated pseudomemories. This development is dependent on fantasy proneness as well as on sociocognitive and sociocultural efficient causes, and final causes such as the wish to be special or to be seen more. Particularly phase-oriented treatment of dissociative disorders and traumatic memories lead to an increase of dissociative symptoms.

Hypothesis of T-Models

Dissociative+ reactions during and following an adverse event dissipate over time as affected individuals integrate their traumatic experiences. Phase-oriented treatment of dissociative disorders and traumatic memories leads to a decrease of dissociative symptoms. However, the reported and actual symptoms initially increase when the individual becomes more consciously aware of the symptoms and the dissociative parts, and as he or she is therapeutically exposed to trauma-related cues. The best way to proceed is to balance the individual's developing integrative capacity and motivation to integrate, and the stress-level that exposure to trauma-related cues entails. Therapeutic efforts to integrate traumatic memories should not be pursued when there is reasonable doubt regarding the authenticity of the involved events.

More Specific TSDP-Based Hypotheses

Dissociative phenomena are resolved with the (re)integration of the personality and traumatic memories associated with EPs. This integration more specifically involves a (re)integration of one or more ANPs and one or more EPs, thus involves the resolution of the formal cause of the disorder. The final cause of this integrative tendency is the desire to function more efficiently in life.

Time and Social Support: Short-Term Effects

For most individuals, dissociative+ reactions that emerged during or briefly after an adverse event dissipate over time and without treatment (Cardeña & Spiegel, 1993; Carlson et al., 2011; Feeny, Zoellner, Fitzgibbons, & Foa, 2000). This also applies to a degree of amnesia (Mechanic, Resick, & Griffin, 1998). The injury of the involved individuals was apparently not so deep that they were unable or unwilling to integrate the traumatizing event into their story, that is, into their personality. They may also have received adequate social support to recover, in that a lack of social support is a predictor of trauma-related pathology following a variety of adverse events (e.g., Chivers-Wilson, 2006; Dimitry, 2013; Heron-Delaney, Kenardy, Charlton, & Matsuoka, 2013).

As reviewed by Holt, Buckley, and Whelan (2008), children and adolescents living with domestic violence are at risk of experiencing emotional, physical, and sexual abuse. The risk of their developing emotional and behavioral problems is also increased, as is the risk that their being exposed to other adversities in their lives. However, in particular a strong relationship with and attachment to a caring adult – usually the mother – can mitigate the injurious impact of these adverse events. To reiterate, in a sample of children aged between 8 to 18 years who experienced accidental injury, youths in more cohesive family environments evidenced decreased symptoms of dissociation after six weeks (Nugent et al., 2011).

The Short-Term Effects of Exposure to Trauma-Related Cues

In addition to what was already said with regard to peritraumatic dissociation+, exposing traumatized individuals to trauma-related cues may cause an increase of dissociative+ symptoms in experimental settings (Lanius et al., 2005; Reinders et al., 2006; Zoellner, Sacks, & Foa, 2007). Special forces soldiers also reported an increase of dissociative+ reactions in relation to a highly stressful survival training (Morgan et al., 2001).

Emergent Treatment Effects

According to TSDP, ASD and PTSD constitute dissociative disorders. The treatment of these conditions is typically geared toward the integration of traumatic memories. This is evident from the well-known and evaluated treatment methods and protocols (e.g., EMDR, cognitive behavioral exposure therapy). When the patient's integrative capacity is insufficient to achieve the goal of integrating traumatic memories, clinicians first aim to increase this capacity, including the development of adaptive affect regulation skills. There is thus major overlap between phase-oriented treatment of complex PTSD (Cloitre et al.,

2011; Ford, Courtois, Steele, Van der Hart, & Nijenhuis, 2005; Landes et al., 2013) and complex dissociative disorders (Van der Hart et al., 2006). This commonality is not accidental, but reflects the shared material, efficient, formal, and final causation of these closely related disorders.

Some clinicians disregard dissociative parts, whereas others more aggressively discourage or forbid patients to talk about or show them. These clinicians commonly tell the patients that these dissociative parts and symptoms are 'not real' or 'imaginary' and often concern iatrogenic constructions. There is no clinical or scientific evidence that treatment that does not acknowledge or include the different dissociative parts of the personality causes symptomatic improvements, leads to the integration of dissociative parts, or resolves the patients' distorted memories. In fact, many patients experienced that these kinds of treatment were not helpful to them or were detrimental to their condition. Further, it is also known that patients with complex dissociative disorders have a suboptimal response to standard exposure-based treatments for PTSD disorder as well as high levels of attrition from treatment (Brand et al., 2012).

In contrast, there is clinical evidence that treatments that specifically focus on the patients' integrative challenges and attachment disruptions are often effective (e.g., Ellason & Ross, 1997; Hirakata, 2009; Kluft, 1984b, 1996; Myrick et al., 2012; Pearlman & Courtois, 2005; Putnam, 1992, 1993, 1997; Ross, 1997; Van der Hart et al., 2006). Emergent systematic treatment effectiveness studies support these collective clinical findings. Patients with complex dissociative disorders who receive specialized treatment addressing their dissociative symptoms and traumatic memories show improved functioning and reduced symptoms (Brand et al., 2009a; Brand et al., 2012). This treatment is associated with decreased symptoms of dissociation+, depression, PTSD, distress, and suicidality (Brand et al., 2009a). Patients with dissociative disorder who have integrated their dissociated parts have reduced symptomatology compared with those who have not integrated. The effect sizes, based on pre/post measures, are in the medium to large range across studies and are comparable to pre/post effect sizes in treatment studies of complex PTSD. The research to date primarily involved naturalistic and open trials, and included methodological limitations such as regression to the mean, limited sample sizes, and nonrandomized research designs. Still, its findings are in full consonance with collective clinical findings.

Using a prospective, naturalistic design, Brand and Stadnik (2013) collected reports of symptoms from a sample of therapists and their patients diagnosed with major and minor DID who participated in the Treatment Outcome of Patients with Dissociative Disorders study (TOP-DD). The patients completed surveys upon entering the study and at a 30-month follow-up. Dissociative+ symptoms, including amnesia, depersonalization/derealization, and absorption were at intake related to initial levels of PTSD and general distress. Changes in dissociative+ symptoms at follow-up were related to changes in PTSD and general distress.

When controlling for length of time for follow-up, length of time practicing therapy, and length of time treating dissociative patients, dissociative+ symptoms at intake were a significant predictor of change in dissociative+ symptoms at follow-up. The results of the study indicate that a reduction in dissociative+ symptoms in patients with major and minor DID is associated with reductions in the overall severity of dissociative+, posttraumatic stress, and distress symptoms. The patients who were enrolled in the TOP-DD also had less destructive behaviors and symptomatology at follow-up (Myrick et al., 2012). Another finding was that young patients (18–30 years) were initially more impaired than older adult patients, but that their treatment progressed at a faster pace.

Myrick et al. (2013) examined the rates of revictimization and victimization of others using therapist-DD patient pairs from the TOP-DD study. They also considered the role of revictimization and life stressors among patients who greatly improved or worsened from enrollment in the study to follow-up after 30 months of treatment. According to the therapists, sexual (3.5%–7.0%) and physical revictimization (4.1%–7.1%) in the previous 6 months were high in the overall TOP-DD sample. Emotional revictimization was particularly high (29%-36%). Still, revictimization tended to decrease during the period of measurement. The therapists reported that more than a quarter of the patients who were revictimized were also occasionally emotionally or physically abusive to others. The patients more often reported sudden improvement in symptoms than sudden worsening at one or more time points. Patients who experienced sudden improvements had fewer revictimizations and stressors overall than patients who worsened. These findings suggest that revictimization and/or stressors may contribute to worsening in treatment, which is not all surprising, of course.

Merskey (1992) asserted that dissociative symptoms may be a misinterpretation of bipolar mood disorder. Upon examining the issue, we found that, in contrast to minor and major DID, bipolar mood disorder is not associated with high DES and SDQ-20 scores (Nijenhuis et al., 1997a). We also documented that only 9.8% (DES) and 4% (SDQ-5; Nijenhuis et al., 1997b) of patients with bipolar mood disorder obtained scores beyond the cutoff in the screening for dissociative disorders. The results clearly contradict Merskey's hypothesis. While individuals with complex dissociative disorders reported extreme dissociative+ symptoms, individuals with bipolar mood disorder hardly experienced these.

Merskey (1997) replied that we had misinterpreted the natural phenomena of bipolar mood disorder. He also claimed that the therapists had educated suggestible patients with bipolar mood disorder into producing what we regard as dissociative states. We compared unindoctrinated subjects with others whom we considered to be dissociative. We rebutted that his assumptions were incorrect (Nijenhuis et al., 1998e). For the patients with dissociative disorders we had two groups: One completed the SDQ-20 prior to the administration of the SCID-D and the diagnosis of minor or major DID, the other after assessment and during the phase-oriented treatment of their dissociative disorder. According to Merskey, the latter group should have more dissociative symptoms than the first. Yet the results did not confirm this presumption: Patients from the first group had higher SDQ-20 scores than patients who were aware of their psychiatric status and who were exposed to therapists who in Merskey's view indoctrinated them. This finding not just contradicts the idea that dissociative symptoms and disorders are iatrogenic phenomena;

it also indicates that phase-oriented treatment of dissociative disorders tends to reduce sensorimotor dissociative symptoms.

Preliminary Conclusion

The studies that have been considered so far do not provide convincing empirical evidence for the various hypotheses of the SC- and F-models of dissociative symptoms and disorders. To the extent that the involved hypotheses of these models differ from the hypotheses of trauma models of dissociative symptoms and disorders, they have not been confirmed by studies with general population and clinical samples. A most serious problem of SC- and F-models of DID is that supporters of these persuasions did not test their hypotheses in samples with DID patients.

In contrast, the empirical evidence presented in this chapter is generally consistent with or supportive of T-models and TSDP. There is also supportive evidence for T-models and specifically for TSDP from functional and structural biopsychosocial studies of DID, whereas the findings of these studies are at odds with SC-and F-models. This evidence is included in the next three chapters.

Chapter 16

Dissociation of the Personality in a Biopsychosocial Perspective

The brain may be regarded as a kind of parasite of the organism, a pensioner, as it were, who dwells with the body.
Arthur Schopenhauer

Personality is only ripe when a man has made the truth his own.
Søren Kierkegaard

In Chapter 12, personality was primarily defined as *a more or less integrated organization of assorted dynamic systems.* It was added that *the organization as a whole as well as its composing systems encompass biological, psychological, and psychosocial attributes.* In consonance with this definition and its philosophical monistic foundation, different prototypes of Janet's "dissociative subsystems of ideas and functions that constitute," which we refer to as *dissociative conscious and self-conscious subsystems* or parts of the personality, should include their own physiological and neurophysiological features.

Let us recall that, according to TSDP, (self-)conscious dissociative parts of the personality are comprehended as systems that are insufficiently integrated, but nonetheless embedded in individuals' whole personality as a higher-order system. Personality does not involve an isolated system though, but it is *an intrinsic component of the individual's organism-environment system.* This even higher-order system *is historical and ever-evolving within limits.* And it was stated that *this organism-environment system determines the individual's characteristic mental and behavioral actions.* The particular organization of an individual's personality involves its *formal cause.* While formal causation is obviously important, knowing this organization does not suffice to understand, assist, and change dissociative parts. To achieve these scientific and clinical goals, it is crucial to grasp what the different dissociative parts wish to achieve. The definition of personality therefore includes the statement that *the conjoint wills that typify the component systems are the personality's final causes.* In this context *the material and efficient causes* of the different prototypical dissociative parts and the dissociative personality as a whole environmentally embedded system can be studied. That is, it should not be overlooked or ignored that the involved material and efficient causes are intermediates.

Criteria for Conscious and Self-Conscious Dissociative Subsystems or Parts of the Personality

What kind of subsystems are ANP, fragile EP, and controlling EP? It seems that there are at least five criteria that can be formulated:

1) What stands out is that, once activated, dissociative parts do not engage in random actions and commonly remain present for at least some period of time (in exceptional situations, they can very rapid alternate, a phenomenon known as 'revolving door switching'). These subsystems are, thus, *self-organizing and self-stabilizing within windows of homeostasis, time, and context* to control and integrate all the rather coherent complexes of biopsychosocial phenomena that they exhibit. This raises the question what drives this self-organization and self-stabilization.
2) Given the existence of several prototypical dissociative parts in dissociative disorders, dissociative subsystems of the personality do not seem to be random, coincidental constructions. ANPs primarily engage in essential tasks of daily life such as reproduction, attachment, caretaking, and socialization, and avoidance of traumatic memories that support focus on daily life issues. In contrast, fragile EPs foremost display basic defensive and emotional reactions to the (perceived) threat on which they seem to be fixated. Controlling EPs consistently seek power; they hunger to have a major influence on their fate. These are essential biopsychosocial functions we share with other mammals, so that it seems likely that dissociative parts are *mediated by basic, functional systems that mammals have developed in the course of evolution.*
3) Whatever systems strongly influence dissociative parts, they should be *very susceptible to classical conditioning*, because EP and ANP strongly respond to classically conditioned threat cues.
4) ANP, fragile EPs and controlling EPs exhibit both invariant and idiosyncratic variations. The systems that affect them should therefore not just provide dissociative parts with some stable characteristics, but they should also *allow for case-dependent variation.*
5) Finally, these influential systems should be *available early in life*, since dissociative disorders can manifest from a very early age. The personality of patients with DID who were traumatized from a very young age may not even have been able to develop a coherent and cohesive personality. Nonetheless they do develop prototypical ANPs, fragile EPs, and controlling EPs.

To address the question of what systems within the personality mediate the functioning of ANP and EP, we would like to discuss the concept of 'personality' and explore whether personality entails certain systems that meet the five criteria.

The Study of Personality

Many authors have proposed that an individual's personality involves a set of distinctive psychological traits, that is, psychological characteristics relatively invariant across contexts such as mental states and environmental situations. More specifically, these traits concern features known as an individual's *temperament*. Temperament indicates affective qualities of an individual's functioning and denotes, for example, to what extent an individual is generally cheerful, optimistic, sad, fearful, or angry; that individual's common interest in exploring the social and material environment, and how responsible that person usually feels for his or her actions.

The study of personality aims to assess the range of psychological traits that distinguish among different individuals. As Davis, Panksepp, and Normansell (2003, p. 57) note, "there is no agreement whether personality should be studied without any theoretical preconceptions or whether theoretical views of human nature are essential to identify the most important psychological dimensions that need to be evaluated." For example, the currently popular Five-Factor Model that includes Neuroticism – also described as Emotional Stability – Extraversion, Openness to Experience, Agreeableness, and Conscientiousness, was derived empirically without a priori theorizing (Hofstee, De Raad, & Goldberg, 1992).

This radical positivistic approach has its drawbacks. In a meta-analytic study of the Five-Factor Model and personality disorder empirical literature, Saulsman and Page (2004, p. 1080) conclude that "a chief factor limiting the progress of [research of the nature of trait maladaptivity] is that the Five-Factor Model is a descriptive account of personality structure, and it does not reveal how personality traits are related to specific behaviors (Benjamin, 1994)." Progress in the study of personality, Saulsman and Page suggest, "requires seeking guidance from existing theories and hypotheses of personality dynamics that complement the Five-Factor Model" (p. 1081).

What theories seem particularly worthwhile to extending our understanding of personality? More specifically, what psychophysical systems would personality entail? McCrae and Costa (1996) suggested that the Five-Factor Model represents 'genotypic' personality traits. Consistent with this position, various authors demonstrated a genetic basis for these factors (Cattell, 1986; Eysenck, 1990; Loehlin, 1992; Pedersen, Plomin, McClearn, & Friberg, 1988; Viken, Rose, Kaprio, & Kowkenvuo, 1994). According to Cattell (1986), the 'source' traits of personality have physiological roots, and other studies also suggest that biological factors rather than social ones predominantly determine personality traits (Bouchard & Loehlin, 2001; Lucas, Diener, Suh, Shao, & Grob, 2000).

Important as it is, the role of biology for personality must not be overstated. First, genetic and developmental processes produce phenotypic attributes jointly (Heyes, 2003; Mayr, 1974). As Heyes (2003) notes,

> [t]he information obtained through natural selection and stored in the genotype cannot produce a phenotype without developmental [i.e., ontogenetic] processes of some kind, and de-

> velopment is not always tightly genetically constrained or canalized (Waddington, 1959) such that it does all and only what natural selection "desires." Development can produce outcomes, some of them adaptive, that were not anticipated (not specifically favored) by natural selection, and these outcomes may be said to have an ontogenetic source (Campbell, 1974; Karmiloff-Smith, 1998).

Animal studies demonstrated that major stress can completely and permanently alter the phenotypic expression of an animal's genotype (Cools & Ellenbroek, 2002). Thus, an animal of a breed that is extraverted by nature can become introverted for life after major traumatization. On a more general plane, there is mounting evidence that emotional neglect and abuse can significantly or even dramatically affect neurobiological (neurogenesis, neuron migration and differentiation, apoptosis, arborization, synaptogenesis, synaptic sculpting, and myelination) and psychological development, relative to age/developmental windows (Perry, 2002). Genes are required for this development as well as macro- and microenvironmental stimulation. Thus, development is both gene-dependent and user-dependent.

Genetic Factors in Personality

The heritable component of personality is associated with variations in multiple alleles and cannot be attributed to a single gene (Livesley & Jang, 2000). It is nonetheless striking that almost every personality dimension studied has been found to have a heritable component, with genetic factors accounting for nearly half the variance on every trait (Plomin, DeFries, McClearn, & Rutter, 1997). Especially adoption studies and twin research have contributed to this conclusion (Kendler, Neale, Kessler, Heath, & Eaves, 1993). Adoption studies (Plomin et al., 1997) as well as studies of twins separated at birth (Tellegen et al., 1988) confirm the heritability of personality traits. It therefore seems justified to conclude that individual differences in personality and temperament have a strong basis in heredity.

Associations between personality traits and genetic variations derive from many different genes and are therefore measurable as quantitative trait loci. But, thus far, this line of investigation has been disappointing. Promising earlier reports (e.g., Lesch et al., 1996) could not be consistently replicated (Gelernter, Kranzler, & Lacobelle, 1998). The main reason is that single alleles account for only a small percentage of the variance on any trait. These studies also suffer from the lack of a precise phenotype for personality traits. The presence of a genetic component in personality also implies that traits are linked to biological markers, but research in this area is at an early stage. Thus far, the strongest finding has been a strong relationship, established in clinical populations, between low levels of central serotonin activity and impulsivity.

Gene-Environment Interaction

The other half of the variance in personality derives from the environment. As recent studies show, environmental factors do not occur in isolation; there exists a gene-environment interaction. Genetic factors may also contribute to the vulnerability for environmental events, and genetic factors also appear to contribute to personality characteristics, which may influence the person's risk for entering into potentially hazardous situations (Jang, Stein, Taylor, Asmundson, & Livesley, 2003). Maltreatment at a young age, although causally involved in predicting either PTSD, DID, or antisocial behavior increases the likelihood of different subtypes of psychopathology even more when a certain genetic or biological predisposition is present (Raine, 2002a, 2002b).

In a prospective study of male children it was found that a functional polymorphism of the gene encoding for monoamine-oxidase-A (MAO-A plays a role in the enzymatic degradation of noradrenalin and serotonin) predicted the occurrence of antisocial behavior only if the children had been maltreated (Caspi et al., 2002). This study shows that a specific genotype (low activity of the MAO-A gene) can influence children's sensitivity and behavioral response toward environmental events. In addition, a polymorphism of the gene for the 5-HT transporter, which determines the availability of serotonin in the synaptic cleft (e.g., in the amygdala) influences the activity of the amygdala (leading to greater activity of the amygdala) when confronted with fearful faces (Hariri et al., 2002). In short, subjects with the short allele (leading to more serotonin in the amygdala) are more prone to anxiety and to feeling threatened even in nonthreatening situations, which may lead to a tendency toward dysfunctional sociability.

The implication of these findings is that our sensitivity for, and interpretation of, environmental events do not occur in a cognitive-emotional vacuum but can be modified by genetic and biological factors.

Personality and Action Systems

People's personality manifests itself in, and can only be inferred from, their predominant affectively charged mental and behavioral actions. Hence, their personality is theoretically perhaps best analyzed in terms of the (constellation of) biopsychosocial systems that essentially mediate their actions. Many human mental and behavioral actions constitute manifestations of innate, but experience-dependent and in many cases maturation-dependent will systems that are founded in primitive subcortical neural systems that we share with many other creatures, and that in us have become linked with higher cortical functions (Damasio et al., 2000; Lang, 1995; Lang, Davis, & Ohman, 2000; Panksepp, 1998, 2003; Panksepp & Biven, 2012). Defense, attachment of offspring to parents, parental attachment to and care for offspring, procreation, sociability, energy management, exploration, and play constitute the major action systems (Panksepp, 1998), and each of these may encompass a range of subsystems (e.g., Fanselow & Lester, 1988). Panksepp argued that basic emotional processes arise from distinct psychobiological systems that reflect coherent integrative processes of the nervous system (cf. Ciompi, 1991). In his view, the essence of emotionality is organized on subcortical and precognitive levels, and each of the action systems involves specific patterns of activation of neural networks and associated neurochemical activity in the brain. Lang (1995) suggests that emotions are driven by two major evolutionarily derived will systems (i.e., appetitive and aversive subcortical circuits that mediate reactions to primary reinforcers). Carver, Sutton, and Scheier (2000) similarly propose that personality involves the approach of rewarding social and material resources, and escape from and avoidance of threat.

Panksepp and colleagues (Davis et al., 2003, p. 58) assert that "optimal personality evaluation should be based on empirically based viewpoints that attempt to carve personality along the lines of emerging brain systems that help generate the relevant psychological attributes." In their original study, Davis et al. hypothesized that a great deal of variability of personality relates to the strengths and weaknesses found in six major action systems, three of which involve appetitive, approach action systems: Play (playing games with physical contact, making jokes, laughing, expressing joy and happiness), Seek (feeling curious, feeling like exploring, seeking solutions for problems and puzzles, positively anticipating new experiences), and Care (nurturing, being drawn to young children and pets, feeling softhearted toward people and animals in need, feeling empathy, liking to care for the sick, feeling affection for and liking to care for others, liking to be needed by others). Three other action systems pertain to aversion-related, avoidance/escape action tendencies: Fear (feeling anxious or tense, worrying, struggling with decisions, ruminating about past decisions and statements, losing sleep, not typically being courageous), Anger (feeling hotheaded, being easily irritated and frustrated leading to anger, expressing anger verbally or physically, and remaining angry for long periods), and Sadness (feeling lonely, crying frequently, thinking about loved ones and past relationships, and feeling distress when not with loved ones). Sadness thus denotes frustrated attachment needs.

Davis et al. (2003) added a seventh category they described as Spirituality, because of their interest in the highest human emotions. I am not aware of psychobiological evidence for Spirituality (feeling "connected" to humanity and creation as a whole, feeling a sense of "oneness" with creation, striving for inner peace and harmony, searching for meaning in life) as an action system. The essential qualities of religious experience include a direct sensory awareness of some higher power, but also a feeling of having touched the ultimate ground of reality and the sense of the incommunicability of the experience of unity. As all human experience is brain-related, the same should be true for these experiences. Available evidence indicates that the dorsolateral prefrontal, dorsomedial frontal, and medial parietal cortices play a role in religious experiences (Azari et al., 2001). Others have suggested that religious experience is associated with the limbic system including the temporal lobe (for review see Saver & Rabin, 1997).

Davis et al. (2003) found strong relationships between scales measuring approach and avoidance/escape will systems and the Big Five. The most robust correlations were Extraversion with Play, Agreeableness with Care and inversely with Anger, Openness to Experience with Seek, and Emotional Stability was inversely associated with the three aversive emotions. Conscientiousness was more weakly correlated with these emotions. Spirituality only correlated (positively) with the Caring and Seeking scales. Davis et al. concluded that each of the six will systems is closely related to at least one of the Big Five personality factors, and that each of the action systems may form a substantial part of the adult five-factor personality structure.

The avoidance/escape action systems (Fear, Sadness, and Anger) were moderately to strongly correlated, and loaded on one factor "low emotional stability." With regard to these findings, Davis et al. (2003) suggested that "negative affect" may emerge as a superordinate personality factor. I speculate that this factor could represent a complex defense system grounded in primitive subcortical brain structures, which we share with many other species. It would include hypervigilance, startle, flight, freeze, tonic immobility (Fear), fight (Anger), and attachment cry (Sadness).

Davis et al. (2003) do not claim that the action systems they studied provide a comprehensive view of human personality. They rather argue that these ancient psychobiological action systems involve defensible core elements of emotional experience and may serve as a foundation for many "higher" mental attributes and faculties. They also point out that there may be other will systems in the human brain and in some other mammals, such as those for dominance, guilt, greed, disgust, and shame. Yet Davis et al. feel that current neurobiological evidence is insufficient to include these potential factors, and they believe that many of those feelings are derived largely through social learning.

However, it is questionable whether the emotion of disgust is acquired solely through social learning. The most direct experience of disgust is related to taste aversion, which immediately leads to a characteristic facial expression and sometimes a vomiting response. The second type relates to our animal origin and is disgust of bodily products such as saliva and excretions. Finally, disgust may play a role in moral and legal judgments (Nussbaum, 2004). The emotion of disgust (the literal meaning of disgust is: bad taste) is based on the role that objects or events can be potential sources of contamination and transmission of disease (Rozin, Lowery, & Ebert, 1994). Fear and disgust may serve different evolutionary purposes: fear as part of the appraisal of danger (LeDoux, 1996), and disgust to deal with the risk of contamination and disease (Rozin et al.). Moreover, the importance of basic emotions such as disgust in psychiatry prompted some authors to speak of disgust as the "forgotten emotion" (Phillips, Senior, Fahy, & David, 1998).

Using fMRI and electrophysiological techniques, several studies showed that facial expressions of fear activated the amygdala, whereas expressed disgust specifically activated the anterior insula, together with the medial frontal cortex, thalamus, and putamen (Krolak-Salmon et al., 2003; Phillips et al., 1997; Schienle et al., 2002; Wicker et al., 2003). Another study showed that facial expressions of disgust activated the anterior insula (and caudate and putamen), whereas vocal expression of disgust did not (Phillips et al., 1998). This latter finding differs from studies of other groups who documented that the neural system for the recognition of disgust can recognize signals of disgust from different sensory modalities (Lavenu, Pasquier, Lebert, Petit, & Van der Linden, 1999). Finally, it appears that it is indeed the same sectors of the insula responding to the recognition of disgust in others and in the participants' own experience of disgust (Wicker et al., 2003), supporting the idea that our brain transforms the sight of someone else's facial expression of disgust into our own experience of disgust (Gallese, Keysers, & Rizolatti, 2004). It is conceivable, but at present unknown, whether DID patients who have been sexually abused during childhood show greater signs of disgust and insula activation than DID patients who suffered from physical abuse. I present evidence later in this chapter that patients with major DID tend to experience disgust when they listen to a personal trauma script as EP, but not as ANP, and that this emotion is associated with potent insula and caudate activation. The scripts pertained to a range of traumatic experiences, including sexual and physical abuse.

Davis et al. (2003) did not include other ancient action systems in their study, notably Reproduction/Lust, Energy Management, and Safety Seeking. However, it can be speculated that greed for food and other resources could relate to extremes of energy management and safety-seeking (e.g., collecting too much food, overeating; collecting/buying/possessing too many objects [e.g., for shelter, i.e., a house too big]). Sexual predation could involve a mixture of action tendencies of dominance and sexual lust, and oftentimes anger. It seems worthwhile to include these tendencies in future research of personality.

In sum, personality crucially involves two major groups of evolutionarily derived but maturation-dependent action systems: those for approach of rewarding social and material resources and those for escape/avoidance of perceived threat. More specifically, there is an approach regarding positive social and environmental rewards (Play, Seek, Care), and a fear-related approach of safety cues (Care in the form of seeking reunion with a caretaker when feeling threatened). And there is active physical withdrawal from real or perceived threat or resistance (Anger/Fight) as well as physically passive defense in the form of total submission, which is characterized by mental escape and avoidance.

Dissociative Parts and Action Systems

As discussed before, TSDP holds that ANP and EP are essentially mediated by (constellations of) these two basic groups of will systems. Action systems closely meet the five criteria of dissociative parts of the personality previously described. They are organizational, evolutionarily derived, functional, flexible within limits, and inborn but epigenetic. Action systems are functional in that they activate various types of affective feelings, which help identify events in the world which are either biologically useful or harmful, and generate adaptive responses to many life-challenging circumstances. Although the resulting behavior is unconditionally summoned by the appropriate cues, approach and avoidance are adaptable to prevailing environmental conditions within limits, rather than being mere inflexible responses. For example, flight involves not just running away from threat, but running that is adapted to the current situation in form, direction, and duration. Thus, threat as an unconditional stimulus does not evoke a single unconditional response, but an integrated series of biopsychosocial responses that can be adapted to prevailing external and internal conditions within limits.

Action systems are epigenetic, that is, the result of influences by nature and nurture. Experiences, especially early ones, can change the fine details of the brain forever. These experiences include learning associations between events. Action systems are susceptible to classical conditioning, for instance, learning that some previously neutral events predict or refer to unconditioned stimuli. These conditioned stimuli tend to reactivate a memory of the unconditioned stimuli, and this association generates action tendencies described as conditioned responses. The conditioned response that an individual develops when perceiving a conditioned stimulus may, but need not, be identical or even similar to the original unconditioned response to the unconditioned stimulus. For example, the original, unconditioned response may have been flight, whereas the conditioned response may be freezing. However, the emitted response still belongs to a particular category of will systems – in the example, defense. Classical conditioning allows in many cases for some flexibility of response, which allows for adaptation to changeable internal and external conditions.

Subsystems of the action system of defense are of particular interest in trauma-related dissociation because of exposure to threat. Each defensive subsystem controls a pattern of biopsychosocial reactions that is adapted to meet a particular degree of threat imminence (Fanselow & Lester, 1988). This degree of imminence can be expressed in terms of the time and space that separate the subject from the threat (i.e., the distance between predator and prey) as well as in terms of an evaluation of the defensive abilities of the subject (e.g., the subject's psychosocial influence and physical force). *Pre-encounter defense* involves an apprehensive state with increased arousal, potentiated startle response, interruption of "normal life" behaviors, and nearly exclusive attentional focus on the potential threat. *Postencounter defense* includes several subsystems: flight, freezing with associated analgesia, and fight. *Poststrike defense* involves tonic immobility and bodily as well as emotional anesthesia. Upon survival, a *recuperative subsystem* is activated which allows for a return of affective awareness and body sensations (e.g., pain, fatigue), and which drives wound care and rest through social isolation as well as sleep. Upon recovery, there will be a reactivation of (sub)systems that control daily life interests such as consumption of food, reproduction, and taking care of offspring.

EP: Primarily Mediated by Actions Systems of Mammalian Defense and Attachment Cry

According to TSDP and as discussed above, EPs are primarily, but not exclusively, manifestations of the action system that mediates defense in the face of threat – particularly threat to the integrity of the body by a person – and potentially also of the will system that controls separation panic in relation to caretakers. Both systems serve survival interests and strongly influence the mental and physical experiences and actions of the EP. While EPs essentially rely on evolutionarily derived will systems, their manifest form will be shaped by environmental conditions, especially traumatic experiences that evoke threat, in particular those that occurred in early childhood, and subsequent external and internal conditions. These conditions include the degree and quality of social support in the aftermath of trauma, repetition of traumatization, and the degree of dissociation between EP and ANP.

ANP: Primarily Mediated by Action Systems for Managing Daily Life

As also discussed above, clinical observations suggest that action systems of the ANP primarily function to direct performance of daily tasks necessary to living (work, social interaction, energy control) and some of the tasks related to survival of the species (caretaking of children). ANPs approach attractive stimuli and mentally avoid EPs and their aversive mental contents. The ANP's escapism from reminders of traumatic experiences may involve an extreme of the normative and adaptive tendency of will systems to inhibit each other (e.g., we do not tend to eat, sleep, fight, or totally submit *simultaneously*). Some ANPs may execute daily life action systems with passion, while others do so in more or less depersonalized and automatic ways (e.g., caretaking). This depersonalization probably relates to the ANP's avoidance of emotional and bodily feelings that have become conditioned stimuli for re-experiencing traumatic memories, a hypothesis that will be explored in more detail later.

It should be mentioned in passing that detached, depersonalized functioning in caretaking and attachment may interfere with synchronizations of physiological processes between adult and child which assist the child in regulating states (Field, 1985), potentially leading to dissociation in the offspring of dissociative parents (Schore, 2003).

A Dimension of Trauma-Related Structural Dissociation

Primary dissociation of the personality involves one major ANP and one much more limited EP. This organization would be the formal cause of simple PTSD and simple cases of somatoform dissociative disorders (i.e., the ICD-10 dissociative disorders of sensation and movement, described in DSM-5 as conversion disorder); a single EP can include all defensive subsystems.

Secondary dissociation involves one major ANP and two or more EPs that are mediated by different defensive subsystems that have not, or insufficiently, been integrated among each other. Different EPs may thus exert different defensive functions. Some EPs typically display freezing and are analgesic, whereas others are inclined to physically resist threat and experience anger, or totally submit to threat while being severely anesthetic. This threat often consists of re-experiencing (traumatic) memories of severe and chronic childhood abuse and neglect or in responding to cues that are salient reminders of these events. Insecure attachment to caretakers can also become associated with one or more EPs in secondary dissociation. This level of integrative failure is mediated by traumatization that is more severe than that associated with simple PTSD. Clinical observations suggest that secondary dissociation is characteristic of complex acute stress disorder, complex PTSD, complex forms of somatoform dissociative disorders, many cases of minor DID, and perhaps some cases of borderline personality disorder (APA, 1994) as well.

Many authors refer to states of hypoarousal, as in tonic immobility, as dissociative, but exclude sympathetic hyperarousal states from this category (Perry, Pollard, Blakely, Baker, & Vigilante, 1995; Schore, 2003). However, defining dissociation as a lack of integration among dissociative parts mediated by will systems that may include single states or clusters of states implies that hyperarousal states can also be dissociative. But these states as well as states involving analgesia and motor inhibition (freezing), bodily and emotional anesthesia, detachment from environmental cues, and submission (tonic immobility, regulated by the parasympathetic nervous system; Porges, 2001, 2003; Schore, 2003) may all be manifestations of insufficiently integrated or nonintegrated subsystems of defense.

In addition to secondary dissociation (division of the defensive system, thus of the EP), division of the ANP may also occur. Thus, this tertiary dissociation (Nijenhuis, Van der Hart, Kruger, & Steele, 2004; Steele, Van der Hart, & Nijenhuis, 2005; Van der Hart et al., 2004; Van der Hart et al., 2006), characteristic only of DID, involves a division among two or more action systems that serve functions in daily life and in survival of the species. For example, one ANP regarded herself as the mother of her children, and another ANP engaged in a job. Remaining as the mother, the patient did not appreciate or understand the interests that she had as a worker and vice versa. A lack of integration of daily life will systems probably does not occur during traumatization, but rather emerges when certain inescapable aspects of daily life become associated with past traumatization. Apart from extreme generalization of stimuli that reactivate traumatic memories, tertiary dissociation of the personality can also result from traumatization that started before the individual had been able to create a cohesive personality. Early and chronic traumatization may lead to some unclear mix of ANP/EP, where neither can be clearly distinguished. Such complexes are clinically observed in more dysfunctional patients with major DID.

Dissociation and Disorganized Attachment

When traumatization by caretakers begins early in the life of the child, he or she may develop 'disorganized/disoriented' attachment (Liotti, 1999; Main & Morgan, 1996). In normal, middle-class families, about 15% of the infants develop this attachment style, but in cases of maltreatment its prevalence may lie up to three times higher (Van IJzendoorn, Schuengel, & Bakermans-Kranenburg, 1999). Thus frightened or frightening parental behavior predicted infant disorganized attachment (Schuengel, Bakermans-Kranenburg, & Van IJzendoorn, 1999). As mentioned above, prospective longitudinal research demonstrated that disorganized and avoidant attachment in early childhood, along with age of onset, chronicity, and severity of abuse, predicted dissociation in various developmental stages, up to late adolescence (Ogawa et al., 1997). Both ANP and EP may be insecurely attached to original abusive caretakers or to (positive or negative) substitute caretakers.

Disorganized attachment may be neither disorganized nor disoriented; rather, it may involve concurrent or rapid successive activation of the attachment system and the defense system when primary attachment figures are both the source of protection from threat and the threat itself for the traumatized child. Separation from attachment figures activates the innate attachment system, which evokes a mental and behavioral approach to the caregiver. However, approach yields an increasing degree of imminence of threat and therefore evokes a succession of defensive subsystems (flight, freeze, fight, tonic immobility). This approach and avoidance conflict cannot be resolved by the child and promotes a dissociation of the attachment and the defensive system.

A lack of parental affect regulation, so common in chronic traumatization, leaves children who are abused, maltreated and emotionally neglected by their parents or other primary caretakers to their own immature affect regulation and integrative devices. This factor contributes to the lack of integration of conflicting action systems and thereby promotes the dissociation of these children's personality (see below for a further discussion of this crucial dynamic).

Similarities Between the Human and Animal Defensive System

At a general level, we (Nijenhuis et al., 1998d) drew a parallel between animal defensive/recuperative systems and characteristic sensorimotor dissociative responses of trauma-reporting patients with dissociative disorders. We suggested that there are similarities between animal and human disturbances of normal eating patterns and other normal behavioral patterns in the face of diffuse threat; freezing and stilling when serious threat materializes; analgesia and anesthesia when strike is about to occur; and acute pain when threat has subsided and recuperation is at stake. Next, we (Nijenhuis et al., 1998a) performed a first empirical test of the hypothesized similarity between animal defensive reactions and certain sensorimotor dissociative symptoms of dissociative disorder patients who reported traumatization. All 12 sensorimotor dissociative symptom clusters tested were found to discriminate between patients with dissociative disorders and patients with other psychiatric diagnoses. The clusters expressive of the hypothesized similarity between animal and human models – freezing, anesthesia-analgesia, and disturbed eating – belonged to the five most characteristic symptom clusters of dissociative disorder patients. Anesthesia-analgesia, urogenital pain, and freezing symptom clusters independently predicted the presence of dissociative disorder. Using an independent sample, we found that anesthesia-analgesia best predicted the presence of dissociative disorder after controlling for symptom severity. The indicated symptom clusters correctly classified 94% of cases in the original sample and 96% of cases in the second sample. These results were largely consistent with the hypothesized similarity to animal defense systems.

Among Dutch and Flemish dissociative disorders patients, the severity of sensorimotor dissociation – as measured by the SDQ-20 – was best predicted by a threat to the integrity of the body in the form of childhood physical abuse and childhood sexual trauma (Nijenhuis et al., 1998b). The particularly strong association between the SDQ-20 – which includes several items that assess anesthesia, analgesia, and motor inhibitions – and physical abuse was also found in a range of other populations: nonclinical subjects (Waller et al., 2000), gynecology patients with chronic pelvic pain (Nijenhuis et al., 2003), women reporting CSA (Nijenhuis et al., 2001), psychiatric outpatients (Nijenhuis et al., 2004) as well as North American (Dell, 1997) and Ugandan patients with dissociative disorders (Van Duyl et al., 2010). Bodily threat from a person and threat to life somatoform disorders also predicted somatoform dissociation in patients with somatoform disorders (Roelofs et al., 2002b) and nonclinical subjects (Maaranen et al., 2004).

Next, I discuss the following experimental research suggesting that (1) animal defense-like reactions particularly characterize the fragile EP, and that (2) ANPs and fragile EPs have different psychophysiological and neural reactions to perceived threat cues, even if these stimuli are presented preconsciously. Future research needs to decipher whether various EP-subtypes have the hypothesized features of animal defensive subsystems.

Psychobiological Interferences with Integration of ANP and EP

Peritraumatic Integrative Deficits

Evocation of the defense system or any other biopsychosocial system is not dissociative in itself. What constitutes dissociation is a lack of integration between various systems and subsystems. Extremely high levels of arousal may interfere with the execution of normal integrative mental and behavioral actions (Krystal, Woods, Hill, & Charney, 1991; Ludwig, Brandsma, Wilbur, Bendtfeldt, & Jameson, 1972; Siegel, 1999), and relate to long-lasting neuroendocrine instability induced by severe stress in early childhood.

It is likely that some will systems can be integrated more readily than others. As Panksepp (1998) argued, multiple feedbacks within and across will systems promote the synthesis of components of a system (e.g., perceptions, feelings, thoughts, behaviors, sense and conception of self) and integration across action systems. However, integration across action systems that involve quite different and sometimes conflicting functions may be far more demanding than synthesizing components of a particular will system or integrating functionally related systems.

If this idea is correct, the integration of will systems dedicated to daily life and survival of the species as well as action systems dedicated to survival of the individual in the face of that threat will fail more readily than integration across subsystems of these two complex systems. Dissociation between one ANP and one fragile EP – primary dissociation of the personality – is thus the basic type of integrative deficit when overwhelming experiences occur. With more enduring and even higher organism-environment defined stress levels, integration of subsystems of defense may be compromised as well, manifesting in secondary dissociation of the personality that involves more than one EP (i.e., lack of integration of different subsystems of defense; attachment cry).

Posttraumatic Integrative Deficits

Since living organisms have a natural tendency toward integration (Siegel, 1999), what maintains dissociation of the personality when traumatizing events have ceased and when stress-induced monoaminergic reactivity has returned to baseline? According to TSDP, apart from integrative deficiency that relates to enduring neuroendocrine changes induced by stress in early life, integrative failure in the aftermath of traumatizing events also relates to fear conditioning.

Traumatization and Classical Conditioning

Trauma-related classical conditioning involves association of stimuli that saliently signaled or accompanied the overwhelming event. As a result, these previously neutral cues thereafter tend to reactivate a version of the traumatic experience. Thus, the essence of Pavlovian or classical conditioning is the development of an anticipatory (conditioned stimulus signals unconditioned stimulus) or referential (conditioned stimulus refers to unconditioned stimulus) response. For example, the specific mood (e.g., anger) of the caretaker when abusive as well as the stimuli that apparently tended to elicit this mood tend to become conditioned stimuli.

Phobias of Traumatic Memories and Dissociative Parts

Classical trauma conditioning can also generate effects that support continued dissociation (Nijenhuis et al., 2002, 2004b). First of all, dissociation is less than perfect: When the traumatic memories of fragile EPs are reactivated by potent external (e.g., certain smells, sounds, sights) or internal (e.g., feelings or body sensations) conditioned stimuli, they can intrude on the experiential domain of ANPs. Since traumatic memories are reconceptions of the traumatic experience, they are formally conditioned stimuli. But the sensorimotor and highly affectively charged properties of these unintegrated experiences are inherently aversive for ANPs and therefore act as unconditioned stimuli. Indeed, when traumatized patients re-experience their terror, it is as if the traumatizing event happens "here and now to the self (i.e., PCS) of the time." When the integrative capacity and motivation to integrate of ANPs does not suffice for the integration of the intruding traumatic memory, these dissociative parts respond to intrusions (unconditioned stimuli) with typical behavioral and mental defensive action tendencies (unconditioned reactions). ANPs cannot escape from the highly stressful intrusions by behavioral means, but mental escape can be effective, as applies to factual (inescapable) traumatizing events. Thus, typical mental (re)actions of ANPs include retracting the perceptual field, lowering the intensity of conscious contents (with pseudoepileptic loss of consciousness as an extreme) manifesting as detachment, and mental avoidance of fragile EPs and the traumatic memories of these dissociative parts. At the same time, ANPs learn to fear and avoid internal and external conditioned stimuli that signal or refer to EPs. As time progresses and the dissociative condition continues, there is an ever-widening range of conditioned stimuli that ANPs behaviorally and mentally avoid due to stimulus generalization.

Evaluative Conditioning

In addition to classical fear conditioning, evaluative conditioning (Baeyens, Hermans, & Eelen, 1993) of external and internal stimuli may occur. This type of associative learning produces robust effects and involves the presentation of two stimuli conjointly: a neutral stimulus and a stimulus that the individual evaluates in a negative (or positive) manner. As a result of this simple procedure, the previously neutral stimulus adopts a similar negative (or positive) tone. ANPs and EPs evaluate traumatic memories differently, and clinical observations strongly suggest that evaluative conditioning applies to trauma-related dissociation. For example, when the traumatic experience pertained to a shameful event, ANPs may learn to be ashamed of EPs and to despise them, and EPs may learn to despise themselves.

In cases of secondary and tertiary dissociation, fragile EPs, controlling EPs, and ANPs may learn to fear, reject, and avoid each other along similar pathways of evaluative and classical conditioning. In tertiary dissociation, avoidance of different ANPs may be based on similar trauma-related issues and conflicts. In summary, many dissociative personalities become phobic of each other. These conditioned effects interfere with normal integrative action tendencies. Hence, trauma-related dissociation involves a strong tendency toward chronicity when the individual's integrative capacity and motivation to integrate the traumatic past is low, and the social environment does not help the individual to integrate this past – or even fosters mental avoidance of recollections of traumatizing events.

In some individuals, alternations between ANPs and EPs manifest from the acute phase onward, though other individuals function apparently well for extended periods of time before displaying posttraumatic stress symptoms. However, upon closer scrutiny it often appears that the latency period was marked by avoidance of the traumatic memories and associated internal and external cues, yielding a condition of chronic depersonalization. In cases of trauma-related dissociative amnesia as a disorder (APA, 1994), access to the memory of the trauma and to other parts of one's previous nontraumatic life seem to be inhibited (Markowitsch, 1999; Markowitsch et al., 2000; Van der Hart & Brom, 2000; Van der Hart, Nijenhuis, & Brown, 2001; Van der Hart, Brown, & Graafland, 1999).

Relational Factors that Maintain Dissociation

When significant others deny trauma instead of assisting in the integration of the painful experience or prohibit talking about it, dissociative tendencies are enhanced. These adverse social influences prevail in intrafamilial CSA (Freyd, 1996) and seem to promote dissociative amnesia (Vanderlinden, Van Dyck, Vandereycken, & Vertommen, 1993). PTSD has been associated with lack of support in the aftermath of traumatizing events (King, King, Fairbank, Keane, & Adams, 1998), and in another study, patients with complex dissociative disorders reported total absence of support and consolation when abused (Nijenhuis et al., 1998b). As TSDP predicts, social support can buffer negative effects of exposure to potentially traumatizing events (Elklit, 1997; Runtz & Schallow, 1997). It might be that social support provides safety cues, assists the individual in modulating the affective state and biological stress levels, and thus promotes the integration of emergent dissociative parts of the personality.

Different Individuals – Different Biopsychosocial Reactions to Perceived Threat

Most researchers of traumatic stress assume that all survivors have in principle similar (abnormal) reactions to natural and experimental cues, and that their functioning is relatively stable over time. These assumptions are convenient because they allow for straightforward group comparisons between individuals who lived through potentially traumatizing events and nonexposed controls. However, these points of departure are at odds with 150 years of clinical observations and associated theoretical analyses suggesting that the biopsychosocial condition of those exposed to identical or similar potentially traumatizing events can be very different for different individuals – and are inherently changeable for each individual (see Volume I).

TSDP holds that this changeability is to a certain extent systematic, that is, the biopsychosocial functioning of survivors alternates with the part(s) of the personality activated at the time of measurement. The functioning of each of these parts would also alternate to some extent or change with temporary or chronic changes of available mental energy and integrative capacity. For example, ANPs would generally have more integrative capacity than EPs. Some traumatized individuals may predominantly display ANPs during measurement, others EPs, and still others may alternate among these different parts, or have parallel activation of different parts.

Indeed, an increasing number of studies suggest that different individuals can display different, sometimes even opposite, psychobiological features. Such differences also appear in animals (Cohen, Zohar, & Matar, 2003; Cools & Ellenbroek, 2002). They include contrasting cortisol levels and autonomic nervous system reactions as well as different patterns of cerebral blood flow.

Arousal, Polyvagal Theory, and Dissociation

Most psychobiological trauma research is based on the assumption that 'arousal,' and with it traumatic stress, is regulated by the sympathetic branch of the autonomic nervous system. This view, originally proposed by Cannon (1927, 1932), predicts that stress reactions involve fight and flight behaviors and concomitant increases in heart rate, blood pressure, sweat gland activity, and circulating catecholamines. However, researchers of the animal defensive responses (e.g., Fanselow & Lester, 1988) and several authors on trauma-related dissociation observed that defense is not limited to increases in 'arousal' and active defensive motor actions, but also involves passivity and losses (e.g., immobilization, bodily and emotional anesthesia, and physiological deactivation).

As Porges (2003) notes, the rather exclusive focus on the sympathetic nervous system neglects the role of the parasympathetic branch of the nervous system in survival. His *polyvagal theory* is more differentiated and details essential neural structures and neurobehavioral systems we share with, or have adapted from, our phylogenetic ancestry (Porges, 2001, 2003). Polyvagal theory proposes three response systems that relate to different branches of the autonomic nervous system (i.e., the ventral and dorsal vagal branches of the parasympathetic nervous system and the sympathetic-catecholaminergic branch). These systems are related to their own adaptive strategies. In this paradigm, a state can be changed in a predictable manner, and specific state changes are associated with potentiating or limiting the range of specific behaviors.

The functions of the phylogenetically most recent system are social communication, self-soothing, and calming (i.e., a major component of self-regulation and affect-regulation) as well as inhibition of sympathetic-catecholaminergic influences. This mammalian signaling system for motion, emotion, and communication involves cranial nerve regulation of the striated facial muscles, coordinated by a myelinated vagus that inhibits sympathetic activity at the level of the heart. Porges described this ventral vagal control as the *vagal brake.* This brake regulates the heart and allows the individual to stay calm in safe environments. The lower motor neurons of this social engagement system are situated in the nucleus ambiguous. This system involves pathways that originate in the frontal cortex. Hence, there are cortical influences on these medullary motor neurons.

The second, phylogenetically older system serves active defense from threat and is dependent on the sympathetic nervous system. This adaptive system innervates the heart to provide the energy required to focus on threat cues, to run, or to fight. The lower neurons are found in the spinal cord. However, individuals can achieve mobilization in two ways: The quickest way is to release the vagal brake, which instantly activates the heart and thus provides energy for active defense. Individuals can rapidly calm themselves by re-engaging the ventral vagal system that decreases metabolic output. The sympathetic system can assist in energy mobilization under prolonged challenge.

The third and phylogenetically oldest system is the dorsal vagal system that serves major immobilization under threat. It provides inhibitory input to the sinoatrial node of the heart (i.e., the heart's 'pacemaker') via unmyelinated fibers and also provides low tonic influences on the bronchi. Massive bradycardia (i.e., low heart rate) may thus be determined by the unmyelinated dorsal vagal fibers. I hold that this system serves tonic immobility rather than mere immobilization. It seems that Porges (e.g., 2001) does not distinguish between freezing and tonic immobility. However, freezing is very different from dorsal vagal immobilization. Freezing marks being immobile and silent and being ready to explode into motor action. It occurs in close proximity to hypervigilance, flight, and fight, and is probably under ventral vagal and sympathetic control (Nijsen et al., 2000; Nijsen, Croiset, Diamant, De Wied, & Wiegant, 2001). However, the autonomic nervous system is differentially involved in heart rate regulation in fear-conditioned rats and in nonshocked controls (Nijsen et al., 1998). In nonshocked controls a predominant sympathetic nervous system activation results in an increase in heart rate, whereas in fear-conditioned rats the tachycardic response is attenuated by a simultaneous activation of sympathetic nervous system and parasympathetic nervous system. Freezing involves rapid, shallow breathing, high heart rate, increase of norepinephrine and epinephrine, and high muscle tone. Tonic immobility is associated with low heart rate and blood pressure, and slow breathing. Freezing is associated with analgesia (i.e., insensitivity to painful stimulation), whereas tonic immobility runs parallel to bodily and emotional anesthesia (Nijenhuis et al., 1998a, 1998d). While freezing consumes much energy, tonic immobility conserves energy.

Porges (2001, 2007, 2009) proposes a hierarchical response strategy to environmental challenges with the most recently developed system employed first and the most primitive last. This idea is consistent with Jackson's dissolution theory (Jackson, 1958), and with Janet's ideas on vehement emotions (Janet, 1928b). Jackson proposes that "[t]he higher nervous arrangements inhibit (or control) the lower, and thus, when the higher are suddenly rendered functionless, the lower rise in activity" (Jackson, 1958, quoted in Porges, 2001, p. 132). However, Porges (2001) adds that "the neurophysiological substrate of specific behavioral states and coping strategies may incorporate activation of a sequence of response systems representing more than one phylogenetic stage" (p. 132). Thus, the response strategies may include transitional blends between the boundaries of the different stages. These may be mediated by visceral feedback and higher brain structures, including the hypothalamus-pituitary-adrenal cortex axis (HPA axis), and vasopressin and oxytocinergic pathways that communicate between the hypothalamus and the dorsal vagal system.

Porges (2001) maintains that these three systems are not per se activated as a result of dissolution, but rather involve adaptive biobehavioral response strategies to different environmental challenges. When the tone of the ventral vagal complex is high, individuals are able to communicate via facial expressions, vocalizations, and gestures (i.e., via verbal and nonverbal motor actions). When the tone of this system is low, the sympathetic-catecholaminergic system is unopposed and easily expressed to support defensive mobilization or freezing. Finally, when the tone of the dorsal vagal complex is high, there is immobilization in the sense of tonic immobility.

I agree that these systems involve adaptation, but I also suggest that integration of the three systems is required for adaptive behavior beyond threat exposure (i.e., for adaptation once the threat has passed). Thus, I hypothesize that trauma-related dissociation includes a lack of integration of the three systems and their blends (see Table 16.1). Unless ANP is considerably or very physically and emotionally numbed (e.g., depersonalized), ANP would be associated with activation of the ventral vagal complex as well as EPs, which can engage in attachment behaviors, play, and some explo-

Table 16.1. Dissociative parts and the polyvagal theory: Some hypotheses.

Ventral vagal parasympathetic system	Social communication, exploration of the environment attachment, play	ANP to the degree that they are not depersonalized and emotionally and physically numb; EPs when feeling safe
Sympathetic-catecholaminergic system	Defensive actions such as taking care in traffic and becoming angry when insulted	ANP
Sympathetic-catecholaminergic system	Hypervigilance, freeze, flight, fight	(Hyperaroused) EPs when threatened; (Hyperaroused) ANPs who are intruded on by EPs and associated traumatic memories
Dorsal vagal parasympathetic system	Tonic immobility	(Hypoaroused) EPs when threatened; (Hypoaroused) ANPs who consciously or preconsciously avoid imminent intrusions of EPs and associated traumatic memories

ration when they feel safe. However, ANPs also encompass the sympathetic system to a degree in that they engage in defensive actions when they feel threatened, for example, by threatening internal experiences that relate to EPs such as intrusions of traumatic memories that EP retrieves. The active defensive actions of EPs would be predominantly associated with the sympathetic-catecholamine system and their passive defensive actions with the dorsal vagal complex. Primary dissociation involves a certain lack of integration of the ventral vagal complex and the two older phylogenetic systems. Secondary dissociation reflects a lack of integration of the sympathetic-catecholamine system and the dorsal vagal complex, or even a lack of integration within the sympathetic-catecholamine system. Tertiary dissociation additionally involves lack of integration among different subsystems of the ventral vagal complex. Vehement emotions denote individuals' failure to engage in efficacious, goal-directed mental and motor actions within or across any of these three psychophysiological complexes. To the extent that these emotions dominate, the individual does not manage to use energy supplies, such as mental and physical energy, for adaptive, creative actions within any psychophysiological system.

Porges (2001) argues that mobilization is associated with increases in cortisol, whereas immobilization (i.e., tonic immobility) involves reduced cortisol secretion because the dorsal vagal complex has an inhibitory influence on the HPA axis. Furthermore, oxytocin is associated with vagal processes and vasopressin with sympathetic processes. Vasopressin stimulates the HPA axis during chronic stress (Aguilera & Rabadan-Diehl, 2000) and is involved in active behavioral strategies aimed at coping with threat (Ebner, Wotjak, Holsboer, Landgraf, & Engelmann, 1999). Release of oxytocin would be associated with perceiving the environment as safe (e.g., with recognition of familiar individuals and attachment) and hence would promote the ventral vagal system. Release of vasopressin may be a component of a response profile related to the perception that the environment is unsafe, and that active behavioral defense is required. Interactions among cortisol, oxytocin, vasopressin, and norepinephrine do occur (Haller, Albert, & Makara, 1997).

To the degree that polyvagal theory is correct, it can be hypothesized that ANPs and EPs have different biopsychosocial profiles, including neuroendocrine and psychophysiological profiles. EPs would theoretically have different neuroendocrine profiles compared to ANPs and healthy controls, and some types of EPs would have different neuroendocrine profiles than other EPs. For example, notably when they perceive threat do fragile EPs typically engage in freezing, flight, or fight and would have increased cortisol and catecholamine levels; totally submissive fragile EPs would have decreased cortisol (cf. Porges, 2001). ANPs that feel safe would have higher levels of oxytocin, as would fragile EPs that are essentially mediated by attachment (cf. Uvnas-Moberg, 1997), whereas most EPs would have higher levels of vasopressin (Teicher, Andersen, Polcari, Anderson, & Navalta, 2002; cf. Porges, 2001). ANPs would likely have low basal levels of norepinephrine, as is suggested by low basal norepinephrine in depersonalization disorder (Simeon, Guralnik, Knutelska, Yehuda, & Schmeidler, 2003).

The theory also suggests that fragile EPs that engage in active defense when they feel threatened have increased HR, blood pressure, and decreased skin conductance response compared to ANPs. It also maintains that tonic immobile fragile EPs have decreased HR and blood pressure when exposed to (perceived) threat. Furthermore, 'sympathetically mediated' EPs, 'parasympathetically mediated' EPs, and ANPs would all have different patterns of cerebral metabolism. For example, EPs would have more activity in the amygdala, insula as well as somatosensory cortex and basal ganglia. These brain structures are known to be involved in emotional and sensorimotor reactions to perceived threat.

ANPs would have more activity in the anterior cingulate and the medial prefrontal cortex (mPFC) when exposed to major reminders of traumatizing events (i.e., brain structures that exert inhibitory influences on the 'emotional brain'). ANPs would also have more activity in parietal multimodal sensory association areas under such circumstances. However, all dissociative parts would have less frontal activity compared to mentally healthy controls because dissociative patients have lower integrative capacity than mentally healthy individuals. The theory proposes that ANPs tend to become depersonalized and feel detached when exposed to reminders of traumatizing events, and that depersonalization is associated with surplus metabolism in the parietal multisensory association areas. This detachment/depersonalization could relate to conscious as well as preconscious mental actions – conscious and subconscious inhibition of emotional reactions, including perception of trauma-related internal (e.g., sensations) and external stimuli. As clinical observations suggest, many ANPs display efforts to evade reminders of traumatizing events and other trauma-related stimuli. Their mental escapism prominently includes the narrowing of attention of these parts to concerns of daily life, which might include conscious or unconscious effort to keep the ventral vagal system online. In the next chapter, several research findings will be discussed in the light of these hypotheses.

Chapter 17

Dissociation of the Personality: Functional Biopsychosocial Findings I

The root of all health is in the brain.
The trunk of it is in emotion.
The branches and leaves are the body.
The flower of health blooms
when all parts work together.
Kurdish folk wisdom

According to TSDP, different traumatized individuals may have different biopsychosocial reactions to actual or perceived threat cues. The theory states that these differences are not random, but relate to the different will systems that may mediate their functioning. For example, one traumatized individual could be predominantly influenced by the action system of flight and freezing in this circumstance, another by the will system of tonic immobility. It is also possible that at one point in time they are guided by a single action system, say, active defense, and at a different point in time by a different action system, say, a particular will system for functioning in daily life.

The idea is that these differences tend to relate to the activation and deactivation of the different (types of) dissociative parts of the individual's personality during measurement. There may be state-dependent biopsychosocial differences *within* different ANPs, hyperaroused fragile EPs, hypoaroused fragile EPs, and controlling EPs. For example, an ANP may not always be able to focus on daily life interests, and in that sense may stay at a mental distance of threat cues. This may apply when the ANP is exhausted or under extreme pressure. However, according to TSDP, far more outspoken biopsychosocial differences will exist *between* these different prototypical parts of the personality.

To date, our focus of research has been on ANP and hyperaroused fragile EP. First, this division is the most basic; second, it is very difficult for patients with complex dissociative disorders to activate a hypoaroused fragile EP and a controlling EP on demand in a controlled research setting. Future research must nonetheless include these other prototypical parts as well. It could well be that they can only be studied in clinical or other even more natural settings.

Different Reaction Patterns in Different Survivors

Different Neuroendocrinological Features in Different Individuals: Cortisol

Some scientists maintain that survivors have elevated cortisol levels compared to controls. Others hold that cortisol in traumatized individuals is depressed. Very few of them, however, have hypothesized that different survivors can have different cortisol levels across time, situation, and state. Yet this possibility is suggested by early and more recent neuroendocrine studies. Price, Thaler, and Mason (1957) found that most patients anticipating high-risk elective cardiac surgery had relatively low preoperative cortisol levels. These patients used disengagement coping strategies such as emotional avoidance, denial, and withdrawal in the face of the impending surgery. Parents of fatally ill children with low cortisol levels also used disengagement as a coping style (Friedman, Mason, & Hamburg, 1963; Wolff, Friedman, Hofer, & Mason, 1964). In 1967, Bourne, Rose and Mason, documented that special forces soldiers who used disengagement coping had lower cortisol levels on the day they expected a massive overrunning by the Vietcong than on the days before and after the expected attack, whereas men who were forced to remain engaged with the life-threatening situation because of the nature of their duties (the officer and the radio operator) showed increased cortisol levels. (cited in Mason et al., 2001, p. 388).

Vietnam veterans with PTSD who felt guilty over their military actions in Vietnam were for that reason emotionally engaged in their trauma history at the time of measurement. They had elevated cortisol levels, whereas veterans with PTSD who were emotionally numb, avoidant, and generally disengaged had low cortisol levels (Mason et al., 2001). Mason et al. suggested that emotional engagement and disengagement may involve primary (i.e., immediate) and secondary (i.e., subsequent avoidant) emotional responses to traumatizing events. In terms of TSDP, the immediate reactions could denote EPs engaging in flight, freezing, or fight, and the avoidant reactions could pertain to ANPs or fragile EPs under dorsal vagal control. I am not aware of any direct studies of cortisol levels in ANPs and EPs.

Recent studies showed that genetic factors influence HPA axis functioning. There is accumulating evidence that variants of the glucocorticoid (GR) receptor affect the cell's sensitivity for glucocorticoids and thus contribute to the large intraindividual variability of HPA-axis reactivity in nonclinical samples (DeRijk, Schaaf, & de Kloet, 2002). However, it is questionable whether different GR polymorphisms also contribute to the cortisol response in PTSD and DID. Only one study in PTSD found that subtypes of GR polymorphisms were not more frequent in PTSD compared to controls. The only positive association was a reduced cortisol baseline level in a subset of PTSD patients associated with the presence a GR polymorphism (Bachmann et al., 2005). Whether this relationship also holds for minor and major DID is at present not known.

Different Psychophysiological Features in Different Individuals

Several studies found that individuals with a trauma-related disorder tend to have elevated heart rate and blood pressure in the acute stage of the disorder (Bryant, Harvey, Guthrie, & Moulds, 2000; Shalev et al., 1998). They may also have these psychophysiological reactions when exposed to perceived threat cues such as script-driven imagery (Kinzie et al., 1998; Orr, 1997; Orr et al., 1997; Shalev, Peri, Gelpin, Orr, & Pitman, 1997) or loud tones (Orr et al., 2003). The effects could be due to sympathetic control and/or to release of the vagal brake. Some preliminary findings indeed suggest that elevated sympathetic tone in individuals in response to mild cognitive challenge can relate to a dysfunctional parasympathetic system (Sahar, Shalev, & Porges, 2001).

As mentioned in Chapter 5, Osuch et al. (2001) found that only a proportion of survivors had increased psychophysiological responses to general emotional challenge and to trauma cue exposure (see also Kinzie et al., 1998). These subgroups have been labeled 'physiologic responders' and 'physiological nonresponders.' Lack of heart-rate increases in response to challenge in a substantial proportion of PTSD patients may not suggest a flight or fight, but rather a 'giving-up response' that involves inhibition (i.e., tonic immobility). This inhibition could be related to dorsal vagal parasympathetic control in these survivors. In terms of TSDP, the absence of heart-rate increases (or rather heart-rate decreases) to emotional challenge may mark fragile EPs that engage in tonic immobility. The absence of heart-rate changes to such challenge may also involve ANPs. EPs engaging in flight, freezing, or fight should increase heart rate.

Heart rate reflects both sympathetic and parasympathetic nervous system activity and can be measured both tonically (i.e., beats per minute at rest) or phasically (i.e., change in response to a stimulus). Accelerations in heart rate as reaction to a stimulus are thought to reflect sensory rejection or a 'tuning out' of noxious environmental events, while decelerations are thought to reflect sensory intake or an environmental openness (Lacey & Lacey, 1974). Emotionally speaking, heart rate has been associated with the experience of anxiety. As such, high-tonic heart rate is thought to reflect fear, while low-tonic heart rate may reflect fearlessness.

One of the most consistent findings is the reduced resting heart rate in antisocial behavior in children and adolescents with externalizing behavior (Ortiz & Raine, 2004). Raine (1993) noted that all 14 relevant studies replicated the finding of reduced resting heart rate in antisocial groups. Low heart rate is a robust marker independent of cultural context, the relationship having been established in the United States (e.g., Rogeness, Cepeda, Macedo, Fisher, & Harris. 1990), Germany (Schmeck & Poustka, 1993), the United Kingdom (e.g., Farrington, 1997), Canada (Mezzacappa et al., 1997), Mauritius (Raine, Venables, & Mednick, 1997), and New Zealand (Moffit & Caspi, 2001). In light of these findings, it would be of interest to assess the resting heart rate of controlling EPs.

Lack of heart rate changes to emotional challenge may relate to negative dissociative symptoms, suggesting parasympathetic dominance. Thus, adult raped women with a high degree of negative dissociative symptoms had lower heart rate when talking about their rape compared to survivors with a low degree of negative dissociative symptoms (Griffin, Resick, & Mechanic, 1997). In general, there was a suppression of autonomic physiological responses in the high dissociation+ group. Delinquent, traumatized adolescents with many negative dissociative symptoms also had lower heart rate compared to those with few negative dissociative symptoms (Koopman, Carion, Sudhakar, Palmer, & Steiner, 2000). This effect was more pronounced when the individuals spoke in a free association task, compared to who talked about their most stressful life experience. However, higher mean heart rate was found among youths reporting greater frequency and intensity of adverse childhood experiences. These differences could relate to the activation of different types of dissociative parts.

Schmahl, Elzinga, and Bremner (2002) also reported that individuals who were abused as children can have very different subjective psychological and physiological reactions to trauma scripts. During their experiment, a woman with PTSD and a woman with histrionic personality disorder had elevated heart rate and blood pressure, but a woman with borderline personality disorder and a "dissociative" reaction (i.e., negative symptoms) in response to an abandonment script had an extreme drop in physiological reactivity.

Different Neural Activity in Different Individuals

Lanius et al. (2002) studied the neural circuitry associated with response patterns of sexual-abuse-related PTSD patients to trauma scripts using fMRI. They found that reactivity depended on whether the patients tended to re-experience the traumatizing event or become detached from them. They did not describe re-experiencing the traumatizing event as a positive dissociative response but did describe detachment as a dissociative response, although this response might involve some different kind of alteration of consciousness. Compared to controls, the PTSD patients who became detached showed more activation in the superior and middle temporal gyri (Brodmann area [BA] 38), inferior frontal gyrus, occipital lobe (BA 19), mPFC (BA 10), parietal lobe (BA 7), medial cortex (BA 9), and anterior cingulate gyrus (BA 24 and BA 32). However, the PTSD patients who re-experienced traumatizing events showed significantly less activation of the thalamus, anterior cingulate gyrus (BA 32), and medial frontal gyrus (BA 10/11) than did the comparison subjects. In terms of TSDP, re-experiencing constitutes a positive dissociative response and probably a fragile EP engaging in active defense. What Lanius et al. called a dissociative response pertains to negative symptoms and possibly to a detached ANP or EP.

Similarly, Lanius et al. (2003) described a husband and wife who had developed PTSD in the context of a very serious motor vehicle accident in which they saw a child burn to death and in which they feared they too would die. Whereas both reported peritraumatic dissociative + symptoms, they exhibited very different subjective, psychophysiological, and neurobiological responses to trauma-script-driven imagery that caused them to re-experience the accident. The husband successfully had managed to rescue himself and his wife by breaking the windshield while feeling extremely aroused. She could hardly move because she was frozen. When re-experiencing the accident, he was very psychologically and physically aroused, and she felt numb and frozen. They thus re-engaged in their original response patterns. His heart rate increased 13 beats per minute from baseline, and he had increased activity in the anterior frontal, anterior cingulate, superior and medial temporal, thalamic, parietal, and occipital brain regions. She had no heart rate change from baseline and had only increased activity in occipital regions. Lanius et al. (2003) concluded that their "fMRI results demonstrate that PTSD patients can have very different responses, both subjectively and biologically, while re-experiencing traumatic events" (p. 668).

Different Biopsychosocial Reactions for Different Types of Dissociative Parts

The studies discussed so far demonstrate that different survivors can have very different psychobiological profiles. A range of studies of major DID patients suggest that different types of dissociative parts of the personality can have different psychobiological profiles that are not reproduced by DID-simulating controls. Differences have been reported in:

- electrodermal activity (skin conductance; Ludwig et al., 1972; Larmore, Ludwig, & Cain, 1977),
- EEG, in particular in the beta 2 band (Coons, Milstein, & Marley, 1982; Hughes, Kuhlman, Fichtner, & Gruenfeld, 1990; Ludwig et al., 1972; Putnam, Buchsbaum, & Post, 1993),
- visual evoked potentials (Putnam et al., 1992),
- regional cerebral bloodflow (Mathew, Jack, & West, 1985; Saxe, Vasile, Hill, Bloomingdale, & Van der Kolk, 1992),
- autonomic nervous system variables (Putnam et al., 1993),
- optical variables (Birnbaum & Thomann, 1996; Miller, 1989; Miller, Blackburn, Scholes, White, & Mammalis, 1991; Miller & Triggiano, 1992), and
- arousal (Putnam, Zahn, & Post, 1990).

While these studies are valuable, it is difficult to say what the data actually tell us beyond suggesting that these physiological data sets "are most parsimoniously explained by regarding the alter personalities [i.e., dissociative parts of the personality] as discrete states of consciousness" (Putnam, 1997, p. 138). Advances in the field critically depend on theoretical predictions with respect to the kind of differences that exist among different types of dissociative parts of the personality. Because TSDP offers such predictions, from the early 1990s on I developed several ideas on how psychophysiological and neural reaction patterns of ANP and EP in women with carefully diagnosed and clinically confirmed major DID could be explored.

One hurdle was to find colleagues who were courageous enough to engage in this work, and another problem was to get such studies funded. The basic belief among researchers and many colleagues at the time was (and in part still is) that major DID is a fabrication due to suggestion, suggestibility, fantasy proneness, and motivated-role playing. They did not seem to care much that their beliefs are hypotheses in need of empirical testing, and that there was – and to the best of my knowledge to date still is – not a single study with major DID patients showing that their hypotheses regarding individuals with this severe mental disorder hold. When it comes to DID, strange things can happen to the mind of gifted individuals.

It was a deep relief to find colleagues at the University of Groningen, The Netherlands, and later also at the University of Zürich, such as Simone Reinders, Johan den Boer, Yolanda Schlumpf, and Lutz Jäncke who were willing to test several basic biopsychosocial hypotheses of TSDP. The involved colleagues took a courageous step, because studying DID commonly harvests ridicule and rejection more than professional praise and rewards, particularly but not exclusively in a university setting. I thus am most grateful that they stayed true to the essence of science, and that they were willing to engage with me in tests of TSDP and extend the work in a later phase. TSDP was grounded on the phenomena of severe dissociation, which had filled my clinical practice for many years, as well as on that of the two other parents of TSDP, Onno van der Hart and Kathy Steele. TSDP was also based in emergent research using systematic self-report. No matter how stable and powerful these clinical and self-report based scientific data may have been, they obviously needed more formal testing. Psychophysiological and neuroimaging research would be one major way to do this.

The first TSDP-inspired hypothesis I proposed was that ANP and EP in women with major DID have different subjective, psychophysiological, and neural reaction patterns to reminders of a traumatizing event they had experienced. Based on extensive clinical experiences with DID patients, I realized this research would be most challenging to them. The women had to be able to alternate between ANP and EP in a controlled and demanding setting. They had to lie down for approximately 3 hours in a positron emission tomography scanner, and they had to remain immobile each time they were confronted with trauma-related cues. These are exceptional challenges given the histories of chronic sexual, physical, and emotional abuse and emotional neglect patients with major DID typically report. The patients who participated in our studies were thus the most courageous of all.

We applied several inclusion and exclusion criteria. The basic design of our biopsychosocial studies of major DID involves the sequential presence of a single ANP and a single fragile, hyperaroused EP. For this reason, we could only include women with major DID who were able to alternate between one of their ANPs and one of their hyperaroused fragile EPs on demand. Before women with DID can meet this requirement, they have already come a considerable way in their treatment. For ethical reasons, candidate participants could only be entered into studies involving confrontations with traumatic memories or other trauma-specific cues if they had reached a phase of treatment in which the focus was on the integration of their traumatic memories. This difficult therapeutic work requires the controlled co-activation and co-participation of ANPs and EPs.

We tried to prevent overburdening of the patients in our experiments. To this end, we refrained from including fragile EPs with a subjective age younger than 10 years and from using the patients' most severe traumatic memories. We also made sure that the trauma scripts included only situational descriptions. The decision to exclude descriptions of the patients' reactions to the traumatizing events was also motivated by our wish to avoid suggestive experimental influences as much as possible. Response descriptions are common in psychophysiological research, but might be seen as response instructions.

The implication of these various inclusion and exclusion criteria is that our studies involved women who are less dissociative than they were when they entered treatment and who did not tap into their strongest trauma-related reactions. In sum, our methodological and ethical restrictions were certainly not favoring the hypotheses derived from TSDP.

Psychophysiological and Subjective Reactivity

In Reinders et al. (2003, 2006), we studied the psychophysiological reactions of major DID patients to auditory scripts while functioning as ANP and as fearful fragile EP. In this study of ANP- and fearful fragile EP-dependent psychophysiological functioning, each participant listened to two audiorecorded scripts. One script involved a neutral personal memory that the ANPs and fearful, and thus emotionally engaged, EPs experienced as a personal narrative memory; the other script described a traumatic experience that fragile EPs but not ANPs regarded as a personal experience. The TSDP-based hypotheses were that, compared to controls, fragile EPs would only have increased physiological activity as well as subjective emotional and sensorimotor reactions to the trauma scripts.

The results supported the hypotheses. ANPs and fragile EPs did not have increased heart rate and blood pressure in response to neutral memories, compared both to each other and to baseline. However, fragile EPs (but not ANPs) had highly significant increases of heart rate and systolic blood pressure compared to baseline and neutral script exposure when listening to the trauma scripts. As we also hypothesized, fragile EPs had significantly less heart rate variability compared to ANPs when these dissociative parts listened to the trauma scripts. Fragile EPs but not the ANPs had strong subjective emotional and sensorimotor reactions to the trauma scripts. Only fragile

EPs reported a spectrum of primary emotions, including fear, anger, and disgust, and experienced many positive and negative sensorimotor dissociative symptoms such as being physically touched, having visual images of the traumatic experience, smelling smells, and bodily paralysis.

In 2004, I was able to document heart rate and bodily movements in response to perceived threat cues of ANPs and fragile EPs of patients with complex dissociative disorders in a clinical setting. The exposure constituted a therapeutic exercise designed to help the patients to develop the courage and assertive skills to stop ongoing abuse or threats of further traumatization. The 'threat' cue constituted a small, insignificant object such as a tea bag that the therapist moved in the direction of the patient's face. As ANPs, the patients did not have heart-rate changes, looked composed, and reported that they had felt at ease during the exposure. As EPs who engaged in freezing or who experienced an inclination to ward off the 'threat' cue, the patients had strong heart-rate increases. As these EPs, they had very fearful facial expressions, were totally fixated on the moving object, and reported intense fear, inability to move (freezing), or a strong impulse to run (flight). Some tended to assume a fetal body posture. Sometimes 'fight' EPs became activated during the exposure, but these parts did not dare to execute their impulses to ward off the approaching object. Finally, as fragile EPs engaged in tonic immobility, the patients had decreasing heart rate, averted their gaze, and later reported they had mentally left their body. Some of these EPs reported amnesia for the phase in which the object had come close to their face.

Figures 17.1 to 17.5 provide some examples of heart-rate responsiveness of ANPs and fragile EPs to this test. Emotional support during 'threat' exposure in the form of a hand of a trusted person on the back prevented extreme increases and decreases of psychophysiological activity, and promoted assertive defense (Nijenhuis, 2004; see Figure 17.5). This support likely activates the ventral vagal nervous system, more specifically, the attachment will system. The ventral vagal system implies the vagal brake, which inhibits full activation of defensive system in response to potent reminders of traumatic experience (i.e., conditioned stimuli). In other words, emotional support raises the patients' integrative capacity.

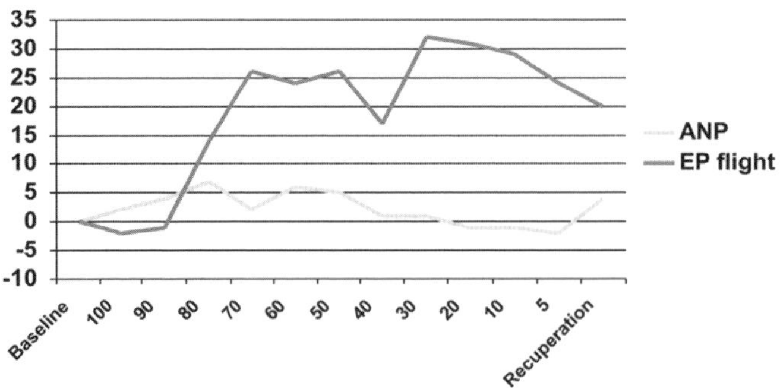

Figure 17.1. Heart-rate changes compared to baseline for different dissociative parts in a DID patient upon exposure to approaching picture of a man with an angry facial expression.

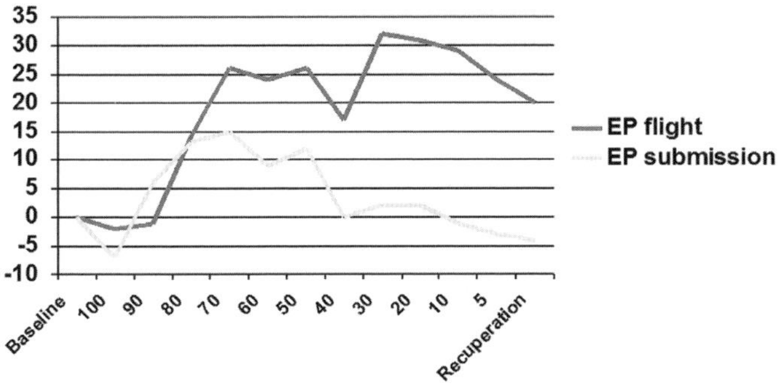

Figure 17.2. Heart-rate changes compared to baseline for different dissociative parts in a patient with major DID upon exposure to approaching picture of a man with an angry facial expression.

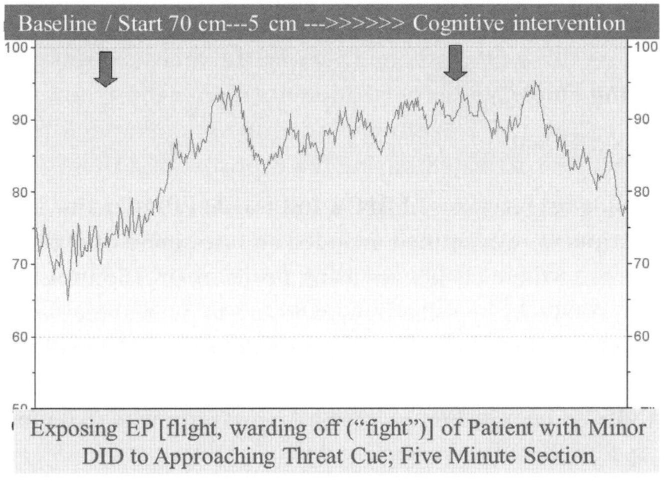

Figure 17.3. Heart-rate frequency in a patient with minor DID during exposure to approaching perceived threat cue: hyperaroused fragile EP.

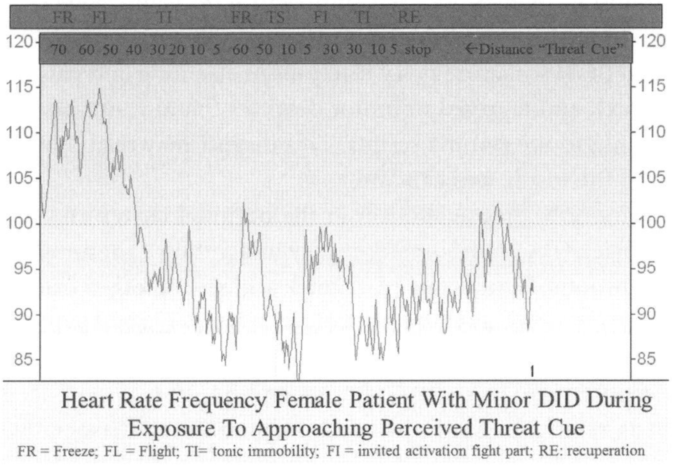

Figure 17.4. Heart-rate frequency in a patient with minor DID during exposure to approaching perceived threat cue: hypoarousal following initial increase of arousal.

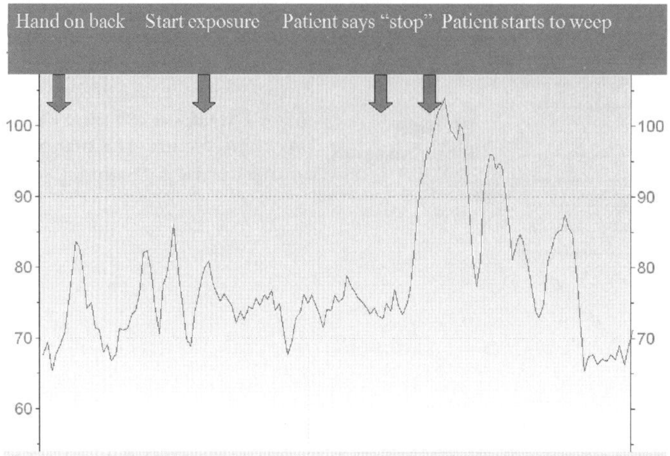

Figure 17.5. Heart-rate frequency of DID patient from Figures 17.1 and 17.2 in response to a picture of a male with an angry facial expression that is moved from 70 cm to 5 cm distance in the direction of the patient's face in a therapy session. This time, the hand of the cotherapist, whom the patient had learned to trust, was on the patient's back as a token of social support. The activated parts were fragile EPs that otherwise engage in flight and freeze. The experienced support was associated with a stable heart rate, an effect that may reflect dominance of the ventral vagal system.

ANP- and EP-Dependent Neural Activity

Supraliminal Exposure to Perceived Threat

The study in which psychophysiological reactions of ANPs and fragile EPs in major DID patients to neutral and trauma scripts were examined included an assessment of regional cerebral bloodflow (rCBF) patterns to these challenges using positron emission tomography (PET; Reinders et al., 2003, 2006). As hypothesized, exposure to neutral memories that ANPs and fragile EPs regarded as a shared personal memory did not yield any difference in regional cerebral bloodflow patterns. However, as we also hypothesized, major differences emerged between ANPs' and fragile EPs' psychobiological responses to trauma scripts that only EPs regarded as a personal memory.

Compared to ANPs, fragile EPs had more activity (i.e, more rCBF) in the amygdala, insular cortex, somatosensory areas I and II in the parietal cortex, and the basal ganglia. This activity is consistent with clinical observations and subjective reports of fragile EPs. These parts had somatosensory reactions to trauma scripts (somatosensory areas I and II), responded to these scripts and these somatosensory reactions in alarming and painful ways (amygdala and insular cortex), and engaged in motor defenses (basal ganglia). EPs also reported disgust when listening to the trauma scripts. This disgust may relate to the observed increase of activation in the insula and caudate.

Compared to EPs, ANPs had more brain metabolism in the occipital cortex (BA 19: visual perception), the parietal cortex (BA 7/40: somatosensory integration), the anterior cingulate (BA 24 and BA 32: inhibition of emotional reactions), and several other frontal areas, including BA 10 (planning, self-awareness). Many of these areas were also involved in the detachment that some PTSD patients displayed in Lanius et al's (2002) study. As suggested before, the major activity for ANPs in BA 7, BA 40, and BA 19 may be linked with depersonalization, which is related to several negative somatoform dissociative symptoms, for example, experiencing the body as a foreign object. Simeon et al. (2000)

reported that depersonalization disorder was associated with functional abnormalities along sequential hierarchical areas, secondary and cross-modal areas of the sensory cortex (visual, auditory, and somatosensory) as well as areas responsible for an integrated body schema. More specifically, they found less bloodflow in the right temporal cortex (auditory association area) and more metabolism in the parietal somatosensory association area and the multimodal association area. Dissociation and depersonalization scores among the sample were strongly correlated with activation patterns in the posterior parietal association area (BA 7).

It seems that failure to integrate bodily sensations – integration of these sensations may lie at the heart of basic forms of consciousness (Damasio, 1999) – is related to dysfunctional temporal, parietal, and occipital association areas. Indeed, "[t]here is a hierarchy of sensory processing in the brain, from primary sensory areas to unimodal and then polymodal association areas and finally to the PFC" (Simeon et al., 2000, p. 1786). Depersonalization and negative sensorimotor dissociative symptoms may thus relate to dysfunctional posterior association areas. This dysfunction might negatively affect the transfer of signals to these posterior areas to the prefrontal cortex. ANPs indeed report low body awareness and feel generally more or less detached from their body.

To return to Reinders et al.'s (2003, 2006) symptom provocation study of DID, reduced activity in the PFC for fragile EPs suggests lack of inhibition regarding emotional reactivity. Stress hormones also interfere with the activation of the mPFC. Thus, elevated levels of norepinephrine were associated with dysfunction of the PFC (Arnsten, 1999). Interestingly, reduced activity in neural networks in the PFC has been shown to increase c-FOS expression (one of the immediate early genes responding to environmental stimuli) in the paraventricular nucleus, leading to increased stress vulnerability (Gerrits et al., 2003).

Interference of the mPFC related to stress hormones presents a major problem of affect regulation in that hippocampal activity (McCormick & Thompson, 1982) and medial prefrontal 'information processing' (Armony & LeDoux, 1997) are crucially involved in inhibiting the amygdala. Bremner et al. (1999a) documented mPFC and anterior cingulate dysfunction in women with and without PTSD who reported CSA. The participants were exposed to neutral personal memories and to descriptions of personalized CSA events. CSA scripts were associated with greater increases in rCBF in portions of the PFC, posterior cingulate, and motor cortex in women with PTSD than in women without PTSD. Listening to these scripts was also associated with alterations in rCBF in the mPFC (i.e., decreased bloodflow in subcallosal gyrus and the anterior cingulate). Compared with women who had not developed PTSD, those with PTSD also had decreased bloodflow in the right hippocampus, fusiform/inferior temporal gyrus, supramarginal gyrus, and visual association cortex.

"Host" parts of the personality in patients with DID (i.e., ANPs) had less cerebral bloodflow in the orbitofrontal cortex bilaterally than did healthy controls (Sar et al., 2007c). They also had more bloodflow in median and superior frontal regions and occipital regions. These findings are generally consistent with TSDP.

Chapter 18

Dissociation of the Personality: Functional Biopsychosocial Findings II

Biology gives you a brain. Life turns it into a mind.
Jeffrey Eugenides (2002, p. 479)

Proponents of the sociocognitive and fantasy models of complex dissociation and DID in particular (SC- and F-models) expressed doubt that the different psychophysiological and neural reaction patterns to trauma memory scripts for ANPs and fragile EPs (Reinders et al., 2003, 2006) demonstrate the reality of DID as an authentic mental disorder. They suggested that high fantasy-prone, mentally healthy women, motivated and instructed to simulate an ANP and a fragile EP, could easily simulate the involved response patterns. As Spanos (1994, 1996) contended, few suggestions would suffice and little role practice would be needed. However, neither Spanos nor other SC- and F-model theorists had actually tested their hypotheses in studies with DID patients. Whereas the documented biopsychosocial differences for ANP and EP fit various kernal hypotheses TSDP, it is true that Reinders et al. (2003, 2006) did not control for suggestion and fantasy proneness. We thus examined whether the findings were upheld when controlling for fantasy proneness, suggestion, and instructed and motivated role-playing in follow-up study (Reinders et al., 2012).

The different hypotheses can be formulated as follows:

- *Hypothesis SC- and F-models:* High fantasy- but not low fantasy-prone individuals can effectively simulate ANP and fragile EP as they appear in patients with psychophysiological and neurobiological regards, when they have received role instructions and have practiced these roles. Few suggestions and little practice suffice, because ANP and fragile EP in DID concern suggested roles.
- *Hypothesis TSDP:* High and low fantasy-prone individuals who do not have a dissociative disorder and who are instructed, motivated, and trained to simulate an authentic ANP and a fragile EP as they appear in DID cannot effectively simulate these different prototypical parts of the personality in psychophysiological and neurobiological regards under test conditions that evoke different biopsychosocial reactions in real ANPs and fragile EPs.

- *Additional hypothesis TSDP:* ANPs and fragile EPs in patients with DID do not have different biopsychosocial reactions to cues or situations that are not of particular relevance to these different dissociative parts, or that are not associated with dissimilar theoretically predicted and clinically observed phenomenal reactions of these different prototypes of dissociative parts. The ecological validity of experimental cues, thus, should be meticulously considered.

Subjective and Psychophysiological Reactions of Authentic and Simulated ANPs and Fragile EPs to an Adverse Personal Memory Script

Non-PTSD patients have difficulty simulating physiological responses of traumatized patients (Gerardi, Keane, & Penk, 1989; Orr & Pitman, 1993). Whereas simulating controls are generally unable to produce psychophysiological state changes equivalent to those in DID patients (Putnam, 1997), according to SC-/F-models carefully instructed and highly suggestible individuals would readily simulate dissociative parts in DID. TSDP in turn states that neither low nor high fantasy-prone healthy controls who are carefully instructed and highly motivated to simulate the biopsychosocial reactions patterns of prototypical dissociative parts can simulate fragile EPs who engage in active mammalian defenses such as freezing and flight in reaction to threat signals. In contrast to authentic fragile EPs, simulated fragile EPs do not have an increased heart rate and systolic blood pressure when they listen to an audiotaped description of a painful autobiographical memory. SC-/F-models and TSDP have the same hypotheses with respect to heart rate and blood pressure for ANP.

In order to test the opposite physiological hypotheses for fragile EPs, we asked high and low fantasy-prone, mentally healthy controls to provide their most painful memory to serve as an analogue for the patients' personal trauma memories (Reinders et al., 2012). We also asked them to provide a neutral personal episodic memory. The controls received detailed descriptions and explanations regarding the core features of ANPs and fragile EPs in DID as well as templates on how to switch between these different dissociative parts. We checked whether they had understood the simulation instructions and assisted them when they had difficulty simulating these dissociative parts during practice. We also checked whether they sufficiently practiced their roles. Controls were included in the study only when they were convinced that they could play their roles well. The participating controls reported that they had tried to simulate an ANP and a fragile EP as well as switching between these simulated dissociative parts to the best of their abilities.

Consistent with this, both high and low fantasy-prone DID-simulating controls reported phenomenal emotional reactions of these two different prototypes of dissociative parts that fit those of the DID patients (Reinders & Nijenhuis, 2012). High fantasy-prone DID simulating controls were better at this simulation than low fantasy-prone controls. The results were obtained after relatively brief practice and are in line with the SC- and F-models of DID with respect to subjective emotional reactions. Holders of trauma-related models of DID including TSDP do not deny that simulation of phenomenal reports is to some degree possible. However, they emphasize that subjective reports do not imply phenomenal experiences. Furthermore, high and low fantasy-prone controls had difficulty imitating the DID patients' (reports of) sensorimotor reactions to trauma scripts despite careful role instructions. As remarked before, SC- and F-models have difficulty explaining the sensorimotor reactions of different dissociative parts. There is much more to the phenomenal sensorimotor experiences of DID patients than these models presume.

Psychophysiological Findings

The high and low fantasy-prone controls had similar levels of heart rate and blood pressure whether they simulated an ANP or a fragile EP, or when they listened to audiotapes with descriptions of neutral or painful personal memories (Reinders et al., 2012). These findings strongly suggest that the psychophysiological reactions of authentic ANPs and EPs in DID to the trauma script are not due to suggestion, fantasy, fantasy proneness, and motivated role-playing.

Neural Reactions of Authentic and Simulated ANPs and EPs to an Adverse Personal Memory Script

Hypothesis TSDP

Neurobiological differences for ANPs and fearful fragile EPs in DID patients that remain after controlling for the potential effects of simulating these dissociative parts include subcortical activity (e.g., activation of the amygdala and caudate) for EP, and hyperactivation of the cortical multimodal posterior association areas (e.g., the intraparietal sulcus and [pre-]cuneus) for ANPs when listening to personal trauma scripts that are personal for fearful fragile EPs.

Neither high nor low fantasy-prone healthy controls mimicked ANPs' and fragile EPs' neural reactions. If there was any effect at all, the fantasy-prone controls simulated the performance of DID patients better than high fantasy-prone controls. These results contrast completely with the hypotheses of the SC-/F-models of DID.

Brain Activation Patterns for Authentic ANPs, Compared to that of High or Low Fantasy-Prone Controls[1]

Compared to the controls, authentic ANPs activated more cerebral cortical areas. It is of interest that their pattern of brain activation significantly overlapped with that of mentally healthy individuals who suppressed emotional unwanted memories (Anderson et al., 2004). The overlap included several frontal areas (BA 4, 6, 8, 10, 47), a part of the cingulate cortex (BA 32), the intraparietal sulcus (BA 7/40), and the lingual gyrus/cuneus (BA 18). ANPs were associated with the activation of an even larger number of brain areas than memory suppressing individuals in Anderson et al.'s study.

ANPs also activated posterior association areas such as the (pre-)cuneus (BA 7/39, 18/19), fusiform gyrus (BA 18/19/37), lingual gyrus (BA 18), occipital gyrus (BA 18/19/37), and the parahippocampal gyrus (BA 35/36). These brain areas overlap in part with those of PTSD patients who respond with negative dissociative+ symptoms such as depersonalization in response to trauma scripts (Lanius et al., 2002). Compared with controls, the individuals with PTSD and negative symptoms had more activation in the superior and middle temporal gyri (BA 38), inferior frontal gyrus (**BA 47**), occipital lobe (**BA 19**), parietal lobe (**BA** 7), medial frontal gyrus (**BA 10**), medial cortex (BA 9), and anterior cingulate gyrus (BA 24 and **BA 32**). The overlap in activated brain structures for patients with PTSD with negative symptoms and for ANP in DID is indicated in **bold**.

As the term 'ANP' indicates, according to TSDP, this prototypical dissociative part's normality is apparent. For example, as ANP, individuals with dissociative disorders tend to be more or less depersonalized and emotionally and physically numb when they are confronted with reminders of traumatic memories in which fragile EPs are fixed, so that the involved ANP is not intruded on by pertinent reactions to these reminders of one or more EPs. Parietal and occipital areas (BA 7, 19, 39) that patients with major DID activated as ANP were also hyperactivated in patients with depersonalization disorder. As noted above, hypermetabolism in BA 7b was correlated with the severity of depersonalization and dissociative+ symptoms in patients with depersonalization disorder (Simeon et al., 2000). Simeon et al. concluded that depersonalization is linked with functional abnormalities along sequential hierarchical areas – secondary and cross-modal – of the sensory cortex as well as with areas responsible for an integrated body schema. Indeed, these parieto-occipital areas are involved in multimodal sensory integration, particularly in re-

1 The discussion includes brain areas that are specific to DID. The comparisons pertain to four kinds of comparisons (for more specific descriptions, see Reinders et al., 2012): (1) brain areas found in the DID within-group analysis, in the DID versus high fantasy-prone controls (CH) between-group analysis and in the DID versus low fantasy-prone controls (CL) between-group analysis; (2) brain areas found in the DID within-group analysis and in the DID versus CH between-group analysis; (3) brain areas found in the DID within-group analysis and in the DID versus CL between-group analysis; (4) brain areas not found in the DID within-group analysis but found in the between-group analysis DID versus CH or DID versus CL.

lation to attention and perceptual awareness (Driver & Vuilleumier, 2001; Pavani, La'davas, & Driver, 2003; Wallace, 2004). The posterior cortices play a pivotal role in sensory perception. This mental action is associated with primary sensory areas, unimodal and multimodal association areas as well as with the prefrontal cortex (Fuster, 2003).

Brain Activation Patterns for Authentic Fragile EPs, Compared to that of High or Low Fantasy-Prone Controls

Compared to the controls, fragile EPs had more activation in two brain areas that were also activated in mentally healthy individuals who did not suppress memories (Anderson et al., 2004): the insula (BA 13) and the parietal operculum (BA 40/43). There were also differences between EPs and controls. These were to be expected in that EPs do not tend to recall their traumatic memories in a symbolized, verbal form, but rather as sensorimotor, affectively charged experiences. Consistent with this, fragile EPs did not activate the hippocampus when they listened to the trauma-memory scripts but rather the caudate nucleus. This finding fits previous observations that exposure to an acute stressor can be associated with a shift from involvement of the hippocampus to that of the caudate nucleus (Schwabe, Dalm, Schächinger, & Oitzl, 2008; White, 2009). Confrontation with an acute stressor was linked with the more rigid caudate nucleus-related stimulus-response type of reactivity at the expense of hippocampus-related spatial learning and memory – in mice as well as in man (Schwabe et al., 2008; Schwabe, Schächinger, de Kloet, & Oitzl, 2010). As Schwabe, Oitzl, and Schächinger (2007, p. 112) detailed,

> [i]n stressful situations, attention has to be diverted, and fast reactions are required. Hesitation, delays, might endanger the organism. Stimulus-response learning is more rigid, and thus, reduces ambiguity and interfering conflict. It is cognitively less demanding than spatial learning, leaving more cognitive capacities for coping with the current stress and its consequences. Stimulus-response learning may not depend on an explicit cognitive reflection, but rather a "habit" formation. It appears reasonable to assume that these are accessible more quickly than "cognitive" (e.g., spatial) memories. The lack of cognitive reflection inherent to stimulus-response learning and memory is paralleled by a relative insensitivity to situational changes that may prompt for change of behavior. This idea is in line with the concept of "bounded rationality" (Simon, 1982; Gigerenzer & Goldstein, 1996) postulating that participants often use heuristics, that is, relatively simple rules, which lead to cognitive relief and correct decisions in many situations – but not in all. In general, the arguments above underline stimulus-response strategies as adaptive behavioral response to stress.

We also found more putamen activation for fragile EPs. The putamen and caudate both belong to a group of brain areas known as the basal ganglia. This group is associated with a variety of functions, including voluntary motor control, procedural learning involving routine behaviors, and cognitive coordination (Stocco, Lebiere, & Anderson, 2010). The structures are also centrally involved in memory, cognition, action selection, reinforcement learning, and emotions (Rosen & Levenson, 2009). Mediated by signals from many other brain areas, the basal ganglia can activate a particular motor system by inhibiting others. It has also been suggested that the basal ganglia play an important role in threat assessment and self-defense (Flannelly, Koenig, Galek, & Ellison, 2007).

The hippocampus seems to have an inhibitory role toward classically conditioned stimuli. This capacity to inhibit conditioned reactions relates to hippocampal-related evaluation of the context in which a conditioned cue is perceived (Bouton, 2004; Holland & Bouton, 1999). Apart from the hippocampal and basal ganglia memory systems, the amygdala may be part of a third memory system (White & McDonald, 2002). This complex structure fulfills an important role in emotional learning and in memory in many instances (e.g., LeDoux, 2000), and fragile EPs exhibited more amygdala activation than high fantasy-prone controls. The three different memory systems (hippocampus, basal ganglia, amygdala) seem to run in parallel, and can influence as well as compete with (i.e., inhibit) each other.

Fragile EPs fit these various ideas very well. As these parts, DID patients have fixed and fast stimulus response like defensive actions to perceived threat. These reactions are efficient during actual threat, but maladaptive when there is no real threat – as a clear perception of contextual cues would tell. But EPs are insufficiently aware of the current spatiotemporal context. For them the 'past' is the 'present,' 'there' is 'here,' and former person perspectives are EPs' present conceptions of self, world, and self-of-the-world.

The findings of our study are clearly opposite to the hypotheses of the SC- and F-models of DID. As we detailed in the article on the study (Reinders et al., 2012), one might argue that the minimal duration of 2 weeks of practice was insufficient to simulate the biopsychosocial features of authentic ANP and fragile EP. However, this argument is weak on several major counts. First, the SC-/F-models claim that few suggestions and little practice suffice to generate dissociative parts. Second, low fantasy-prone controls simulated the features of DID – in a relative sense – better than high fantasy-prone, mentally healthy women. Third, if proponents of the SC- and F-models would adapt their view and argue that years of practice are needed to generate the biopsychosocial features of ANP and EP, then they would have to demonstrate that individuals with DID actually engage in this *tour de force*. And if they choose to go this way, they must also explain what the final cause of these individuals' presumed long-term efforts to enact dissociative parts would be. To date, not a single study of true positives has showed that they trained themselves for years to play the roles of different prototypical parts. The final causes for true positive cases' role-playing these dissociative parts have also remained mysterious. Clinicians who are unaware of DID, or who regard the disorder as factitious, do not tend to receive patients with major DID with sympathy. So, why would these individuals role-play DID? Fourth, if the hypothesis is that therapists who 'believe in' DID must provide DID-fostering suggestions for many years before the patients become good at their simulation, then proponents of the SC- and F-models must demonstrate that these therapists actually engage in these unethical behaviors. They must also explain what the final causes of these therapists' suggestive actions would be. There are no studies showing that therapists of true positive cases of DID actually engage in these actions. In contrast, phase-oriented treatment of DID is focused on integration (e.g., Van der Hart et al., 2006), and emergent treatment evaluation studies demonstrate that this treatment is associated with reductions of dissociative pathology (see Chapter 15). Moreover, therapists who apply phase-oriented treatment to DID patients were often ignored, rejected, or ridiculed by their colleagues. Why would they still go on suggesting DID for years?

Memory Transfer Between Dissociative Parts

Our finding that ANPs and EPs are associated with different explicit reactions to identical trauma scripts suggests that these prototypical parts reconceive ('recollect') past traumatic experiences in different ways. Dissociative parts can also have different memories of non-traumatic events. For example, Elzinga et al. (2003) tested implicit and explicit memory in major DID using a directed forgetting task. They asked the participants to switch from one dissociative part to an 'amnesic' dissociative part in the time between (1) the presentation of to-be-remembered or to-be-forgotten neutral and emotional words, and (2) memory testing. The patients demonstrated selective forgetting of to-be-forgotten, but not of to-be-remembered words in the amnesic state. They did not exhibit directed forgetting within the same dissociative part, and implicit memory was fully preserved across different dissociative parts. Furthermore, independent of the kind of dissociative parts (i.e., amnesic or not amnesic), patients recalled more emotional than neutral words. The authors interpreted the findings in terms of retrieval inhibition.

Other studies of memory in DID found that learned stimuli, affective evaluations, and emotionally neutral episodic memories that one dissociative part had recently gained in a recent experimental setting can become transferred to another dissociative part (Huntjens, Peters, Woertman, Van der Hart, & Postma, 2007; Huntjens, Postma, Peters, Woertman, Van der Hart, 2003; Huntjens et al., 2002, 2005, 2006). This transfer occurred even though the dissociative part who had not been activated during the learning reported that they had not learned the involved stimulus.

Huntjens and colleagues also studied the transfer between dissociative parts for procedural learning (Huntjens, Postma, Woertman, Van der Hart, & Peters, 2005). Whereas there was a lack of transfer between authentic dissociative parts, simulators mimicked this pattern. It was therefore impossible to say whether the findings for the DID patients involved a form of amnesia or a different effect such as simulation.

Huntjens, Verschuere, and McNally (2012) examined memory transfer between two dissociative parts with respect to nontrauma related autobiographical details. The dependent variable was the time it took a dissociative part to press a button indicating recognition or nonrecognition of the personal relevance of a stimulus word, which might pertain to a personal feature, a feature of the other dissociative part, or an irrelevant word.

The experiment included two types of dissociative parts: The 'amnestic' part had to be subjectively amnestic for a memory of CSA that the 'trauma' dissociative part recalled as a personal memory. The 'amnestic' dissociative part's reaction times for personally relevant words, words pertaining to the 'trauma' dissociative part, and irrelevant words were assessed. Huntjens et al. found that the 'amnestic' dissociative part had similar reaction times for the 'trauma' part-dependent words and the irrelevant words. They interpreted the similar reaction times as an indication that the 'amnestic' dissociative part was not amnestic of the autobiographical details of the 'trauma' part, even though they subjectively said that this was the case. The researchers did not consider that the 'amnestic' part may mentally avoid features of the 'trauma' part, and that this avoidance takes time. It is also important to realize that there is a difference between phenomenal experience in the first-person perspective and physical judgment in the third-person perspective.

How can the discrepancies between the studies of Reinders et al. and Huntjens et al. be understood? According to TSDP, there is biopsychosocial overlap between different dissociative parts of the personality. They are often not fully ignorant of each other, occasionally intrude on each other, and can interact with each other. They also tend to share a number of implicit and explicit memories, including autobiographical memories. ANPs' mental avoidance of fragile EPs depends on ANPs' final cause, that is, on ANPs' will to evade fragile EPs and the traumatic memories in which these EPs are fixed. EPs' final cause is to defend against the threat they perceive. Whereas Reinders et al. examined ANPs and fragile EPs' reactions to trauma-related cues, Huntjens et al. tested the effects of memory transfer for words and other simple cues that did not have a negative emotional meaning for either dissociative part. That is a crucial difference. The ecological validity of tests involving cues that do not have a particular aversive meaning for one type or both types of dissociative parts is dubious.

Still, the fact remains that the 'amnestic' dissociative parts in Huntjens et al.'s studies were subjectively amnestic – or at least claimed amnesia for personal features of the 'trauma' dissociative parts – whereas the applied tests suggested transfer of memories from the 'trauma' parts to the 'amnestic' parts. The difference between subjective amnesia and transfer of memory on tests needs clarification. It could be studied if participants in these studies report amnesia for some reason (e.g., due to demand characteristics of the study), or if they experience, and are therefore subjectively convinced, that they are amnestic.

There are good reasons to emphasize that the phenomenology of the reported amnesia in experimental studies of DID requires more attention. For example, from a clinical point of view, it is uncommon that 'amnestic' dissociative parts are unaware of features of 'trauma' parts when they have reached a treatment stage in which they have become able to switch between these different parts on command. This is typically the phase of treatment that is geared toward the integration of traumatic memories. This second phase is preceded by a first phase in which the different dissociative parts become more acquainted with each other, learn to appreciate each other, and are stimulated to cooperate with each other. In this regard, it is of note that the DID patients in Huntjens et al. (2012) had already been in treatment for a very long time ($M = 8.9$ years, SD = 5.89).

In any case, in order to test biopsychosocial differences between dissociative parts in DID, it is in TSDP important to include the prototypes of dissociative parts that at the time of measurement are theoretically and clinically expected to have different biopsychosocial reactions while executing ecologically valid experimental tasks. These studies should also carefully and deeply examine the phenomenology and meaning of the patients' reports of their phenomenal experiences during and immediately after the experimental trials. Our own studies can also be improved in the latter regard.

Subliminal Exposure to Perceived Threat

Preconscious mental actions play a key role in responding to unconditioned and conditioned threat cues and in fear-related learning (Davies, 2000; Dolan, 2000; LeDoux, 1996; Morris, Ohman, & Dolan, 1998). TSDP includes the idea that ANPs preconsciously and consciously aim to avoid this actual or perceived threat, and that EPs preconsciously and consciously – and selectively – attend to these cues to the extent that these different parts have not yet integrated the traumatic memories and have not yet overcome their various phobias (e.g., of attachment, detachment, body sensations, affects, other dissociative parts, traumatic memories, other trauma-related conditioned stimuli). Because dissociative parts are comprehended as biopsychosocial subsystems of the personality as a whole system, ANPs and EPs have different preconscious neural and behavioral reactions to significant trauma-related cues.

It is worthwhile to use pictures of facial expression in studies of preconscious mental reactivity. Facial expressions are an important means of interpersonal communication. Their meaning is quite stable across cultures and is very rapidly assessed. A general trend is to quickly assess the meaning of the expression and then to look away (Becker & Detweiler-Bedell, 2009). However, high-anxious individuals gaze at negative facial expressions more than low-anxious individuals (Georgiou et al., 2005; Mogg, Garner, & Bradley, 2007).

First Step

In our first study on the topic, we hypothesized that dissociative part-dependent reactivity to intact (un)conditioned threat will be evident following cues that are presented very briefly in order to preclude conscious perception (Hermans et al., 2006). We more specifically tested the effects of exposing an ANP and a hyperaroused fragile EP in DID patients to masked neutral, fearful, and angry facial expressions.

The patients were instructed to indicate an observed shift of the color of a centrally placed dot on a computer screen (e.g., to say when a blue dot turned yellow). What they did not know was that this change followed a subliminally presented face. Preconsciously exposed to angry faces, ANPs named the color change more quickly than when they had preconsciously 'seen' neutral facial expressions. Fragile EPs did not show these differences. DID-simulating controls had the reverse pattern: They showed a tendency toward longer response latencies after exposure to angry faces as a simulated ANP, and a tendency toward faster reactions to preconsciously presented angry faces as a simulated fragile EP. The interaction "group (genuine DID vs. DID-simulators) × condition (angry vs. neutral faces)" was statistically significant. This effect was specific to cues (i.e., angry faces) that signal an increased possibility of attack, because it was absent when comparing fearful and neutral faces.

The results are consistent with the hypothesis that ANPs avoid subliminal threat cues by means of gaze aversion or some other form of avoidance, and that fragile EPs particularly attend to bodily threat from a person with increased sympathetic tone. The response of the EP is pathological, because angry faces represent social threat that can be reduced by gaze aversion: a social cue that signals submission to a dominant individual. The results of the study are inconsistent with SC- and F-models of DID, because the controls were unable to produce the reactions of an authentic ANP and EP.

Second Step

Given the results of Hermans et al. (2006), we decided to examine which brain areas ANP and hyperaroused fragile EP activate when they are subliminally exposed to facial expressions (Schlumpf et al., 2013). To control for possible effects of suggestion and fantasy proneness, we included actors as controls. They were carefully instructed, highly motivated, and trained to simulate an ANP and a fragile EP as they appear in patients with DID. The actors received detailed written and video information on DID, the core features of ANPs and hyperaroused fragile EPs, and switching between these prototypical dissociative parts. We instructed the controls to practice simulating ANP and EP as often as they deemed necessary to adequately enact the two roles, but at least three times before the MRI measurement.

During the experiment, the participants were consecutively exposed to neutral and angry faces. The exposure time per face was only 16.7 ms. The projection of the faces was preceded and immediately followed by the projection of a black-and-white dotted mask. The procedure was designed to preclude conscious awareness of the faces. Posthoc tests confirmed that the participants had indeed not consciously perceived the faces. The masks preceding and following the faces had a centered colored dot, but in a different color. It was the participants' task to immediately press a button when they observed a color change. Their reaction time was recorded. Final statistical analyses were conducted on 11 DID patients and 15 controls for differences in neural activity, and 13 DID patients and 15 controls for differences in behavior and psychometric measures.

Hypotheses

Based on TSDP as well as our own and others' prior research, we hypothesized that compared to (1) patients as ANP, and (2) actors as simulated fragile EP patients as a fragile EP have a different pattern of neural activity in response to subliminally presented faces. We particularly predicted that these EPs would display more activity in primary and higher-order visual areas, face-sensitive areas including extrastriate occipito-temporal regions, limbic structures including the amygdala and hippocampal/parahippocampal region, and motor-related areas comprising the cortical motor system, basal ganglia, and cerebellum. We also hypothesized that (3) these differences are more pronounced following angry faces, that (4) DID patients have longer reaction times to these faces as fragile EP than as ANP, and also longer than controls as fragile EP, and that (5) comparisons of ANP and EP in controls yield different neural and behavioral reactivity patterns than comparisons of ANP and EP in DID patients.

Results: Subjective Report of Fear and Brain Activation

Consistent with our first three hypotheses, we found that the DID patients had dissociative part-dependent biopsychosocial reactions to masked neutral and angry faces. They were overactivated as a fragile EP that typically engages in active forms of mammalian defense, and underactivated as an ANP. These findings are clearly supportive of TSDP. The actors effectively simulated reported phenomenal fear as simulated fragile EP. SC-/F-models as well as T-models of DID predict this effect. However, the controls were unable to simulate authentic EPs' reaction times and neural activation patterns. The latter result is inconsistent with SC- and F-models of DID.

Fragile EP Versus ANP: Fragile EPs in DID patients demonstrated more activation in the right parahippocampal gyrus during the masked presentation of neutral and angry faces than authentic ANPs. This gyrus has been implicated in recall of autobiographical memories (Fink et al., 1996), with a right hemispheric predominance (Tulving et al., 1994) and in re-experiencing symptoms in PTSD (Osuch et al., 2001; Sakamoto et al., 2005). The observed enhanced activation in the parahippocampal gyrus fits core features of hyperaroused fragile EPs, that is, their fixation in traumatic memories, their tendency to perceive safe individuals as dangerous, and their tendency to reactivate traumatic memories when confronted with reminders of traumatic experiences.

ANP Versus Fragile EP. Comparing hyperaroused fragile EP and ANP in DID, we did not find the hypothesized differences with respect to visual areas, face sensitive areas, amygdala, and motor areas. This negative finding may at least in part relate to limitations of the study. Our sample size was relatively small, mainly because of the difficulty of finding DID patients who are able to alternate between ANP and fragile EP at request and to remain activated, particularly as this EP, for a substantial period of time in an fMRI environment. As ANP quite a few DID patients will meet the challenge of lying on their back in a narrow and noisy scanner for a substantial period of time with their head fixated. However, for many hyperaroused fragile EPs, many of whom are fixed in horrible memories of sexual and physical abuse, this experimental setting can be too demanding. DID patients who are willing and able to meet the requirements of the study are ones who have been in treatment for at least several years. Because treatment of DID fosters the integration of traumatic memories and the subsequent integration between different dissociative parts, studies such as the present one are prone to underestimate naturally existing biopsychosocial differences between these subsystems of the personality (as indicated, this limitation also applies to Huntjens et al.'s various studies).

Fragile EP in DID Versus Fragile EP in Controls: Differences in neural activation patterns were much more pronounced for EPs in DID patients compared to the simulated EPs in controls. However, in contrast to our third hypothesis, the subliminal perception of EPs of *neutral* and not their perception of angry faces revealed these strong differences. In reaction to subliminally presented angry faces, hyperaroused EPs in DID were associated with enhanced activity in the precentral gyrus and in the temporal pole of the superior temporal gyrus. These areas are involved in the analysis of faces, and the temporal pole is particularly involved in analyzing the semantic knowledge of a face (Haxby, Hoffman, & Gobbini, 2000).

In response to masked neutral faces, fragile EPs activated a cluster of brain areas. These included the dorsal brainstem, the parahippocampal gyrus, and the mainly left lateralized areas positioned in the occipito-temporal junction as well as several motor-related areas. The dorsal brainstem activity indicates arousal (Jones, 2003) and associated vigilance. It is also associated with basic motivations or will (Panksepp & Biven, 2012). The occipito-temporal junction is a face-sensitive region (Gorno-Tempini et al., 2001; Haxby et al., 2001; Nakamura et al., 2000). The occipital fusiform gyrus is activated in a very early phase in the face-processing stream and is associated with the initial representation of a face (Pitcher, Walsh, Yovel, & Duchaine, 2007). The mainly left lateralized activation pattern for hyperaroused fragile EPs is consistent with previous findings of left hemispheric involvement in subliminal perception of faces (Henke, Landis, & Markowitsch, 1994). Activation of motor areas could indicate defensive reactions to perceived threat.

We did not find abnormal amygdala activation for these EPs in DID. However, an increase of amygdala activation in reaction to angry or neutral faces is not a consistent finding (Fusar-Poli et al., 2009), nor is it consistently found in PTSD neuroimaging studies. For still other possible explanations, see Schlumpf et al. (2013).

ANP in DID Versus Fragile EP in Controls: We thus found increased activation in many a priori defined brain regions for fragile EPs in DID patients compared to fragile EPs in controls. There were fewer differences for ANPs in DID patients compared to EPs in these patients. We therefore decided to check posthoc whether the documented differences for authentic versus simulated fragile EPs also existed for authentic ANPs versus these simulated fragile EPs. We found enhanced activity in the dorsal brainstem, the lingual gyrus, and motor-related areas such as the putamen and the (pre-)supplementary motor area. This pattern resembles that for authentic fragile EPs, though less pronounced. ANPs' decreased involvement in consciously perceived trauma-related cues (Reinders et al., 2003, 2006) thus seems to have roots in this part's subdued preconscious reactivity to trauma-related cues.

Are Consciously Perceived Neutral Faces Neutral? The conscious perception of emotional and of neutral faces is associated with activation of several similar brain areas (Carvajal et al., 2013). This similarity may relate to the fact that neutral faces are ecologically not necessarily neutral; individuals tend to assign them an emotional content. Whereas little effort is needed to assess the affective significance of emotional faces, assessing the meaning of a neutral face requires lengthier evaluative attention. Social judgment of neutral faces was particularly associated with frontal brain activation and longer reaction times in mentally healthy individuals. This recent finding is consistent with our findings for reaction times in DID.

Results: Reaction Times

Consistent with the neural findings and our fourth hypothesis, fragile EPs in DID patients showed significantly slower reaction times to neutral faces and a tendency toward slower reaction times to angry faces, compared to ANP in DID patients and simulated fragile EPs in controls (see Figure 18.1). This face- and dissociative part-specific effect could also be

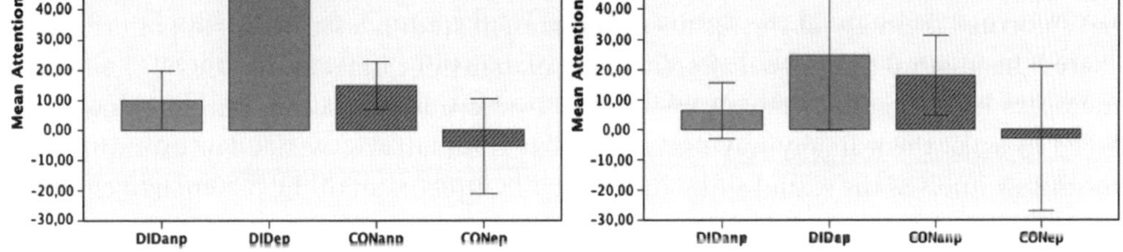

Figure 18.1. Mean attentional bias score (reaction times for facial expressions minus reaction times for scrambled stimuli) for (A) neutral faces (attentional bias neutral faces minus scrambled stimuli) and (B) angry faces (attentional bias angry faces minus scrambled stimuli) in ms (±SEM). A positive attentional bias indicates vigilance, a negative attentional bias indicates avoidance, $^{*}p < .00625$ (Bonferroni corrected).

observed in the direct comparison between reaction times related to neutral and angry faces. The comparison only yielded statistically significant longer reaction times in the neutral face condition for the involved fragile EPs of DID patients.

Neutral faces may be threatening to hyperaroused fragile EPs for a variety of reasons. First, they may find it hard to disambiguate these facial expressions ("What does this face mean?"), particularly following emotional neglect ("This person may not care about me") and abuse ("this person seems calm, but for how long? What emotion will he or she show next?"). Consistent with this interpretation, patients with borderline personality disorder regarded neutral faces as threatening, and their amygdala became hyperactivated when they were supraliminally confronted with these faces (Donegan et al., 2003). Borderline personality disorder, DID, and dissociative symptoms are all intimately related to a context of unstable and disrupted interpersonal relationships (Benjamin, 1993; Dutra et al., 2009; Kelley et al., 2002; Korol, 2008; Linehan, 1993; Ogawa et al., 1997). As a dissociative part of the personality fixed in the traumatic past, fragile EPs may regard neutral faces as untrustworthy and threatening, and thus becomes hypervigilant when confronted with them, and prepares motor defensive reactions.

Our results fit those of detrimental effects of still (i.e., neutral, unengaged) faces for children (Mesman, Van IJzendoorn, & Bakermans-Kranenburg, 2009; Tronick et al., 1978), particularly for those who are neglected, abused, and insecurely attached. Faces that are physically judged as neutral in third-person perspective need not be phenomenally neutral in the other person perspectives. For example, neutral faces may communicate affective unavailability of other individuals such as primary caretakers to a traumatized child. This unavailability applied to the DID patients who participated in the study, all of whom reported emotional neglect and abuse by family members. As discussed above, the quality of the early caregiving relationship is linked to dissociation: Affective parental unavailability and disorganized attachment in childhood are major predictors of dissociative symptoms in adulthood (Dutra et al., 2009; Ogawa et al., 1997). The findings of Schlumpf et al. (2013) add to the evidence for a pivotal role of emotional neglect and emotional unavailability of caretakers in DID.

When discussing the significance and meaning of neutral and angry facial expressions with several women with DID who were in treatment with me, they spontaneously (I had not informed them about the results of the present study) described both patterns. They shared that neutral faces signal affective unavailability of caretakers for them. Their family members had generally been aware of the chronic traumatization, but all or most had failed to assist them in any way during or after traumatizing events. For example, some mothers witnessed the sexual abuse or physical maltreatment of the patient as a child, but showed a blank face and did not interfere with the abuse and neglect. A flat face may also reveal emotional uninvolvement of the perpetrator during or after the abuse. A common remark of DID patients was that there is little need to attend for long to an angry face. Things are clear once a face has turned angry. However, only an open eye can track the loss of neutrality.

Our findings fit the words of the Dutch author, poet, and biologist Dirk Hillenius (1927–1987; Beurskens, 2013, p. 74):

> Looking is never neutral
> Even lions evade your gaze
> Watching only as run-up
> to fight or sex

Controls

Our fifth and last hypothesis was that the identified behavioral and neural differences for an ANP and a fragile EP in DID patients would not be matched by controls, who were instructed and motivated to simulate an ANP and EP. Controls showed a tendency toward inverse reaction times and neural activation patterns for these different prototypical parts. As a simulated ANP, the actors tended to react like an authentic EP in DID patients and as a simulated EP like an authentic ANP in these patients. The actors were thus unable to simulate DID with respect to behavioral and neural reactivity, a finding that contradicts the sociocognitive model of DID. Compared to a simulated EP, as a simulated ANP controls had amygdala activity in the neutral face condition, but neither brainstem activity nor longer reaction times. Whereas the neutral faces were thus salient (Davis & Whalen, 2001; LeDoux, 1998) for ANP-simulating controls, the pictures did not arouse them or attract much preconscious attention, as happened for authentic EPs. These findings add to the biopsychosocial evidence that DID is neither an effect of suggestion and fantasy, nor of role-playing.

Clinical Implications

The findings suggest that therapists of DID patients must be emotionally and behaviorally engaged. Therapeutic neutrality likely scares patients, particularly when they function as fragile EPs: It triggers and reinforces conditioned emotional and defensive reactions. For example, as this type of part the patients may perceive an emotionally neutral therapist as an emotionally unavailable caretaker. As ANPs, they may notice and report that this neutrality negatively affects one or more EPs. It may seem that nothing is wrong when one or more ANPs are dominant and out of touch with fragile EPs. The therapist's neutrality can nonetheless affect as one or more EPs that may be activated in parallel. This possibility is consistent with clinical observations (Van der Hart et al., 2006). It also happens that ANPs do not notice EPs' emotional reactions straight away. However, these reactions can surface when the involved trauma-fixated parts come forward more and express feelings of rejection, confusion, or fear.

Conclusion

The study showed that two prototypical parts of the personality in DID patients, ANP and hyperaroused fragile EP, have different biopsychosocial reaction patterns to backward-masked neutral and angry faces. It also demonstrated that controls were unable to simulate these different conscious subsystems of the personality. Fixed in active defense, as a fragile EP DID patients engaged in early, automatic, and intense scanning of facial expressions. Avoiding threat cues, as an ANP they were underinvolved in the faces. These results and interpretations are consistent with clinical observations and supportive of TSDP, but inconsistent with the SC- and F-models of DID.

Hermans et al. (2006) Versus Schlumpf et al. (2013)

The data from Schlumpf et al. (2013) and Hermans et al. (2006) differ in some regards. In the first study, but not in the latter, we found faster reaction times to angry faces compared to neutral faces for fragile EPs. This conflicting finding might be related to several methodological differences between these studies. For example, in Schlumpf et al. we presented facial stimuli for 16.7 ms, and in Hermans et al. we presented them for 25 ms. Cognitive theories of anxiety maintain that the attentional bias toward threatening material occurs at a preconscious level (Cisler & Koster, 2010). The stage of sensory reactivity at which this bias emerges in DID has not been systematically investigated to date. There is neurophysiological evidence showing that the signals transmitted by neurons in the visual cortex increase as a function of stimulus length (Rolls, Tovee, & Panzeri, 1999). In other words, the shorter the presentation time, the less sensory signals for the discrimination of a face are provided. Neutral faces have an uncertain emotional valence and therefore require deeper processing demands. It might be speculated that the slightly shorter presentation time in Schlumpf et al. (2013) particularly increased early preconscious fixation of EPs on neutral facial expressions, because hyperaroused fragile EPs are focused on threat or potential threat cues from their earliest perception of these cues. Future studies are needed to test this hypothesis.

ANP and Fragile EP in DID: What Catches the Eye?

In a pioneering further study, Simona Seidmann and Yolanda Schlumpf (2014) examined eye-movement patterns of an ANP and a fragile EP in a woman with DID, a female actor who was instructed and motivated to simulate these dissociative parts of the personality, and mentally healthy controls who were not playing a role. They were presented three pairs of photographs of faces with contrasting emotional expressions (see Figure 18.2), and rated the faces with respect to arousal, threat, and valence (Table 18.1).

Table 18.1. Face ratings of the DID patient and the DID-simulating actress for fearful, happy, and neutral faces.

			DID					
			Arousal		Threat		Valence	
			ANP Median	EP Median	ANP Median	EP Median	ANP Median	EP Median
Face	Fearful	Female	4	3	3	4	2	2
		Male	4	5	2	5	2	1
	Happy	Female	5	3	1	3	5	3
		Male	4	3	1	4	5	3
	Neutral	Female	3	4	3	4	2	2
		Male	4	5	4	5	2	1
			SIM					
			Arousal		Threat		Valence	
			ANP Median	EP Median	ANP Median	EP Median	ANP Median	EP Median
Face	Fearful	Female	4	4	4	3	2	2
		Male	4	4	4	4	2	2
	Happy	Female	3	1	1	1	3	5
		Male	4	3	1	1	4	4
	Neutral	Female	3	3	3	3	3	3
		Male	3	4	3	2	2	2

Note. DID: ANP and EP in a woman with DID; SIM: ANP and fragile EP in a DID-simulating actress. Arousal ratings: 1 = "very calming," 2 = "rather calming," 3 = "neutral," 4 = "rather activating," 5 = "very activating." Threat ratings: 1 = "not threatening," 2 = "hardly threatening," 3 = "neutral," 4 = "rather threatening," 5 = "very threatening. " Valence ratings: 1 = "very displeasing," 2 = "rather displeasing," 3 = "neutral," 4 = "rather pleasing," 5 = "very pleasing"

As Table 18.1 shows, the DID patient and the DID-simulating actress rated the fearful face in a similar fashion, but they evaluated the happy and neutral faces in different ways. For example, as EP the actress felt that the female happy face was very calming, whereas it was neither calming nor activating for the real EP. Consistent with EPs' subliminal reactions to neutral faces (Schlumpf et al., 2013), neutral faces were activating, threatening, and displeasing to the authentic EP in the present study, but less activating, threatening, and displeasing to the simulated EP. Compared with the simulated ANP, the real ANP rated fearful faces as less threatening, whereas the simulated EP experienced these faces as less threatening than the authentic EP. In all, the actress found it difficult to simulate the phenomenal evaluations of faces by real dissociative parts, and neutral faces are not at all neutral to the real EP.

Figure 18.2 clearly shows that, in contrast to mentally healthy individuals, the real fragile EP had hardly been looking at happy faces, but had spent an abnormal lot of time looking at fearful and neutral faces. The authentic ANP had engaged in the opposite pattern, and had been looking a lot at happy faces. It could well be that this dissociative part avoids fearful and neutral faces by focusing on happy faces. A comparison of Figure 18.3 and Figure 18.4 makes it clear that the simulated ANP had been looking less at happy faces than at fearful and neutral faces, and had attended to happy faces far less than the real

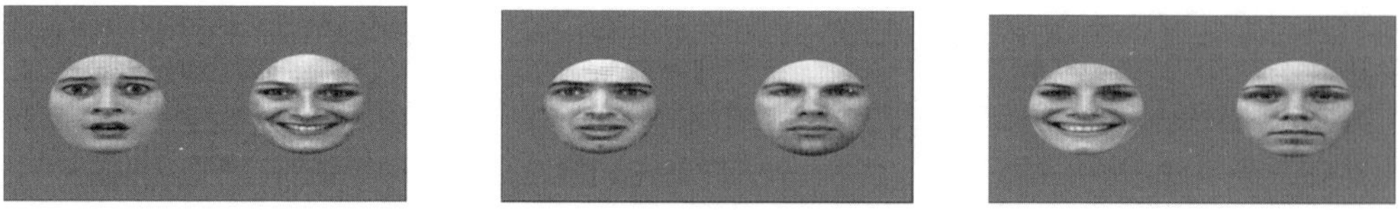

Figure 18.2. Three contrasts: fearful female face vs. happy female face (left), fearful male face vs. neutral male face (middle), and happy female face vs. neutral female face (right).

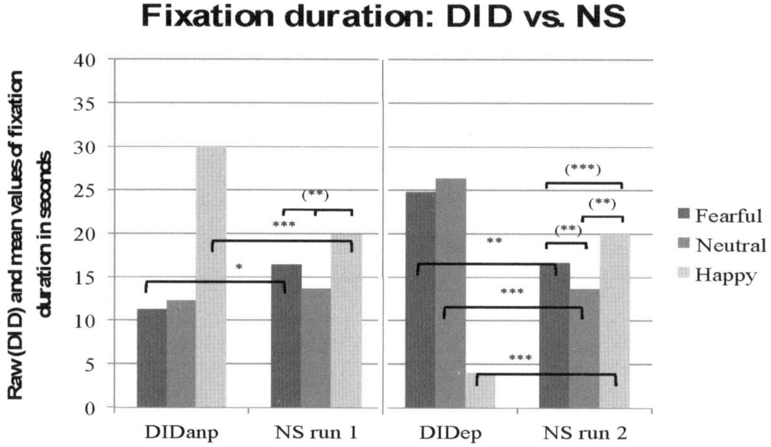

Figure 18.3. How long do ANP and fragile EP in DID and mentally healthy women look at fearful, happy, and neutral faces? *Note:* DID: dissociative identity disorder, measured as an ANP and a fragile EP; NS: mentally healthy controls who were not simulating ANP or EP. Raw values of DID and mean values of NS for fixation duration: *$p < .05$, $p < .01$, *$p < .001$.

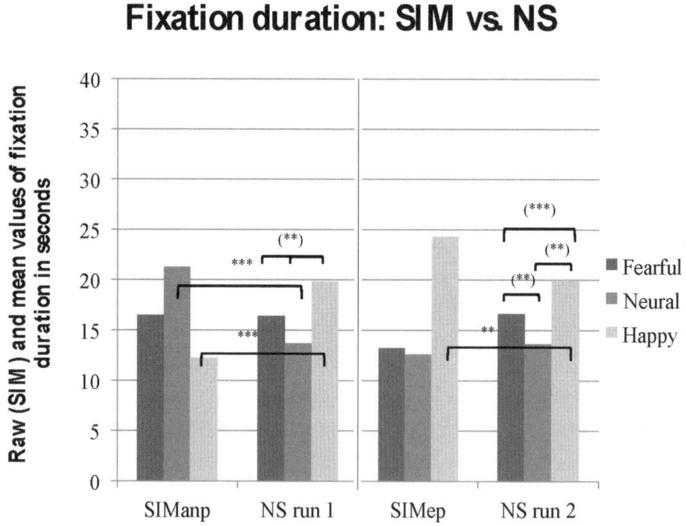

Figure 18.4. How long do a simulated ANP and fragile EP and mentally healthy women look at fearful, happy, and neutral faces? *Note.* SIM: actress instructed and motivated to simulate an ANP and a fragile EP; NS: mentally healthy controls who were not simulating ANP or EP. Raw values of SIM and mean values of NS for fixation duration: $p < .01$, *$p < .001$

ANP. Ineffective simulation of DID also showed in the results for the simulated and the real EP. The simulated EP had been looking at happy faces a lot, whereas the authentic EP had hardly looked at these faces.

These conjoint findings are fully consistent with previous findings as well as TSDP, but completely at odds with SC- and F-models of DID. According to TSDP, real EPs are fixated on threat cues (fearful and neutral faces), and real ANPs mentally avoid threat cues by focusing on cues that they do not perceive as threatening (happy faces). As in previous studies, simulating controls tend to "guess wrong." This pioneering controlled case study will be followed up by a group comparison study.

ANP and fragile EP in DID in Response to Rest Instructions

Having shown that women with DID as ANPs and hyperaroused fragile EPs have different biopsychosocial reactions to ecologically valid (i.e., trauma-related) supraliminal and subliminal cues, we took a next scientific step. This time, we wanted to examine how women with DID respond to rest instructions in a challenging environment. As indicated above, lying in an fMRI scanner in operation is always a difficult task for patients with DID. Instructions to relax, close the eyes, and stay motionless on one's back with one's head fixated in a narrow tube of a loud machine is challenging for patients with DID who have been chronically sexually abused and physically maltreated in their childhood and adolescence – and particularly for fragile EPs. The task includes powerful reminders of this abuse (e.g., being fixated, lying on one's back) and maltreatment (e.g., being tied up in a closet) that may elicit conditioned defensive reactions. In this context, rest instructions constitute a contradictory assignment for these individuals. They are invited to relax in a situation in which they feel an urgent need to be on guard, and in which there are no exteroceptive cues that signal what is going to happen next.

Based on TSDP, we hypothesized that this situation would generate different neural reactions in ANPs and fragile EPs, and that actors who are motivated, instructed, and trained to simulate these different prototypical dissociative parts would have different patterns of brain activation. We included actors who simulated ANPs and fragile EPs in DID to control for suggestion, fantasy, and motivated role-playing. Considering that playing a role is a task, simulation of ANP and fragile EP does not control for rest. We therefore also included mentally and physically healthy controls who did not simulate DID and who received rest instructions as a second control group (Schlumpf et al., 2014).

Hypotheses

Developing the hypotheses for the study, based on TSDP and prior research we reasoned as follows.

Default Mode Network

The study of resting-state neural activity has become an important area of neuroimaging. Of special interest is the so-called default mode network. This network consists of a set of brain areas made up of the medial prefrontal cortex, the posterior cingulate cortex in addition to midline parietal structures, lateral parietal regions, and the medial and lateral temporal lobes (Raichle & Snyder, 2007). Individuals activate it when they receive rest instructions and deactivate it when they execute goal-directed tasks (Fox et al., 2005; Fransson, 2005; Greicius, Krasnow, Reiss, & Menon, 2003; Grecius & Menon, 2004; Mazoyer et al., 2001; Shulman et al., 1997; Tian et al., 2007). Converging evidence suggests that the network is critically associated with general self-referential processing, such as autobiographical memory, self-reflection, self-awareness (i.e., introspection), and stimulus-independent thoughts (Andrews-Hanna, Reidler, Huang, & Buckner, 2010; Buckner, Andrews-Hanna, & Schacter, 2008; Mason et al., 2007; Northoff et al., 2006).

There is relationship between a number of mental disorders and atypical default mode activity (Broyd et al., 2009). Compared to healthy controls, individuals with PTSD had abnormal activity in some areas of the network following rest-instructions in two studies (Bonne et al., 2003; Sachinvala, Kling, Suffin, Lake, & Cohen, 2000). However, the findings for PTSD are heterogeneous, and the abnormalities are not restricted to the default mode activity (Bonne et al., 2003; Lucey et al., 1997; Mirzaei et al., 2001; Sachinvala et al., 2000; Yin et al., 2011). Since our rest instruction study of DID was the first ever done, we derived our hypotheses from TSDP and consistent clinical observations of patients with DID.

Because self-referencing is clearly abnormal in DID, we expected to find abnormal default mode activity. In this light, our most general hypotheses were that ANP and EP in women with DID have different neural activation patterns in response to rest instructions in an fMRI environment, and that ANP and EP simulating controls have different reactions, as have nonsimulating controls. Seeking to formulate more specific hypotheses, we more specifically reasoned as follows.

Fragile EP

According to TSDP, fragile EPs fixed in active mammalian defense focus on exteroceptive threat and alarming bodily and emotional cues. The brain region most consistently involved in the interoceptive awareness of potentially distressing emotional and bodily states is the anterior insula (Craig, 2009; Critchley, 2004; Critchley, Wiens, Rothstein, Ohman, & Dolan, 2004). The somatosensory cortex, in conjunction with the anterior insula, plays a central role in mediating the primary cortical conception of bodily states (Critchley, Mathias, & Dolan, 2001; Damasio, 1999). This conception is associated with subjective feeling states (Damasio, 1994; Damasio et al., 2000). A meta-analysis suggested that self-awareness is particularly linked to the dorsomedial prefrontal cortex (Gusnard & Raichle, 2001). This area also mediates the evaluation and monitoring of emotions, and gates the conscious subjective experience of an emotion (Etkin, Egner, & Kalisch, 2011).

There are intimate links between brain structures involved in emotions and motor actions, and emotions that activate motor actions (Baumgartner, Willi, & Jäncke, 2007, Damasio et al., 2000; Hajcak et al., 2007; Oliveri et al., 2003). TSDP proposes that hyperaroused fragile EPs are primarily mediated by the mammalian action system of mammalian defense. They are prone to engage in flight and freezing. As documented in our prior studies, these EPs indeed activate the motor system when they consciously and preconsciously perceive trauma-related cues – including the basal ganglia and cerebellum (Reinders et al., 2006, 2012). They were also associated with activation of cortical motor areas comprising the primary motor cortex, premotor cortex, and presupplementary motor cortex (Schlumpf et al., 2013). We thus expected that as fragile EPs, DID patients activate motor-related brain structures when they receive rest instructions in a situation that is scary to them.

ANP

In contrast, as ANPs DID patients attempt to avoid experiencing and knowing exteroceptive and interoceptive threats. When they succeed in this regard, they are bodily and emotionally numbed and depersonalized. We thus expected that ANPs would be underengaged following rest instructions in an MRI environment, and that this underengagement would manifest itself in a brain perfusion pattern reflecting low somatosensory awareness and inhibition of emotions. This pattern might well include increased perfusion in parietal somatosensory association cortex (i.e., BA 7). As discussed above, this area was overactivated in depersonalization disorder (Simeon et al., 2000), in a symptom-provocation study including PTSD patients with negative dissociative symptoms (Lanius et al., 2002), and in DID patients when exposed as ANPs to a personal trauma script (Reinders et al., 2006). Negative dissociative responses to reminders of the trauma were also associated with emotional overmodulation mediated by the medial prefrontal cortex including the anterior cingulate cortex (Lanius et al., 2002, 2010; Reinders et al., 2006).

In sum, we hypothesized that (1) DID patients and DID simulating controls engage in different patterns of brain activity after rest instructions. We particularly predicted (1a) that compared to the actors, women with DID activate the default mode network more, i.e., the medial prefrontal cortex, posterior cingulated cortex/precuneus, medial and lateral parietal areas, and medial and lateral temporal regions (DID-actors; the '–' stands for 'minus'; fMRI analysis is based on subtraction of the brain activity for one group compared to that of another group). Looking at the comparison from the other side (i.e., actors-DID), we hypothesized (1b) that actors compared to patients engage in decreased default mode activity because simulating an ANP and EP involves a goal-directed task. We furthermore hypothesized (2a) that in response to the described rest instructions, compared to genuine ANPs, genuine fragile EPs attend more to their bodily and emotional states as well as prepare for motor defensive actions. This awareness and preparedness is associated with increased activation of the dorsomedial prefrontal cortex, anterior insula, somatosensory cortex, and motor-related areas comprising of the cerebellum, basal ganglia, and cortical motor regions including the primary motor cortex, premotor cortex, and presupplementary motor cortex. For ANPs, we hypothesized (2b) that, compared to fragile EPs, these parts will mentally avoid threat cues and therefore become depersonalized and emotionally overmodulated, revealed in increased bloodflow in the somatosensory association cortex (i.e., BA 7) and the medial prefrontal cortex including the anterior cingulate cortex. We finally hypothesized (3) that ANP and fragile EP simulating controls generate different neural reactivity patterns than authentic ANPs and fragile EPs.

Results

We found differences between DID patients and DID simulating actors (hypotheses 1, 1a, 1b) as well as between ANPs and fragile EPs in DID patients (hypotheses 2a, 2b). We also found the hypothesized different perfusion patterns for DID and nonsimulating controls (hypothesis 3).

Hypothesis 1a

Compared to actors, DID patients showed higher resting-state metabolism in several areas belonging to the default mode network (i.e., temporal pole of the middle temporal gyrus, precuneus, angular gyrus, and dorsomedial prefrontal cortex; Gusnard & Raichle, 2001). DID patients were more involved in attending to their phenomenal selves when instructed to rest than actors.

Hypothesis 1b

The actors did not have more blood perfusion in any brain area to our predefined statistical thresholds. The default mode network is also known as the "task-negative" network (Tian et al., 2007). Individuals activate this network when they are at rest or are engaging in self-referential mental action (Buckner et al., 2008; Critchley et al., 2004; Mazoyer et al., 2001; Mason et al., 2007; Northoff et al., 2006; Raichle et al., 2001). However, the activity in these brain structures decreases when they engage in goal-directed tasks (Andrews et al., 2010; Fox et al., 1997; Fransson, 2005; Greicius et al., 2003; Greicius & Menon, 2004; Shulman et al., 1997; Tian et al., 2007). Enacting an ANP and a fragile EP involves a goal-directed task, which can explain the relative lower default mode activity for DID simulating controls compared to DID patients.

The comparisons between fragile EP/ANP in women with DID and actors fit these interpretations. Of special interest is the increased activity in the precuneus and the angular gyrus for ANPs and EPs in DID patients when contrasted with the corresponding simulated ANPs and EPs. Both brain areas are part of the default mode network (Raichle et al.,

2001). The precuneus is even the area of the brain with the highest resting-state perfusion and with perfusion decreases during non-self-referential, goal-directed actions (Kjaer, Nowak, & Lou, 2002). We therefore concluded that, in contrast to the DID simulating controls, as ANPs and fragile EPs DID patients were engaged in self-referential mental activity following our resting-state instructions.

Hypothesis 2a

The comparison of ANPs and fragile EPs in women with DID (DIDanp-DIDep) did not result in any perfusion differences that reached our predefined statistical thresholds. This finding is in line with Schlumpf et al. (2013), whereas ANP women with DID had less activity throughout the brain in reaction to threat-related stimuli than as EP. In the inverse contrast (DIDep-DIDanp), we found increased bloodflow in the primary somatosensory cortex, several motor-related brain areas (i.e., the primary motor cortex, premotor cortex, and presupplementary motor cortex, and the dorsomedial prefrontal cortex (see Figure 18.5).

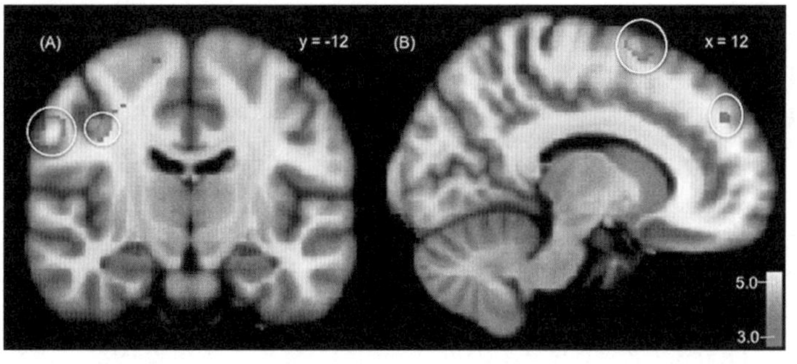

Figure 18.5. Significant regional cerebral blood flow increases (encircled) in genuine fragile EPs compared to genuine ANPs in (A) the primary somatosensory cortex, primary motor cortex, premotor cortex, and (B) the presupplementary motor cortex and dorsomedial prefrontal cortex.

Consistent with TSDP, DID, as fragile EP patients specifically reported not having a more explicit task to focus on while lying in the scanner was threatening. As EP but not as ANP, several women with DID experienced an urge to get out of the scanner, and one of them actually fled in a sudden and powerful reflex. The treating clinician had to reassure some women as EP, by being present during the actual scan, or even by gently holding one of their feet as they were scanned.

These findings fit the postulate of TSDP that women with DID as fragile EP are more self-aware and experience more bodily sensations than as ANP. In a number of independent studies, self-referential action was associated with activity in the dorsomedial prefrontal cortex (Gusnard, Akbudak, Shulman, & Raichle, 2001; Kjaer et al., 2002; Macrae, Moran, Heatherton, Banfield, & Kelley, 2004). We also found increased activity in this brain area for EPs in or backward masking study (Schlumpf et al., 2013). The primary motor cortex and the premotor cortex are involved in action planning and action execution (Kawashima, Rolland, & O'Sullivan, 1994), and the presupplementary motor cortex in the inhibition of motor responses (Neubert & Klein, 2010). Combining these findings, we interpret that, as EP, the patients were mediated by the will system of mammalian defense. In this sense, they focused on their phenomenal self, which prominently included bodily-emotional cues in an environment that they conceived as threatening, and experienced an urge to flee. However, they had to inhibit this will to run to meet their will to fulfill the experimental task.

Hypothesis 2b

Compared to EPs, ANPs did not show elevated perfusion in any brain region. As ANP, the women with DID may also have conceived our instructions to relax, close their eyes, and stay immobile in a loud narrow space as threatening. In response to this, they may have mobilized their mental avoidance strategy, which made them bodily and emotionally numb and depersonalized.

Hypothesis 3

Consistent with our third hypothesis, comparisons of ANP and EP in controls yielded different neural reactivity patterns than comparisons of ANP and EP in DID patients. However, compared to simulating EP, when simulating ANP the actors did not involve perfusion differences that reached our predefined statistical thresholds.

As the simulated EP, the actors had increased activity in many a priori defined regions. Of particular interest is the increased perfusion in the anterior insula. Based on the idea that actors had to try to experience another person's feelings, the increased activity in the anterior insula might be discussed in the framework of empathy in the sense of *einfühlen*, that is "feeling into someone" (Barnes & Thagard, 1997; Eisenberg & Strayer, 1987). The anterior insula are associated with empathy for pain (Jackson, Meltzhoff, & Deceity, 2005; Singer et al., 2004). Furthermore, pain can occur beyond nociception. It can be generalized to mental suffering of any sort (Craig, 2003), such as lying in a scanner as a very scared dissociative part of a traumatized individual's personality.

Hypothesis 4

Upon comparing DID patients and nonsimulating controls, we found that the women with DID, both as ANP and as EP, activated the temporal lobe more. Prior neuroimaging studies as well as electrophysiological investigations had already suggested a link between dissociation and temporal lobe functioning (Hughes et al., 1990; Sar, Unal, Kiziltan, Kundakci, & Ozturk, 2001). The temporal lobe was also implicated in several studies investigating the relationship between temporal lobe epilepsy and DID (Benson, Miller, & Signer,1986; Mesulam, 1981). Some authors regard the temporal lobe as the generator of 'dissociative states' (e.g., Bob, 2003), but they do not seem to comprehend and define ANP as a 'dissociative state.' Moreover, studies show that dissociation of the personality involves much more than an abnormally functioning temporal lobe.

Still, the temporal lobe has strong anatomical connections to the limbic system (e.g., amygdala and is involved in emotions, whereas the hippocampus is involved in episodic memory [Bob, 2003]. Emotional and mnemonic functions are disturbed in trauma stressor-related disorders such as dissociative disorders. Dissociative parts of the personality involve biopsychosocial subsystems that involve their own feelings and conceptions of who they are, what the world is like, and how they relate to that world. This selectivity might be associated in part with temporal lobe activity, which would be in accordance with a previous single-case study showing that temporal lobe functioning may mediate "switches" between dissociative parts of the personality (Tsai, Condie, Wu, & Chang, 1999).

DID as EP Versus Nonsimulating Controls

Compared to nonsimulating healthy participants, women with DID had as hyperaroused fragile EP but not as ANP more activity in the right-sided orbitofrontal and dorsolateral medial prefrontal cortex. As Schlumpf et al. (2013) found, fragile EPs were also associated with more activation of the dorsomedial prefrontal cortex in response to subliminally perceived faces. In line with TSDP, increased orbitofrontal and dorsomedial prefrontal activation for hyperaroused fragile EP might be associated with this dissociative part's ongoing tendency toward mind threat.

Many functional neuroimaging studies of PTSD patients have suggested abnormalities of brain regions implicated in affect regulation, including the ventral parts of the medial prefrontal cortex (Etkin et al., 2011) and the orbitofrontal cortex (Bremner et al., 2003; Rauch et al., 1996). Still, in the light of the cortico-limbic inhibition model of PTSD (Lanius et al., 2010), our finding for fragile EP is unsuspected. This model proposes that re-experiencing together with hyperarousal symptoms in reaction to reminders of traumatizing events are due to hypoactivity of the prefrontal areas. This hypoactivity is thought to reflect a lack of prefrontal control of the limbic system, that is, the 'emotional brain,' leading to hyperemotionality. For example, Bremner et al. (2003) found a decrease of orbitofrontal activity during the retrieval of emotionally valenced word-pairs as compared to the brain activation in this area for neutrally valenced word-pairs. Underregulation of the emotional brain with structures such as the amygdala would thus mark the DSM-5 hyperarousal subtype of PTSD. The cortico-limbic inhibition model also postulates that subjective disengagement from the emotional content of reactivated traumatic memories in the form of depersonalization, derealization, and/or emotional numbing is associated with hyperactivity of prefrontal areas. This response pattern characterizes the 'dissociative subtype of PTSD.' In sum, the idea of the cortico-limbic model of trauma is that prefrontal structures can – and should – inhibit the emotional brain. Put in psychological terms, reason can control affect, for better or worse.

Whereas the cortico-limbic inhibition model predicts that hyperaroused and scared fragile EPs are associated with hypoactive prefrontal areas, we found hyperactive orbitofrontal and dorsomedial prefrontal activation. How can the apparent inconsistency be reconciled? First, with Myers-Schulz and Koenigs (2012, p. 138), it holds that

> [a]ny theoretical framework, which assumes that an 'increase' or 'decrease' in the activity of a particular brain area would have a straightforward effect on an individual's subjective emotional state may be a gross oversimplification of a complex and dynamic network. Rather, the effect of modifying activity in any particular brain area may depend critically on the exact conditions of the rest of the network.

Second, there are conflicting findings regarding prefrontal activity in traumatized individuals (Myers-Schulz & Koenigs, 2012). War veterans with damage to ventromedial prefrontal cortex were less likely to develop PTSD (Koenigs et al., 2008), and at least two neuroimaging studies of PTSD found an increase of ventromedial prefrontal activation (Morey, Petty, Cooper, Labar, & McCarthy, 2008; Pannu Hayes, Labar, Petty, McCarthy, & Morey, 2009). Abnormalities in response to trauma scripts versus neutral scripts included more right orbitofrontal activation in one study (Rauch, Shin, & Phelps, 1996). Patients with borderline personality disorder – with or without PTSD – also had an increase of the orbitofrontal cortex in response to trauma-related words (Driessen et al., 2004).

The infralimbic cortex and the ventromedial prefrontal cortex can be involved in checking stress reactions by inhibiting central amygdala output, but these prefrontal structures can also play a role in the *enhancement* of stress-related reactions (Myers-Schulz & Koenigs, 2012). This augmentation might work (i.e., efficient causation) by enhancing the output of the central amygdala or by directly stimulating particular autonomic regions that lie outside of the amygdala. One explanation of these different effects is that the ventromedial prefrontal cortex encompasses different structures (Ongür, Ferry, & Price, 2003) and is not only associated with affect regulation. For example, it is also crucially involved in assessing the affective value of an external sensory stimulus and in linking this perception to appropriate guidance of behavior (Damasio, 1994, 1999). The right-sided sector of the ventromedial part of the frontal cortex mediates the assessment of the aversive value of an external cue (Kawasaki et al., 2001), and is sensitive to threat-related cues (Davidson, 2004). Activation of the left orbitofrontal cortex was positively correlated with heart rate variability in PTSD, but not in individuals who had experienced adverse events but who did not develop PTSD (Barkay et al., 2012). The dorsal parts of the medial prefrontal cortex are not involved in regulating the emotional brain, but rather are involved in the evaluation and monitoring of negative emotions (Etkin et al., 2011). The brain structure also has a pivotal role in conscious perceptual awareness (Lau & Passingham, 2006). Third, there is evidence suggesting that the orbitofrontal cortex encompasses different components, each with their own functions: The medial orbitofrontal cortex and the ventromedial prefrontal cortex seem to be implicated in fear extinction, whereas the anterolateral orbitofrontal cortex is associated more with negative affects and obsessions (Milad & Rauch, 2007).

Taken together, it seems that the cortico-limbic inhibition model of PTSD needs modification to explain the inconsistent findings regarding the role of prefrontal brain regions in trauma-related disorders. More activation of the right-sided orbitofrontal and dorsolateral medial prefrontal cortex for fragile EP in comparison to mentally healthy controls who did not simulate DID may be implied in the sharp conscious awareness, assessment, and evaluation of adversity, threat, and negative emotions. This interpretation is fully consistent with the subjective experiences of fragile EPs during the rest instruction fMRI challenge, and consistent observations of fragile EPs in clinical situations and real life.

Nonsimulating Controls Versus DID as ANP/EP

In the inverse contrasts, mentally healthy individuals who did not simulate DID showed a tendency toward elevated neural activity in posterior parietal regions, the medial prefrontal cortex, and the hippocampus. This perfusion pattern resembles the one that subserves scene construction and that includes a temporo-parietal-frontal network (Hassabis & Maguire, 2007, 2009; Schacter & Addis, 2007). Scene construction describes episodic simulation or imagery of future and past events (Hassabis & Maguire, 2007). Scene construction and default mode activity share internally directed attention (Hassabis & Maguire, 2009), and brain networks mediating future thinking and episodic memory overlap (Addis, Wong, & Schacter, 2007; Hassabis & Maguire, 2009; Schacter & Addis, 2007; Okuda et al., 2003; Szpunar, Watson, & McDermott, 2007). The medial temporal lobe system, which has long been considered to be uniquely involved in remembering the past, and which has been observed in nonsimulating healthy controls as well (i.e., hippocampus), is also required to flexibly recombine details from the past in order to simulate future episodes (Hassabis, Kumaran, Vann, & Maguire, 2007; Okuda et al., 1998; Sznupar et al., 2007). The idea that the mentally (non-DID-simulating) healthy participants were mentally travelling in time is further supported by elevated activity within the frontopolar cortex involved in future imagery and prospective thinking (Addis et al., 2007; Burgess, Quayle, & Frith, 2001; Okuda et al., 1998, 2003) as well as increased perfusion in the extrastriate visual cortex associated with remembering past events (Addis & Schacter, 2008).

Based on these interpretations and empirical foundations, we suggested that, under resting instructions as ANP and EP, DID patients activate left temporal regions more than mentally healthy controls who do not simulate ANP and EP. These controls may have been less involved in the task ("rest") and scanner environment, allowing them to let their mind wander to their personal past and imagined future.

As ANP and fragile EP, DID patients had less perfusion in brain areas involved in imagination than the non-DID-simulating healthy controls. These findings are at odds with the idea that fantasy proneness and actual fantasizing explain DID.

Conclusion

The study was the first to show that the different prototypes of dissociative parts are associated with different patterns of brain activity after rest instructions. It also demonstrated for the first time that, in this context and in contrast to DID-simulating actors particularly but not exclusively as EP, DID patients activated brain structures involved in self-consciousness. These findings are supportive of clinical observations of DID patients and of TSDP. Following rest instructions, neural activation associated with motivated role-playing of ANP and EP by mentally healthy controls was different from neural activation associated with being an authentic ANP and EP. The study thus adds to the evidence from supraliminal and subliminal neuroimaging studies of ANP and EP in DID that suggestion, role-playing, and fantasy proneness do not explain the disorder. The results also suggest that dissociative parts of the personality do not particularly activate brain structures associated with imagination. Imagination and absorption are thus not only different from dissociation of the personality conceptually, the difference is also biopsychosocial.

Profound Overlap in Brain Area Activation in Hyperaroused (Fragile EP) and Nonaroused or Hypoaroused (ANP/Fragile EP) Patients with PTSD and DID

According to TSDP, there should be major overlap in the dynamic causation of PTSD and major as well as minor DID. Dissociation of the personality constitutes the formal cause of trauma. This division, the theory postulates, characterizes the full continuum of trauma-related disorders. The simplest formal cause of trauma would be found in simple ASD, simple PTSD, and simple sensorimotor dissociative disorders. The most complex formal cause entails more than one ANP, more than one EP – some of which can be quite elaborate and emancipated – and particular mixtures of ANP and EP. This complexity would mark DID involving the major symptoms of hysteria, that is, intense and manifold cognitive-emotional and sensorimotor dissociative symptoms!sensorimotor dissociative symptoms.

Dissociation of the personality manifests itself in positive and negative symptoms. The complexity of this division should therefore be proportional to the severity of these symptoms. The involved disorders may also involve other symptoms and phenomena, but these will not be specific to mental disorders that basically involve a dissociation of the personality.

TSDP furthermore states that these mental disorders also share material and efficient causation. Shared material causation of PTSD as well as minor and major DID are presented in the next chapter on structural brain abnormalities in trauma-related disorders. The last part of the present chapter examines the postulated common efficient causality of PTSD and DID.

As detailed in Volume I, material and efficient causation do not explain a mental disorder in the absence of an understanding of the condition's formal and, most of all, final causes. What do traumatized individuals want to achieve, not in terms of reason, but in terms of basic will? That is the essential question. In accordance with Spinoza and Schopenhauer, I postulate in this book that it is the will to survive horrible events and to live daily live. Chronic abuse, maltreatment, and neglect also include the will to attach to caretakers. It is this collection of various deep existential desires that are extremely hard to integrate when children are traumatized by their parents or other primary caretakers on whom they are totally dependent – and to whom they, by their very nature, must and will attach.

Schopenhauer suspected that the will relates to the depth of our brain. Consistent with this intuition, Panksepp (1998; Panksepp & Biven, 2012) emphasizes that mammalian will systems are rooted in the periaquaductal gray and adjacent brainstem structures and have links with the emotional brain, also described as the limbic system. Affect often precedes cognition.

Rejecting philosophical dualism and adhering to philosophical monism that is not philosophical materialism and naïve realism, TSDP holds that, at the level of the brain, the different epistemic person-perspectives of dissociative parts and their involved affects, behaviors, and cognitions (conceptions, ideas) should be associated with particular patterns of brain activity as one form of material and efficient causation. Some of the more specific hypotheses regarding experimental exposure to reminders of traumatic experiences are schematically presented in Table 18.2.

Table 18.2. Several hypotheses regarding prototypical ANPs, hyperaroused fragile EPs, and hypoaroused fragile EPs' reactions to reminders of traumatic experiences.

	Mental and behavioral states	Psychophysiological states	Brain states
ANP	Emotionally numbed. Physically numbed. Depersonalized. Focused on wills of daily life. Underengaged in physical defense.	No significant changes in: heart rate, heart rate variability, and blood pressure. At least some degree of ventral vagal control.	General underengagement in presented cues. More activation of neocortical structures such as medial prefrontal cortex and anterior cingulate. More activation of multimodal association areas.
Fragile EP, hyperaroused	High emotionality. Strong sensory reactions. Behavioral engagement in active kinds of mammalian defense.	High heart rate. Low heart rate variability. High blood pressure as well as other markers of sympathetic nervous system dominance.	More activation of brain stem, emotional brain structures such as amygdala, basal ganglia, and neocortical areas such as insula and sensorimotor cortex.
Fragile EP-hypoaroused	Low emotionality. Analgesia-anesthesia. Paralysis. Low consciousness. Out-of-body phenomena. Behavioral engagement in tonic immobility/death feigning.	Low heart rate. Low heart rate variability. Low blood pressure. Still other markers of dorsal vagal dominance.	Extreme underengagement in cues. Involvement of the periaquaductal gray and the basolateral amygdala.

Note. ANP: Apparently normal part of the personality. Fragile EP, hyperaroused: Emotional part of the personality that as consistently observed by the patient's psychotherapist typically engages in *flight and freeze* in reaction to perceived threat. Fragile EP, hypoaroused: Emotional part of the personality that, consistently observed by the patient's psychotherapist, typically engages in *tonic immobility/death feigning* in reaction to perceived threat.

Psychophysical Reactions

In terms of TSDP, hyperarousal (e.g., increase of heart rate and blood pressure; decrease of heart rate variability and galvanic skin response) in PTSD and other trauma-related disorders involve a sympathetically mediated EP engaging in active types of mammalian defense that is dominant or that intrudes on ANP. It might also be an angry, controlling EP. Unaffected psychophysiology would involve the dominance of an ANP who keeps traumatic memories at bay. A decrease of heart rate would characterize a fragile EP engaging in tonic immobility/death feigning, or an ANP intruded on by this prototypical EP. Intrusions of EP into ANP's domain imply the parallel activation of two different dissociative parts of the personality. PTSD patients as well as patients with DID can thus have an increase or decrease of heart rate or an unaltered heart rate when they are confronted with reminders of traumatizing events.

These various hypotheses are supported by consistent research findings (Bremner et al. 1999a, 1999b; Frewen & Lanius, 2006; Hopper et al., 2007; Lanius et al., 2002, 2003, 2005, 2006, 2010, 2012; Osuch et al., 2001; Pissiota et al., 2002; Rauch et al., 1996; Reinders et al., 2006, 2012; Shin et al 1999; Wolf et al., 2012a, 2012b). Some PTSD patients became psychophysiologically hyperaroused and relived traumatic experiences, whereas others were not affected much, or became hypoaroused. In agreement with our work (Nijenhuis, Vanderlinden, & Spinhoven, 1998d; Nijenhuis et al., 1998b; Nijenhuis et al., 2002), Frewen and Lanius (2006) proposed that hyperaroused reliving of traumatic experiences pertains to sympathetically related mammalian flight and freeze. They also concurred with us that detached responding may relate to tonic immobility or to emotional numbing as a means of avoiding traumatic memories. Indeed, it is important to reiterate that *correlations* between patterns of brain activations and psychological phenomena do not necessarily demonstrate that brain activation *causes* the psychological phenomena. Descartes' error should be avoided, and philosophical materialism has its serious flaws (see Volume I). A crucial question, of course, is why the prefrontal cortex of some traumatized individuals is *hypoactive* and why it is *hyperactive* in others? The brain in itself does not and cannot tell the whole story. And *why* would some traumatized individuals have an increase, some a decrease, and still others an unaltered heart rate following confrontations with trauma-related cues? This book claims that there are intrinsic relationships between the brain, the body, and the environment. Embedded in an adverse environment, individuals have a deep will to survive and to have a daily life. As whole embodied and embedded organisms, they select a course of action that represents their effort to live and to continue to exist under the environmental conditions they find, conceive, and create. Evolution has given them various basic options that constitute the heart of the action or will systems, and these primary urges includes attachment cry, flight, freezing, or feigning death. Their will to survive and live life in one way or another generally constitute their final causes. However, some give up, wish to escape their pain forever, and commit suicide (dissociative symptoms are strongly associated with suicidal thoughts and acts).

Bremner (1999) and Lanius et al. (2010, 2012) suggested that these different reaction patterns involve the two subtypes of PTSD that have become included in the DSM-5. Individuals with the "re-experiencing/hyperarousal subtype" become hyperaroused and tend to relive traumatic experiences when they are confronted with reminders of these experiences. Those with the "dissociative subtype" of PTSD – the current DSM-5 "PTSD with dissociative symptoms" – remain physiologically relatively stable or become hypoaroused. They may also become subjectively detached.

Lanius et al. (2010, 2012) also suggested that these different response patterns can alternate in individuals with PTSD. They did not provide empirical evidence for this hypothesis, but the phenomenon is clinically observed and fully consistent with TSDP. We empirically demonstrated this alternation in women with DID (Reinders et al., 2006, 2012). Again, fearful fragile EPs for whom the trauma script pertained to a personal event respond with a major increase of heart rate and systolic blood pressure. ANPs who had not personalized the involved memory remained mentally and physiologically unaffected. Measurements of heart rate during my psychotherapy sessions with male and female DID patients indicate that fragile EPs who engage in death feigning when they feel threatened tend to have a significant drop in heart rate. They become absent minded, more or less emotionally and physically numb, may lose muscle tone, do not try to ward off an approaching perceived threat cue, and may experience that they float out of their body.

Neural Activation Patterns

PTSD studies have found different neural activation patterns for PTSD patients who respond to trauma-related cues with hyperarousal to the point of full-blown flashbacks, and PTSD patients who respond with depersonalization, derealization and emotional detachment.

According to TSDP, the hyperarousal reaction involves a hyperaroused EP or an ANP that is intruded on by this type of EP. The numbing reaction may involve an EP who more or less feigns death, an ANP who is intruded on by an EP of this nature, or a mentally avoidant ANP. Patients with PTSD and DID should therefore have largely similar ANP-dependent and EP-dependent neural reaction patterns to cues that remind them of the traumatizing events they lived. I am not aware of studies exploring neural activation patterns associated with tonic immobility/death feigning. Animal studies suggest involvement of parts of the periaquaductal gray (Vieira, Menescal-de-Oliveira, & Leite-Panissi, 2010) and the dorsal raphe nucleus (Ferreira & Menescal-de-Oliveira, 2009, 2012), two brain stem structures. This activation is consistent with the idea that, mediated by the dorsal vagal parasympathetic system, death feigning is the evolutionarily eldest type of vertebrate defense. The basolateral amygdala may play a role in the regulation of tonic immobility (Donatti & Leite-Panissi, 2009, 2011; Huang & Lin, 2006).

Table 18.3 summarizes the various findings.

Table 18.3. Profound overlap in brain area activation in hyperaroused (fragile EPs) and nonaroused or hypoaroused (ANPs or fragile EPs) patients with PTSD and DID.

Disorder, experimental condition	Brain area activation	Studies
18.3.1. Hyperactivation: fragile EP in PTSD	*In italics*, shared brain area hyperactivation in PTSD as fragile EP (18.3.1) and DID as fragile EP (18.3.2)	
Exposure to reminders of traumatizing events: (PTSD as hyperaroused fragile EP) – (HC)	+ *amygdala* + anterior paralimbic regions (e.g., *insula*) + R sensorimotor cortex, BA 1–4, 6 + *cerebellum*, cerebellar vermis + brainstem: periaquaductal gray	Frewen & Lanius, 2006; Lanius et al., 2006, 2010; Pissiota et al., 2002; Rauch et al., 2006; Schmahl et al., 2010
Positive correlations with PTSD flashback intensity	brainstem, lingula, *LR insula* R *basal ganglia, putamen* L hippocampal and perihippocampal regions L *somatosensory regions* *cerebellar regions*	Osuch et al., 2001
18.3.2. Hyperactivation: EP in DID		
Exposure to personal trauma memory in DID: (EP) – (ANP)	+ RL *insula* + RL *amygdala* + RL *basal ganglia*, caudate + R lateral fissure/postcentral gyrus: *somatosensory cortex* SII, BA43 + inferior temporal gyrus, BA 20 + middle temporal gyrus, BA 21 + L *cerebellum*, ventral-medial and lateral part	Reinders et al., 2003, 2006
Exposure to personal trauma* memory script: EP and ANP in DID versus EP and ANP simulating, high fantasy-prone HC. The comparison was: ([DID as EP] – [DID as ANP]) – ([HC as EP] – [HC as ANP])	+ L orbitofrontal cortex, BA11 + R postcentral gyrus, BA43 + L *amygdala* + RL *basal ganglia*, caudate + L *basal ganglia, putamen* + L *cerebellum*	Reinders et al., 2012
DID as fragile EP minus high fantasy-prone HC who simulate fragile EP. The comparison was (EP exposure to trauma* memory script) – (EP exposure to neutral memory script)	+ L *insula* + R inferior temporal gyrus, BA 20 + R *basal ganglia*, caudatus, dorsal/dorsal-lateral + L *basal ganglia,* caudatus, tail + L *basal ganglia, putamen*	Reinders et al., 2012
18.3.3. Hypoactivation: ANP (or EP tonic immobility in some cases) in PTSD	In **bold**, shared brain area activation for PTSD as ANP or fragile EP in tonic immobility (18.3.3), DID as ANP, DID as EP neutral memory (18.3.4), and depersonalization disorder (18.3.5); relative *de*activation for hyperaroused fragile EP in PTSD has also been found for these regions (18.3.3)	

Disorder, experimental condition	Brain area activation	Studies
Exposure to trauma-related cues: (PTSD hypoarousal [i.e., as ANP, or as fragile EP in tonic immobility]) – (HC)	+ **superior and middle temporal gyri**, BA 38 + inferior, middle, and superior frontal gyrus (e.g., BA 47) + R **medial frontal gyrus, BA 10** + medial prefrontal cortex, BA 9 + R **anterior cingulate gyrus, BA 24, 32** + ventral prefrontal cortex BA + insula + **parietal lobe, BA 7** + RL **occipital lobe, cuneus BA 19** – dorsomedial prefrontal regions	Felmingham et al., 2008; Frewen & Lanius, 2006; Lanius et al., 2002; Schmahl et al., 2010
Exposure to reminders of traumatizing events: (PTSD as hyperaroused fragile EP) – (HC), relative *de*activation for PTSD as hyperaroused EP	– ventro**medial prefrontal regions** – **anterior cingulated gyrus, BA 32** – L inferior frontal gyrus, BA 47 – **medial frontal gyrus, BA 10**, 11 – L **middle temporal cortex** – R **retrosplenial cortex, BA 21**, 29, 30, and in part 23 – **parietal cortex, BA 40** – **occipital visual association cortex, BA 19** – R **inferior temporal gyrus**, BA 20 – R hippocampus – thalamus	Frewen & Lanius, 2006; Lanius et al., 2006; Lanius et al., 2010; Pissiota et al., 2002; Rauch et al., 2006; Schmahl et al., 2010
Negative correlations with PTSD flashback intensity	LR dorsolateral prefrontal cortex R **fusiform cortex (occipitotemporal cortex)** R **middle temporal cortex**	Osuch et al., 2001
18.3.4. Hypoactivation: ANP in DID		
Exposure to trauma memory script in DID: (ANP) minus (hyperaroused fragile EP)	+ LR **inferior parietal sulcus, transition superior and inferior parietal lobule, BA 7, 40** + R **superior parietal lobule, BA 7** + L **medial occipital gyrus, BA** 18, **19** + R **fusiform gyrus, BA 19**, 37 + L **(pre-)cuneus, BA 7, 18, 19** + R **superior frontal gyrus**, BA 6, 8 + LR **medial frontal gyrus**, BA 6 + **medial prefrontal cortex, BA 10** + LR **cingulate gyrus**, BA 6, **24**, 31, **32** + R **inferior, middle and superior temporal gyri, BA 21, 32,** 37 + LR parahippocampal gyrus, BA35 (hippocampus activated in PTSD ANP) + R globus pallidus, + L caudate, ventral part	Reinders et al., 2003, 2006
Exposure to trauma* memory script ([DID as ANP] minus [DID as EP]) minus ([high fantasy-prone HC as ANP] minus [high fantasy-prone HC as EP])	+ R angular gyrus, BA 39 + R **anterior cingulate, BA 32** + L posterior cingulate, BA 31 + LR **cuneus**, BA 18, **19** + R **superior frontal gyrus**, BA 4, 6 + R **occipitotemporal cortex, BA 20**, 37 + LR parahippocampal gyrus, BA 35, 36 (hippocampus activated in PTSD ANP) + LR **intra-parietal sulcus, parietal lobule, BA 7, 40**	Reinders et al., 2012

Disorder, experimental condition	Brain area activation	Studies
Exposure to neutral and trauma* memory script: ([DID as EP, neutral script] – [DID as EP, trauma script]) – ([high fantasy-prone HC as EP, neutral script] – [high fantasy-prone HC as EP, trauma* script])	+ L **cuneus**, BA 18, **19** + R **occipito-temporal sulcus**, BA 20, 37 + R **intra parietal sulcus, BA 7, 40** + L **precuneus, BA 7**, 31 + R **middle temporal gyrus, BA 21**	Reinders et al., 2012
18.3.5. Depersonalization disorder		
Depersonalization disorder versus HC	+ LR **parietal cortex, BA 7B**, 39 + L **occipital cortex, BA 19** – R superior and middle temporal gyri, BA 21, 22 Dissociation and depersonalization scores among the subjects with depersonalization disorder were significantly positively correlated with metabolic activity in **BA 7B**	Simeon et al., 2000
18.3.6. Masking paradigm PTSD	Overlap between PTSD and DID is indicated by *italics*	
Masked images of adverse and benign events/cues: within PTSD and between PTSD and HC	+ L *parahippocampal gyrus* + L hippocampus, tail	Sakamoto et al., 2005
18.3.7. Masking paradigm DID		
Angry faces as well as neutral faces: (DID as fragile EP) – (DID as ANP) Neutral faces: (DID as fragile EP) – (fragile EP-simulating actors)	+ R *parahippocampal gyrus* + L brain stem + R *parahippocampal gyrus* + LR middle frontal gyrus + R middle temporal gyrus + L presupplementary motor area + LR precentral gyrus (primary motor area) + posterior middle cingulate/dorsal posterior cingulate + R dorsal medial prefrontal cortex + R middle temporal gyrus + L superior temporal gyrus + R lateral occipital cortex, inferior part + R occipital pole	Schlumpf et al., 2013

General remarks: Based on the reasons provided in this book, hyperarousal in PTSD involves an intruding hyperaroused EP or a switch to a hyperaroused EP; nonarousal or hypoarousal in PTSD in most cases pertains to a mentally avoidant ANP, an intruding EP in tonic immobility, or a switch to this type of fragile EP. In the case of a switch, one dissociative part takes executive control, whereas one or more other dissociative parts become deactivated. In the case of an intrusion, one dissociative part strongly influences another dissociative part.

ANP: apparently normal part of the personality; EP: emotional part of the personality; DID: dissociative identity disorder. In Reinders et al. (2003, 2006, 2012) and Schlumpf et al. (2013) all participants were women; HC: mentally healthy controls; HC in Reinders et al., 2012: extremely fantasy-prone women; HC in Schlumpf et al., 2013: female actors; L: left hemisphere; R: right hemisphere.

In the first column, '–' stands for 'minus' (fMRI and PET results are based on subtraction); in the second column '+' stands for more neural activity, and '–' for less neural activity. *Trauma memory scripts with respect to HC in Reinders et al. (2012) involved the worst adverse events HC were willing to share with the investigators

Table 18.3.1 and Table 18.3.2: Hyperaroused Fragile EP in PTSD and DID

Exposed to reminders of traumatizing events, hyperaroused EP in PTSD (Table 18.3.1) and DID patients as EP (Table 18.3.2) activate strikingly similar parts of the brain. The documented areas include the amygdala, insula, parts of the basal ganglia (the caudate, putamen), the sensory cortex, the inferior and middle temporal gyrus, portions of the cerebellum, and the orbitofrontal cortex. These various structures have major roles in unconditioned and conditioned emotional and motor defensive reactions to actual or perceived threat cues as well as in the evaluation of (alarming) bodily sensations and the state of the body.

This hyperreactivity of the brain is linked with a relative underactivation of several frontal cortical areas, including the anterior cingulated gyrus. This underactivation suggests a lack of inhibition of conditioned emotional reactions to former threat (e.g., Rauch et al., 2006). Underactivation of the hippocampal regions may indicate a lack of context evaluation (Rauch et al., 2006) that contributes to perseverance of alarm reactions to reminders of traumatizing events.

Table 18.3.3, Table 18.3.4, and Table 18.3.5: Hypoarousal in PTSD, DID, and Depersonalization Disorder

PTSD patients who react to reminders of traumatizing events with depersonalization, derealization, and emotional numbing in PTSD had brain activation patterns (Table 18.3.3) that closely match those for DID patients who function as ANP (Table 18.3.4). The brain structures include frontal (BA 9, 10, 24, 32), parietal (BA 7, 40), occipital (BA 19) as well as hippocampal regions. Many of these areas are activated during emotional memory suppression in mentally healthy individuals such as frontal areas (BA 4, 6, 8, 10/47), the anterior cingulate cortex (BA 32), and the intraparietal sulcus (BA 7, 40) (see above and Reinders et al., 2006). In patients with depersonalization disorder, BA 7 and 19 are also more activated than in healthy controls (Table 18.3.5).

Several of the brain areas that were activated for the above conditions in mentally healthy controls and patients with PTSD, DID, and depersonalization disorder were relatively *de*activated for hyperaroused fragile EP in patients with PTSD (Table 18.3.3).

Table 18.3.6 and Table 18.3.7: Masked Reminders of Traumatizing Events in PTSD and DID

Sakamoto et al. (2005) exposed patients with PTSD to masked images of traumatizing events and then performed a whole brain analysis (other masking studies of PTSD did not include this analysis) (Table 18.3.6). Activation in the ventral frontoparietal network, which is commonly associated with visual attention, was attenuated in these patients. The left hippocampal area – commonly associated with episodic and autobiographical memory – was abnormally easily activated. Sakamoto et al. noted that this brain activation pattern "corresponds well to the clinical characteristics of PTSD, in which even slight traumatic stimuli tend to induce intrusive recollection or flashbacks, despite a general decrease in attention and ability to concentrate" (p. 813).

Hyperaroused EP in DID also activated the parahippocampal gyrus in reaction to masked neutral faces (Table 18.3.7). This area as well as the hippocampus were correlated with flashback intensity in hyperaroused PTSD patients (Osuch et al., 2001, see Table 18.3.1). Both areas are implicated in the recall of autobiographical memories. Consistent with clinical observations, neutral faces may be threatening and ambiguous to EPs. The masked faces seem to elicit an instant search for meaning, as is suggested by the activation of the temporal pole of the superior temporal gyrus (see above; Schlumpf et al., 2013). This gyrus is part of a semantic system.

The brain areas that were more activated for EP in DID as compared to EP in actors who simulated these dissociative parts have functions in early phases of face perception as well as functions in behavioral defense to perceived threat. A comparison of ANP in DID and EP in the actors yielded a similar but less pronounced pattern of neural activation. The lesser involvement of ANP in consciously perceived trauma-related cues (see above; Reinders et al., 2003, 2006, 2012) could therefore have roots in the subdued preconscious reactivity of ANP to trauma-related cues.

If ANPs (can) already preconsciously avoid *externally* presented (un)conditioned threat cues, it is reasonable to assume that they can also preconsciously avoid *internal* (un)conditioned threatening stimuli. Hence, as TSDP states, ANPs may preconsciously attempt to avoid EPs, these parts' traumatic memories and other trauma-related cues to the degree that they are (still) phobic of these memories and cues. Some neurobiological data are consistent with the interpretation that dissociative amnesia involves inhibited access to episodic memory. Markowitsch and colleagues demonstrated that trauma-related dissociative amnesia as a disorder (APA, 1994) can be associated with reduced bloodflow in parts of the brain that are normally activated during retrieval of autobiographical memories (Markowitsch, 1999; Markowitz, Fink, Thone, Kessler, & Heiss, 1997; Markowitsch et al., 1998, 2000). Moreover, regaining these memories was correlated with a return to normal bloodflow in these brain areas (Markowitz et al., 2000).

Conclusion

There is a major and striking commonality between hyperaroused re-enactment of traumatizing events in PTSD – which according to the present analysis involves an EP – and an EP in DID which engages in active mammalian defense in reaction to these reminders and perceived threat. The match pertains to supraliminally as well as subliminally presented cues. The commonality also pertains to unaltered arousal/hypoarousal in PTSD and unaltered arousal/hypoarousal for ANP in DID. A direct comparison of biopsychosocial reactions of individuals with PTSD and individuals with DID to emotional and other cues is in order. In fact, such a study is underway.

The profound overlap strengthens trauma-related perspectives on complex dissociative disorders, particularly TSDP, and constitutes another falsification of SC- and F-models of these disorders.

Chapter 19

Dissociation of the Personality: Structural Brain Abnormalities

Picture the Mind

It's not a pretty sight – Vesalius's folded surface
of the brain. Or da Vinci's ventricles, spinal cord

trailing down like a braided afterthought.
Or each hemisphere bed down in its cubicle,

parted by the corpus callosum, crossing guard
for traffic back and forth. Now Descartes comes

on stage, appoints the pineal gland – trusty messenger
between matter and mind. Hard to say when beauty

slipped into this equation. Axon and dendrite.
Molecules dancing across synaptic space.

Receptors hungry for their messages.
Cascade of ions in their chrysalis of light.

Myra Sklarew[1]

Childhood maltreatment can affect the structure of the brain, and this structure influences how its owner lives his or her life. For example, structural brain features such as the volume of an individual's hippocampus may increase the risk of developing a dissociation of the personality when life turns dark (Gilbertson et al., 2002). When we seek to com-

1 Myra Sklarew worked in the 1950s at Yale Medical School under Karl Pribram studying frontal lobe function and delayed response memory of Rhesus monkeys. A collection of her poetry, *Harmless*, was published in 2010.

prehend trauma, one important reflection is that the structure of the brain constitutes one material cause in a web of other material causes. The brain is embodied, just as the (rest of the) body is embrained, and the body-brain unit is intrinsically embedded in a material environment with inorganic and organic matter. For example, an isolated gene is impotent. That it works, and how it works, is co-dependent on the environment of that gene: its material surroundings (e.g., other parts of the brain, a material exteroceptive environment), the individual's psychological milieu (e.g., the way in which an individual conceives the environment), and the individual's social *Umwelt.*

Another challenge is understanding the systemic level of material causation. There is a tendency to think that 'small is beautiful.' In seeking to answer the eternal riddle 'What is matter?,' physics has hunted for ever smaller particles. But can human action eventually be explained by quantum particles? By mystically vibrating superstrings? Is there any end to the Babushka race at all? Any system is a system within a system, and these systems influence each other. Genes affect experience but experience affects genes. Cells are influenced by their inner features, and these are influenced by the cell as a whole. Cells guide other cells and are guided by them. Brain structures such as the hippocampus, the amygdala, and the prefrontal cortices sway and are swayed by each other. A neural network does not exist in isolation either, but is bathed in numerous others. All of these material connections clearly do not stop there. There is the brain as a whole, but that whole belongs to the body as another material whole, and the body in turn is embedded in the material environment. So, here is the problem: What systemic level of material causation must one choose in order to understand trauma? One particular level, several different levels, or all of them? Where to begin, where to stop?

Another stumbling-block on the materialist's path is the realization that knowing the material causes of human sensations, affects, thoughts, memories, plans, dreams, fantasies, movements, and behaviors is absolutely insufficient to understanding these phenomena. As pointed out before, material causes in themselves do not explain mental and behavioral actions, but are situated in the framework of the organism-environment system that is dynamically caused. Material causation at any systemic level is intermediate causation – no more and no less. No matter how exciting and helpful it is to know the material causes of trauma, psychotraumatologists would be better off not being envious of the splendid successes of physics and its methods. They should also better not fall in love with physics: The mental cannot be completely 'naturalized' (i.e., reduced to matter). Still, nothing need prevent psychotraumatologists (and psychologists more generally) from being *inspired* by physics. For example, is it not intriguing that at the quantum level perception and perceiver affect each other? So, why not accept that subject and object are generally co-constitutive, co-dependent, and ever co-occurring?

And is it not equally strange and fascinating that at the subatomic level the world is quantified, i.e., split in parts? At the atomic and subatomic level, there is no such thing as continuous distribution of energy. Imagine that one can drive either at 100 or 150 kilometers per hour in the sense that these two speeds are absolutely discrete. Push the accelerator and in one timeless jump you are moving at the other speed. Impossible? Experiments prove otherwise. For a variety of reasons, it is inadmissible to transfer our understanding of the quantum world to a host of other phenomena, including the level of dissociative parts of the personality. A clinical and empirically demonstrated ground is that dissociative parts are not fully discrete: They are divided, not totally split. They are different but to some degree and in some way in touch with each other. Physical metaphors should not be thoughtlessly embraced by psychology. Though some of them may not be transportable at all, they may inspire. One inspiration of the magical quantum world is to avoid saying too soon that something "must" or "cannot" be the case. Human 'reason' and 'logic' can be quite fallible. With respect to dissociation of the personality, many feel that no one can have more than one 'I.' But the belief in the one 'I' is neither a conceptual necessity nor an empirical fact. Some individuals include, so to speak, different 'quanta of person perspectives.'

That said, there is evidence that there are relationships between exposure to adverse life events, mental disorders, and deviations of total and regional brain volume (Hart & Rubia, 2012; Karl et al., 2006)[2]. These findings are consistent with animal models of trauma-related disorders. For example, mice had smaller hippocampal and amygdalar volume after adverse events; these effects might be due to shrinkage of axonal extensions (Golub et al., 2010). The abnormalities found for human subjects pertain to gray and white matter of several regions that sometimes include and sometimes exclude the hippocampus and the amygdala. TSDP includes the general idea that simple, more complex, and very complex trauma-related divisions of the personality share structural brain abnormalities. Some of these abnormalities may be proportional to the complexity of this dissociation as well as to the severity and timing of the adverse events. Emergent findings for PTSD and DID are consistent with these hypotheses. They also include surprises.

Gray Matter Abnormalities

Childhood traumatization is associated with a host of functional problems. These include (brain areas playing an important role in the functions are in parentheses):

- motor inhibition, working memory, attention, planning (dorsolateral prefrontal cortex),
- social cognition including self-conceptions and conceptions of other individuals (medial prefrontal cortex),
- emotion regulation, motivation, evaluation of reward, and affect (frontolimbic system including the medial prefrontal and orbitofrontal cortex, amygdala, cerebellum),
- classical conditioning (amygdala),
- learning, memory, context evaluation (hippocampal areas), and
- executive functions, including attention and timing (cerebellum).

2 To prevent an overload of literature references, I only list a few pertinent studies. See Hart and Rubia (2012) and Karl and colleagues' (2006) excellent reviews for a large number of studies.

Region of Interest Studies

Whereas there may be links between the functions and the structures of the listed brain areas, it is important to avoid a new kind of phrenology. The brain constitutes a whole embodied and environmentally embedded system, and parts of the brain are always parts of that whole system. When evaluating the meaning and validity of functional and structural brain research, it is important to keep this perspective prominently in mind.

Studies of children, adolescents, and adults who experienced adverse events during childhood have documented gray matter abnormalities that prominently include the dorsolateral and ventromedial prefrontal cortex. Further, cortisol levels were negatively correlated with volume in the prefrontal cortex (Carrion & Wong, 2012).

The volumetric deviations also concern the hippocampus, the amygdala, the corpus callosum, and the cerebellum. For example, adolescents with PTSD had higher cortisol levels, and prebedtime levels of cortisol predicted decreases in hippocampal volume longitudinally. A meta-analysis of hippocampal volumes in adults with trauma-related PTSD (Kitayama, Vaccarino, Kutner, Weiss, & Bremner, 2005) documented that small hippocampal volume in maltreated individuals was related to PTSD rather than to the adversity itself in that the volumetric deviation was more profound in individuals who developed PTSD.

Based on several meta-analyses (Karl et al., 2006; Kitayama et al., 2005; Smith, 2005), it seems safe to conclude that PTSD patients who were abused and neglected as children have a smaller hippocampal volume than healthy controls as well as controls who experienced childhood abuse and neglect, but who do not have PTSD. Whereas fronto-limbic networks seem to be affected most, most studies examined only *a priori* hypothesized regions of interest. Other areas might be affected as well, limiting the conclusions that can be drawn from region-of-interest studies (Friston, Rotshtein, Geng, Sterzer, & Henson, 2006). We are whole organisms indeed.

Very few region-of-interest studies have examined structural gray matter features of the fronto-striatal system. Only one study found smaller caudate nuclei in adults with a history of traumatic adverse childhood events (Cohen et al., 2006). Studies using whole-brain analysis did not report basal ganglia changes in maltreated subjects (Carrion et al., 2009; Hanson et al., 2010; Tomoda et al., 2009, 2010; Treadway et al., 2009). But, see below too.

Whole Brain Studies

Whole brain analyses have found smaller gray matter volume of similar areas as those found in region-of-interest studies with maltreated subjects (Hart & Rubia, 2012). They particularly include the orbitofrontal, dorsolateral, and medial prefrontal cortex as well as the anterior cingulate. However, more areas than these prefrontal areas appeared to be abnormally small, including the thalamus, and the parietal, temporal, and superior frontal lobes (Tomoda et al., 2009, 2010; Hanson et al., 2010). Some other areas were abnormally large in some studies. They include the cerebellum, the cingulate cortex, the prefrontal cortex, the superior temporal gyrus, the occipital lobe, and the parahippocampal gyrus (Tomoda et al., 2009, 2010; Hanson et al., 2010). Hart and Rubia (2012) did not find whole brain studies showing the structural hippocampal or amygdala abnormalities reported in region-of-interest studies of individuals who had been abused and maltreated as children. But, again, see below.

Whole brain and region-of-interest studies with unmedicated individuals who experienced childhood adverse events but who did not have PTSD demonstrated similar volumetric abnormalities. The areas included the medial, dorsolateral, and orbitofrontal prefrontal cortex, the anterior cingulate, the caudate, the thalamus, the parietal lobe, and the superior frontal lobe. These studies also documented that the cerebellum, the cingulate, and the prefrontal cortex might be abnormally large in these samples. The hippocampal and amygdalar volumes were normal.

Comorbidity

Hart and Rubia (2012) note that in many studies insufficient distinctions are made between the influences on the structure of the brain of childhood adverse events as such, and those of a trauma-related mental disorder such as PTSD and/or the comorbidity of the examined disorder. It is therefore hard to say whether the documented structural abnormalities are due to the adverse events, PTSD, other disorders, or a particular interaction between these two factors.

However, what is comorbidity in the context of trauma? For example, De Bellis and colleagues (1999, 2002) documented that, compared to controls, maltreated children had smaller cerebral volumes and total lateral ventricles and larger cortical and prefrontal cortical cerebrospinal fluid (CSF) volumes. The volume of their brain was positively associated with age of onset of the adverse events and negatively correlated with duration of abuse. All maltreated children had PTSD, but near 90% had other mental disorders as well. This comorbidity fits the common finding that childhood adverse events tend to evoke more complex pathology than is captured in simple PTSD. However, clinicians and scientists would do better not be content with assessing comorbidity. They might even consider rejecting the very concept and seeking to fully describe and comprehend the biopsychosocial troubles of individuals who experienced adverse events. It makes no sense to cut a disorder into pieces.

Such complete understanding requires an analysis of the links between the various symptoms. According to TSDP, the core problem in chronic childhood traumatization lies in the difficulty to integrate dreadful experiences. This problem becomes particularly massive when the afflicted individual is torn between two major wills: One will is to approach and trust the parents or other caretakers on which they are dependent, whereas the other is to avoid them because they are dangerous. This dilemma divides the personality, and this dissociation manifests itself in a wide variety of biopsychosocial characteristics.

Moreover, according to the philosophical grounding of TSDP, any event exists in the framework of the organism-environment system: Subject and object are co-constitutive, co-dependent, and co-occurrent. There is not an event 'out there' and there are no isolated biopsychosocial troubles 'in here' (i.e., 'in the subject'). Hart and Rubia (2012) reached a converging conclusion on empirical grounds: As they observe, chronic childhood adverse events are so strongly tied to PTSD that it is very hard to separate between these events and this disorder.

Gray Matter and Features of Adverse Events

It might well be that there are relationships between variables such as the age at onset, severity, chronicity, (lack of) social support, and the kind and degree of structural brain abnormalities. Consistent with this idea, some studies reported correlations between structural brain abnormalities and age and onset of potentially traumatizing childhood events. The areas included the volume of the cerebral cortex, the hippocampus, the anterior cingulate cortex, the amygdala, and the caudate. Two studies did not find a correlation between these events and hippocampal volume. Studying maltreated children, De Bellis and colleagues (1999, 2002) found correlations of early childhood adverse events and volumetric brain differences. The children had smaller cerebral volumes and total lateral ventricles as well as larger volumes of cortical and prefrontal cortical cerebrospinal fluid. In addition to PTSD the children had comorbid psychiatric disorders that may have confounded the findings. However, the diagnosis of PTSD does not capture the full complexity of an individual's traumatic condition. De Bellis and colleagues documented that total brain volume was positively associated age of onset of the traumatizing events, and negatively associated with duration of abuse. In a longitudinal study with adults who did not have a formal diagnosis, Papagni and colleagues (2010) found that reductions of the anterior cingulate, the hippocampus, and the parahippocampal gyrus were related to the number of stressful life events that individuals had lived during the study.

Gray Matter and Maternal Features

Gray matter may also relate to the quality of maternal affiliation. Maternal affiliation was positively associated with hippocampal and orbitofrontal gray matter density in mentally healthy adolescents (Schneider et al., 2012), and maternal support in early childhood predicted larger hippocampal volume at the children's school age (Luby et al., 2012). These findings extend those of animal studies that demonstrated causal relations (Teicher, Tomoda, & Andersen, 2006). For example, low maternal licking and grooming – let me conveniently call it 'care' – was associated with shorter dendritic branch length and lower spine density in the hippocampal CA1 cells of adult offspring of low-care offspring than in adult offspring who had received high care (Champagne et al., 2008). Relative to high-care offspring, low-care offspring displayed impaired memory in basal conditions, but enhanced memory in response to experimental administration of high corticosterone as an analogue of a natural stressful event. They demonstrated this enhanced memory in a hippocampal-dependent contextual fear-conditioning paradigm. Offspring of high- and low-care mothers showed enhanced learning under contexts of low and high stress, respectively. Champagne and colleagues concluded that maternal effects may modulate optimal functioning in environments varying in demand in later life. Children neglected from early childhood might prepare themselves for a stressful life, just as well-raised, loved children get ready for adaptive and creative functioning in peaceful daily life.

Humans share with other species remarkable capacities to adapt to stress, including the ability to adjust the neuroendocrine stress system. However, factors such as inappropriate timing and/or duration of stress may have harmful effects. For example, a group of French researchers documented profound impairment of hippocampal functioning in the offspring of mothers exposed to prenatal stress (Amiel-Tison et al., 2004). Reviewing the evidence, they suggested that fetal changes are likely one of the risk factors for a number of diseases in adulthood. For example, prenatally stressed subjects have a lower performance in hippocampal-mediated learning tasks, particularly during aging, and have difficulty coping with novelty and stressful environments. They are also more prone to self-administer drugs of abuse, and to develop drug-induced adaptations implied in the development of drug dependence.

Similar features can mark children whose mothers experienced psychological stress or adverse life events during pregnancy. In this light, it is important to recall the work of Trickett and colleagues (2011) (see Chapter 6), whose prospective study of the long-term impact of CSA documented deleterious sequelae across a host of biopsychosocial domains into adulthood, although there was also substantial variability among the women in this regard. The sad fact was that children born to abused mothers were at increased risk for childhood abuse, maltreatment, and neglect as well as overall maldevelopment. Most abused mothers did not abuse their children, but those that had children involved in Child Protective Service interventions "were either neglectful (mostly attributable to substance use issues) or in other ways recreated environmental conditions in which abuse was allowed to persist across generations" (p. 468).

Gray Matter and Attachment Style

Research has also documented relationships between hippocampal features and attachment style (Vrticka & Vuilleumier, 2012). For example, attachment avoidance was associated with smaller bilateral hippocampal volume in one study (Quirin, Gillath, Pruessner, & Eggert, 2010). Attachment anxiety was related to reduced cell concentration in the left hippocampus. Another study found associations between anxious attachment and the volumes of the temporal anterior pole and the left lateral orbital gyrus (Benetti et al., 2010).

The more pleasant part of the 'care-brain' story is that there are ways to improve maternal behavior, and that improved motherhood can reverse the long-term effects of prenatal stress (cf. Amiel-Tison et al., 2004). Enhancement of somatosensory stimulation of the pup by the mother seems to be a major importance in this regard (Vallee et al., 1999). This finding could be an inspiration for the treatment of human trauma.

The collective findings suggest one reason why emotional neglect constitutes a potentially traumatizing event. Lack of physical warmth should also be added to this category. Good care includes warm and sound bodily interaction that is adapted to the child's needs. It is strange that for ages professionals have not generally realized this, and it seems that Harlow's and Bowlby's messages are still not fully integrated in the trauma field. Look at the mothers and fathers of thriving children and see how they interact. This is not separate brains 'processing information.' These are living organisms enacting a safe environment. Then take a look at emotionally neglectful and physically distant parenting and see what is missing. How could professionals in general have missed such obvious differences and their implications for child development for so long?

Gray Matter Deviance in Minor and Major DID

Hart and Rubia (2012) did not report on structural brain deviations in individuals with DSM-IV and ICD-10 dissociative disorders. Again, psychiatry mostly neglects these disorders (e.g., Sar, 2011; see Chapter 6). For example, the assessment of comorbidity hardly ever considers the (co-)presence of a more complex dissociative disorders than PTSD. Still, according to TSDP, the comorbidity of PTSD can often be understood in the framework of a more complex dissociation of the personality (e.g., Van der Hart et al., 2005, 2006).

Hippocampus, Parahippocampal Gyrus, and Amygdala

The absence of hippocampal abnormalities in abused and neglected children suggests that the hippocampal abnormalities associated with chronic traumatization may evolve over time. This long-term effect might be related to chronic abnormal cortisol levels (Carrion, Weems, & Reiss, 2007). If there is a connection between trauma and abnormal cortisol, and if minor and major DID are like PTSD trauma-related conditions, it makes sense to hypothesize

- that complex dissociative disorders are associated with small hippocampal volume,
- that these disorders involve smaller hippocampal volume than simple and complex PTSD,

- that there are negative correlations between hippocampal volume and cognitive-emotional as well as sensorimotor dissociative symptoms, including PTSD symptoms,
- that there are negative correlations between hippocampal volume and cumulative adverse events.

There have been seven multisubject gray matter studies of DID to date (Chalavi, 2013; Chalavi et al., 2014; Chalavi et al., in press; also Reinders, 2014; Ehling et al., 2008; Irle, Lange, Sachsse, & Weniger, 2009; Vermetten, Schmahl, Lindner, Loewenstein, & Bremner, 2006; Weniger, Lange, Sachsse, & Irle, 2008). Two of these studies included, apart from patients with dissociative amnesia as a disorder, only few individuals with DID (Irle et al.: 2; Weniger et al.: 4), and will therefore not be considered here.

Compared to healthy controls matched for sex, age, and education, women with major DID had smaller hippocampi (Chalavi et al., 2014, also Reinders, 2014; Ehling et al., 2008; Vermetten et al., 2006), parahippocampal gyri (Ehling et al., 2008), and amygdala (Ehling et al., 2008; Vermetten et al., 2006). Women with minor DID also had smaller hippocampal and parahippocampal volumes than healthy controls, but their hippocampi were larger than those of women with major DID (Ehling et al., 2008). This difference did not exist for the parahippocampal gyri. In this study, we also found that the volumes of the left and right hippocampal were strongly and negatively correlated with cognitive-emotional and sensorimotor dissociative symptoms, PTSD symptoms, and multifaceted chronic childhood traumatization. The correlations with general psychiatric symptoms were moderate. Fantasy proneness was not associated with the volumetric deviations. The left and right parahippocampal gyrus were also associated with the indicated symptoms and reported childhood adverse events, but not with fantasy proneness.

Whole Brain Analysis

In the only whole brain study of DID to date, Chalavi and colleagues (2013; Chalavi et al., in press) examined women with DID and women with PTSD, and mentally healthy women as controls. Compared with controls, women with DID and women with PTSD had less cortical gray matter for the whole brain as well as for frontal, temporal, and insular cortices. The subcortical analyses documented smaller hippocampal (Chalavi et al., 2014) and larger caudate and palladium volumes for the patients with DID relative to the controls (Chalavi et al., in press). The volume of the caudate and palladium in patients with DID was also larger than in the PTSD patients. Chalavi and colleagues (2013; Chalavi et al., in press) proposed that the large dorsal striatum volume in DID may relate to the involvement of the striatum in the frequent switching between different dissociative parts in this disorder as well as to the maintenance of this organization of the personality.

Small Hippocampus, Adverse Events, and Complexity of Personality Dissociation

Women with DID reported more childhood adverse events than women with PTSD, and they also had smaller hippocampal volume (Chalavi et al., 2014). Smaller hippocampal volume may be associated with the severity, chronicity, and age at onset of childhood adverse events as well as with adult age at the time of the measurement of the brain. This association may be due to hippocampal dendritic atrophy or even cell loss. Given the high density of glucocorticoid hippocampal receptors, this damage could result from prolonged exposure to stress hormones. In this light, and from the perspective of TSDP, across studies hippocampal volume seems to be incrementally smaller for increasing complexity of the dissociation of the personality. It tends to be smaller in adult childhood-based PTSD, still smaller in minor adult DID, and the smallest in major adult DID.

Not all hippocampal subfields may be affected in PTSD. For example, Wang et al. (2010) reported that only area CA-3/dentate gyrus was smaller in combat veterans with PTSD compared to combat veterans without PTSD. Exposure to proximate and distal adverse events may also be associated with different abnormal hippocampal shapes.

Consistent with these various hypotheses, in Chalavi et al. (in press), the left and right hippocampus were smaller in persons with DID compared to those with PTSD and healthy controls. Compared to healthy controls, right hippocampal volume of PTSD patients who reported moderate to severe childhood traumatization tended to be smaller. Hippocampal volume and shape were negatively correlated with the severity of childhood adverse events. Shape analysis revealed contractions in the CA-1, CA2–3, and subiculum subfields. The subiculum plays an important role in the formation of explicit memories, and CA2–3 is involved in their reconstruction. CA1 is involved in both memory functions. The correlations were stronger for childhood adverse events as reported by EPs compared to ANPs. Studies with adults with a history of early-life adverse events also found correlations between the severity of these events and the volumes of CA2–3 and the subiculum (Teicher, Anderson, & Polcari, 2012). Similar results have also been reported for other mammals. Finally, cognitive-emotional (DES) and sensorimotor dissociative symptoms (SDQ-20) were correlated with the left (pre)subiculum (Chalavi et al., 2014).

DID and PTSD: Gray Matter Commonalities and Differences

Taken together, the findings for gray matter volume show gray matter links between PTSD and DID and thereby support the interpretation that PTSD and DID are related trauma-related disorders. The Chalavi et al. studies specifically demonstrate striking gray matter volumetric commonalities between DID and PTSD. Had there only been volumetric commonalities, one might have concluded that these existed because all women with DID in these studies also met the criteria for DSM-IV PTSD – which was the case. However, there were also gray matter differences between PTSD and DID such as different hippocampal volume. The latter difference indicates that hippocampal volume may, as hypothesized above, be negatively related to the complexity of the dissociative disorder with simple PTSD as the simplest form and major DID as the most complex. It may also be that chronic and more limited adverse events, different kinds and contexts, and different developmental timing of adverse events affect the hippocampal structure differently.

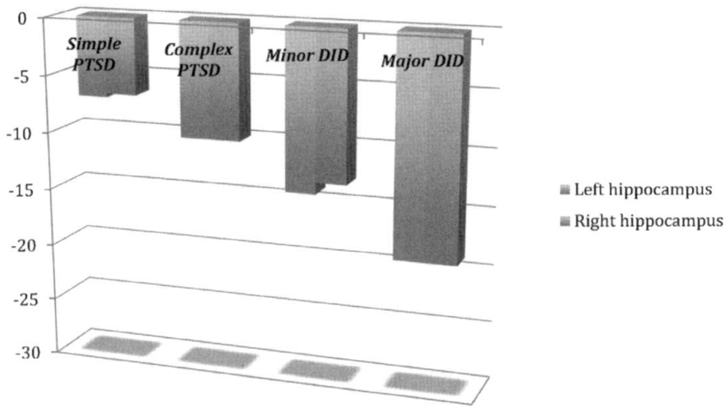

Figure 19.1. Hippocampal volume for different dissociative disorders: the more complex the dissociation of the personality, the less hippocampal volume. *Note.* Complex PTSD: Values of Thomaes et al. (2010). Minor DID: Values of Ehling et al. (2008). Major DID: Simple means of the values reported in three studies (Chalavi et al., 2014; Ehling et al., 2008; Vermetten et al., 2006).

The negative values in the graph stand for the deviations in hippocampal volume in individuals with dissociative disorders compared to mentally healthy controls. The differences are expressed in percentages. The values for simple PTSD are taken from a meta-analysis by Smith (2005). Very similar values were reported by Wang et al. (2010) and by Shu et al. (2013) for a Chinese population.

This TSDP perspective fits the conclusions of Karl et al.'s (2006) meta-analysis on structural brain abnormalities in PTSD, who said that exposure to adverse events, regardless of the absence or presence of PTSD, is associated with age- and sex-mediated smaller hippocampal volumes. However, compared to individuals who were exposed to adverse events but who did not develop PTSD, individuals with severe PTSD in unmedicated adult samples had smaller hippocampal volumes. The effect size of the association of hippocampal volume and PTSD increased with PTSD severity. (Karl et al. also noted that the volumetric abnormalities are not restricted to the hippocampus, and that adults and minors exhibit different types of structural abnormalities.) In summary, in adults the severity of (childhood) adverse event exposure, of dissociative symptoms including PTSD symptoms, and of the complexity of the dissociation of the personality, and the volume of the hippocampus are correlated phenomena, as was hypothesized above.

Another difference between gray matter in PTSD and DID involves the striatum. A larger striatum in combination with smaller neocortical volume might be specific to DID and might be related to frequent alternations among different dissociative parts (Chalavi, 2013) and implied different basic desires. It may also be associated with frequent and long-term basal ganglia activation during reactivations of traumatic memories for EP.

The studies reviewed above demonstrate that PTSD and DID have many gray matter deviations in common. Together with the shared efficient, formal, and final causation of these disorders, this common material causation makes a strong case for the postulate in TSDP that PTSD and DID are intimately related conditions: Major DID constitutes a severe form of PTSD, just as PTSD is a simple form of DID; minor DID is lesser form of major DID, and thereby closer to Complex PTSD.

Hippocampal Treatment-Related Repair

The hippocampus is a plastic structure. Several findings suggest that effective treatment can be associated with 'hippocampal repair' in patients with PTSD and more complex dissociative disorders.

PTSD

Clinical improvement in individuals with PTSD after cognitive behavior therapy was associated with increased expression of FKBP5 – a key modulator of the glucocorticoid receptor – and increased hippocampal volume (Levy-Gigi, Szabo, Kelemen, & Keri, 2013). The increased FKBP5 expression and the increased hippocampal volume were positively correlated.

Major DID

Ehling et al. (2008) also compared women with florid major DID as well as Dutch, German, and Belgian women who had fully recovered from this disorder as a result of long-term phase-oriented treatment. The recovered women had originally been as disturbed as those with florid major DID, but at the time of the study had integrated all previously existing dissociative ANPs and EPs. They did not meet the SCID-D criteria anymore, and their scores on the DES, SDQ-20 and scales measuring general psychopathology and depression were in the range of those of mentally healthy women. They had more hippocampal volume than the women with florid DID (left + 9%, right + 18%), but not more parahippocampal volume.

Longitudinal and Prospective Assessment: A Single Case Study

In a case study, we found that the patient's left and right hippocampal volume had significantly increased by the time she had integrated all ANPs and EPs (Ehling, Nijenhuis, & Krikke, unpublished data). At first assessment the left and right hippocampal volume were fully within the range of the DID patients that participated in Ehling et al. (2008), with left 26% and right 25% smaller than controls. The first assessment was performed 6 years after the start of her treatment with me (T1). Previously, she had been in treatment for years with a different therapist who had not helped her and who had in fact sexually abused her. At T1 the patient was working hard to integrate chronic sexual, physical, and emotional abuse as well as the emotional neglect by her father and mother experienced from early childhood onward until she ran away from home when she was 18 years old. One of her sisters told me that she had observed many of these adverse events, and that she had been abused and neglected by her parents as well. It was widely known in the family that her mother was severely mentally disturbed. Still, the family had not undertaken any action to protect the children.

After 8 years of treatment with me, the patient was fully recovered from her major DID (T2). By this time, she was completely free of symptoms and was able to successfully study and work. Currently, 10 years later, she continues to be completely healthy, speaks at conferences about her long and winding road to recovery, and assists other patients with DID. At T2 her left and right hippocampal volume, but not her parahippocampal volume, had significantly increased. The gain in hippocampal volume – left + 20%, and right + 19% – was fully preserved at follow-up 1.5 years later (T3). At T3 her parahippocampal volume was as it had been at T1 and T2. For the recovered DID patients in Ehling et al. (2008), the figures for this structure were left -19%, and right -20%. A change in parahippocampal volume was not predicted because the neocortex is not known to be plastic. The finding of increased hippocampal volume following successful treatment of DID is promising, but obviously needs replication with groups of DID patients.

White Matter Abnormalities

White brain matter is involved in the transmission of signals from one region of the cerebrum to another as well as between the cerebrum and the lower brain regions, and vice versa. Long axonal connections are formed in early childhood, but the diameter and structure of axons and their myelination develop into adulthood. Emergent evidence suggests that adverse events might negatively affect this development.

Whereas gray matter abnormalities are assessed with structural MRI, white matter is studied using diffusion tensor imaging (DTI). Individuals who have experienced adverse events have smaller white matter volume more often than larger white matter volume (Daniels, Lamke, Gaebler, Walter, & Scheel, 2013). Daniels et al.'s meta-analysis of seven studies with adults identified significantly smaller and larger clusters in several structures, particularly the cingulum and the superior longitudinal fasciculus. Abnormalities of the uncinate fasciculus were also reported (Choi et al., 2009; Eluvathingal et al., 2006). The uncinate fasciculus as well as the cingulum link the anterior temporal pole (that includes the amygdala) with the cingulate and the orbitofrontal cortex. Both bundles play a role in affect regulation.

In the first ever study of white matter integrity in DID, Chalavi (2013; also Reinders, 2014) found differences between PTSD, DID (all women with this disorder also met criteria for PTSD), and mentally healthy controls. Compared with mentally healthy controls, women with PTSD had statistically significant disruptions of white matter integrity. These included commissural tracts, several association tracts, including the bilateral superior longitudinal fasciculus and the right cingulum as well as several projection tracts. The women with DID also had lower levels of white matter integrity in several fiber tracts than the healthy controls, most prominently in the genu of the corpus callosum (differences between groups uncorrected for multiple comparisons; $p < .05$). Comparisons of women with DID and women with PTSD demonstrated a small number of regions with lower white matter integrity for the women with PTSD.

The white matter integrity differences between DID and PTSD were thus smaller than the differences between these two clinical groups and the controls. In light of TSDP this finding is not surprising: Core postulates of this theory are that both disorders involve a division of the personality as a whole biopsychosocial system, and that this division is more complex in DID than in PTSD. However, the fact that PTSD was associated with more pronounced disrupted of white matter integrity than DID was remarkable.

What could explain the lower white matter integrity in PTSD than in DID? One speculation is that women with DID used more psychotropic drugs (Chalavi, 2013). There is some evidence that medication can have positive effects on white matter integrity, but the findings are not consistent. A different speculation Chalavi and colleagues (2013) offered is that DID patients have earlier and more substantial training in the mental avoidance of traumatic memories and the associated evolving EPs. Chronic mental avoidance may implicate the use of axonal connections, which may save them from 'pruning'[3]. Learning to live as an (at least partly) trauma-ignorant ANP would seem to be very necessary, given the earlier, more complex, and more severe childhood traumatization the women with DID had to endure. Still another speculation is that white matter has become reorganized in the women with DID in order to compensate for the loss of gray matter, as discussed above. For example, low hippocampal volume in these women may have become balanced by a reorganization of the right cingulum-parahippocampal fiber tract (Chalavi, 2013). This idea is consistent with the positive correlation between the severity of reported childhood traumatization and the fractional anisotropy of this tract. Fractional anisotropy is believed to reflect the degree of fiber organization, fiber directional coherence, or white matter integrity.

Corpus Callosum: Abnormal Genu (DID) and Splenium (PTSD)

The corpus callosum is the largest commissural or transverse white matter pathway. The most rostral region (rostral = toward the tip of the frontal lobe), the genu, contains axons that link the left and right prefrontal cortices. The caudal region (caudal = toward the feet; the Latin word 'cauda' means tail, extreme part) connects the bilateral occipital, parietal, temporal, and insular cortices. This region encompasses the body and the splenium.

The lower white matter integrity of the corpus callosum in PTSD and DID that Chalavi and colleagues (2013) found is consistent with the results of DTI studies in children (Jackowski et al., 2008; Rinne-Albers, Van der Wee, Lamers-Winkelman, & Vermeiren, 2013),

---

3 In neuroscience, the terms synaptic pruning, neuronal pruning, and axon pruning stand for a reduction of the overall number of synapses, neurons, and axons. Pruning is a general feature of mammalian brain development which leaves more efficient structural configurations. In humans the process starts near the time of birth and is thought to be completed by the time of sexual maturation. Mediated by environmental events (in terms of the present book, the brain is intrinsically related to the environment), pruning relates to learning. For the present discussion, it is important to realize that the maintenance of axonal connections is activity-dependent ("use them or lose them").

adolescents (Huang, Gundapuneedi, & Rao, 2012; Rinne et al., 2013), and adults (Teicher et al., 2010) who experienced childhood maltreatment. Compared to healthy controls, abused and neglected children also had a smaller corpus callosum volume in several studies (De Bellis et al., 2002; Teicher et al., 2004).

PTSD and DID were associated with different kinds of corpus callosum deviations. Chalavi (2013) and collaborators offer several interpretations of this finding. A worthwhile speculation in need of further research addresses the maturational track of the structure. In DID the cluster with lower fractional anisotropy was located in the genu, whereas in PTSD it was situated in the splenium. The most significant increase in the myelination in the corpus callosum occurs between 6 months and 3 years, and the myelination continues into the third decade of life. The genu starts to mature at an early age. Thereafter the maturation of the corpus callosum spreads in the caudal direction and reaches the splenium. Teicher et al. (2002) suggested that the different subfields of the corpus callosum have differing sensitive maturational periods, that is, there might be a relationship between the timing of adverse events and the degree of white matter integrity of the corpus callosum subregions. Early life adversity would affect the genu more and adverse events in later childhood the splenium. Consistent with this, the women with DID reported that their chronic, severe, and complex traumatization had started in early childhood, whereas the women with PTSD stated that their sexual harassment and sexual abuse had occurred between 7 and 12 years. It is of note in this context that sexual abuse was the strongest traumatizing factor associated with smaller corpus callosum in girls (Teicher et al., 2004), and that borderline personality disorder – another disorder related in many cases to childhood traumatization – was also associated with less fractional anisotropy in the genu and other rostral subregions of the corpus callosum (Carrasco et al., 2012).

Conclusion

PTSD and DID share many gray and white matter abnormalities. There are also structural brain differences between DID and PTSD, but these are generally smaller than the differences between these two disorders and mentally healthy controls. Some gray matter differences such as smaller hippocampal volume relate to the complexity of the dissociation of the personality and the severity, duration, timing, and context of traumatizing events. In other regards, there may be use-dependent features such as a larger caudate in DID (frequent alternating between different and highly evolved dissociative parts) and less severe lack of white matter integrity in DID compared to PTSD (a lifetime of training to life as different dissociative parts in DID). The major structural brain commonalities of PTSD and DID reinforce the findings regarding common functional brain abnormalities in these two disorders. The shared material and efficient causation constitutes strong evidence that DID is a trauma-related condition, which is similar to PTSD, but also more complex.

Dissociative Symptoms and Mild Neurological Impairment

- *Hypothesis of SC- and F-models:* Mild neurological impairment causes 'dissociation.'
- *Hypothesis of F-models:* 'Dissociation' may be related to neurological impairment, which may be a consequence of adverse life events.
- *Hypothesis of TSDP:* Structural and functional neurobiological impairments can be a risk factor for dissociative disorders, but are also a dose-dependent consequence of adverse life events.

The proposal that dissociative symptoms can be a sign of neurological impairment (Giesbrecht et al., 2007) includes several problems. Because it is a material defect – a neurological impairment involves an intermediate cause – a more complete understanding of dissociation needs to detail the environmental efficient causes, and the formal and final causes of this neurological impairment. It must thus be asked what the cause or causes of this material defect are? The brain is not a thing in itself, but exists as a component of intrinsic relations between the brain, the body, and the environment. In light of this philosophical grounding, TSDP holds that chronic environmental stress can damage the evolving brain, and that the brain of patients with dissociative disorders, including PTSD, will include structural (the present chapter) and functional brain abnormalities (Chapters 16 to 18). A related problem of the view that mild neurological impairment causes dissociation as a mental phenomenon is that it implies philosophical dualism, that is, the idea that a material defect causes a mental phenomenon. TSDP does not rely on philosophical dualism, but regards matter and mind as two attributes of one substance (see Volume I).

Chapter 20

The Trinity of Trauma in Survivors, Perpetrators, Families, Psychiatry, and Society

Ignorance is the night of the mind, but a night without moon and star.
Confucius

If blood will flow when flesh and steel are one
Drying in the colour of the evening sun
Tomorrow's rain will wash the stains away
But something in our minds will always stay

On and on the rain will fall
On and on the rain will fall

Perhaps this final act was meant
To clinch a lifetime's argument
That nothing comes from violence
and nothing ever could
For all those born beneath an angry star
Lest we forget how fragile we are

On and on the rain will fall
Like tears from a star
Like tears from a star
On and on the rain will say
How fragile we are
How fragile we are
Sting

Within confines, dissociation of the personality can be a creative adaptation and adaptive creation to an adverse environment. It serves survival when adversities are still ongoing, when the biopsychosocial capacity of individuals to integrate the involved experiences and events are limited. Such limitations have various causes, such as a lack of modeling of integrative skills and a lack of integrative help from others. In these circumstances, there is meaning and value to cope with one's fragility by remaining as ignorant and emotionally distant as possible of this fragility and the traumatizing events as one or more ANPs. But the mental avoidance of ANPs of traumatic memories, associated EPs, bodily and emotional feelings, their use of drugs, alcohol and medication, their self-cutting and self-burning, their avoidance of intimacy, and still other evasions these dissociative parts employ also truncate their life. These actions maintain the dissociation of the personality and prevent the healing of the injury that trauma truly is.

Whereas effective dissociation of the personality is a blessing for ANPs, it is a sheer disaster for EPs. The view that dissociation constitutes a defense mechanism is superficial and mistaken. It completely overlooks that the gain implies ongoing pain. Any ignorance of the ANP is adverse to fragile and controlling EPs. In the context of a history of chronic intrafamilial traumatization, it mirrors and reinforces the emotional neglect and rejection of prime caretakers. For EPs, chronically avoidant ANPs become another enemy. EPs in fact need the ANPs' help to integrate traumatic experiences, but with the ANPs gone, EPs remain stuck in traumatic experiences. Neither the traumatizing world nor EPs age over time. In EPs' eyes, ANPs may not even mature. EPs remain more or less ignorant of change. Being or feeling chronically endangered, EPs try to control enacted or re-enacted adverse life events by engaging in attachment cry, by being prepared for attack at any time, or by defending physical integrity when real or perceived disasters happen. The more EPs are stuck in these conceptions of the self, the world, and the self-of-the-world, the more EPs pose a threat to ANPs, the more ANPs mentally avoid EPs – and the worse EPs' existence gets.

Fragile EPs are stuck in traumatic life. Ignorant of personal aging and environmental change, for them the world and its inhabitants pose a chronic threat. Their best option is to defend: to startle, flee, freeze, ward off perpetrators, feign death. Some attempt to befriend perpetrators by meeting these individuals' wishes; these actions may include initiating sexual acts, clearly not for the sake of sexual arousal, but to control perpetrators.

Controlling EPs commonly start their existence from a will to have at least some grip on life. They often initially attempt to assist fragile EPs by being brave. Frustrated by their limited power to control their traumatic life, they drift toward imitating perpetrators. They may also identity with them. Who wants to be a victim? Who would not rather be in charge? And who shows the child how to control one's world? Searching for power, controlling EPs start to despise fragile EPs. They abhor the vulnerability and helplessness of these parts, and they detest EPs who engage in an ongoing, but useless cry for attachment. Like fragile EPs, most controlling EPs do not age. Many conceive of themselves as adolescents. Some act as if they have reached that phase of life and hide their younger phenomenal age. Given this fixation in the past, controlling EPs tend to conceive ANPs as weak children or adolescents, as sissies who try to have some kind of daily life, but who cannot save themselves. Denying their own fragility, including their need for attachment and safety, controlling EPs seek shelter in a display of power. To that end, they may call ANPs and fragile EPs names, cut or burn the bodies of these parts, take on the perpetrators voice, manners, and looks as well as forbid relationships, including relationships with clinicians. They may also continue traumatizing relationships and actions such as prostitution in an effort to keep things clear: ANPs and fragile EPs should know that they are *bad* and that they should have no hopes for a better future. They annoyed their perpetrators and therefore deserve punishment. In this sense, some EPs grow so despondent that death becomes a most appealing escape.

The division of the personality in trauma is thus a way to live an impossible life, a way to deal with intense and persistent conflicts between the opposite desires to have a daily life, to defend, to attach, and to maintain the power to influence one's own fate. However, because of ANPs' mental avoidance, fragile and controlling EPs remain imprisoned in past trauma-focused conceptions of the self, the world, and the self-of-the-world. With EPs' growing frustration and ANPs' increasing exhaustion – their avoidance is effortful, and over time ANPs may lose power – EPs and their mental and behavioral contents may intrude on ANPs ever more. When ANP's ignorance falters, these dissociative parts tend to come for professional help. This does not at all mean that they generally come to integrate EPs and traumatic memories. What most ANPs want is simply relief from ongoing intrusions that they may or may not understand. What they want is to end the voices, pains, nightmares, self-mutilation, panic attacks, and episodic loss of consciousness.

When the integrative capacity is sufficiently high, traumatized individuals would better substitute the dissociation of their personality for an integrative approach. The first person, quasi-second-person, and third-person perspectives of EPs and ANPs linger to the very day that ANPs start to recognize, acknowledge, and contact them – and eventually integrate the traumatic memories of these parts. With this commonly stepwise therapeutic approach, re-enactments of the traumatic past, including relational re-enactments, start to come to an end and become replaced by a growing symbolization and realization of this past (Van der Hart et al., 2006). The previously re-enacted traumatic life becomes an integrated dark chapter of the book of the individual's life, a horrible story told. And this chapter may be a long one. The integrative actions are higher-level actions that replace traumatized individuals' actions that served as lower-level substitutes for these far more difficult actions that were previously unattainable.

The trinity of trauma is not exclusive to traumatized individuals. Ignorance, fragility, and control also characterize perpetrators, families in which the traumatization occurs, psychology and psychiatry, and indeed society at large. This view is based in part on consistent reports of traumatized individuals and several witnesses I have met over the last three decades. It is also inspired by observations of perpetrators and empirical data as well as by more general observations. The formulations are general and preliminary, describe prototypical patterns, and are only meant to provide a heuristic framework that can guide us to far deeper analyses of the possible generality of the trinity of trauma. In order to focus the discussion, I emphasize child sexual abuse. The studies cited serve to illustrate the idea of a general trinity of trauma; no attempt is made to give a complete review of the literature.

Figure 20.1 captures the trinity of trauma. The photographs depict Charcot's patient Augustine.

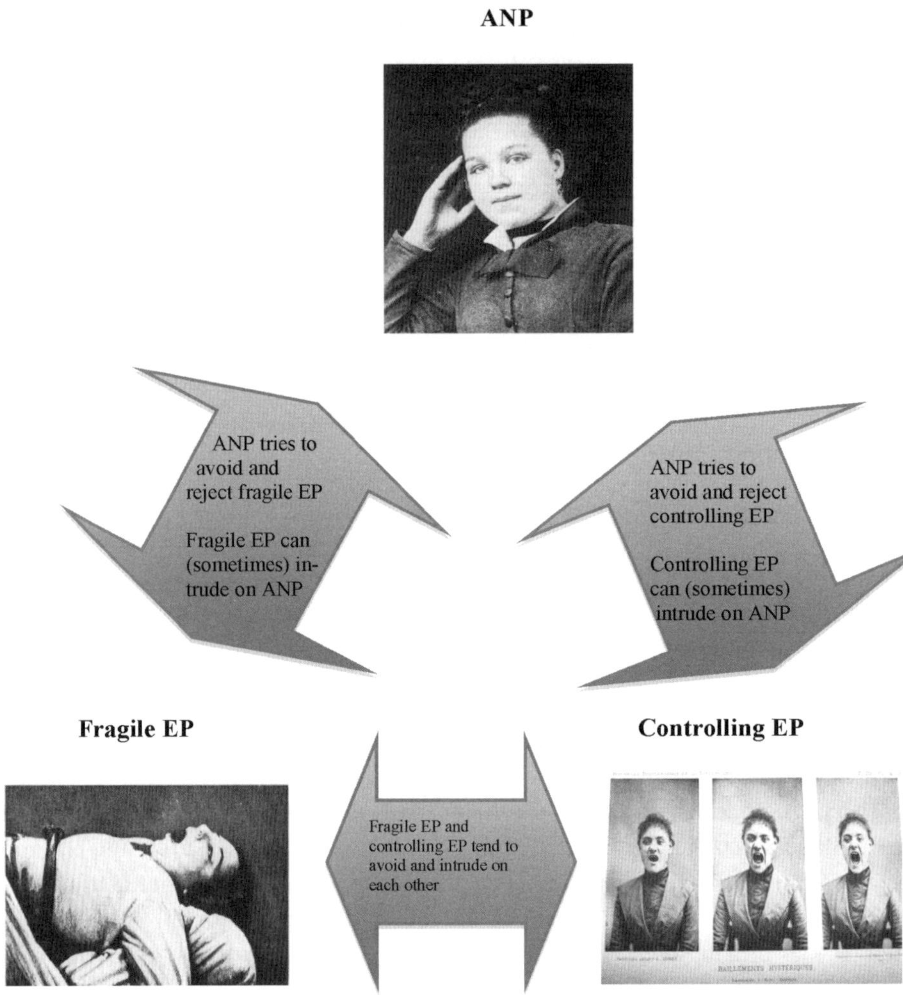

Figure 20.1. The trinity of trauma.

Perpetrators

Violence and emotional neglect are global and multifaceted. For example, as Watts and Zimmermann (2002) summarized, violence against women may take the form of intimate partner violence, sexual abuse by nonintimate partners, trafficking, forced prostitution, exploitation of labor, and debt bondage of women and girls, physical and sexual violence against prostitutes, sex-selective abortion, female infanticide, the deliberate neglect of girls, and rape during wartimes. They observed that

> [t]here are many potential perpetrators, including spouses and partners, parents, other family members, neighbors, and men in positions of power or influence. Most forms of violence are

> not unique incidents but are ongoing, and can even continue for decades. Because of the sensitivity of the subject, violence is almost universally under-reported. Nevertheless, the prevalence of such violence suggests that globally, millions of women are experiencing violence or living with its consequences. (p. 1232)

Indeed, to speak with Dartnall and Jewkes (2012, p. 3),

> [r]ape and sexual violence occur in all societies, and cut across all social classes. Prevalence estimates of rape victimisation range between 6 and 59% of women having experienced sexual abuse from their husbands or boyfriends in their lifetime. Two population-based studies from South Africa have found that 28% and 37% of men, respectively, have perpetrated rape. Estimates of rape perpetration from high-income countries seem to be lower than those from low- and middle-income countries; however, current data make it impossible to confirm this.

The *World Report on Violence Against Children* (Paulo Sérgio Pinheiro, Independent Expert for the United Nations Secretary-General's Study on Violence against Children, 2006) presents the situation for children. It includes the following statement from Kofi Annan, United Nations Secretary-General October (Pinheiro, 2006, p. XI):

> Violence against children cuts across boundaries of geography, race, class, religion and culture. It occurs in homes, schools and streets; in places of work and entertainment, and in care and detention centres. Perpetrators include parents, family members, teachers, caretakers, law enforcement authorities and other children. Some children are particularly vulnerable because of gender, race, ethnic origin, disability or social status. And no country is immune, whether rich or poor.

Pinheiro (2006, p. XVIII) emphasized that the international community mostly ignores the violence against children:

> Some forms of violence, such as sexual exploitation and trafficking and the impact of armed conflict on children, have provoked international condemnation over the past decade. The recognition of these extreme situations has helped to bring children's concerns high on the international agenda. However attention to violence against children in general continues to be fragmented and very limited – different forms of violence in the home, schools, institutions and the community are largely ignored in current debates in the international community ... As Nelson Mandela has reminded us, violence thrives in the absence of democracy and respect for human rights. Violence against children persists as a permanent threat where authoritarian relationships between adults and children remain. The belief that adults have unlimited rights in the upbringing of a child compromises any approach to stop and prevent violence committed within the home, school or state institution. For lasting change, attitudes that condone or normalise violence against children, including stereotypical gender roles, need to be challenged. Our failure to listen to children has resulted in a failure to respond to their needs. It is hard to understand why and how adults can continue to argue that children should have less protection from violence than adults do: in law, in policy and in practice.

The following examples may serve to give some idea of the range and scale of violence against children that the report (p. 11–12) covered:

- The World Health Organization estimates that almost 53,000 child deaths in 2002 were homicides.
- In the Global School-Based Student Health Survey carried out in a wide range of developing countries, between 20% and 65% of school-aged children reported having been verbally or physically bullied in school in the previous 30 days. Similar rates of bullying have been found in industrialized countries.
- An estimated 150 million girls and 73 million boys under 18 have experienced forced sexual intercourse or other forms of sexual violence involving physical contact.
- UNICEF estimates that in sub-Saharan Africa, Egypt, and Sudan, 3 million girls and women are subjected to female genital mutilation/cutting every year.
- The International Labor Organization estimates that 218 million children were involved in child labor in 2004, of whom 126 million were engaged in hazardous work. Estimates from 2000 suggest that 5.7 million were in forced or bonded labor, 1.8 million in prostitution and pornography, and 1.2 million were victims of trafficking.
- Only 2.4% of the world's children are legally protected from corporal punishment in all settings.

Of all sexual offences, CSA may be the commonest type and is associated with a high risk of re-offending (Balasundaram, Frazer, & Wood, 2009). Child sexual abuse is certainly not an exclusive Western phenomenon. For example, child sexual abuse cases formed between 40–60% of the rape cases brought to the attention of hospitals, police, and court in Zimbabwe (Meursing et al., 1995). Many more cases probably go unreported. Often detected through sexually transmitted diseases including HIV, in the majority of cases the sexual abuse was committed by mature men known to the child. Rape and attempted rape, particularly of young girls, constituted the majority of reported incidents of violence against children in Bangladesh (Fattah & Kabir, 2013). The perpetrators included men from all walks of life.

Child sexual abuse takes different, not mutually exclusive forms. As Lanning (2010, p. 2) reported,

> [t]he sexual victimization of children involves varied and diverse dynamics. It can range from one-on-one intrafamilial abuse to multioffender/multivictim extrafamilial sex rings and from nonfamily abduction of toddlers to prostitution of teenagers. Sexual victimization of children can run the gamut of "normal" sexual acts from fondling to intercourse. The victimization can also include deviant sexual behavior involving more unusual conduct (e.g., urination, defecation, playing dead) that often goes unrecognized, including by statutes, as possibly being sexual in nature.

Perpetrator Types

More socially isolated, assaultive, and resentful than general offenders (Valliant & Bergeron, 1997), sex offenders do not constitute one class. Some are pedophiles – i.e., individuals who abuse children outside the family – and others are not (Glasser et al., 2001; Walters, Marcus, Edens, Knight, & Sanford, 2012). Some are psychopaths (Kolla et al., 2013), some commit incest, and some abuse children inside as well as outside the family (Glasser et al., 2001). The distinction between pedophiles and nonpedophiles is associated with different correlates. For example, pedophiles had lower psychopathy scores (Walters, Marcus, Edens, Knight, & Sanford, 2012).

Child sex offenders were similar to other sex offenders with respect to family factors, externalizing behaviors, internalizing behaviors, social deficits, sexual problems, and attitudes and beliefs (Whitaker et al., 2008). Both groups were different from nonoffenders in this regard. Some child molesters have low levels of self-esteem and intimacy, and have difficulty regulating negative emotions (Mandeville-Norden & Beech, 2009). Others were characterized more by a poor understanding of the harm they caused to the children they abused. Still others had more global, offense-specific, and socioaffective problems.

The estimates of the prevalence of mental disorders in male perpetrators vary. For example, one study suggested that only some men who were charged with sexual offences abused children who presented before criminal courts met the criteria of a mental disorder (e.g., Balasundaram et al., 2009). Only some have significant personality factors. However, many sexual offenders against minors referred to forensic psychiatric evaluation in Sweden had severe mental health and behavioral problems that had already started in childhood (Carlsted et al., 2009). In one study, men who abused very young children (0–5 years) did not have more mental health and psychosocial problems than those who victimized older children. They also did not have a different sexual orientation, but had more often abused both boys and girls. However, another study found that, compared with incest offenders whose victims were 12 to 16 years of age, incest offenders whose youngest victims were less than 6 years had a greater history of substance abuse and more current problems with alcohol (Firestone, Dixon, Nunes, & Bradford, 2005). Their sexual functioning was poorer, they were more psychiatrically disturbed, and they were more likely to have a male victim, to have abused a nephew/niece or grandson/granddaughter, and to have denied their offense(s).

Female Perpetrators

CSA is not limited to male offenders. In fact, abuse by females is less rare than it was once thought. For example, many Swedish psychiatric patients reported parental abuse that often included the mother (Nilsson, Bengtsson-Tops, & Persson, 2005). Sexual abuse by females often goes underreported, unrecognized, or is considered ethically more acceptable than male abuse (Tsopelas, Tsetsou, & Douzenis, 2011; Tsopelas, Tsetsou, Ntounas, & Douzenis, 2012). Tsopelas and colleagues documented that women who had engaged in sexual abuse were mainly young (age up to 36 years old), friends or relatives of the victim, and had experienced abuse themselves. They used more persuasion and psychological coercion, but were legally charged in a lesser extent compared with male abusers. However, the psychological consequences for the victim might be even more severe than the sequelae of male sexual abuse.

Among all adult female sex offenders known to the Dutch criminal justice authorities between 1994 and 2005, 77% had abused children (Wijkman, Bijleveld, & Hendriks, 2010). Approximately two thirds had abused children – commonly their own – in collaboration with an intimate male partner. Many of these women had mental disorders, and one third of them had been sexually abused themselves.

Juvenile Perpetrators

Sex offenders are not limited to adults either. It is unclear to date whether male juvenile sex offenders resemble nonsexual juvenile offenders with respect to individual, familial, and environmental characteristics. A review suggests that they have different personality characteristics, behavioral problems, history of sexual abuse, nonsexual offending, and peer functioning (Van Wijk et al., 2006). With respect to demographic factors, family functioning and background, antisocial attitudes, and intellectual and neurological functioning the results were inconsistent.

A recent study of incarcerated adolescent boys addressed callous-unemotional traits in youth (Kimonis, Fanti, Isoma, & Donoghue, 2013). These traits can be seen as developmental precursors to adult psychopathy. Consistent with prior research, boys with high scores for this insensitivity and cold-heartedness had greater neglect and sexual abuse histories, violent and property delinquency, and a sexually motivated index offense.

Nearly all incarcerated male and female youths in Canada met the criteria for at least one mental disorder (Gretton & Clift, 2011). Substance abuse and dependence disorders were highly prevalent, and aggressive forms of conduct disorder common, as were own physical and sexual abuse. Female adolescents were more likely to present with substance abuse/dependence disorders, current suicide ideation, sexual abuse, PTSD, symptoms of depression and anxiety, oppositional defiant disorder, and multiple mental disorder diagnoses. The male youths had higher odds of presenting with aggressive symptoms of conduct disorder.

Dissociation

Dissociation is seldom evaluated in perpetrators of childhood adversities. Emergent evidence nonetheless suggests that the psychiatric evaluation of offenders with or without antisocial personality disorder should include an assessment of dissociative symptoms. Indeed, in a review of the limited literature, Moskowitz (2004) concluded that dissociation+ predicts violence in a wide range of populations, and that consideration of this kind of psychopathology may contribute to an understanding of violent behavior. For example, a considerable number of child molesters may have a dissociative disorder or at least significant dissociative symptoms (Friedrich et al., 2001). Compared to controls, pedophiles used more dissociation+, displacement, denial, autistic fantasy, splitting of object, projective identification, acting out, and passive aggressive behavior, but less intellectualization and rationalization (Drapeau, Beretta, de Roten, Koerner, & Despland, 2008). Case reports suggest that individuals who have committed serious sexual assaults or who had killed may have major DID[1] (Lewis et al., 1997; Nijenhuis, 1995; Ross, 2008). However, DID may be missed in forensic psychiatry because several of many of its characteristics are – on the surface – similar to the symptoms associated with antisocial personality (Lewis & Bard, 1991, p. 741):

> For example, amnesia for behaviors is dismissed as lying, fugue states appear to be attempts to evade justice; finding things in one's possession looks like stealing; self-mutilation and suicide attempts seem manipulative; and the use of different names at different times and in different circumstances is interpreted as the conscious use of aliases in order to evade the law. Even the dramatic, at times heart-wrenching emotional catharses relating to abuse revealed during hypnosis are so painful that the average person has difficulty accepting that they happened and, therefore, dismisses them as exaggeration or total fabrication. Most often, the diagnosis is missed because the clinician does not even consider it a possibility.

Dissociative Symptoms/Disorders and Childhood Adverse Events in Offenders

Dissociative conditions in offenders including PTSD, thus, remain severely underresearched. A substantial proportion of young offenders of child maltreatment have PTSD, though in a recent study the diagnosis was more common in women (40%) than in men (17%) (Moore, Gaskin, & Indig, 2013). Whereas over half of them reported a form of childhood abuse or neglect, the risk of reporting three of more kinds of severe childhood traumatization was almost ten times higher for the women – and this risk was the main correlate of a PTSD diagnosis. Another study documented that intentional and accidental perpetration of serious injury or death was associated with high levels of mental disorders (Nickerson, Aderka, Bryant, Litz, & Hofmann, 2011). However, compared to accidental perpetration, intentional perpetration was associated with more PTSD symptoms; and compared to accidental perpetrators, intentional perpetrators were more likely to have experienced interpersonal adverse events in adulthood and childhood.

Very few studies have investigated possible associations between PTSD symptoms and reoffending risk in perpetrators of violence. In a study of prisoners, Ardino, Milani, and Di Blasio (2013) documented that two thirds of prisoners had PTSD symptoms, and that approximately one third was at risk of reoffending. Their analyses suggested that there

1 Volume III of this book series includes a description of the successful treatment of a man with DID who had committed murder. His DID had gone unnoticed during 12 years of incarceration and psychiatric treatment, but was in fact not hard to diagnose with the SCID-D.

could be a pathway from PTSD to worry and a negative perception of other individuals' support to an increased risk of reoffending.

As in other populations, offenders with dissociative symptoms tend to have experienced adverse events. For example, compared to mentally healthy military controls, individuals with antisocial personality disorder who had been admitted to a military psychiatric hospital reported more CSA, physical abuse, neglect, and early separation from parents (Semiz et al., 2007). Each of these adverse events predicted the personality disorder. The patients also had more dissociative symptoms. Half of them reported a pathological level of these symptoms, and this level was associated with childhood adverse events and comorbid psychopathological features relevant to antisocial personality. In a study on inmates, Dietrich (2003) did not find differences between sex offenders and nonsexual offenders in terms of probable PTSD, probable DID, cognitive-emotional (DES), and sensorimotor (SDQ-20) dissociative symptoms. However, inmates who had been sexually abused as a child had more sensorimotor dissociative symptoms than those who had not been abused. Among offenders, cognitive-emotional dissociation+ scores were correlated with trauma-related variables even after controlling for negative affectivity (Ruiz, Poythress, Lilienfeld, & Douglas, 2008). Sexual offenders and nonsexual offenders had similar scores for dissociation+ and psychopathology in one study, but the former group had experienced more CSA (Dudeck et al., 2008). Lewis et al. (1997) in a study on 12 convicted murderers documented signs and symptoms of major DID in childhood and adulthood which were corroborated independently and from several sources in all cases. Objective evidence of severe childhood abuse was gathered in 11 cases. The subjects had amnesia for most of their own abuse and they underreported it.

Dissociative Amnesia and Offending

Offenders can have many reasons for denying their perpetration, including dissociative amnesia (Becker-Blease & Freyd, 2007; Nijenhuis, 1995; Ross, 2008). For example, half of 17 convicted sex offenders reported some forgetting of instances when they had sexually abused another person (Becker-Blease & Freyd, 2007). This forgetting was related to both dissociative symptoms at the time of the offense and in daily life. Also, dissociative symptoms during their own physical or sexual abuse in childhood was related to both dissociative symptoms during later perpetration and everyday dissociative symptoms as an adult. Whereas the dissociation+ symptoms were also related to measures of antisocial behavior and aggression, they did not predict recidivism.

TSDP and Offending

In light of TSDP, offenders with a dissociative disorder probably encompass controlling EPs, ignorant/ignoring ANPs, and fragile EPs. This formal causation may foremost pertain to offenders with high dissociation+ scores. Others perpetrators do not have a dissociative disorder, but the different patterns of mental and behavioral actions they can engage in over time seem phenomenologically comparable. These action patterns can be described as controlling EP-like, ANP-like, and fragile EP-like. For the sake of convenience, below I do not apply the distinction between real dissociative parts and dissociative part-like organism-environment subsystems. Remember that in the latter cases not real dissociative parts but dissociative part-like modes are intended; once in a while I use the terms 'apparently normal perpetrator mode,' 'fragile emotional perpetrator mode,' and 'controlling emotional perpetrator mode.' I also use the shorthands 'apparently normal perpetrator,' 'fragile emotional perpetrator,' and 'controlling emotional perpetrator.'

The Controlling Emotional Perpetrator

The idea that committing sexual abuse alleviates the perpetrators' negative affects does not seem to hold (McCoy & Fremouw, 2010). Their will, their final goal, thus, does not pertain to affect regulation, but concerns different desires.

Driven by a will to dominate others, get sexual gratification, express anger, or fulfil still other personal desires at the expense of those of other individuals, perpetrators are clearly controlling and emotional when they are abusive. In the controlling emotional perpetrator mode, they are led by these final goals. For example, male sex offenders were mainly led by sexual motivation and substance abuse (Balasundaram et al., 2009). Substance abuse can be a precipitant of the abuse, but it can also serve as an excuse. The urge to control others extends to postabuse behaviors. As Scott and King (2007) documented, perpetrators of abuse and violence against women and children were often reluctant participants in intervention programs. They frequently missed scheduled appointments, were sometimes openly hostile to intervention staff, and often judged program materials as irrelevant to their situation.

Cognitive Distortions. Lanning (2010, p. 3) emphasizes that there are serious reasons to be skeptical of research that relies strongly on uncorroborated perpetrator self-report. He details that

> [t]his [view] may be due in part to a professional lifetime spent interviewing and talking with individuals who repeatedly lie about, misrepresent, and rationalize their behavior for a wide variety of reasons.

Reviewing 10 years of qualitative research, Lawson (2003) documented in line with Lanning's observations that child molesters commonly use cognitive distortions to meet their personal needs, including the need to protect themselves from aversive self-awareness. They also tend to engage in cognitive distortions to overcome internal inhibitions against engaging children in sexual activity. To justify themselves, offenders commonly make excuses and redefine their actions as tokens of love and mutuality. However, in full contrast with the meaning of the term 'pedophile[2],' pedophiles are motivated more by sexual gratification than by an emotional or relationship interest in their victims or children (Wilson, 1999). In fact, perpetrators exploit the power imbalance that characterizes all adult-child relationships. They do not tend to commit their abusive acts impulsively, but often groom their victims. This preparation reveals how well planned and controlled child sexual abuse commonly is.

First-Person and Quasi-Second-Person Perspective

As a controlling emotional perpetrator, the first-person perspective of perpetrators of childhood abuse and neglect seems to be dominated by their lust, hunger for control, and anger. These urges imply their own kinds of phenomenal sensations, affects, thoughts, and behaviors. The involved wills are the heart of the actions systems of lust – sexual arousal, the desire for preferred sexual acts, sexual thoughts, and behaviors – social dominance, and fight (see Figure 20.2 below; Dutton & Starzomsky, 1997). For example, compared to healthy controls, offenders with antisocial personality disorder attended more violence-related and negative words in a Stroop test (Domes, Mense, Vohs, & Habermeyer, 2012). Offenders who reported childhood maltreatment attended more to violence-related words than offenders who did not report such maltreatment.

Perpetrators' thoughts commonly include the idea of being *entitled* to engage in abusive and neglectful actions that meet their particular constellation of desires. In quasi-second-person perspective, their phenomenal judgment might be something like "I can serve my needs"; "My actions are justified."

Second-Person Perspective

Perpetrators' second-person perspective lacks empathy and sympathy for their victims. To the degree that perpetrators of CSA (initially) show friendliness or later regrets, these feelings may be more apparent than real. Lia (53 years; major DID) had long believed that her father's tears after his vicious rapes and his promises that "it would never happen again" were sincere. Later, she realized that his regrets and promises had merely been a means to keep her mouth shut. "Never" lasted a day or two. Perpetrators' second-person perspective often includes the well-known 'blaming the victim.' Many patients report that their perpetrators accused them of being seductive, bad, unmanageable, "difficult," and the like. These judgments can be seen as efficient causes that serve the perpetrators' final causes.

Consistent with these clinical impressions, child-molesting men demonstrated more cognitive distortions than nonsexual offenders and nonoffending men (Marshall, Ham-

2 The term pedophila stems from the Greek 'pais' (genitive 'paidos') that means 'child,' plus 'philos' that stands for 'loving.'

ilton, & Fernandez, 2001). Their greatest empathy deficits were toward their victims. There were also differences within the group of child molesters in that violent child molesters were significantly more likely to make statements denigrating their victims than were the child molesters classified as seductive (Eisenman, 1997).

The variable 'cognitive distortions' was one of four features that characterized high-risk offenders (Coxe & Holmes, 2009). These distortions were associated with greater denial or minimization of one's own guilt and deviance, of harm to one's victims, of one's need for treatment, and of responsibility for one's sexual offenses (Nunes & Jung, 2012). For perpetrators of incest, denial was associated with increased sexual recidivism (Nunes et al., 2007). However, this relationship did not apply to offenders with unrelated victims in this study.

Some sexual offenders were traumatized as children themselves, and this personal history may influence their second-person perspective. Among men convicted for sexual offences, personal CSA was associated with higher total scores for psychopathy as well as with facets tapping a grandiose and manipulative interpersonal style, impulsive-irresponsible lifestyle, and antisocial behavior (Graham, Kimonis, Wasserman, & Kline, 2012). Child molesters' antisocial behavior was associated with their own childhood physical abuse and neglect, and their lack of empathy and shallow affect correlated with their own childhood emotional neglect. Rapists, however, scored higher on these traits irrespective of their own neglect history. A prospective longitudinal study showed that CSA predicted abnormal physiological responses to stress in late adolescence, and this stress predicted higher levels of depression and antisocial behaviors in young adulthood (Shenk, Noll, Putnam, & Trickett, 2010).

Third-Person Perspective

To the degree that perpetrators lack empathy and sympathy for their victims, they regard their victims as objects more than as subjects when they are abusive. In other words, they do not engage in a second-person perspective with their victims (anymore), but rather take on a third-person perspective in which their victims appear as objects. What should be an I-You relationship becomes an I-Object relationship. For example, they may regard the child as a "dirty thing," a "whore" in the sense of a thing one can use as one pleases, or a slave. These judgments, thus, are not phenomenal. They are physical.

The second-person and third-person perspective associated with the controlling emotional perpetrator mode are reflected in the *Power & Control Wheel of Child Abuse* (Domestic Abuse Intervention Project; www.duluth-model.org; Figure 20.2).

Perpetrators have an obvious interest in silencing their victims. Whereas silencing actions suggest a second-person perspective, offenders may, as mentioned above, in fact regard their victims as dangerous objects more than as dangerous subjects. To silence them, perpetrators engage in a variety of actions. Patients with dissociative disorders provide a host of examples of these behaviors, including enticing the victim ("What you and I have

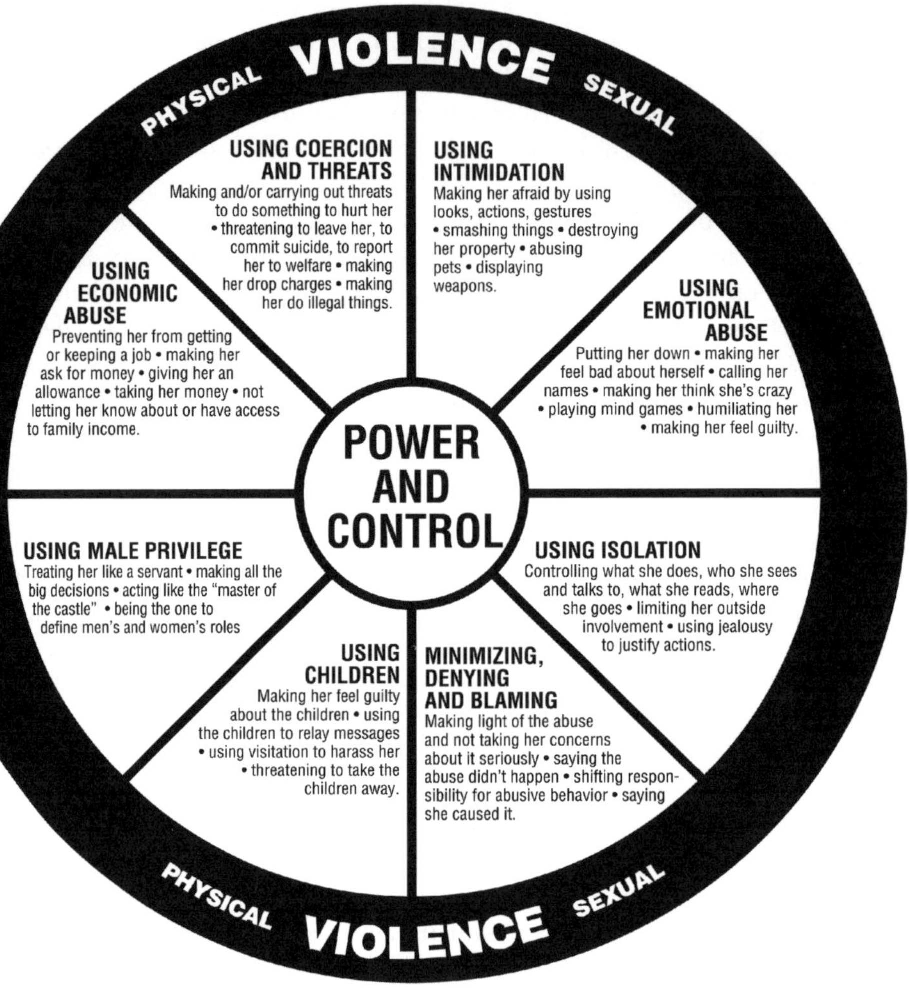

Figure 20.2. The Power & Control Wheel of Child Abuse.

is so special; it's our little secret"), threats of punishment ("If you tell anyone, I will kill you," or "You don't want anything to happen to your child, will you?"), abandonment ("No one will love you anymore"), and suffering of the family ("Mommy will be in pain"). Some use threat of judicial actions against them ("I will go to jail, and that will be your fault;" "Mommy will be sad and will have no money") and legal actions against their victims ("I will see you in court and ruin you"), rejection ("Everyone will know you are a whore"), and ridicule ("Who's ever gonna believe you?"). Real objects must also be silenced, that is, traces of abuse and neglect must be wiped out. For example, Ineke (50 years, major DID) reported that her father had instructed her to clean the blood and semen stained sheets and clothes each time he had raped her.

Apparently Normal Perpetrator

Many perpetrators are not necessarily controlling in public. Their societal behavior may impress as more or less 'normal.' Indeed, they generally are psychiatrically otherwise 'normal' men who are skilled at both planning their offending behaviors and denying their existence (Glaser, 1998). Their normality is only apparent. As apparently normal perpetrators, they may effectively hide their position as controlling emotional perpetrators. Offenders may thus try to make a favorable impression on others, and particularly child molesters exhibit a strong tendency to 'fake good' (Tan & Grace, 2008). Some of the Big Five personality traits as well as state features characterizing emotional adjustment may characterize different types of sexual offenders (Carvalho & Nobre, 2013). Individuals convicted for rape and child sexual abuse had more neuroticism than nonconvicted sexual offenders. However, child sex molesters presented significantly less openness and less hostility than rapists and nonconvicted sexual offenders, and they had less marked psychopathological features than convicted rapists.

Two thirds of sexual offenders did not have a psychiatric history prior to their conviction, but about half of them appeared to have a personality disorder, mainly borderline personality disorder (Curtin & Niveau, 1998). Whereas offenders against adults were socially isolated and had a low socioeconomic status, child molesters had a relatively normal psychosocial profile in this Swiss study. Even two thirds of severe sexual sadists – individuals with a sexual preference that focuses on humiliation and subjugation of the victim, sometimes causing grievous injury or death – went undetected prior to the crime that brought them into a high-security forensic setting (Nitschke, Blendl, Ottermann, Osterheider, & Mokros, 2009).

Ineke (50 years, major DID) had been sexually abused, physically abused, and emotionally neglected by both her father and mother. From the age of 6 years, she ran the household, cooked the meals, did the laundry, and cleaned the house. Visitors would meet a well-kept, friendly, and caring mother. When they had left, Ineke's mother would as a rule instantly switch to her existence as controlling emotional perpetrator. Her existence as apparently normal perpetrator and controlling emotional perpetrator had probably been more than modes, because Ineke's descriptions of her mother suggested that she had had major DID. As controlling emotional part/perpetrator, her mother had been abusive, untidy, accusative, and rejecting. Ineke realized in the course of her treatment that her vulnerability and dependency as a child and adolescent may have triggered mother's traumatic memories of her own childhood abuse and neglect.

Apparently normal perpetrators may thus go unrecognized as controlling emotional perpetrators in the extended family or society more generally. Their social face need not match the face of their controlling emotional perpetrator. Ineke's public mother and private mother were miles apart. However, some perpetrators are publicly controlling and emotional. For example, Ineke's father "had many women" and there was nothing he loved more than talking about sex – and everyone who knew him knew that.

Confronted with their abusive and neglectful actions, many perpetrators deny their truth. A problem in itself, denial also predicts continuation of incest. As documented by Nunes et al. (2007), denial was positively related to increased sexual recidivism for incest offenders. It was not associated with increased recidivism for offenders with unrelated victims.

Fragile Emotional Perpetrator: Own History of Adverse Childhood Events

There are two different ways in which perpetrators of childhood abuse and neglect function in the mode of fragile emotional perpetrator. One pertains to an own history of childhood traumatization, and the other involves taking the victim position.

Adverse Childhood Events

Adverse childhood events are associated with a wide range of negative outcomes in adolescence and adulthood such as physical and mental health disorders, including personality disorders (Hengartner, Ajdacic-Gross, Rodgers, Muller, & Rossler, 2013), social dominance (Teisl, Rogosch, Oshri, & Cicchetti, 2011), and aggressive behavior. For example, the risk that parents physically abuse their children is higher when they have a psychiatric disorder or when they were abused as a child (Medley & Sachs-Ericsson, 2009).

Several studies suggest that a high percentage of committed sex offenders were exposed to CSA and/or other adverse childhood events (Hulme & Middleton, 2013). Compared to adult normative samples, they had significantly higher scores for eight of ten adverse childhood events, and convicted sexual offenders and child abusers reported more sexual abuse in childhood than other offender types (Reavis, Looman, Franco, & Rojas, 2013). Based on a review of the literature and on their own findings, the authors concluded that criminal behavior is to be added to the host of negative outcomes associated with scores on the Adverse Childhood Events Questionnaire.

One third of pedophiles had a history of CSA (Balasundaram et al., 2009). Incarcerated individuals and psychologically disturbed sexual offenders have generally lived a high degree of traumatic experiences (Duceck et al., 2006). Some studies even suggest that the majority of rapists and child sexual abusers were abused as children (Simons, Wurtele, & Durham, 2008). Compared to rapists, child sexual abusers reported more frequently child sexual abuse, early exposure to pornography, an earlier onset of masturbation, and sexual activities with animals. Rapists reported more frequent experiences of physical abuse, parental violence, emotional abuse, and cruelty to animals. Further, almost all child sexual abusers and rapists had been frequently exposed to violent media during their childhood. Among offenders with an intellectual disability, some sexual offenders were sexually abused in their childhood (Lindsay, Law, Quinn, Smart, & Smith, 2001). Physical abuse stood out more in the history of the nonsexual offenders.

Both psychopathic and nonpsychopathic criminals experienced more traumatic childhood experiences than a control group in a study by Cima, Smeets, and Jelicic (2008). Whereas childhood traumatization was associated with high levels of aggression in the nonpsychopaths and control participants, this relationship did not exist for the psychopaths. Another study also found that childhood abuse exerted no direct or indirect effect on the core interpersonal and affective features of psychopathy, but documented that this abuse was directly related to the aspect of psychopathy associated with an impulsive and irresponsible lifestyle (Poythress, Skeem, & Lilienfeld, 2006). However, the research findings are inconsistent. For example, Bailey and Shelton (2014) found that childhood separations, physical abuse, and indifferent parenting styles were more prominent in self-reports of incarcerated male psychopaths than in those of incarcerated males who were not psychopathic. Childhood physical abuse was associated with reactive aggression in violent offenders, including those with high scores for psychopathy (Kolla et al., 2013).

Serious female offenders at a maximum-security correctional facility with and without Cluster B personality pathology had also experienced substantial early maltreatment (Loper, Mahmoodzadegan, & Warren, 2008). Women with Cluster B pathology reported higher levels and a greater variety of maternal and paternal physical and psychological abuse, but not more CSA. Both groups of women had experienced more physical and psychological abuse from maternal than paternal caregivers. Studying large samples of men and women with antisocial personality disorder, Alegria et al. (2013) found that, compared to the men, the women reported more frequent childhood emotional neglect and sexual abuse, parent-related adverse event(s) during childhood (e.g., parental substance use disorder), and adverse events during adulthood. The women were more impaired and received less social support. They were also less violent, but displayed more aggressiveness and irritability than the men.

Adolescent sibling-incest offenders were more often victims of CSA, and they were more likely to have a younger child in their families than offenders who abused nonsibling children (Worling, 1995). The offenders had experienced more marital discord, parental rejection, physical discipline, negative family atmosphere, and general dissatisfaction with family relationships. There is also evidence that juvenile offenders who had been emotionally neglected in their childhood and who were still emotional neglected were more likely to reoffend compared to adolescents who had no official history of emotional neglect (Ryan, Williams, & Courtney, 2013).

There is limited support for the hypothesis of a "cycle of abuse," that is, a link between childhood traumatization and the risk of becoming an offender (Glasser et al., 2001). In a study of individuals who attended a forensic psychotherapy clinic for antisocial and sexually deviant subjects, Glasser et al. found that there are at least two subgroups of adult perpetrators of child sexual abuse. Approximately one third reported childhood adverse experiences, yet two thirds did not. It is clear that the notion of a cycle of sexual abuse could apply only to the smaller group. The risk of becoming a perpetrator was higher for individuals who had had adverse childhood experiences, including parental loss in childhood. This risk was doubled for incest, still higher for pedophilia, and the highest for those exposed to both pedophilia and incest. A high percentage of male subjects abused in childhood by a female relative became perpetrators. Another study similarly suggested that the cycle of abuse may particularly pertain to being the victim and perpetrator of sexual abuse rather than to any kind of childhood adversity (Reckdenwald, Mancini, & Beauregard, 2013).

Whereas the findings support the idea of a victim-to-victimizer cycle in a subgroup of male perpetrators, the relationship did not apply to the female victims studied. My own clinical observations with respect to help-seeking, chronically traumatized women are consistent with the notion that most women who were sexually abused and otherwise traumatized as a child do not necessarily become sex offenders. All who had children tried their utmost to be good mothers. This did not mean that all of them succeeded in all regards, and with treatment for childhood traumatization and dissociation of the personality they became better mothers. The "cycle of abuse" is thus by no means inevitable – and it does not explain why some victims but not others become victimizers or why it applies to men more than women.

Attachment

Many sexual offenders are insecurely attached. In one study child molesters were more likely to be preoccupied, whereas rapists, violent offenders, and, to a lesser degree, incest offenders were more likely to be dismissive (Stirpe, Abracen, Stermac, & Wilson, 2006). Childhood attachment problems may present in adulthood more in adult state attachment than in adult trait attachment (McKillop, Smallbone, Wortley, & Andjic, 2012). Thus among men who had been sexually abused as children and had been in an intimate relationship prior to the onset of their sexual offence, childhood attachment problems, particularly with fathers, were more clearly reflected in state adult attachment (i.e., in the month preceding sexual offending onset) than in trait adult attachment. Research suggests that male adolescents with attachment anxiety, but with positive attitudes toward others may develop feelings of personal inadequacy (Miner et al., 2009). Socially isolated from peers, they may be prone to turn to children to fulfill their intimacy and sexual needs (Miner et al., 2009).

Most offenders experience insecure parental attachment bonds (Simons, Wurtele, & Durham, 2008). For rapists, avoidant parental attachments stand out, and for child sexual abusers anxious parental attachments. The parent-child attachment relationships of men who sexually abused children were most frequently characterized by affectionless control, that is, by low parental care and high overprotection and control (McKillop et al., 2012).

A review of the literature documented the relationships between adolescent sex offending and histories of family violence, parental depression and child maltreatment, problematic communication patterns, parental psychological inaccessibility, inconsistent discipline, and failure of the family to acknowledge the youth's offending behavior (Worley, Church, & Clemmons, 2011).

The research findings regarding attachment are not fully consistent though. For example, in a study of large groups of adolescent sexual and nonsexual offenders, Seto and Lalumiere (2010) did not find support for explanations of sexual offending focusing on family communication problems, poor parent-child attachment, exposure to nonsexual violence, or socially incompetent attitudes and beliefs about women or sexual offending. They also did not find that adolescent sexual offending could be parsimoniously explained as a simple manifestation of general antisocial tendencies. Correlates that stood out in their study were that, compared with nonsexual offenders, adolescent sex offenders had much less extensive criminal histories, fewer antisocial peers, and fewer substance use problems. The largest group difference was obtained for atypical sexual interests, followed by sexual abuse history, and, in turn, criminal history, antisocial associations, and substance abuse.

Fragile Emotional Perpetrator: Taking the Victim Position

Perpetrators tend to take the fragile emotional perpetrator position when their victims openly accuse them. For example, they may plea innocence and complain that the accusers deeply hurt their feelings and other interests. Trying to save their face and regain control, they may enter the controlling emotional perpetrator mode and protest that the accusers must have pseudomemories of the abuse and neglect due to the accusers' fantasy, suggestibility, and viciousness. In this context, they prefer to believe that delayed memories of childhood traumatization are false per definitionem or unreliable, because – as they inaccurately claim – memories of true childhood traumatization are continuous. They may also discredit accusers by stating that memories of alleged traumatizing events and dissociative disorders are fabrications due to suggestive therapy.

Apart from denial, perpetrators may say that they simply do not remember. In many cases there were no witnesses or witnesses remained silent or have since died. Some witnesses have been sexually abusive themselves and may therefore be motivated to deny and withhold testimony (Worley et al., 2011). These actions immensely complicate the accusers' efforts to find recognition and justice.

Hypothesis

Like their victims, perpetrators seem to alternate between three major modes. In public, they may function in the mode of apparently normal perpetrator. They operate in the mode of controlling emotional perpetrator when they engage in abusive acts that they do insufficiently integrate as an apparently normal perpetrator. When accused, they tend to become more controlling (an example is given below), attempt to keep up their apparently normal face, and/or enter the fragile emotional perpetrator mode. In the latter position, they present themselves as victims and commonly portray accusers and individuals who work with accusers as the perpetrators. In a considerable number of cases, the existence and alternations between these three different prototypical modes may relate to the perpetrators' own childhood traumatization and attachment disruptions. For example, as a fragile emotional perpetrator, they may phenomenally experience the pain of their own traumatization that they overcompensate for by becoming a controlling emotional perpetrator. As the apparently normal perpetrators, they hide their fragility and control – and hence fail to integrate and realize these. This sad dissociative existence keeps their injuries, defects, and injurious actions intact, all the more when their social environment supports the perpetration more than inhibits it.

Partners in Crime

Apparently Normal Partners in Crime, Apparently Normal Families

The abuse and neglect of perpetrators are commonly at least partly known within the families in which the traumatization happens. Offenders tend to have active or passive accomplices. For example, many individuals who were traumatized in the core family report that one parent knew what the other parent was doing, simply because the deeds were done in public (e.g., physical abuse), or because they were accidentally observed (e.g., "Mother entered the room and saw that my father was raping me. She turned, walked away, and never touched the subject"). Some also state that the other parent must or should have known because of traces of blood and semen, vaginal or other wounds, or their efforts to remove the traces (Lia's father instructed her to wash the bedlinen and her pants after the rapes. Her mother never asked why she did these things as a young child). Else (55, major DID) was more than once hardly able to walk after gang rapes that her father had arranged for his friends and himself. Nina's (46, fully recovered from major DID) father who abused her sexually for 17 years was an accomplice to his wife's sexual, physical, and emotional abuse and neglect of their daughter. He knew that his wife was recurrently psychotic and always sexually obsessed. They often abused Nina together. He often left Nina alone with his wife, found excuses why she could not attend primary school, and never asked what happened during all the hours that Nina was alone with her mother. The extended family also knew that Nina's mother had a severe mental disorder. Still, no one ever showed concern what she might do to Nina. It had not occurred to the headmaster of the primary school or the family's physician that Nina's frequent and extended absences from school were a matter of grave concern. They may also have chosen just to turn it a blind eye. Knowing trouble and responsibilities and realizing them are very different actions.

Mediated by final causes such as avoiding family scandals, shame, perpetrator revenge, and realization of personal childhood trauma, apparently normal partners in crime thus tend to act as if nothing is seriously wrong, and as if they have no responsibility in bringing perpetrations to light.

Controlling Emotional Partners in Crime, Controlling Emotional Families

In a defensive reflex, the apparently normal family becomes the controlling emotional family when traumatized individuals eventually speak out. Many traumatized individuals report how the controlling emotional family tends to join with and imitate the perpetrator's defensive actions. Without ever talking to the accusers, without ever examining what might have happened, the family typically turns against them as in a defensive reflex.

For example, guided by the final goal of saving apparent normality, the whole family, including two elderly sisters who had not been abused, instantly accused Nina of lying when she eventually spoke out and completely rejected her. The fact that everyone knew how 'weird' Nina's mother had been did not seem to have made any difference. It took years before a single nephew even wanted to listen to Nina's story. The controlling emotional family was paralleled by the fragile emotional family. Had the family taken a serious interest in examining Nina's reports, they would have uncovered a dreadful history that implicated them as partners in crime. Rather than integrating and realizing their shameful role, they felt hurt by Nina: Nina had jeopardized the interests of the family.

Ineke had been in psychiatric care for many years. She had not talked with her father or any other family members about the sexual abuse experienced from her father. Observing Ineke's fear of her father, Anja, one of her sisters, got the idea that he might have sexually abused Ineke and asked her if that might be the case. As ANP, Ineke honestly replied that she did not know for sure (her EPs definitely knew), that she was carefully examining the issue in therapy, and that she needed time. Anja was not content. She pressured Ineke even more, which reactivated a second ANP who was trained to obey. At this juncture, Ineke gave in on the condition that Anja would keep the matter to herself. When Anja promised to meet this request, Ineke shared with her that she experienced many intrusions that pertained to incest. The next day, Anja betrayed the arrangement and spread the news in the family, which then massively and aggressively attacked Ineke.

Her father first entered the mode of the fragile emotional perpetrator, showed hurt, and played innocent. A few days later, he switched to the controlling emotional perpetrator mode and asked Ineke to sign a document he had composed. It involved a statement that he had never touched his daughter in any indecent way. Ineke gave in after 3 hours of intense pressure. On the next occasion, the family intruded on her house. In the mode of controlling emotional partners in crime, they accused her in no friendly words of ruining them, leaving Ineke in a prepsychotic state.

When her father was dying, she wished to take her leave from him in the best possible way she could think of. She had hoped that he would talk about the traumatization with her, if only with minor hints. But he kept up the apparently normal perpetrator mode and perfectly avoided the topic. As a last gesture of peacemaking, Ineke wanted to kiss him briefly on his forehead. He took her head, kissed her fully on the mouth, and worked his tongue inside. The controlling emotional perpetrator would not give up. Ineke fled from the hospital. Her father died the next day. Confused, she contacted me, and shared as ANP what had happened. We were able to prevent a dissociative psychotic episode (i.e., an episode in which one or more bewildered fragile EPs became dominant for several days). In fact, and quite paradoxically, her father's final abusive action had helped her to finally start taking the reality of the incest into herself.

Fragile Emotional Partners in Crime, Fragile Emotional Families

Some family members may have been traumatized themselves. For example, her mother had also sexually abused Ineke's brother. Many years after Nina's revelations of chronic parental incest and other forms of parental traumatization the family had thoughtlessly and stubbornly discredited, it turned out that one of her mother's sisters had committed incest as well.

The disclosure of inner family abuse, maltreatment, and emotional neglect may pose a threat to other traumatized family members who try to cope with life as ANPs. It also poses a threat to other controlling emotional perpetrators in the family. And it poses a threat to apparently normal partners in crime who knew, could have known, or should have known the fact of the traumatization. Accurate accusations of traumatization confront them with the painful drama and their failure to act responsibly.

Fragile Emotional Partners in Crime, Emotional Families: Taking the Victim Position

When the intrafamilial childhood abuse and neglect gets uncovered, the apparently normal family tends to shift into the mode of the fragile emotional family, and commences to defend its interests as the controlling emotional family. In the first-person perspective there is phenomenal hurt. The quasi-second-person perspective involves the phenomenal judgment that "bad things are happening to us," and in the second-person perspective this judgment is that there is an individual, a "You" assisted by one or more "accomplices" such as therapists, who "do it to them." These second-person perspectives show at least strong features of a third-person physical judgment, when the accuser's story is not examined, but rejected in a reflex. If the defense works, the final goals of evading hurt, shame, and responsibility are reached. Then, the family may become the apparently normal family again.

Medicine, Psychology, and Psychiatry

As shown in Volume I, trauma and particularly childhood adversity and traumatization have had a troubled role in the history of medicine, psychology and psychiatry. For ages, childhood and other kinds of traumatization were mostly overlooked or ignored. This observation also applies to a trauma-related understanding of dissociative disorders with the exception of a temporary understanding in some quarters of 19th-century French and, in its trail, North American psychiatry. Lost ground was reclaimed from the 1980s onward. Since this time ever more physicians, psychologists, and psychiatrists have started to lift the veil of professional ignorance. However, even amid increasing recognition, acknowledgment, and realization of trauma and the spectrum of trauma-related disorders, some seem to remain stuck in ignorance and aggressive opposition, at least in some regards.

Apparently Normal Healthcare Providers

Would it be too strong to say that medicine, psychology, and psychiatry have often taken, and in some regards still do take, an ANP-like position regarding child abuse and neglect and dissociative disorders? To illustrate, let me reiterate some previously discussed facts and add a few scattered observations:

- Generally speaking, the recognition, acknowledgment, and realization of childhood traumatization in medicine, psychology, and psychiatry have followed rather than initiated societal developments.
- Psychology and psychiatry have often resisted the acknowledgment, recognition, assessment, and treatment of childhood traumatization.
- There continues to be a lack of general knowledge and education regarding childhood abuse, maltreatment, and emotional neglect (Vandeven & Newton, 2006).
- There is a major lack of knowledge to date about individuals who sexually abuse children and adolescents while working in organizations such as daycare centers, primary schools, high schools, churches, and sporting clubs (Colton, Roberts, & Vanstone, 2010).
- Ongoing incestuous abuse during adulthood has never been addressed in a systematic way in the professional literature (Middleton, 2013). However, as Middleton (p. 184) reported, "Accounts of such cases have been appearing for many years. The Josef Fritzl case added a new impetus to reporting such abuses in the popular press. The current study presents 44 such cases from 24 countries that appeared in English-language press accounts over 5 years commencing January 2007. These cases are discussed in light of the minimal coverage of such issues in the professional literature. The results of this study suggest that cases of enduring incest are not rare and typically incorporate decades of sexual abuse, frequently result in pregnancies, and commonly incorporate ongoing violence and death threats."
- Many psychologists, psychiatrists, and physicians believe that delayed memories of adverse events are pseudomemories. However, there is no empirical evidence that delayed memories are less reliable and valid than continuously available memories of adverse events.
- Dissociative disorders are dramatically underrepresented and underresearched. To this day, childhood and adolescent dissociative disorders are even less studied than adult

dissociative disorders (Boysen, 2011; Sar, Middleton, & Dorahy, 2012). Many psychiatric studies do not include an assessment of dissociative disorders as a differential diagnosis. One can only wonder how many individuals diagnosed with complex PTSD, borderline personality disorder, and psychosis were in fact suffering from a dissociative disorder or 'comorbid' dissociative disorder? A similar concern is that general psychiatric assessment instruments do not cover DSM-IV (DSM-5) dissociative disorders, so that the results of many large-scale epidemiological studies are biased in this regard. This bias is a major fault, because studies using reliable and valid tools to assess dissociative disorders yielded lifetime prevalence rates around 10% in clinical and general population samples.

The clinical and scientific neglect of dissociative disorders constitutes a most deplorable and unacceptable state of affairs given the strong evidence that in particular complex PTSD, minor DID, and major DID have their roots in childhood traumatization. The lack of attention for childhood dissociative disorders is not due to the difficulty of diagnosing the conditions. Ignoring dissociative disorders involves a different dynamic causation.

– Emotional neglect has attracted far less attention than the adverse act of commission. PubMed, an online scientific library and search engine comprising more than 23 million citations for biomedical literature, produced 25,787 citations for 'sexual abuse,' 26,432 for physical abuse, and 13,865 for emotional abuse. The figure for 'emotional neglect' (1,218), however, was far lower. The term 'childhood abuse' resulted in 8,707 references, 4,246 for 'childhood sexual abuse,' 2,670 for 'childhood physical abuse,' and 1,148 for 'childhood neglect.' Many patients who report adverse acts of commission as well as adverse acts of omission feel that chronic emotional neglect was the worst of them all. The term 'adult trauma,' which basically generates publications on physical injuries, yielded 396,635 citations. This figure clearly reveals that medicine is clearly far more concerned with the attribute of matter than with the attribute of mind.

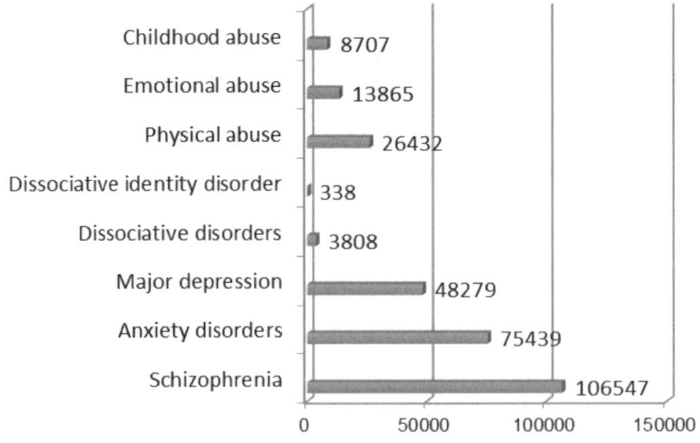

Figure 20.3. Numbers of PubMed citations for various mental disorders and adverse events (see also Chapter 7).

Controlling Emotional Healthcare Providers

It seems that medicine, psychology, and psychiatry have long tried to control rather than gain more knowledge about complex dissociative disorders and chronic childhood traumatization. This desire for control was guided by emotion more than by reason. Rather than studying the phenomena, many clinicians and researchers reflexively felt that the disorders were somehow not real, that they had to be fabrications driven by incestuous wishes, desire for money, cowardice, suggestion, fantasy, or still other shameful personal features. They typically did not study the literature before reaching their conclusions, though, and they did not seem to care that the involved ideas had not been tested in the population of concern.

Many patients reported that these professionals did not believe or accept their condition, and that they were not taken seriously in medicine and psychiatry. Some were laughed in the face and told that their condition did not really exist. The patients also experienced that 'treatment as usual' – which commonly implied disregard of dissociative symptoms and dissociative parts – had not helped them. Although utterly ineffective, these approaches continued for years. Their complaints and suggestions for improvement were commonly not welcomed. Many were given to understand that they would better leave their suggestive therapists.

A considerable number of peers gave clinicians who did take complex dissociative disorders seriously, who applied reliable and valid self-reporting questionnaires and diagnostic tools as well as the nowadays rather generally accepted phase-oriented treatment model (e.g., Van der Hart et al., 2006) a hard time. They portrayed them as dangerous individuals who in fact were suggesting the dissociative phenomena and the traumatic memories they treated. These clinicians would only worsen their patients' health and life, and that complex dissociative disorders existed only in those parts of the country where these professionals operated, that DID, in fact, was extremely rare. These and related claims were commonly presented with great confidence, despite a lack of empirical data and despite mounting evidence to the contrary. Some even tried to prevent the dissociative disorders from entering the DSM-5.

When patients had to be admitted for some time to a psychiatric hospital, admission requests were more than once rejected off hand. When they were admitted, many forfeited their original SCID-D based diagnosis and received a new one (e.g., schizophrenia, borderline personality disorder, generalized anxiety disorder). When it became clear that the diagnosis did not fit clinical realities, it was seldom withdrawn and exchanged for the correct diagnosis. Good advice from the treating and referring outpatient clinician was not commonly appreciated or used. Fragile EPs were often ignored or punished, and controlling EPs were commonly seen as manipulators to the extent that these dissociative parts of the personality were recognized and acknowledged at all. Many clinicians seemed content that patients as ANPs suppressed EPs, and some actively trained ANPs to become more effective avoiders of these emotional, trauma-fixated parts.

The university climate regarding complex dissociative disorders has generally speaking been similarly antagonistic. Scientific peers gave researchers of DID a hard time (ridicule, rejection, isolation, outright aggression). Another way to control dissociative disorders was to reject respective sound research proposals, or deny funding this work needs. The university training of psychologists, psychiatrists, and psychotherapists did not commonly include education in the existence, assessment, and treatment of complex dissociative disorders and chronic traumatization.

The policy of some scientific journals constitutes another kind of control mechanism of the problem of complex dissociative disorders. For example, one may wonder how it can be that papers including strong opinions regarding DID continue to be accepted despite the examination of the hypotheses in samples of individuals with DID? Would reviewers also accept articles presenting strong claims regarding other severe mental disorders, say schizophrenia, that are not supported by empirical data obtained in studies with the population of concern? And would editors-in-chief accept such papers? Would they be inclined to accept general survey studies of mental disorders that do not include anxiety disorders, major depression, and schizophrenia?

Fragile Emotional Healthcare Providers

Why are complex dissociative disorders an exception to the clinical and scientific rules? Why are dissociative disorders so strongly underrepresented, misrepresented, and understudied? Could these facts flow not from reason, but from emotional fragility?

The reality of complex dissociative disorders implies the general reality of chronic childhood traumatization that commonly occurs in the families in which the child is raised. This realization confronts clinicians and researchers with most painful facts that they might have rather avoided by staying ignorant and emotionally controlling. It also confronts them with the painful reality that the models of mental disorders and their treatment they were taught may fail to explain complex dissociative disorders; they realize that they have probably missed numerous cases, that they have failed to understand the involved individuals, and that they have applied the wrong kind of treatment, in some cases for years. It confronts them with the need for major additional education and training. Realizing the existence of authentic complex dissociative disorders may also be threatening by implying a confrontation with the fragility of our cherished, presumably singular 'I.' The idea that an individual can encompass more than one 'I' may be so scary that it seems safer to simply deny the possibility.

Therapists

It is not exceptional that at some point therapeutic teams become divided regarding a dissociative patient in their care. The positions different team members may take can generally be cast in terms of sympathy and antipathy for ANPs, fragile EPs, and controlling

EPs. For example, mirroring a particular ANP's mediation by action systems of daily life, one team member may sympathize mostly with this part's interests. He or she may accordingly phenomenally and physically judge that the patient should foremost learn to cope with daily life more. In this context, the traumatic memories of EPs and these parts would best be ignored or suppressed. The involved clinician thus copies ANP's mental avoidance of these dissociative parts and the traumatic memories in which they are stuck. Another team member may feel that the patient is a highly vulnerable individual. Mediated by the caretaking will system, this individual foremost phenomenally judges how important it is to acknowledge and respond to EPs' fragility. In reaction to controlling EPs, a third team member might phenomenally judge that the patient is above all resistant, manipulative, and controlling, and therefore physically judges that the team should put strict boundaries on these behaviors. These phenomenal and physical judgments and the associated reactions are often predominantly guided by the social dominance will system. A fourth colleague may feel that the case is in the end hopeless. This depressive position can be seen as joining the patient's fixation in the recuperation action system as a suicidal EP. When the different team members take these contrasting positions, they end up struggling with the patient and with each other in ways that more or less reflect those of the different dissociative parts. Unresolved conflicts among the different dissociative parts of the patient then become unresolved conflicts among the team members. As applies to each dissociative part, each colleague responds only to some of the patient's desires and interests, but fails to appreciate others. This is the dissociative therapeutic team lost in 'follies' that primarily mark the patient.

Clinicians may also become *internally* divided when working with dissociative patients. For example, they may initially be mediated by the caretaking action system. Being highly empathic with suffering fragile EPs, they risk becoming the regulator of the patient's fears and pains. Controlling EPs do not accept this one-sided sympathy for what they regard as the weak, needy EPs and are therefore inclined to fight back. ANPs are content that the therapist takes care of the fragile EPs, so that they do not need to do the job. The fragile EP-focused therapist sooner or later becomes overloaded and frustrated. The needs of fragile EPs seem endless, ANPs fail to make progress, and controlling EPs interfere ever more. These developments activate the therapist's own defense will system. Instead of exploring the whole personality system and stimulating this system to exchange inner avoidance and rejection, the therapist may start to fight with the "impossible and dangerous" controlling EPs, blame the "weak and avoidant" ANPs for being neglectful of fragile EPs, and abandon or reject the "needy and inconsolable" fragile EPs.

Clinicians who mostly or even singularly focus on the patient's interests of daily life collude with ANPs' tendencies to avoid fragile and controlling EPs. In resonance with the action systems for daily life functioning, they are prone to neglect the interests of fragile EPs and to reject the interests of controlling EPs. Fragile EPs feel continued emotional neglect and rejection, which reinforces their inability to thrive. Controlling EPs feel misunderstood and angry, and act out at some point. Colliding with despondent EPs that the patient may encompass, they become suicidal and attempt to end their impossible existence. Some controlling EPs are in turn phenomenally homicidal: They feel that they can kill ANPs and fragile EPs and still survive themselves. The lack of progress frustrates the ANP-focused therapists, and the suicidal actions will clearly scare them. Their defense action system now awakened, they tend to flee from the patient (e.g., feel relieved when the patient misses appointments, wish to end therapy, or feel tempted to refer the patient to a colleague) – or they start to fight with the patient for dominance (e.g., out of a wish to control controlling EPs), to become even more avoidant of fragile EPs and controlling EPs, or to become despondent. Compassion-fatigue and more general burnout become serious risks.

Clinicians who feel a need to control controlling EPs are mediated by the social dominance and/or the defense will system. This approach entails a recurrent power struggle. A therapeutic display of power reactivates the perpetrator-victim dynamic. Controlling EPs become more dominant, and frustrate the felt need for therapeutic control. ANPs and fragile EPs grow more scared of the controlling EPs, may lose trust in the therapist's ability to assist. This leaves these parts more isolated: Fragile EPs feel abandoned once more.

For example, having correctly diagnosed the 40-year-old Loes as a case of major DID, the caring and sympathetic therapeutic team felt that Loes as the eldest ANP should first of all become more functional in daily life. To that end, the team stimulated suppressing her various EPs and taking on the jobs of two other ANPs. The team's instruction to suppress Bert, the singular controlling EP, was mostly evoked by the therapists' fear of this part. Loes appreciated their help and tried hard to reach the therapeutic goals. She became a stronger ANP over the course of 5 years of therapy and learned to trust the team. These were major advancements. However, the fragile EPs felt completely rejected and refused ever less be suppressed or just "disappear." In fact they intruded on Loes ever more. Bert also felt totally discarded and opposed. Despondent and furious, he engaged in a very serious suicide attempt. Loes and the team were shocked and did not know what to do. Loes, other ANPs, the fragile EPs and the therapeutic team became even more afraid of Bert.

It was decided to refer the patient to me. I was impressed by the team's dedication and care, valued the progress, and sympathized with their fears and frustration. I also felt and stated that it would be important to fully include all dissociative parts in the treatment. Loes could relate to this, but reiterated how dangerous Bert was. I empathized with her fear of Bert, but emphasized how important he and the other dissociative parts were. Assuming that the EPs listened in, I specifically addressed Bert and sincerely invited him to tell me about his tasks and (final) goals when he was ready. Loes was surprised and apprehensive by this approach but she did not run from therapy. Bert came prudently forward after some 15 sessions. Time and again, I stimulated all parts to show an interest in Bert and to value him as they slowly started to understand him more. When Bert eventually dared to speak freely, he stated how decisive it had been that I had treated all dissociative parts, including him, so evenhandedly from the first session. Loes and the patient's other parts stressed how my sincere interest in and will to understand all dissociative parts had been an inspiration for a new way of relating to each other. It soon became clear how Bert had been of major importance to safeguard at least some sense of autonomy amid the chronic traumatization, that, in Bert's perception, was still ongoing; he did not know or realize that Loes had turned 40 years, that she did not live with her parents anymore, etc. Helping Bert to get acquainted with the facts of 'now' and stimulating him to engage in autonomous actions that fit this world meant major therapeutic progress. (A more detailed account of the therapeutic steps of Loes' complete treatment follows in Volume III.)

When dissociative parts are treated unevenly, the therapist-patient dyad easily slips into an ongoing re-enactment of the original traumatic relationships characterized by patterns of domination, rejection, neglect, blaming, and the like. This imbalance often relates to undue activation of a particular final goal in the therapist(s) such as the wish to take care of fragile EPs, the need to control controlling EPs, and the urge to side with ANPs' phobias of EPs, traumatic memories, and related phobic cues. These limitations can be associated with personal features such as the therapists' phobias of strong affects (e.g., fear, shame, sadness, anger and rage, desires of revenge), traumatic horror, and insufficiently integrated personal painful or traumatic memories. They can also relate to still other features such as a lack of experience and training in working with complex dissociative systems, a lack of professional peer support, or actual or feared professional peer rejection.

Realization

Whereas the road to general recognition of childhood traumatization and complex dissociative disorders has been long and winding – and remains insufficiently paved to this day – significant progress has been made. A growing number of clinicians and researchers realize that childhood traumatization is common, that dissociative disorders are authentic conditions that in many cases relate to an adverse life history, and that their prevalence is considerable. They also realize and acknowledge now that 'treatment as usual' (e.g., medication, ignoring, dismissing, or suppressing dissociative parts, focusing on comorbidities) does not work. Many clinicians are attending workshops and courses on chronic traumatization and on dissociative disorders, and the number of researchers who study chronic traumatization and dissociation is increasing. As clinicians learn more, they typically report that they start to understand their patients much better, and that they become more effective in helping them. Many patients quickly notice their treating clinicians' advancements and value their courage and investments. The work can be difficult, though, and the learning does not always come easy. Many trainees feel that continuing education is a must. Scientists detect that patients with dissociative disorders are generally very willing to cooperate in biopsychosocial research of their condition and have the experience that the patients are generally grateful when researchers engage in this work.

Unknown, unloved is the antinomy of science. Guided by a deep desire to explore terra incognita, scientists should be like the Viking Leif Ericksson (c. 970–c. 1020), who was the first to set foot on current North America; the Dutchman Abel Tasman (1603–1659), who found Tasmania, New Zealand, and Tongatapu; and the Italian Cristoforo Colombo. These brave men sailed the seas with tiny ships to discover "The West" or "The East," knowing that projects can fail. Trying to find a Northern route to the East, Willem Barentsz (c. 1550–1597, Nova Zembla), Jacob van Heemskerck (1567–1607), and their men got stuck in pack ice, and were forced to survive the extreme Nova Zembla winter – alas, Barentsz did not make it. Scientists should be as inquisitive and daring.

Prof. Dr. Lutz Jäncke, holder of the Chair in Neuropsychology at the Zurich University and Yolanda Schlumpf are exemplary. Our paths crossed when I was looking for neuropsychologists with access to neuroimaging devices who might be interested to explore how patients with DID respond as ANP and as fragile EP to subliminally presented facial expression (Schlumpf et al., 2013, 2014). A Swiss colleague had advised me to have a talk with him; she also knew Yolanda, a gifted young psychologist who wished to dedicate her dissertation to the biopsychosocial research of DID. There was a torrential rainfall on the day of my appointment. My wife and I accidentally got off the bus one stop too early and arrived soaked to the bone. An energetic, busy man, Prof. Jäncke kept my wife and me waiting for quite a while. We were thankful for that, as it allowed us to dry off a bit and present ourselves more decently. During our conversation, I showed Prof. Jäncke the results of our studies (Reinders et al., 2003, 2006; Hermans et al., 2006) and invited him to examine some videos of a DID patient. The video showed an ANP, a fragile EP engaging in flight and freeze, and a fragile EP engaging in tonic immobility. These different dissociative parts had very different phenomenal and psychophysiological reactions to a photo of an angry man that was brought in the direction of the patient's face. Prof. Jäncke listened, watched, and inquired. After an hour or so, he promised to look for the budget to finance a functional MRI study and a dissertation take. And he found it. Yolanda defended her dissertation in 2012. Her time at the university had not been easy. Most of her colleagues did not take DID very seriously, but Prof. Jäncke supported her all the way, and I did my share. Her defense was brilliant, and the committee unanimously decided that she deserved to get her doctor title summa cum laude. Chatting a bit after the formalities, Prof. Jäncke confessed with a laugh that, despite my efforts to convince him of the reality of DID the day we met, I had failed to achieve that aim. His face grew serious as he added that now, however, based on the results of our conjoint work, there was no doubt in his mind that DID is a real mental disorder. I wish universities would harbor more open-minded professors who seek, assess, and judge facts rather than follow prejudice or engage in studies of doubtful ecological validity or studies that do not even include the patients of concern. Isn't this what the science of dissociative disorders should be about?

Society

Apparently Normal Peoples

Childhood traumatization and dissociative disorders largely remained societal terra incognita in the past. The most common societal pattern can be described as the 'apparently normal peoples mode,' or, for the sake of brevity, as 'apparently normal peoples.' For example, as Lanning (2010, p. 4) put it,

> [i]n the United States, society's historical attitude about the sexual victimization of children can generally be summed up in one word: denial. Most people do not want to hear about it and would prefer to pretend such victimization just does not occur.

Apparently normal peoples include institutions and professionals such as general physicians and pediatricians with a low degree of suspicion of childhood traumatization and its sequelae. Other contributors to apparent societal normality are law enforcement agents, lawyers, judges, and politicians with little or confused knowledge or appreciation of the facts – and little wish to become better educated. It also includes citizens who turn childhood traumatization a blind eye.

Although knowledge and recognition of childhood traumatization and its consequences are presently increasing among many professional and other individuals, several myths regarding childhood traumatization persist. They include minimizations or exaggerations of the extent of the harm child sexual abuse poses, denials of the extent of child sexual abuse, diffusions of perpetrator blame, and perpetrator stereotypes (Cromer & Goldsmith, 2010). The biases involved are influenced by general societal phenomena such as traditional sexual scripts, including the perception of females as sexually passive, harmless, and innocent (Denov, 2003). These perspectives have influenced broader societal views concerning sexuality and sexual abuse, and they have affected criminal law, victim-reporting practices, and professional responses to female sex offending (see also Knoll, 2010). The general societal knowledge, understanding, and appreciation of complex dissociative disorders remain severely wanting (e.g., Dorahy et al., 2005; Ross, 2009).

Is there a rational final cause or set of final causes of apparently normal peoples' ignorance and biases? A rational attitude would involve serious consideration of the huge costs of childhood adversities in terms of mental and physical health problems, including psychosis, substance abuse, and suicidality, reduced academic and occupational achievements, teenage and unwanted pregnancy, miscarriages, sexually transmitted disease as well as intergenerational transference of childhood adversities, increased risk of criminality, and still other costs (e.g., Bebbington et al., 2004; Freyd et al., 2005; Janssen et al., 2004; Newmann, Greenley, & Sweeney, 1998; Reza et al., 2009; Trickett et al., 2011; Zielinski, 2009).

The economic costs are as extreme as the emotional and relational ones (Fang, Brown, Florence, & Mercy, 2011; Florence, Brown, Fang, & Thompson, 2013; Galbraith & Neubauer, 2000; Meerding, 2005; Murray et al., 2013; Wickizer, 2013). Fang et al. (2011) estimated that the total lifetime economic burden resulting from new cases of fatal and nonfatal child maltreatment in the United States in 2008 was approximately $124 billion. Studying a large representative sample of the general population in the Netherlands, Cuijpers et al. (2011) calculated the disability weight for each participant, reflecting the severity of a disease or condition. The disability weight indicates the proportion of a healthy lifeyear reduced by the specific health state of the individual. This weight allows the calculation of the total number of years lost due to disability in the population. Cuijpers et al. calculated the disability weight and the years lived with disability for nine different childhood adversities in the areas of parental psychopathology, abuse and neglect, and major life events. They also calculated the two factors for major categories of mental disorders and general medical disorders. All nine adversities were associated with a significantly increased disability weight, except death of a parent before the age of 16. The highest disability weights existed for adversities in the category of abuse and neglect, followed by parental psychopathology, and life events during childhood.

All adversities together were associated with 20.7 years lost to disability/1,000. Among these, the category of abuse/neglect had the highest loss (15.8 years lost/1,000). Both losses were more severe than the loss for all mental disorders together (12.9 years lost/1,000). Cuijpers et al. (2011) thus concluded that childhood adversities are more important from a public health point of view than all common mental disorders together. They should therefore be a priority for public health interventions.

The costs of complex dissociative disorders are also very high (Galbraith & Neubauer, 2000). Sar et al. (2007b) documented that one third of the patients who attended an emergency psychiatric ward had a dissociative disorder. As Van der Kolk (2008) communicated, patients suffering from DID had by far the highest healthcare utilization of any psychiatric diagnosis in Massachusetts during 1997/1998, making it the most expensive psychiatric diagnosis. However, treatment does not imply *effective* treatment: Many patients with complex dissociative disorders – if they are accurately diagnosed at all – are not treated according to a phase-oriented treatment model that constitutes the state-of-the-art treatment specialists apply and recommend (Van der Hart et al., 2006).

Healthcare insurers tend to feel that long-term psychotherapy for complex dissociative disorders is unduly expensive, so that the disorder remains undertreated in most cases. However, this view is probably inaccurate as some simple calculations reveal. Most patients with minor and major DID function much better after, say, 10 years of weekly trauma- and dissociation-focused psychotherapy sessions. The total costs of this treatment come out to approximately 45 sessions per year × 10 years × (approximately) EUR 125 = EUR 56,250. If this steady outpatient treatment is not offered, changes are high that these patients will someday be admitted to a psychiatric hospital for a considerable period of time, consume other forms of mental and physical healthcare, and remain relationally, socially, academically, and occupationally disabled. This is because 'treatment as usual' is just ineffective. The costs of this approach are far higher. For example, it is not unreasonable to assume that a DID patient would be admitted for a total of 1 year over a period of 10 years. This will cost 300 days × (approximately) EUR 350 = EUR 105,000. The probability that the patient will have improved is minimal, though, so that more costs are to be expected in the years following these 10 years.

Taken together, these and related facts strongly suggest that the final cause of the "apparently normal peoples" is not rational. It is emotional. Indeed, knowing and realizing the facts about childhood adversity implies major consequences. The prevalence is high, and it commonly involved abuse, maltreatment, and/or neglect by the child's parents or other family members. What should be the safest place on earth for a developing child – and what society generally portrays as the child's best place – is in fact a wretched place for a considerable number of children, and it is this place where they often must stay until they are old and strong enough to flee.

These facts imply that peoples must discuss how the safety of children can be better protected. A deep and fair discussion is bound to have major implications. For example, democracy, personal safety, and societal safety are based on the core idea that any form of power needs to be checked. So, how secluded, how private can family life in a fair society be given the fact that things go horribly wrong in far too many cases? How open should it become to protect children? How should these societal checks be organized? How can we prevent controllers from becoming an institution that serves its own interests more than the interests of the children they are supposed to protect? What constraints can be placed on the legal rights of parents? Who should control and guide families who abuse their power regarding their own children? How, when, and how often? How can perpetrators be effectively stopped and treated? How can society deal with the high number of abusive and neglectful families? How can national and international funds be redirected to allow a profound and lasting effort to limit childhood traumatization, and to treat its consequences more effectively? What priority do we give this funding? Given that every cent can only be spent once, what currently higher ranked priorities are to be given a lower priority?

Fragile and Controlling Emotional Peoples

These questions are some of the essential hard problems that apparently normal peoples tend to evade. However, protecting emotional fragility by ignoring, downplaying, or otherwise avoiding feared realities may not work well with all the continuing media reports, victim testimonies, and clinical as well as scientific findings of childhood traumatization and its sequelae for mental and physical health. Undeniable, dramatic cases that reach the media particularly intrude on the cherished pretense of normality. A shocked fragile and emotional people erupts and remains dominant for some time. Trying to fix the problem, a fragile emotional people (including institutions within society) may be paralleled by, or turn into, a controlling emotional people (including societal institutions) that may, among others, try to silence, attack, or otherwise reject and attempt to control victims and other messengers such as clinicians and researchers who bring the bad news (e.g., Smith & Freyd, 2014).

For example, several journalists and citizens heavily attacked Nel Draijer in 1988 when she published the unnerving findings of her empirical study on CSA in the Netherlands. She was marked as a hysterical, lesbian, frigid scientist. Media sociologist Professor Brouwer wrote in a widely read magazine that Draijer "took sexual morals back to the dark fifties . . ." In a newspaper interview, Hans Crombag, Professor of Law Psychology, depicted Van der Hart, Boon, and me as "sloppy thinkers who spread dangerous psychological theories" (De Groene Amsterdammer, April 26, 1996). He felt that Van der Hart should never have become a professor, and he portrayed me as a liar and as a disturbed individual uttering nonsense. Unfortunately, we did not get the chance to present our case or to comment.

Another strategy of a controlling emotional people is to accuse authorities and mental healthcare workers of neglecting or failing to solve the issues at stake. Doing so tends to disregard major concerns such as lack of funding of mental and physical healthcare and research regarding the prevention and treatment of childhood traumatization, insufficient professional education, legal limitations, and the difficulty of detecting, predicting, and preventing intrafamilial human malicious behavior. A general trend is to allow the veil of resurfacing apparent normality to cover fragile and controlling emotional people, which prevents the problem of child abuse and neglect from becoming a priority in mental and physical healthcare and in society more generally.

Realization

The problem is thus coming to the forefront of the societal reality of childhood adversity – and staying there. Because our professional knowledge of child maltreatment is still inadequate, education must be incorporated into the undergraduate and graduate curricula in medicine and other professions dealing with children (Johnson, 2002), adolescents, and adults. Because in particular child victims are generally unable to represent themselves, government and private organizations must assume this task. Johnson also proposed that countries that do not protect children from maltreatment including the ravages of war must be seen as perpetrators of child maltreatment and answerable to the international community.

The problem is also taking action. Increased knowledge of childhood adversity (Abbey, 2005; Ellis, 1997) does not automatically mean realizing its ramifications. Realization – the complicated action of becoming fully aware of a fact, of its implications, and of what needs to be done – is still wanting. There is currently a fissure between (1) our knowledge of childhood adversities and their sequelae, and (2) our realization of societal action needed to prevent or at least limit childhood adversities, realization of the consequences of these adversities for mental and physical health, including risks of intergenerational transfer of psychopathology, and realization of the need to treat the consequences. As James A. Mercy, Editorial Board of the UN Secretary-General's Study on Violence against Children Mercy (cited in Pinheiro, 2006, p. 5) asserted,

> [t]here is a large gap between what we know about violence against children and what we know should be done. We know that violence against children often causes lifelong physical and mental harm. We also know that violence erodes the potential for children to contribute to society by affecting their ability to learn and their social and emotional development. Given the importance of children to our future the current complacency cannot continue – we must place "preventing" violence against children among our highest priorities.

And Thomas Hammarberg, Commissioner for Human Rights of the Council of Europe (cited in Pinheiro, 2006, p. 10) raised a crucial question:

> How can we expect children to take human rights seriously and to help build a culture of human rights,, while we adults not only persist in slapping, spanking, smacking and beating them, but actually defend doing so as being 'for their own good'? Smacking children is not just a lesson in bad behaviour; it is a potent demonstration of contempt for the human rights of smaller, weaker people.

That question and statement obviously pertains to all forms of childhood adversity.

Chapter 21

150 Concise Propositions

Taken together, Volumes I and II constitute a long text. This closing chapter lists its propositions in a more concise form.

Matter and Mind: One Substance, Two Attributes, Countless Modi

1. There exists one substance. Two of its attributes are known to man: mind and matter.
2. Mind and matter cannot be reduced to each other. It makes no sense to say that matter 'causes' mind or that mind 'causes' matter, or that matter and mind are correlates of two independent phenomena.
3. Mind and matter manifest themselves in countless modi.
4. There is a trinity of the brain, the body, and the environment. That is, the brain, the body, and the environment are intrinsically related. The brain cannot exist without a (wider) body, the (wider) body not without a brain, and the brain/body not without a material and social environment.
5. Mind depends on the trinity of the brain, the body, and the environment, just as the concepts of the brain, the body, and the environment depend on experiencing and knowing minds. One implication is that the mind is not in the head.
6. The concept of *mental disorder* is strictly speaking a misnomer, since any mental phenomenon presupposes an embrained body and and embodied brain. A mental disorder implies a material disorder (just as a material disorder implies the mind in embrained and embodied beings), but mental phenomena cannot be reduced to material phenomena. Statements such as "you are your synapses" and "you are your brain" are nonsensical.
7. Psychiatry and psychology are still dominated by the mistaken view that matter and mind are two substances.

Subject and Object

8. There is a trinity of ways in which subject and object are intrinsically related: They are co-constitutive, co-dependent, and co-occurrent.
9. There are neither objects nor events without experiencing and knowing subjects, and there is no subject without a material and social world.
10. 'Subjects' and 'objects' exist as dynamic organism-environment systems.
11. In accordance with the foregoing, psychology and psychiatry become advanced when they move from the still predominant isolation of subject and object to an understanding and realization of the principled relativity of subject and object. This principle constitutes the core notion of what can be called relativity ontology, relativity epistemology, relativity psychology, or relativity psychiatry.

Events

12. Events do not exist in isolation of experiencing and knowing individuals. Hence, they cannot be defined in subject-independent ways.
13. Events do not exist in isolation of a material and social environment. Hence, they cannot be defined in object-independent ways.
14. Events emerge with the existence of phenomenal, that is, conscious organism-environment systems.
15. Individuals experience and know events as changes in the environment that exist in the context of other past, present, and anticipated events: "What happens now relates to what was and will be." They thus experience and know adverse events as environmentally and historically embedded ones. It follows that the meaning of the adverse event for the individual who lives it is necessarily co-dependent on the context of the current environment as well as on the embedded events that preceded and are anticipated to follow the current one.
16. Ontology and epistemology are intimately related. Any experience and any form of knowledge and realization of what exists and happens depends on the experiencing, knowing, and realizing subject, and on this individual's (currently active) first-, quasi-second-, second-, and/or third-person perspective(s).

Science and Science-Driven Practice

17. There is no objectively existing world, because subject and object are co-dependent and co-constitutive.
18. There is no view from nowhere, any view is someone's view.
19. Science, thus, does not and cannot uncover an objectively existing world.

20. Science is a human enactive enterprise in third-person perspective.
21. The third-person physical judgment is grounded in the first-person, quasi-second-person, and second-person perspectives that involve phenomenal experience and phenomenal judgment.
22. In other words, scientists and science-driven professionals such as psychologists and psychiatrists do not know 'objective reality' because their third-person perspective which involves an "I-object" relationship includes them as experiencing and knowing subjects. Third persons cannot perform miracles like the Baron Von Münchhausen, who pulled himself out of a moor by holding on to the tail of his wig. Third persons do not find such sky-hooks.
23. Nonetheless, many of them seem to ignore or overlook that their physical judgment in third-person perspective includes their phenomenal experience and judgment in first-person, quasi-second, and second-person perspective.
24. This flaw generates the illusion that man's knowledge can be 'objective.'
25. Scientific and clinical evidence lies in the eye of the beholder. Hence, the term 'evidence-based clinical practice' stands at best for relative knowledge.
26. Neuroscience is unable to explain consciousness, because like any science neuroscience starts and ends by presupposing consciousness, self-consciousness, and a will to explore.
27. Philosophical materialism as well as sciences and practices built upon this persuasion are flawed because they overlook that these projects depart from and must always return to mind (i.e., consciousness).
28. Practitioners, scientists, and neuroscientists who wish to study the phenomena of consciousness and self-consciousness must include and seriously consider the phenomenal experiences and phenomenal judgments of the agents and owners of these experiences and judgments.
29. Refusing or forgetting to consider, value, and use the phenomenal experiences and judgments of the subjects of their investigations (i.e., the subjects they physically judge), the practioners and scientists are like individuals who stubbornly or thoughtlessly search a key to wisdom in the dark refusing to turn on the flashlight in their hand.

Will and Action or Will Systems

30. Will is a final cause.
31. Like all organisms, humans are willing.
32. Considered under the attribute of mind (and with Spinoza), human will involves an unrelenting and unstoppable mental appetite and phenomenal desire to obtain what the subject phenomenally experiences and phenomenally conceives as attractive as

well as an equally unrelenting and unstoppable desire to escape from or avoid what the subject phenomenally experiences and phenomenally conceives as adverse.

33. Considered under the attribute of matter, will is strongly associated with evolutionarily primitive brain structures. These predominantly include the brain stem and the 'emotional brain.'
34. The will has become differentiated in evolution.
35. These wills constitute the 'heart' of action systems that mammals have developed over evolutionary time.
36. Any form human will takes is partly mental (i.e., unconscious) and partly phenomenal (i.e., conscious).
37. Human beings involve different wills, and these wills can be more or less complementary or contrary.
38. One will (hence will system) can conflict with one or more other wills (and the associated action or will systems).
39. The more different wills and associated action systems are contrary, the harder it is to integrate them.
40. Conflict involves a clash of contrary wills and associated action systems (e.g., attachment; physical defense) or modes of action systems (e.g., flight, tonic immobility).
41. The modulation and integration of contrary wills is a developmental task and achievement.
42. Considered under the attribute of mind, the ability to modulate and integrate contrary wills is strongly dependent on benign and stimulating social interaction and support.
43. Considered under the attribute of matter, this ability is in part dependent on the maturation of the brain.

Action

44. An action is something an individual does for a reason.
45. Action includes mental and behavioral actions.
46. Mental action is simulated behavioral action. It is, so to speak, behavioral action minus actual physical movement.
47. Action tendencies involve integrated clusters of action planning (which need not be conscious), initiation, cycles of evaluation and continuation, and completion.
48. Action tendencies can be more or less efficient, and more or less energetic.
49. The fulfillment of a particular will requires one or more actions involving particular degrees of mental and behavioral efficiency and energy.
50. A perfect action involves an optimal balance of efficiency and energy.
51. The degrees of mental and physical energy that an individual invests in a particular action may not match the levels that the perfect action would take.

52. The levels of mental and physical efficiency of an executed action may not match the levels that the perfect action would take.
53. When perfect actions are beyond individuals' reach, they engage in substitute actions.
54. Substitute actions involve actions that do not optimally fit the realization of a will.
55. Relative to the involved objective of the action, substitute actions can be too low (e.g., too explosive, too impulsive, too nonverbal, too nonreflected, too rigid), or too high (e.g., too reflected, as in obsessive-compulsive disorder, too verbal, when an individual talks about matters on end that require more immediate behavioral action) in the hierarchy of action tendencies (Van der Hart et al., 2006; see Volume III).
56. Symptoms of biopsychosocial pathology are actions. More specifically, symptoms are substitute actions that an individual engages in to fulfill some will, that is, some appetite (mental urge) that may also be a desire (phenomenal striving).
57. Symptoms may involve too little or too much energy and/or efficiency.
58. Studying and assisting traumatized individuals, including the dissociative parts these individuals encompass, scientists and clinicians explore: *Who does what and why*?

Enaction and Meaning

59. Organisms including human subjects enact themselves and their world.
60. Enaction is the idea that organisms create their own experience, thoughts, and meaning through their mental, phenomenal, and behavioral actions.
61. They neither receive 'input' from an objectively existing environment nor do they generate 'output.' Rather, they are embrained and embodied individuals embedded in a material and social environment. In enaction, subject (individual) and object (objects of experience, perception, and conception) constitute each other, depend on each other, and occur together.
62. In other words, "[o]rganisms do not passive receive information from their environment, which they then translate into internal representations. Natural cognitive systems ... participate in the generation of meaning through their bodies and action often engaging in transformational and not merely informational interactions: *they enact a world* ... it is always an activity with a *formative* trace, never merely about the innocent extraction of information as if this was already present to a fully realized (and thus inert) agent" (Di Paolo, De Jaegher, & Rhohde, 2014, p. 33).
63. Hence, there is no pre-given 'information' to human beings, and they do not 'process information.'
64. Humans are not a 'headtop.'
65. Humans must and do make meaning. Anything that exists, exists for an individual and is conceived of in a particular way and is accordingly evaluated by that individual.
66. Meaning is affected by will. Hence, different primal desires (urges, strivings) imply different meanings.

Causation

67. Human experience, thought, and behavior involve dynamic causation.
68. Dynamic causation involves a complex of material, efficient, formal, and final causes.
69. Material and efficient causality are intermediates. They do not completely explain organism-environment systems. For example, stones, nails, and wood (material cause) must be brought together (efficient cause) in a particular way (formal cause) to be a house, but none of these causes explains why there is a thing that is a house. Humans put matter together according to a plan (formal cause) because a house provides what humans desire (final cause): protection from predators, villains, frost, heat, moisture as well as privacy. Similarly, patterns of physiological and brain activity reveal and explain neither what its owner was willing, feeling, thinking, or doing, nor what it is like to will, feel, think, and act.
70. Human personality involves a particular dynamic organization as a formal cause that relates to our wills as our final causes.

Personality

71. Personality is an 'embrained,' embodied, and environmentally (materially, socially) embedded system. Hence, it constitutes a biopsychosocial organism-environment system.
72. Personality can be described and studied in terms of biology, psychology, and psychosocial relationships.
73. These disciplines consider different attributes and modi, not different substances. None fully captures personality in isolation of the other attributes and modi.
74. Personality is dynamic, that is, it is in a constant flux.
75. Personality includes unconscious and preconscious as well as conscious action.
76. Unconscious and preconscious action is mental; conscious action is mental as well as phenomenal.

Person Perspectives

77. To have a particular person-perspective, humans must engage in a particular action: no action, no consciousness, no person perspectives. Hence, when individuals are asleep and do not dream, they do not phenomenally exist in the first-person and/or quasi-second-person perspective.
78. Phenomenal action is generally tied to phenomenal experience, which involves a first-person perspective: the phenomenal experience of being or having an 'I.'
79. Phenomenal action can also be tied to phenomenal judgment, which involves a quasi-second-perspective, that is, the phenomenal judgment of being or having an 'I' that relates to 'me, myself, mine' in terms of agency and ownership.

80. Phenomenal experience and judgment are centered in the body of the experiencing subject.
81. The phenomenal experience of having or being an 'I,' together with the phenomenal judgment of having or being and 'I' that relates to 'me, myself, mine' in terms of agency and ownership, involves the combined generation of a phenomenal experience and conception of self.
82. Phenomenal action can also pertain to the phenomenal judgment that 'I' have a particular kind of unilateral or bilateral relationship with one or more 'You's.' This is a second-person perspective, which involves a relationship of a phenomenal conception of self and one or more phenomenal conceptions of other 'I's.' This relationship is a phenomenal conception of an intentionality relationship, of an 'I' intentionally related to one or more other individuals. In the second-person perspective, there is a self, one or more other selves, and a self that is a part of a social world.
83. Grounded in phenomenal experience and phenomenal judgment, 'I' can also physically judge that there are one or more 'things' with particular properties (e.g., warm, soft, red, small). This third-person perspective involves a relationship of a phenomenal conception of self and one or more physically conceived objects. The relationship is a phenomenal conception of an intentionality relationship, of an 'I' who is intentionally related to an object or set of objects. In the third-person perspective, there is a self, a material world, and a self existing in or being a part of this material world.

The Terms Traumatic and Traumatizing Experiences and Events

84. Some experiences and events are adverse to humans.
85. Adverse events are potentially injurious. The terms and concepts 'adverse events' and 'potentially traumatic/traumatizing events' are synonyms.
86. Traumatic/traumatizing events are adverse events that an individual has not integrated – that is, synthesized, personified, and presentified – and realized – that is, responsibly responded to – at least not sufficiently.
87. The terms 'potentially traumatic experience' and 'traumatic experience' pertain to the first-person perspective.
88. The terms 'potentially traumatic event' and 'traumatic event' pertain to the phenomenal judgment of a particular event in the quasi-second- and second-person perspective.
89. The terms 'potentially traumatizing event' and 'traumatizing event' pertain to the physical judgment of an event in the third-person perspective.
90. Traumatic experiences are sensorimotor, emotional, and behavioral.
91. (Reactivated) traumatic memories are icons, that is, re-enactments and reconceptions of traumatic experiences. They lack (sufficient) symbolization. The re-enactments and reconceptions include relational re-enactments.

92. The integration and subsequent realization of traumatic experiences and memories involves turning these icons into symbols. When traumatic memories constitute re-enactments, integrated and realized traumatic experiences and memories are stories involving "clear and distinct ideas" (Spinoza, 1677) that recount most adverse and painful past experiences.

Trauma and Dissociation in Trauma

93. Trauma is an injury that implies recurrent re-enactment.
94. The term 'trauma' does not and cannot pertain to an event as such, because any event as an object is co-constituted by, co-dependent on, and co-occurrent with one or more experiencing and knowing individuals.
95. The injury that trauma is involves dynamic causation, that is, a constellation of material, efficient, formal and final causes.
96. Material and efficient causes include a trinity of the living brain, body, and adverse environmentally perceived and conceived material and social events.
97. The formal cause of trauma is a dissociation of the personality as a whole system. This system can be conceived of in terms of different attributes: psychological, psychosocial, and biological. It does not involve different substances.
98. The final cause of this formal organization is an unresolved conflict and the implied lack of integration of two or more (groups of) evolutionarily derived appetites and desires (Spinoza) or wills (Schopenhauer), and associated (sets of) will systems.
99. The most general conflict is an opposition of the will to live one's daily life following traumatic/traumatizing events and the will to defend one's mental and physical existence in the face of traumatic/traumatizing events in which one is fixed.
100. This conflict exists in proportion to one's ability to integrate traumatic experiences/memories in one's personality.
101. Dissociation of the personality in trauma involves the existence of two or more insufficiently integrated mental, phenomenal – i.e., unconscious and conscious – and behavioral subsystems.
102. Each of these phenomenal dissociative subsystems is a dynamic, though in at least some regards too rigid organization (re)generated in ongoing action. That is, each exists to the degree that an individual engages in particular creative actions, and ceases to exist when the individual ceases to engage in these actions.
103. Phenomenal dissociative subsystems or 'dissociative parts' are predominantly mediated by basic desires (will).
104. Some phenomenal dissociative subsystems or 'dissociative parts' are primarily mediated by the will to live daily life as well as the will to evade traumatic memories. These prototypical phenomenal subsystems are metaphorically referred to as 'apparently normal parts' of the personality (ANPs).

105. ANPs, thus, can have desires such as rest, sleep, eat, explore, play, relate to others, give care to others, receive care from others, and reproduce. These wills are associated with action systems for daily life and the different modi they encompass.
106. Whereas ANPs desire to evade traumatic memories and dissociative parts who are directly or indirectly associated with these memories as much as possible, they can be intruded on by these other dissociative parts and the traumatic memories they re-enact.
107. These intrusions manifest themselves in symptoms. They are not seldom mistaken for being possessed/influenced by strange forces in the first-person and quasi-second-person perspective, and for psychotic symptoms in the third-person perspective. These misperceptions lead to fears and false phenomenal judgments of being 'mad' (and the like) in the first-person and quasi-second-person perspective, and to false physical judgments (e.g., to false positive cases of psychosis, schizophrenia, mania) in the third-person perspective (e.g., see Read, Van Os, Morrison, & Ross, 2005; dissociative psychosis has only been briefly discussed so far, but will be more deeply considered in Volume III).
108. Other dissociative parts are primarily mediated by the will to survive adverse/traumatizing events. They tend to be fixed in one or more modi of the mammalian defense system and/or attachment cry. These prototypical dissociative parts are metaphorically referred to as 'fragile emotional parts' of the personality (fragile EP). Mediated by active mammalian defense (e.g., flight, freeze) or attachment cry, they are hyperaroused. Mediated by passive mammalian defense (tonic immobility), they are hypoaroused.
109. The conflict and dissociation between at least one ANP and at least one fragile EP is typical of rather simple forms of trauma.
110. In chronic child abuse, maltreatment, and emotional neglect, the conflict of wills is more complicated. This trauma prototypically involves a trinity of major wills: (1) various wills associated with living daily life, (2) the complex of wills to survive major adversity, and (3) the will to influence one's fate in an adverse material and social environment.
111. Predominantly mediated by the will and implied will system of social dominance, the latter prototypical dissociative subsystem can be described as a controlling EP. These dissociative parts tend to imitate and to a degree identify with perpetrators or their partners in crime.
112. ANPs are more or less phenomenally trauma *ignorant*. This experiential and epistemic effect is due to *controlling* actions that are driven by *fragility*: avoidance of fragile and controlling EPs trauma-fixated dissociative parts and these phenomenal subsystems' traumatic memories. In this context, they may also avoid other phenomenal contents such as particular body sensations, affects, thoughts, fantasies, postures, movements, and behaviors.
113. Fragile EPs experience per definition *fragility*. Trying to *control* perceived or feared

(further) adversity, they engage in physical defensive actions and/or attachment cry. Because they remain stuck in trauma-time, trauma-land, and trauma-identity, they remain *ignorant* of the 'dividual's' actual time, place, and identity.

114. Controlling EPs desire and enact *control* to compensate *fragility*. They are generally more or less consciously aware of this fragility. However, they tend to feel that they should not experience it for what is it, let alone show it, because it would interfere with their primary will. Like a fragile EP, they remain stuck in trauma-time, trauma-land, and trauma-identity, and are largely *ignorant* of the actual time, place, and identity.
115. All dissociative parts can thus be described as subsystems involving three major features: *ignorance*, *fragility*, and *control*. The relative phenomenal dominance of this trinity differs per prototypical part:
116. ANP: (1) ignorance, (2) fragility, (3) control;
117. Fragile EP: (1) fragility, (2) control, (3) ignorance;
118. Controlling EP: (1) control, (2) fragility, (3) ignorance.

The Concept of Dissociation in Trauma

119. To be scientifically and clinically useful, concepts must be sensitive and specific.
120. To honor the principle of sensitivity, the concept of 'dissociation' must capture positive and negative manifestations of a dissociation of the personality, each of which can pertain to cognitive-emotional and sensorimotor manifestations.
121. To honor the principle of specificity, the concept of 'dissociation in trauma' must be delimited. Many forms of psychopathology involve a certain lack of integration, but it is not helpful to regard all integrative problems as manifestations of dissociation. If too many integrative problems are allowed to enter the domain of dissociation, the concept becomes meaningless, hence useless.
122. The generic concept of 'dissociation in trauma' involves a lack of integration of two or more phenomenally experienced (in first-person perspective), phenomenally known (in quasi-second and second-person perspective), and physically observed (in third-person perspective) subsystems of the personality as an organism-environment system.
123. The concept of 'dissociative subsystem of the personality' or 'part of the personality' in trauma is best delimited to conscious and self-conscious subsystems of the personality, each with their own person perspectives, that include apart from these specific phenomenal features specific mental features.
124. When awake and not dreaming, these dissociative subsystems or 'parts' generate their own phenomenal conceptions of self, world, and self-of-the-social/material world.
125. Including phenomena into the domain of dissociation because they pertain to dissociation of the personality fosters their better understanding and distinction from

other phenomena (e.g., such as psychotic symptoms that do not relate to a dissociation of the personality).

126. Excluding phenomena that do not pertain to dissociation of the personality from the domain of dissociation fosters their deeper theoretical analysis, conceptual understanding, and empirical study.
127. Of all constraints on the concept of 'consciousness,' only multiple perspectivalness counts as dissociative. Problems with global coherence, phenomenal now, situatedness, convolved holism, dynamicity, transparency, online and offline activation, intensity, homogeneity, adaptivity, and degree of reality are sensitive but not specific to dissociative disorders.

The Spectrum of Dissociative Disorders

128. There is a spectrum of dissociative disorders, each with its own dynamic organization of dissociative parts of the personality.
129. This organization can be more or less complex. For example, it tends to be simple in simple PTSD, more complex in complex PTSD, still more complex in minor DID, and is the most complex in major DID.
130. Ego-states disorders do not constitute a dissociative disorder, because individuals with ego-states regard these states as their own. Although these states are insufficiently integrated, their owners in quasi-second-person perspective still personify them. This fact has clinical implications that will be detailed in Volume III.
131. The dissociative disorder is the general frame in which the patient's symptoms are to be studied, understood, and treated.
132. 'Comorbid' diagnoses are to be studied, understood, and treated in the framework of the existing dissociative disorder.
133. Since this 'comorbidity' is not coincidental but an inherent part of the patient's disorder, the term 'comorbidity' is of little use.
134. The 'hyperarousal' and the 'dissociative + subtype' of PTSD both involve a dissociation of the personality. Hence, both qualify as a dissociative disorder. This conclusion should have consequences for the understanding and classification of PTSD.
135. Comparisons of biopsychosocial research findings for PTSD and DID support the present position that PTSD is a dissociative disorder and that DID is a complex form of PTSD.
136. The psychiatric term 'conversion' involves, and is therefore to be replaced by, the term 'dissociation.' Conversion disorder as described in DSM-5 and as used more generally is a dissociative disorder and nothing else.

The Sociocognitive Model and Trauma Models of DID

137. There is no evidence from biopsychosocial studies with DID that this disorder results from suggestibility and suggestion, from fantasy proneness and fantasy, or from role-playing talents and actual role-playing.
138. DID patients are not fantasy prone.
139. Lacking empirical support to date, the sociocognitive model of DID involves a set of unsubstantiated ideas in third-person perspective or, as one might also say, a set of third-person suggestions and fantasies.
140. The scientific and clinical evidence consistently, coherently, and strongly supports trauma models of complex dissociative disorders as well as phase-oriented treatment models of trauma-related dissociation of the personality (to be detailed and discussed in Volume III).
141. The evidence for ANP and fragile EP as biopsychosocial subsystems of the personality is consistent, coherent, and strong. Controlling EPs are clinically observed, but scientifically severely understudied to date.
142. The current data base should cause a major increase in the empirical research of complex dissociative disorders if the science of major psychopathology is to be more scientific rather than strongly politically biased as it is to date.

Costs

143. The prevalence and moral as well as economical costs of dissociative disorders are high.
144. The prevalence and moral as well as economical costs of chronic childhood traumatization are huge.
145. Ignoring dissociative disorders and chronic childhood traumatization is morally unacceptable and economically unwise.

The General Trinity of Trauma

146. The trinity of trauma applies to traumatized individuals, victims, perpetrators, partners in crime, professionals including psychologists and psychiatrists, and peoples.
147. Traumatized individuals involve a dynamic constellation of insufficiently integrated conscious and self-conscious dissociative organism-environment subsystems, with ANPs, fragile EPs, and controlling EPs as the major prototypes.
148. When it comes to the problems of chronic childhood traumatization and complex dissociative disorders, the other listed individuals and groups of individuals are quite

susceptible to functioning in ANP-like, fragile EP-like, and controlling EP-like modi, insofar as they do not have a dissociative disorder.

149. The general problem of trauma, notably including and most strongly pertaining to chronic childhood traumatization, is the difficulty and lack of will to integrate and realize its existence and implications.
150. Volume III of the present trilogy, *Enactive Trauma Treatment*, details and discusses ways to act on childhood trauma and traumatization, primarily at the level of treatment, but also on the societal level. Overcoming these major problems takes a trinity of actions: (1) substitute ignorance for integrative knowledge and realization; (2) balance naturally given fragility with adaptive and creative ways to prevent further harm, to protect and to heal; and (3) raise control by putting these new-found ways into dedicated, thoughtful, and lasting action.

References

Abbey, A. (2005). Lessons learned and unanswered questions about sexual assault perpetration. *Journal of Interpersonal Violence, 20*, 39–42.

Abram, H. S. (Ed.). (1970). *Psychological aspects of stress.* Springfield, IL: C. C. Thomas.

Abrams, M. P., Carleton, R. N., Taylor, S., & Asmundson, G. J. (2009). Human tonic immobility: Measurement and correlates. *Depression and Anxiety, 26*, 550–556.

Addis, D. R., & Schacter, D. L. (2008). Constructive episodic simulation: Temporal distance and detail of past and future events modulate hippocampal engagement. *Hippocampus, 18*, 227–237.

Addis, D. R., Wong, A. T., & Schacter, D. L. (2007). Remembering the past and imagining the future: Common and distinct neural substrates during event construction and elaboration. *Neuropsychologia, 45*, 1363–1377.

Agamben, G. (2004). *The open: Man and animal.* Stanford, CA: Stanford University Press.

Aguilera, G., & Rabadan-Diehl, C. (2000). Vasopressinergic regulation of the hypothalamic-pituitary-adrenal axis: Implications for stress adaptation. *Regulatory Peptides, 96*, 23–29.

Akyuz, G., Sar, V., Kugu, N., & Dogan, O. (2005). Reported childhood trauma, attempted suicide and self-mutilative behavior among women in the general population. *European Psychiatry, 20*, 268–273.

Alegria, A. A., Blanco, C., Petry, N. M., Skodol, A. E., Liu, S. M., Grant, B., & Hasin. D. (2013). Sex differences in antisocial personality disorder: Results from the National Epidemiological Survey on Alcohol and Related Conditions. *Personal Disorders, 4*, 214–222.

Allen, J. G., & Coyne, L. (1995). Dissociation and vulnerability to psychotic experience: The Dissociative Experiences Scale and the MMPI-2. *Journal of Nervous and Mental Disease, 183*, 615–622.

Allen, J. G., Coyne, L., & Console, D. A. (1996). Dissociation contributes to anxiety and psychoticism on the Brief Symptom Inventory. *Journal of Nervous and Mental Disease, 184*, 639–641.

Allen, J. G., Coyne, L., & Console, D. A. (1997). Dissociative detachment relates to psychotic symptoms and personality decompensation. *Comprehensive Psychiatry, 38*, 327–334.

Allen, J. G., Fultz, J., Huntoon, J., & Brethour, J. R., Jr. (2002). Pathological dissociative taxon membership, absorption, and reported child- hood trauma in women with trauma-related disorders. *Journal of Trauma & Dissociation, 3*, 89–110.

Allport, G. W. (1961). *Pattern and growth in personality*. New York: Holt, Rinehart, Winston.

Amdur, R., & Liberzon, I. (1996). Dimensionality of dissociation in subjects with PTSD. *Dissociation, 9*, 118–124.

American Psychiatric Association (APA). (1952). *Diagnostic and statistical manual: Mental disorders.* Washington, DC: American Psychiatric Association Mental Hospital Service.

American Psychiatric Association (APA). (1968). *Diagnostic and statistical manual of mental disorders II.* Washington, DC: Author.

American Psychiatric Association (APA). (1980). *Diagnostic and statistical manual of mental disorders III.* Washington, DC: Author.

American Psychiatric Association (APA). (1994). *Diagnostic and statistical manual of mental disorders IV.* Washington, DC: Author.

American Psychiatric Association (APA). (2013). *Diagnostic and statistical manual of mental disorders, 5th edition DSM-5*. Washington, DC: American Psychiatric Publishing.

Amiel-Tison, C., Cabrol, D., Denver, R., Jarreau, P. H., Papiernik, E., & Piazza, P. V. (2004). Fetal adaptation to stress: Part II. Evolutionary aspects; stress-induced hippocampal damage; long-term effects on behavior; consequences on adult health. *Early Human Development, 78*, 81–94.

Anda, R. F., Brown, D. W., Dube, S. R., Bremner, J. D., Felitti, V. J., & Giles, W. H. (2008). Adverse childhood experiences and chronic obstructive pulmonary disease in adults. *American Journal of Preventive Medicine, 34*, 396–403.

Anda, R. F., Felitti, V. J., Bremner, J. D., Walker, J. D., Whitfield, C., Perry, B. D., . . . Giles, W. H. (2006). The enduring effects of abuse and related adverse experiences in childhood: A convergence of evidence from neurobiology and epidemiology. *European Archives of Psychiatry and Clinical Neuroscience, 256*, 174–186.

Anderson, M. C., Ochsner, K. N., Kuhl, B., Cooper, J., Robertson, E., Gabrieli, S.W, . . . Gabrieli, J. D. (2004). Neural systems underlying the suppression of unwanted memories. *Science 303*, 232–235.

Andrew, E. M., Gray, N. S., & Snowden, R. J. (2008). The relationship between trauma and beliefs about hearing voices: A study of psychiatric and non-psychiatric voice hearers. *Psychological Medicine, 38*, 1409–1417.

Andrews, B., Brewin, C. R., & Rose, S. (2003). Gender, social support, and PTSD in victims of violent crime. *Journal of Traumatic Stress, 16*, 421–427.

Andrews-Hanna, J. R., Reidler, J. S., Huang, C., & Buckner, R. L. (2010). Evidence for the default network's role in spontaneous cognition. *Journal of Neurophysiology, 104*, 322–335.

Anketell, C., Dorahy, M. J., Shannon, M., Elder, R., Hamilton, G., Corry, M., . . . O'Raw, B. (2010). An exploratory analysis of voice hearing in chronic PTSD: Potential associated mechanisms. *Journal of Trauma & Dissociation, 11*, 93–107.

Anketell, C., Dorahy, M. J., & Curran, D. (2011). A preliminary qualitative investigation of voice hearing and its association with dissociation in chronic PTSD. *Journal of Trauma & Dissociation, 12*, 88–101.

Ardino, V., Milani, L., & Di Blasio, P. (2013). PTSD and re-offending risk: The mediating role of worry and a negative perception of other people's support. *European Journal of Psychotraumatology, 4*.

Armony, J. G., & LeDoux, J. E. (1997). How the brain processes emotional information. *Annals of the New York Academy of Sciences, 821*, 259–270.

Armstrong, J. G., Putnam, F. W., Carlson, E. B., Libero, D. Z., & Smith, S. R. (1997). Development and validation of a measure of adolescent dissociation: The Adolescent Dissociative Experiences Scale. *Journal of Nervous and Mental Disease, 185*, 491–497.

Arnsten, A. (1999). Development of the prefrontal cortex: XIV. Stress impairs prefrontal cortical function. *Journal of the American Academy of Child and Adolescent Psychiatry, 38*, 220–222.

Augustine. (1950). The character of the human will. Chapter VI in *The city of God. Book XIV* (transl. M. Dodds). New York: The Modern Library.

Azari, N. P., Nickel, J., Wunderich, G., Niedeggen, M., Hefter, H., Tellman, L., . . . Seitz, R. J. (1997). Neural correlates of religious experience. *European Journal of Neuroscience, 13*, 1649–1652.

Babinski, J. (1901). Definition de l'hysteìrie [The definition of hysteria]. *Revue Neurologique, 9*, 1074–1080.

Babinski, J. (1909). Demembrement de l'hystèrie traditionelle: Phitiathisme [Breaking up of traditional hysteria: Phytiatism]. *La Semaine Médicale, 59*, 3–8.

Bachmann, A. W., Sedgley, T. L., Jackson, R. V., Gibson, J. N., Young, R. M., & Torpy, D. J. (2005). Glucocorticoid receptor polymorphisms and posttraumatic stress disorder. *Psychoneuroendocrinology, 30*, 297–306.

Badour, C. L., Bown, S., Adams, T. G., Bunaciu, L., & Feldner, M. T. (2012). Specificity of fear and disgust experienced during traumatic interpersonal victimization in predicting posttraumatic stress and contamination-based obsessive-compulsive symptoms. *Journal of Anxiety Disorders, 26*, 590–598.

Bailey, C., & Shelton, D. (2014). Self-reports of faulty parental attachments in childhood and criminal psychopathy in an adult-incarcerated population: An integrative literature review. *Journal of Psychiatry and Mental Health Nursing, 21*, 365–374.

Bailey, H. N., Moran, G., & Pederson, D. R. (2007). Childhood maltreatment, complex trauma symptoms, and unresolved attachment in an at-risk sample of adolescent mothers. *Attachment and Human Development, 9*, 139–161.

Balasundaram, B., Frazer, J. B., & Wood, P. J. (2009). Who are sexual offenders? A survey of pretrial psychiatric reports. *Medical Science Law, 49*, 33–40.

Banks, G., Short, P., Martinez, A. J., Latchaw, R., Ratcliff, G., & Boller, F. (1989). The alien hand syndrome: Clinical and postmortem findings. *Archives of Neurology, 46*, 456–459.

Baranyi, A., Leithgob, O., Kreiner, B., Tanzer, K., Ehrlich, G., Hofer, H. P., & Rothenhausler, H. B. (2010). Relationship between posttraumatic stress disorder, quality of life, social support, and affective and dissociative status in severely injured accident victims 12 months after trauma. *Psychosomatics, 51*, 237–247.

Barkay, G., Freedman, N., Lester, H., Louzoun, Y., Sapoznikov, D., Luckenbaugh, D., ... Bonne, O. (2012). Brain activation and heart rate during script-driven traumatic imagery in PTSD: Preliminary findings. *Psychiatry Research, 204*, 155–160.

Barnes, A., & Thagard, P. (1997). Empathy and analogy. *Dialogue Canadian Philosophical Review, 36*, 705–720.

Barrett, D. (1992). Fantasizers and dissociators: Data on two distinct subgroups of deep trance subjects. *Psychological Reports, 71*(3 Pt 1), 1011–1014.

Barrett, D. (1996). Fantasizers and dissociators: Two types of high hypnotizables, two different imagery styles. In R. G. Kunzendorfer, N. P. Spanos, & B. Wallace (Eds.), *Hypnosis and imagination* (pp. 123–135). Amityville, NY: Baywood.

Baumgartner, T., Willi, M., & Jäncke, L. (2007). Modulation of corticospinal activity by strong emotions evoked by pictures and classical music: A transcranial magnetic stimulation study. *Neuroreport, 18*, 261–265.

Baxter, A. J., Scott, K. M., Vos, T., & Whiteford, H. A. (2012). Global prevalence of anxiety disorders: A systematic review and meta-regression. *Psychological Medicine, 43*, 897–910.

Baeyens, F., Hermans, D., & Eelen, P. (1993). The role of CS-UCS contingency in human evaluative conditioning. *Behavior Research and Therapy, 31*, 731–737.

BBC. (2001–01–10). Porn ring "was real child abuse." Retrieved from http://news.bbc.co.uk/2/hi/uk_news/1109787.stm

Beard, G. (1869). Neurasthenia, or nervous exhaustion. *The Boston Medical and Surgical Journal*. April 28, 217–221.

Bebbington, P. E., Bhugra, D., Brugha, T., Singleton, N., Farrell, M., Jenkins, R., ... Metzler, H. (2004). Psychosis, victimisation and childhood disadvantage: Evidence from the second British National Survey of Psychiatric Morbidity. *British Journal of Psychiatry, 185*, 220–226.

Becker, M. W., & Detweiler-Bedell, B. (2009). Early detection and avoidance of threatening faces during passive viewing. *Quarterly Journal of Experimental Psychology (Hove), 62*, 1257–1264.

Becker-Blease, K. A., Deater-Deckard, K., Eley, T., Freyd, J. J., Stevenson, J., & Plomin. R. (2004). A genetic analysis of individual differences in dissociative behaviors in childhood and adolescence. *Journal of Child Psychology and Psychiatry 45*, 522–532.

Becker-Blease, K. A., & Freyd, J. J. (2007). Dissociation and memory for perpetration among convicted sex offenders. *Journal of Trauma & Dissociation, 8*, 69–80.

Bedard-Gilligan, M., & Zoellner, L. A. (2008). The utility of the A1 and A2 criteria in the diagnosis of PTSD. *Behavior Research and Therapy, 46*, 1062–1069.

Benetti, S., McCrory, E., Arulanantham, S., De Sanctis, T., McGuire, P., & Mechelli, A. (2010). Attachment style, affective loss and gray matter volume: A voxel-based morphometry study. *Human Brain Mapping, 31*, 1482–1489.

Benjamin, L. S. (1993). *Interpersonal diagnosis and treatment of personality disorders* (2nd ed.). New York: Guilford.

Benjamin, L. S. (1994). SASB: A bridge between personality theory and clinical psychology. *Psychological Inquiry, 5*, 273–316.

Bennett, J. (2005). *Correspondence between Descartes and Princess Elisabeth.* Retrieved from www.earlymoderntexts.com/pdfbits/desel2.pdf

Bennett, M. R., & Hacker, P. M. S. (2003). *Philosophical foundations of neuroscience.* Oxford: Blackwell.

Benson, D. F., Miller, B. L., & Signer, S. F. (1986). Dual personality associated with epilepsy. *Archives of Neurology, 43*, 471–474.

Bernard, P. (1886). *Des attentats à la pudeur sur les petites filles* [Indecent assaults on young girls]. Paris: Octave Doin.

Bernstein, R. (2003, Sept. 27). Germany says it uncovered huge child pornography ring. *New York Times.* http://www.nytimes.com/2003/09/27/world/germany-says-it-uncovered-huge-child-pornography-ring.htm

Bernstein, E. M., & Putnam, F. W. (1986). Development, reliability, and validity of a dissociation scale. *Journal of Nervous and Mental Disease, 174*, 727–735.

Bernstein, D. P., Stein, J. A., Newcomb, M. D., Walker, E., Pogge, D., Ahluvalia, T., ... Zule, W. (2003). Development and validation of a brief screening version of the Childhood Trauma Questionnaire. *Child Abuse and Neglect, 27*, 169–190.

Beurskens, H. (2013). *Het Artisbestuarium* [The artisbestiary]. Amsterdam: Nieuw Amsterdam Uitgevers.

Bilodeau, D. (1996). Physics, machines, and the hard problem. *Journal of Consciousness Studies, 3*, 381–401.

Birnbaum, M. H., & Thomann, K. (1996). Visual function in multiple personality disorder. *Journal of the American Optometric Association, 67*, 327–334.

Bitbol, M. (2002). Science as if situation mattered. *Phenomenology and the Cognitive Science, 1*, 181–224.

Bitbol, M. (2008). Is consciousness primary? *NeuroQuantology, 6*, 53–72.

Bleuler, E. (1911/1950). *Dementia praecox or the group of schizophrenias* (Translation: J. Zinkin). Madison: International Universities Press.

Bliss, E. L. (1984). Spontaneous self-hypnosis in multiple personality disorder. *Psychiatric Clinics of North America, 7*, 135–148.

Blizard, R. A., (1997). The origins of dissociative identity disorder from an object relations theory and attachment theory perspective. *Dissociation, 10*, 223–229.

Blizard, R. A. (2003). Disorganized attachment, development of dissociated self-states, and a relational approach to treatment. *Journal of Trauma & Dissociation, 4*(3), 27–50.

Block, N. (1998). On a confusion about the function of consciousness. In N. Block, O. Flanagan, & G. Guzeldere (Eds.), *The nature of consciousness: Philosophical debates* (pp. 375–415). Cambridge, MA: MIT.

Boals, A., & Schuettler, D. (2009). PTSD symptoms in the response to traumatic and non-traumatic events: The role of respondent perception and A2 criterion. *Journal of Anxiety Disorders, 23*, 458–462.

Bob, P. (2003). Dissociation and neuroscience: History and new perspectives. *International Journal of Neuroscience, 113*, 903–914.

Bob, P., Golla, M., Epstein, P., & Konopka, L. (2011). EEG complexity and attentional processes related to dissociative states. *Clinical EEG and Neuroscience, 42*, 175–179.

Bob, P., Selesova, P., Raboch, J., & Kukla, L. (2013). "Pseudoneurological" symptoms, dissociation and stress-related psychopathology in healthy young adults. *BMC Psychiatry, 13*, 149.

Bohn, D., Bernardy, K., Wolfe, F., & Hauser, W. (2013). The association among childhood maltreatment, somatic symptom intensity, depression, and somatoform dissociative symptoms in patients with fibromyalgia syndrome: A single-center cohort study. *Journal of Trauma & Dissociation, 14*, 342–358.

Bolles, R. C. (1970). Species-specific defense reactions and avoidance learning. *Psychological Review, 71*, 32–48.

Bolles, R.C. F., & Fanselow, M. S. (1980). A perceptual-defensive-recuperative model of fear and pain. *Behavioral Brain Science, 3*, 291–301.

Bonhoeffer, K. (1911). Wie weit kommen psychogene Krankheitszustände und Krankheitsprozesse vor, die nicht der Hysterie zuzurechnen sind? [To what degree do psychogenic states and processes of illness exist which are not due to hysteria?] *Allgemeine Zeitschrift für Psychiatrie, 68*, 371–386.

Bonne, O., Gilboa, A., Louzoun, Y., Brandes, D., Yona, I., Lester, H., . . . Shalev, A. Y. (2003). Resting regional cerebral perfusion in recent posttraumatic stress disorder. *Biological Psychiatry, 54*, 1077–1086.

Boon, S., & Draijer, N. (1993a). Multiple personality disorder in The Netherlands: A clinical investigation of 71 patients. *American Journal of Psychiatry, 150*, 489–494.

Boon, S., & Draijer, N. (1993b). The differentiation of patients with MPD or DDNOS from patients with a cluster B personality disorder. *Dissociation, 6*, 126–135.

Boroske-Leiner, K., Hofmann, A., & Sack, M. (2008). Assessment of complex PTSD: Internal and external validity of a diagnostic interview. *Psychotherapie, Psychosomatik, medizinische Psychologie, 58*, 192–199.

Bourneville, D. (Ed.). (1886). *La possession de Jeanne Fery, religieuse professe du couvent des soeures noires de la ville de Mons (1584)* [The possession of Jeanne Fery, nun at the convent of the black sisters of the city of Mons]. Paris: Progrès Médicale/A. Delahaye & Lescrosnier (Bibliotheque diabolique).

Bos, A. P. (1998, August). *Aristotle's psychology: The traditional (hylomorphistic) interpretation refuted.* Presented at the Twentieth World Congress of Philosophy, Boston, MA.

Bos, A. P. (2003). *The soul and its instrumental body: A reinterpretation of Aristotle's philosophy of living nature.* Leiden: Koninklijke Brill.

Bouchard, T. J. Jr., & Loehlin, J. C. (2001). Genes, evolution, and personality. *Behavior Genetics, 31*, 243–273.

Bourne, P. G., Rose, R. M., & Mason, J. W. (1967). 17-OHCS levels in combat: Special Forces "A" Team under threat of attack. *Archives of General Psychiatry, 19*, 135–140.

Bouton, M. E. (2004). Context and behavioral processes in extinction. *Learning and Memory, 11*, 485–494.

Bovin, M. J., Jager-Hyman, S., Gold, S. D., Marx, B. P., & Sloan, D. M. (2008). Tonic immobility mediates the influence of peritraumatic fear and perceived inescapability on posttraumatic stress symptom severity among sexual assault survivors. *Journal of Traumatic Stress, 21*, 402–409.

Bovin, M. J., & Marx, B. P. (2010). The importance of the peritraumatic experience in defining traumatic stress. *Psychological Bulletin, 137*, 47–67.

Bowlby, J. (1980). *Attachment and loss, Vol. 3: Loss: Sadness and depression.* New York: Basic Books.

Bowman, E. S. (2006). Why conversion seizures should be classified as a dissociative disorder. *Psychiatric Clinics of North America, 29*, 185–211.

Bowman, E. S. (2011). Nijenhuis and Van der Hart: One view of the elephant. *Journal of Trauma & Dissociation, 12*, 446–449.

Boysen, G. A. (2011). The scientific status of childhood dissociative identity disorder: A review of published research. *Psychotherapy and Psychosomatics, 80*, 329–334.

Bracken, P. (2001). Post-modernity and post-traumatic stress disorder. *Social Science and Medicine, 53*, 733–743.

Braffman, W., & Kirsch, I. (1999). Imaginative suggestibility and hypnotizability: An empirical analysis. *Journal of Personality and Social Psychology, 77*, 578–587.

Brand, B. L., Classen, C. C., Lanius, R., Loewenstein, R., McNary, S., Pain, C., & Putnam, F. W. (2009). A naturalistic study of dissociative identity disorder and dissociative disorder not otherwise specified patients treated by community clinicians. *Psychological Trauma: Theory, Research, Practice, and Policy, 1*, 153–171.

Brand, B. L., Classen, C. C., McNary, S. W., & Zaveri, P. (2009a). A review of dissociative disorders treatment studies. *Journal of Nervous and Mental Disease, 197*, 646–654.

Brand, B. L., Lanius, R., Vermetten, E., Loewenstein, R. J., & Spiegel, D. (2012). Where are we going? An update on assessment, treatment, and neurobiological research in dissociative disorders as we move toward the DSM-5. *Journal of Trauma & Dissociation, 13*(1), 9–31.

Brand, B. L., McNary, S. W., Loewenstein, R. J., Kolos, A. C., & Barr, S. R. (2006). Assessment of genuine and simulated dissociative identity disorder on the structured interview of reported symptoms. *Journal of Trauma & Dissociation, 7*(1), 63–85.

Brand, B. L., & Stadnik, R. (2013). What contributes to predicting change in the treatment of dissociation: Initial levels of dissociation, PTSD, or overall distress? *Journal of Trauma & Dissociation, 14*, 328–341.

Braude, S. E. (1979). *ESP and psychokinesis: A philosophical examination.* Philadelphia: Temple University Press.

Braude, S. E. (1995). *First person plural: Multiple personality and the philosophy of mind.* Lanham: Rowman and Littlefield.

Braude, S. E. (1997). *The limits of influence: Psychokinesis and the philosophy of science.* Lanham: University Press of America.

Braude, S. E. (2002). *ESP and psychokinesis: A philosophical examination* (rev. ed.). Parkland, FL: Brown Walker.

Braude, S. E. (2006). Memory without a trace. *European Journal of Parapsychology, 21*, 182–202.

Breh, D. C., & Seidler, G. H. (2007). Is peritraumatic dissociation a risk factor for PTSD? *Journal of Trauma & Dissociation, 8*(1), 53–69.

Breland, K., & Breland, M. (1961). The misbehavior of organisms. *American Psychologist, 16*, 681–684.

Bremner, J. D. (1999). Acute and chronic responses to psychological trauma: Where do we go from here? (Editorial). *American Journal of Psychiatry, 156*, 349–351.

Bremner, J. D., & Vermetten, E. (2001). Stress and development: Behavioral and biological consequences. *Development and Psychopathology, 13*, 473–489.

Bremner, J. D. (2010). Cognitive processes in dissociation: Comment on Giesbrecht et al. (2008). *Psychological Bulletin, 136*, 1–6, 7–11.

Bremner, J. D., Narayan, M., Staib, L. H., Southwick, S. M., McGlashan, T., & Charney, D. S. (1999a). Neural correlates of memories of childhood sexual abuse in women with and without posttraumatic stress disorder. *American Journal of Psychiatry, 156*, 1787–1795.

Bremner, J. D., Staib, L., Kaloupek, D., Southwick, S. M., Soufer, R., & Charney, D. S. (1999b). Neural correlates of exposure to traumatic pictures and sound in Vietnam combat veterans with and without posttraumatic stress disorder: A positron emission tomography study. *Biological Psychiatry, 45*, 806–816.

Bremner, J. D., Steinberg, M., Southwick, S. M., Johnson, D. R., & Charney, D. S. (1993). Use of the Structured Clinical Interview for DSM-IV Dissociative Disorders for systematic assessment of dissociative symptoms in posttraumatic stress disorder. *American Journal of Psychiatry, 150*, 1011–1014.

Bremner, J. D., Vythilingam, M., Vermetten, E., Southwick, S. M., McGlashan, T., Staib, L. H., . . . Charney, D. S. (2003). Neural correlates of declarative memory for emotionally valenced words in women with posttraumatic stress disorder related to early childhood sexual abuse. *Biological Psychiatry, 53*, 879–889.

Brennen, T., Dybdahl, R., & Kapidzic, A. (2007). Trauma-related and neutral false memories in war-induced posttraumatic stress disorder. *Consciousness and Cognition, 16,* 877–885.

Breuer, J., & Freud, S. (1893–1895/1955). *Studies on hysteria. Complete psychological works, standard edition, Volume 2.* London: Hogarth.

Brewin, C. R., Andrews, B., & Valentine, J. D. (2000). Meta-analysis of risk factors for posttraumatic stress disorder in trauma-exposed adults. *Journal of Consulting and Clinical Psychology, 68,* 748–766.

Brewin, C. R., Dalgleish, T., & Joseph, S. (1996). A dual representation theory of posttraumatic stress disorder. *Psychological Review, 103,* 670–686.

Brewin, C. R., Lanius, R. A., Novac, A., Schnyder, U., & Galea, S. (2009). Reformulating PTSD for DSM-V: Life after Criterion A. *Journal of Traumatic Stress, 22,* 366–373.

Brewin, C. R., McNally, R. J., & Taylor, S. (2004). Point-counterpoint: Two views on traumatic memory and posttraumatic stress disorder. *Journal of Cognitive Psychotherapy, 18,* 99–114.

Brewin, C. R., & Patel, T. (2010). Auditory pseudohallucinations in United Kingdom war veterans and civilians with posttraumatic stress disorder. *Journal of Clinical Psychiatry, 71,* 419–425.

Briere, J. (1996). Psychometric review of the Trauma Symptom Checklist-40. In B. H. Stamm (Ed.), *Measurement of stress, trauma, and adaptation* (pp. 381–383), Lutherville MD: Sidran.

Briere, J., & Spinazzola, J. (2009). Assessment of the sequelae of complex trauma: Evidence-based measures. In C. A. Courtois & J. D. Ford (Eds.), *Treating complex traumatic stress disorders* (pp. 104–123). New York: Guilford.

Briquet, P. (1859). *Traité clinique et thérapeutique de l'hystérie, Tome I* [Clinical and therapeutic treatise on hysteria, Vol. 1]. Paris: J-B Baillière et Fils.

Brodie, B. (1837). Injuries to the spinal cord. *Medico-Chirurgical Transactions, 20,* 118.

Brooks, R., Bryant, R. A., Silove, D., Creamer, M., O'Donnell, M., McFarlane, A. C., & Marmar, C. R. (2009). The latent structure of the Peritraumatic Dissociative Experiences Questionnaire. *Journal of Traumatic Stress, 22,* 153–157.

Broyd, S. J., Demanuele, C., Debener, S., Helps, S. K., James, C. J., & Sonuga-Barke, E. G. (2009). Default-mode brain dysfunction in mental disorders: A systematic review. *Neuroscience and Biobehavioral Reviews, 33,* 279–296.

Brown, L. S., & Freyd, J. J. (2008). PTSD criterion A and betrayal trauma: A modest proposal for a new look at what constitutes danger to self. *Trauma Psychology, Division 56, American Psychological Association, Newsletter,* 3(1), 11–15.

Brown, R. J. (2006). Different types of "dissociation" have different psychological mechanisms. *Journal of Trauma & Dissociation, 7*(4), 7–28.

Brown, R. J. (2011). Commentary on "Dissociation in trauma: A new definition and comparison with previous formulations" by Nijenhuis and Van der Hart. *Journal of Trauma & Dissociation, 12,* 450–453.

Brown, R. J., Cardeña, E., Nijenhuis, E., Sar, V., & Van der Hart, O. (2007). Should conversion disorder be reclassified as a dissociative disorder in DSM-V? *Psychosomatics, 48,* 369–378.

Brown, R. J., & Lewis-Fernandez, R. (2011). Culture and conversion disorder: Implications for DSM-5. *Psychiatry, 74,* 187–206.

Brown, W. (1919a). War neuroses: A comparison of early cases seen in the field with those seen at the base. *The Lancet, 193*(4994), *May 17,* 833–836.

Brown, W. (1919b). Hypnosis, suggestion, and dissociation. *The British Medical Journal, June 14,* 734–736.

Bryant, R. A. (2007). Does dissociation further our understanding of PTSD? *Journal of Anxiety Disorders, 21,* 183–191.

Bryant, R. A. (2012). Simplifying complex PTSD: Comment on Resick et al. (2012). *Journal of Traumatic Stress, 25,* 252–253, 260–263.

Bryant, R. A., Brooks, R., Silove, D., Creamer, M., O'Donnell, M., & McFarlane, A. C. (2011). Peritraumatic dissociation mediates the relationship between acute panic and chronic posttraumatic stress disorder. *Behavior Research & Therapy, 49*, 346–351.

Bryant, R. A., Guthrie, R. M., & Moulds, M. L. (2001). Hypnotizability in acute stress disorder. *American Journal of Psychiatry, 158*, 600–604.

Bryant, R. A., Harvey, A. G., Guthrie, R. M., & Moulds, M. L. (2000). A prospective study of psychophysiological arousal, acute stress disorder, and posttraumatic stress disorder. *Journal of Abnormal Psychology, 109*, 341–344.

Buber, M. (1983). *Ich und Du* [I and Thou]. Heidelberg: Reclam.

Buckner, R. L., Andrews-Hanna, J. R., & Schacter, D. L. (2008). The brain's default network: Anatomy, function, and relevance to disease. *Annals of the New York Academy of Science, 1124*, 1–38.

Burgess, P. W., Quayle, A., & Frith, C. D. (2001). Brain regions involved in prospective memory as determined by positron emission tomography. *Neuropsychologia, 39*, 545–555.

Bursen, H. A. (1978). *Dismantling the memory machine: A philosophical investigation of machine theories of memory*. Dordrecht: Reidel.

Butler, L. D. (2001). Must dissociation be unusual? *Journal of Trauma & Dissociation, 12*, 454–456.

Butler, L. D. (2004). Editorial: The dissociation of everyday life. *Journal of Trauma & Dissociation, 5*(1), 1–11.

Butler, L. D. (2006). Normative dissociation. *Psychiatric Clinics of North America, 29*, 45–62.

Campbell, D. T. (1974). Evolutionary epistemology. In P. A. Schlipp (Ed.), *The philosophy of Karl Popper* (pp. 413–463). LaSalle, IL: Open Court.

Cannon, W. B. (1927). The James-Lange theory of emotions. *American Journal of Psychology, 39*, 115–124.

Cannon, W. B. (1932). *The wisdom of the body* (2nd ed., 1939). New York: Norton.

Cantor, C. (2009). Posttraumatic stress disorder: Evolutionary perspectives. *Australian and New Zealand Journal of Psychiatry, 43*, 1038–1048.

Caplan, E. (1995). Trains, brains, and sprains: Railway spine and the origin of psychoneuroses. *Bulletin of the History of Medicine, 69*, 387–419.

Caplan, E. (2010). Trains and trauma in the American gilded age. In M. S. Micale & P. Lerner (Eds.), *Traumatic pasts: History, psychiatry, and trauma in the modern age, 1870–1930* (pp. 57–77). Cambridge: Cambridge University Press.

Cardeña, E. (1994). The domain of dissociation. In S. J. Lynn & J. W. Rhue (Eds.), *Dissociation: Clinical and theoretical aspects* (pp. 5–31). New York: Guilford.

Cardeña, E. (2011). One split too many . . . *Journal of Trauma & Dissociation, 12*, 457–460.

Cardeña, E., & Spiegel, D. (1993). Dissociative reactions to the San Francisco Bay Area earthquake of 1989. *American Journal of Psychiatry, 150*, 474–478.

Cardyn, L. (2001). The construction of female sexual trauma in turn-of-the-century American mental medicine. In M. S. Micale & P. Lerner (Eds.), *Traumatic pasts: History, psychiatry and trauma in the modern age, 1870–1930* (pp. 172–201). Cambridge: Cambridge University Press.

Carlson, E. B. (2014, March). *Progress in the conceptualization and assessment of dissociation and its relation to posttraumatic disorders.* Keynote address at the 2014 International Conference of the European Society for Trauma and Dissociation, Copenhagen, Denmark.

Carlson, E. B., & Dalenberg, C. (2009, November). *The role of dissociation in PTSD: Empirical findings on dissociation, traumatic stress exposure, and PTSD.* Paper presented at the International Society of Traumatic Stress Studies, Atlanta, GA.

Carlson, E. B., Dalenberg, C., & McDade-Montez, E. (2012). Dissociation in Posttraumatic Stress Disorder, Part I: Definitions and review of research. *Psychological Trauma: Theory, Research, Practice, and Policy. 4(5)*, 479–489.

Carlson, E. B., Field, N. P., Ruzek, J. I., Bryant, R. A., Dalenberg, C. J., Keane, T. M., & Spain, D. A. (submitted). *Psychometric study of proximal intensive assessment of psychological phenomena and behaviors.* Manuscript submitted for publication.

Carlson, S. M., Tahiroglu, D., & Taylor, M. (2008). Links between dissociation and role play in a nonclinical sample of preschool children. *Journal of Trauma & Dissociation, 9*, 149–171.

Carrasco, J. L., Tajima-Pozo, K., Diaz-Marsa, M., Casado, A., Lopez-Ibor, J. J., Arrazola, J., & Yus, M. (2012). Microstructural white matter damage at orbitofrontal areas in borderline personality disorder. *Journal of Affective Disorders, 139*, 149–153.

Carrion V. G., Weems C. F., & Reiss A. L. (2007). Stress predicts brain changes in children: A pilot longitudinal study on youth stress, posttraumatic stress disorder, and the hippocampus. *Pediatrics, 119*, 509–516.

Carrion, V. G., Weems, C. F., Watson, C., Eliez, S., Menon, V., & Reiss, A. L. (2009). Converging evidence for abnormalities of the prefrontal cortex and evaluation of midsagittal structures in pediatric posttraumatic stress disorder: An MRI study. *Psychiatry Research, 172*, 226–234.

Carrion, V. G., & Wong, S. S. (2012). Can traumatic stress alter the brain? Understanding the implications of early trauma on brain development and learning. *Journal of Adolescent Health, 51*(Suppl. 2), S23-S28.

Carter, R. B. (1853). *On the psychology and treatment of hysteria*. London: Churchill.

Carvajal, F., Rubio, S., Serrano, J. M., Rios-Lago, M., Alvarez-Linera, J., Pacheco, L., & Martin, P. (2013). Is a neutral expression also a neutral stimulus? A study with functional magnetic resonance. *Experimental Brain Research, 228*, 467–479.

Carvalho, J., & Nobre, P. J. (2014). Five-Factor Model of personality and sexual aggression. *International Journal of Offender Therapy and Comparative Criminology.*

Carver, C. S., & Scheier, M. F. (2000). Scaling back goals and recalibration of the affect system are processes in normal adaptive self-regulation: Understanding 'response shift' phenomena. *Social Science & Medicine, 50*, 1715–1722.

Carver, C. S., Sutton, S. K., & Scheier, M. F. (2000). Action, emotion, and personality: Emerging conceptual integration. *Personality and Social Psychology Bulletin, 26*, 741–751.

Caspi, A., McClay, J., Moffitt, T. E., Mill, J., Martin, J., Craig, I. W., ... Poulton, R. (2002). Role of genotype in the cycle of violence in maltreated children. *Science, 297*, 851–854.

Caston, V. (1997). Epiphenomenalisms, ancient and modern. *The Philosophical Review, 106*, 309–363.

Cattell, R. B. (1986). Structured tests and functional diagnoses. In R. B. Cattell & R. C. Johnson (Eds.), *Functional psychological testing: Principles and Instruments* (pp. 3–14). New York: Brunner/Mazel.

Chalavi, S. (2013). *The traumatized brain: Gray and white matter morphology in dissociative identity disorder and posttraumatic stress disorder*. Dissertation, Rijksuniversiteit Groningen.

Chalavi, S., Vissia, E. M., Giesen, M. E., Nijenhuis, E. R. S., Draijer, N., Cole, J. H., ... Reinders, A. A. T. S. (2014). Abnormal hippocampal morphology in dissociative identity disorder and posttraumatic stress disorder correlates with childhood trauma and dissociative symptoms. *Human Brain Mapping* (published online December 29, 2014).

Chalavi, S., Vissia, E. M., Giesen, M. E., Nijenhuis, E. R. S., Draijer, N., Barker, G. J., ... Reinders, A. A. T. S. (in press). Similar cortical but not subcortical gray matter abnormalities in women with posttraumatic stress disorder with or without dissociative identity disorder. *Psychiatry Research: Neuroimaging.* doi 10.1016/j.psychresns.2015.01.014i

Chalmers, D. J. (1996). *The conscious mind: In search of a fundamental theory*. New York: Oxford University Press.

Champagne, D. L., Bagot, R. C., van Hasselt, F., Ramakers, G., Meaney, M. J., de Kloet, E. R., ... Krugers, H. (2008). Maternal care and hippocampal plasticity: Evidence for experience-dependent structural plasticity, altered synaptic functioning, and differential responsiveness to glucocorticoids and stress. *Journal of Neuroscience, 28*, 6037–6045.

Charcot, J.-M. (1889). *Clinical lectures on diseases of the nervous system: Volume III* (transl. T. Savill). London: New Sydenham Society.

Chaturvedi, S. K., Desai, G., & Shaligram, D. (2009). Dissociative disorders in a psychiatric institute in India: A selected review and patterns over a decade. *International Journal of Social Psychiatry, 56*, 533–539.

Chen, J., & Shi, S. (2011). A review of neuroimaging studies of anxiety disorders in China. *Journal of Neuropsychiatric Disease and Treatment, 7*, 241–249.

Cheyne, G. (1733). *The English malady.* (Reprint: Tavistock classics in the history of psychiatry, R. Porter (Ed.). London: Routledge, 1991).

Chivers-Wilson, K. A. (2006). Sexual assault and posttraumatic stress disorder: A review of the biological, psychological and sociological factors and treatments. *Mcgill J Med, 9*, 111–118.

Choi, J., Jeong, B., Rohan, M. L., Polcari, A. M., & Teicher, M. H. (2009). Preliminary evidence for white matter tract abnormalities in young adults exposed to parental verbal abuse. *Biological Psychiatry, 65*, 227–234.

Chu, J. A., Frey, L. M., Ganzel, B. L., & Matthews, J. A. (1999). Memories of childhood abuse: Dissociation, amnesia, and corroboration. *American Journal of Psychiatry, 156*, 749–763.

Cima, M., Smeets, T., & Jelicic, M. (2008). Self-reported trauma, cortisol levels, and aggression in psychopathic and nonpsychopathic prison inmates. *Biological Psychology, 78*, 75–86.

Ciompi, L. (1991). Affects as central organizing and integrating factors: A new psychosocial/biological model of the psyche. *British Journal of Psychiatry, 159*, 97–105.

Cisler, J. M., & Koster, E. H. (2010). Mechanisms of attentional biases towards threat in anxiety disorders: An integrative review. *Clinical Psychology Review, 30*, 203–216.

Cloitre, M., Courtois, C. A., Charuvastra, A., Carapezza, R., Stolbach, B. C., & Green, B. L. (2011). Treatment of complex PTSD: Results of the ISTSS expert clinician survey on best practices. *Journal of Traumatic Stress, 24*, 615–627.

Cloitre, M., Garvert, D. W., Brewin, C. R., Bryant, R. A., & Maercker, A. (2013). Evidence for proposed ICD-11 PTSD and complex PTSD: A latent profile analysis. *European Journal of Psychotraumatology, 4*, 20706.

Cobben, J. J. (1976). *Jan Wier, devils, witches, and magic.* Philadelphia: Dorrance.

Cohen, R. A., Grieve, S., Hoth, K. F., Paul, R. H., Sweet, L., Tate, D., & Williams, L. M. (2006). Early life stress and morphometry of the adult anterior cingulate cortex and caudate nuclei. *Biological Psychiatry, 59*, 975–982.

Cohen, H., Zohar, J., & Matar, M. (2003). The relevance of differential response to trauma in an animal model of posttraumatic stress disorder. *Biological Psychiatry, 53*, 463–473.

Collin-Vézina, D., & Hébert, M. (2005). Comparing dissociation and PTSD in sexually abused school-aged girls. *Journal of Nervous and Mental Disease, 193*(1), 47–52.

Colton, M., Roberts, S., & Vanstone, M. (2010). Sexual abuse by men who work with children. *Journal of Child Sexual Abuse, 19*, 345–364.

Combe, A. (1831). *Observations on mental derangement: Being an application of the principles of phrenology to the elucidation of the causes, symptoms, nature and treatment of insanity.* Edinburgh: Anderson.

Cooley, C. H. (1902). *Human nature and the social order.* New York: Scribner's. See www. http://media.pfeiffer.edu/lridener/DSS/Cooley/LKGLSSLF.HTML

Cools, A. R., & Ellenbroek, B. A. (2002). Animal models of personality. In H. D'Haenen, J. A. den Boer, & P. Willner (Eds.), *Biological psychiatry* (pp. 1333–1344). London: Wiley.

Coons, P. M. (1992). Dissociative disorder not otherwise specified: A clinical investigation of 50 cases with suggestions for typology and treatment. *Dissociation, 5*(1), 187–195.

Coons, P. M. (2005). Re: The persistence of folly: A critical examination of dissociative identity disorder. *Canadian Journal of Psychiatry, 50*, 813.

Coons, P. M., & Milstein, V. (1986). Psychosexual disturbances in multiple personality: Characteristics, etiology, and treatment. *Journal of Clinical Psychiatry, 47*, 106–110.

Coons, P. M., Milstein, V., & Marley, C. (1982). EEG studies of two multiple personalities and a control. *Archives of General Psychiatry, 39*, 823–825.

Copleston, F. C. (1955). *Aquinas*. Harmondsworth: Penguin.

Corr, P. J., & McNaughton, N. (2012). Neuroscience and approach/avoidance personality traits: A two stage (valuation-motivation) approach. *Neuroscience and Biobehavioral Reviews, 36*, 2339–2354.

Coxe, R., & Holmes, W. (2009). A comparative study of two groups of sex offenders identified as high and low risk on the static-99. *Journal of Child Sexual Abuse, 18*, 137–153.

Craig, A. D. (2003). Pain mechanisms: Labeled lines versus convergence in central processing. *Annual Review of Neuroscience, 26*, 1–30.

Craig, A. D. (2009). How do you feel–now? The anterior insula and human awareness. *Natural Review of Neuroscience, 10*, 59–70.

Crick, F. H. C. (1994). *The astonishing hypothesis: The scientific search for the soul*. New York: Scribner.

Critchley, H. D. (2004). The human cortex responds to an interoceptive challenge. *Proceedings of the National Academy of Sciences USA, 101*, 6333–6334.

Critchley, H. D., Mathias, C. J., & Dolan, R. J. (2001). Neuroanatomical basis for first- and second-order representations of bodily states. *Nature Neuroscience, 4*, 207–212.

Critchley, H. D., Wiens, S., Rothstein, P., Ohman, A., & Dolan, R. J. (2004). Neural systems supporting interoceptive awareness. *Nature Neuroscience, 7*, 189–195.

Cromer, L. D., & Goldsmith, R. E. (2010). Child sexual abuse myths: Attitudes, beliefs, and individual differences. *Journal of Child Sexual Abuse, 19*, 618–647.

Currie, J., & Widom, C. S. (2010). Long-term consequences of child abuse and neglect on adult economic well-being. *Child Maltreatment, 15*, 111–120.

Currier, J. M., Holland, J. M., & Allen, D. (2012). Attachment and mental health symptoms among U. S. Afghanistan and Iraq veterans seeking health care services. *Journal of Traumatic Stress, 25*, 633–640.

Curtin, F., & Niveau, G. (1998). Psychosocial profile of Swiss sexual offenders. *Journal of Forensic Sciences, 43*, 755–759.

Cuijpers, P., Smit, F., Unger, F., Stikkelbroek, Y., Ten Have, M., & de Graaf, R. (2011). The disease burden of childhood adversities in adults: A population-based study. *Child Abuse and Neglect, 35*, 937–945.

Cyr, C., Euser, E. M., Bakermans-Kranenburg, M. J., & Van IJzendoorn, M. H. (2010). Attachment security and disorganization in maltreating and high-risk families: A series of meta-analyses. *Development and Psychopathology, 22*, 87–108.

Da Costa, J. M. (1871). On irritable heart: A clinical study of a form of functional heart disorder and its consequences. *The American Journal of the Medical Sciences, 121*, 17–52.

Dale, K. Y., Berg, R., Elden, A., Odegard, A., & Holte, A. (2009). Testing the diagnosis of dissociative identity disorder through measures of dissociation, absorption, hypnotizability and PTSD: A Norwegian pilot study. *Journal of Trauma & Dissociation, 10*(1), 102–112.

Dalenberg, C. J. (1996). Accuracy, timing, and circumstances of disclosure in therapy of recovered and continuous memories of abuse. *Journal of Psychiatry and Law, 24*, 229–275.

Dalenberg, C. (2006). Recovered memory and the Daubert criteria: Recovered memory as professionally tested, peer reviewed, and accepted in the relevant scientific community. *Trauma Violence & Abuse, 7*, 274–310.

Dalenberg, C. J., Brand, B. L., Gleaves, D. H., Dorahy, M. J., Loewenstein, R. J., Cardeña, E., & Spiegel, D.

(2012). Evaluation of the evidence for the trauma and fantasy models of dissociation. *Psychological Bulletin, 138*, 550–588.

Dalenberg, C., & Paulson, K. (2009). The case for the study of "normal" dissociation processes. In P. F. Dell & J. A. O'Neil (Eds.), *Dissociation and the dissociative disorders: DSM-IV and beyond* (pp. 145–154). New York: Routledge.

Daly, R. J. (1983). Samuel Pepys and posttraumatic stress disorder. *British Journal of Psychiatry, 1443*, 64–68.

Damasio, A. R. (1994). *Descartes' error: Emotion, reason, and the human brain*. London: Vintage.

Damasio, A. R. (1999). *The feeling of what happens: Body and emotion in the making of consciousness*. Orlando, FL: Harcourt Brace.

Damasio, A. R., Grabowski, T. J., Bechara, A., Damasio, H., Ponto, L. L., Parvizi, J., & Hichwa, R. D. (2000). Subcortical and cortical brain activity during the feeling of self-generated emotions. *Nature Neuroscience, 3*, 1049–1056.

Dana, C. L. (1892). *Textbook of the nervous diseases, being a compendium for the use of students and practitioners of medicine*. New York: William Wood & Co.

D'Andrea, W., Ford, J. D., Stolbach, B., Spinazzola, J., & Van der Kolk, B. A. (2012). Understanding interpersonal trauma in children: Why we need a developmentally appropriate trauma diagnosis. *American Journal of Orthopsychiatry, 82*, 187–200.

Daniels, J. K., Lamke, J. P., Gaebler, M., Walter, H., & Scheel, M. (2013). White matter integrity and its relationship to PTSD and childhood trauma–a systematic review and meta-analysis. *Depression and Anxiety, 30*, 207–216.

Dartnall, E., & Jewkes, R. (2012). Sexual violence against women: The scope of the problem. *Best Practice and Research in Clinical Obstetrics and Gynaecology, 27*(1), 3–13.

Davey, G. C. L. (1989). UCS revaluation and conditioning models of acquired fears. *Behaviour Research and Therapy, 27*, 521–528.

David, A. C., Akerib, V., Gaston, L., & Brunet, A. (2010). Consistency of retrospective reports of peritraumatic responses and their relation to PTSD diagnostic status. *Journal of Traumatic Stress, 23*, 599–605.

Davidson, R. J. (2004). What does the prefrontal cortex "do" in affect: Perspectives on frontal EEG asymmetry research. *Biological Psychology, 67*, 219–233.

Davies, M. (2000). The role of the amygdala in conditioned and unconditioned fear and anxiety. In J. P. Aggleton (Ed.), *The amygdala* (pp. 213–288). New York: Oxford University Press.

Davis, K. L., & Panksepp, J. (2011). The brain's emotional foundations of human personality and the Affective Neuroscience Personality Scales. *Neuroscience and Biobehavioral Reviews, 35*, 1946–1958.

Davis, K. L., Panksepp, J., & Normansell, L. (2003). The Affective Neuroscience Personality Scales: Normative data and implications. *Neuro-Psychoanalysis, 5*, 57–69.

Davis, M., & Whalen, P. J. (2001). The amygdala: Vigilance and emotion. *Molecular Psychiatry, 6*, 13–34.

Deacon, T. W. (1997). *The symbolic species: The co-evolution of language and the brain*. New York: Norton.

De Bellis, M. D., Baum, A. S., Birmaher, B., Keshavan, M. S., Eccard, C. H., Boring, A. M., . . . Ryan, N. D. (1999). Developmental traumatology, Part I: Biological stress systems. *Biological Psychiatry, 45*, 1259–1270.

De Bellis, M. D., Keshavan, M. S., Shifflett, H., Iyengar, S., Beers, S. R., Hall, J., & Moritz, G. (2002). Brain structures in pediatric maltreatment-related posttraumatic stress disorder: A sociodemographically matched study. *Biological Psychiatry, 52*, 1066–1078.

Delbo, C. (1985). *La mémoire et les jours* [Days and memory]. Paris: Berg International.

Dell, P. F. (1997, November). Somatoform dissociation and reported trauma in DID and DDNOS. In *Proceedings of the 14th International Conference of the International Society for the Study of Dissociation*, Montreal, Quebec.

Dell, P. F. (1998). Axis II pathology in outpatients with dissociative identity disorder. *Journal of Nervous and Mental Disease, 186*, 352–356.

Dell, P. F. (2006a). A new model of dissociative identity disorder. *Psychiatric Clinics of North America, 29*, 1–26.

Dell, P. F. (2006b). The multidimensional inventory of dissociation (MID): A comprehensive measure of pathological dissociation. *Journal of Trauma & Dissociation, 7*, 77–106.

Dell, P. F. (2009a). The long struggle to diagnose multiple personality disorder (MPD): Partial MPD. In P. F. Dell & J. A. O'Neil (Eds.), *Dissociation and the dissociative disorders: DSM-IV and beyond* (pp. 403–428). New York: Routledge.

Dell, P. F. (2009b). Understanding dissociation. In P. F. Dell & J. A. O'Neil (Eds.), *Dissociation and the dissociative disorders: DSM-IV and beyond* (pp. 709–826). New York: Routledge.

Dell, P. F. (2011). An excellent definition of structural dissociation and a dogmatic rejection of all other models. *Journal of Trauma & Dissociation, 12*, 461–464.

Dell, P. F., & O'Neil, J. (2009). *Dissociation and the dissociative disorders: DSM-V and beyond.* London: Routledge.

Denov, M. S. (2003). The myth of innocence: sexual scripts and the recognition of child sexual abuse by female perpetrators. *Journal of Sex Research, 40*, 303–314.

Denton, J., Newton, A. W., & Vandeven, A. M. (2011). Update on child maltreatment: Toward refining the evidence base. *Currents Opinion in Pediatry, 23*, 240–248.

Depraz, N., Varela, F. J., & Vermersch, P. (2003). *On becoming aware: A pragmatics of experiencing.* Amsterdam/Philadelphia: John Benjamins.

DePrince, A. P. (2001). *Trauma and posttraumatic responses: An examination of fear and betrayal.* Dissertation, University of Oregon.

DePrince, A. P., Chu, A., & Visvanathan, P. (2006). Dissociation and posttraumatic stress disorder (PTSD). *PTSD Quarterly, 17*, 1–7.

DePrince, A. P., & Freyd, J. J. (2007). Trauma-induced dissociation. In M. J. Friedman, T. M. Keane, & P. A. Resick (Eds.), *Handbook of PTSD: Science and practice* (pp. 135–150). New York: Guilford.

Descartes, R. (1637). *Discourse on the method of rightly conducting one's reason and seeking truth in the sciences* (transl. J. Bennett, 2007). Retrieved from http://www.earlymoderntexts.com/pdfs/descartes1637.pdf

DeRijk, R. H., Schaaf, M., & de Kloet, E. R. (2002). Glucocorticoid receptor variants: Clinical implications. *Journal of Steroid Biochemistry and Molecular Biology, 81*, 103–122.

Dewhurst, K. (1966). *Sir Thomas Sydenham: His life and original writings.* Berkeley/Los Angeles: University of California Press.

Dickinson, E. (1975). *The complete poems of Emily Dickinson.* Edited by T. H. Johnson. London: Faber & Faber.

Dienes, Z., Brown, E., Hutton, S., Kirsch, I., Mazzoni, G., & Wright, D. B. (2009). Hypnotic suggestibility, cognitive inhibition, and dissociation. *Consciousness and Cognition, 18*, 837–847.

Dietrich, A. (2003). Characteristics of child maltreatment, psychological dissociation, and somatoform dissociation of Canadian inmates. *Journal of Trauma & Dissociation, 4*(1), 81–100.

DiGangi, J. A., Gomez, D., Mendoza, L., Jason, L. A., Keys, C. B., & Koenen, K. C. (2013). Pretrauma risk factors for posttraumatic stress disorder. A systematic review of the literature. *Clinical Psychology Review, 33*, 728–744

Dimitry, L. (2013). A systematic review on the mental health of children and adolescents in areas of armed conflict in the Middle East. *Child: Care, Health, and Development, 38*, 153–161.

Di Paolo, E. A., De Jaegher, H., & Rhohde, M. (2010). Horizons for the enactive mind: Values, social interaction, and play. In J. Stewart, O. Gapenne, & E. A. Di Paolo (Eds.), *Enaction: Toward a new paradigm for cognitive science* (pp. 33–87). Cambridge, MA: MIT.

Diseth, T. H. (2005). Dissociation in children and adolescents as reaction to trauma: An overview of conceptual issues and neurobiological factors. *Nordic Journal of Psychiatry, 59*, 79–91.

Diseth, T. H. (2006). Dissociation following traumatic medical treatment procedures in childhood: A longitudinal follow-up. *Developmental Psychopathology, 18*, 233–251.

Dolan, R. J. (2000). Functional neuroimaging of the amygdala during emotional processing and learning. In J. P. Aggleton (Ed.), *The amygdala* (pp. 631–655). New York: Oxford University Press.

Domes, G., Mense, J., Vohs, K., & Habermeyer, E. (2012). Offenders with antisocial personality disorder show attentional bias for violence-related stimuli. *Psychiatry Research, 209*(1), 78–84.

Domjan, M. (2012). Biological and evolutionary constraints on learning. In N. M. Seel (Ed.), *Encyclopedia of the sciences of learning* (pp. 461–463). New York: Springer-Verlag.

Donatti, A. F., & Leite-Panissi, C. R. (2009). GABAergic antagonist blocks the reduction of tonic immobility behavior induced by activation of 5-HT2 receptors in the basolateral nucleus of the amygdala in guinea pigs. *Brain Research Bulletin, 79*, 358–364.

Donatti, A. F., & Leite-Panissi, C. R. (2011). Activation of corticotropin-releasing factor receptors from the basolateral or central amygdala increases the tonic immobility response in guinea pigs: An innate fear behavior. *Behavioural Brain Research, 225*(1), 23–30.

Dong, M., Giles, W. H., Felitti, V. J., Dube, S. R., Williams, J. E., Chapman, D. P., & Anda, R. F. (2004). Insights into causal pathways for ischemic heart disease: Adverse Childhood Experiences Study. *Circulation, 110*, 1761–1766.

Dorahy, M. J., Corry, M., Shannon, M., Webb, K., McDermott, B., Ryan, M., & Dyer, K. F.(2013). Complex trauma and intimate relationships: The impact of shame, guilt and dissociation. *Journal of Affective Disorders, 147*(1–3), 72–79.

Dorahy, M. J., & Huntjens, R. J. C. (2007). Memory and attentional processes in dissociative identity disorder: A review of the empirical literature. In E. Vermetten, M. J. Dorahy, & D. Spiegel (Eds.), *Traumatic dissociation: Neurobiology and treatment* (pp. 55–75). Arlington, VA: American Psychiatric Publishing.

Dorahy, M. J., Lewis, C. A., & Mulholland, C. (2005). The detection of dissociative identity disorder by Northern Irish clinical psychologists and psychiatrists: A clinical vignettes study. *Journal of Trauma & Dissociation, 6*(4), 39–50.

Dorahy, M. J., & Van der Hart, O. (2007). Relationship between trauma and dissociation: A historical analysis. In E. Vermetten, M. J. Dorahy, & D. Spiegel (Eds.), *Traumatic dissociation: Neurobiology and treatment* (pp. 3–30). Arlington, VA: American Psychiatric Publishing.

Dorrepaal, E., Thomaes, K., Smit, J. H., Hoogendoorn, A., Veltman, D. J., Van Balkom, A. J., & Draijer, N. D. (2013). Clinical phenomenology of childhood abuse-related complex PTSD in a population of female patients: Patterns of personality disturbance. *Journal of Trauma & Dissociation, 13*, 271–290.

Draijer, N., & Boon, S. (1999). The imitation of dissociative identity disorder: Patients at risk, therapists at risk. *The Journal of Psychiatry and Law*, 27, 423–458.

Draijer, N., & Langeland, W. (1999). Childhood trauma and perceived parental dysfunction in the etiology of dissociative symptoms in psychiatric inpatients. *American Journal of Psychiatry, 156*, 379–385.

Draijer, N., & Van Zon, P. (2013). Transference-focused psychotherapy with former child soldiers: meeting the murderous self. *Journal of Trauma & Dissociation, 14*, 170–183.

Drapeau, M., Beretta, V., de Roten, Y., Koerner, A., & Despland, J. N. (2008). Defense styles of pedophilic offenders. *International Journal of Offender Therapy and Comparative Criminology, 52*, 185–195.

Driessen, M., Beblo, T., Mertens, M., Piefke, M., Rullkoetter, N., Silva-Saavedra, A., … Woermann, F. G. (2004). Posttraumatic stress disorder and fMRI activation patterns of traumatic memory in patients with borderline personality disorder. *Biological Psychiatry, 55*, 603–611.

Driver, J., & Vuilleumier, P. (2001). Perceptual awareness and its loss in unilateral neglect and extinction. *Cognition, 79*, 39–88.

Dube, S. R., Fairweather, D., Pearson, W. S., Felitti, V. J., Anda, R. F., & Croft, J. B. (2009). Cumulative childhood stress and autoimmune diseases in adults. *Psychosomatic Medicine, 71*, 243–250.

Dudeck, M., Barnow, S., Spitzer, C., Stopsack, M., Gillner, M., & Freyberger, H. J. (2006). The relevance of personality and sexual traumata for sexual offenders in forensic psychiatry. *Psychotherapie, Psychosomatik, medizinische Psychologie, 56*, 147–153.

Duffy, C. (2000). *Prevalence of undiagnosed dissociative disorders in an inpatient setting* (Doctoral dissertation). Available from ProQuest Dissertations and Theses database. (AAT No. 3041898)

Dutra, L., Bureau, J. F., Holmes, B., Lyubchik, A., & Lyons-Ruth, K. (2009). Quality of early care and childhood trauma: A prospective study of developmental pathways to dissociation. *Journal of Nervous and Mental Disease, 197*, 383–390.

Dutton, D. G., & Starzomsky, A. J. (1997). Personality predictors of the Minnesota Power and Control Wheel. *Journal of Interpersonal Violence, 12*, 70–82.

Eadie, M. J. (2003a). A pathology of the animal spirits: The clinical neurology of Thomas Willis (1621–1675), Part I: Background, and disorders of intrinsically normal animal spirits. *Journal of Clinical Neuroscience, 10*, 14–29.

Eadie, M. J. (2003b). A pathology of the animal spirits: The clinical neurology of Thomas Willis (1621–1675), Part II: Disorders of intrinsically abnormal animal spirits. *Journal of Clinical Neuroscience*, 10, 146–157.

Ebner, K., Wotjak, C. T., Holsboer, F., Landgraf, R., & Engelmann, M. (1999). Vasopressin released within the septal brain area during swim stress modulates the behavioural stress response in rats. *European Journal of Neuroscience, 11*, 997–1002.

Edelman, G. (1989). *The remembered present.* New York: Basic Books.

Edelman, G. M. (1992). *Bright air, brilliant fire: On the matter of mind.* New York: Basic Books.

Edelman, G. M., & Tononi, G. (2000). *A universe of consciousness: How matter becomes imagination.* New York: Basic Books.

Ehlers, A., & Clark, D. M. (2000). A cognitive model of posttraumatic stress disorder. *Behaviour Research and Therapy, 38*, 319–345.

Ehling, T., Nijenhuis, E. R. S., & Krikke, A. P. (2008). Volume of discrete brain structures in complex dissociative: Preliminary findings. In E. R. de Kloet, M. S. Oitzl, & E. Vermetten (Eds.), *Progress in brain research* (Vol. 167, pp. 301–310). Amsterdam: Elsevier.

Eisenberg, N., & Strayer, J. (1987). Critical issues in the study of empathy. In: N. Eisenberg, & J. Strayer (Eds.), *Empathy and its development* (pp. 3–13). New York: Cambridge University Press.

Eisenman, R. (1997). Denigration of a victim in individual psychotherapy by violent vs seductive child molesters. *Psychological Reports, 81*, 1276–1278.

El-Hage, W., Darves-Bornoz, J.-M., Allilaire, J.-F., & Gaillard, P. (2002). Posttraumatic somatoform dissociation in French psychiatric outpatients. *Journal of Trauma & Dissociation, 3*(3), 59–73.

Elklit, A. (1997). The aftermath of an industrial disaster. *Acta Psychiatrica Scandinavica, 96*, 1–25.

Ellason, J. W., & Ross, C. A. (1997). Two-year follow-up of inpatients with dissociative identity disorder. *American Journal of Psychiatry, 154*, 832–839.

Ellason, J. W., Ross, C. A., & Fuchs, D. L. (1995). Assessment of dissociative identity disorder with the Millon Clinical Multiaxial Inventory-II. *Psychological Reports, 76*, 895–905.

Ellenberger, H. F. (1970). *The discovery of the unconscious.* New York: Basic Books.

Ellis, P. S. (1997). The pathology of fatal child abuse. *Pathology, 29*, 113–121.

Eluvathingal, T. J., Chugani, H. T., Behen, M. E., Juhasz, C., Muzik, O., Maqbool, M., . . . Makki, M. (2006).

Abnormal brain connectivity in children after early severe socioemotional deprivation: A diffusion tensor imaging study. *Pediatrics, 117*, 2093–2100.

Ely, F. A. (1903). Traumatic neuroses. *Medical Age, 21*, 928.

Elzinga, B. M., Phaf, R. H., Ardon, A. M., & Van Dyck, R. (2003). Directed forgetting between, but not within, dissociative personality states. *Journal of Abnormal Psychology, 112*, 237–243.

Engel, G. L. (1977). The need for a new medical model: A challenge for biomedicine. *Science, 196*, 129–136.

Engel, G. L. (1997). From biomedical to biopsychosocial: Being scientific in the human domain. *Psychotherapy & Psychosomatics, 66*, 57–62.

Erichsen, J. E. (1866). *On railway and other injuries of the nervous system.* London: Walton & Maberly.

Erichsen, J. E. (1875). *On concussion of the spine, nervous shock, and other obscure injuries of the nervous system in their classical clinical and medico-legal aspects.* London: Longmans Green.

Amaral do Espirito-Santo, H. M., & Pio-Abreu, J. L. (2007). Dissociative disorders and other psychopathological groups: Exploring the differences through the Somatoform Dissociation Questionnaire (SDQ-20). *Revista Brasileira de Psiquiatria, 29*, 354–358.

Etkin, A., Egner, T., & Kalisch, R. (2011). Emotional processing in anterior cingulate and medial prefrontal cortex. *Trends in Cognitive Science, 15*, 85–93.

Eugenides, J. (2002). *Middlesex.* New York: St. Martin.

Eulenburg, A. (1878). *Lehrbuch der Nervenkrankheiten, Bde. 1, 2* [Textbook of nervous diseases, Vols. 1, 2]. Berlin: August Hirschwald.

Eysenck, H. J. (1990). Genetic and environmental contributions to individual differences: The three major dimensions of personality. *Journal of Personality, 58I*, 245–261.

Falcon, A. (2008). Aristotle on causality. In *Stanford Encyclopedia of Philosophy*. Retrieved from http://plato.stanford.edu/entries/aristotle-causality

Fang, X., Brown, D. S., Florence, C. S., & Mercy, J. A. (2012). The economic burden of child maltreatment in the United States and implications for prevention. *Child Abuse and Neglect, 36*, 156–165.

Fanselow, M. S., & Lester, L. S. (1988). A functional behavioristic approach to aversively motivated behavior: Predatory imminence as a determinant of the topography of defensive behavior. In R. S. Bolles & M. D. Beecher (Eds.), *Evolution and learning* (pp. 185–212). Hillsdale, NJ: Erlbaum.

Farina, B., Ceccarelli, M., & Di Gionnantonio, M. (2005). Henri Ey's Neojacksonism and the psychopathology of the disintegrated mind. *Psychopathology, 38*, 285–290.

Farina, B., Mazzotti, E., Pasquini, P., & Mantione, M. G. (2011a). Somatoform and psychoform dissociation among women with orgasmic and sexual pain disorders. *Journal of Trauma & Dissociation, 12*, 526–534.

Farina, B., Mazzotti, E., Pasquini, P., Nijenhuis, E., & Di Giannantonio, M. (2011b). Somatoform and psychoform dissociation among students. *Journal of Clinical Psychology, 67*, 665–672.

Farrington, D. P. (1997). The relationship between low resting heart rate and violence. In A. Raine, P. A. Brennan, D. P. Farrington, & S. A. Mednick (Eds.), *Biosocial bases of violence* (3rd ed., pp. 89–106). New York: Plenum.

Fattah, K. N., & Kabir, Z. N. (2013). No place is safe: Sexual abuse of children in rural Bangladesh. *Journal of Child Sexual Abuse, 22*, 901–914.

Feeny, N. C., Zoellner, L. A., Fitzgibbons, L. A., & Foa, E. B. (2000). Exploring the roles of emotional numbing, depression, and dissociation in PTSD. *Journal of Traumatic Stress, 13*, 489–498.

Felitti, V. J., & Anda, R. F. (2009). The relationship of adverse childhood experiences to adult medical disease: Implications for healthcare. In R. Lanius & E. Vermetten (Eds.), *The hidden epidemic: The impact of early life trauma on health and disease* (pp. 77–87). Cambridge: Cambridge University Press.

Felmingham, K., Kemp, A. H., Williams, L., Falconer, E., Olivieri, G., Peduto, A., & Bryant, R. (2008). Dissociative responses to conscious and non-conscious fear impact underlying brain function in post-traumatic stress disorder. *Psychological Medicine, 38*, 1771–1780.

Fendt, M., & Fanselow, M. S. (1999). The neuroanatomical and neurochemical basis of conditioned fear. *Neuroscience and Biobehavioral Reviews, 23*, 743–760.

Ferenczi, S. (1919). Die Psychoanalyse der Kriegsneurosen [The psychoanalysis of war neuroses]. In S. Freud, S. Ferenczi, K. Abraham, & E. Simmel (Eds.), *Zur Psychoanalyse der Kriegsneurosen* [On psychoanalysis of war neuroses] (pp. 9–30). Leipzig and Vienna: Internationaler Psychoanalytischer Verlag.

Ferenczi, S. (1929). *Final contributions to the problems and methods of psycho-analysis.* London: H. Karnac Books.

Ferenczi, S. (1932, September). *Sprachverwirrung zwischen den Erwachsenen und dem Kind: Die Sprache der Zärtlichkeit und der Leidenschaft* [Confusion of tongues between adults and the child: The language of tenderness and of passion]. Presented at the XXII. Internationalen Psychoanalytischen Kongress. Wiesbaden. In *Schriften zur Psychoanalyse* [Texts on psychoanalysis]. Auswahl in Zwei Bänden. Frankfurt/M.: Fischer Taschenbuch Verlag, 1982, pp. 303–313.

Ferenczi, S. (1933). Sprachverwirrung zwischen den Erwachsenen und dem Kind (Die Sprache der Zärtlichkeit und der Leidenschaft) [Confusion of tongues between adults and the child: The language of tenderness and of passion]. *Internationale Zeitschrift für Psychoanalyse, XIX Band*, Heft 1/2, S. 5–15. In *Selected Writings* (1999, pp. 293–303). London: Penguin.

Ferenczi, S. (1949). Confusion of the tongues between the adults and the children. *International Journal of Psycho-Analysis, 30*, 225–230.

Ferreira, M. D., & Menescal-de-Oliveira, L. (2009). Role of dorsal raphe nucleus 5-HT(1A) and 5-HT(2) receptors in tonic immobility modulation in guinea pigs. *Brain Research, 1285*, 69–76.

Ferreira, M. D., & Menescal-de-Oliveira, L. (2012). Opioidergic, GABAergic, and serotonergic neurotransmission in the dorsal raphe nucleus modulates tonic immobility in guinea pigs. *Physiology and Behavior, 106*, 109–116.

Field, T. M. (1985). Attachment as psychobiological attunement: Being on the same wavelength. In M. Reite & T. M. Fields (Eds.), *The psychobiology of attachment and separation* (pp. 415–454). Orlando, FL: Academic Press.

Fink, D. (1991). The comorbidity of multiple personality disorder and DSM-III-R axis II disorders. *Psychiatric Clinics of North America, 14*, 547–566.

Fink, G. (2011). Stress controversies: Post-traumatic stress disorder, hippocampal volume, gastroduodenal ulceration. *Journal of Neuroendocrinology, 23*, 107–117.

Fink, G. R., Markowitsch, H. J., Reinkemeier, M., Bruckbauer, T., Kessler, J., & Heiss, W. D., (1996). Cerebral representation of one's own past: Neural networks involved in autobiographical memory. *Journal of Neuroscience, 16*, 4275–4282.

Firestone, P., Dixon, K. L., Nunes, K. L., & Bradford, J. M. (2005). A comparison of incest offenders based on victim age. *Journal of the American Academy of Psychiatry and Law, 33*, 223–232.

Fischer-Homburger, E. (1975). *Die traumatische Neurose: Vom somatischen zum sozialen Leiden* [Traumatic neurosis: From somatic to social suffering]. Bern: Huber.

Fischer-Homburger, E. (1999). Zur Medizingeschichte des Traumas [Toward a medical history of trauma]. *Gesnerus, 56*, 260–294.

Fiszman, A., Mendlowicz, M. V., Marques-Portella, C., Volchan, E., Coutinho, E. S., Souza, W. F., ... Figueira, I. (2008). Peritraumatic tonic immobility predicts a poor response to pharmacological treatment in victims of urban violence with PTSD. *Journal of Affective Disorders, 107*, 193–197.

Flannelly, K. J., Koenig, H. G., Galek, K., & Ellison, C. G. (2007). Beliefs, mental health, and evolutionary threat assessment systems in the brain. *Journal of Nervous and Mental Disease, 195*, 996–1003.

Florence, C., Brown, D. S., Fang, X., & Thompson, H. F. (2013). Health care costs associated with child maltreatment: Impact on medicaid. *Pediatrics, 132*, 312–318.

Flynn, E. G., Laland, K. N., Kendal, R. L., & Kendal, J. R. (2013). Target article with commentaries: Developmental niche construction. *Developmental Sciences, 16*, 296–313.

Foote, B., Smolin, Y., Kaplan, M., Legatt, M. E., & Lipschitz, D. (2006). Prevalence of dissociative disorders in psychiatric outpatients. *American Journal of Psychiatry, 163*, 623–629.

Foote, B., Smolin, Y., Neft, D. I., & Lipschitz, D. (2008). Dissociative disorders and suicidality in psychiatric outpatients. *Journal of Nervous and Mental Disease, 196*, 29–36.

Ford, J. D., Connor, D. F., & Hawke, J. (2009). Complex trauma among psychiatrically impaired children: A cross-sectional, chart-review study. *Journal of Clinical Psychiatry, 70*, 1155–1163.

Ford, J. D., & Courtois, C. A. (2009). Defining and understanding complex trauma and complex traumatic stress disorders. In C. A. Courtois & J. D. Ford (Eds.), *Treating complex traumatic stress disorders: An evidence-based guide* (pp. 13–31). New York: Guilford.

Ford, J. D., Courtois, C. A., Steele, K., Van der Hart, O., & Nijenhuis, E. R. S. (2005). Treatment of complex posttraumatic self-dysregulation. *Journal of Traumatic Stress, 18*, 437–447.

Fox, M. D., Snyder, A. Z., Vincent, J. L., Corbetta, M., Van Essen, D. C., & Raichle, M. E. (2005). The human brain is intrinsically organized into dynamic, anticorrelated functional networks. *Proceedings of the National Academy of Sciences USA, 102*, 9673–9678.

Fransson, P. (2005). Spontaneous low-frequency BOLD signal fluctuations: An fMRI investigation of the resting-state default mode of brain function hypothesis. *Human Brain Mapping, 26*, 15–29.

Fraser, G. A. (2005). Re: The persistence of folly: A critical examination of dissociative identity disorder. *Canadian Journal of Psychiatry, 50*, 814.

Freedman, A. M., Kaplan, H. I., & Sadock, B. J. (1975). *Comprehensive textbook of psychiatry* (2nd ed.). Baltimore: Williams and Wilkins.

Freud, S. (1895/1962). Entwurf einer Psychologie [Design of a psychology]. In *Aus der Anfängen der Psychoanalyse 1887–1902: Briefe an Wilhelm Fliess* [From the beginnings of psychoanalysis 1887–1902: Letters to Wilhelm Fliess]. Frankfurt/M: S. Fisher Verlag.

Freud, S. (1905/1958). Remembering, repeating, and working through (further recommendations on the technique of psycho-analysis II). *The standard edition of the complete psychological works of Sigmund Freud, Volume 12*. London: Hogarth.

Freud, S. (1919/1954). *Introduction to psychoanalysis and the war neuroses. Standard Edition, Vol. 17* (transl. and ed. by J. Strachey). London: Hogarth Press.

Freud, S. (1928/1956). *Beyond the pleasure principle.* New York: Liveright.

Freud, S. (1933/1960). New introductory lessons on psychoanalysis and other works. *Standard edition, Volume 22* (transl. by J. Stracey). London: The Hogarth Press.

Frewen, P. A., & Lanius, R. A. (2006). Toward a psychobiology of posttraumatic self-dysregulation: Reexperiencing, hyperarousal, dissociation, and emotional numbing. *Annals of the New York Academy of Science, 1071*, 110–124.

Frewen, P. A., Pain, C., Dozois, D. J., & Lanius, R. A. (2006). Alexithymia in PTSD: Psychometric and FMRI studies. *Annals of the New York Academy of Sciences, 1071*, 397–400.

Freyd, J. J. (1996). *Betrayal trauma: The logic of forgetting childhood trauma.* Cambridge, MA: Harvard University Press.

Freyd, J. J. (2008). Betrayal trauma. In G. Reyes, J. D. Elhai, & J. D. Ford (Eds), *Encyclopedia of psychological trauma* (p. 76). New York: Wiley.

Freyd, J. J., & Birrell, P. J. (2013). *Blind to betrayal: Why we fool ourselves. We aren't being fooled.* Hoboken, NJ: Wiley.

Freyd, J. J., DePrince, A. P., & Gleaves, D. (2007). The state of betrayal trauma theory. Reply to McNally (2007): Conceptual issues and future directions. *Memory, 15*, 295–311.

Freyd, J. J., Putnam, F. W., Lyon, T. D., Becker-Blease, K. A., Cheit, R. E., Siegel, N. B., & Pezdek, K. (2005). Psychology: The science of child sexual abuse. *Science, 308*(5721), 501.

Friedman, M. J., Resick, P. A., Bryant, R. A., Strain, J., Horowitz, M., & Spiegel, D. (2011). Classification of trauma and stressor-related disorders in DSM-5. *Depression and Anxiety, 28*, 737–749.

Friedman, S. B., Mason, J. W., & Hamburg, D. A. (1963). Urinary 17-hydroxycorticoisteroid levels in parents of children with neoplastic disease. *Psychosomatic Medicine, 25*, 364–376.

Friedrich, W. N., Gerber, P. N., Koplin, B., Davis, M., Giese, J., Mykelbust, C., & Franckowiak, D. (2001). Multimodal assessment of dissociation in adolescents: Inpatients and juvenile sex offenders. *Sexual Abuse, 13*, 167–177.

Frischholz, E. J., Braun, B. G., Sachs, R. G., Hopkins, L., Shaeffer, D. M., Lewis, J., . . . Schwartz, D. R. (1990). The Dissociative Experiences Scale: Further replication and validation. *Dissociation: Progress in the Dissociative Disorders, 3*, 151–153.

Friston, K. J., Rotshtein, P., Geng, J. J., Sterzer, P., & Henson, R. N. (2006). A critique of functional localisers. *Neuroimage, 30*, 1077–1087.

Fryers, T., & Brugha, T. (2013). Childhood determinants of adult psychiatric disorder. *Clinical Practice & Epidemiology in Mental Health, 9*, 1–50.

Fuchs, T. (2008). *Leib und Lebenswelt: Neue philosophisch-psychiatrische Essays* [Body and life-world: New philosophical-psychiatric essays]. Kusterdingen: Die Graue Edition.

Fuchs, T. (2010). *Das Gehirn–ein Beziehungsorgan: Eine phänomenologisch-ökologische Konzeption* (3. aktual. und erw. Auflage) [The brain–a relational organ: A phenomenological-ecological conception. 3rd updated and extended edition]. Stuttgart: Kohlhammer.

Fuchs, T., & DeJaeger, H. (2010). Non-representational subjectivity. In T. Fuchs, H. C. Sattel, & P. Henningsen (Eds.), *The embodied self: Dimensions, coherence and disorders* (pp. 203–214). Stuttgart: Schattauer.

Fusar-Poli, P., Placentino, A., Carletti, F., Landi, P., Allen, P., Surguladze, S., . . . Politi, P. (2009). Functional atlas of emotional faces processing: A voxel-based meta-analysis of 105 functional magnetic resonance imaging studies. *Journal of Psychiatry and Neuroscience, 34*, 418–432.

Fuster, J. M. (2003). *Cortex and mind: Unifying cognition*. New York: Oxford University Press.

Galbraith, P. M., & Neubauer, P. J. (2000). Underwriting considerations for dissociative disorders. *Journal of Insurance Medicine, 32*, 71–78.

Gallagher, S. (2005). *How the body shapes the mind.* Oxford: Oxford University Press.

Gallagher, S. (2005). Metzinger's matrix: Living the virtual life with a real body. *Psyche, 11*(5), 1–9.

Gallagher, S., & Zahavi, D. (2008). *The phenomenological mind: An introduction to philosophy of mind and cognitive science.* London/New York: Routledge.

Gallese, V. (2007). Before and below 'theory of mind': Embodied simulation and the neural correlates of social cognition. *Philosophical Transactions of the Royal Society of London, Series B, Biological Sciences, 362*, 659–669.

Gallese, V., Keysers, C., & Rizzolatti, G. (2004). A unifying view of the basis of social cognition. *Trends in Cognitive Sciences, 8*, 396–403.

Garcia, J. (1981). Tilting at the paper mills of academia. *American Psychologist, 36*, 149–158.

Garcia, J., Kimeldorf, D. J., & Koelling, R. A. (1955). Conditioned taste aversion to saccharin resulting from exposure to gamma radiation. *Science, 122*(3160), 157–158.

Garcia, J., Lasiter, P. S., Bermudez-Rattoni, F., & Deems, D. A. (1985). A general theory of aversion learning. *Annals of the New York Academy of Science, 443*, 8–21.

Gaupp, R. (1911). Über den Begriff der Hysterie [On the concept of hysteria]. *Zeitschrift für die gesamte Neurologie und Psychiatrie, 5*, 458.

Gaupp, R. (1918). Krieg und Seelenleben [War and the life of the soul]. *Deutsche Revue, 43*, 162–178.

Gelernter, J., Kranzler, H., & Lacobelle, J. (1998). Population studies of polymorphisms at loci of neuropsychiatric interest (tryptophan hydroxylase (TPH), dopamine transporter protein (SLC6A3), D3 dopamine receptor (DRD3), apolipoprotein E (APOE), mu opioid receptor (OPRM1), and ciliary neurotrophic factor (CNTF)). *Genomics, 52*, 289–297.

Georgiou, G. A., Bleakley, C., Hayward, J., Russo, R., Dutton, K., Eltiti, S., & Fox, E. (2005). Focusing on fear: Attentional disengagement from emotional faces. *Vision Cognition, 12*(1), 145–158.

Geraerts, E., Merckelbach, H., Jelicic, M., Smeets, E., & Van Heerden, J. (2006). Dissociative symptoms and how they relate to fantasy proneness in women reporting repressed or recovered memories. *Personality and Individual Differences, 40*, 1143–1151.

Geraerts, E., Schooler, J. W., Merckelbach, H., Jelicic, M., Hauer, B. J. A., & Ambadar, Z. (2007). The reality of recovered memories: Corroborating continuous and discontinuous memories of childhood sexual abuse. *Psychological Science, 18*, 564 –568.

Geraerts, E., McNally, R. J., Jelicic, M., Merckelbach, H., & Raymaekers, L. (2008). Linking thought suppression and recovered memories of childhood sexual abuse. *Memory, 16*, 22–28.

Gerardi, R., Keane, T. M., & Penk, W. (1989). Utility: Sensitivity and specificity in developing diagnostic tests of combat-related post-traumatic stress disorder (PTSD). *Journal of Clinical Psychology, 45*, 691–703.

Gerrits, M., Westenbroek, C., Fokkema, D. S., Jongsma, M. E., Den Boer, J. A., & Ter Horst, G. (2003). Increased stress vulnerability after a prefrontal cortex lesion in female rats. *Brain Research Bulletin, 61*, 627–635.

Ghin, M. (2005). What a self could be. *Psyche, 11*(5), 1–10.

Gibbs, R. W. (2005). *Embodiment and cognitive science.* New York: Cambridge University Press.

Gibson, J. J. (1977). The theory of affordances. In R. Shaw & J. Bransford (Eds.), *Perceiving, acting and knowing* (pp. 67–82). Hillsdale, NJ: Erlbaum.

Gibson, J. J. (1979). *The ecological approach to visual perception.* New York: Houghton Mifflin.

Giesbrecht, T., Lynn, S. J., Lilienfeld, S. O., & Merckelbach, H. (2008). Cognitive processes in dissociation: An analysis of core theoretical assumptions. *Psychological Bulletin, 134*, 617–647.

Giesbrecht, T., Lynn, S. J., Lilienfeld, S. O., & Merckelbach, H. (2010). Cognitive processes, trauma, and dissociation–misconceptions and misrepresentations: Reply to Bremner (2010). *Psychological Bulletin, 136*, 7–11.

Giesbrecht, T., & Merckelbach, H. (2006). Dreaming to reduce fantasy? Fantasy proneness, dissociation, and subjective sleep experiences. *Personality and Individual Differences, 41*, 697–706.

Giesbrecht, T., Merckelbach, H., Kater, M., & Sluis, A. F. (2007). Why dissociation and schizotypy overlap: The joint influence of fantasy proneness, cognitive failures, and childhood trauma. *Journal of Nervous and Mental Disease, 195*, 812–818.

Gigerenzer, G., & Goldstein, D. G. (1996). Reasoning the fast and frugal way: Models of bounded rationality. *Psychological Review, 103*, 650–669.

Gilbertson, M. W., Shenton, M. E., Ciszewski, A., Kasai, K., Lasko, N. B., Orr, S. P., & Pitman, R. K. (2002). Smaller hippocampal volume predicts pathologic vulnerability to psychological trauma. *Nature Neuroscience, 5*, 1242–1247.

Gillespie, C. F., Phifer, J., Bradley, B., & Ressler, K. J. (2009). Risk and resilience: Genetic and environmental influences on development of the stress response. *Depression and Anxiety, 26*, 984–992.

Glas, J. (2012). *Dubbel glas: Alle gedichten.* [Double glazing: All poems.] Groningen, The Netherlands: Uitgeverij kleine Uil.

Glaser, B. (1998). Psychiatry and paedophilia: A major public health issue. *Australian and New Zealand Journal of Psychiatry, 32*, 162–167.

Glasser, M., Kolvin, I., Campbell, D., Glasser, A., Leitch, I., & Farrelly, S. (2001). Cycle of child sexual abuse:

Links between being a victim and becoming a perpetrator. *British Journal of Psychiatry, 179*, 482–494, 495–487.

Gleaves, D. H. (1996). The sociocognitive model of dissociative identity disorder: A re-examination of the evidence. *Psychological Bulletin, 120*, 42–59.

Goethe, J. W. von (1808/1959). *Faust* (transl. J. Shawcross). London: Allan Wingate.

Goldsmith, R. E., Freyd, J. J., & DePrince, A. P. (2011). Betrayal trauma: Associations with psychological and physical symptoms in young adults. *Journal of Interpersonal Violence, 27*, 547–567.

Goldstein, L. H., Drew, C., Mellers, J., Mitchell-O'Malley, S., & Oakley, D. A. (2000). Dissociation, hypnotizability, coping styles and health locus of control: Characteristics of pseudoseizure patients. *Seizure, 9*, 314–322.

Golub, Y., Kaltwasser, S. F., Mauch, C. P., Herrmann, L., Schmidt, U., Holsboer, F., . . . Wotjak, C. T. (2010). Reduced hippocampus volume in the mouse model of posttraumatic stress disorder. *Journal of Psychiatric Research, 45*, 650–659.

Gonen, T., Admon, R., Podlipsky, I., & Hendler, T. (2012). From animal model to human brain networking: Dynamic causal modeling of motivational systems. *Journal of Neuroscience, 32*, 7218–7224.

Goodman, M. (2012). Complex PTSD is on the trauma spectrum: Comment on Resick et al. (2012). *Journal of Traumatic Stress, 25*, 254–255, 260–253.

Gorno-Tempini, M. L., Pradelli, S., Serafini, M., Pagnoni, G., Baraldi, P., Porro, C., . . . Nichelli, P. (2001). Explicit and incidental facial expression processing: An fMRI study. *Neuroimage, 14*, 465–473.

Gosling, F. G. (1987). *Before Freud: Neurasthenia and the American Medical Community 1870–1910*. Urbana: University of Illinois Press.

Graham, G., Horgan, T., & Tienson, J. (2009). Phenomenology, intentionality, and the unity of mind. In A. Beckermann & B. McLaughlin (Eds.), *Oxford handbook of philosophy of mind* (pp. 512–540). Oxford: Oxford University Press.

Graham, N., Kimonis, E. R., Wasserman, A. L., & Kline, S. M. (2012). Associations among childhood abuse and psychopathy facets in male sexual offenders. *Personal Disorders, 3*(1), 66–75.

Greene, B. (1999). *The elegant universe*. New York: Vintage.

Greene, B. (2004). *The fabric of the cosmos: Space, time and the texture of reality*. New York: Knopf.

Greicius, M. D., Krasnow, B., Reiss, A. L., & Menon, V. (2003). Functional connectivity in the resting brain: a network analysis of the default mode hypothesis. *Proceedings of the National Academy of Sciences USA, 100*, 253–258.

Greicius, M. D., & Menon, V. (2004). Default-mode activity during a passive sensory task: Uncoupled from deactivation but impacting activation. *Journal of Cognitive Neuroscience, 16*, 1484–1492.

Gretton, H. M., & Clift, R. J. (2011). The mental health needs of incarcerated youth in British Columbia, Canada. *International Journal of Law and Psychiatry, 34*, 109–115.

Griffin, M. G., Resick, P. A., & Mechanic, M. B. (1997). Objective assessment of peritraumatic dissociation: Psychophysiological indicators. *American Journal of Psychiatry, 154*, 1081–1088.

Grinker, R. R., & Spiegel, J. P. (1945). *Men under stress*. Philadelphia: Blakiston.

Gudjonsson, G. H. (Ed.). (2003). *The psychology of interrogations and confessions: A handbook*. West Sussex, UK: Wiley.

Gusnard, D. A., Akbudak, E., Shulman, G. L., & Raichle, M. E. (2001). Medial prefrontal cortex and self-referential mental activity: Relation to a default mode of brain function. *Proceedings of the National Academy of Sciences USA, 98*, 4259–4264.

Gusnard, D. A., & Raichle, M. E. (2001). Searching for a baseline: Functional imaging and the resting human brain. *Natural Review of Neuroscience, 2*, 685–694.

Gutner, C. A., Pineles, S. L., Griffin, M. G., Bauer, M. R., Weierich, M. R., & Resick, P. A. (2011). Physiological predictors of posttraumatic stress disorder. *Journal of Traumatic Stress, 23*, 775–784.

Hacking, I. (1995). *Rewriting the soul: Multiple personalities and the sciences of memory.* Princeton: Princeton University Press.

Hacking, I. (2002), *Mad travelers: Reflections on the reality of transient mental illness.* Cambridge, MA: Harvard University Press.

Hajcak, G., Molnar, C., George, M. S., Bolger, K., Koola, J., & Nahas, Z. (2007). Emotion facilitates action: A transcranial magnetic stimulation study of motor cortex excitability during picture viewing. *Psychophysiology, 44*, 91–97.

Haller, J., Albert, I., & Makara, G. B. (1997). The effects of the alpha 2 adrenoceptor blocker idazoxan on defeat-induced immobility and plasma corticosterone in rats is antagonized by administration of adrenocorticotrophin-antiserum. *Behavioural Pharmacology, 8*, 269–273.

Hanson, J. L., Chung, M. K., Avants, B. B., Shirtcliff, E. A., Gee, J. C., Davidson, R. J., & Pollak, S. D. (2010). Early stress is associated with alterations in the orbitofrontal cortex: A tensor-based morphometry investigation of brain structure and behavioral risk. *Journal of Neuroscience, 30*, 7466–7472.

Hariri, A. R., Mattay, V. S., Tessitore, A., Kolachana, B., Fera, F., Goldman, D., . . . Weinberger, D. R. (2002). Serotonin transporter genetic variation and the response of the human amygdala. *Science, 297*, 400–403.

Harman, G. (2011). Cosmos and history. *The Journal of Natural and Social Philosophy*, *7*(1), 7–36.

Harrington, R. (1994). The neuroses of the railway. *History Today, 44*, 15–21.

Harrington, R. (2010). The railway accident: Trains, trauma, and technological crises in nineteenth-century Britain. In M. S. Micale & P. Lerner (Eds.), *Traumatic pasts: History, psychiatry, and trauma in the modern age, 1870–1930* (pp. 31–56). Cambridge: Cambridge University Press.

Hart, B. (1926). The conception of dissociation. *British Journal of Medical Psychology, 6*, 241–257.

Hart, H., & Rubia, K. (2012). Neuroimaging of child abuse: A critical review. *Frontiers of Human Neuroscience, 6*, 52.

Hassabis, D., Kumaran, D., Vann, S. D., & Maguire, E. A. (2007). Patients with hippocampal amnesia cannot imagine new experiences. *Proceedings of the National Academy of Sciences USA, 104*, 1726–1731.

Hassabis, D., & Maguire, E. A. (2007). Deconstructing episodic memory with construction. *Trends in Cognitive Science, 11*, 299–306.

Hassabis, D., & Maguire, E. A. (2009). The construction system of the brain. *Philosophical Transactions of the Royal Society of London. Series B: Biological Sciences, 364*, 1263–1271.

Hauschildt, M., Peters, M. J., Jelinek, L., & Moritz, S. (2011). Veridical and false memory for scenic material in posttraumatic stress disorder. *Consciousness and Cognition, 21*, 80–89.

Haxby, J. V., Hoffman, E. A., & Gobbini, M. I. (2000). The distributed human neural system for face perception. *Trends in Cognitive Science, 4*, 223–233.

Hayes, S. C., Wilson, K. G., Gilford, E. V., Follette, V. M., & Strosahl, K. (1996). Experiential avoidance and behavioral disorders: A functional dimensional approach to diagnosis and treatment. *Journal of Consulting and Clinical Psychology, 64*, 1152–1168.

Heiberg, P. A., & Kuhr, V. (Eds.). (1909). *Søren Kierkegaards papirer* [The papers of Søren Kierkegaard]. Volume 11, part 1, sect. 352. (Reprint: *In The Last Years: Journals 1853–55*, edited and translated by Ronald G. Smith (1965).

Heidegger, M. (1986). *Sein und Zeit.* Tübingen: Max Niedermeyer. (engl. *Being and time,* transl. J. Stambaugh, 1996). Albany: SUNY.

Heil, J. (1978). Traces of things past. *Philosophy of Science 45*, 60–67.

Heil, J. (2011). Language and thought. In B. P. McLaughlin, A. Beckermann, & S. Walter (Eds.), *The Oxford handbook of philosophy of mind* (pp. 631–647). Oxford: Oxford University Press.

Hengartner, M. P., Ajdacic-Gross, V., Rodgers, S., Muller, M., & Rossler, W. (2013). Childhood adversity in association with personality disorder dimensions: New findings in an old debate. *European Psychiatry, 28*, 476–482.

Henke, K., Landis, T., & Markowitsch, H. J. (1994). Subliminal perception of words and faces. *International Journal of Neuroscience, 75*, 181–187.

Herman, J. L. (1992). *Trauma and recovery.* New York: Basic Books.

Herman, J. (2012). CPTSD is a distinct entity: Comment on Resick et al. (2012). *Journal of Traumatic Stress, 25*, 256–257, 260–253.

Hermans, E. J., Nijenhuis, E. R. S., Van Honk, J., Huntjens, R. J. C., & Van der Hart, O. (2006). Identity state-dependent attentional bias for facial threat in dissociative identity disorder. *Psychiatry Research 141*, 233–236.

Heron-Delaney, M., Kenardy, J., Charlton, E., & Matsuoka, Y. (2013). A systematic review of predictors of posttraumatic stress disorder (PTSD) for adult road traffic crash survivors. *Injury, 44*, 1413–1422.

Heyes, C. (2003). Four routes to cognitive evolution. *Psychological Review, 110*, 713–727.

Hilgard, J. R. (1970). *Personality and hypnosis: A study of imaginative involvement.* Chicago: University of Chicago Press.

Himma, K. E. (2005). The problem of explaining phenomenal selfhood: A comment on Thomas Metzinger's self-model theory of subjectivity. *Psyche, 11*(5), 1–19.

Hirakata, P. (2009). Narratives of dissociation: Insights into the treatment of dissociation in individuals who were sexually abused as children. *Journal of Trauma & Dissociation, 10*, 297–314.

Hobson, A. (2005). Finally some one: Reflections on Thomas Metzinger's *Being no one. Psyche, 11*(5), 1–8.

Hofer, J. (1678). *Nostalgia: Heimwehe oder Heimsehnsucht* [Nostalgia: Homesickness or longing for home]. Basel.

Hofstee, W.K. B. (1980). *De empirische discussie: Theorie van sociaal-wetenschappelijk Onderzoek* [The empirical discussion: Theory of social-scientific research]. Meppel: Boom.

Hofstee, W. K., De Raad, B., & Goldberg, L. R. (1992). Integration of the big five and circumplex approaches to trait structure. *Journal of Personality and Social Psychology, 63*, 146–163.

Holland, P. C., & Bouton, M. E. (1999). Hippocampus and context in classical conditioning. *Current Opinions in Neurobiology, 9*, 195–202.

Hollender, M. H., & Hirsch, S. J. (1964). Hysterical psychosis. *American Journal of Psychiatry, 120*, 1066–1074.

Holmes, E., Brown, R. J., Mansell, W., Fearon, R. P., Hunter, E., Frasquilho, F., & Oakley, D. A. (2005). Are there two qualitatively distinct forms of dissociation? A review and some clinical implications. *Clinical Psychology Review, 25*, 1–23.

Holt, S., Buckley, H., & Whelan, S. (2008). The impact of exposure to domestic violence on children and young people: A review of the literature. *Child Abuse and Neglect, 32*, 797–810.

Hopper, J. W., Frewen, P. A., Van der Kolk, B. A., & Lanius, R. A. (2007). Neural correlates of reexperiencing, avoidance, and dissociation in PTSD: Symptom dimensions and emotion dysregulation in responses to script-driven trauma imagery. *Journal of Traumatic Stress, 20*, 713–725.

Hornstein, N. L., & Putnam, F. W. (1992). Clinical phenomenology of child and adolescent disorders. *Journal of the American Academy of Child and Adolescent Psychiatry, 31*, 1077–1085.

Horowitz, M. J. (1976). *Stress response syndromes.* New York: Aronson.

Horowitz, M. J. (1988). *Introduction to psychodynamics: A new synthesis.* New York: Basic Books.

Horselenberg, R., Merckelbach, H., Muris, P., Rassin, E., Sijsenaar, M., & Spaan, V. (2000). Imagining fictitious childhood events: The role of individual differences in imagination inflation. *Clinical Psychology & Psychotherapy, 7*, 128–137.

Hovens, H. (2007). Psychopathologische gevolgen van trauma en comorbiditeit [Psychopathological sequelae of trauma and comorbidity]. In P. G. H. Aarts & W. D. Visser (Eds.), *Trauma: Diagnostiek en behandeling* (2nd rev. ed., pp. 91–105). Houten: Bohn Stafleu Van Loghum.

Howell, E. F. (2005). *The dissociative mind.* Hillsdale, NJ: The Analytic Press.

Huang, H., Gundapuneedi, T., & Rao, U. (2012). White matter disruptions in adolescents exposed to childhood maltreatment and vulnerability to psychopathology. *Neuropsychopharmacology, 37*, 2693–2701.

Huang, T. Y., & Lin, C. H. (2006). Role of amygdala MAPK activation on immobility behavior of forced swim rats. *Behavioral Brain Research, 173*(1), 104–111.

Hughes, J. R., Kuhlman, D. T., Fichtner, C. G., & Gruenfeld, M. J. (1990). Brain mapping in a case of multiple personality. *Clinical Electroencephalography, 21*, 200–209.

Hulme, P. A., & Middleton, M. R. (2013). Psychosocial and developmental characteristics of civilly committed sex offenders. *Issues in Mental Health Nursing, 34*, 141–149.

Huntjens, R. J. C., Peters, M. L., Postma, A., Woertman, L., Effting, M., & Van der Hart, O. (2005). Transfer of newly acquired stimulus valence between identities in dissociative identity disorder (DID). *Behaviour Research and Therapy, 43*, 243–255.

Huntjens, R. J. C., Peters, M. L., Woertman, L., Bovenschen, L. M., Martin, R. C., & Postma, A. (2006). Inter-identity amnesia in dissociative identity disorder: A simulated memory impairment? *Psychological Medicine, 36*, 857–863.

Huntjens, R. J. C., Peters, M. L., Woertman, L., Van der Hart, O., & Postma, A. (2007). Memory transfer for emotionally valenced words between identities in dissociative identity disorder. *Behaviour Research and Therapy, 45*, 775–789.

Huntjens, R. J. C., Postma, A., Hamaker, E. L., Woertman, L., Van der Hart, O., & Peters, M. (2002). Perceptual and conceptual priming in patients with dissociative identity disorder. *Memory and Cognition, 30*, 1033–1043.

Huntjens, R. J. C., Postma, A., Peters, M. L., Woertman, L., & Van der Hart, O. (2003). Interidentity amnesia for neutral, episodic information in dissociative identity disorder. *Journal of Abnormal Psychology, 112*, 290–297.

Huntjens, R. J. C., Postma, A., Woertman, L., Van der Hart, O., & Peters, M. L. (2005). Procedural memory in dissociative identity disorder: When can inter-identity amnesia be truly established? *Consciousness and Cognition, 14*, 377–389.

Huntjens, R. J. C., Verschuere, B., & McNally, R. J. (2012). Inter-identity autobiographical amnesia in patients with dissociative identity disorder. *PLoS One, 7*(7), e40580.

Hurley, S. L., (1998). *Consciousness in action.* London: Harvard University Press.

Hurley, S. L., & Noë, A. (2003). Neural plasticity and consciousness. *Biology and Philosophy, 18*, 131–168.

Husserl, E. (1970). *The crisis of European sciences and transcendental phenomenology: An introduction to phenomenological philosophy.* Evanston, IN: Northwestern University Press. (Posthumous German publication, *Die Krisis der europäischen Wissenschaften und die transzendentale Phänomenologie: Eine Einleitung in die phänomenologische Philosophie*, W. Biemel (Ed.) (1954). The Hague: Martinus Nijhoff).

Hut, P., & Shepard, R. (1996). Turning the hard problem upside down and sideways. *Journal of Consciousness Studies, 3*, 313–329.

Hutto, D. D. (2010). Radical enactivism and narrative practice. In T. Fuchs, H. C. Sattel, & P. Henningsen (Eds.), *The embodied self: Dimensions, coherence and disorders* (pp. 43–65). Stuttgart: Schattauer.

Hutto, D. D., & Myin, E. (2013). *Radicalizing enactivism: Basic minds without content.* Cambridge, MA: MIT.

Huxley, T. H. (1893/2011). On the hypothesis that animals are automata. In *Collected essays* (Vol. 1, pp. 199–250). Cambridge: Cambridge University Press.

Huxley, T. H., & Youmans, W. J. (1868). *The elements of physiology and hygiene: A text-book for educational instructions.* New York: D. Appleton & Co.

International Society for the Study of Dissociation, Chu, J. A., Loewenstein, R., Dell, P. F., Barach, P. M., Somer, E., Kluft, R. P., . . . Howell, E.]. (2005). Guidelines for treating Dissociative Identity Disorder in adults. *Journal of Trauma & Dissociation,* 6(4), 69–149. Retrieved from http://www.haworthpress.com/web/JTD.

International Society for the Study of Dissociation. (2011). Guidelines for treating dissociative identity disorder in adults, third revision. *Journal of Trauma & Dissociation, 12,* 115–187.

Ingemann-Hansen, O., Brink, O., Sabroe, S., Sorensen, V., & Charles, A. V. (2008). Legal aspects of sexual violence: Does forensic evidence make a difference? *Forensic Science International, 180,* 98–104.

Irle, E., Lange, C., Sachsse, U., & Weniger, G. (2009). Further evidence that post-traumatic stress disorder but not dissociative disorders are related to amygdala and hippocampal size reduction in trauma-exposed individuals. *Acta Psychiatrica Scandinavica, 119,* 330–331; discussion 331.

Israel, J. I. (2001). *Radical enlightenment: Philosophy and the making of modernity 1650–1750.* Oxford: Oxford University Press.

Jackson, J. H. (1958). Evolution and dissolution of the nervous system. In J. Taylor (Ed.), *Selected writings of John Hughlings Jackson* (pp. 45–118). London, Stapes.

Jackson, P. L., Meltzoff, A. N., & Decety, J. (2005). How do we perceive the pain of others? A window into the neural processes involved in empathy. *Neuroimage, 24,* 771–779.

Jackson, S. W. (1987). *Melancholia and depression.* New Haven, CN: Yale University Press.

Jackowski, A. P., Douglas-Palumberi, H., Jackowski, M., Win, L., Schultz, R. T., Staib, L. W., . . . Kaufmann, J. (2008). Corpus callosum in maltreated children with posttraumatic stress disorder: A diffusion tensor imaging study. *Psychiatry Research, 162,* 256–261.

Jackson, J. H. (1958). Evolution and dissolution of the nervous system. In J. Taylor (Ed.), *Selected writings of John Hughlings Jackson* (pp. 45–118). London: Stapes.

Jacobson, C. M., & Gould, M. (2007). The epidemiology and phenomenology of non-suicidal self-injurious behavior among adolescents: A critical review of the literature. *Archives of Suicide Research, 11,* 129–147.

James, W. (1890). *Principles of psychology. Volume I.* New York: Cosimo, 2007. Available at http://psychclassics.yorku.ca/James/Principles/index.htm

Janet, P. (1889). *L'automatisme psychologique: Essai de psychologie expérimentale sur les formes inférieures de l'activité humaine* [Psychological automatism: An experimental psychological essay on the inferior forms of human action]. Paris: Felix Alcan; Paris, Société Pierre Janet/Payot, 1973.

Janet, P. (1901/1977). *The mental state of hystericals: A study of mental stigmata and mental accidents* (edited and with prefaces by D. N. Robinson). Washington DC: University Publications of America.

Janet, P. (1904/1911). L'amnésie et la dissociation des souvenirs par l'émotion [Amnesia and emotion-related dissociation of memories]. *Journal de Psychologie, 1,* 417–453. Also in P. Janet, *L'état mental des hystériques* [The mental state of hystericals] (second ed., pp. 506– 544). Paris: Félix Alcan (Reprint: Lafitte Reprints, Marseilles, 1983).

Janet, P. (1904/1983). L'amnésie et la dissociation des souvenirs par l'émotion [Amnesia and the dissociation of memories through emotion]. In P. Janet, *L'état mental des hystériques* (second print, pp. 506–544). Marseille: Lafitte. Reprint Paris: L'Harmattan 2007.

Janet, P. (1907). *The major symptoms of hysteria.* London/New York: Macmillan.

Janet, P. (1909). Problèmes psychologiques de l'émotion [Psychological problems of emotion]. *Revue Neurologique, 17,* 1551–1687.

Janet, P. (1911). *L'état mental des hystériques* [The mental state of hystericals (2nd ed.)]. Paris: Félix Alcan. (Reprint: Lafitte Reprints, Marseilles, 1983).

Janet, P. (1928a). *L'évolution de la mémoire et de la notion du temps* [The evolution of memory and the notion of time]. Paris: A. Chahine.

Janet, P. (1928b). *De l'angoisse à l'extase, Vol 2: Les sentiments fondamentaux* [From fear to ecstasy: The fundamental feelings]. Paris: Félix Alcan. New edition: Paris: Société Pierre Janet, 1975.

Janet, P. (1935). Réalisation et interpretation [Realization and interpretation]. *Annales Médico-Psychologiques, 93*, 329–366.

Jang, K. L., Paris, J., Zweig-Frank, H., & Livesley, W. J. (1998). Twin study of dissociative experience. *Journal of Nervous and Mental Disease, 186*, 345–351.

Jang, K. L., Stein, M. B., Taylor, S., Asmundson, G. J., & Livesley, W. J. (2003). Exposure to traumatic events and experiences: Aetiological relationships with personality function. *Psychiatry Research, 120*, 61–69.

Janssen, I., Krabbendam, L., Bak, M., Hanssen, M., Vollebergh, W., de Graaf, R., & Van Os, J. (2004). Childhood abuse as a risk factor for psychotic experiences. *Acta Psychiatrica Scandinavica, 109*, 38–45.

Järvilehto, T. (1998a). The theory of the organism-environment system: I. Description of the theory. *Integrative Physiological and Behavioural Sciences, 33*, 321–334.

Järvilehto, T. (1998b). The theory of the organism-environment system: II. Significance of nervous activity in the organism-environment system. *Integrative Physiological and Behavioural Sciences, 33*, 335–342; discussion 343.

Järvilehto, T. (1999). The theory of the organism-environment system: III. Role of efferent influences on receptors in the formation of knowledge. *Integrative Physiological and Behavioural Sciences, 34*, 90–100.

Järvilehto, T. (2000a). Theory of the organism-environment system: IV. The problem on mental activity and consciousness. *Integrative Physiological and Behavioural Sciences, 35*, 35–57.

Järvilehto, T. (2000b). Consciousness as cooperation. *Advances in Mind Body Medicine, 16*, 89–92; discussion 97–101.

Järvilehto, T. (2000c). Feeling as knowing. *Consciousness & Emotion, 1(2)*, 53–65.

Järvilehto, T. (2001a). Feeling as knowing, Part 2. Emotion, consciousness, and brain activity. *Consciousness & Emotion, 2(1), 75–102.*

Järvilehto, T. (2001b). *The self and free will in the framework of the organism-environment theory.* Karl Jaspers Forum, target article 36b. Retrieved from www.kjf.ca/36B-TAJA.html

Järvilehto, T. (2004). Consciousness and the ultimate essence of matter. *NeuroQuantology, 2*, 210–218. Retrieved from www.neuroquantology.com/2004/03/ToC2004_3.htm

Jeannerod, M. (1997). *The cognitive neuroscience of action.* Wiley-Blackwell.

Jelinek, L., Hottenrott, B., Randjbar, S., Peters, M. J., & Moritz, S. (2009). Visual false memories in post-traumatic stress disorder (PTSD). *Journal of Behavior Therapy and Experimental Psychiatry, 40*, 374–383.

Jinkins, W. E. (1905). Robbed of her work basket. *Louisville Monthly Journal of Medicine and Surgery, 12*, 115.

Johnson, C. F. (2002). Child maltreatment 2002: Recognition, reporting and risk. *Pediatrics International, 44*, 554–560.

Jonas, H. (1966). *The phenomenon of life: Towards a philosophical biology.* New York: Harper and Row.

Jonas, H. (1973). *Organismus und Freiheit: Ansätze zu einer philosophischen Biologie* [Organism and freedom: Towards a philosophical biology]. Göttingen: Vandenhoeck & Ruprecht.

Jones, B. E. (2003). Arousal systems. *Frontiers in Bioscience, 8*, s438–451.

Jones, D. P. (1986). Individual psychotherapy for the sexually abused child. *Child Abuse & Neglect, 10*, 377–385.

Jones, E., Vermaas, R. H., McCartney, H., Beech, C., Palmer, I., Hyams, K., & Wessely, S. (2003). Flashbacks and post-traumatic stress disorder: The genesis of a 20th century diagnosis. *British Journal of Psychiatry, 182*, 158–163.

Jordan, J. F. (1873). *Surgical inquiries.* London: J. and A. Churchill.

Joubert, D., Webster, L., & Hackett, R. K. (2012). Unresolved attachment status and trauma-related symptomatology in maltreated adolescents: An examination of cognitive mediators. *Child Psychiatry and Human Development, 43,* 471–483.

Juarrero, A. (1999). *Dynamics in action: Intentional behavior as a complex system.* Cambridge, MA: MIT.

Kant, I. (1781/1998). *Critique of pure reason.* Cambridge, MA: Cambridge University Press.

Karl, A., Schaefer, M., Malta, L. S., Dorfel, D., Rohleder, N., & Werner, A. (2006). A meta-analysis of structural brain abnormalities in PTSD. *Neuroscience and Biobehavioral Reviews, 30,* 1004–1031.

Kalin, N. H., & Shelton, S. E. (1989). Defensive behaviors in infant rhesus monkeys: Environmental cues and neurochemical regulation. *Science, 243*(4899), 1718–1721.

Kalin, N. H., Shelton, S. E., & Takahashi, L. K. (1991). Defensive behaviors in infant rhesus monkeys: Ontogeny and context-dependent selective expression. *Child Development, 62,* 1175–1183.

Kardiner, A. (1941). *The traumatic neuroses of war.* New York: Paul Hoeber.

Kardiner, A., & Spiegel, H. (1947). *War, stress and neurotic illness.* New York: Paul Hoeber.

Karl, A., Schaefer, M., Malta, L. S., Dorfel, D., Rohleder, N., & Werner, A. (2006). A meta-analysis of structural brain abnormalities in PTSD. *Neuroscience and Biobehavioral Reviews, 30,* 1004–1031.

Karmiloff-Smith, A. (1998). Development itself is the key to understanding developmental disorders. *Trends in Cognitive Sciences, 2,* 389–398.

Kawasaki, H., Kaufman, O., Damasio, H., Damasio, A. R., Granner, M., Bakken, H., & Adolphs, R. (2001). Single-neuron responses to emotional visual stimuli recorded in human ventral prefrontal cortex. *Nature Neuroscience, 4,* 15–16.

Kawashima, R., Rolland, P. E., & O'Sullivan, B. T. (1994). Fields in human motor areas involved in preparation for reaching, actual reaching, and visumotor learning: A positron emission tomography study. *Journal of Neuroscience, 14,* 3462–3474.

Keane, T., Kolb, L., Kaloupek, D., Orr, S., Blanchard, E., Thomas, R., Hsieh, F., & Lavori, P. (1998). Utility of psychophysiological measurement in the diagnosis of posttraumatic stress disorder: Results from a Department of Veterans Affairs cooperative study. *Journal of Consulting and Clinical Psychology, 66,* 914–923.

Kelley, L. P., Weathers, F. W., Mason, E. A., & Pruneau, G. M. (2012). Association of life threat and betrayal with posttraumatic stress disorder symptom severity. *Journal of Traumatic Stress, 25,* 408–415.

Kelley, W. M., Macrae, C. N., Wyland, C. L., Caglar, S., Inati, S., & Heatherton, T. F. (2002). Finding the self? An event-related fMRI study. *Journal of Cognitive Neuroscience,* 14, 785–794.

Kempe, C. H., Silverman, F. N., Steele, B. F., Droegemueller, W., & Silver, H. K. (1962). The battered-child syndrome. *Journal of the American Medical Association, 181,* 17–24.

Kendler, K. S., Neale, M. C., Kessler, R. C., Heath, A. C., & Eaves, L. J. (1993). A test of the equal-environment assumption in twin studies of psychiatric illness. *Behavioral Genetics, 23,* 21–27.

Keuroghlian, A. S., Butler, L. D., Neri, E., & Spiegel, D. (2010). Hypnotizability, posttraumatic stress, and depressive symptoms in metastatic breast cancer. *International Journal of Clinical and Experimental Hypnosis, 58*(1), 39–52.

Kihlstrom, J. F. (1998). Dissociations and dissociation theory in hypnosis: Comment on Kirsch and Lynn (1998). *Psychological Bulletin, 123,* 186–191.

Kilpatrick, D. G., Resnick, H. S., & Acierno, R. (2009). Should PTSD Criterion A be retained? *Journal of Traumatic Stress, 22,* 374–383.

Kilpatrick, D. G., Saunders, B. E., Amick-McMullan, A., Best, C. L., Veronen, L. J., & Resnick, H. S. (1989). Victim and crime factors associated with the development of crime-related posttraumatic stress disorder. *Behavior Therapy, 20,* 199–214.

Kim, D., Park, S. C., Yang, H., & Oh, D. H. (2011). Reliability and validity of the Korean version of the childhood trauma questionnaire-short form for psychiatric outpatients. *Psychiatry Investigation, 8*, 305–311.

Kimonis, E. R., Fanti, K. A., Isoma, Z., & Donoghue, K. (2013). Maltreatment profiles among incarcerated boys with callous-unemotional traits. *Child Maltreatment, 18*, 108–121.

King, H. (1993). One-Once upon a text: Hysteria from Hippocrates. In S. L. Gilman, H. King, R. Porter, G. S. Rousseau, & E. Showalter (Eds.), *Hysteria beyond Freud* (pp. 3–90). Berkeley: University of California Press.

King, L. A., King, D. W., Fairbank, J. A., Keane, T. M., & Adams, G. A. (1998). Resilience-recovery factors in posttraumatic stress disorder among female and male Vietnam veterans: Hardiness, postwar social support study of reactivation of posttraumatic stress disorder symptoms. American and Cambodian psychophysiological response to viewing traumatic video scenes. *Journal of Nervous and Mental Disease, 186*, 670–676.

Kinsey, A., Pomeroy, W., Martin, C., & Gebhard, P. (1953). *Sexual behavior in the human female*. Philadelphia: Saunders.

Kinzie, J. D., Denney, D., Riley, C., Boehnlein, J., McFarland, B., & Leung, P. (1998). A cross-cultural study of reactivation of posttraumatic stress disorder symptoms: American and Cambodian psychophysiological response to viewing traumatic video scenes. *Journal of Nervous and Mental Disease, 186*, 670–676.

Kirmayer, L. J. (2011). Defining and delimiting trauma-related dissociation: A view from cultural psychiatry. *Journal of Trauma & Dissociation, 12*, 465–468.

Kirsch, I., & Lynn, S. J. (1998). Dissociating the wheat from the chaff in theories of hypnosis: Reply to Kihlstrom (1998) and Woody and Sadler (1998). *Psychological Bulletin, 123*, 198–202.

Kitayama, N., Vaccarino, V., Kutner, M., Weiss, P., & Bremner, J. D. (2005). Magnetic resonance imaging (MRI) measurement of hippocampal volume in posttraumatic stress disorder: A meta-analysis. *Journal of Affective Disorders, 88*(1), 79–86.

Kjaer, T. W., Nowak, M., & Lou, H. C. (2002). Reflective self-awareness and conscious states: PET evidence for a common midline parietofrontal core. *Neuroimage, 17*, 1080–1086.

Kluft, R. P. (1984a). An introduction to multiple personality disorder. *Psychiatric Annals, 14*, 19–24.

Kluft, R. P. (1984b). Treatment of multiple personality disorder: A study of 33 cases. *Psychiatric Clinics of North America, 7*(1), 9–29.

Kluft, R. P. (1985). The natural history of multiple personality disorder. In R. P. Kluft (Ed.), *Childhood antecedents of multiple personality disorder* (pp. 167–196). Washington, DC: American Psychiatric Press.

Kluft, R. P. (1987). An update on multiple personality disorder. *Hospital and Community Psychiatry, 38*, 363–373.

Kluft, R. P. (1996). Treating the traumatic memories of patients with dissociative identity disorder. *American Journal of Psychiatry, 153*(Suppl 7), 103–110.

Knoll, J. (2010). Teacher sexual misconduct: Grooming patterns and female offenders. *Journal of Child Sexual Abuse, 19*, 371–386.

Koenigs, M., Huey, E. D., Raymont, V., Cheon, B., Solomon, J., Wassermann, E. M., & Grafman, J. (2008). Focal brain damage protects against post-traumatic stress disorder in combat veterans. *Nature Neuroscience, 11*, 232–237.

Kolla, N. J., Malcolm, C., Attard, S., Arenovich, T., Blackwood, N., & Hodgins, S. (2013). Childhood maltreatment and aggressive behaviour in violent offenders with psychopathy. *Canadian Journal of Psychiatry, 58*, 487–494.

Koopman, C., Carion, V., Sudhakar, S., Palmer, L., & Steiner, H. (2000, November). *Dissociation, childhood abuse and heart rate during a stressful speech*. Poster presented at the 16th Conference of the International Society for Traumatic Stress Studies, San Antonio, TX.

Korol, S. (2008). Familial and social support as protective factors against the development of dissociative identity disorder. *Journal of Trauma & Dissociation, 9*, 249–267.

Korzekwa, M. I., Dell, P. F., Links, P. S., Thabane, L., & Fougere, P. (2009). Dissociation in borderline personality disorder: A detailed look. *Journal of Trauma & Dissociation, 10*, 346–367.

Kouwer, B. J. (1963). *Het spel van de persoonlijkheid: Theorieën en systemen in de psychologie van de menselijke persoon.* [The play of the personality: Theories and systems in the psychology of the human individual.]. Utrecht: Erven J. Bijleveld.

Kreisler, F. (1915). *Four weeks in the trenches: The war story of a violinist.* Boston and New York: Houghton Mifflin. Retrieved from http://net.lib.byu.edu/estu/wwi/memoir/kreisler/kreisler.htm

Kretschmer, E. (1923). *Über Hysterie* [On hysteria]. Leipzig: Thieme. Reprinted as *Hysterie, Reflex, und Instinkt* [Hysteria, reflex, and instinct], 1927, 1944.

Krolak-Salmon, P., Henaff, M. A., Isnard, J., Tallon-Baudry, C., Guenot, M., Vighetto, A., . . . Mauguière, F. (2003). An attention modulated response to disgust in human ventral anterior insula. *Annals of Neurology, 53*, 446–453.

Krueger, J. (2010). Comment: Radical enactivism and inter-corporeal affectivity. In T. Fuchs, H. C. Sattel, & P. Henningsen (Eds.), *The embodied self: Dimensions, coherence and disorders* (pp. 43–65). Stuttgart: Schattauer.

Krystal, H. (1968). *Massive psychic trauma.* New York: International Universities Press.

Krystal, J. H., Woods, S. W., Hill, C. L., & Charney, D. S. (1991). Characteristics of panic attack subtypes: Assessment of spontaneous panic, situational panic, sleep panic, and limited symptom attacks. *Comprehensive Psychiatry, 32*, 474–478.

Kubany, E. S. (1994). A cognitive model of guilt typology in combat-related PTSD. *Journal of Traumatic Stress, 7*, 3–19.

Kukules, P. (1955). *Life and civilization of the Byzantines, Volume 6.* Athens, Greece: Papazeses.

Kumar, V. K., Marcano, G., & Pekala, R. J. (1996). Behavioral and subjective scoring of the Harvard Group Scale of Hypnotic Susceptibility: further data and an extension. *American Journal of Clinical Hypnosis, 38*, 191–199.

Kumpula, M. J., Orcutt, H. K., Bardeen, J. R., & Varkovitzky, R. L. (2011). Peritraumatic dissociation and experiential avoidance as prospective predictors of posttraumatic stress symptoms. *Journal of Abnormal Psychology, 120*, 617–627.

Kuyk, J., Spinhoven, P., Van Emde Boas, M. D., & Van Dyck, R. (1999). Dissociation in temporal lobe epilepsy and pseudo-epileptic seizure patients. *The Journal of Nervous and Mental Disease, 187*, 713–20.

Labbé, Jean (2005). Ambroise Tardieu: The man and his work on child maltreatment a century before Kempe. *Child Abuse & Neglect, 29*, 311–324.

Lacey, B. C., & Lacey, J. I. (1974). Studies of heart rate and other bodily processes in sensorimotor behavior. In P. A. Orbist, A. H. Black, J. Brener, & L. DiCara (Eds.), *Cardiovascular psychophysiology: Current issues in response mechanisms, biofeedback, and methodology* (pp. 538–564). Chicago: Aldine.

Lakoff, G., & Johnson, M. (1980). *Metaphors we live by.* Chicago: The University of Chicago Press.

Lakoff, G., & Johnson, M. (1999). *Philosophy in the flesh: The embodied mind and its challenge to Western thought.* New York: Basic Books.

Lalor, K. (2001). *The end of innocence: Child sexual abuse in Ireland.* Cork: Oak Tree Press.

Lalor, K. (1998). Child sexual abuse in Ireland: An historical and anthropological note. *Irish Journal of Applied Social Studies, 1*(1), 37–54.

Laland, K. N., & Brown, J. R. (2006). Niche construction, human behavior, and the adaptive-lag hypothesis. *Evolutionary Anthropology, 15*, 95–104.

Landes, S. J., Garovoy, N. D., & Burkman, K. M. (2013). Treating complex trauma among veterans: Three stage-based treatment models. *Journal of Clinical Psychology, 69*, 523–533.

Lang, P.J. (1995). The emotion probe: Studies of motivation and attention. *American Psychologist, 50,* 372–385.

Lang, P.J., & Bradley, M.M. (2009). Emotion and the motivational brain. *Biological Psychology, 84,* 437–450.

Lang, P.J., Bradley, M.M., & Cuthbert, B.N. (1998). Emotion, motivation, and anxiety: Brain mechanisms and psychophysiology. *Biological Psychiatry, 44,* 1248–1263.

Lang, P.J., Davis, M., & Ohman, A. (2000). Fear and anxiety: animal models and human cognitive psychophysiology. *Journal of Affective Disorders, 61,* 137–159.

Lanius, R.A., Bluhm, R., Lanius, U., & Pain, C. (2006). A review of neuroimaging studies in PTSD: Heterogeneity of response to symptom provocation. *Journal of Psychiatric Research, 40,* 709–729.

Lanius, R.A., Brand, B., Vermetten, E., Frewen, P.A., & Spiegel, D. (2012). The dissociative subtype of posttraumatic stress disorder: Rationale, clinical and neurobiological evidence, and implications. *Depression and Anxiety, 29,* 701–708.

Lanius, R.A., Hopper, J.W., & Menon, R.S. (2003). Individual differences in a husband and wife who developed PTSD after a motor vehicle accident: A functional MRI case study. *American Journal of Psychiatry, 160,* 667–669.

Lanius, R.A., Vermetten, E., Loewenstein, R.J., Brand, B., Schmahl, C., Bremner, J.D., & Spiegel, D. (2010). Emotion modulation in PTSD: Clinical and neurobiological evidence for a dissociative subtype. *American Journal of Psychiatry, 167,* 640–647.

Lanius, R.A., Vermetten, E., & Pain, C. (2010). *The impact of early life trauma on health and disease: The hidden epidemic.* Cambridge, UK: Cambridge University Press.

Lanius, R.A., Williamson, P.C., Bluhm, R.L., Densmore, M., Boksman, K., Neufeld, R.W.J., … Menon, R.S. (2005). Functional connectivity of dissociative response in posttraumatic stress disorder: A functional magnetic resonance imaging investigation. *Biological Psychiatry, 57,* 873–884.

Lanius, R.A., Williamson, P.C., Boksman, K., Densmore, M., Gupta, M., Neufeld, R.W., … Menon, R.S. (2002). Brain activation during script-driven imagery induced dissociative responses in PTSD: A functional magnetic resonance imaging investigation. *Biological Psychiatry, 52,* 305–311.

Lanning, K.V. (2010). *Child molesters: A behavioral analysis for professionals investigating the sexual exploitation of children* (5th ed.). Arlington, VA: National Center for Missing & Exploited Children.

Larmore, K., Ludwig, A.M., & Cain, R.L. (1977). Multiple personality: An objective case study. *British Journal of Psychiatry, 131,* 35–40.

Lascaratos, J., & Poulakou-Rembelakou, E. (2000). Child sexual abuse: Historical cases in the Byzantine Empire (324–1453 A.D.). *Child Abuse & Neglect, 8,* 1085–1090.

Lau, H.C., & Passingham, R.E. (2006). Relative blindsight in normal observers and the neural correlate of visual consciousness. *Proceedings of the National Academy of Sciences USA, 103,* 18763–18768.

Laub, D., & Auerhahn, N.C. (1993). Knowing and not knowing massive psychic trauma: Forms of traumatic memory. *International Journal of Psychoanalysis, 74,* 287–302.

Lavenu, I., Pasquier, F., Lebert, F., Petit, H., & Van der Linden, M. (1999). Perception of emotion in frontotemporal dementia and Alzheimer disease. *Alzheimer Disease and Associated Disorders, 13,* 96–101.

Lawn, B. (Ed.). (1979). *The prose Salernitan questions.* London: Oxford University Press.

Lawson, L. (2003). Isolation, gratification, justification: Offenders' explanations of child molesting. *Issues in Mental Health Nursing, 24,* 695–705.

Lawton, G., Baker, G.A., & Brown, R.J. (2008). Comparison of two types of dissociation in epileptic and nonepileptic seizures. *Epilepsy and Behavior, 13,* 333–336.

Leavitt, F. (1997). False attribution of suggestibility to explain recovered memory of childhood sexual abuse following extended amnesia. *Child Abuse & Neglect, 21,* 265–272.

Leavitt, F. (2001). MMPI profile characteristics of women with varying levels of normal dissociation. *Journal of Clinical Psychology, 57*, 1469–1477.

LeDoux, J. E. (1995). Emotion: Clues from the brain. *Annual Review of Psychology, 46*, 209–235.

LeDoux, J. E. (1996). *The emotional brain: The mysterious underpinning of emotional life*. New York: Simon and Schuster.

LeDoux, J. E. (2000). Emotion circuits in the brain. *Annual Review of Neuroscience, 23*, 155–184.

LeDoux, J. E. (2002). *Synaptic self: How our brains become who we are*. New York: Viking Penguin.

Lees-Grossmann, L. (2010). Comment: A common ground approach to selfhood. In T. Fuchs, H. C. Sattel & P. Henningsen, & (Eds.), *The embodied mind: Dimensions, coherence, and disorders* (pp. 71–76). Stuttgart: Schattauer.

Legrand, D. (2005). Transparently oneself. *Psyche, 11*(5), 1–19.

Le Gros Clark, E. (1868). Lectures on the principle of surgical diagnosis: Lecture VI. *British Medical Journal, 2* (459), 409. Retrieved from https://archive.org/stream/lecturesonprinc00clargoog/lecturesonprinc00clargoog_djvu.txt

Leibniz, G. W. (1714). *La Monadologie*. (transl. Rescher (1991), *The monadology: An edition for students*). Pittsburgh, PA: University of Pittsburgh Press.

Lensvelt-Mulders, G., Van der Hart, O., Van Ochten, J. M., Van Son, M. J. M., Steele, K., & Breeman, L. (2008). Relations among peritraumatic dissociation and posttraumatic stress: A meta-analysis. *Clinical Psychology Review, 28*, 1138–1151.

Leopold, D. A., & Logothetis, N. K. (1999). Multistable phenomena: Changing views in perception. *Trends in Cognitive Sciences, 3*, 254–264.

Lerner, P. (2001). From traumatic neurosis to male hysteria: The decline and fall of Hermann Oppenheim, 1889–1919. In M. S. Micale & P. Lerner (Eds.), *Traumatic pasts: History, psychiatry, and trauma in the modern age, 1870–1930* (pp. 140–171). New York: Cambridge University Press.

Lerner, P. (2003). *Hysterical men: War, psychiatry, and the politics of trauma in Germany, 1890–1930*. Ithaca/London: Cornell University Press.

Lesch, K. P., Bengel, D., Heils, A., Sabol, S. Z., Greenberg, B. D., Petri, S., . . . Murphy, D. L. (1996). Association of anxiety-related traits with a polymorphism in the serotonin transporter gene regulatory region. *Science, 274*, 1527–1531.

Levin, R., & Spei, E. (2004). Relationship of purported measures of pathological and nonpathological dissociation to self-reported psychological distress and fantasy immersion. *Assessment, 11*, 160–168.

Levy-Gigi, E., Szabo, C., Kelemen, O., & Keri, S. (2013). Association among clinical response, hippocampal volume, and FKBP5 gene expression in individuals with posttraumatic stress disorder receiving cognitive behavioral therapy. *Biological Psychiatry, 74*, 793–800.

Lewis, D. O., Yeager, C. A., Swica, Y., Pincus, J. H., & Lewis, M. (1997). Objective documentation of child abuse and dissociation in 12 murderers with dissociative identity disorder. *American Journal of Psychiatry, 154*, 1703–1710.

Lilienfeld, S. O., Lynn, S. J., Kirsch, I., Chaves, J. F., Sarbin, T. R., Ganaway, G. K., & Powell, R. A. (1999). Dissociative identity disorder and the sociocognitive model: Recalling the lessons of the past. *Psychological Bulletin, 125*, 507–523.

Lima, A. A., Fiszman, A., Marques-Portella, C., Mendlowicz, M. V., Coutinho, E. S., Maia, D. C., . . . Figueira, I. (2010). The impact of tonic immobility reaction on the prognosis of posttraumatic stress disorder. *Journal of Psychiatric Research, 44*, 224–228.

Lindauer, R. J. (2012). Child maltreatment–Clinical PTSD diagnosis not enough?!: Comment on Resick et al. (2012). *Journal of Traumatic Stress, 25*, 258–259, 260–253.

Lindsay, W. R., Law, J., Quinn, K., Smart, N., & Smith, A. H. (2001). A comparison of physical and sexual abuse: Histories of sexual and nonsexual offenders with intellectual disability. *Child Abuse and Neglect, 25*, 989–995.

Linehan, M. M. (1993). *Cognitive-behavioral treatment of borderline personality disorder.* New York: Guilford.

Liotti, G. (1999). Disorganization of attachment as a model for understanding dissociative psychopathology. In J. Solomon & C. George (Eds.), *Disorganization of attachment* (pp. 297–317). New York: Guilford.

Liotti, G. (2004). Trauma, dissociation and disorganized attachment: Three strands of a single braid. *Psychotherapy: Theory, Research, Practice and Training, 41*, 472–486.

Liotti, G. (2006). A model of dissociation based on attachment theory and research. *Journal of Trauma & Dissociation, 7*(4), 55–73.

Lipsanen, T., Korkeila, J., Peltola, P., Jarvinen, J., Langen, K., & Lauerma, H. (2004). Dissociative disorders among psychiatric patients comparison with a nonclinical sample. *European Psychiatry, 19*, 53–55.

Litt, L. (2013). Clinical decision making in the treatment of complex PTSD and substance misuse. *Journal of Clinical Psychology, 69*, 534–542.

Littré, E. (1851–1853). *Oeuvres complètes d'Hippocrate* [The complete works of Hippocrates, 10 vols.]. Paris: Baillière.

Livesley, W. J., & Jang, K. L. (2000). Toward an empirically based classification of personality disorder. *Journal of Personality Disorders, 14*, 137–151.

Livet, P. (2005). What is transparency? *Psyche, 11*(5), 1–15.

Lochner, C., Seedat, S., Hemmings, S. M., Moolman-Smook, J. C., Kidd, M., & Stein, D. J. (2007). Investigating the possible effects of trauma experiences and 5-HTT on the dissociative experiences of patients with OCD using path analysis and multiple regression. *Neuropsychobiology, 56*(1), 6–13.

Locke, J. (1690/1836). *Essay concerning human understanding.* London: Tegg & Son.

Loehlin, J. C. (1992). *Genes and environment in personality.* Newbury Park, CA: Sage.

Loevinger, J. (1976). *Ego development.* San Francisco: Jossey-Bass.

Loewenstein, R. J. (2007). Dissociative identity disorder: Issues in the iatrogenesis controversy. In E. Vermetten, M. Dorahy, D. Spiegel (Eds.), *Traumatic dissociation: Neurobiology and treatment* (pp. 275–299). Washington, DC: American Psychiatric Press.

Loftus, E., & Ketcham, K. (1994). *The myth of repressed memory: False memories and allegations of sexual abuse.* New York: St. Martin.

Longden, E., Madill, A., & Waterman, M. G. (2011). Dissociation, trauma, and the role of lived experience: Toward a new conceptualization of voice hearing. *Psychological Bulletin, 138*, 28–76.

Loper, A. B., Mahmoodzadegan, N., & Warren, J. I. (2008). Childhood maltreatment and Cluster B personality pathology in female serious offenders. *Sexual Abuse: A Journal of Research and Treatment, 20*, 139–160.

Lorenz, K. (1937). On the formation of the concept of instinct. *Natural Sciences, 25*, 289–300.

Luby J. L., Barch, D. M., Belden, A., Gaffrey, M. S., Tillman, R., Babb, C., . . . Botteron, K. N. (2012). Maternal support in early childhood predicts larger hippocampal volumes at school age. *Proceedings of the National Academy of Sciences USA, 109*, 2854–2859.

Lucas, R. E., Diener, E., Suh, E. M., Shao, L., & Grob., A. (2000). Cross-cultural evidence for the fundamental features of extraversion. *Journal of Personality and Social Psychology, 79*, 452–468.

Lucey, J. V., Costa, D. C., Adshead, G., Deahl, M., Busatto, G., Gacinovic, S., . . . Kerwin, R. W. (1997). Brain blood flow in anxiety disorders. OCD, panic disorder with agoraphobia, and posttraumatic stress disorder on 99 mTcHMPAO single photon emission tomography (SPET). *British Journal of Psychiatry, 171*, 346–350.

Ludwig, A. M., Brandsma, J. M., Wilbur, C. B., Bendtfeldt, F., & Jameson, D. H. (1972). The objective study of a multiple personality. *Archives of General Psychiatry, 26*, 298–310.

Luppa, M., Sikorski, C., Luck, T., Ehreke, L., Konnopka, A., Wiese, B., . . . Riedel-Heller, S. G. (2011). Age- and gender-specific prevalence of depression in latest-life: Systematic review and meta-analysis. *Journal of Affective Disorders, 136*, 212–221.

Lutz, A., Greishar, L. L., Rawlings, N. B., Ricard M., & Davidson, R. J. (2004). Long-term meditators self-induce high-amplitude gamma synchrony during mental practice. *Proceedings of the National Academy of Sciences USA, 101*, 16369–16373.

Lynn, S. J., & Rhue, J. W. (1988). Fantasy proneness: Hypnosis, developmental antecedents, and psychopathology. *American Psychologist, 43*, 350–444.

Lynn, S. J., Rhue, J. W., Myers, B. P., & Weekes, J. R. (1994). Pseudomemory in hypnotized and simulating subjects. *International Journal of Clinical and Experimental Hypnosis, 42*, 118–129.

Lyons-Ruth, K. (2008). Contributions of the mother-infant relationship to dissociative, borderline, and conduct symptoms in young adulthood. *Infant Mental Health Journal, 29*, 203–218.

Lyons-Ruth, K., Dutra, L., Schuder, M. R., & Bianchi, I. (2006). From infant attachment disorganization to adult dissociation: Relational adaptations or traumatic experiences? *Psychiatric Clinics in North America, 29*, 63–86.

Maaranen, P., Tanskanen, A., Honkalampi, K., Haatainen, K., Hintikka, J., & Viinamaki, H. (2005a). Factors associated with pathological dissociation in the general population. *Australian and New Zealand Journal of Psychiatry, 39*, 387–394.

Maaranen, P., Tanskanen, A., Haatainen, K., Honkalampi, K., Koivumaa-Honkanen, H., Hintikka, J., & Viinamaki, H. (2005b). The relationship between psychological and somatoform dissociation in the general population. *Journal of Nervous and Mental Disease, 193*, 690–692.

Maaranen, P., Tanskanen, A., Haatainen, K., Koivumaa-Honkanen, H., Hintikka, J., & Viinamaki, H. (2004). Somatoform dissociation and adverse childhood experiences in the general population. *Journal of Nervous and Mental Disease, 192*, 337–342.

Macfie, J., Cicchetti, D., & Toth, S. L. (2001a). The development of dissociation in maltreated preschool-aged children. *Development and Psychopathology, 13*, 233–254.

Macfie, J., Cicchetti, D., & Toth, S. L. (2001b). Dissociation in maltreated versus nonmaltreated preschool-aged children. *Child Abuse and Neglect, 25*, 1253–1267.

Mackowiak, P. A., & Batten, S. V. (2008). Post-traumatic stress reactions before the advent of post-traumatic stress disorder: Potential effects on the lives and legacies of Alexander the Great, Captain James Cook, Emily Dickinson, and Florence Nightingale. *Military Medicine, 173*, 1158–1163.

MacMillan, M. B. (1990). Freud and Janet on organic and hysterical paralyses: A mystery solved? *International Review of Psycho-Analysis, 17*, 189–203.

Macrae, C. N., Moran, J. M., Heatherton, T. F., Banfield, J. F., & Kelley, W. M. (2004). Medial prefrontal activity predicts memory for self. *Cerebral Cortex, 14*, 647–654.

Main, M., & Morgan, H. (1996). Disorganization and disorientation in infant Strange Situation behavior: Phenotypic resemblance to dissociative states? In L. Michelson & W. Ray (Eds.), *Handbook of dissociation* (pp. 107–137). New York: Plenum.

Malcolm, N. (1977). *Memory and mind.* Ithaca, NY: Cornell University Press.

Mandeville-Norden, R., & Beech, A. R. (2009). Development of a psychometric typology of child molesters: Implications for treatment. *Journal of Interpersonal Violence, 24*, 307–325.

Manzano-Mojica, J., Martinez-Taboas, A., Sayers-Montalvo, S. K., Cabiya, J. J., & Alicea-Rodriguez, L. E. (2012). Dissociation in sexually abused Puerto Rican children: A replication utilizing social workers as informers. *Journal of Trauma & Dissociation, 13*, 330–344.

Marchetti, C., & Della Sala, S. (1998). Disentangling the alien and the anarchic hand. *Cognitive Neuropsychiatry, 3*, 191–207.

Marchetti, R. L., Kurcgant, D., Gallucci Neto, J., von Bismark, M. A., & Fiore, L. A. (2009). Evaluating patients with suspected nonepileptic psychogenic seizures. *Journal of Neuropsychiatry and Clinical Neurosciences, 21*, 292–298.

Markowitsch, H. J. (1999). Functional neuroimaging correlates of functional amnesia. *Memory, 7*, 561–583.

Markowitsch, H. J., Calabrese, P., Fink, G. R., Durwen, H. F., Kessler, J., Harting, C., . . . Gehlen, W. (1997). Impaired episodic memory retrieval in a case of probably psychogenic amnesia. *Psychiatry Research: Neuroimaging Section, 74*, 119–126.

Markowitsch, H. J., Fink, G. R., Thone, A., Kessler, J., & Heiss, W.-D. (1997). A PET study of persistent psychogenic amnesia covering the whole life span. *Cognitive Neuropsychiatry, 2*, 135–158.

Markowitsch, H. J., Kessler, J., Van der Ven, C., Weber-Luxenburger, G., Albers, M., & Heiss, W.-D. (1998). Psychic trauma causing grossly reduced brain metabolism and cognitive deterioration. *Neuropsychologica, 36*, 77–82.

Markowitsch, H. J., Kessler, J., Weber-Luxenburger, G., Van der Ven, C., Albers, M., & Heiss, W.-D. (2000). Neuroimaging and behavioral correlates of recovery from mnestic block syndrome and other cognitive deteriorations. *Neuropsychiatry, Neuropsychology, and Behavioral Neurology, 13*, 60–66.

Marmar, C. R., Weiss, D. S., & Metzler, T. J. (1998). Peritraumatic dissociation and posttraumatic stress disorder. In J. D. Bremner & C. R. Marmar (Eds.), *Trauma, memory, and dissociation* (pp. 229–252). Washington, DC: American Psychiatric Press.

Marmar, C. R., Weiss, D. S., Schlenger, W. E., Fairbank, J. A., Jordan, K., Kulka, R. A., & Hough, R. L. (1994). Peritraumatic dissociation and posttraumatic stress in male Vietnam theater veterans. *American Journal of Psychiatry, 151*, 902–907.

Marshall, W. L., Hamilton, K., & Fernandez, Y. (2001). Empathy deficits and cognitive distortions in child molesters. *Sexual Abuse, 13*, 123–130.

Martin, C. G., Cromer, L. D., Deprince, A. P., & Freyd, J. J. (2013). The role of cumulative trauma, betrayal, and appraisals in understanding trauma symptomatology. *Psychological Trauma, 52*, 110–118.

Marquis, C. (2001). US says it broke ring that peddles child pornography. *New York Times*, September 8. Retrieved from http://www.nytimes.com/2001/08/09/us/us-says-it-broke-ring-t hat-peddled-child-pornography.html

Marx, B. P., & Sloan, D. M. (2002). The role of emotion in the psychological functioning of adult survivors of childhood sexual abuse. *Behavior Therapy, 33*, 563–578.

Marysko, M., Reck, C., Mattheis, V., Finke, P., Resch, F., & Moehler, E. (2010). History of childhood abuse is accompanied by increased dissociation in young mothers five months postnatally. *Psychopathology, 43*, 104–109.

Mason, M. F., Norton, M. I., Van Horn, J. D., Wegner, D. M., Grafton, S. T., & Macrae, C. N. (2007). Wandering minds: The default network and stimulus-independent thought. *Science, 315*, 393–395.

Mason, J. W., Wang, S., Yehuda, R., Riney, S., Charney, D. S., & Southwick, S. M. (2001). Psychogenic lowering of urinary cortisol levels linked to increased emotional numbing and a shame-depressive syndrome in combat-related posttraumatic stress disorder. *Psychosomatic Medicine, 63*, 387–401.

Masson, J. M. (1984). *Assault on the truth*. New York: Farrar Straus.

Mathew, R. J., Jack, R. A., & West, W. S. (1985). Regional cerebral blood flow in a patient with multiple personality. *American Journal of Psychiatry, 142*, 504–505.

Mauritz, M. W., Goossens, P. J., Draijer, N., & Van Achterberg, T. (2013). Prevalence of interpersonal trauma exposure and trauma-related disorders in severe mental illness. *European Journal of Psychotraumatology, 4*, 19985.

Mayr, E. (1974). Behavior programs and evolutionary strategies. *American Scientist, 62*, 650–659.

Mazoyer, B., Zago, L., Mellet, E., Bricogne, S., Etard, O., Houdé, O., . . . Tzourio-Mazoyer, N. (2001). Cortical networks for working memory and executive functions sustain the conscious resting state in man. *Brain Research Bulletin, 54*, 287–298.

McConkey, K. M., Glisky, M. L., & Kihlstrom, J. F. (1989). Individual differences between hypnotic virtuosos. *Australian Journal of Clinical and Experimental Hypnosis, 17*, 131–140.

McCormick, D. D., & Thompson, R. F. (1982). Locus coeruleus lesions and resistance to extinction of a classically conditioned response: Involvement of the neocortex and hippocampus. *Brain Research, 245*, 239–249.

McCoy, K., & Fremouw, W. (2010). The relation between negative affect and sexual offending: A critical review. *Clinical Psychology Review, 30*, 317–325.

McCrae, R. R., & Costa, P. T. (1996). Toward a new generation of personality theories: Theoretical contexts for the five-factor model. In J. S. Wiggins (Ed.), *The Five-Factor Model of Personality: Theoretical perspectives* (pp. 51–87). New York: Guilford.

McDougall, W. (1926). *An outline of abnormal psychology*. London: Methuen & Co.

McGinn, C. (1989). *Mental content*. Oxford: Blackwell.

McGinn, C. (1999). *The mysterious flame: Conscious minds in a material world*. Oxford, Cambridge, MA: Blackwell.

McKillop, N., Smallbone, S., Wortley, R., & Andjic, I. (2012). Offenders' attachment and sexual abuse onset: A test of theoretical propositions. *Sexual Abuse, 24*, 591–610.

McNally, R. J. (2003a). Progress and controversy in the study of posttraumatic stress disorder. *Annual Review of Psychology, 54*, 229–252.

McNally, R. J. (2003b). *Remembering trauma*. Cambridge, MA: Harvard University Press.

Mead, G. H. (1925). The genesis of the self and social control. *International Journal of Ethics, 35*, 251–277.

Mechanic, M. B., Resick, P. A., & Griffin, M. G. (1998). A comparison of normal forgetting, psychopathology, and information processing models of reported amnesia for recent sexual trauma. *Journal of Consulting and Clinical Psychology, 66*, 948–957.

Medley, A., & Sachs-Ericsson, N. (2009). Predictors of parental physical abuse: The contribution of internalizing and externalizing disorders and childhood experiences of abuse. *Journal of Affective Disorders, 113*, 244–254.

Meerding, W. J. (2005). De maatschappelijke kosten van kindermishandeling [The societal costs of child abuse]. In H. Baartman, R. Bullens, & J. Willems (Eds.), *Kindermishandeling: de politiek een zorg* (pp. 46–62). Amsterdam: SWP.

Merckelbach, H., à Campo, J., Hardy, S., & Giesbrecht,T. (2005). Dissociation and fantasy proneness in psychiatric patients: A preliminary study. *Comprehensive Psychiatry, 46*, 181–185.

Merckelbach, H., Devilly, G. J., & Rassin, E. (2002). Alters in dissociative identity disorder: Metaphors or genuine entities? *Clinical Psychology Review, 22*, 481–497.

Merckelbach, H., Horselenberg, R., & Muris P. (2001). The Creative Experiences Questionnaire (CEQ): A brief self-report measure of fantasy proneness. *Personality and Individual Differences, 31*, 987–995.

Merckelbach, H., Horselenberg, R., & Schmidt, H. (2002). Modeling the connection between self-reported trauma and dissociation in a student sample. *Personality and Individual Differences, 32*, 695–705.

Merckelbach, H., & Muris, P. (2001). The causal link between self-reported trauma and dissociation: A critical review. *Behaviour, Research, & Therapy, 39*, 245–254.

Merckelbach, H., Muris, P., Horselenberg, R., & Stougie, S. (2000). Dissociative experiences, response bias, and fantasy proneness in college students. *Personality and Individual Differences, 28*, 49–58.

Merckelbach, H., Muris, P., & Rassin, E. (1999). Fantasy proneness and cognitive failures as correlates of dissociative experiences. *Personality and Individual Differences, 26*, 961–967.

Merckelbach, H., Rassin, E., & Muris, P. (2000). Dissociation, schizotypy, and fantasy proneness in undergraduate students. *Journal of Nervous and Mental Disease, 188*, 428–431.

Mercy, J. A. (1999). Having new eyes: Viewing child sexual abuse as a public health problem. *Sexual Abuse, 11*, 317–321.

Merleau-Ponty, M. (1945/1962). *Phenomenology of perception.* London: Routledge & Kegan. (Translation of *Phénomenologie de la perception*. Paris: Éditions Gallimard).

Merskey, H. (1992). The manufacture of personalities: The production of multiple personality disorder. *British Journal of Psychiatry, 160*, 327–340.

Merskey, H. (1997). Tests of 'dissociation' and mood disorder. *British Journal of Psychiatry, 171*, 487.

Mesman, J., Van IJzendoorn, M. H., & Bakermans-Kranenburg, M. J. (2009). The many faces of the Still-Face Paradigm: A review and meta-analysis. *Developmental Review, 29*, 120–162.

Mesulam, M. M. (1981). Dissociative states with abnormal temporal lobe EEG: Multiple personality and the illusion of possession. *Archives of Neurology, 38*, 176–181.

Metzinger, T. (2003). *Being no one: The self-model theory of subjectivity.* Cambridge, MA: MIT.

Metzinger, T. (2005). Précis: Being no one. *Psyche, 11*(5), 1–35.

Metzinger, T. (2006). Conscious volition and mental representation: Towards a more fine-grained analysis. In N. Sebanz & W. Prinz (Eds.), *Disorders of volition* (pp. 19–48). Cambridge, MA: MIT.

Metzinger, T. (2006a). Reply to Zahavi: The value of historical scholarship. *Psyche, 12*(4), 1–9.

Metzinger, T. (2006b). Reply to Ghin: Self-sustainment on the level of global availability. *Psyche, 12*(4), 1–2.

Metzinger, T. (2006c). Reply to Himma: Personal identity and Cartesian intuitions. *Psyche, 12*(4), 1–5.

Metzinger, T. (2006d). Reply to Hobson: Can there be a first-person science of consciousness? *Psyche, 12*(4), 1–5.

Metzinger, T. (2006e). Reply to Legrand: Content from the inside out. *Psyche, 12*(4), 1–6.

Metzinger, T. (2006f). Reply to Livet: Meta-abeyance? *Psyche, 12*(4), 1–3.

Metzinger, T. (2006 g). Reply to Weisberg: No direction home–searching for neutral ground. *Psyche, 12*(4), 1–6.

Meursing, K., Vos, T., Coutinho, O., Moyo, M., Mpofu, S., Oneko, O., ... Sibindi, F. (1995). Child sexual abuse in Matabeleland, Zimbabwe. *Social Science & Medicine, 41*, 1693–1704.

Mezzacappa, E., Tremblay, R. E., Kindlon, D., Saul, J. P., Arseneault, L., Seguin, J., ... Earls, F. (1997). Anxiety, antisocial behavior, and heart rate regulation in adolescent males. *Journal of Child Psychology and Psychiatry, 38*, 457–469.

Middleton, W. (2013). Parent-child incest that extends into adulthood: A survey of international press reports, 2007–2011. *Journal of Trauma & Dissociation, 14*, 184–197.

Milad, M. R., & Rauch, S. L. (2007). The role of the orbitofrontal cortex in anxiety disorders. *Annals of the New York Academy of Science, 1121*, 546–561.

Miller, S. D. (1989). Optical differences in cases of multiple personality disorder. *Journal of Nervous and Mental Disease, 177*, 480–486.

Miller, S. D., Blackburn, T., Scholes, G., White, G. L., & Mammalis, N. (1991). Optical differences in multiple personality disorder: A second look. *Journal of Nervous and Mental Disease, 179*, 132–135.

Miller, S. D., & Triggiano, P. J. (1992). The psychophysiological investigation of multiple personality disorder: Review and update. *American Journal of Clinical Hypnosis, 35*, 47–61.

Miner, M. H., Robinson, B. E., Knight, R. A., Berg, D., Romine, R. S., & Netland, J. (2009). Understanding sexual perpetration against children: Effects of attachment style, interpersonal involvement, and hypersexuality. *Sex Abuse, 22*, 58–77.

Mirzaei, S., Knoll, P., Keck, A., Preitler, B., Gutierrez, E., Umek, H., ... Pecherstorfer, M. (2001). Regional cerebral blood flow in patients suffering from posttraumatic stress disorder. *Neuropsychobiology, 43*, 260–264.

Mitchell, S. W. (1885). *Lectures on diseases of the nervous system: Especially in women* (2nd ed.). Philadelphia: Lea Brothers.

Mitchell, T. W. (1922). *Medical psychology and psychical research.* London: Methuen.

Moffitt, T. E., & Caspi, A. (2001). Childhood predictors differentiate life-course persistent and adolescence-limited antisocial pathways among males and females. *Development and Psychopathology, 13,* 355–375.

Mogg, K., Garner, M., & Bradley, B. P. (2007). Anxiety and orienting of gaze to angry and fearful faces. *Biological Psychology, 76,* 163–169.

Montero, B. (2009). What is the physical? In B. P. McLaughlin, A. Beckermann, & S. Walter (Eds.), *The Oxford handbook of philosophy of mind* (pp. 173–188). Oxford: Clarendon.

Moore, E., Gaskin, C., & Indig, D. (2013). Childhood maltreatment and post-traumatic stress disorder among incarcerated young offenders. *Child Abuse and Neglect, 37,* 861–870.

Moreira-Almeida, A., Neto, F. L., & Cardeña, E. (2008). Comparison of Brazilian spiritist mediumship and dissociative identity disorder. *Journal of Nervous and Mental Disease, 196,* 420–424.

Morey, R. A., Petty, C. M., Cooper, D. A., Labar, K. S., & McCarthy, G. (2008). Neural systems for executive and emotional processing are modulated by symptoms of posttraumatic stress disorder in Iraq War veterans. *Psychiatry Research, 162,* 59–72.

Morgan, C. A., Wang, S., Rasmusson, A., Hazlett, G., Anderson, G., & Charney, D. S. (2001). Relationship among plasma cortisol, catecholamines, neuropeptide Y, and human performance during exposure to uncontrollable stress. *Psychosomatic Medicine, 63,* 412–422.

Morris, J. S., Ohman, A., & Dolan, R. J. (1998). Conscious and unconscious emotional learning in the human amygdala. *Nature, 393,* 467–470.

Moskowitz, A. (2004). Dissociation and violence: A review of the literature. *Trauma Violence & Abuse, 5*(1), 21–46.

Moskowitz, A. (2014, March). Trauma, dissociation, attachment, and psychosis: Toward a new paradigm of psychopathology. *Trauma, dissociation and attachment in the 21st century.* European Society for Trauma and Dissociation, ESTD, 2014 Conference. Copenhagen.

Moskowitz, A., Schäfer, I., & Dorahy, M. (2008). *Psychosis, trauma and dissociation: Emerging perspectives on severe psychopathology.* Chichester: Wiley.

Mott, F. W. (1916, January). Special discussion on shell shock without visible signs of injury. *Proceedings of the Royal Society of Medicine: Section of Neurology and Psychiatry, 9,* i-xxiv.

Motta, R. W. (2008). Secondary trauma. *International Journal of Emergency Mental Health, 10,* 291–298.

Müller-Pfeiffer, C., Schumacher, S., Martin-Soelch, C., Pazhenkottil, A. P., Wirtz, G., Fuhrhans, C., . . . Rufer, M. (2010). The validity and reliability of the German version of the Somatoform Dissociation Questionnaire (SDQ-20). *Journal of Trauma & Dissociation, 11,* 337–357.

Müller-Pfeiffer, C., Rufibach, K., Wyss, D., Perron, N., Pitman, R., & Rufer, M. (2013). Screening for dissociative disorders in psychiatric out- and daycare patients. *Journal of Psychopathology and Behavioral Assessment, 35,* 592–602.

Murray, C. J., Richards, M. A., Newton, J. N., Fenton, K. A., Anderson, H. R., Atkinson, C., . . . Davis, A. (2013). UK health performance: Findings of the Global Burden of Disease Study 2010. *Lancet, 381*(9871), 997–1020.

Myers, C. S. (1940). *Shell shock in France 1914–18.* Cambridge: Cambridge University Press.

Myers-Schulz, B., & Koenigs, M. (2012). Functional anatomy of ventromedial prefrontal cortex: Implications for mood and anxiety disorders. *Molecular Psychiatry, 17,* 132–141.

Myrick, A. C., Brand, B. L., McNary, S. W., Classen, C. C., Lanius, R., Loewenstein, R. J., & Putnam, F. W. (2012). An exploration of young adults' progress in treatment for dissociative disorder. *Journal of Trauma & Dissociation, 13,* 582–595.

Myrick, A. C., Brand, B. L., & Putnam, F. W. (2013). For better or worse: The role of revictimization and stress in the course of treatment for dissociative disorders. *Journal of Trauma & Dissociation, 14*, 375–389.

Nadler, S. (1999). *Spinoza, a life.* Cambridge: Cambridge University Press.

Nakamura, K., Kawashima, R., Sato, N., Nakamura, A., Sugiura, M., Kato, T., . . . Zilles, K. (2000). Functional delineation of the human occipito-temporal areas related to face and scene processing. A PET study. *Brain, 123*, 1903–1912.

Näring, G. W. B., & Nijenhuis, E. R. S. (2005). Relationships between self-reported potentially traumatizing events, psychoform and somatoform dissociation, and absorption, in two nonclinical populations. *Australian and New Zealand Journal of Psychiatry, 39*, 982–988.

Näring, G. W. B., Van Lankveld, W. G. H. M., & Geenen, R. (2007). Somatoform dissociation and traumatic experiences in patients with rheumatoid arthritis and fibromyalgia. *Clinical and Experimental Rheumatology, 25*, 872–877.

Natsoulas, T. (1983). Concepts of consciousness. *The Journal of Mind and Behavior, 4*(1), 13–59.

Nash, M. R., & Lynn, S. J. (1986). Child abuse and hypnotic ability. *Imagination, Cognition, and Personality, 5*, 211–218.

Nash, M. R., Lynn, S. J., & Givens, D. L. (1984). Adult hypnotic susceptibility, childhood punishment and child abuse. *International Journal of Clinical and Experimental Hypnosis, 32*, 6–11.

Nasio, J.-D. (1998). *Hysteria from Freud to Lacan: The splendid child of psychoanalysis.* New York: Other Press.

Nejad, A. G., & Farahati, H. (2007). Dissociative disorders and dissociative symptoms among veterans of the Iraq-Iran war suffering from chronic post-traumatic disorder. *Neurosciences (Riyadh), 12*, 318–321.

Neubert, F. X., Klein, M. C. (2010). What is driving inhibition-related activity in the frontal lobe? *Journal of Neuroscience, 30*, 4830–4832.

Newmann, J., Greenley, D., & Sweeney, J. K. (1998). Abuse histories, severe mental illness and the cost of care. In: B. K. Leven, A. K. Blanch, A. Jennings (Eds.), *Women's mental health services: A public health perspective* (pp. 279–308). London, UK: Sage.

Niebuhr, B. G. (1828). *Agathiae historiarum* [Agathias' histories]. Bonn: I. Weber.

Nickerson, A., Aderka, I. M., Bryant, R. A., Litz, B. T., & Hofmann, S. G. (2011). Accidental and intentional perpetration of serious injury or death: Correlates and relationship to trauma exposure. *Journal of Trauma, 71*, 1821–1828.

Nietzsche, F. (1886). *Jenseits von Gut und Böse* (engl. *Beyond good and evil,* transl. Walter Kaufmann, 1996). New York: Vintage Books.

Nietzsche, F. (1968). *The will to power: In science, nature, society and art.* New York: Random House.

Nijenhuis, E. R. S. (1995). Dissociatieve stoornissen als gevolg van incest [Dissociative disorders as a consequence of incest]. In H. Baartman (Ed.), *Op gebaande paden? Ontwikkelingen in diagnostiek, hulpverlening en preventie met betrekking tot seksueel misbruik van kinderen* (pp. 61–85). Utrecht, The Netherlands: SWP.

Nijenhuis, E. R. S. (2004). *Somatoform dissociation: Phenomena, measurement, and theoretical issues.* New York: Norton.

Nijenhuis, E. R. S. (2009). Somatoform dissociation and somatoform dissociative disorders. In P. F. Dell & J. O'Neil (Eds.), *Dissociation and dissociative disorders: DSM-IV and beyond* (pp. 259–277). New York: Routledge.

Nijenhuis, E. R. S. (2012). Consciousness and self-consciousness in dissociative disorders. In V. Sinason (Ed.), *Attachment, trauma and multiplicity: Working on identity and selves* (pp. 115–153). London: Routledge.

Nijenhuis, E. R. S. (2014a). Dissociation in the DSM-5: Your view S'Il Vous Plait, Docteur Janet? *Journal of Trauma & Dissociation, 15*, 245–253.

Nijenhuis, E. R. S. (2014b). Ten reasons for conceiving and categorizing posttraumatic stress disorder as a dissociative disorder. *Psichiatra e Psicoterapia, 33*(1), 74–106.

Nijenhuis, E. R. S., & Den Boer, J. A. (2009). Psychobiology of traumatization and trauma-related structural dissociation of the personality. In P. F. Dell & J. A. O'Neil (Eds.), *Dissociation and the dissociative disorders: DSM-V and beyond* (pp. 337–367). New York: Routledge.

Nijenhuis, E. R. S., Lewis-Fernandez, R., Moskowitz, A., & Moreira-Almeida, A. (2014, September). *Proposals and evidence for the ICD-11 classification of dissociative disorders.* World Health Organization, ICD-11 Symposium Series, World Congress of Psychiatry, Madrid.

Nijenhuis, E. R. S., & Reinders, A. A. T. S. (2012). Fantasy proneness in dissociative identity disorder. *PLoS ONE 7*(6), e39279. Supporting information S1.

Nijenhuis, E. R. S., Spinhoven, P., Vanderlinden, J., Van Dyck, R., & Van der Hart, O. (1998a). Somatoform dissociative symptoms as related to animal defensive reactions to predatory imminence and injury. *Journal of Abnormal Psychology, 107*, 63–73.

Nijenhuis, E. R. S., Spinhoven, P., Van Dyck, R., Van der Hart, O., de Graaf, A. M. J., & Knoppert, E.A. M. (1997a). Dissociative pathology discriminates between bipolar mood disorder and dissociative disorder (letter). *British Journal of Psychiatry, 170*, 581.

Nijenhuis, E. R. S., Spinhoven, P., Van Dyck, R., Van der Hart, O., & Vanderlinden, J. (1996). The development and the psychometric characteristics of the Somatoform Dissociation Questionnaire (SDQ-20). *Journal of Nervous and Mental Disease, 184*, 688–694.

Nijenhuis, E. R. S., Spinhoven, P., Van Dyck, R., Van der Hart, O., & Vanderlinden, J. (1997b). The development of the Somatoform Dissociation Questionnaire (SDQ–5) as a screening instrument for dissociative disorders. *Acta Psychiatrica Scandinavica, 96*, 311–318.

Nijenhuis, E. R. S., Spinhoven, P., Van Dyck, R., Van der Hart, O., & Vanderlinden, J. (1998b). Degree of somatoform and psychological dissociation in dissociative disorder is correlated with reported trauma. *Journal of Traumatic Stress, 11*, 711–730.

Nijenhuis, E. R. S., Spinhoven, P., Van Dyck, R., Van der Hart, O., & Vanderlinden, J. (1998c). Psychometric characteristics of the Somatoform Dissociation Questionnaire: A replication study. *Psychotherapy and Psychosomatics, 67*(1), 17–23.

Nijenhuis, E. R. S., & Van der Hart, O. (2011a). Dissociation in trauma: A new definition and comparison with previous formulations. *Journal of Trauma & Dissociation, 12*, 416–445.

Nijenhuis, E. R. S., & Van der Hart, O. (2011b). Defining dissociation in trauma. *Journal of Trauma & Dissociation, 12*, 469–473.

Nijenhuis, E. R. S., Van der Hart, O., & Kruger, K. (2002). The psychometric characteristics of the Traumatic Experiences Questionnaire (TEC): First findings among psychiatric outpatients. *Clinical Psychology and Psychotherapy*, 9, 200–210.

Nijenhuis, E. R. S., Van der Hart, O., Kruger, K., & Steele, K. (2004). Somatoform dissociation, reported abuse and animal defence-like reactions. *Australian and New Zealand Journal of Psychiatry, 38*, 678–686.

Nijenhuis, E. R. S., Van der Hart, O., & Steele, K. (2002). The emerging psychobiology of trauma-related dissociation and dissociative disorders. In H. D'Haenen, J. A. Den Boer, & P. Willner (Eds.), *Biological psychiatry* (pp. 1079–1098). London: Wiley.

Nijenhuis, E. R. S., Vanderlinden, J., & Spinhoven, P. (1998d). Animal defensive reactions as a model for trauma-induced dissociative reactions. *Journal of Traumatic Stress, 11*, 243–260.

Nijenhuis, E. R. S., Van Dyck, R., Ter Kuile, M. M., Mourits, M. J., Spinhoven, P., & Van der Hart, O. (2003). Evidence for associations among somatoform dissociation, psychological dissociation and reported trauma in patients with chronic pelvic pain. *Journal of Psychosomatic Obstetrics and Gynecology, 24*, 87–98.

Nijenhuis, E. R. S., Van Dyck, R., Spinhoven, P., Van der Hart, O., Chatrou, M., Vanderlinden, J., & Moene, F. (1999). Somatoform dissociation discriminates between diagnostic categories over and above general psychopathology. *Australian and New Zealand Journal of Psychiatry, 33*, 512–520.

Nijenhuis, E. R. S., Van Dyck, R., Van der Hart, O., & Spinhoven, P. (1998e). Somatoform dissociation is unlikely to be a result of indoctrination by therapists (letter). *British Journal of Psychiatry, 172*, 452.

Nijenhuis, E. R. S., Van Engen, A., Kusters, I., & Van der Hart, O. (2001). Peritraumatic somatoform and psychological dissociation in relation to recall of childhood sexual abuse. *Journal of Trauma & Dissociation, 2*, 49–68.

Nijsen, M. J., Croiset, G., Diamant, M., De Wied, D., & Wiegant, V. M. (2001). CRH signalling in the bed nucleus of the stria terminalis is involved in stress-induced cardiac vagal activation in conscious rats. *Neuropsychopharmacology, 24*, 1–10.

Nijsen, M. J., Croiset, G., Diamant, M., Stam, R., Delsing, D., De Wied, D., & Wiegant, V. M. (1998). Conditioned fear-induced tachycardia in the rat: Vagal involvement. *European Journal of Pharmacology, 350*, 211–222.

Nijsen, M. J., Croiset, G., Diamant, M., Stam, R., Kamphuis, P. J., Bruijnzeel, A., . . . Wigant, V. M. (2000). Endogenous corticotropin-releasing hormone inhibits conditioned-fear-induced vagal activation in the rat. *European Journal of Pharmacology, 389*, 89–98.

Nilsson, G., Bengtsson-Tops, A. B., & Persson, L. (2005). Childhood abuse in Swedish female users of psychiatric services. *Journal of Psychiatric and Mental Health Nursing, 12*, 365–371.

Nitschke, J., Blendl, V., Ottermann, B., Osterheider, M., & Mokros, A. (2009). Severe sexual sadism–An underdiagnosed disorder? Evidence from a sample of forensic inpatients. *Journal of Forensic Sciences, 54*, 685–691.

Noë, A. (2009). *Out of our heads.* New York: Hill and Wang.

Nonne, M. (1915). Soll man wieder traumatische Neurosen diagnostizieren? [Should one diagnose traumatic neuroses again?] *Archiv für Psychiatrie und Nervenkrankheiten, 56*, 337–339.

Nonne, M. (1971). *Anfang und Ziel meines Lebens* [Beginning and goal of my life]. Hamburg: Hans Christians Verlag.

Northoff, G. (2003). *Philosophy of the brain: The brain problem.* Amsterdam/Philadelphia: John Benjamins.

Northoff, G. (2012). *Das disziplinlose Gehirn: Was nun Herr Kant?* [The unruly brain: What now, Mister Kant?]. München: Irisiana.

Northoff, G., Heinzel, A., de Greck, M., Bermpohl, F., Dobrowolny, H., & Panksepp, J. (2006). Self-referential processing in our brain: A meta-analysis of imaging studies on the self. *Neuroimage, 31*, 440–457.

Nugent, N. R., Sledjeski, E. M., Christopher, N. C., & Delahanty, D. L. (2011). The influence of family environment on dissociation in pediatric injury patients. *Clinical Child Psychology and Psychiatry, 16*, 485–497.

Nunes, K. L., Hanson, R. K., Firestone, P., Moulden, H. M., Greenberg, D. M., & Bradford, J. M. (2007). Denial predicts recidivism for some sexual offenders. *Sexual Abuse, 19*, 91–105.

Nunes, K. L., & Jung, S. (2012). Are cognitive distortions associated with denial and minimization among sex offenders? *Sexual Abuse, 25*, 166–188.

Nussbaum, M. C. (2004). *Hiding from humanity: Disgust, shame and the law.* Princeton/Oxford: Princeton University Press.

Odling-Smee, J., Erwin, D. H., Palkovacs, E. P., Feldman, M. W., & Laland, K. N. (2013). Niche construction theory: A practical guide for ecologists. *Quarterly Review of Biology, 88*(1), 4–28.

Ogawa, J. R., Sroufe, L. A., Weinfield, N. S., Carlson, E. A., & Egeland, B. (1997). Development and the fragmented self: Longitudinal study of dissociative symptomatology in a nonclinical sample. *Developmental Psychopathology, 9*, 855–879.

Okuda, J., Fujii, T., Ohtake, H., Tsukiura, T., Tanji, K., Suzuki, K., . . . Yamadori, A. (2003). Thinking of the future and past: the roles of the frontal pole and the medial temporal lobes. *Neuroimage, 19*, 1369–1380.

Okuda, J., Fujii, T., Yamadori, A., Kawashima, R., Tsukiura, T., Fukatsu, R., . . . Fukuda, H. (1998). Participation of the prefrontal cortices in prospective memory: Evidence from a PET study in humans. *Neuroscience Letters, 253*, 127–130.

Oliveri, M., Babiloni, C., Filippi, M. M., Caltagirone, C., Babiloni, F., Cicinelli, P., . . . Rossini, P. M. (2003). Influence of the supplementary motor area on primary motor cortex excitability during movements triggered by neutral or emotionally unpleasant visual cues. *Experimental Brain Research, 149*, 214–221.

O'Neil, J. A. (1997). Expanding the psychoanalytic view of the intrapsychic: Psychic conflict in the inscape. *Dissociation, 10*, 192–202.

Ongür, D., Ferry, A. T., & Price, J. L. (2003). Architectonic subdivision of the human orbital and medial prefrontal cortex. *Journal of Comparative Neurology, 460*, 425–449.

Oppenheim, H. (1884). Über einen sich an Kopfverletzungen und allgemeinen Erschütterungen anschliessenden cerebralen Symptomencomplex [On a complex of cerebral symptoms subsequent to brain injuries and general concussions]. *Berliner klinische Wochenschrift, 21*, 725.

Oppenheim H. (1889). *Die traumatischen Neurosen, nach den in der Nervenklinik der Charité in den letzten 5 Jahren gesammelten Beobachtungen* [The traumatic neuroses, according to the collected observations during the last 5 years in the psychiatric clinic Charité]. Berlin: Hirschwald.

Orr, S. P. (1997). Psychophysiologic reactivity to trauma-related imagery in PTSD: Diagnostic and theoretical implications of recent findings. *Annals of the New York Academy of Sciences, 821*, 114–124.

Orr, S. P., Lasko, N. B., Metzger, L. J., Berry, N. J., Ahern, C. E., & Pitman, R. K. (1997). Psychophysiologic assessment of PTSD in adult females sexually abused during childhood. *Annals of the New York Academy of Sciences, 821*, 491–493.

Orr, S. P., Metzger, L. J., Lasko, N. B., Macklin, M. L., Hu, F. B., Shalev, A. Y., & Harvard/Veterans Affairs Posttraumatic Stress Disorder Twin Study. (2003). Physiologic responses to sudden, loud tones in monozygotic twins discordant for combat exposure: Association with posttraumatic stress disorder. *Archives of General Psychiatry, 60*, 283–288.

Orr, S. P., & Pitman, R. K. (1993). Psychophysiologic assessment of attempts to simulate posttraumatic stress disorder. *Biological Psychiatry, 33*, 127–129.

Ortiz, J., & Raine, A. (2004). Heart rate level and antisocial behavior in children and adolescents: A meta-analysis. *Journal of the American Academy of Child and Adolescent Psychiatry, 43*, 154–162.

Osei-Bonsu, P. E., Spiro III, A., Schultz, M. R., Ryabchenko, K. A., Smith, E., Herz, L., & Eisen, S. V. (2012). Is DMS-IV Criterion A2 associated with PTSD diagnosis and symptom severity? *Journal of Traumatic Stress, 25*, 368–375.

Osuch, E. A., Benson, B., Geraci, M., Podell, D., Herscovitch, P., McCann, U. D., & Post, R. M. (2001). Regional cerebral blood flow correlated with flashback intensity in patients with posttraumatic stress disorder. *Biological Psychiatry, 50*, 246–253.

Out, D., Bakermans-Kranenburg, M. J., & Van IJzendoorn, M. H. (2009). The role of disconnected and extremely insensitive parenting in the development of disorganized attachment: Validation of a new measure. *Attachment and Human Development, 11*, 419–443.

Ozcetin, A., Belli, H., Ertem, U., Bahcebasi, T., Ataoglu, A., & Canan, F. (2009). Childhood trauma and dissociation in women with pseudoseizure-type conversion disorder. *Nordic Journal of Psychiatry, 63*, 462–468.

Ozer, E. J., Best, S. R., Lipsey, T. L., & Weiss, D. S. (2003). Predictors of posttraumatic stress disorder and symptoms in adults: A meta-analysis. *Psychological Bulletin, 129*, 52–73.

Ozturk, E., & Sar, V. (2008). Somatization as a predictor of suicidal ideation in dissociative disorders. *Psychiatry and Clinical Neuroscience, 62*, 662–668.

Papagni, S. A., Benetti, S., Arulanantham, S., McCrory, E., McGuire, P., & Mechelli, A. (2010). Effects of stressful life events on human brain structure: A longitudinal voxel-based morphometry study. *Stress, 14*, 227–232.

Page, H. W. (1891). *Railway injuries: With special reference to those of the back and nervous system, in their medico-legal and clinical aspects.* London: Charles Griffin.

Panksepp, J. (1998). *Affective neuroscience: The foundations of human and animal emotions.* New York: Oxford University Press.

Panksepp. J. (2003). At the interface of affective, behavioral, and cognitive neurosciences: Decoding the emotional feelings of the brain. *Current Directions in Psychological Sciences, 7*, 91–98.

Panksepp, J., & Biven, L. (2012). *The archeology of mind: Neuroevolutionary origins of human emotions.* New York: Norton.

Pannu Hayes, J., Labar, K. S., Petty, C. M., McCarthy, G., & Morey, R. A. (2009). Alterations in the neural circuitry for emotion and attention associated with posttraumatic stress symptomatology. *Psychiatry Research, 172*, 7–15.

Parvin, T. (1885). Foreign bodies in the vagina. *Medical and Surgical Reporter, 53*, 29.

Pasternak, T., Bisley, J. W., & Calkins, D. (2003). Visual information processing in the primate brain. In M. Gallagher & R. J. Nelson (Eds.), *Biological psychology* (pp. 139–185). New York: Wiley.

Pavani, F., La'davas, E., & Driver, J. (2003). Auditory and multisensory aspects of visuospatial neglect. *Trends in Cognitive Science (Regul Ed), 7*, 407–414.

Pavlov, I. (1927). *Conditioned reflexes: An investigation of the physiological activity of the cerebral cortex* (transl. G. V. Anrep). London: Oxford University Press.

Payer, P. J. (1984). *Sex and the Penitentials: The development of a sexual code 550–1150.* Toronto: University of Toronto Press.

Pearlman, L. A., & Courtois, C. A. (2005). Clinical applications of the attachment framework: Relational treatment of complex trauma. *Journal of Traumatic Stress, 18*, 449–459.

Pedersen, N. L., Plomin, R., McClearn, G. E., & Friberg, L. (1988). Neuroticism, extraversion, and related traits in adult twins reared apart and reared together. *Journal of Personality and Social Psychology, 55*, 950–957.

Pederson, C. L., & Wilson, J. F. (2009). Childhood emotional neglect related to posttraumatic disorder symptoms and body mass index in adult women. *Psychological Reports, 105*(1), 111–126.

Peirce, C. S. (1978). *Collected papers, Vol. II: Elements of logic.* (C. Hartshorne & P. Weiss, Eds.). Cambridge, MA: Belknap.

Pekala, R. J., Angelini, F., & Kumar, V. K. (2001). The importance of fantasy-proneness in dissociation: A replication. *Contemporary Hypnosis, 18*, 204–214.

Pekala, R. J., Kumar, V. K., Ainslie, G., Elliott, N. C., Mullen, K. J., Salinger, M. M., & Masten, E. (1999–2000). Dissociation as a function of child abuse and fantasy proneness in a substance abuse population. *Imagination, Cognition and Personality, 19*, 105–129.

Perry, B. D. (2002). Childhood experience and the expression of genetic potential: What childhood neglect tells us about nature and nurture. *Brain and Mind, 3*, 79–100.

Perry, B. D., & Pollard, R. (1998). Homeostasis, stress, trauma, and adaptation: A neurodevelopmental view of childhood trauma. *Child and Adolescent Psychiatric Clinics of North America, 7*, 33–51, viii.

Perry, B. D., Pollard, R. A., Blakely, T. L., Baker, W. L., & Vigilante, D. (1995). Childhood trauma, the neurobiology of adaptation, and "use dependent" development of the brain: How "states" become "traits." *Infant Mental Health Journal, 16*, 271–291.

Petitmengin, C. (2007). Towards the source of thoughts: The gestural and transmodal dimension of lived experience, *Journal of Consciousness Studies, 14*(3), 54–82.

Phillips, M. L., Senior, C., Fahy, T., & David, A. S. (1998). Disgust–The forgotten emotion of psychiatry. *British Journal of Psychiatry, 172,* 373–375.

Phillips, M. L., Young, A. W., Senior, C., Brammer, M., Andrew, C., Calder, A. J., . . . David, A. S. (1997). A specific neural substrate for perceiving facial expressions of disgust. *Nature, 389,* 495–498.

Piaget, J. (1959). *The language and thought of the child* (3rd ed.). London: Routledge & Kegan Paul.

Pineda, J. A. (2008). Sensorimotor cortex as a critical component of an 'extended' mirror neuron system: Does it solve the development, correspondence, and control problems in mirroring? *Behavioral & Brain Functions, 4,* 47.

Pinheiro, P. S. (2006). *World report on violence against children. United Nations Secretary-General's Study on Violence Against Children.* Geneva: ATAR Roto Presse. Retrieved from http://www.unicef.org

Piper, A., & Merskey, H. (2004a). The persistence of folly: A critical examination of dissociative identity disorder, Part I: The excesses of an improbable concept. *Canadian Journal of Psychiatry, 49,* 592–600.

Piper, A., & Merskey, H. (2004b). The persistence of folly: Critical examination of dissociative identity disorder, Part II: The defence and decline of multiple personality or dissociative identity disorder. *Canadian Journal of Psychiatry, 49,* 678–683.

Piper, A., & Merskey, H. (2005). The persistence of folly: A critical examination of dissociative identity disorder. *Canadian Journal of Psychiatry, 50,* 814.

Pissiota, A., Frans, O., Fernandez, M., von Knorring, L., Fischer, H., Fredrikson, M. (2002). Neurofunctional correlates of posttraumatic stress disorder: A PET symptom provocation study. *European Archives of Psychiatry and Clinical Neuroscience, 252,* 68–75.

Pitcher, D., Walsh, V., Yovel, G., & Duchaine, B. (2007). TMS evidence for the involvement of the right occipital face area in early face processing. *Current Biology, 17,* 1568–1573.

Pitta, J. C., & Blay, S. L. (1997). Psychogenic (reactive) and hysterical psychoses: A cross-system reliability study. *Acta Psychiatrica Scandinavica, 95,* 112–118.

Platt, R. D., Lacey, S. C., Iobst, A. D., & Finkelman, D. (1998). Absorption, dissociation, and fantasy-proneness as predictors of memory distortion in autobiographical and laboratory-generated memories. *Applied Cognitive Psychology, 12,* S77–S89.

Pliny. *Natural history*. 20.87.238 (cited in H. King, 1993).

Plomin, R., DeFries, J. C., McClearn, G. E., & Rutter, M. (1997). *Behavioral genetics* (3rd ed.). New York: Freeman.

Porges, S. W. (1995). Orienting in a defensive world: Mammalian modifications of our evolutionary heritage: A polyvagal theory. *Psychophysiology, 32,* 301–318.

Porges, S. W. (2001). The polyvagal theory: Phylogenetic substrates of a social nervous system. *International Journal of Psychophysiology, 42,* 123–146.

Porges, S. W. (2003). The polyvagal theory: Phylogenetic contributions to social behavior. *Physiology of Behavior, 79,* 503–513.

Porges, S. W. (2007). The polyvagal perspective. *Biological Psychology, 74,* 116–143.

Porges, S. W. (2009). The polyvagal theory: New insights into adaptive reactions of the autonomic nervous system. *Cleveland Clinical Journal of Medicine, 76*(Suppl 2), S86-S90.

Poulsen, B. C., & Matthews, Jr. W. J. (2003). Correlates of imaginative and hypnotic suggestibility in children. *Contemporary Hypnosis, 20,* 198–208.

Poythress, N. G., Skeem, J. L., & Lilienfeld, S. O. (2006). Associations among early abuse, dissociation, and psychopathy in an offender sample. *Journal of Abnormal Psychology, 115,* 288–297.

Price, D. B., Thaler, M., & Mason, J. W. (1957). Preoperative emotional states and adrenal contrical activity. *Archives of General Psychiatry, 77,* 646–656.

Prince, M. (1897–1898). Traumatic neurosis. In A. L. Loomis & W. G. Thompson (Eds.), *A system of practical medicine by American authors* (4 volumes). Philadelphia: Lea Brothers.

Prinquet, G. (1977). À propos d'un cas de psychose hystérique [On a case of hysterical psychosis]. *Nouvelle Presse Médicale, 6,* 441–443.

Proenca, I. C., Castro, L. H., Jorge, C. L., & Marchetti, R. L. (2011). Emotional trauma and abuse in patients with psychogenic nonepileptic seizures. *Epilepsy and Behavior, 20,* 331–333.

Putnam, F. W. (1988). The switch process in multiple personality disorder. *Dissociation, 1*(1), 24–32.

Putnam, F. W. (1992). Using hypnosis for therapeutic abreactions. *Psychiatric Medicine, 10*(1), 51–65.

Putnam, F. W. (1993). Dissociative disorders in children: Behavioral profiles and problems. *Child Abuse and Neglect, 17*(1), 39–45.

Putnam, F. W. (1997). *Dissociation in children and adolescents: A developmental perspective.* New York: Guilford.

Putnam, F. W., Buchsbaum, M. S., & Post, R. M. (1993). *Differential brain electrical activity in multiple personality disorder.* Unpublished manuscript.

Putnam, F. W., Buchsbaum, M. S., Howland, F., & Post, R. M. (1992, May). *Evoked potentials in multiple personality disorder (abstract #137).* Presented at the Annual Meeting of the American Psychiatric Association, New Orleans.

Putnam, F. W., & Carlson, E. B. (1998). Hypnosis, dissociation, and trauma: Myths, metaphors, and mechanisms. In J. D. Bremner, & C. R. Marmar (Eds.), *Trauma, memory, and dissociation* (pp. 27–55). Washington DC: American Psychiatric Press.

Putnam, F. W., Helmers, K., & Trickett, P. K. (1993). Development, reliability and validity of a child dissociation scale. *Child Abuse and Neglect, 17,* 731–741.

Putnam, F. W., Helmers, K., Horowitz, L. A., & Trickett, P. K. (1995). Hypnotizability and dissociativity in sexually abused girls. *Child Abuse and Neglect, 19,* 645–655.

Putnam, F. W., Zahn, T. P., & Post, R. M. (1990). Differential autonomic nervous system activity in multiple personality disorder. *Psychiatry Research, 31,* 251–260.

Putnam, H. (1981). *Reason, truth and history.* Cambridge: Cambridge University Press.

Queller, D. C., & Strassmann, J. E. (2002). The many selves of social insects. *Science, 296,* 311–313.

Quirin, M., Gillath, O., Pruessner, J. C., & Eggert, L. D. (2010). Adult attachment insecurity and hippocampal cell density. *Social Cognitive and Affective Neuroscience, 5,* 39–47.

Radden, J. (2000). *The nature of melancholia: From Aristotle to Kristeva.* New York: Oxford University Press.

Raftery, J. (2003). *Marks of war: War neurosis and the legacy of Kokoda.* Adelaide: Lythrum.

Raichle, M. E., MacLeod, A. M., Snyder, A. Z., Powers, W. J., Gusnard, D. A., & Shulman, G. L. (2001). A default mode of brain function. *Proceedings of the National Academy of Sciences USA, 98,* 676–682.

Raichle, M. E., & Snyder, A. Z. (2007). A default mode of brain function: A brief history of an evolving idea. *Neuroimage, 37,* 1083–1090, 1097–1099.

Raine, A. (1993). *The psychopathology of crime: Criminal behavior as a clinical disorder.* San Diego, CA: Academic Press.

Raine, A. (2002a). Annotation: the role of prefrontal deficits, low autonomic arousal, and early health factors in the development of antisocial and aggressive behavior in children. *Journal of Child Psychology and Psychiatry, 43,* 417–434.

Raine, A. (2002b). Biosocial studies of antisocial and violent behavior in children and adults: A review. *Journal of Abnormal Child Psychology, 30,* 311–326.

Raine, A., Venables, P. H., Mednick, S. A. (1997). Low resting heart rate at age 3 years predisposes to aggression at age 11 years: Evidence from the Mauritius Child Health Project. *Journal of the American Academy of Child and Adolescent Psychiatry, 36,* 1457–1464.

Rassin, E., Merckelbach, H., & Spaan, V. (2001). When dreams become a royal road to confusion: Realistic dreams, dissociation, and fantasy proneness. *Journal of Nervous and Mental Disease, 189*, 478–481.

Rauch, S. L., Shin, L. M., & Phelps, E. A. (2006). Neurocircuitry models of posttraumatic stress disorder and extinction: Human neuroimaging research–Past, present, and future. *Biological Psychiatry, 60*, 376–382.

Rauch, S. L., Van der Kolk, B. A., Fisler, R. E., Alpert, N. M., Orr, S. P., Savage, C. R., & Pitman, R. K. (1996). A symptom provocation study of posttraumatic stress disorder using positron emission tomography and script-driven imagery. *Archives of General Psychiatry, 53*, 380–387.

Raulin, J. (1758). *Traité des affections vaporeuses du sexe* [Treatise on the vaporous affections of the female organ]. Paris.

Rauschenberger, S. L., & Lynn, S. J. (1995). Fantasy proneness, DSM-III-R axis I psychopathology, and dissociation. *Journal of Abnormal Psychology, 104*, 373–380.

Read, J., van Os, J., Morrison, A. P., & Ross, C. A. (2005). Childhood trauma, psychosis and schizophrenia: A literature review with theoretical and clinical implications. *Acta Psychiatrica Scandinavica, 112*, 330–350.

Reavis, J. A., Looman, J., Franco, K. A., & Rojas, B. (2013). Adverse childhood experiences and adult criminality: How long must we live before we possess our own lives? *The Permanente Journal, 17*(2), 44–48.

Reckdenwald, A., Mancini, C., & Beauregard, E. (2013). The cycle of violence: Examining the impact of maltreatment early in life on adult offending. *Violence and Victims, 28*, 466–482.

Reed, S. F., Ohel, G., David, R., & Porges, S. W. (1999). A neural explanation of fetal heart rate patterns: A test of the polyvagal theory. *Developmental Psychobiology, 35*, 108–118.

Reinders, A. A. T. S. (2014, March). Neurostructural correlates of trauma and dissociation: A magnetic resonance imaging study in PTSD and DID. In *Trauma, dissociation, and attachment in the 21st Century: Where are we heading?* Fourth Bi-annual International Conference of the European Society for Trauma and Dissociation, Copenhagen.

Reinders, A. A. T. S., & Nijenhuis, E. R. S. (2012). How well are the dissociative identity disorder simulating healthy controls doing? Supporting information SII. *PLoS ONE 7*(6), e39279.

Reinders, A. A. T. S., Nijenhuis, E. R. S., Paans, A. M. J., Korf, J., Willemsen, A. T. M., & Den Boer, J. A. (2003). One brain, two selves. *NeuroImage, 20*, 2119–2125.

Reinders, A. A. T. S., Nijenhuis, E. R. S., Quak, J., Korf, J., Paans, A. M. J., Haaksma, J., . . . Den Boer, J. A. (2006). Psychobiological characteristics of dissociative Identity disorder: A symptom provocation study. *Biological Psychiatry, 60*, 730–740.

Reinders, A. A. T. S., Willemsen, A. T. M., Vos, H. P. J., Den Boer, J. A., & Nijenhuis, E. R. S. (2012). Fact or factitious? A psychobiological study of authentic and simulated dissociative identity states. *PLoS ONE 7*(6), e39279.

Resick, P. A., Bovin, M. J., Calloway, A. L., Dick, A. M., King, M. W., Mitchell, K. S., . . . Wolf, E. J. (2012). A critical evaluation of the complex PTSD literature: Implications for DSM-5. *Journal of Traumatic Stress, 25*, 241–251.

Resick, P. A., & Miller, M. W. (2009). Posttraumatic stress disorder: Anxiety or traumatic stress disorder? *Journal of Traumatic Stress, 22*, 384–390.

Resnick, H. S., Best, C. L., Kilpatrick, D. G., Freedy, J. R., & Falsetti, S. A. (1993). *Trauma Assessment for Adults – Self-Report Version (TAA SR)*. Unpublished assessment instrument. Charleston, SC. National Crime Victims Research and Treatment Center, Medical University of South Carolina.

Reza, A., Breiding, M. J., Gulaid, J., Mercy, J. A., Blanton, C., Mthethwa, Z., & Anderson, M. (2009). Sexual violence and its health consequences for female children in Swaziland: A cluster survey study. *Lancet, 373*(9679), 1966–1972.

Rhue, J. W., & Lynn, S. J. (1987). Fantasy proneness: Developmental antecedents. *Journal of Personality, 55,* 121–137.

Rhue, J. W., & Lynn, S. J. (1987). Fantasy proneness and psychopathology. *Journal of Personality and Social Psychology, 53,* 327–336.

Rilke, R. M. (2005). *Book of hours: Love poems to God* (transl. A. Barrows and J. Macy). New York: Riverhead Trade.

Rinne-Albers, M. A., van der Wee, N. J., Lamers-Winkelman, F., & Vermeiren, R. R. (2013). Neuroimaging in children, adolescents and young adults with psychological trauma. *European Child and Adolescent Psychiatry, 22,* 745–755.

Rivers, W.H. R. (1920). *Instinct and the unconscious: A contribution to a biological theory of the psycho-neuroses.* Cambridge: Cambridge University Press. Retrieved from http://psychclassics.yorku.ca/Rivers/chap15.htm

Rizzolatti, G., & Sinigaglia, C. (2007). Mirror neurons and motor intentionality. *Functional Neurology, 22,* 205–210.

Robb, H. (1892). Hippocrates on hysteria. *John Hopkins Hospital Bulletin, 3,* 78–79.

Robinson, N. (1729). *A new system of the spleen.* London. Cited in Rousseau (1993).

Robinson, H. (2009). Idealism. In B. P. McLaughlin, A. Beckermann, & S. Walter (Eds.), *The Oxford handbook of philosophy of mind* (pp. 189–205). Oxford: Clarendon.

Robinson, W. J. (1917). *Woman: Her sex and love life.* New York: Critic and Guide Co.

Robinson, W. J. (1931). *America's sex, marriage, and divorce problem.* New York: Eugenics Publishing Co.

Rodewald, F., Wilhelm-Goling, C., Emrich, H. M., Reddemann, L., & Gast, U. (2011). Axis-I comorbidity in female patients with dissociative identity disorder and dissociative identity disorder not otherwise specified. *Journal of Nervous and Mental Disease, 199,* 122–131.

Rodriguez-Srednicki, O. (2001). Childhood sexual abuse, dissociation, and adult self-destructive behavior. *Journal of Child Sexual Abuse, 10,* 75–90.

Roelofs, K., Hoogduin, K. A., Keijsers, G. P., Naring, G. W., Moene, F. C., & Sandijck, P. (2002a). Hypnotic susceptibility in patients with conversion disorder. *Journal of Abnormal Psychology, 111,* 390–395.

Roelofs, K., Keijsers, G. P., Hoogduin, K. A., Naring, G. W., & Moene, F. C. (2002b). Childhood abuse in patients with conversion disorder. *American Journal of Psychiatry, 159,* 1908–1913.

Rogeness, G. A., Cepeda, C., Macedo, C. A., Fischer, C., & Harris, W. R. (1990). Differences in heart rate and blood pressure in children with conduct disorder, major depression, and separation anxiety. *Psychiatry Research, 33,* 199–206.

Rolls, E. T. (1999). *The brain and emotion.* Oxford, UK: Oxford University Press.

Rolls, E. T., Tovee, M. J., & Panzeri, S. (1999). The neurophysiology of backward visual masking: Information analysis. *Journal of Cognitive Neuroscience, 11,* 300–311.

Rosch, E. (1977). Human categorization. In N. Warren (Ed.), *Advances in cross-cultural psychology* (Vol. 1, pp. 1–49). London: Academic Press.

Rosen, H. J., & Levenson, R. W. (2009). The emotional brain: Combining insights from patients and basic science. *Neurocase, 15,* 173–181.

Ross, C. A. (1997). *Dissociative identity disorder: Diagnosis, clinical features, and treatment of multiple personality.* New York: Wiley.

Ross, C. A. (2008). Case report: A convicted sex offender with dissociative identity disorder. *Journal of Trauma & Dissociation, 9,* 551–562.

Ross, C. A. (2009). Errors of logic and scholarship concerning dissociative identity disorder. *Journal of Child Sexual Abuse, 18,* 221–231.

Ross, C. A. (2011). Possession experiences in dissociative identity disorder: A preliminary study. *Journal of Trauma & Dissociation, 12,* 393–400.

Ross, C. A., Anderson, G., Fraser, G. A., Reagor, P., Bjornson, L., & Miller, S. D. (1992). Differentiating multiple personality disorder and dissociative disorder not otherwise specified. *Dissociation, 5,* 88–91.

Ross, C. A., Duffy, C. M. M., & Ellason, J. W. (2002). Prevalence, reliability, and validity of dissociative disorders in an inpatient setting. *Journal of Trauma & Dissociation, 3,* 7–17.

Ross, C. A., & Ellason, J. W. (2005). Discriminating among diagnostic categories using the Dissociative Disorders Interview Schedule. *Psychological Reports, 96,* 445–453.

Ross, C. A., Keyes, B. B., Yan, H., Wang, Z., Zou, Z., Zheng, Z., . . . Xiao, Z. (2008). A cross-cultural test of the trauma model of dissociation. *Journal of Trauma & Dissociation, 9,* 35–49.

Ross, C. A., & Ness, L. (2010). Symptom patterns in dissociative identity disorder patients and the general population. *Journal of Trauma & Dissociation, 11,* 458–468.

Ross, J. M. (1882). On some medico-legal aspects of wounds of the external female genitals. *New England Medical Monthly, 2,* 348–353.

Ross, T. A. (1941). *Lectures on war neuroses.* Baltimore: Williams & Wilkins.

Rousseau, G. S. (1993). A strange pathology: Hysteria in the early modern world, 1500–1800. In S. L. Gilman, H. King, R. Porter, G.S. Rousseau, & E. Showalter (Eds.), *Hysteria beyond Freud* (pp. 91–221). Berkeley, CA: University of California Press.

Rozin, P., Lowery, L., & Ebert, R. (1994). Varieties of disgust faces and the structure of disgust. *Journal of Personality and Social Psychology, 66,* 870–881.

Ruethling, G. (2006). 27 charged in international online child pornography ring. *New York Times*, March 16. Retrieved from http://www.nytimes.com/2006/03/16/national/16porn.html?_r=0&adxnnl=1&adxnnlx=1416121369-YjVAqOmy9t57 Fxq6WAPcsw

Ruiz, M. A., Poythress, N. G., Lilienfeld, S. O., & Douglas, K. S. (2008). Factor structure and correlates of the dissociative experiences scale in a large offender sample. *Assessment, 15,* 511–521.

Ruiz Zafón, C. (2005). *The shadow of wind* (L. Graves, trans.). London: Phoenix.

Runtz, M. G., & Schallow, J. R. (1997). Social support and coping strategies as mediators of adult adjustment following childhood maltreatment. *Child Abuse and Neglect, 21,* 211–226.

Ryan, J. P., Williams, A. B., & Courtney, M. E. (2013). Adolescent neglect, juvenile delinquency and the risk of recidivism. *Journal of Youth and Adolescence, 42,* 454–465.

Sachinvala, N., Kling, A., Suffin, S., Lake, R., & Cohen M. (2000). Increased regional cerebral perfusion by 99mTc hexamethyl propylene amine oxime single photon emission computed tomography in posttraumatic stress disorder. *Military Medicine, 165,* 473–479.

Sacks, O. (1984). *A leg to stand on.* London: Duckworth.

Saha, S., Chant, D., Welham, J., & McGrath, J. (2005). A systematic review of the prevalence of schizophrenia. *PLoS Medicine, 2*(5), e141.

Sahar, T., Shalev, A. Y., & Porges, S. W. (2001). Vagal modulation of responses to mental challenge in posttraumatic stress disorder. *Biological Psychiatry, 49,* 637–643.

Sakagami, M., & Niki, H. (1994). Encoding of behavioral significance of visual stimuli by primate prefrontal neurons: Relation to relevant task conditions. *Experimental Brain Research, 97,* 423–436.

Sakamoto, H., Fukuda, R., Okuaki, T., Rogers, M., Kasai, K., Machida, T., . . . Kato, N. (2005). Parahippocampal activation evoked by masked traumatic images in posttraumatic stress disorder: A functional MRI study. *Neuroimage, 26,* 813–821.

Sar, V. (2005). Re: The persistence of folly: A critical examination of dissociative identity disorder: What are Dr. Piper and Dr. Merskey trying to do? *Canadian Journal of Psychiatry, 50,* 813.

Sar, V. (2011a). Epidemiology of dissociative disorders: An overview. *Epidemiology Research International Volume 2011.* Article ID 404538, http://dx.doi.org/10.1155/2011/404538

Sar, V. (2011b). Developmental trauma, complex PTSD, and the current proposal of DSM-5. *European Journal of Psychotraumatology, 2,* 56222

Sar, V., Akyuz, G., & Dogan, O. (2007a). Prevalence of dissociative disorders among women in the general population. *Psychiatry Research, 149,* 169–176.

Sar, V., Akyuz, G., Kugu, N., Ozturk, E., & Ertem-Vehid, H. (2006). Axis I dissociative disorder comorbidity in borderline personality disorder and reports of childhood trauma. *Journal of Clinical Psychiatry, 67,* 1583–1590.

Sar, V., Akyuz, G., Kundakçi, T., Kiziltan, E., & Dogan, O. (2004). Childhood trauma, dissociation, and psychiatric comorbidity in patients with conversion disorder. *American Journal of Psychiatry, 161,* 2271–2276.

Sar, V., Koyuncu, A., Ozturk, E., Yargic, L. I., Kundakçi, T., Yazici, A., . . . Aksü, D. (2007b). Dissociative disorders in the psychiatric emergency ward. *General Hospital Psychiatry, 29,* 45–50.

Sar, V., Kundakçi, T., Kiziltan, E., Bakim, B., & Bozkurt, O. (2000). Differentiating dissociative disorders from other diagnostic groups through somatoform dissociation in Turkey. *Journal of Trauma & Dissociation, 1*(4), 67–80.

Sar, V., Middleton, W., & Dorahy, M. J. (2012). The scientific status of childhood dissociative identity disorder: A review of published research. *Psychotherapy and Psychosomatics, 81,* 183–184, 185.

Sar, V., Onder, C., Kilicaslan, A., Zoroglu, S. S., & Alyanak, B. (2014). Dissociative identity disorder among adolescents: Prevalence in a university psychiatric outpatient unit. *Journal of Trauma & Dissociation, 15,* 402–419.

Sar, V., Unal, S. N., Kiziltan, E., Kundakçi, T., & Ozturk, E. (2001). HMPAO SPECT study of regional cerebral blood flow in dissociative identity disorder. *Journal of Trauma & Dissociation, 2,* 5–25.

Sar, V., Unal, S. N., & Ozturk, E. (2007c). Frontal and occipital perfusion changes in dissociative identity disorder. *Psychiatry Research, 156,* 217–223.

Sassoon, S. (1961). *Collected poems 1908–1956.* London: Faber & Faber.

Saulsman, L. M., & Page, A. C. (2004). The five-factor model and personality disorder empirical literature: A meta-analytic review. *Clinical Psychology Review, 23,* 1055–1085.

Savitz, J. B., van der Merwe, L., Newman, T. K., Solms, M., Stein, D. J., & Ramesar, R. S. (2008). The relationship between childhood abuse and dissociation: Is it influenced by catechol-O-methyltransferase (COMT) activity? *International Journal of Neuropsychopharmacology, 11,* 149–161.

Saver, J. L., & Rabin, J. (1997). The neural substrates of religious experience. In S. Salloway, P. Malloy, & J. L. Cummings (Eds.), *The neuropsychiatry of limbic and subcortical disorders* (pp. 195–207). Washington: American Psychiatric Press.

Saxe, G. N., Vasile, R. G., Hill, T. C., Bloomingdale, K., & Van der Kolk, B. A. (1992). SPECT imaging and multiple personality disorder. *Journal of Nervous and Mental Disease, 180,* 662–663.

Scevola, L., Teitelbaum, J., Oddo, S., Centurion, E., Loidl, C. F., Kochen, S., & D'Allesio, L. (2013). Psychiatric disorders in patients with psychogenic nonepileptic seizures and drug-resistant epilepsy: A study of an Argentine population. *Epilepsy and Behavior, 29*(1), 155–160.

Schacter, D. L., & Addis, D. R. (2007). The cognitive neuroscience of constructive memory: Remembering the past and imagining the future. *Philosophical Transactions of the Royal Society of London. Series B: Biological Sciences, 362,* 773–786.

Schäffner, W. (2003). Events, series, trauma: The probabilistic revolution of the mind in the late nineteenth and early twentieth centuries. In M. S. Micale & P. Lerner (Eds.), *Traumatic pasts: History, psychiatry and trauma in the modern age, 1870–1930* (pp. 81–91). Cambridge: Cambridge University Press.

Schienle, A., Stark, R., Walter, B., Blecker, C., Ott, U., Kirsch, P., . . . Vaitl, D. (2002). The insula is not specifically involved in disgust processing: An fMRI study. *Neuroreport, 13,* 2023–2026.

Schlumpf, Y. R., Reinders, A. A. T. S., Nijenhuis, E. R. S., Luechinger, R., Van Osch, M.J. P., & Jäncke, L. (2014). Dissociative part-dependent resting-state activity in dissociative identity disorder: A controlled fMRI perfusion study. *PLoS ONE, 9*(6), e98795.

Schlumpf, Y. R., Nijenhuis, E. R. S., Chalavi, S., Weder, E. V., Zimmermann, E., Luechinger, R., & Jäncke, L. (2013). Dissociative-part dependent biopsychosocial reactions to backward masked angry and neutral faces: An fMRI study of dissociative identity disorder. *Neuroimage: Clinical, 3*, 54–64.

Schlumpf, Y. R., Reinders, A. A. T. S., Nijenhuis, E. R. S., Luechinger, R., Van Osch, M.J. P., & Jäncke, L. (2014). Dissociative part-dependent resting-state activity in dissociative identity disorder: A controlled fMRI perfusion study. *PLoS ONE, 9*(6), e98795.

Schmahl, C. G., Elzinga, B. M., & Bremner, J. D. (2002). Individual differences in psychophysiological reactivity in adults with childhood abuse. *Clinical Psychology and Psychotherapy, 9*, 271–276.

Schmahl, C., Lanius, R. A., Pain, C., & Vermetten, E. (2010). Biological framework for traumatic dissociation related to early life trauma. In R. A. Lanius, E. Vermetten, & C. Pain (Eds.), *The impact of early life trauma on health and disease: The hidden epidemic* (pp. 178–188). Cambridge: Cambridge University Press.

Schmeck, K., & Poustka F. (1993). Psychophysiologische Reaktionsmuster und psychische Auffälligkeiten im Kindesalter [Psychophysiological reaction patterns and mental peculiarities in childhood]. In P. Baumann (Ed.), *Biologische Psychiatrie der Gegenwart* [Contemporary biological psychiatry] (pp. 359–364). Vienna: Springer-Verlag.

Schneider, S., Brassen, S., Bromberg, U., Banaschewski, T., Conrod, P., Flor, H., . . . Consortium, I. (2012). Maternal interpersonal affiliation is associated with adolescents' brain structure and reward processing. *Translational Psychiatry, 2*, e182.

Schnurr, P. P., Spiro III, A., Vielhauer, M. J., Findler, M.N, & Hamblen, J. L. (2002). Trauma in the lives of older men: Findings from the Normative Aging Study. *Journal of Clinical Gerontopsychology, 8*, 175–187.

Schopenhauer, A. (1958). *The world as will and representation, Vol. I (1818) and Vol. II (1844)* (transl. Richard Burdon Haldane Haldane & John Kemp). Clinton, MA: The Falcon's Wing.

Schopenhauer, A. (1813/2007). *On the fourfold root of the principle of sufficient reason.* New York: Cosima.

Schore, A. N. (2001). The effects of relational trauma on right brain development, affect regulation, and infant mental health. *Infant Mental Health Journal 2001, 22*, 201–269.

Schore A. N. (Ed.). (2003). *Affect dysregulation and disorders of the self.* New York: Norton.

Schubert, C. (2011). Soziopsychoneuroimmunologie: Integration von dynamic und subjektiver Bedeutung in die Psychoneuroimmunologie [Sociopsychoneuroimmunology: Integration of dynamic and subjective meaning in psychoimmunology]. In C. Schubert (Ed.), *Psychoneuroimmunologie und Psychotherapie* [Psychoimmunology and psychotherapy](pp. 374–405). Stuttgart: Schattauer.

Schuengel, C., Bakermans-Kranenburg, M. J., & Van IJzendoorn, M. H. (1999). Frightening maternal behavior linking unresolved loss and disorganized infant attachment. *Journal of Consulting and Clinical Psychology, 67*, 54–63.

Schultze, (1890). Internationaler Kongress in Berlin. [International conference in Berlin.] *Neurologisches Centralblatt, 9*, 509–512.

Schwabe, L., Dalm, S., Schächinger, H., & Oitzl, M. S. (2008). Chronic stress modulates the use of spatial and stimulus-response learning strategies in mice and man. *Neurobiological Learning and Memory, 90*, 495–503.

Schwabe, L., Oitzl, M. S., & Schächinger, H. (2007). Stress modulates the use of spatial versus stimulus-response learning strategies in humans. *Learning & Memory, 14*, 109–116.

Schwabe, L., Schächinger, H., de Kloet, E. R., & Oitzl, M. S. (2010). Stress impairs spatial but not early stimulus response learning. *Behavioral Brain Research, 213*(1), 50 55.

Scott, K. L., & King, C. B. (2007). Resistance, reluctance, and readiness in perpetrators of abuse against women and children. *Trauma Violence & Abuse, 8*, 401–417.

Seeligmüller, A. (1890). Erfahrungen und Gedanken zur Folge der Simulation bei Unfallverletzten [Experiences and thoughts due to simulation in accident victims]. *Deutsche medizinische Wochenschrift, 16,* 663–665, 960–963, 980–982.

Seidmann, S., Schlumpf, Y. R., & Jäncke, L. (2014). *When one look is all it takes: A single-case eye-tracking study in a patient with dissociative identity disorder, a simulant, and healthy controls.* Master thesis, University of Zürich, Philosophical Faculty.

Semiz, U. B., Basoglu, C., Ebrinc, S., & Cetin, M. (2007). Childhood trauma history and dissociative experiences among Turkish men diagnosed with antisocial personality disorder. *Social Psychiatry and Psychiatric Epidemiology, 42,* 865–873.

Seto, M. C., & Lalumiere, M. L. (2010). What is so special about male adolescent sexual offending? A review and test of explanations through meta-analysis. *Psychological Bulletin, 136,* 526–575.

Shalev, A. Y., Peri, T., Gelpin, E., Orr, S. P., & Pitman, R. K. (1997). Psychophysiologic assessment of mental imagery of stressful events in Israeli civilian posttraumatic stress disorder patients. *Comprehensive Psychiatry, 38,* 269–273.

Shalev, A. Y., Sahar, T., Freedman, S., Peri, T., Glick, N., Brandes, D., . . . Pitman, R. K. (1998). A prospective study of heart rate response following trauma and the subsequent development of posttraumatic stress disorder. *Archives of General Psychiatry, 55,* 553–559.

Shapiro, F., & Maxfield, L. (2002). Eye Movement Desensitization and Reprocessing (EMDR): Information processing in the treatment of trauma. *Journal of Clinical Psychology, 58,* 933–946.

Shay, J. (1995). *Achilles in Vietnam: Combat trauma and the undoing of character.* New York: Touchstone.

Shenk, C. E., Noll, J. G., Putnam, F. W., & Trickett, P. K. (2010). A prospective examination of the role of childhood sexual abuse and physiological asymmetry in the development of psychopathology. *Child Abuse and Neglect, 34,* 752–761.

Shewmon, D. A., Holmes, G. L., & Byrne, P. A. (1999). Consciousness in congenitally decorticate children: Developmental vegetative state as self-fulfilling prophecy. *Developmental Medicine and Child Neurology, 41,* 364–374.

Shin, L. M., McNally, R. J., Kosslyn, S. M., Thompson, W. L., Rauch, S. L., Alpert, N. M., . . . Pitman, R. K. (1999). Regional cerebral blood flow during script-driven imagery in childhood sexual abuse-related PTSD: A PET investigation. *American Journal of Psychiatry, 156,* 575–584.

Shu, X. J., Xue, L., Liu, W., Chen, F. Y., Zhu, C., Sun, X. H., . . . Zhao, H. (2013). More vulnerability of left than right hippocampal damage in right-handed patients with posttraumatic stress disorder. *Journal of Psychiatry Research, 212,* 237–244.

Shulman, G. L., Fiez, J. A., Corbetta, M., Buckner, R. L., Miezin, F. M., Raichle, M. E., & Petersen, S. E. (1997). Common blood flow changes across visual tasks: II. Decreases in cerebral cortex. *Journal of Cognitive Neuroscience, 9,* 648–663.

Siegel, D. J. (1999). *The developing mind: Toward a neurobiology of interpersonal experience.* New York: Guilford.

Silberg, J. L. (1998). Dissociative symptomatology in children and adolescents as displayed on psychological testing. *Journal of Personality Assessment, 71,* 421–439.

Silberg, J. L. (2000). Fifteen years of dissociation in maltreated children: Where do we go from here? *Child Maltreatment, 5,* 119–136.

Silva, C. E., & Kirsch, I. (1992). Interpretive sets, expectancy, fantasy proneness, and dissociation as predictors of hypnotic response. *Journal of Personality and Social Psychology, 63,* 847–856.

Simeon, D. (2004). Depersonalisation disorder: A contemporary overview. *CNS Drugs, 18,* 343–354.

Simeon, D., Greenberg, J., Nelson, D., Schmeidler, J., Hollander, E., & Buchsbaum, M. S. (2005). Dissociation and posttraumatic stress 1 year after the World Trade Center disaster: Follow-up of a longitudinal survey. *Journal of Clinical Psychiatry, 66,* 231–237.

Simeon, D., Guralnik, O., Hazlett, E. A., Spiegel-Cohen, J., Hollander, E., & Buchsbaum, M. S. (2000). Feeling unreal: A PET study of depersonalization disorder. *American Journal of Psychiatry, 157*, 1782–1788.

Simeon, D., Guralnik, O., Knutelska, M., Yehuda, R., & Schmeidler, J. (2003). Basal norepinephrine in depersonalization disorder. *Psychiatry Research, 121*, 93–97.

Simeon, D., Smith, R. J., Knutelska, M., & Smith, L. M. (2008). Somatoform dissociation in depersonalization disorder. *Journal of Trauma & Dissociation, 9*, 335–348.

Simmel, E. (1919). Zweites Koreferat [Second co-report]. In S. Freud, S. Ferenczi, K. Abraham, & E. Simmel (Eds.), *Zur Psychoanalyse der Kriegsneurosen* [Psychoanalysis of the war neuroses] (pp. 42–60). Leipzig and Vienna: Internationaler Psychoanalytischer Verlag.

Simon, B. (1978). *Mind and madness in ancient Greece: The classical roots of modern psychiatry*. Ithaca, NY: Cornell University Press.

Simon, H. A. (1982). *Models of bounded rationality*. MIT: Cambridge, MA.

Simons, D. A., Wurtele, S. K., & Durham, R. L. (2008). Developmental experiences of child sexual abusers and rapists. *Child Abuse & Neglect, 32*, 549–560.

Singer, T., Seymour, B., O'Doherty, J., Kaube, H., Dolan, R. J., & Frith, C. D. (2004). Empathy for pain involves the affective but not sensory components of pain. *Science, 303*, 1157–1162.

Smith, C. P., & Freyd, J. J. (2014). Institutional betrayal. *American Psychologist, 69*, 575–587.

Smith, M. E. (2005). Bilateral hippocampal volume reduction in adults with post-traumatic stress disorder: A meta-analysis of structural MRI studies. *Hippocampus, 15*, 798–807.

Somer, E., & Dell, P. F. (2005). Development of the Hebrew-Multidimensional Inventory of Dissociation (H-MID): A valid and reliable measure of pathological dissociation. *Journal of Trauma & Dissociation, 6*, 31–53.

Sommerville, J. A., Woodward, A. L., & Needham, A. (2005). Action experience alters 3-month-old infants' perception of others' actions. *Cognition, 96*, B1-B11.

Soukup, J., Papezova, H., Kubena, A. A., & Mikolajova, V. (2010). Dissociation in nonclinical and clinical sample of Czech adolescents: Reliability and validity of the Czech version of the Adolescent Dissociative Experiences Scale. *European Psychiatry, 25*, 390–395.

Southard, E., & Jarrett, M. C. (1922). *The kingdom of evils: Psychiatric social work presented in one hundred case histories together with a classification of social divisions of evil.* New York: Macmillan.

Spanos, N. P. (1994). Multiple identity enactments and multiple personality disorder: A sociocognitive perspective. *Psychological Bulletin, 116*, 143–165.

Spanos, N. P. (1996). *Multiple identities and false memories: A sociocognitive perspective.* Washington, DC: American Psychological Association.

Spertus, I. L., Yehuda, R., Wong, C. M., Halligan, S., & Seremetis, S. V. (2003). Childhood emotional abuse and neglect as predictors of psychological and physical symptoms in women presenting to a primary care practice. *Child Abuse & Neglect, 27*, 1247–1258.

Spiegel, D. (1984). Multiple personality as a post-traumatic stress disorder. *Psychiatric Clinics of North America, 7*, 101–110.

Spiegel, D., & Cardeña, E. (1991). Disintegrated experience: The dissociative disorders revisited. *Journal of Abnormal Psychology, 100*, 366–378.

Spiegel, D., Hunt, T., & Dondershine, H. E. (1988). Dissociation and hypnotizability in posttraumatic stress disorder. *American Journal of Psychiatry, 145*, 301–305.

Spiegel, D., Loewenstein, R. J., Lewis-Fernandez, R., Sar, V., Simeon, D., Vermetten, E., … Dell, P. (2011). Dissociative disorders in DSM-5. *Depression and Anxiety, 28*, 17–45.

Spinhoven, P., Roelofs, K., Moene, F., Kuyk, J., Nijenhuis, E., Hoogduin, K., & Van Dyck, R. (2004). Trauma and dissociation in conversion disorder and chronic pelvic pain. *International Journal of Psychiatry Med, 34*, 305–318.

Spinoza, B. (1670). *Theologico-political treatise.* Available at http://www.yesselman.com/ttpelws1.htm

Spinoza, B. (1677/1996). *Ethics* (transl. and ed. E. Curley). London: Penguin.

Spitzer, C., Barnow, S., Freyberger, H. J., & Grabe, H. J. (2006). Recent developments in the theory of dissociation. *World Psychiatry, 5,* 82–86.

Steele, R. S. (1982). *Freud and Jung: Conflicts of interpretation.* London: Routledge & Kegan Paul.

Steele, K., Dorahy, M., Van der Hart, O., & Nijenhuis, E. R. S. (2009). Dissociation versus alterations in consciousness: Related but different concepts. In P. F. Dell & J. A. O'Neil (Eds.), *Dissociation and the dissociative disorders: DSM-V and beyond* (pp. 155–170). New York: Routledge.

Steele, K., Van der Hart, O., & Nijenhuis, E. R. S. (2005). Phase-oriented treatment of structural dissociation in complex traumatization: Overcoming trauma-related phobias. *Journal of Trauma & Dissociation, 6*(3), 11–53.

Steinberg, M. (1995). *Handbook for the assessment of dissociation: A clinical guide.* Washington DC: American Psychiatric Press.

Steinberg M. (2000). Advances in the clinical assessment of dissociation. The SCID-D-R. *Bulletin of the Menninger Clinic, 64,* 146–163.

Stirpe, T., Abracen, J., Stermac, L., & Wilson, R. (2006). Sexual offenders' state-of-mind regarding childhood attachment: A controlled investigation. *Sexual Abuse, 18,* 289–302.

Stocco, A., Lebiere, C., & Anderson, J. R. (2010). Conditional routing of information to the cortex: A model of the basal ganglia's role in cognitive coordination. *Psychological Review, 117,* 541–574.

Stone, M. (1985). Shellshock and the psychologists. In W. F. Bynum, R. Porter & M. Shepherd (Eds.), *The anatomy of madness, Vol. II: Institutions and society* (pp. 242–271). London: Tavistock.

Strümpell, A. (1895). Über die Untersuchung, Beurtheilung und Behandlung von Unfallkranken: Praktische Bemerkungen. [On the examination, judgment, and treatment of accident patients: Practical remarks.] *Münchener medizinische Wochenschrift, 42,* 1137–1140, 1165–1168.

Sugar, J., & Ford, J. D. (2012). Peritraumatic reactions and posttraumatic stress disorder in psychiatrically impaired youth. *Journal of Traumatic Stress, 25*(1), 41–49.

Suomi, S. J., Van der Horst, F. C., & Van der Veer, R. (2008). Rigorous experiments on monkey love: An account of Harry F. Harlow's role in the history of attachment theory. *Integrative Psychological and Behavioral Science, 42,* 354–369.

Svevo-Cianci, K. A., Hart, S. N., & Rubinson, C. (2010). Protecting children from violence and maltreatment: A qualitative comparative analysis assessing the implementation of U. N. CRC Article 19. *Child Abuse and Neglect, 34*(1), 45–56.

Schwabe, L., Dalm, S., Schächinger, H., & Oitzl, M. S. (2008). Chronic stress modulates the use of spatial and stimulus-response learning strategies in mice and man. *Neurobiology of Learning and Memory, 90,* 495–503.

Szpunar, K. K., Watson, J. M., & McDermott, K. B. (2007). Neural substrates of envisioning the future. *Proceedings of the National Academy of Sciences USA, 104,* 642–647.

Tagliabue, J. (2005). World Briefing Europe: Child pornography raid in 8 countries. *New York Times,* July 5. Retrieved from http://query.nytimes.com/gst/fullpage.html?res=9C05E1DC1530F934A35756C0A9639C8B63.

Talmey, B. S. (1919). *Love: A treatise on the science of sex-attraction for the use of physicians and students of medical jurisprudence* (4th rev. ed.). New York: Practitioners' Publishing Co.

Tamar-Gurol, D., Sar, V., Karadag, F., Evren, C., & Karagoz, M. (2008). Childhood emotional abuse, dissociation, and suicidality among patients with drug dependency in Turkey. *Psychiatry and Clinical Neuroscience, 62,* 540–547.

Tan, L., & Grace, R. C. (2008). Social desirability and sexual offenders: A review. *Sexual Abuse, 20*(1), 61–87.

Tardieu, A. (1857). Études médico-légale sur les attentats aux moeurs [Medical-legal studies of assaults on decency]. In *Annales d'Hygiène Publique et de Médicine Légale, deuxième series*, VIII, 133–208, 379–429, IX, 137–198.

Tardieu, A. (1860). Études médico-légale sur les sévices et mauvaise traitement exercés sur les enfants [Medical-legal studies of cruelty and brutal treatment inflicted on children]. *Annales d'Hygiène Publique et de Médicine Légale, deuxième series*, 8, 361–398.

Tardieu, A. (1878). *Études médico-légale sur les attentats aux moeurs* [Medical-legal studies of assaults on decency]. Paris: Librairie Baillières et Fils.

Taylor, J., Baldwin, N., & Spencer, N. (2008). Predicting child abuse and neglect: Ethical, theoretical and methodological challenges. *Journal of Clinical Nursing, 17*, 1193–1200.

Teicher, M. H., Anderson, C. M., & Polcari, A. (2012). Childhood maltreatment is associated with reduced volume in the hippocampal subfields CA3, dentate gyrus, and subiculum. *Proceedings of the National Academy of Sciences USA, 109*, E563–572.

Teicher, M. H., Andersen, S. L., Polcari, A., Anderson, C. M., & Navalta, C. P. (2002). Developmental neurobiology of childhood stress and trauma. *Psychiatric Clinics of North America, 25*, 397–426, vii-viii.

Teicher, M. H., Dumont, N. L., Ito, Y., Vaituzis, C., Giedd, J. N., & Andersen, S. L. (2004). Childhood neglect is associated with reduced corpus callosum area. *Biological Psychiatry, 56*, 80–85.

Teicher, M. H., Tomoda, A., & Andersen, S. L. (2006). Neurobiological consequences of early stress and childhood maltreatment: Are results from human and animal studies comparable? *Annals of the New York Academy of Science, 1071*, 313–323.

Teisl, M., Rogosch, F. A., Oshri, A., & Cicchetti, D. (2011). Differential expression of social dominance as a function of age and maltreatment experience. *Developmental Psychology, 48*, 575–588.

Tellegen, A., Lykken, D. T., Bouchard, T. J., Jr., Wilcox, K. J., Segal, N. L., Rich, S. (1988). Personality similarity in twins reared apart and together. *Journal of Personality and Social Psychology, 54*, 1031–1039.

Terhune, D. B., Cardeña, E., & Lindgren, M. (2010). Dissociative tendencies and individual differences in high hypnotic suggestibility. *Cognitive Neuropsychiatry, 16*, 113–135.

Tezcan, E., Atmaca, M., Kuloglu, M., Gecici, O., Buyukbayram, A., & Tutkun, H. (2003). Dissociative disorders in Turkish inpatients with conversion disorder. *Comprehensive Psychiatry, 44*, 324–330.

The Lancet (1862). The influence of railway travelling on public health. London: Robert Hardwicke.

Thoinot, L. H. (1919). *Medicolegal aspects of moral offenses.* Philadelphia: F. A. Davis.

Thomaes, K., Dorrepaal, E., Draijer, N., de Ruiter, M. B., van Balkom, A. J., Smit, J. H., & Veltman, D. (2010). Reduced anterior cingulate and orbitofrontal volumes in child abuse-related complex PTSD. *Journal of Clinical Psychiatry, 71*, 1636–1644.

Thomas, E., Saumier, D., & Brunet, A. (2012). Peritraumatic distress and the course of posttraumatic stress disorder symptoms: A meta-analysis. *Canadian Journal of Psychiatry, 57*, 122–129.

Thompson, E. (2007). *Mind in life: Biology, phenomenology, and the sciences of mind.* Cambridge, MA: Belknap Harvard.

Thomson, P., Keehn, E. B., & Gumpel, T. P. (2009). Generators and interpretors in a performing arts population: Dissociation, trauma, fantasy proneness, and affective states. *Creativity Research Journal, 21*, 72–91.

Thorndike, E. L. (1911). *Animal intelligence.* New York: Macmillan. (Reprint Bristol: Thoemmes, 1999).

Tian, L., Jiang, T., Liu, Y., Yu, C., Wang, K., Zhou, Y., . . . Li, K. (2007). The relationship within and between the extrinsic and intrinsic systems indicated by resting state correlational patterns of sensory cortices. *Neuroimage, 36*, 681–690.

Timberlake, W. (1993). Behavior systems and reinforcement: An integrative approach. *Journal of Experimental Analysis of Behavior, 60*(1), 105–128.

Timberlake, W., & Lucas, G. A. (1989). Behavior systems and learning: From misbehavior to general principles. In S. B. Klein & R. R. Mowrer (Eds.), *Contemporary learning theories* (pp. 237–275). Hillsdale, NJ: Erlbaum.

Tinbergen, N. (1951). *The study of instinct.* Oxford: Clarendon.

Tinbergen, N. (1953). *The Herring Gull's world.* London: Collins.

Tolmunen, T., Rissanen, M. L., Hintikka, J., Maaranen, P., Honkalampi, K., Kylma, J., & Laukkanen, E. (2008). Dissociation, self-cutting, and other self-harm behavior in a general population of Finnish adolescents. *Journal of Nervous and Mental Disease, 196*, 768–771.

Tomasello, M. (1999). *The cultural origin of human cognition.* Cambridge, MA: Harvard University Press.

Tomoda, A., Sheu, Y. S., Rabi, K., Suzuki, H., Navalta, C. P., Polcari, A., & Teicher, M. H. (2010). Exposure to parental verbal abuse is associated with increased gray matter volume in superior temporal gyrus. *Neuroimage, 54*(Suppl 1), S280-S286.

Tomoda, A., Suzuki, H., Rabi, K., Sheu, Y.-S., Polcari, A., & Teicher, M. H. (2009). Reduced prefrontal cortical gray matter volume in young adults exposed to harsh corporal punishment. *Neuroimage, 47*(Suppl 2), T66–T71.

Tomoda, A., Sheu, Y. S., Rabi, K., Suzuki, H., Navalta, C. P., Polcari, A., & Teicher, M. H. (2010). Exposure to parental verbal abuse is associated with increased gray matter volume in superior temporal gyrus. *Neuroimage, 54*(Suppl. 1), S280–S286.

Toronchuk, J. A., & Ellis, G. F. (2012). Affective neuronal selection: The nature of the primordial emotion systems. *Frontiers of Psychology, 3*, 589.

Treadway, M. T., Grant, M. M., Ding, Z., Hollon, S. D., Gore, J. C., & Shelton, R. C. (2009). Early adverse events, HPA activity and rostral anterior cingulate volume in MDD. *PLoS One, 4*, e4887.

Trembinski, D. (2011). Comparing premodern melancholy/mania and modern trauma: An argument in favor of historical experiences of trauma. *History of Psychology, 14(1),* 80–99.

Trickett, P. K., Noll, J. G., & Putnam, F. W. (2011). The impact of sexual abuse on female development: Lessons from a multigenerational, longitudinal research study. *Development and Psychopathology 23*, 453–476.

Trickett, P. K., Noll, J. G., Reiffman, A., & Putnam, F. W. (2001). Variants of intrafamilial sexual abuse experience: Implications for short- and long-term development. *Development and Psychopathology, 13*, 1001–1019.

Trimble, M. R. (1981). *Post-traumatic neurosis: From railway spine to the whiplash.* Chichester, UK: Wiley.

Trimble, M. R. (1982). Functional diseases. *British Medical Journal, 285*, 1768–1770.

Trillat, E. (1986). *Histoire de l'hystérie* [The history of hysteria]. Paris: Seghers.

Tronick, E., Als, H., Adamson, L., Wise, S., Brazelton, T. B. (1978). The infant's response to entrapment between contradictory messages in face-to-face interaction. *Journal of the American Academy of Child Psychiatry, 17*, 1–13.

Tsai, G. E., Condie, D., Wu, M. T., & Chang, I. W. (1999). Functional magnetic resonance imaging of personality switches in a woman with dissociative identity disorder. *Harvard Review of Psychiatry, 7*, 119–122.

Tsopelas, C., Tsetsou, S., & Douzenis, A. (2011). Review on female sexual offenders: Findings about profile and personality. *International Journal of Law and Psychiatry, 34*, 122–126.

Tsopelas, C., Tsetsou, S., Ntounas, P., & Douzenis, A. (2012). Female perpetrators of sexual abuse of minors: What are the consequences for the victims? *International Journal of Law and Psychiatry, 35*, 305–310.

Tulving, E., Kapur, S., Craik, F. I., Moscovitch, M., Houle, S. (1994). Hemispheric encoding/retrieval asymmetry in episodic memory: positron emission tomography findings. *Proceedings of the National Academy of Sciences USA, 91*, 2016–2020.

Udolf, R. (1981). *Handbook of hypnosis for professionals.* Ontario: Van Nostrand Reinhold Company.

Uexküll, T. von (1994). Was ist und was will Integrierte Psychosomatische Medizin? [What is integrated psychosomatic medicine and what does it want?]. In T. von Uexküll (Ed.), *Integrierte Psychosomatische Medizin in Klinik und Praxis* (pp. 17–34). Stuttgart, New York: Schattauer.

Uvnas-Moberg, K. (1997). Physiological and endocrine effects of social contact. *Annals of the New York Academy of Sciences, 807*, 146–163.

Vaitl, D., Birbaumer, N., Gruzelier, J., Jamieson, G. A., Kotoubey, B., Kübler, A., . . . Weiss, T. (2005). Psychobiology of altered states of consciousness. *Psychological Bulletin, 131*, 98–127.

Vallee, M., MacCari, S., Dellu, F., Simon, H., Le Moal, M., & Mayo, W. (1999). Long-term effects of prenatal stress and postnatal handling on age-related glucocorticoid secretion and cognitive performance: A longitudinal study in the rat. *European Journal of Neuroscience, 11*, 2906–2916.

Valliant, P. M., & Bergeron, T. (1997). Personality and criminal profile of adolescent sexual offenders, general offenders in comparison to nonoffenders. *Psychological Reports, 81*, 483–489.

Van Bergen, L. (1999). *Zacht en eervol: Lijden en sterven in een Grote Oorlog* [Tender and honorable: Suffering and dying in a Great War]. Nijmegen: SUA.

Van der Boom, K. J., Van den Hout, M. A., & Huntjens, R. J. C. (2010). Psychoform and somatoform dissociation, traumatic experiences, and fantasy proneness in somatoform disorders. *Personality and Individual Differences,* 48, 447–451.

Van Derbur, M. (2003). *Miss America by day: Lessons learned from ultimate betrayals and unconditional love.* Denver: Oak Hill.

Van Derbur, M. (2012, April). *Miss America by day*. Presentation at Zwanzig Jahre Villa Lindenfels: Gesichter der Gewalt, Fellbach.

Van der Hart, O., Bolt, H., & Van der Kolk, B. A. (2005). Memory fragmentation in dissociative identity disorder. *Journal of Trauma & Dissociation, 6*(1), 55–70.

Van der Hart, O., & Broeze, A. (2012). Posttraumatische stress en de posttraumatische stress-stoornis: Een historisch overzicht [Posttraumatic stress and the posttraumatic stress disorder: A historical review]. In E. Vermetten, R. J. Kleber, & O. van der Hart (Eds.), *Handboek posttraumatische stress stoornissen* (pp. 25–44). Utrecht: De Tijdstroom.

Van der Hart, O., & Brom, D. (2000). When the victim forgets: Trauma-induced amnesia and its assessment in Holocaust survivors. In A. Y. Shalev, R. Yehuda, & A. C. McFarlane (Eds.), *International handbook of human response to trauma* (pp. 223–248). New York: Kluwer Academic/Plenum.

Van der Hart, O., & Brown, P. (1990). Concept of psychological trauma. *American Journal of Psychiatry, 147*, 1691.

Van der Hart, O., Brown, P., & Graafland, M. (1999). Trauma-induced dissociative amnesia in World War I combat soldiers. *Australian and New Zealand Journal of Psychiatry, 33*, 37–46.

Van der Hart, O., & Dorahy, M. (2009). Dissociation: History of a concept. In P. F. Dell & J. A. O'Neil (Eds.), *Dissociation and the dissociative disorders: DSM-IV and beyond* (pp. 3–26). New York: Routledge.

Van der Hart, O., & Friedman, B. (1989). A reader's guide to Pierre Janet on dissociation: A neglected intellectual heritage. *Dissociation, 2*, 3–16.

Van der Hart, O., Lierens, R., & Goodwin, J. (1996). Jeanne Fery: A sixteenth-century case of dissociative identity disorder. *The Journal of Psychohistory, 24*, 1–12.

Van der Hart, O., & Nijenhuis, E. R. S. (2008). Dissociative disorders. In P. H. Blaney & T. Millon (Eds.), *Oxford textbook of psychopathology* (2nd ed., pp. 452–481). New York, Oxford: Oxford University Press.

Van der Hart, O., Nijenhuis, E. R. S., & Brown, P. (2001). Loss and recovery of different memory types in generalized dissociative amnesia. *Australian and New Zealand Journal of Psychiatry, 35*, 589–600.

Van der Hart, O., Nijenhuis, E. R. S., Steele, K. (2005). Dissociation: An insufficiently recognized major feature of complex PTSD. *Journal of Traumatic Stress, 18*, 413–425.

Van der Hart, O., Nijenhuis, E. R. S., & Steele, K. (2006). *The haunted self: Structural dissociation and the treatment of chronic traumatization.* New York: Norton.

Van der Hart, O., Nijenhuis, E. R. S., Steele, K., & Brown, D. (2004). Trauma-related dissociation: Conceptual clarity lost and found. *Australian and New Zealand Journal of Psychiatry, 38*, 906–914.

Van der Hart, O., Van Dijke, A., Van Son, M., & Steele, K. (2000). Somatoform dissociation in traumatized World War I combat soldiers: A neglected heritage. *Journal of Trauma & Dissociation, 1*(4), 33–66.

Van der Hart, O., Van Ochten, J. M., Van Son, M. J., Steele, K., & Lensvelt-Mulders, G. (2008). Relations among peritraumatic dissociation and posttraumatic stress: A critical review. *Journal of Trauma & Dissociation, 9*, 481–505.

Van der Hart, O., Witztum, E., & Friedman, B. (1993). From hysterical psychosis to reactive dissociative psychosis. *Journal of Traumatic Stress, 6*(1), 43–63.

Van der Kolk, B. A. (2003). The neurobiology of childhood trauma and abuse. *Child and Adolescent Psychiatric Clinics of North America, 12*, 293–317, ix.

Van der Kolk, B. A. (2005). Developmental trauma disorder: Toward a rational diagnosis for chronically traumatized children. *Psychiatric Annals, 35*, 401–408.

Van der Kolk, B. (2008, April). *120 years of dissociation: A history of brilliant insights, lost awareness and stunning disconnections.* Paper presented at the Biannual Conference of the European Society for Trauma and Dissociation, Amsterdam, Netherlands.

Van der Kolk, B. A. (2009). Developmental trauma disorder: Towards a rational diagnosis for chronically traumatized children. *Praxis der Kinderpsychologie und Kinderpsychiatrie, 58*, 572–586.

Van der Kolk, B. A. (2010). Towards a developmental trauma disorder diagnosis for childhood interpersonal trauma. In R. A. Lanius, E. Vermetten, & C. Pain (Eds.), *The impact of early life trauma on health and disease: The hidden epidemic* (pp. 57–68). Cambridge: Cambridge University Press.

Van der Kolk, B. A., & d'Andrea, W. (2010). Towards a developmental trauma disorder diagnosis for childhood interpersonal trauma. In R. A. Lanius, E. Vermetten, & C. Pain (Eds.), *The impact of early life trauma on health and disease: The hidden epidemic* (pp. 57–68). Cambridge MA: Cambridge University Press.

Van der Kolk, B. A., & Van der Hart, O. (1989). Pierre Janet and the breakdown of adaptation in psychological trauma. *American Journal of Psychiatry, 146*, 1530–1540.

Van der Kolk, B. A., Perry, J. C., & Herman, J. L. (1991). Childhood origins of self-destructive behavior. *American Journal of Psychiatry, 148*, 1665–1671.

Van der Kolk, B. A., Roth, S., Pelcovitz, D., Sunday, S., & Spinazzola, J. (2005). Disorders of extreme stress: The empirical foundation of a complex adaptation to trauma. *Journal of Traumatic Stress, 18*, 389–399.

Vanderlinden, J. (1993). *Dissociative experiences, trauma, and hypnosis.* Delft: Eburon.

Vanderlinden, J., Van Dyck, R., Vandereycken, W., & Vertommen, H. (1993). Dissociation and traumatic experiences in the general population of The Netherlands. *Hospital and Community Psychiatry, 44*, 786–788.

Van der Velden, P. G., Kleber, R. J., Christiaanse, B., Gersons, B. P., Marcelissen, F. G., Drogendijk, A. N., . . . Meewisse, M. L. (2006). The independent predictive value of peritraumatic dissociation for postdisaster intrusions, avoidance reactions, and PTSD symptom severity: A 4-year prospective study. *Journal of Traumatic Stress, 19*, 493–506.

Vandeven, A & Newton, A. W. (2006). Update on child physical abuse, sexual abuse, and prevention. *Current Opinions in Pediatrics, 18*, 201–205.

Van Dongen, J., & Boomsma, D. I. (2013). The evolutionary paradox and the missing heritability of schizophrenia. *American Journal of Medical Genetics, Part B: Neuropsychiatric Genetics, 162B*, 122–136.

Van Duijl, M., Cardeña, E., & De Jong, J. T. (2005). The validity of DSM-IV dissociative disorders categories in South-West Uganda. *Transcultural Psychiatry, 42*, 219–241.

Van Duijl, M., Nijenhuis, E., Komproe, I. H., Gernaat, H. B., & de Jong, J. T. (2010). Dissociative symptoms and reported trauma among patients with spirit possession and matched healthy controls in Uganda. *Culture, Medicine, and Psychiatry, 34*, 380–400.

Van Gelder, T. (1995). What might cognition be, if not computation? *Journal of Philosophy, 91*, 345–381.

Van Haute, P., & Geyskens, T. (2004). *Confusion of tongues: The primary of sexuality in Freud, Ferenczi, and Laplanche*. New York: Other Press.

Van Ommeren, M., De Jong, J. T., Sharma, B., Komproe, I., Thapa, S. B., & Cardeña, E. (2001a). Psychiatric disorders among tortured Bhutanese refugees in Nepal. *Archives of General Psychiatry, 58*, 475–482.

Van Ommeren, M., Sharma, B., Komproe, Poudyal, B. N., Sharma, G. K., Cardeña, E., & De Jong, J. T. (2001b). Trauma and loss as determinants of medically unexplained epidemic illness in a Bhutanese refugee camp. *Psychological Medicine, 31*, 1259–1267.

Van Wijk, A., Vermeiren, R., Loeber, R., Hart-Kerkhoffs, L., Doreleijers, T., & Bullens, R. (2006). Juvenile sex offenders compared to non-sex offenders: A review of the literature 1995–2005. *Trauma Violence & Abuse, 7*, 227–243.

Van IJzendoorn, M. H., Schuengel, C., & Bakersman-Kranenburg, M. (1999). Disorganized attachment in early childhood: Meta-analysis of precursors, concomitants, and sequelae. *Development & Psychopathology, 11*, 225–249.

Varela, F. (1996). Neurophenomenology: A methodological remedy for the hard problem. *Journal of Consciousness Studies, 3*, 330–349.

Varela, F. J., Thompson, E., & Rosch, E. (1993). *The embodied mind: Cognitive science and human experience*. Cambridge, MA: MIT.

Varese, F., Barkus, E., & Bentall, R. P. (2011). Dissociation mediates the relationship between childhood trauma and hallucination-proneness. *Psychological Medicine, 42*, 1025–1036.

Veith, I. (1965). *Hysteria: The history of a disease*. Chicago: University of Chicago Press.

Vermetten, E., Schmahl, C., Lindner, S., Loewenstein, R. J., & Bremner, J. D. (2006). Hippocampal and amygdalar volumes in dissociative identity disorder. *American Journal of Psychiatry, 163*, 630–636.

Verhaeghe, P. (2001). Trauma and psychopathology in Freud and Lacan. In *Beyond gender: From subject to drive*. New York: Other Press.

Vicedo, M. (2010). The evolution of Harry Harlow: From the nature to the nurture of love. *Hist Psychiatry, 21*(82 Pt 2), 190–205.

Vicedo, M. (2012). Playing the game: Psychology textbooks speak out about love. *Isis, 103*(1), 111–125.

Vieira, E. B., Menescal-de-Oliveira, L., & Leite-Panissi, C. R. (2010). Functional mapping of the periaqueductal gray matter involved in organizing tonic immobility behavior in guinea pigs. *Behavioral Brain Research, 216*(1), 94–99.

Viken, R. J., Rose, R. J., Kaprio, J., & Kowkenvuo, M. (1994). A developmental genetic analysis of adult personality extraversion and neuroticism from 18 to 59 years of age. *Journal of Personality and Social Psychology, 47*, 127–144.

Vogel, M., Braungardt, T., Grabe, H. J., Schneider, W., & Klauer, T. (2013). Detachment, compartmentalization, and schizophrenia: Linking dissociation and psychosis by subtype. *Journal of Trauma & Dissociation, 14*, 273–287.

Voisin, A. (1883). *Lecons cliniques sur les maladies mentales and les maladies nerveuses* [Clinical lessons on the mental and the nervous diseases]. Paris: J. B. Balliere & Fils.

Vrticka, P., & Vuilleumier, P. (2012). Neuroscience of human social interactions and adult attachment style. *Frontiers of Human Neuroscience, 6*, 212.

Vygotsky, L. S. (1934/1986). Thought and language. (A. Kozulin, trans. and ed.). Cambridge, MA: MIT.

Wade, D., Hardy, R., Howell, D., & Mythen, M. (2013). Identifying clinical and acute psychological risk factors for PTSD after critical care: A systematic review. *Minerva Anestesiologica 79*, 944–963.

Waddington, C. H. (1959). Canalization of development and the inheritance of acquired characters. *Nature, 183*, 1654–1655.

Wallace, B. A. (2000). *The taboo of subjectivity: Toward a new science of consciousness.* Oxford: Oxford University Press.

Wallace, M. T. (2004). The development of multisensory processes. *Cognitive Processing, 5*, 69–83.

Waller, G., Babbs, M., Wright, F., Potterton, C., Meyer, C., & Leung, N. (2003). Somatoform dissociation in eating-disordered patients. *Behavior Research & Therapy, 41*, 619–627.

Waller, G., Hamilton, K., Elliott, P., Lewendon, J., Stopa, L. Waters, A., . . . Bashford, V. (2000). Somatoform dissociation, psychological dissociation and specific forms of trauma. *Journal of Trauma & Dissociation, 1*(4), 81–98.

Waller, N. G., Putnam, F. W., & Carlson, E. B. (1996). Types of dissociation and dissociative types: A taxonomic analysis of dissociative experiences. *Psychological Methods, 1*, 300–321.

Walters, G. D., Marcus, D. K., Edens, J. F., Knight, R. A., & Sanford, G. M. (2012). In search of the psychopathic sexuality taxon: Indicator size does matter. *Behavioral Science and Law, 29*(1), 23–39.

Wang, S., Wilson, J. P., & Mason, J. W. (1996). Stages of decompensation in combat-related posttraumatic stress disorder: A new conceptual model. *Integrative Physiology & Behavioral Science, 31*, 237–253.

Wang, Z., Neylan, T. C., Mueller, S. G., Lenoci, M., Truran, D., Marmar, C. R., . . . Schuff, N. (2010). Magnetic resonance imaging of hippocampal subfields in posttraumatic stress disorder. *Archives of General Psychiatry, 67*, 296–303.

War Office Committee. (1922). *Report of the War Office Committee of enquiry into "shell-shock."* London: His Majesty's Stationary Office.

Watson, B. (1968). *The complete works of Chuang Tzu.* New York: Columbia University Press.

Watson, J. B. (1913). Psychology as the behaviorist views it. *Psychological Review, 20*, 158–177.

Watson, J. B. (1930). *Behaviorism* (rev. ed.). Chicago: University of Chicago Press.

Watson, S., Chilton, R., Fairchild, H., & Whewell, P. (2006). Association between childhood trauma and dissociation among patients with borderline personality disorder. *Australian and New Zealand Journal of Psychiatry, 40*, 478–481.

Watts, C., & Zimmerman, C. (2002). Violence against women: Global scope and magnitude. *Lancet, 359*(9313), 1232–1237.

Weathers, F., & Keane, T. (2007). The Criterion A problem revisited. *Journal of Traumatic Stress, 20*, 107–121.

Weber, A. (2002). Feeling the signs: Organic experience, intrinsic teleology and the origins of meaning in the biological philosophy of Hans Jonas and Susanne K. Langer. *Sign System Studies, 30*(1), 183–200.

Weber, C., Wermter, S., & Elshaw, M. (2006). A hybrid generative and predictive model of the motor cortex. *Neural Networks, 19*, 339–353.

Weinberg, S. K. (1955). *Incest behavior.* New York: Citadel.

Weisberg, D. (2005). Consciousness constrained: A commentary on *Being no one. Psyche, 11*(5), 1–22.

Weniger, G., Lange, C., Sachsse, U., & Irle, E. (2008). Amygdala and hippocampal volumes and cognition in adult survivors of childhood abuse with dissociative disorders. *Acta Psychiatrica Scandinavica, 118*, 281–290.

Whitaker, D. J., Le, B., Karl Hanson, R., Baker, C. K., McMahon, P. M., Ryan, G., . . . Rice, D. D. (2008). Risk factors for the perpetration of child sexual abuse: A review and meta-analysis. *Child Abuse and Neglect, 32*, 529–548.

White, N. M. (2009). Some highlights of research on the effects of caudate nucleus lesions over the past 200 years. *Behavioral Brain Research, 199*, 3–23.

White, N. M., & McDonald, R. J. (2002). Multiple parallel memory systems in the brain of the rat. *Neurobiological Learning and Memory, 77*, 125–184.

Wicker, B., Keysers, C., Plailly, J., Royet, J. P., Gallese, V., & Rizzolatti, G. (2003). Both of us disgusted in My insula: The common neural basis of seeing and feeling disgust. *Neuron, 40*, 655–664.

Wickizer, T. M. (2013). State-level estimates of the economic costs of alcohol and drug abuse. *Journal of Healthcare Finance, 39*(3), 71–84.

Widom, C. S. (1999). Posttraumatic stress disorder in abused and neglected children grown up. *American Journal of Psychiatry, 156*, 1223–1229.

Widom, C. S., Czaja, S. J., Bentley, T., & Johnson, M. S. (2012). A prospective investigation of physical health outcomes in abused and neglected children: New findings from a 30-year follow-up. *American Journal of Public Health, 102*, 1135–1144.

Widom, C. S., Czaja, S. J., & Paris, J. (2009). A prospective investigation of borderline personality disorder in abused and neglected children followed up into adulthood. *Journal of Personality Disorders, 23*, 433–446.

Wijkman, M., Bijleveld, C., & Hendriks, J. (2010). Women don't do such things! Characteristics of female sex offenders and offender types. *Sexual Abuse, 22*, 135–156.

Williams, G. (1913). Rape in children and young girls. *International Clinics, 23*, 250.

Williams, L. M. (1995). Recovered memories of abuse in women with documented child sexual victimization histories. *Journal of Traumatic Stress, 8*, 649–673.

Wilson, J. P. (1995). Traumatic events and PTSD and prevention. In B. Raphael & J. Barrows (Eds.), *The handbook on studies of preventive psychiatry* (pp. 281–296). Amsterdam: Elsevier.

Wilson, J. P., Drozdek, B., & Turkovic, S. (2006). Posttraumatic shame and guilt. *Trauma Violence & Abuse, 7*, 122–141.

Wilson, J. P., & Walker, A. (1986). The psychobiology of trauma. In J. P. Wilson (Ed.), *Trauma transformation and healing* (pp. 21–37). New York: Brunner/Mazel.

Wilson, J. P., & Zigelbaum, S. D. (1986). PTSD and the disposition to criminal behavior. In C. R. Figley (Ed.), *Trauma and its wake, Volume II* (pp. 305–321). New York: Brunner/Mazel.

Wilson, R. J. (1999). Emotional congruence in sexual offenders against children. *Sexual Abuse, 11*, 33–47.

Wilson, S. C., & Barber, T. X. (1983). Fantasy-prone personality: Implications for understanding imagery, hypnosis, and parapsychological phenomena. In A. A. Sheikh (Ed.), *Imagery: Current theory, research, and application* (pp. 340–387). New York: Wiley.

Wittgenstein, L. (1953). *Philosophical investigations.* New York: MacMillan.

Wittmann, L., Moergeli, H., & Schnyder, U. (2006). Low predictive power of peritraumatic dissociation for PTSD symptoms in accident survivors. *Journal of Traumatic Stress, 19*, 639–651.

Witztum, E., & Van der Hart, O. (2008). The return of the diagnosis of hysterical psychosis. In A. Moskowitz, I. Schäfer, & M. Dorahy (2008). *Psychosis, trauma and dissociation: Emerging perspectives on severe psychopathology* (pp. 21–33). Chichester: Wiley.

Wolf, E. J., Lunney, C. A., Miller, M. W., Resick, P. A., Friedman, M. J., & Schnurr, P. P. (2012a). The dissociative subtype of PTSD: A replication and extension. *Depression and Anxiety, 29*, 679–688.

Wolf, E. J., Miller, M. W., Reardon, A. F., Ryabchenko, K. A., Castillo, D., & Freund, R. (2012b). A latent class analysis of dissociation and posttraumatic stress disorder: Evidence for a dissociative subtype. *Archives of General Psychiatry, 69*, 698–705.

Wolff, C. T., Friedman, S. B., Hofer, M. A., & Mason, J. W. (1964). Relationship between psychological defenses and mean urinary 17-OHCS excretion rates: A predictive study of parents of fatally ill children. *Psychosomatic Medicine, 26*, 576–591.

Wong, M., Looney, E., Michaels, J., Palesh, O., & Koopman, C. (2006). A preliminary study of peritraumatic dissociation, social support, and coping in relation to posttraumatic stress symptoms for a parent's cancer. *Psychooncology, 15*, 1093–1098.

Woon, F. L., Sood, S., & Hedges, D. W. (2010). Hippocampal volume deficits associated with exposure to psychological trauma and posttraumatic stress disorder in adults: A meta-analysis. *Progress in Neuro-psychopharmacology and Biological Psychiatry, 34,* 1181–1188.

World Health Organization. (1977). *International classification of diseases, 9th revision.* Geneva, Switzerland: Author.

World Health Organization. (1992). *The ICD-10 classification of mental and behavioural disorders: Clinical descriptions and diagnostic guidelines.* Geneva, Switzerland: Author.

Worley, K. B., Church, J. K., & Clemmons, J. C. (2011). Parents of adolescents who have committed sexual offenses: Characteristics, challenges, and interventions. *Clinical Child Psychology and Psychiatry, 17,* 433–448.

Worling, J. R. (1995). Adolescent sibling-incest offenders: Differences in family and individual functioning when compared to adolescent nonsibling sex offenders. *Child Abuse and Neglect, 19,* 633–643.

Wright, M. O., Crawford, E., & Del Castillo, D. (2009). Childhood emotional maltreatment and later psychological distress among college students: The mediating role of maladaptive schemas. *Child Abuse & Neglect, 33,* 59–68.

Xie, P., Kranzler, H. R., Poling, J., Stein, M. B., Anton, R. F., Brady, K., . . . Gelernter, J. (2009). Interactive effect of stressful life events and the serotonin transporter 5-HTTLPR genotype on posttraumatic stress disorder diagnosis in two independent populations. *Archives of General Psychiatry, 66,* 1201–1209.

Xiao, Z., Yan, H., Wang, Z., Zou, Z., Xu, Y., Chen, J., . . . Keyes, B. B. (2006). Trauma and dissociation in China. *American Journal of Psychiatry, 163,* 1388–1391.

Yang, B. Z., Zhang, H., Ge, W., Weder, N., Douglas-Palumberi, H., Perepletchikova, F., . . . Kaufmann, J. (2013). Child abuse and epigenetic mechanisms of disease risk. *American Journal of Preventive Medicine, 44,* 101–107.

Yard, S. S., DuHamel, K. N., & Galynker, I. I. (2008). Hypnotizability as a potential risk factor for posttraumatic stress: A review of quantitative studies. *International Journal of Clinical and Experimental Hypnosis, 56,* 334–356.

Yasan, A., Guzel, A., Tamam, Y., & Ozkan, M. (2009). Predictive factors for acute stress disorder and posttraumatic stress disorder after motor vehicle accidents. *Psychopathology, 42,* 236–241.

Young, A. (1997). *The harmony of illusions: Inventing post-traumatic stress disorder.* New York: Princeton University Press.

Yargic, L. I., Sar, V., Tutkun, H., & Alyanak, B. (1998). Comparison of dissociative identity disorder with other diagnostic groups using a structured interview in Turkey. *Comprehensive Psychiatry 39,* 345–351.

Yin, Y., Li, L., Jin, C., Hu, X., Duan, L., Eyler, L. T., . . . Li, W. (2011). Abnormal baseline brain activity in posttraumatic stress disorder: A resting-state functional magnetic resonance imaging study. *Neuroscience Letters, 498,* 185–189.

Yu, J., Ross, C. A., Keyes, B. B., Li, Y., Dai, Y., Zhang, T., . . . Xiao, Z. (2010). Dissociative disorders among Chinese inpatients diagnosed with schizophrenia. *Journal of Trauma & Dissociation, 11,* 358–372.

Yücel, B., Özyalçın, S., Sertel, H. O., Çamlıca, H., Ketenci, A., & Talu, G. K. (2002). Childhood traumatic events and dissociative experiences in patients with chronic headache and low back pain. *Clinical Journal of Pain, 18,* 394–401.

Zahavi, D. (2005). Being someone. *Psyche, 11*(5), 1–20.

Zielinski, D. S. (2009). Child maltreatment and adult socioeconomic well-being. *Child Abuse and Neglect, 33,* 666–678.

Zilberg, N. J., Weiss, D. S., & Horowitz, M. J. (1982). Impact of Events Scale: A cross-validation study and some empirical evidence supporting a model of stress response syndromes. *Journal of Consulting and Clinical Psychology, 50,* 407–414.

Zlotnick, C., Shea, M. T., Zakriski, A., Costello, E., Begin, A., Pearlstein, T., & Simpson, E. (1995). Stressors and close relationships during childhood and dissociative experiences in survivors of sexual abuse among inpatient psychiatric women. *Comprehensive Psychiatry, 36*, 207–212.

Zoellner, L. A., Foa, E. B., Brigidi, B. D., & Przeworski, A. (2000). Are trauma victims susceptible to "false memories"? *Journal of Abnormal Psychology, 109*, 517–524.

Zoellner, L. A., Sacks, M., & Foa, E. B. (2007). Dissociation and serenity induction. *Journal of Behavior Therapy and Experimental Psychiatry, 38*, 252–262.

Zoroglu, S. S., Sar, V., Tuzun, U., Tutkun, H., & Savas, H. A. (2002). Reliability and validity of the Turkish version of the Adolescent Dissociative Experiences Scale. *Psychiatry and Clinical Neuroscience, 56*, 551–556.

Zoroglu, S. S., Tuzun, U., Sar, V., Tutkun, H., Savacs, H. A., Ozturk, M., . . . Kora, M. E. (2003). Suicide attempt and self-mutilation among Turkish high school students in relation with abuse, neglect and dissociation. *Psychiatry and Clinical Neuroscience, 57*(1), 119–126.

Zucker, M., Spinazzola, J., Blaustein, M., & Van der Kolk, B. A. (2006). Dissociative symptomatology in posttraumatic stress disorder and disorders of extreme stress. *Journal of Trauma & Dissociation, 7*, 19–31.

Author Index

I

J

K

L

M

N

O

P

Q

R

S

T

Subject Index

D

T

W